T0336842

Handbook of Research on High Performance and Cloud Computing in Scientific Research and Education

Marijana Despotović–Zrakić
University of Belgrade, Serbia

Veljko Milutinović
University of Belgrade, Serbia

Aleksandar Belić
University of Belgrade, Serbia

A volume in the Advances in Systems Analysis, Software Engineering, and High Performance Computing (ASASEHPC) Book Series

An Imprint of IGI Global

Managing Director:	Lindsay Johnston
Production Editor:	Jennifer Yoder
Development Editor:	Erin O'Dea
Acquisitions Editor:	Kayla Wolfe
Typesetter:	Deanna Jo Zombro
Cover Design:	Jason Mull

Published in the United States of America by
Information Science Reference (an imprint of IGI Global)
701 E. Chocolate Avenue
Hershey PA 17033
Tel: 717-533-8845
Fax: 717-533-8661
E-mail: cust@igi-global.com
Web site: http://www.igi-global.com

Library of Congress Cataloging-in-Publication Data

Handbook of Research on High performance and cloud computing in scientific research and education / Marijana Despoto-vic-Zrakic, Veljko Milutinovic, and Aleksandar Belic, editors.
    pages cm
 Includes bibliographical references and index.
 ISBN 978-1-4666-5784-7 (hardcover) -- ISBN 978-1-4666-5785-4 (ebook) -- ISBN 978-1-4666-5787-8 (print & perpetual access) 1. Cloud computing. 2. High performance computing. I. Despotovic-Zrakic, Marijana, 1977- editor of compilation. II. Milutinovic, Veljko editor of compilation. III. Belic, Aleksandar, 1962- editor of compilation.
 QA76.585.H55 2014
 004.67'82--dc23
                                    2013050675

This book is published in the IGI Global book series Advances in Systems Analysis, Software Engineering, and High Performance Computing (ASASEHPC) (ISSN: 2327-3453; eISSN: 2327-3461)

British Cataloguing in Publication Data
A Cataloguing in Publication record for this book is available from the British Library.

Advances in Systems Analysis, Software Engineering, and High Performance Computing (ASASEHPC) Book Series

Vijayan Sugumaran
Oakland University, USA

ISSN: 2327-3453
EISSN: 2327-3461

MISSION

The theory and practice of computing applications and distributed systems has emerged as one of the key areas of research driving innovations in business, engineering, and science. The fields of software engineering, systems analysis, and high performance computing offer a wide range of applications and solutions in solving computational problems for any modern organization.

The **Advances in Systems Analysis, Software Engineering, and High Performance Computing (ASASEHPC) Book Series** brings together research in the areas of distributed computing, systems and software engineering, high performance computing, and service science. This collection of publications is useful for academics, researchers, and practitioners seeking the latest practices and knowledge in this field.

COVERAGE

- Computer Graphics
- Computer Networking
- Computer System Analysis
- Distributed Cloud Computing
- Enterprise Information Systems
- Metadata and Semantic Web
- Parallel Architectures
- Performance Modeling
- Software Engineering
- Virtual Data Systems

IGI Global is currently accepting manuscripts for publication within this series. To submit a proposal for a volume in this series, please contact our Acquisition Editors at Acquisitions@igi-global.com or visit: http://www.igi-global.com/publish/.

Titles in this Series

For a list of additional titles in this series, please visit: www.igi-global.com

Systems and Software Development, Modeling, and Analysis New Perspectives and Methodologies
Mehdi Khosrow-Pour (Information Resources Management Association, USA)
Information Science Reference • copyright 2014 • 400pp • H/C (ISBN: 9781466660984) • US $215.00 (our price)

Handbook of Research on Emerging Advancements and Technologies in Software Engineering
Imran Ghani (Universiti Teknologi Malaysia, Malaysia) Wan Mohd Nasir Wan Kadir (Universiti Teknologi Malaysia, Malaysia) and Mohammad Nazir Ahmad (Universiti Teknologi Malaysia, Malaysia)
Engineering Science Reference • copyright 2014 • 478pp • H/C (ISBN: 9781466660267) • US $395.00 (our price)

Advancing Embedded Systems and Real-Time Communications with Emerging Technologies
Seppo Virtanen (University of Turku, Finland)
Information Science Reference • copyright 2014 • 308pp • H/C (ISBN: 9781466660342) • US $235.00 (our price)

Handbook of Research on High Performance and Cloud Computing in Scientific Research and Education
Marijana Despotović-Zrakić (University of Belgrade, Serbia) Veljko Milutinović (University of Belgrade, Serbia) and Aleksandar Belić (Institute of Physics, Serbia)
Information Science Reference • copyright 2014 • 350pp • H/C (ISBN: 9781466657847) • US $195.00 (our price)

Agile Estimation Techniques and Innovative Approaches to Software Process Improvement
Ricardo Colomo-Palacios (Universidad Carlos III de Madrid, Spain) Jose Antonio Calvo-Manzano Villalón (Universidad Politécnica De Madrid, Spain) Antonio de Amescua Seco (Universidad Carlos III de Madrid, Spain) and Tomás San Feliu Gilabert (Universidad Politécnica De Madrid, Spain)
Information Science Reference • copyright 2014 • 399pp • H/C (ISBN: 9781466651821) • US $215.00 (our price)

Enabling the New Era of Cloud Computing Data Security, Transfer, and Management
Yushi Shen (Microsoft, USA) Yale Li (Microsoft, USA) Ling Wu (EMC, USA) Shaofeng Liu (Microsoft, USA) and Qian Wen (Endronic Corp, USA)
Information Science Reference • copyright 2014 • 336pp • H/C (ISBN: 9781466648012) • US $195.00 (our price)

Theory and Application of Multi-Formalism Modeling
Marco Gribaudo (Politecnico di Milano, Italy) and Mauro Iacono (Seconda Università degli Studi di Napoli, Italy)
Information Science Reference • copyright 2014 • 314pp • H/C (ISBN: 9781466646599) • US $195.00 (our price)

Pervasive Cloud Computing Technologies Future Outlooks and Interdisciplinary Perspectives
Lucio Grandinetti (University of Calabria, Italy) Ornella Pisacane (Polytechnic University of Marche, Italy) and Mehdi Sheikhalishahi (University of Calabria, Italy)
Information Science Reference • copyright 2014 • 325pp • H/C (ISBN: 9781466646834) • US $190.00 (our price)

IGI GLOBAL
DISSEMINATOR of KNOWLEDGE

www.igi-global.com

701 E. Chocolate Ave., Hershey, PA 17033
Order online at www.igi-global.com or call 717-533-8845 x100
To place a standing order for titles released in this series, contact: cust@igi-global.com
Mon-Fri 8:00 am - 5:00 pm (est) or fax 24 hours a day 717-533-8661

Table of Contents

Section 1
Cloud Computing Concepts

Section 2
Cloud Computing in Education

Section 3
High Performance and Cloud Computing in Scientific Research

Section 4
Security Issues

Chapter 16

Detailed Table of Contents

Section 1
Cloud Computing Concepts

Chapter 1

Božidar Radenković, University of Belgrade, Serbia

Petar Kočović, Calisto Adriatic/Gartner, Serbia

The adoption of cloud computing accelerated significantly over the past few years, and this trend will remain. As cloud-computing technologies and vendors mature, more educational institutions will adopt the Internet-based computing style. Organizations will use cloud computing to reduce the cost of e-mail, IT infrastructure, data centers and storage, and business applications. Cloud computing is a model for enabling ubiquitous, convenient, on-demand network access to a shared pool of configurable computing resources (e.g., networks, servers, storage, applications, and services) that can be rapidly provisioned and released with minimal management effort or service provider interaction. This cloud model promotes availability and is composed of five essential characteristics, three service models, and four deployment models. The absence of a clear definition of cloud computing is slowing the adoption of cloud computing by needlessly increasing user apprehension and obscuring the cloud's benefits. Organizations need to understand cloud computing before they can realize its benefits and avoid its risks. This chapter clears up confusion about the cloud by defining cloud computing and its characteristics, architectural model, benefits, and shortcomings. This chapter provides the definition of the concept of cloud computing and cloud computing as a service. Subsequently, it explores the characteristics of different types of clouds, as well as the security aspect of this technology. Major trends of cloud computing, such as social computing, context-aware computing, and pattern based strategy, are described. In a conclusion, the authors provide an overview of future use of cloud computing.

This chapter is focused on the business model of scientific research, theoretically analysing managerial, organizational, and financial, rather than technical aspects of this concept. Theoretic explanation is based on an organizational networking platform. In practice, this platform is presented by Seven Bridges Genomics software solution, and the new opportunities for the organizational network broker are illustrated both in theory and practice. The impact that cloud computing has upon organizational performances is theoretically explained by costs of the ICT infrastructure, as well as of transactional and opportunity costs of operations. Through cloud computing, approach opportunity costs are reduced and efficiency is increased. The business model is presented in the framework of Osterwalder and Pigneur. By means of theoretical analysis and practical example, the authors demonstrate the development of a business model related to scientific research in bioinformatics. Cloud computing enables organizational separation of two distinct parts of the scientific research business model: core research and IT support. From the perspective of efficiency, network achieves a higher level of capital utilisation, better resistance to business risks, lower transaction costs, and in general, better efficiency, while the core research part has the opportunity to focus its structure on effectiveness and creativity.

Chapter 3

Existing approaches for management of digital identities within e-learning ecosystems imply defining different access parameters for each service or application. However, this can reduce system security and lead to insufficient usage of the services by end-users. This chapter investigates various approaches for identity management, particulary in a cloud computing environment. Several complex issues are discussed, such as cross-domain authentication, provisioning, multi-tenancy, delegation, and security. The main goal of the research is to provide a highly effective, scalable identity management for end-users in an educational private cloud. A federated identity concept was introduced as a solution that enables organizations to implement secure identity management and to share information on the identities of users in the cloud environment. As a proof of concept, the identity management system was implemented in the e-learning system of Faculty of Organizational Sciences, University of Belgrade.

Chapter 4

Applications are often multi-tier and require application servers, workflow engines, and database management systems. Cloud computing is a computing paradigm wherein the resources such as processors, storage, and software applications are provided as services via the Internet. Moving an enterprise application to the cloud can be a challenge. This application needs to be split into the components that then automatically deploy on the cloud. In this chapter, the authors introduce a way to automatically derivate the main architecture components from the software requirements that can serve as a basis for an architecture diagram in the MOCCA method. The proposed approach is model and use case driven.

Section 2
Cloud Computing in Education

Chapter 5

Zorica Bogdanović, University of Belgrade, Serbia
Aleksandar Milić, University of Belgrade, Serbia
Aleksandra Labus, University of Belgrade, Serbia

With rapid increase in the number of users, services, educational content, and required resources, educational institutions face new challenges in design and deployment of IT infrastructure for e-education. This chapter deals with defining and developing a model of IT infrastructure for e-learning by using cloud computing concept. The first challenge is adoption and implementation of digital identity management systems and the second is providing support for a system that would be able to use all advantages of federation systems for digital identities management. The experimental part of the chapter consists of a study directed towards the validation of the proposed IT infrastructure model for e-learning. Research was conducted in the Laboratory for E-Business at the Faculty of Organizational Sciences. The results of the research show that the implemented model of IT infrastructure enables the system of e-learning to be more efficient, flexible, and more economical.

Chapter 6

Dušan Barać, University of Belgrade, Serbia
Miloš Radenković, Union University, Serbia
Branislav Jovanić, University of Belgrade, Serbia

This chapter discusses providing mobile learning services on cloud. Mobile cloud computing brings numerous benefits and enables overcoming technical constraints of mobile learning. The main techniques and approaches in mobile cloud computing are analyzed. A model for mobile learning services delivering through cloud computing is proposed. Several examples of mobile learning services implementations on cloud are presented: Android native application that provides Moodle learning management system features and a SMS service and mobile application for managing the infrastructure of e-learning system.

Chapter 7

Marko Vulić, University of Belgrade, Serbia
Pavle Petrović, University of Belgrade, Serbia
Ivanka Kovačević, CT Computers, Serbia
Vanjica Ratković Živanović, Radio Television Serbia (RTS), Serbia

A new vision of higher education systems, in which the student is the central subject of the teaching process, opens up new learning opportunities that include customization of teaching methods to the students' needs, and new modes of communication both between teachers and students and among students themselves. The main subject of this chapter is the implementation and improvement of the Student Relationship Management (SRM) concept as a cloud service in an e-education system by using social media. The experimental part of the chapter presents the design and implementation of an e-education model based on cloud computing. The proposed model is implemented at the Faculty of Organizational Sciences, University of Belgrade, by using the existing cloud computing infrastructure of the Laboratory for E-Business.

L2 language learning is an activity that is becoming increasingly ubiquitous and learner-centric in order to support lifelong learning. Applications for learning are constrained by multiple technical and educational requirements and should support multiple platforms and multiple approaches to learning. This chapter investigates the possibility of applying ontology-based, dynamically generated learning objects implemented on a cloud computing infrastructure in order to satisfy these requirements. Previous work on using mobile learning objects is used as a starting point in an attempt to design a system that will preserve all of the advantages of utilizing learning objects, while eliminating any flaws and maximizing compatibility with existing systems. A model of a highly modular, flexible, multiplatform language learning system is presented along with some implementation remarks and advices for future implementation.

Section 3
High Performance and Cloud Computing in Scientific Research

This chapter introduces applications of High Performance Computing (HPC), Grid computing, and development of electronic infrastructures in Serbia, in the South Eastern Europe region, and in Europe as a whole. Grid computing represents one of the key enablers of scientific progress in many areas of research. Main HPC and Grid infrastructures, initiatives, projects and programs in Europe, Partnership for Advanced Computing in Europe (PRACE) and European Grid Initiative (EGI) associations, as well as Academic and Educational Grid Initiative of Serbia (AEGIS) are presented. Further, the chapter describes some of the applications related to the condensed matter physics, developed at the Scientific Computing Laboratory of the Institute of Physics, University of Belgrade.

Chapter 10

In modern computer systems, the effect known as the memory gap has become a serious bottleneck. It is becoming increasingly difficult to bridge this gap with traditional solutions, and much effort is put into developing new and more effective solutions to this problem. An earlier design, the Dual Data Cache (DDC), is a cache design that implies separation of data into two different cache subsystems so as to increase effectiveness of the cache. Data are separated accordingly to their predominant type of locality. The modified DDC, described here, introduces different internal organizations of the temporal and spatial parts, for better utilization of data characteristics. Conducted simulations show substantial improvements over traditional cache systems, with little increase in surface area and power consumption.

Meta-heuristics represent powerful tools for addressing hard combinatorial optimization problems. However, real life instances usually cannot be treated efficiently in "reasonable" computing times. Moreover, a major issue in meta-heuristic design and calibration is to provide high performance solutions for a variety of problems. Parallel meta-heuristics aim to address both issues. The objective of this chapter is to present a state-of-the-art survey of the main parallelization ideas and strategies, and to discuss general design principles applicable to all meta-heuristic classes. To achieve this goal, the authors explain various paradigms related to parallel meta-heuristic development, where communications, synchronization, and control aspects are the most relevant. They also discuss implementation issues pointing out the characteristics of shared and distributed memory multiprocessors as target architectures. All these topics are illustrated by the examples from recent literature related to the parallelization of various meta-heuristic methods. Here, the authors focus on Variable Neighborhood Search and Bee Colony Optimization.

This chapter is a review of the literature related to the use of cloud-based computer simulations in scientific research. The authors examine the types and good examples of cloud-based computer simulations, offering suggestions for the architecture, frameworks, and runtime infrastructures that support running simulations in cloud environment. Cloud computing has become the standard for providing hardware and software infrastructure. Using the possibilities offered by cloud computing platforms, researchers can efficiently use the already existing IT resources in solving computationally intensive scientific problems. Further on, the authors emphasize the possibilities of using the existing and already known simulation models and tools in the cloud computing environment. The cloud environment provides possibilities to execute all kinds of simulation experiments as in traditional environments. This way, models are accessible to a wider range of researchers and the analysis of data resulting from simulation experiments is significantly improved.

In this chapter, the authors discuss issues surrounding High Performance Computing (HPC)-driven science on the example of Peta science Monte Carlo experiments conducted at the Brookhaven National Laboratory (BNL), one of the US Department of Energy (DOE) High Energy and Nuclear Physics (HENP) research sites. BNL, hosting the only remaining US-based HENP experiments and apparatus, seem appropriate to study the nature of the High-Throughput Computing (HTC) hungry experiments and short historical development of the HPC technology used in such experiments. The development of parallel processors, multiprocessor systems, custom clusters, supercomputers, networked super systems, and hierarchical parallelisms are presented in an evolutionary manner. Coarse grained, rigid Grid system parallelism is contrasted by cloud computing, which is classified within this chapter as flexible and fine grained soft system parallelism. In the process of evaluating various high performance computing options, a clear distinction between high availability-bound enterprise and high scalability-bound scientific computing is made. This distinction is used to further differentiate cloud from the pre-cloud computing technologies and fit cloud computing better into the scientific HPC.

Chapter 14

Slađana Janković, University of Belgrade, Serbia
Snežana Mladenović, University of Belgrade, Serbia
Slavko Vesković, University of Belgrade, Serbia

This chapter analyzes the possibilities of applying the cloud concepts in the realization of the interoperable electronic business of traffic and transport subjects. Special attention is paid to defining the Business-to-Business (B2B) model of integrating the traffic business subjects in cloud computing technological environment. It describes the design, implementation, and application of the cloud concepts on the examples of B2B integration in the field of traffic. The examples demonstrate the usage of Platform-as-a-Service (PaaS) and Software-as-a-Service (SaaS) by traffic business subjects in the Republic of Serbia. The examples of PaaS are the databases created and hosted on Microsoft SQL Azure platform. The examples of SaaS are Web services hosted on Microsoft Windows Azure platform. The defined model of B2B integration allows interoperability of the traffic business subjects on the syntactic, conceptual, and semantic level.

Chapter 15

Boban Stojanović, Faculty of Science, University of Kragujevac, Serbia
Nikola Milivojević, "Jaroslav Černi" Institute for the Development of Water Resources, Serbia
Miloš Ivanović, Faculty of Science, University of Kragujevac, Serbia
Dejan Divac, "Jaroslav Černi" Institute for the Development of Water Resources, Serbia

Real-world problems often contain nonlinearities, relationships, and uncertainties that are too complex to be modeled analytically. In these scenarios, simulation-based optimization is a powerful tool to determine optimal system parameters. Evolutionary Algorithms (EAs) are robust and powerful techniques for optimization of complex systems that perfectly fit into this concept. Since evolutionary algorithms require a large number of time expensive evaluations of candidate solutions, the whole process of optimization can take huge CPU time. In this chapter, .NET platform for distributed evaluation using WCF (Windows Communication Foundation) Web services is presented in order to reduce computational time. This concept provides parallelization of evolutionary algorithms independently of geographic location and platform where evaluation is performed. Hydroinformatics is a typical representative of fields where complex systems with many uncertainties are studied. Application of the developed platform in hydroinformatics is also presented in this chapter.

Section 4
Security Issues

Chapter 16

Miodrag J. Mihaljević, Mathematical Institute, Serbian Academy of Sciences and Arts, Serbia
    & Chuo University, Japan
Hideki Imai, Chuo University, Japan

The main security and privacy issues of cloud computing as well as the related implications are addressed, and a general framework for achieving the goals is summarized. This chapter basically considers scientific and educational employment of a cloud as a particular instance of a public cloud and its security, and as a potentially specific issue, a request for a heavy minimization of the costs implied by security is pointed out. Consequently, the problem of minimization of the overheads implied by security/privacy mechanisms is addressed. The main security requirements are given as well as the main recommendations, providing a framework for the security management. As a particular issue, data protection is considered and significance of data access control and encryption are discussed. Accordingly, an illustrative approach for achieving lightweight and provable secure encryption is shown. The considered encryption is based on joint employment of cryptographic and coding methods.

Foreword

Cloud computing has gained adoption in many areas of general purpose computing, especially for Web service-based applications, productivity applications such as office applications, and for delivering IT from the Cloud. For security-sensitive applications, the notion of private Clouds, offers more secure delivery, and outsourcing—either onsite or offsite—has moved towards Cloud-based platforms such as OpenStack. Even government agencies endeavor using Clouds, as witnessed by the recent contract by US government, and that has been common practice in other parts of the world, especially in Europe. Most traditional IT companies (both hardware and software), such as HP, IBM, and Microsoft, offer Cloud solutions in addition to early providers such as Amazon and Salesforce.

HPC in the Cloud has gained slower acceptance due to the nature of most HPC applications: large scale, but tightly coupled and therefore sensitive to noise introduced by shared infrastructures, un-optimized operating systems, and anything but low latency networks. Virtualization, which is best suited for multi-tenanted Cloud, is another source of noise for HPC applications. Therefore, HPC in the Cloud was limited to a) testing, debugging, and, in general, development of HPC applications, b) small-scale tightly coupled applications, and c) embarrassingly parallel applications. Traditional high-scale, tightly coupled applications continue to run on supercomputers; just as traditional banking has done, transactions software will continue to run on mainframes despite the fact that the sweet spot of computing moved away from mainframes longtime ago.

Nevertheless, the HPC in the Cloud has a very promising future as Cloud providers increasingly offer HPC-friendly hardware (e.g. dedicated clusters with improved networking, such as 10GE and Infiniband), as virtualization gains more maturity and introduces less noise for HPC, and, finally, with the introduction of noise-tolerant HPC applications. Most promising is the introduction of photonic networks, both off chip and on chip that will circumvent some of the most challenging issues of tightly coupled applications. From the economic perspective, supporting onsite IT becomes increasingly cost-prohibitive and requires moving both hardware and software into common shared pools, such as the Cloud.

The book, *High Performance and Cloud Computing in Scientific Research and Education*, is a series of studies systematically introducing general notions of Cloud computing, followed by its application to education, scientific research, and one of the most commonly addressed issue of Clouds: security. The book is written by renowned experts in the field, who bring out the intrinsic challenges, benefits, and intricacies of Cloud computing applied to education and scientific research. The book can be read cover to cover or selectively in areas of interest to audience (four individual parts) or even narrowing down to specific areas, such as mobile Cloud, Cloud-based computer simulation, e-business in traffic sector, and .Net platform for applications in hydro informatics.

The book is intended for a) novel readers who can benefit from understanding general concepts of the Cloud, b) general practitioners who seek guidance into the field of Cloud computing to better understand its opportunities and applicability, and c) experts in the field who can benefit from detailed analysis of specific problems and solutions described in individual studies. The authors introduce a blend of scientific and engineering concepts, benefiting both academics and practitioners audiences.

Dejan Milojičić
HP Labs, USA

Dejan Milojičić *is a senior researcher and senior manager at HP Labs, Palo Alto, CA (1998-), working in the technical areas of systems software, distributed systems, Cloud computing, high performance computing, and service management. He is IEEE Computer Society 2014 President. He has served on many program committees of conferences and on journal editorial boards. He has been a member of IEEE CS, ACM, and USENIX for over 20 years. Prior to HP Labs, he worked in OSF Research Institute, Cambridge, MA (1994-1998), and Institute "Mihajlo Pupin," Belgrade, Serbia (1983-1991). He is teaching a class on Cloud Management at SJSU, San Jose, CA. He received his PhD from University of Kaiserslautern, Germany (1993) and MSc/BSc from Belgrade University, Serbia (1983/86). Dejan is an IEEE Fellow, ACM Distinguished Engineer, and USENIX member. Dejan has published over 130 papers and 2 books; he has 12 patents and 25 patent applications.*

Preface

Requirements for the design and implementation of information systems that are used for educational and research purposes have become more complex. These information systems include a plethora of services, applications, resources, and interactions. The resulting conglomerate of services and solutions is becoming increasingly difficult to deal with and improve further. In addition, new and extremely important concepts, such as mobility, pervasiveness, services on demand, have further fuelled the need for change and improvement of the existing approaches. With a huge growth in the number of users, services, contents, and resources, these systems have become more and more large-scale. One of the basic problems in developing a model of infrastructure for educational and research institutions is how to provide scalability and reliability of applications and services. As a result, efforts to design a new computing architecture, the so-called cloud computing, have been initiated over the last couple of years and are ongoing across the world. New paradigms such as high performance computing and cloud computing will provide a reliable and cost-effective IT infrastructure that enhances the realization of research and educational processes.

The main subject of the book is a high performance computing and cloud computing application in the areas of scientific research and education. Supercomputers are used for compute-intensive tasks such as problems including quantum physics, weather forecasting, climate research, oil and gas exploration, molecular modeling, and physical simulations. Cloud computing is an emerging area that includes a set of disciplines, technologies, and business models used to deliver IT capabilities as an on-demand, scalable, elastic service. This book presents various concepts and applications of high performance and cloud computing in the fields of scientific research and education.

The primary goal of this book is to provide a variety of research and survey articles in the field of modern computer technologies and their application in science and education. Findings and discussion provided within the book should foster potentials and capabilities of research, of the academic community, and of industry as well. The publication is oriented towards making an impact in practice. The research presented in the book will leverage the dissemination of knowledge and awareness of potential benefits of high performance and cloud computing.

The target audience of this book is composed of professionals and researchers working in the field of information and communication technologies and their application in scientific research and education. Researchers and scholars will gain insight onto how modern technologies can be used as a support for scientific research. The book will also provide resources on how cloud technologies can be used to build an effective infrastructure of educational institutions. Administrators, technicians, teachers, and researchers within education and research institutions are the prime target of the book. This book is also beneficial to computer and system infrastructure designers, developers, business managers, entrepreneurs, and investors within the cloud computing-related industry.

The real value of the proposed book is reflected in a variety of experimental studies and case studies within real systems for e-learning, m-learning, high performance computing laboratories, scientific laboratories as well as implementations and solutions within a scope of a few international projects in the area of cloud computing, high performance computing, physics, etc.

The book content is divided into four sections: "Cloud Computing Concepts," "Cloud Computing in Education," "High Performance and Cloud Computing in Scientific Research," and "Security Issues."

The first section of the book discusses the main concepts and implications of cloud computing. In the chapter "From Mainframe to Cloud," the authors define cloud computing, the related types, and models. The major trends of cloud computing, such as social computing, context-aware computing, and pattern-based strategy are described. In the conclusion, the authors provide an overview of the future use of cloud computing. In the chapter "Organizational and Management Aspects of Cloud Computing Application in Scientific Research," the authors discuss the differences between the traditional and the cloud computing approaches to information and communication technologies in the organization. By means of theoretical analysis and practical examples, the authors demonstrate the development of the business model related to scientific research in bioinformatics. The impacts of cloud computing on organizational structure and organizational performance are analyzed. The components of the Seven Bridges Genomics Business model are discussed with respect to cloud computing. The chapter titled "Digital Identity Management in Cloud" investigates various approaches to identity management, particularly in a cloud computing environment. Several complex issues are discussed, such as cross-domain authentication, provisioning, multi-tenancy, delegation, and security. The main goal of the research is to provide a highly effective, scalable identity management for end-users in an educational private cloud. A federated identity concept was introduced as a solution that enables the organization to implement secure identity management and to share information on the identities of users in the cloud environment. As a proof of concept, the identity management system was implemented in an e-learning system. The chapter "From Software Specification to Cloud Model" is related to software design and deployment on cloud computing infrastructure. The method has been described using various steps to be performed and artifacts to be created in order to move the software in the cloud. The move2cloud problem emphasizes the problem of rearranging the software components into groups that might be provisioned into different clouds. The architecture model describes architectural components of the software, and it is the initial model in the MOCCA method. The authors have introduced a model and use case driven transformation that can be used to automatically derive architectural model from software requirements specification.

The second section of the book discusses the possibilities of cloud computing applications in education. The first chapter in this section, titled "Model of E-Education Infrastructure based on Cloud Computing" deals with defining and developing a model of IT infrastructure for e-learning by using the cloud computing concept. The chapter demonstrates a measurable improvement of the e-learning system by developing infrastructure for e-learning through CC. The experimental part of the chapter consists of a study directed towards the validation of the proposed IT infrastructure model for e-learning. The results of the study have shown that the implemented model enabled the e-learning system to be more efficient, more flexible, and more economical. The chapter "Mobile Learning Services on Cloud" discusses mobile learning services in a cloud environment. Mobile cloud computing brings numerous benefits and enables overcoming technical constraints of mobile learning. Cloud computing service models: IaaS, PaaS, and particularly SaaS, provide flexible and efficient ways to augment computing, storage, and communication capabilities of mobile learning services and applications. This chapter investigates the possibilities for delivering mobile learning services through cloud computing. The main techniques and approaches in mobile cloud computing are analyzed, particularly Weblets and cloudlets. A model for mobile learning services delivery through cloud computing is proposed. Further, several examples of mobile learning services implementations on cloud are presented. The next chapter, "Student Relationship Management Using Social Clouds," introduces implementation and improvement of the Student Relationship Management (SRM) concept as a cloud service in an e-education system by using social media. The experimental part of the chapter presents the design and implementation of SRM in e-education based on cloud computing. SRM was provided as SaaS on cloud computing infrastructure for e-learning. The chapter "Ontology-Based Multimodal Language Learning" investigates the possibility of applying ontology-based, dynamically generated learning objects implemented on a cloud computing infrastructure in order to satisfy the requirements for ubiquitous and learner-centric language learning. The authors have designed an ontology-based, modular, flexible, and multiplatform system for mobile language learning that preserves the advantages of utilizing learning objects from learning management systems.

The third section of the book is related to cloud computing applications in scientific research within different areas. The chapter "High Performance and Grid Computing Developments and Applications in Condensed Matter Physics" introduces applications of High Performance Computing (HPC), Grid computing, and development of electronic infrastructures in Serbia, in the South Eastern Europe region, and in Europe as a whole. Grid computing is designed and optimized for large-scale distributed computing, ideally supporting the execution of an enormous numbers of independent tasks (Monte Carlo simulations, search of large, multidimensional parameter spaces). On the other hand, HPC is ideally suited for capability computing, when solving of challenging problems requires highly parallel and scalable systems, able to support simultaneous execution of tens of thousands parallel processes. The main HPC and Grid infrastructures, initiatives, projects and programs in Europe, Partnership for Advanced Computing in Europe (PRACE) and European Grid Initiative (EGI) associations, as well as Academic and Educational Grid Initiative of Serbia (AEGIS) are presented. Further, the chapter describes some of the applications related to the condensed matter physics, developed at the Scientific Computing Laboratory of the Institute of Physics in Belgrade. The chapter "Exploiting Spatial and Temporal Patterns in a High-Performance CPU" introduces an approach to improve traditional cache systems. The main idea behind Dual Data Cache (DDC) is that two different types of locality (spatial and temporal) in data access patterns can be observed, and that data exhibiting predominantly one of these types of localities should be treated differently from the data that exhibit the other. The modified DDC described in the chapter introduces different internal organizations of the temporal and spatial parts, for better utilization of data characteristics. Conducted simulations showed substantial improvements over traditional cache systems, with little increase in the surface area and power consumption. The chapter "Designing Parallel Meta-Heuristic Methods" discusses meta-heuristics as powerful tools for addressing hard combinatorial optimization problems. A major issue in the meta-heuristic design and calibration is to provide high performance solutions for a variety of problems. Parallel meta-heuristics aim to address both issues. The objective of this chapter is to present a state-of-the-art survey of the main parallelization ideas and strategies, and to discuss general design principles applicable to all meta-heuristic classes. To achieve this goal, the authors explain various paradigms related to parallel meta-heuristic development, where communications, synchronization, and control aspects are the most relevant. They also discuss implementation issues pointing out the characteristics of shared and distributed memory multiprocessors as target architectures. All these topics are illustrated by the examples from the literature related to the parallelization of various meta-heuristic methods. The authors focus on the Variable Neighborhood

Search and Bee Colony Optimization. The chapter titled "Application of Cloud-Based Simulation in Scientific Research" is a review of the literature related to the use of cloud-based computer simulations in scientific research. The authors examine the types and good examples of cloud-based computer simulations, offering models for the architecture, frameworks, and runtime infrastructures, which support running simulations in a cloud environment. Using the possibilities offered by cloud computing platforms, researchers can efficiently use the already existing IT resources in solving computationally intensive scientific problems. Further on, the authors emphasize the possibilities of using the existing and already known simulation models and tools in a loud computing environment. The chapter "Grids, Clouds, and Massive Simulations" discusses issues surrounding high performance computing-driven science on the example of the Petascale science Monte Carlo experiments conducted at the Brookhaven National Laboratory. The nature of the HPC hungry experiments is described. The development of parallel processors, multiprocessor systems, custom clusters, supercomputers, networked super systems, and hierarchical parallelisms are presented in an evolutionary manner. A coarse-grained, rigid Grid system parallelism is contrasted by cloud computing which is classified as flexible and fine-grained soft system parallelism. Advantages and disadvantages of using Grid, Cloud, or Grid/Cloud hybrid for Petascale science experiments are comparatively analyzed. In the process of evaluating various high performance computing options, a clear distinction between a high availability-bound enterprise and high scalability-bound scientific computing is made. This distinction is used to further differentiate the cloud from the pre-cloud computing technologies and fit cloud computing better into the scientific HPC. The chapter "Model of Interoperable E-Business in Traffic Sector based on Cloud Computing Concepts" analyzes the possibilities of applying the cloud concepts in the realization of the interoperable electronic business of traffic and transport subjects. Special attention is paid to defining the Business-to-Business (B2B) model of integrating the traffic business subjects in cloud computing technological environment. It describes the design, implementation, and application of the Cloud concepts on the examples of B2B integration in the field of traffic. The examples demonstrate the usage of PaaS and SaaS by traffic business subjects in the Republic of Serbia. The defined model of B2B integration allows for interoperability of the traffic business subjects on the syntactic, conceptual, and semantic levels. The chapter "DotNet Platform for Distributed Evolutionary Algorithms with Application in Hydroinformatics" describes .NET platform for distributed evaluation using WCF (Windows Communication Foundation) Web services in order to reduce computational time. This concept provides a parallelization of evolutionary algorithms independently of the geographic location and platform where evaluation is performed. Hydroinformatics is a typical representative of fields where complex systems with many uncertainties are studied. Application of the developed platform in hydroinformatics is also presented. Two real-world benchmarks were performed with different single individual evaluation complexity and different hardware/software platform to run on. The first one used relatively complex individual evaluation in the environment of ordinary LAN of office PCs. The second used a bit less complex individual evaluation on the real HPC resource – a computational cluster running Mono on top of Linux kernel and libraries. Both benchmarks have shown a significant speedup and good scalability potential. In order to properly quantify how the expense of a single evaluation affects speedup and scalability, the additional benchmarks have been performed, this time with quasi-evaluators simulating various durations. The results of this additional analysis are of practical use – one can take them as a guideline to estimate the duration of a very long EA run in a heuristic fashion.

The concluding section of the book discusses issues related to the security of cloud computing. The chapter "Security Issues of Cloud Computing and an Encryption Approach" considers scientific and educational employment of a cloud as a particular instance of a public cloud and its security, and also as a potentially specific issue; a request for a heavy minimization of the costs implied by security is pointed out. Consequently, the problem of minimization of the overheads implied by security/privacy mechanisms is addressed. The main security requirements are given as well as the main recommendations, providing a framework for the security management. As a particular issue, data protection is considered and the significance of data access control and encryption are discussed. Accordingly, an illustrative approach to achieving lightweight and provable secure encryption is shown. The considered encryption is based on joint employment of cryptographic and coding methods.

This book provides numerous examples, practical solutions, and applications of high performance computing and Cloud computing that can improve capacity, capability, and quality of research, teaching, and learning processes. Setting up new IT infrastructures and services, as well as enabling efficient and cost-effective usage of software and hardware resources, are of significant importance, particularly in developing countries. In addition, the presented works are expected to contribute to introducing cloud computing and high performance application and services in business and industry as well.

Marijana Despotović-Zrakić
University of Belgrade, Serbia

Veljko Milutinović
University of Belgrade, Serbia

Aleksandar Belić
University of Belgrade, Serbia

Acknowledgment

The editors are thankful to the Ministry of Education, Science, and Technological Development, Republic of Serbia, for financial support, grant number 174031.

Marijana Despotović-Zrakić
University of Belgrade, Serbia

Veljko Milutinović
University of Belgrade, Serbia

Aleksandar Belić
University of Belgrade, Serbia

Section 1
Cloud Computing Concepts

Chapter 1
From Mainframe to Cloud

Božidar Radenković
University of Belgrade, Serbia

Petar Kočović
Calisto Adriatic/Gartner, Serbia

ABSTRACT

The adoption of cloud computing accelerated significantly over the past few years, and this trend will remain. As cloud-computing technologies and vendors mature, more educational institutions will adopt the Internet-based computing style. Organizations will use cloud computing to reduce the cost of e-mail, IT infrastructure, data centers and storage, and business applications. Cloud computing is a model for enabling ubiquitous, convenient, on-demand network access to a shared pool of configurable computing resources (e.g., networks, servers, storage, applications, and services) that can be rapidly provisioned and released with minimal management effort or service provider interaction. This cloud model promotes availability and is composed of five essential characteristics, three service models, and four deployment models. The absence of a clear definition of cloud computing is slowing the adoption of cloud computing by needlessly increasing user apprehension and obscuring the cloud's benefits. Organizations need to understand cloud computing before they can realize its benefits and avoid its risks. This chapter clears up confusion about the cloud by defining cloud computing and its characteristics, architectural model, benefits, and shortcomings. This chapter provides the definition of the concept of cloud computing and cloud computing as a service. Subsequently, it explores the characteristics of different types of clouds, as well as the security aspect of this technology. Major trends of cloud computing, such as social computing, context-aware computing, and pattern based strategy, are described. In a conclusion, the authors provide an overview of future use of cloud computing.

DOI: 10.4018/978-1-4666-5784-7.ch001

INTRODUCTION

History of Cloud Computing

The concept of cloud computing dates from the earliest years of computing. The notion of an individual personal computer was laughable; computers were expensive, fragile, and rare. Computers were designed with the assumption they would run many programs for many users. This was simply the most efficient solution to the limited resources of the day. The underlying concept of cloud computing dates back to the 1960s when John McCarthy opined that computation may someday be organized as a public utility (Abelson, 1999). While the introduction of affordable personal computers in the 1970s and 1980s was a huge step forward in many ways, it was a big setback for cloud computing. At that time, most users preferred to store data on floppy drives, rather than in a remote, centralized location. Also, applications were quite platform-dependent; a PC user might have no way of communicating or sharing data with the Apple user next door. It was a big step back for security as well; with system administration the responsibility of data loss, crashes, and virus infections became widespread. With the popularization of the World Wide Web in the 1990s, the world changed. At that time, most users' Internet needs were simple: look up information, send email, etc. But over time, the way people use the Internet has changed. Cloud computing promises a future where the only local application most users will need is a Web browser.

Modern Cloud Computing

The term *cloud* might have originated in the telecommunications industry. The basic idea is that the most efficient path for data to flow from Point A to Point B cannot be pre-determined by a human operator. Rather, you must trust your switching system to route the data efficiently on a moment-by-moment basis. The term *telecom cloud* refers to the following abstract process; the user you broadcasts its message into the cloud and trusts it to come out the other side, without knowing or caring what happens to the data in between. Hence, cloud computing can be seen as a movement to apply the telecom industry's innovations and economies of scale to the computer industry. The first scholarly use of the term *cloud computing* appears in a 1997 lecture by Ramnath Chellappa of the University of Texas (Chellappa, 1997). Key players in cloud computing of the late-twentieth century included IBM, Microsoft, and Amazon.

Cloud computing became widely recognized around the year 2007, when the Google Docs service went mainstream. Google provided a full, virtualized office suite that could be accessed for free from any Internet-connected computer. In a world where an office software suite can cost hundreds of dollars, the appeal of such a service is obvious. Many cloud applications targeted at individual consumers are free to use. However, there is also a growing category of paid cloud applications targeted at scientists. The benefit is to reduce the IT budget by "outsourcing" critical applications to the cloud. Data backup, security, development of new features, etc. become the responsibility of the application's provider, rather than an internal IT department.

Another growing cloud computing application is cloud based customer relationship management. As the idea of "Software as a Service" (SaaS) became widespread, comparisons with other industries became useful. Cell phone users, for example, will gladly sign a service contract and pay a monthly fee, as long as they get the features they want. Having this in mind, it is necessary to think of the many ways in which businesses that provide cloud computing services can deepen and enrich their relationship with the users.

DEFINITION

Cloud computing on-demand, pay-as-you-go service model is transforming IT from massive, cumbersome, internal cost centers into agile, reactive, external services that are used not merely as business tools, but as the medium by which business is conducted. Unfortunately, the absence of a clear definition, in addition to vendor hype, questionable business cases, and indeterminate risks, confuses users and hinders cloud adoption. Organizations that understand cloud computing can take advantage of its strengths and avoid its risks.

Blakley and Reeves (2010) define cloud computing as a set of disciplines, technologies, and business models used to deliver IT capabilities (software, platforms, hardware) as an on-demand, scalable, elastic service. National Institute of Science and Technology (NIST) defines cloud computing as a model for enabling ubiquitous, convenient, on-demand network access to a shared pool of configurable computing resources (e.g., networks, servers, storage, applications, and services) that can be rapidly provisioned and released with minimal management effort or service provider interaction. This cloud model promotes availability and is composed of five essential characteristics, three service models, and four deployment models (Mell & Grance, 2011). This definition is depicted in Figure 1.

From the technical point of view, Cloud computing implies TCP/IP based high development and the integration of computer technologies such as fast microprocessor, huge memory, high-speed network and reliable system architecture. Standard inter-connect protocols and developed data center technologies too represent a necessity for the development of cloud computing.

The term cloud computing became widely heard in October 2007 when IBM and Google announced collaboration in cloud computing (IBM, 2007). Beside the Web email, the Amazon Elastic Compute Cloud (EC2), Google App Engine and Salesforce's CRM largely represent a promising conceptual foundation of cloud services. The services of cloud computing are broadly divided into three categories: Infrastructure-as-a-Service (IaaS), Platform-as-a-Service (PaaS), and Software-as-a-Service (SaaS) (Buyya, Yeo, Venugopal, Broberg, & Brandic, 2009). Cloud computing can also be divided into five layers including clients, applications, platform, infrastructure and servers.

Figure 1. NIST cloud computing model

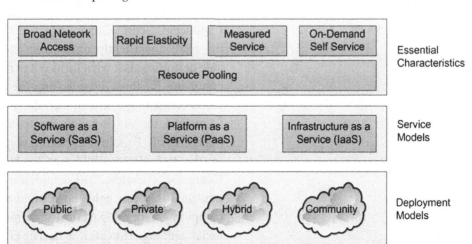

Listing common characteristics found in many cloud computing services will provide scope to the definition and aid in comprehension. As shown in Figure 2, common characteristics include:

1. **Shared Infrastructure:** As a part of doing business, cloud providers invest in and build the infrastructure necessary to offer software, platforms or infrastructure as a service to multiple consumers. The infrastructure and environment necessary to house it represents a large capital expense and ongoing operational expense that the provider must recoup before making a profit. As a result, users should be aware that service providers have a financial incentive to leverage the infrastructure across as many consumers as possible.

2. **On-Demand Self-Service:** On-demand self-service is the cloud user's (i.e., consumer) ability to purchase and use cloud services as the need arises. In some cases, cloud vendors provide an application program-ming interface (API) that enables the user to programmatically (or automatically through a management application) use a service.

3. **Elastic and Scalable:** From a user point of view, cloud computing ability to quickly provide and withdraw IT services creates an elastic, scalable IT resource. Users pay for only the IT services they use. Although no IT service is infinitely scalable, the cloud service provider's ability to meet user's IT needs creates the perception that the service is infinitely scalable and increases its value.

4. **Consumption-Based Pricing Model:** Providers charge the user per amount of service used. For example, cloud vendors may charge for the service by the hour or gigabytes stored per month.

Dynamic and virtualized: The need to leverage the infrastructure across as many users as possible typically drives cloud vendors to create a more agile and efficient infrastructure that can move user workloads, lower overhead and increase service quality. Many vendors choose server virtualization to create this dynamic infrastructure.

Understanding Cloud Computing

A universally accepted cloud computing defini-tion remains elusive. However, definition of cloud computing (Plummer, Smith, Bittman, Cearley, Cappuccio, Scott, Kumar et al., 2009) remains the most consistently unchanged and explain-able definition. But what turns out to be the most confusing for those approaching the subject of cloud computing is not, in fact, the definition. It is, instead, the words people use to describe the phenomenon. To help alleviate this concern, "Us-ing the Right Words Will Ease Cloud Computing Confusion" (Cearley, 2010, para. 4) provides some guidance that can help those discussing cloud computing to develop a consistent framework of understanding. However, a further challenge to

Figure 2. Cloud computing characteristics (Adapted from Kocovic, 2013)

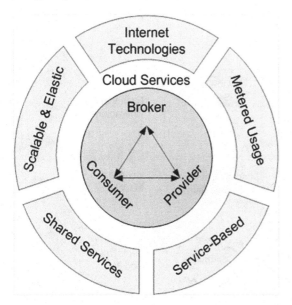

achieve a common understanding of the concept of cloud computing comes from the fact that different constituencies view the cloud from different perspectives. Austin, Smith, and Cappuccio (2009) explore this issue in some detail.

At a high level, understanding the relationship of global class and cloud is also a good foundation for understanding. Global class is primarily a type of thinking (Smith & Plummer, 2009). In terms of technology, this thinking manifests itself in two ways: global-class applications and global-class systems. A global-class application is best described as one that was developed with global-class thinking, and as having attributes such as using WOA, a style of service-oriented architecture (SOA).

Global-class systems provide the necessary elasticity and scalability (upward and downward) to power global-class applications. Enabling technologies and approaches include virtualization, parallel processing, grid computing, extreme transaction processing (XTP), and real-time infrastructure (RTI). Much of the focus in global-class systems is around input/output (I/O) and optimizations in that area. These enabling technologies and approaches are helpful but are not sufficient for an application to be global-class. After all, it is primarily the thinking, rather than the technology, that is the main determinant.

Comparing Cloud Computing and Infrastructure

Utility deals with the differences and synergies between these two concepts. There are many ways to "slice" into cloud computing. A "horizontal" slicing along the lines of public vs. private and hybrid deployment models is one way. Developing further the Spectrum of Public-to-Private Cloud Computing we are taking into account the nuances introduced by the "private cloud" concept. Another way to slice it is "vertically," along the lines of somewhat-traditional layering approaches, but adjusted to meet the realities of the cloud.

Cloud computing is deployed using one or more of five models (Blakley & Reeves, 2010; Plummer, Smith, Reeves, Robertson, Austin, & McDonald, 2010; Kočović, 2012):

- **Public Cloud:** An IT capability as a service that cloud providers offer to any user over the public Internet. Examples: Saleforce.com, Google App Engine, Microsoft Azure, and Amazon EC2.
- **Private Cloud:** An IT capability as a service that cloud providers offer to a selected group of users. The cloud service provider may be an internal IT organization (i.e., the same organization as the user) or a third party. The network used to offer the service may be the public Internet or a private network, but service access is restricted to authorized users. Example: hospitals or universities that band together to purchase infrastructure and build cloud services for their private consumption.
- **Internal Cloud:** A subset of a private cloud, an internal cloud is an IT capability offered as a service by an IT organization to its business. For example, IT organizations building highly virtualized environments can become infrastructure providers to internal application developers. In a typical IT organization, application developers are required to work through the IT infrastructure operations team to procure and provide the development and production application platform (e.g., hardware, OS, and middleware) necessary to house a new application. In this model, the infrastructure team provides cloud-like IT infrastructure to the application development team (or any other IT team) thereby allowing it to provide its own application platform.
- **External Cloud:** An IT capability offered as a service to a business that is not hosted by its own IT organization. An external

cloud can be public or private, but must be implemented by a third party.

- **Hybrid Cloud:** An IT capability offered as a service using both internal and external IT resources.

CLOUD COMPUTING: ".AAS"

Cloud computing sets the stage for a new approach to IT that enables individuals and businesses to choose how they'll acquire or deliver IT services, with reduced emphasis on the constraints of traditional software and hardware licensing models. The emergence of cloud/Web platforms enables the work of composite applications and composite businesses, and has the potential to have a profound impact on IT and business. The push to deliver information, Websites and Web-based applications as a complex Web service is a key catalyst that is driving the delivery of "everything as a service."

In order to clarify the term "everything as a Service," it might be practical to state the USA National Institute of Standards and Technology (part of US Department of Commerce) definitions (Mell & Grance, 2011):

- **Cloud Software as a Service (SaaS):** The user is permitted to use the provider's applications running on a cloud infrastructure. The applications are accessible from various client devices through a thin client interface such as a Web browser (e.g., Web-based email). The user does not manage or control the underlying cloud infrastructure including network, servers, operating systems, storage, or even individual application capabilities, with the possible exception of limited user-specific application configuration settings.

- **Cloud Platform as a Service (PaaS):** The user is permitted to deploy user-created or acquired applications onto the cloud infrastructure. These applications are created using programming languages and tools supported by the provider. The user does not manage or control the underlying cloud infrastructure including network, servers, operating systems, or storage, but has control over the deployed applications and possibly application hosting environment configurations.

- **Cloud Infrastructure as a Service (IaaS):** The user is permitted to provision processing, storage, networks, and other fundamental computing resources where the user is able to deploy and run arbitrary software, which can include operating systems and applications. The user does not manage or control the underlying cloud infrastructure but has control over operating systems, storage, deployed applications, and possibly limited control of select networking components (e.g., host firewalls).

Summary is shown in Table 1.

According to Kocovic (2013) the cloud offers the four categories of services shown in Figure 3.

Three Pillars of Cloud Computing

Three major areas, or pillars, of issues concerning cloud computing includes:

- Finance and economics
- Risk mitigation and management
- Business enablement.

Finance and Economics

Much of the buzz around cloud computing is based on the assumption that it is a less costly way to provide IT-related services to the organization. Cost savings are expected to come largely from paying for cloud-computing resources in proportion to use, rather than by purchasing hardware and software directly. Also, with cloud computing, the

Table 1. Summary of cloud layers

Cloud Layer	Use When	Example
Software as a service (SaaS)	The user's desired functionality is available in a complete form from an external provider. The provider does the development and hosting. The user just uses it.	Salesforce.com
Platform as a service (PaaS)	The user wants to perform the development, but needs a set of pre-built services to accelerate the development work. The user also needs the service of hosting.	Microsoft Azure
Infrastructure as a service (IaaS)	The user doesn't want to host its solution at all. The solution may be something the user built or purchased.	Amazon EC2

Figure 3. Four tiers of services offered by the cloud architecture (Adapted from Kocovic, 2013)

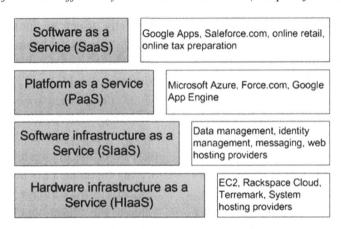

cost is moved from capital expense to operating expense, which means the cash flow impact is spread over the usage of the resource rather than heavily weighted upfront. Therefore, cloud-based services have financial advantages when capital is constrained or cash flow is under pressure. There is also an associated reduction in internal IT support costs and "hard" dollar cost savings in hardware maintenance, data center floor space, energy, or heating, ventilation and air-conditioning, as well as an associated reduction in the carbon footprint. Moreover, most cloud providers have tremendous leverage with hardware vendors and expertise in virtualizing storage, networks, processing and others that even the largest enterprises have difficulty matching.

There are many factors that must be considered when evaluating the financial impact of cloud computing, including license/subscription cost, implementation, infrastructure costs, IT support and upgrade costs. Cloud computing is not always less expensive than on-premises computing. On-premises equipment is usually depreciated or amortized over a three to five-year period. Therefore, the cost of using that equipment drops annually. However, the price of computing in the cloud will not undergo a similar or consistent drop over the same period. In fact, usage may go up, which will lead to the increased cost of computing resources in the cloud. The time horizon and the cost of migration from existing on premises computing to cloud computing must be weighed against the cost savings of moving to cloud computing. These costs include migration, implementation, training and process redesign.

Also, one must take into account the variability of service consumption in a cloud model. Since services will be paid for by subscription or in a "pay as you go" style, there is the possibility that some months will vary wildly above or below other months. C-level executives will need to plan for much more variability in spending to gain the agility inherent in cloud computing. The C-level executives should engage with the CIO to gain a better understanding of the IT service portfolios, service-level requirements and service costs to fully grasp the financial implications of a cloud-computing strategy and to identify and prioritize the highest value opportunities to embrace the cloud computing.

Risk Mitigation and Management

Cloud computing comes with its share of risks that must be considered as part of the development of a cloud-computing strategy. These risks include:

- **Data Security:** Is the data safe outside the firewall?
- **Data Loss:** What happens if the data gets lost? How can it be retrieved?
- **Compliance:** Can regulatory reporting and transparency requirements be met? If data is stored in another country, are there cross-border data transfer issues?
- **Reliability and Performance**: Will it meet the "uptime" availability requirements?
- **Integration:** How will it integrate with our on-premises assets?
- **Process Continuity:** Will we still have "end-to-end" control of our internal processes?
- **Vendor Viability:** What happens if the cloud-computing vendor fails?
- **Privacy:** Is critical data safe from intrusion by competitors?

Viable mitigation plan for each of these risks should be developed. For example, users should ensure that the vendor provides documented uptime guarantees (typically between 99.5% and 99.9%) for mission-critical applications. They should also ensure that the vendor's security procedures for vulnerability management, intru-

sion prevention, incident response, and incident escalation and investigation are well-documented. Some cloud-computing vendors actually have better procedures than many internal IT organizations, but it is imperative that the onus be put on the provider to prove it has documented and tested procedures that address the key risk areas previously outlined.

Enterprise Enablement

Typically, users are more interested in what a service can do for them than in the particular technology used to implement systems. Cloud computing enables agility, speed and flexibility. Cloud computing also minimizes the focus on the technology underpinnings and refocuses it on the services that are delivered. With cloud computing, the role of the IT organization can shift toward driving fundamentally new capabilities and dramatically restructuring processes that deliver more value to the educational institutions, rather than incrementally improving commodity processes.

Cloud computing can also provide educational institutions with the capability to do things that otherwise couldn't be done technologically, were not economically feasible, or would otherwise be deferred due to resource constraints. Cloud computing also frees up technical talent and management resources for more mission-critical applications. In many cases, it improves the quality of service delivered by IT. Shortcomings and bottlenecks in IT service delivery exist and cloud computing could safely address some of these shortcomings.

Many IT organizations own and operate all of the IT resources necessary to conduct business. These organizations are compelled to install complex solutions integrating disparate applications, operating systems, servers, networks and storage. This complexity prevents IT organizations from focusing on strategic initiatives and drives up IT operational costs because they are too busy fighting fires that come with maintaining their complex infrastructure. Thus, enterprises view their IT organizations as "money pits" that consume large sums of capital and return little value to the business.

In a post-modern IT world, enterprises can reduce the size and complexity of their internal IT operations by shifting nonstrategic, yet still essential, IT resources to the cloud. Internal IT resources can then be focused on more-important, higher-level projects that can drive core business initiatives, thus increasing IT (and employee) (Kočović, 2011) (See Figure 4).

Figure 5 clarifies how strong "xaaS" are (Cearley & Smith, 2010). It is important to notice that market sizes of all three segments of the market are not the same. Largest segment is SaaS that is becoming more mainstream. Boom is behind us, slightly slower IT spending ahead is obvious.

PUBLIC VS. PRIVATE CLOUD

Private cloud computing is a style of computing where organizations deliver scalable and elastic IT-enabled capabilities "as a service" to internal users using Internet technologies. The focus on internal is related to who can access or use the services in question, and who owns or coordinates the resources used to deliver the services (Figure 6).

Two characteristics related to conducting private cloud computing, as opposed to public cloud computing are (Plummer, Smith, Bittman, Cearley, Cappuccio, Scott, Kumar et al. 2009):

1. **Limited Membership (that is, exclusive membership):** A private cloud implementation has a bounded membership that is exclusive (that is, only approved members

Figure 4. Post modern IT service ownership (Adapted from Kocovic, 2013)

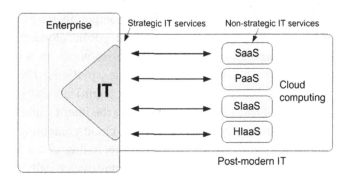

Figure 5. Cloud market per segment: SaaS, PaaS, IaaS

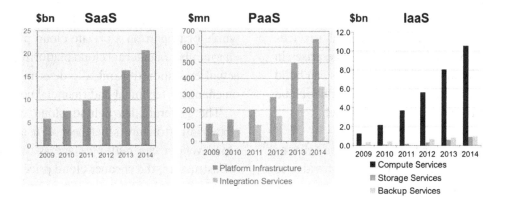

Figure 6. Public-private-hybrid cloud services

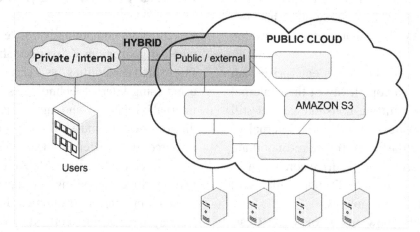

can participate, and approval is contingent on some characteristic that the general public or other general businesses cannot gain easily). For example, membership may be limited to employees and students of a given educational institution. Note that we do not consider a cloud service that only requires users to sign up to be exclusive.

2. **Spectrum of Control/Ownership:** A private cloud service is different from a public cloud service in that an organization implements private cloud services for an exclusive set of users. Zhang, Zhang, Chen, and Huo (2010) noted that there is a spectrum from fully private services to fully public services that blurs distinctions of ownership or control. Many examples fall somewhere between public cloud services and private cloud services, including business partners sharing resources, private cloud services built on top of public cloud services and specialized services limited to a small number of enterprises in a specific industry. Organizations can build private cloud services on top of a public cloud infrastructure or in a hybrid model.

Public cloud computing refers to the delivery of cloud services by a third-party provider to external users. In private cloud computing, the IT organization acts as the provider of services to internal users. Hybrid cloud computing refers to the combination of public cloud-computing services with internal IT services (private cloud services or traditional IT services).

Most companies using public cloud computing will also have some internal IT systems. Hybrid cloud computing refers to the combination of external public cloud-computing services and internal resources in a coordinated fashion to assemble solutions. Hybrid cloud computing implies significant integration or coordination between the internal and external environments. Hybrid cloud computing can take a number of forms, including cloud bursting, where an application is dynamically extended from a private cloud platform to an external public cloud service, based on the need for additional resources. More ambitious approaches define a solution as a series of granular services, each of which can run in whole or in part on a private cloud platform or on a number of external cloud platforms, with the actual execution dynamically determined based on changing technical and financial conditions.

The general idea behind cloud computing shared infrastructure is that the more users a public cloud vendor can multiplex across the massive infrastructure, the cheaper cloud prices become. Cloud vendors who utilize the pay-as-you-go model must roll both capital and operational costs into one price, charging enough to compensate for the huge cash outlay and still make money. To determine total cloud costs, IT organizations must do the same. However, depending on IT personnel efficiency, cost of labor, price of power and space, some IT organizations may find that keeping IT capabilities in house is cheaper in the long run. Thus, "lower operational costs" are classified as a future cloud benefit.

Public cloud computing services - especially SaaS - enable mobile users to access external IT capabilities without incurring additional internal IT overhead. Although cloud computing cannot solve every mobile user's needs, it can address many of their issues, including communication, collaboration and monitoring operational status. Savvy IT organizations will find cloud computing solutions that enable mobile users to perform these actions without tunneling through a VPN or coming into the office.

SECURITY IN CLOUD COMPUTING

Cloud computing security has not been sufficiently investigated, although cloud computing service has. In particular, since the typical technical element of cloud computing is virtual technology, insecurity arises from a user not fully understanding the actual conditions. Thus, in cloud computing, investigating the users' perceptions of security is becoming as important as the investigating quality of service. Below, the main subjects of security based on the social viewpoint in cloud computing are described (Tanimoto, Hiramoto, Iwashita, Sato, & Kanai, 2011):

1. **Existence of Two or More Stakeholders:** Generally, various services are distributed and provided in the cloud environment. Thus, to use a service, identity information must be shown. In this case, the criteria are needed to determine the importance of various kinds

of identity information. For example, in the case of the identity information that is not secure, only unimportant services can be provided. On the other hand, receiving more important information or services requires more detailed identity information. However, these issues have been under investigated.

2. **Security Guarantee in Disclosure Environment:** Users generally do not understand at all about how information is managed in the cloud environment. Until now, studies from a viewpoint of availability have done about storing the information in cloud computing. However, the security of critical information represented by personal information has not been investigated yet. That is, risks have not been fully discussed.

3. **Mission Critical Data Problem:** Because they do not fully trust cloud services' security, users have been reluctant to entrust clouds with mission critical data. Thus, educational institutions build private clouds. However, to do this takes a lot of money and requires specialist knowledge. Therefore, it is desirable that users' insecurity be assuaged so they can confidently store data by using cloud computing.

Cloud computing provides a facility that enable large-scale controlled sharing and interoperation among resources that are dispersedly owned and managed. Security is therefore a major element in any cloud computing infrastructure, because it is necessary to ensure that only authorized access is permitted and secure behavior is accepted. Members in the cloud and the cloud computing environment should be trusted by each other, and the members that have communication should be trusted by each other. Trust is the major concern of the users and provider of services that participate in a cloud computing environment (Shen & Tong, 2010).

Because the cloud computing is composed of different local systems and includes the members from multiple environments, therefore the security in cloud is complicate. In one side, the security mechanism should provide guarantees secure enough to the user, on the other side, the security mechanism should not be too complex to put the users into an inconvenient situation. The openness and flexibility of the computer and popular commercial operating systems have been important factors supporting their widespread adoption. However, that very same openness and flexibility have been proved to be a double edged sword, because it brings complexity, reduces trust degree and threat against security. So there should be a balance between the security and the convenience (Farzad, 2011).

The dependable and secure computing includes not only security and confidentiality, but also reliability, availability, safety and integrity. In order to archive security in cloud computing system, some technologies have been used to build the security mechanism for cloud computing. The cloud computing security can be provided as security services (Ren, Wang, & Wang, 2012). Security messages and secured messages can be transported, understood, and manipulated by standard Web services tools and software. This mechanism is a good choice because the Web service technology has been well established in the network-computing environment. Even the

mechanism for the cloud computing security has many merits now, but there are still some disadvantages. For example, there is short of the mechanism on the hardware to support the trusted computing in cloud computing system.

The trusted root in cloud computing environment has not been defined clearly. The creation and protection of certificates are not secure enough for cloud computing environments. The performance is reduced apparently when the cryptographic computing are processed. There are also lack of some mechanisms to register and classify the participants carefully, such as the tracing and monitoring for them. In the following section, we will analyze the challenge for the cloud computing security in deep.

Cloud Ecosystem Management and Security

Applying security model on platforms defined by Gartner and NIST, we will show the differences between those two models (Figure 7).

Ecosystem management and security services refer to services that manage the access, configuration, consumption, delivery and security of cloud-based services and information, as well as the service-level agreements associated with the

Figure 7. NIST and Gartner terminology (Adapted from Kocovic, 2013)

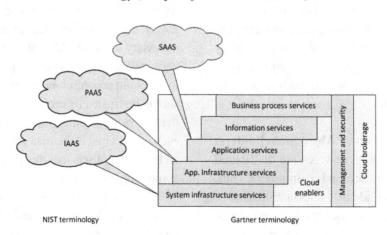

services. The primary and direct values of cloud services are provided by the application, information and process services, insofar as they are the services that touch the end user directly. Ecosystem management and security services deliver value by making it easier, less risky and more effective to use other cloud services. These services are critical for users who plan to use and integrate multiple cloud services from multiple vendors or build applications in the cloud. Often, some level of management and security service is included as part of one or more application infrastructure services. There is no corresponding layer in the NIST terminology, but since these are generally service-based versions of software, they would generally be included under the SaaS category for NIST.

High Risk Factors for Computing

Three basic characteristics are indicative of the risk associated with a digital implementation: accessibility, complexity and extensibility. To an extent, these three factors are related, with an increase in one often resulting in a corresponding increase in another.

Extensibility describes the degree to which new code can be linked into a system. All modern computing environments have some degree of extensibility. Operating systems can easily accept new code, such as device drivers and operating system libraries. The security implication of extensibility is that new risks can be added to a system after it has been assessed. Within the corporate data center, the addition of new code extensions is usually recognized and takes place under a well-understood schedule (and scientific-run clouds should be no exception). Externally provisioned services are rarely so transparent. Users may have minimal ability to control the timing, but they should ask their provider for visibility into the change management practices, the forms of change that are being made and their schedule (Vaquero, Rodero-Merino, & Morán, 2010).

Accessibility refers to the attack surface or exposure. It is a function of the ease and extent to which a system can be touched (who, from where and in what way). A stand-alone workstation in a locked room is relatively inaccessible, while service that is offered over the Internet, especially a user service, must be able to resist every attacker in the world. Internet accessibility is a function of the number of listening ports, the number of types of service that are listening on those ports, and the number of IP addresses serving those listening ports. "Internal accessibility" refers to the degree of exposure to users, including privileged ones. The more access to data that a system administrator has, the easier it is for this person to steal it or to sabotage systems. The greater the level of administrative access, the more effort is needed to vet and monitor administrators and track their activities. Users of cloud computing services should ask for detailed information on how privileged users are controlled, and how the efficacy of these controls is monitored (Grobauer, Walloschek, & Stocker, 2011).

Complexity describes the size and intricacy of a computing environment. "Size" refers to the amount of code. All else being equal, the more lines of code there are, the greater the number of vulnerabilities. Complexity can also create emergent vulnerabilities that are the result of unforeseen interactions between functions that, by themselves, may well be adequately secure. As an example, SQL injection is a form of vulnerability in which a weakness in one service, a Web server, is exploited to direct an attack against a related service, a database that is otherwise shielded from attack. Scalability and elasticity are typically provided by distributed and virtualized platforms that epitomize computing complexity. The cloud computing model takes advantage of multihost/multisite virtualization, which implies continuing increases in size and complexity.

Control Implications of Different Cloud Models

The control implications of different cloud models - IaaS, PaaS and SaaS need to be specifically understood. Different forms and degrees of control and security are provided at each level. In a SaaS model, in which virtually the entire system is externally provisioned, the provider is responsible for virtually all of the security functionality, monitoring and incident response, with the probable exception of user provisioning and access rules (Subashini & Kavitha, 2011).

Furthermore, a SaaS user has almost no ability to add security mechanisms or controls, such as data loss prevention, authentication mechanisms and database activity monitoring (Takabi, Joshi, & Ahn, 2010). Forensic investigation is virtually impossible, and e-discovery is possible only if the vendor has explicitly added the functionality (or is willing to do this itself for a fee). The service provider is responsible for the majority of the security mechanisms, and determines the possible level of investigative access.

In a PaaS model, security controls are usually located within the application and the platform (Ren, Wang, & Wang, 2012), meaning that both the provider and customer have some level of responsibility.

IaaS customers are responsible for the majority of their security functionality, monitoring and investigation. The provider is still responsible for physical security and the hardware, and may play some role as a sort of traffic controller for the network, which is shared by all tenants.

Frameworks for Evaluation of Cloud Computing Security

During the past years, two different initiatives have begun to develop frameworks for the evaluation of cloud computing security. The Cloud Security Alliance has published security guidance (Cloud Security Alliance, 2011). The European Network and Information Security Agency has published "Cloud Computing Security Risk Assessment" (Catteddu & Hogben, 2009). Both of these early documents, which influenced this research report, identify a wide variety of risk areas that need assessment, extending beyond security to address topics such as e-discovery, vendor lock-in and vendor viability. They do not provide useful guidance on how to actually assess these factors, and they barely touch on the lack of design and build transparency of most commercial offerings. They represent today's consensus as to where the significant risks are, but they must be understood as early examples of work that is in progress.

The most prominent groups working on assessment criteria are the financial services BITS consortium, the CSA, the CAMM working group, ENISA, and the U.S. federal government's General Services Administration (GSA). These groups and others are producing a growing body of control standards frameworks and literature.

Over time, standards will stabilize, mature, and map to each other and to existing industry compliance frameworks. For now, security practitioners face hours of manual work mapping criteria themselves. But help from IT governance, risk, and compliance (IT-GRC) vendors such as RSA/Archer and Agilliance is on the way. Soon the webs of mutually cross-referencing spreadsheets will be better-organized using wizards and dashboards. Some of the duplication of effort may also be reduced over time; the work of CSA, CAMM, and other groups may be contributed to the International Organization for Standards (ISO) 27036 (ISO/IEC 27036 – IT Security – Security techniques – Information security for supplier relationships (DRAFT)) efforts.

INFORMATICA POSTMODERNA

IT is becoming post-modern, similar to what the architectural world went through in the 1970s. From the 1930s through the 1960s, modern architects such as Gropius and Mies van der Rohe and Le Corbusier designed boxes that eschewed extra ornamentation in a quest for universal spaces the architectural equivalent of "one size fits all."

The term "Postmodern" was first used around the 1870s. John Watkins Chapman suggested "a postmodern style of painting" as a way to move beyond French Impressionism. J. M. Thompson, in his 1914 article in The Hibbert Journal (a quarterly philosophical review), used it to describe changes in attitudes and beliefs in the critique of religion: "The raison d'etre of Post-Modernism is to escape from the double-mindedness of Modernism by being thorough in its criticism by extending it to religion as well as theology, to Catholic feeling as well as to Catholic tradition." (Thompson, 1914, p. 733).

In 1917, Rudolf Pannwitz used the term to describe a philosophically-oriented culture. His idea of post-modernism drew from Friedrich Nietzsche's analysis of modernity and its end results of decadence and nihilism. Pannwitz's post-human would be able to overcome these predicaments of the modern human. Contrary to Nietzsche, Pannwitz also included nationalist and mythical elements in his use of the term (Thompson, 1914, p. 733).

However, in the anti-establishment 1960s, people grew tired of living in sterile boxes and hearing that architects were the sole arbiters of taste. They struck back, inspired by post-modern architects such as Charles Moore and Robert Venturi. These new tastemakers were sensitive to how people worked as well as to the surrounding environment, thus designing buildings that were both varied and appropriate. Often, these architects hammered out their designs in public forums by showing an initial set of designs to a crowd of future users and using the crowd's reactions to refine the design.

This messier but more inclusive way of creating buildings continues to this day. IT should emulate this strategy in a post-modern world that is characterized by four macro trends:

- **Volatility**: Many of the new technologies used in 3CS - for example virtualization, SaaS, and social software continue to quickly evolve in ways that upset the status quo. Users are less predictable and bring their own devices to work. Meanwhile, fickle users use Facebook and Twitter to complain about institutions and create public relations nightmares within hours.

- **Multiplicity**: User requirements and system options continue to expand. Furthermore, the number of delivery models has grown: Many enterprises now leverage software, virtualization, and SaaS to deliver 3CS systems, all at the same time.

- **Versatility**: Non-technical skills such as writing contracts and interviewing users continue to gain in importance while IT evolves from being the corporate "engine room" into being an IT services broker. This is especially important in the 3CS space because users increasingly want to view IT as an enabler or helper, not as an enforcer.

- **Mobility**: The burgeoning number of devices and the multiple ways that employees want to use them are straining long-used systems and processes. These changes are forcing IT departments to reconsider how they buy and code software so that they can better support mobile devices.

SOCIAL COMPUTING

Basic approach to social networks is good to be taken from the book Nexus, of Mark Buchanan (Buchanan, 2003). The notion of "small worlds" comes from Stanley Milgram's letter experiments on how people are interconnected in the U.S. He sent out letters to randomly selected people in different cities with instructions to send them to some other individual. If they didn't know that person, then they would forward it to someone they felt might know the person. Milligram found that the letters made it to their destination with an average chain length of 5-6 people. This theory has a critique.

Whether or not the six degrees of separation is accurate, the small-world phenomenon apparently is found in many different network systems - for example, food webs, cellular metabolism, the Internet, language, and so on and the organizing principles of social networks are apparently the same as those of other small worlds. This feature has a specific mathematical signature: the power-law or fat-tail pattern for the distribution of elements according to how many links they have. And this signature turns out to be nearly identical from one kind of network to the next. What we see then is a kind of natural order seems to well up in networks of all kinds and that does so despite the complexities of their individual histories.

In this power-law pattern, a few nodes are highly connected, resulting in clusters, while the majority has only a few connections. We can see that in the classroom, too. The teacher is a hub, connecting to all the students, and among the students, some have more connections with classmates than others do. In a small class, this might not play a significant role, but in large lecture classes- 400 students - it might. In addition, the teacher is neither the only hub nor always the biggest one in a particular class.

Some connections between people are obviously stronger than others. Strong ties result from interaction over time and affect (e.g., trust, respect, and friendship). So, another aspect of the small world phenomenon is the notion of strong and weak ties formulated by Mark Granovetter. Both types of ties are important. Strong ties play a role in motivation, support, and identity. Weak ties have a role, too. Granovetter's seminal articles (Granovetter, 1973; Granovetter, 1983) "The Strength of Weak Ties" showed that weak ties acted as bridges to information and sources different from one's networks of strong ties.

Socially-driven processes are disrupting traditional approaches to business. Social technologies allow people to connect, interact and rally together with unprecedented speed and ease, yet there is still confusion about the value that social technologies deliver. Savvy business and IT leaders are not content to watch from the sidelines as these changes unfold. They are getting smart about social and serious about exploring, and possibly exploiting, the opportunities these new relationship dynamics promise.

Four major trends are evolving simultaneously:

1. The artifacts users leave behind in social networks provide a treasure-trove of insight. Given that social networks have gone, enterprises should mine this data to uncover forward-looking intelligence. User enthusiasm can be channeled to drive processes in areas such as innovation, demand generation, marketing, distribution and customer service.
2. Business application vendors are integrating social features into their applications and the dividing lines between transactional tools and social environments are fading.
3. While business opportunity is driving some social initiatives and investments, fear and uncertainty leads to inaction or worse-yet, an attempt to lock-down employee access to social networks. Prudent policies and disciplines are necessary now, as enterprises pace their ventures into a vastly different environment.
4. Social solutions are relevant to business functions beyond marketing and customer service. There are use cases for social media in a broad range of business functions, both internally and externally.

People, on their own, are moving in huge numbers to take advantage of new (Internet-supported) social tools. Witness the billions of "tweets" and social-site memberships as well as the millions of blogs and the explosion of YouTube visits, posts and discussions. There are millions of terabytes of data on the Web that reflect the attitudes, intentions and venues within which both institutions and user are expressing their opinions and influencing the actions of their peers. The accumulation of their conversations, comments, ratings and rankings is already being mined by some for "social intelligence." The mixed nature of the data artifacts, unstructured and rich media, makes mining difficult, but not impossible.

The IT organization has a challenge on its hands. How does it provide leadership in intelligence gathering and other efforts to integrate these collective activities in enterprise processes?

From the other side, we have the exponential growth of social media, from blogs, Facebook and Twitter to LinkedIn and YouTube, offers organizations the chance to join a conversation with millions of customers around the globe every day.

Few research documents (Chard, Caton, Rana, & Bubendorfer, 2010) showing good guidance how to use social network in everyday business (Mahapatra & Banerjee, 2010). Social media is experiencing explosive growth. In a recent survey by Harvard Business Review Analytic Services (Mahapatra & Banerjee, 2010), 79% of the 2,100 organizations surveyed said they are currently using social media channels (58%) or preparing to launch social media initiatives (21%). Despite this high level of interest, most organizations appear poorly prepared for the change that social media will bring about in their organizations. Many efforts are still in the experimentation stage. In the survey, just 12% of organizations described themselves as effective users of social media.

Socially driven processes are disrupting traditional approaches to business. Social technologies allow people to connect, transact, learn and innovate with unprecedented speed and ease, see Figure 8. These interactions can occur with a network of strong ties, but the most exciting potential of social media is the ability to leverage the knowledge and insight from people with whom

we have weaker ties and even exploit relationships with people we do not yet know.

Nonetheless, there is still confusion about the value that social technologies deliver. Savvy business and IT leaders are not content to watch from the sidelines as these changes unfold. They are getting smart about social and serious about exploring, and possibly exploiting, the opportunities these new relationship dynamics promise.

Social media is growing exponentially and isn't just for fun anymore. It is a new channel to connect with current and potential users, partners and influencers. A social presence has become business-critical. Location matters. If you want to interact with other individuals, the best strategy is to go to where they are. And these days, individuals live in social media.

All industries indicate that the primary reason to invest in social media and collaboration tools is to strengthen the relationship with the user (47% of respondents) (Mahapatra & Banerjee, 2010). The second-most-significant reason across industries is to enhance the brand. This is certainly the case for the media industry. However, for transportation respondents, the second-most-important reason identified is to share information and ideas with

Figure 8. Social computing components (Adapted from Kocovic, 2013)

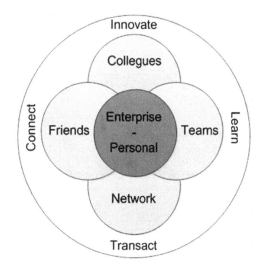

stakeholders. The government identifies all of the aforementioned reasons as equally significant together with enhancing employee productivity.

Many clients are unable to articulate what benefits they hope to achieve by employing social media to become more collaborative. This decreases the likelihood of achieving a successful implementation. The most successful social media initiatives solve real business problems.

Broadcasting messages out via social media is easy. This simplistic approach extends enterprise communication to another set of channels. Greater value and more implementation challenges will come from initiatives designed to participate, learn from and engage with various constituencies using social software tools in the workplace, for externally facing communities and the social Web.

CONTEXT-AWARE COMPUTING

Context-aware computing is about improving the user experience for users, business partners, educational institutions and sciences by using

the information about a person or object's environment, activities, connections and preferences to anticipate the user's needs and proactively serve up the most appropriate content, product or service. Educational institutions can leverage context-aware computing to target prospects better, increase customer intimacy and enhance associate productivity and collaboration. Context-aware computing components are shown in Figure 9.

Without the advances in cloud computing, context-aware experiences will be relegated to siloed, specialized implementations. The cloud is the common fabric in linking context-aware experiences.

Context is not just about the user experience, it also can play a part in shaping the demand for services. Context-aware computing raises significant security and privacy concerns. Conversely, the practice of information security and privacy will be significantly enhanced by contextual information. Context fits in strategically at the convergence of mobile, location, and social business and technology adoption. Context will be a source of differentiation for software, handset, mobile

Figure 9. Context-aware computing components (Adapted from Kocovic, 2013)

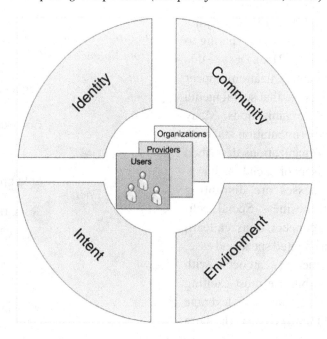

network operators and communications vendors. Because vendors are beginning to develop their positioning regarding context, most educational institutions are arriving at its doorstep through a focus on mobility, location or social platforms.

There are five key issues that need to be addressed by various parts of an enterprise and its IT organization. The first two center on user experience: large-scale, context-enriched commerce and context-enhanced performance. But user experience must be built on applications and content - it cannot exist in a vacuum, thus, one level removed from the user experience. The third key issue of context-aware computing is that it is an information and content-centric phenomenon that will touch many other IT areas, including security, mobile, the cloud, application development and Pattern-Based Strategy. The fourth key issue deals with our belief that context awareness will create new, significant market opportunities for communication service providers, software and technology vendors. Finally, fifth key issues gets down to what educational institutions and scientist will need to put together in implementation plans for context-aware computing.

Context: The Intersection of Mobile, Social, Digital, and Physical Worlds

Context maps the digital world to the physical worlds together. Context-aware computing has been studied and applied since about 1990 and allows experience designers to link physical, electronic and mobile commerce for commercial gain and to enhance knowledge work productivity. Face recognition as a part of context-aware computing is shown in Figure 10. In 2011, a focus on user interface - individual applications, individual platforms relies on manual, sometimes difficult, navigation, redundant inputs, inappropriate or inconvenient channels, and some personalization, with limited integration. In general, today's users do not expect cross-channel experience, and

educational applications are focused on portal access. Practices include optimizing individual experiences and interaction channels.

The main battleground between stakeholders will be where physical and information ecosystems overlap. Application, identity and content awareness are part of an enterprise shift to context-aware security infrastructure. This collection of vendors already possesses vast amounts of information about the digital habits (search habits, devices, apps, UI utilization). Studies of consumer acceptance in the U.K., France, Canada, and the United States indicate that about 27% of the general population willing to exchange personally identifiable information for convenience and an additional 50% will opt-in in some cases. If we assume the base of 27% will be readily opt-in to having their digital habits tracked to make their lives more convenient and that one quarter of the others who conditionally accept, then this equates to about 40% of the installed base of users using these smartphone vendors. Given the overall smartphone base, this equates to about 720 million people, about 10% of the global population. Payment card issuers and retailers currently hold important transactional information per person, and social platforms like Facebook can provide some influence, but the ubiquity of the devices

Figure 10. Face recognition as a part of context-aware computing (Adapted from Kocovic, 2013)

and the convenience of context enriched services means that those providers are sources of context, but cannot deliver "the last contextual moment of choice."

Context-aware computing addresses user experience as a science by linking the science presenting context-aware content and user experience with goals, it is one of the top disruptive trends of this decade. Mobile and network service providers are already investing significantly in this area, and organizations in financial services, healthcare and retail are already beginning to leverage context for revenue opportunities and productivity increases. The disruptions caused by context-aware computing will include major user, technology and business shifts, including changes in model-driven security and application programming, and the interest of governments in regulating contextual information access and control.

Context-Aware Computing and Security

Context-aware computing - technology that uses contextual information (for example, user identity, device location, activity and time) has a complex and interlocking relationship with information security. When implemented appropriately, context-aware technologies hold the potential to deliver increased revenue, enhance productivity and deliver a superior end-user experience. However, the same technologies can also introduce serious data security risks and damage the enterprise's brand reputation. These are all very serious concerns. There are, inevitably, significant security and privacy implications for all individuals and entities participating in context-aware computing, from users, to enterprises, to product and service providers. The creators and users of context-aware services must recognize the potential privacy risks and ensure that the services are used properly.

Context-aware computing has important implications for virtually every aspect of the practice of information security. The recent research

documents in this collection show just how wide-ranging the impact of context-aware computing is, on security. It is important to note, however, that many of these, though focused on the use of context-awareness in security, have implications that extend well beyond security into the general use of context-aware computing. The practice of information security is, in fact, one of the richest areas of opportunity for context-aware computing.

PATTERN BASED STRATEGY

In everyday life, it is common to hear people say: "I think I see a pattern." Patterns are all around us. They are in our speech, writing, pictures, sciences, social behaviors, etc. Patterns are particularly useful when the raw version of what we are looking at is too much to easily handle. When people mention a "pattern," they are going up one or more levels from the basic concept.

In the case of education and IT, there are countless places where looking at the raw data is simply too much to deal with. How can educational institutions make sense of all the data pouring out of applications, content management systems, mobile devices, operational technologies and social networks? We believe the key is to apply basic concepts focused on patterns to answer three key questions:

- What is all the information telling you?
- What should you do about it?
- Are the actions you are taking working?

This led to Pattern-Based Strategy (Figure 11). The economic environment emerging from the recession will force leaders to look at their opportunities for growth and competitive differentiation in a new way. To date, the strategic use of information has been limited to very conventional approaches that only provide obvious indicators of considerations like economic health, emerging opportunities and user preferences.

There are some new sources of information and influence that have to be considered and exploited, the power of an individual to impact an institution's image, the fact that users now buy as communities and the potential demise of classic functions like product design because users are designing their own products.

Tragically, most institutions today are so invested in traditional processes and thinking that they can't hear or sense any of these new signals. But it's not enough to just seek changes in social, economic, political and environmental landscapes. Institutions need a way to evaluate what they are hearing and act appropriately. They also need to seek patterns, not just from information, but also in activities of people and processes.

Not all thinking is geared for recognition of patterns. But those attuned to this phenomenon realize that we live in a world of patterns that can tell us what's likely to happen and can help guide us on what to change as a result. Competitive advantage and survival are about recognizing and acting on these patterns before others. Executing a pattern-based strategy will require institutions to seek patterns, analyze them and establish a repeatable discipline to respond. Pattern-Based Strategy provides a framework to proactively seek patterns from traditional and nontraditional information

sources, model their impact and adapt according to the requirements of the pattern.

A Pattern-Based Strategy enables institutions to identify and respond to risks and opportunities before competitors do. Thus, institutions can seize opportunities first, spot problems, and make other strategic moves that require insight into the future. Institutions can create new opportunities for themselves by applying a Pattern-Based Strategy to new kinds of information, such as social media, mobile data and other pools of "big data" (Khalidi, 2011). Pattern-Based Strategies can come in many different forms, depending on the type of organization that employs them, the goals it has set and the industry it competes in. Pattern-Based Strategy brings together many areas that have not typically joined before into a single framework for business and IT:

- Analytics and business intelligence;
- Enterprise information management, enterprise information architecture;
- Business process management, business applications;
- Governance, risk and compliance;
- Change management;
- Service-oriented architecture, complex events processing, cloud computing.

IT leaders need to focus on four disciplines in successfully adopting a Pattern-Based Strategy: pattern seeking, operational tempo (optempo) advantage, performance-driven culture and transparency, see Figure 12.

Pattern seeking comprises focusing on the competencies, activities, technologies and resources that expose signals that may lead to a pattern that will have a positive or negative impact on strategy or operations focusing on those areas of vulnerability or risk and innovation/opportunity for institution. Seeking patterns can mean looking inside or outside the organization, and involves exploiting the new power of the collective that is, exploiting collective knowledge with

Figure 11. Pattern based strategy components (Adapted from Kocovic, 2013)

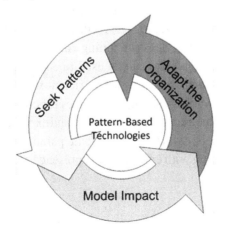

Figure 12. New disciplines supported by technology (Adapted from Kocovic, 2013)

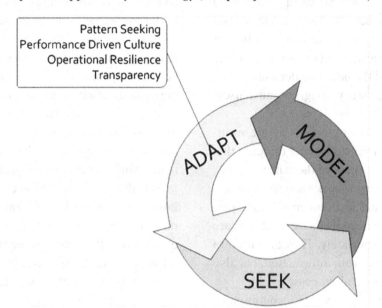

creative activities, and exploiting collective activities as an unexplored source of patterns.

Instilling a performance-driven culture serves as a means to manage the impact of change to organizational patterns, track progress and drive desired behaviors across the organization. A performance-driven culture enables an organization to monitor leading indicators of change, and where performance is used to enable change through the alignment of organizational resources to strategic performance metrics.

In the context of a Pattern-Based Strategy, transparency means the demonstration of institution health and the strategic use of transparency for differentiation. If organizations can proactively evolve transparency from a once-a-quarter financial-results event to using it to set the right expectations of seeking new patterns and responding with consistent results, this proactive use will enable them to enter new markets, gain access to funds that competitors can't access and demonstrate differentiation to customers and suppliers.

FUTURE OF CLOUD COMPUTING

In the past, enterprises supported collaboration through email and highly structured applications only. E-mail is a freewheeling platform for completely unstructured communications. Structured applications, such as ERP systems and workflow applications focus on process-specific needs and tasks. None of them captures the big variety of collaborative interactions characterizing how people work. Today, a wide range of capabilities have emerged in communications, social Web and mobile that enable richer interactions among people and expand collaboration to a broader level. Social networks, blogs and wikis are available on a variety of devices (including smartphones and media tablets) and can be used to enable a truly collaborative, effective and efficient workplace. People want to use mobile devices for collaboration to share content, information and experiences with their communities. Social paradigms are converging with email, IM and presence, creating new collaboration styles. Native email clients on many smartphones already integrate collaboration features.

However, nothing will change until enterprises make these capabilities widely available and users become more comfortable with them. The flexibility of email draws people into using it for just about any purpose but IM is better for quick interactions; discussion boards or wikis for debating issues; and social networks for socializing and sharing experiences. Yet a collaborative environment and culture is a prerequisite for organizations to take advantage of these new capabilities.

Multiple collaboration applications are converging to support several different interaction styles (e.g., email, IM, presence, social networking) from a single client, both on PC, Web and mobile devices. While mobile drives collaboration innovation, collaboration drives mobile innovation. Two groups on mutual task: users and organizations are shown in Figure 13.

One of the most intriguing aspects of the tablet phenomenon is the way it is driving new user behaviors. Tablets do not merely present a new form factor for users, but they also create new opportunities to engage them. Tablets are not used

in the same way as traditional PCs, and they are not replacing other devices, such as smartphones. Instead, they are extending computing capabilities into new locations that were not practical before, and along the way are extending the amount of time users spend in any computing environment. Given that user attention is a scarce commodity, businesses can capitalize on the additional time the tablet screen can offer.

Smartphones and laptops will dominate shipments in mature markets. The tension between portability and flexibility will remain until technologies like flexible screens mature. Increasingly integrated electronics will enable the creation of ever smaller devices, but their limited screen real-estate will restrict the tasks they can perform. Mobile apps and services are as much of a challenge as devices: they provide new ways to communicate and collaborate. Enthusiasm for mobile deployments has run ahead of mobile security.

There are opportunities to innovate and deliver new services and experiences to consumers and to change the way in which devices and applications are supplied to users. The social changes driven by mobility and smartphones apply particularly to the next generation of employees and users.

Figure 13. Two groups on mutual task: users and organizations

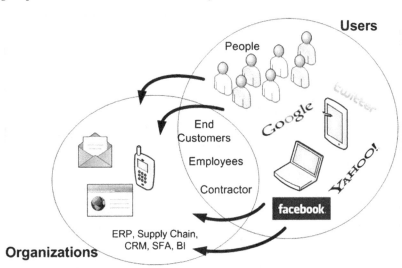

Key market trends (Figure 14) include:

- The rapid growth of smartphone shipments in mature markets.
- Media tablets will remain relatively niche and expensive devices; the limitations of first generation tablets will mean they're unlikely to be viable PC replacements. Many tablets will therefore be additive, not replacements, so increasing support challenges.
- Smartphone adoption varies widely by region and the relatively high price of smartphones means that they will be adopted only slowly in emerging markets.

Mobile platforms remain important although HTML5 and the growth of Web ecosystems and key applications such as Facebook means that for some purposes the Web ecosystems are threatening platform ecosystems. This is particularly so in the case of weak platform ecosystems where developers may not want to write native apps.

In the next few years, Android will remain the platform number 1. Symbian has been abandoned by Nokia so shipments are falling rapidly. All mobile OS platforms will evolve rapidly with several major and minor OS releases every year (Figure 15).

Looking on technologies in mobile technologies - many wireless technologies will coexist (Johnes, 2012). In mobile phones technologies will include HSPA and its variations, LTE, Bluetooth, Wi-Fi, NFC. In consumer electronics ZigBee, WI-Fi and some cellular will be important. Network operators have regained their interest in Wi-Fi recently as a way to offload traffic from cellular networks where demand will exceed supply until BGAN is a satellite technology which will be primarily used in remote locations when cellular coverage is unavailable. 802.15.6 is a technology that is still being defined by the IEEE but is intended for body area networks and implanted sensors. DASH-7 is an open source sensor networking wireless system used extensively by the U.S. department of defense. New versions of 802.11 will push Wi-Fi up to new performance levels and frequency bands.

Google Apple and Microsoft are investing billions of dollars every year, building out data centers to support their cloud offerings, and hoping to be No. 1 in a world where the cloud is central to computing. They are also investing in next-generation devices and strategies that look to leverage the opportunities in emerging consumer markets. And they each have some level of interest in enterprise computing. They each have different strengths and perceptions that comprise

Figure 14. Smartphones as a percentage of handheld shipments (Adapted from Kocovic, 2013)

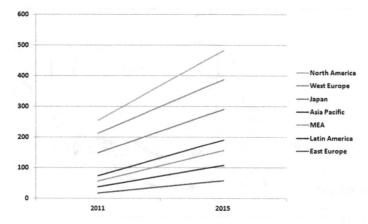

Figure 15. Smartphone platform trends

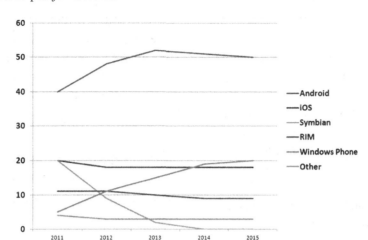

the position that they occupy in various markets. Perception is not always reality, but it has a lot of impact on the ultimate outcomes.

The competition is heating up between these companies as markets are undergoing tremendous upheaval. Disruptive forces of gigantic proportion, like cloud computing and consumerization, stand to change the balance of vendor power in many ways.

Cloud Computing Beyond 2020

In 1863, Jules Verne wrote book with the title: "Paris in the 20th Century." Written in 1863 but first published only in 1994, about a young man who lives in a technologically advanced, but culturally backwards future. Often referred to as

Verne's lost novel, the work, set in August 1960, paints a grim, dystopian view of the future. Many of Verne's predictions are remarkably on target. His publisher, Pierre-Jules Hetzel, did not release the book because he thought it was too unbelievable and inferior to his previous work: "Five Weeks in a Balloon."

He predicted that we will have Moon rockets, which will orbit three days around the Moon, and that will touch down the Earth. He predicted Paris in 1960. He predicted that in 1960 in Paris we will have skyscrapers, gas automobile, we will have fax machines, and something looks like Internet.

As Verne made predictions, based on personal contact with top scientist of his time, Michio Kaku, professor of theoretical physics making the same in his books (Kaku, 2010). He, as well

Figure 16. Contact lenses for eyes that will be able to project computer image

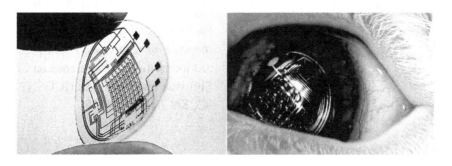

as other authors, is reporting about many projects that will change communication landscape of our planet. For example, researchers at the University of Washington (Parviz, 2009) have developed contact lenses for eyes that will be able to project computer image (Figure 16).

With the advent of the screen in the form of foil, whose prices will fall dramatically, we expect that our rooms and offices are going to be "covered" with these foils. Thus, 360 degrees screens will surround us. Due to these technologies, PCs and tablets will be thin as paper. For such cheap devices, the case will be cardboard made. Such computers are called disposable computers. The windshield will be covered with these foils, and all the necessary information will be visible on them: from the fact how fast we drive, up to information on the distance to adjacent cars, and we will be able to surf the Internet while driving. Problem relating to the speed and distance will take over the computer in our car.

Internet, far more advanced will be in use. Cloud computing, will be the basic working model. Wireless Internet everywhere, cheap workstations and powerful servers and storages in the background it is a picture of the near future.

REFERENCES

Abelson, H. (1999). *Architects of the information society: Thirty-five years of the laboratory for computer science at MIT*. Cambridge, MA: MIT Press.

Blakley, B., & Reeves, D. (Eds.). (2010). *Defining cloud computing*. Washington, DC: Gartner Inc.

Buchanan, M. (2003). *Nexus: Small worlds and the groundbreaking science of networks*. New York: W. W. Norton & Company, Inc.

Buyya, R., Yeo, C. S., Venugopal, S., Broberg, J., & Brandic, I. (2009). Cloud computing and emerging IT platforms: Vision, hype, and reality for delivering computing as the 5th utility. *Future Generation Computer Systems, 25*(6), 599–616. doi:10.1016/j.future.2008.12.001

Catteddu, D., & Hogben, G. (2009). *Cloud computing security risk assessment*. Retrieved April 13, 2013, from http://www.enisa.europa.eu/activities/risk-management/files/deliverables/cloud-computing-risk-assessment/at_download/fullReport

Cearley, D., & Smith, D. M. (2010, November). *The cloud computing scenario*. Paper presented at the Gartner Symposium/ITxpo 2010. Cannes, France.

Cearley, D. W. (2010). *Cloud computing: Key initiative overview*. Retrieved April 13, 2013, from http://www.gartner.com/it/initiatives/pdf/KeyInitiativeOverview_CloudComputing.pdf

Chard, K., Caton, S., Rana, O., & Bubendorfer, K. (2010). *Social cloud: Cloud computing in social networks*. Paper presented at IEEE 3rd International Conference on Cloud Computing (CLOUD). doi: 10.1109/CLOUD.2010.28

Chellappa, R. K. (1997, October). *Intermediaries in cloud-computing: A new computing paradigm*. Paper presented at the INFORMS National Meeting. Dallas, TX.

Cloud Security Alliance. (2011). *Security guidance for critical areas of focus in cloud computing v3.0*. Retrieved from https://cloudsecurityalliance.org/guidance/csaguide.v3.0.pdf

Farzad, S. (2011, May). *Cloud computing security threats and responses*. Paper presented at IEEE 3rd International Conference on Communication Software and Networks (ICCSN). doi: 10.1109/ICCSN.2011.6014715

Granovetter, M. (1983). The strength of weak ties: A network theory revisited. *Sociological Theory*, *1*, 201–233. doi:10.2307/202051

Granovetter, M. S. (1973). The strength of weak ties. *American Journal of Sociology*, *78*(6), 1360–1380. doi:10.1086/225469

Grobauer, B., Walloschek, T., & Stocker, E. (2011). Understanding cloud computing vulnerabilities. *IEEE Security Privacy Magazine*, *9*(2), 50–57. doi:10.1109/MSP.2010.115

IBM. (2007). Google and IBM announced university initiative to address internet-scale computing challenges. Retrieved from http://www-03.ibm.com/press/us/en/pressrelease/22414.wss

ISO/IEC 27036 - IT security - Security techniques - Information security for supplier relationships (Draft). (n.d.). Retrieved from http://www.iso27001security.com/html/27036.html

Johnes, N. (2012, April). *The mobile scenario: Confusion, complexity and opportunity through 2015*. Paper presented at the Gartner IT Infrastructure & Data Center Summit. Tokyo, Japan.

Kaku, M. (2010). *Physics of the future*. New York: Double Day.

Khalidi, Y. (2011). Building a cloud computing platform for new possibilities. *IEEE Computer*. Retrieved from http://ieeexplore.ieee.org/xpls/abs_all.jsp?arnumber=5719573

Kočović, P. (2011). *Informatica postmoderna*. Belgrade, Serbia: Petar Kočović

Kočović, P. (2012). Challenges in cloud computing. *IPSI Transactions of Internet Research*, *8*(1), 24–29.

Mahapatra, S., & Banerjee, D. (2010). The new conversation: Taking social media from talk to action. *Business*, *57*(3), 21.

Mell, P., & Grance, T. (2011). *The NIST definition of cloud computing*. Retrieved from http://csrc.nist.gov/publications/nistpubs/800-145/SP800-145.pdf

Parviz, B. A. (2009). *Augmented reality in a contact lens*. Retrieved from http://spectrum.ieee.org/biomedical/bionics/augmented-reality-in-a-contact-lens

Plummer, D. C., Smith, D. M., Bittman, T. J., Cearley, D. W., Cappuccio, D. J., & Scott, D. et al. (2009, May). Five refining attributes of public and private cloud computing. *Reproduction (Cambridge, England)*, 1–5. Retrieved from http://my.gartner.com/portal/server.pt?open=512&objID=260&mode=2&PageID=3460702&docCode=167182&ref=docDisplay

Plummer, D. C., Smith, D. M., Reeves, D., Robertson, B., Austin, T., & McDonald, M. P. (Eds.). (2010). *Cloud computing, CIO desk reference*. New York: Gartner Inc.

Ren, K., Wang, C., & Wang, Q. (2012). Security challenges for the public cloud. *IEEE Internet Computing*, *16*(1), 69–73. doi:10.1109/MIC.2012.14

Shen, Z. S. Z., & Tong, Q. T. Q. (2010). The security of cloud computing system enabled by trusted computing technology. In *Proceedings of 2nd International Conference on Signal Processing Systems ICSPS 2010*. IEEE. Retrieved from http://ieeexplore.ieee.org/lpdocs/epic03/wrapper.htm?arnumber=5555234

Smith, D. M., & Plummer, D. C. (Eds.). (2009). *Global class: The inspiration for cloud computing*. New York: Gartner Inc.

Subashini, S., & Kavitha, V. (2011). A survey on security issues in service delivery models of cloud computing. *Journal of Network and Computer Applications*, *34*(1), 1–11. doi:10.1016/j.jnca.2010.07.006

Takabi, H., Joshi, J. B. D., & Ahn, G. (2010). Security and privacy challenges in cloud computing environments. *IEEE Security Privacy Magazine*. Retrieved from http://www.ncbi.nlm.nih.gov/pubmed/20703745

Tanimoto, S., Hiramoto, M., Iwashita, M., Sato, H., & Kanai, A. (2011). Risk management on the security problem in cloud computing. In Y. C. Byun, K. Akingbehin, P. Hnetynka, & R. Lee (Eds.), *Proceedings of the First ACIS/J International Conference on Computers, Networks, Systems and Industrial Engineering (CNSI)*. Los Alamitos, CA: IEEE Computer Society.

Thompson, J. M. (1914). Post-modernism. *The Hibbert Journal, 12*(4), 733.

Vaquero, L. M., Rodero-Merino, L., & Morán, D. (2010). Locking the sky: A survey on IaaS cloud security. *Computing, 91*(1), 93–118. doi:10.1007/s00607-010-0140-x

Zhang, S., Zhang, S., Chen, X., & Huo, X. (2010). Cloud computing research and development trend. In B. Werner (Ed.), *Proceedings of the Second International Conference on Future Networks* (pp. 93-97). Los Alamitos, CA: IEEE Computer Society. doi: 10.1109/ICFN.2010.58

ADDITIONAL READING

Abstract, E., Bugiel, S., & Stefan, N. Sadeghi, A.-reza, & Schneider, T. (2011). Twin Clouds: An Architecture for Secure Cloud Computing. *Advances, 7025*, 1-11. Springer. Retrieved from http://www.zurich.ibm.com/~cca/csc2011/submissions/bugiel.pdf

Abualkibash, M., & Elleithy, K. (2012). Cloud computing: the future of it industry. *International Journal of Distributed and Parallel Systems IJDPS, 3*(4), 1–12. doi:10.5121/ijdps.2012.3401

Agudo, I., Nuñez, D., Giammatteo, G., Rizomiliotis, P., & Lambrinoudakis, C. (2011). Cryptography Goes to the Cloud. In C. Lee, J.-M. Seigneur, J. J. Park, & R. R. Wagner (Eds.) *Communications in Computer and Information Science*. Springer. Retrieved from http://www.scopus.com/inward/record.url?eid=2-s2.0-79960257802&partnerID=40&md5=559c26e22f991d3fd27f9b8a37fc5acd

Armbrust, M., Joseph, A. D., Katz, R. H., & Patterson, D. A. (2009). Above the Clouds: A Berkeley View of Cloud Computing. *Science, 53*(UCB/EECS-2009-28), 07-013. Citeseer. Retrieved from http://citeseerx.ist.psu.edu/viewdoc/download?doi=10.1.1.149.7163&rep=rep1&type=pdf

Blum, D. (Ed.). (2010). *Developing a Cloud Computing Security Strategy*. Gartner Inc.

Blum, D., & Heidt, E. T. (Eds.). (2013). *Determining Criteria for Cloud Security Assessment: It's More Than a Checklist*. Gartner Inc.

Che Fauzi, A. A., Noraziah, A., Herawan, T., & Mohd Zin, N. (2012). On cloud computing security issues. *Lecture Notes in Computer Science including subseries Lecture Notes in Artificial Intelligence and Lecture Notes in Bioinformatics*. Retrieved from http://www.scopus.com/inward/record.url?eid=2-s2.0-84858719302&partnerID=40&md5=28ba9343f0d8ffb175827c6453845d29

Chen, Y., Li, X., & Chen, F. (2011). Overview and analysis of cloud computing research and application. *2011 International Conference on EBusiness and EGovernment ICEE*. IEEE. Retrieved from http://ieeexplore.ieee.org/lpdocs/epic03/wrapper.htm?arnumber=5881819

Chu, F. -seng, & Chen, K.-cheng. (2011). Toward Green Cloud Computing. *System*, 0-4. ACM Press. Retrieved from http://portal.acm.org/citation.cfm?id=1968651

Dinh, H. T., Lee, C., Niyato, D., & Wang, P. (2011). A Survey of Mobile Cloud Computing: Architecture, Applications, and Approaches. *Computer*, (Cc), 1-38. Wiley Online Library. Retrieved from http://onlinelibrary.wiley.com/doi/10.1002/wcm.1203/full

Fernando, N., Loke, S. W., & Rahayu, W. (2013). Mobile cloud computing: A survey. *Future Generation Computer Systems, 29*(1), 84-106. Elsevier B.V. Retrieved from http://linkinghub.elsevier.com/retrieve/pii/S0167739X12001318

Furht, B. (2010). Cloud Computing Fundamentals. (B. Furht & A. Escalante, Eds.) *Handbook of Cloud Computing*, (May), 3-19. Springer US. Retrieved from http://www.springerlink.com/index/10.1007/978-1-4419-6524-0

Iyer, B., & Henderson, J. C. (2010). Preparing for the Future: Understanding the Seven Capabilities Cloud Computing. *MIS Quarterly Executive, 9*(2), 117–131.

Jr., S. O. (2011). The Problem with Cloud-Computing Standardization. *Computer*. IEEE. Retrieved from http://dx.doi.org/10.1109/MC.2011.220

Khan, A., & Ahirwar, K. (2011). Mobile cloud computing as a future of mobile multimedia database. *Database*, 2(1), 219–221.

Khan, Q.-tul-ain, Naseem, S., Ahmad, F., & Khan, M. S. (2012). Usage & Issues of Cloud Computing Techniques. *International Journal of Scientific Engineering Research*, 3(5), 1–7.

Kocovic, P. (2013). Informatica Postmoderna. Belgrade, Serbia: Petar Kočović

Kushwaha, D., & Maurya, A. (2013). Cloud Computing-A Tool For Future. *International Journal Of Mathematics, 1*, 09-14. Retrieved from http://www.ijmcr.in/files/writeable/uploads/hostgator97575/file/3-ijmcrin.pdf

Lamba, H. S., & Singh, G. (2011). Cloud Computing-Future Framework for e-management of NGO's. *International Journal of Advancements in Technology, 7*(7), 31–34. Retrieved from arxiv.org/pdf/1107.3217

Liu, W. (2012). Research on cloud computing security problem and strategy. *Consumer Electronics Communications and Networks CECNet 2012 2nd International Conference on*.

Madan, D. (2012). E-learning based on Cloud Computing. *Architecture (Washington, D.C.), 2*(2). Retrieved from http://ijarcsse.com/docs/papers/february2012/volume_2_issue_2/V2I2048.pdf

Mauch, V., Kunze, M., & Hillenbrand, M. (2012). High performance cloud computing. *Future Generation Computer Systems*, Elsevier B.V. Retrieved from http://linkinghub.elsevier.com/retrieve/pii/S0167739X12000647

Mavodza, J. (2013). The impact of cloud computing on the future of academic library practices and services. *New Library World, 114*(3), 132-141. Emerald Group Publishing Limited. Retrieved from http://www.emeraldinsight.com/journals.htm?issn=0307-4803&volume=114&issue=3/4&articleid=17084096&show=html

Mirashe, S. P., & Kalyankar, N. V. (2010). Cloud Computing. In N. Antonopoulos & L. Gillam (Eds.) *Communications of the ACM, 51*(7), 9. ACM. Retrieved from http://arxiv.org/abs/1003.4074

Ramgovind, S., Eloff, M. M., & Smith, E. (2010). The management of security in Cloud computing. *Information Security for South Africa ISSA 2010*. IEEE. Retrieved from http://ieeexplore.ieee.org/xpls/abs_all.jsp?arnumber=5542654

Report, E. G. (2010). The future of cloud computing. In L. Schubert, K. Jeffery, & B. Neidecker-Lutz (Eds.)*Analysis, 1*(1), 1-26. European Commission. Retrieved from http://cordis.europa.eu/fp7/ict/ssai/docs/cloud-report-final.pdf

Tanimoto, S., Hiramoto, M., Iwashita, M., Sato, H., & Kanai, A. (2011). Risk Management on the Security Problem in Cloud Computing. *2011 First ACISJNU International Conference on Computers Networks Systems and Industrial Engineering*, 147-152. IEEE. Retrieved from http://ieeexplore.ieee.org/lpdocs/epic03/wrapper.htm?arnumber=5954300

Tiwari, P. K. (2012). Future of Cloud Computing in India. *International Journal of Advanced Computer Research, 2*(1), 76–80.

Wang, C.-C., Pai, W.-C., & Yen, N. Y. (2011). A sharable e-Learning platform based on Cloud computing. *2011 3rd International Conference on Computer Research and Development*. IEEE.

Xiu-feng, Q., Jian-wei, L., & Peng-chuan, Z. (2011). Secure cloud computing architecture on mobile internet. *2011 2nd International Conference on Artificial Intelligence Management Science and Electronic Commerce AIMSEC*. IEEE. Retrieved from http://ieeexplore.ieee.org/xpls/abs_all.jsp?arnumber=6083853

KEY TERMS AND DEFINITIONS

Cloud Computing: Is Internet based computing whereby shared resources, information and information are provided to other devices with Internet connection on demand.

Cloud Computing Security: Is set of policies, technologies, and controls deployed to protect data, applications, and the associated infrastructure of cloud computing.

Context Aware Computing: Is a style of computing which is aware of its user's state and surroundings, and helps it adapt its behavior.

Infrastructure as a Service (IaaS): Provides access to computing resource, specifically computing infrastructure, in a virtualized environment, through Internet connection.

Multiple Collaboration Applications: Are designed to help people involved in a common task achieve goals.

Pattern-Based Strategy: Is framework that helps companies exploit patterns in the marketplace for competitive advantage.

Platform as a Service (PaaS): Provides a platform and environment to allow developers to build applications and services over the Internet.

Private Cloud: Represents a cloud computing platform that is implemented within the organization firewall.

Public Cloud: Is provided "as a service" over the Internet and the user's infrastructure or applications are hosted by a cloud service provider at the cloud provider's premises. The core infrastructure is shared between many organizations, but each organization's data & application usage is logically segregated so only authorized users are allowed access.

Service-Oriented Architecture (SOA): Is a strategy that proclaims the intention to build all the software assets in the company using the service-oriented programming methodology.

Social Driven Process: Is a set of logically related tasks performed to achieve a defined valuable social outcome.

Social Web: Is a set of social relations that link people through the World Wide Web.

Software as a Service (SaaS): Cloud model enables user to access and use applications hosted on the cloud.

Chapter 2
Organizational and Management Aspects of Cloud Computing Application in Scientific Research

Mladen Čudanov
University of Belgrade, Serbia

Jovan Krivokapić
University of Belgrade, Serbia

ABSTRACT

This chapter is focused on the business model of scientific research, theoretically analysing managerial, organizational, and financial, rather than technical aspects of this concept. Theoretic explanation is based on an organizational networking platform. In practice, this platform is presented by Seven Bridges Genomics software solution, and the new opportunities for the organizational network broker are illustrated both in theory and practice. The impact that cloud computing has upon organizational performances is theoretically explained by costs of the ICT infrastructure, as well as of transactional and opportunity costs of operations. Through cloud computing, approach opportunity costs are reduced and efficiency is increased. The business model is presented in the framework of Osterwalder and Pigneur. By means of theoretical analysis and practical example, the authors demonstrate the development of a business model related to scientific research in bioinformatics. Cloud computing enables organizational separation of two distinct parts of the scientific research business model: core research and IT support. From the perspective of efficiency, network achieves a higher level of capital utilisation, better resistance to business risks, lower transaction costs, and in general, better efficiency, while the core research part has the opportunity to focus its structure on effectiveness and creativity.

DOI: 10.4018/978-1-4666-5784-7.ch002

INTRODUCTION

This article discusses how cloud computing concept is influencing strategic business aspects of scientific research. Other information and communication technologies (hereinafter: ICT) concepts have also influenced strategic management, (Nolan & McFarlan, 2005) increasing competitive advantage of the business systems if applied in accordance with business aspects. Idea of strategic implementation of ICT is based on the assumption that economic performance is directly associated with the management's competence to create strategic feedback between the market position of the organization and the design of the adequate support for achieving goals (Čudanov, Krivokapić, & Krunić, 2011). Therefore, means for achieving adaptable and dynamic competitive advantage are not regarded from a technocratic view, as a set of sophisticated and advanced technological functionalities, but instead as organizational solutions for better technology utilization in comparison with the competitors (Henderson & Venkatraman, 1993). In other words no ICT application, no matter how technically sophisticated and advanced, can ensure competitive advantage (Čudanov, Krivokapić, & Krunić, 2011). Also, it does not represent fully strategic implementation of ICT, if it is applied without analysing organizational aspects and business model (Čudanov, 2011). The real benefit from the strategic implementation of any ICT concept, in this case cloud computing paradigm, is achieved by the organization's ability to make a long-term use of the ICT based functionalities (Čudanov, 2011). Today, companies base their abilities mostly on information and communication technologies, often without contingent planning - risking that the failure of ICT infrastructure leads to breakdown of organizational operations. Therefore organization should strategically analyse implementation of ICT in order to prevent ICT failures without acceptable solution. Strategic implementation of ICT has four suggested categories:

1. Systems that share information through technologically based systems with buyers/consumers and/or suppliers and change the nature of the relationships;
2. Systems that are more effective in integrating the use of information in the process of new value creation;
3. Systems enabling the organization to develop, produce, place on the market and deliver new or improved information-based products or services; and
4. Systems supporting the managers with development and strategy implementation information, especially by integrating the relevant internal and external information obtained from the analysis (Ward & Peppard, 2009).

It is often a case that ICT determine virtual organization and serve as basis for strategy design (Jaško, Čudanov, & Jevtić, 2009). Our practical example of Seven Bridges Genomics generally covers first three categories of strategic ICT implementation.

One of currently very interesting topics of strategic ICT application is Cloud Computing paradigm, defined as the "Model that adequately ensures access to the shared set of computer resources (e.g., networks, servers, memory space, applications or data processing services) that can be configured, promptly protected and used with a minimum effort by the organizational management or interaction with the entity providing the services." Main characteristic of cloud computing are: autonomous use of services at request, broad access to the network, joining resources, fast flexibility (of response to user claim) and measuring of service delivery; it can be used as private, public, hybrid and joined; three manners of service provision are described: software as service, platform as service and infrastructure as service (Mell & Grance, 2009). Companies today face turning-point: to adopt or not to adopt the cloud computing concept and practically set a section of the entire information infrastructure out of the physical area of the company, hiring third party to maintain it, as once was the case with electrical energy (Čudanov, Krivokapić, & Krunić, 2011). Several ICT industry giants, like Amazon, are starting to offer cloud computing services. Presence of such competitors and amounts of invested funds indicate that cloud computing should be counted on in the very near future and that companies should make their best efforts in order to prepare technically, but even more important – organizationally and operationally, for its implementation and to get maximum efficiency and effectiveness in realization of organizational goals from its advantages.

Most of the technologies related to cloud computing, like online data storage, visualisation of computer resources, Web services and applications are already present, discussed in research community and tested to some degree in practice. Currently, one of important, but not sufficiently explained factors might be management perspective on implementation of cloud computing. It offers solution to questions of efficiency, reliability, strategic agility and adaptability through partly or entirely replacing the information resources of the company. This chapter will analyze problem of application of cloud computing in scientific research from organizational and business perspective in order to improve efficiency and effectiveness of main involved parties.

DIFFERENCES BETWEEN THE CLASSICAL AND CLOUD COMPUTING APPROACH TO INFORMATION AND COMMUNICATION TECHNOLOGIES IN THE ORGANIZATION

Growing importance of ICT, which was described earlier, requires more organizational resources allocated to ICT needs for achieving never fully achievable goals of infrastructure development.

ICT infrastructure should meet the needs of scalability, flexibility and organizational changes. It is also important to notice that total costs related to hardware, software, labour and other services are growing steadily on a global scale since 2001 (Cowhey & Aronson, 2009), and have become the subject of great importance in the budget of the companies.

As a consequence, new trends have become popular among managers responsible for information systems (CIOs). That involves outsourcing ICT-related jobs that do not support the major competency of the organization. Outsourcing these activities increases the efficiency of the organization in couple of ways. First of all, it is obvious that the costs are being reduced because the organization does not have to make large investments in some fields it is not expert in, and that is why it uses specialized services, provided by some other organizations, that have ability to perform the same work at significantly lower costs, thus in a position to offer such specialized services at decent prices. Also, the efficiency of the organization's services has increased by allowing organization to focus on what is essential for it and thus improve their business. Having known these facts, it is obvious that "cloud computing," greatly differs from the traditional approach, as it will be shown in following lines. So, main characteristics of traditional approach would be (Skilton, 2010):

- Hardware is inside the organization that not only uses, but also maintains it;
- Information resources (software and hardware) are permanently available at any time in the same quantity of resources – both in "smooth" business conditions and in the moments of highest demand (for example, when it is greatest workload on the system);
- If resources are unused for a longer period of time, traditional methods such as money returns or some kind of compensations can be negotiated at best case;

- Organization is also responsible for and pays for depreciation;
- Organization pays for the maintenance of functionality of infrastructure, is responsible for replacing inappropriate components and must cover all the disparities that can be influenced by unforeseen circumstances,
- Slow introduction of new capacities into production is noticed (includes selection, purchase and installation), this might last several months or a year on average;
- In current business conditions, there is a high risk of huge fixed (capital) expenses which may result into the situation of capital being "trapped" in the means of production (Čudanov, Krivokapić, & Krunić, 2011).

As seen, traditional approach provides some well known concepts, but leaves place for many improvements. On the other hand, the basic characteristics of Cloud computing approach are (Skilton, 2010):

- Hardware remains at the service provider (public cloud) or it is partly with the provider (hybrid), or entirely within the organization (private cloud);
- Services are paid on a short-term principle so that companies can avoid unnecessary payments for unused resources, and that is not possible when the infrastructure is physically owned;
- Information resources (software and hardware) are used as the services, whose capacities decrease or increase depending on the demand or organizational needs;
- While using the "cloud" resources, the organization has chance to abstract all its worries and so can be focused only upon the amount of resources it uses and price per unit of resources which are contracted with the provider of "cloud" services;

- Capacities can be expanded within a couple of seconds, by just a couple of clicks;
- Organization has no concerns about depreciation of infrastructure in the "cloud;"
- The risk of business is by far lower thanks to extremely low capital costs that are transferred into operations costs, and so the organization owns more money that can be used for "core" activity (Čudanov, Krivokapić, & Krunić, 2011).

IMPACT OF "CLOUD COMPUTING" ON ORGANIZATIONAL STRUCTURE

Companies which are using services of cloud computing usually have the organizational structure that is more network-oriented, rather than based on the traditional hierarchal structure (Hugos & Hulitzky, 2010). It will be illustrated in our practical example of Seven Bridges Genomics Company, where large part of activities is outsourced to a network of partners. The main reason for this type of organization is the fact that network structure allows its business units much higher level of autonomy. These companies support the flexibility of the structure by using the shared service model, which has the core unit responsible for coordination, but also sets the objectives, general strategies, and provides support for other business units with its administration, systems support and financial services (Jaško, Jaško, & Čudanov, 2010). This type of organization enables business units to release these jobs, so they can fully concentrate on specialized operations that really earn profit. Focusing on small number of activities allows the benefits of economies of scale, and also provides changes of business processes in the organization. It is pretty obvious that, in addition to their impact on business processes or organizational structures, information and communication technologies affect many other aspects of business. Those aspects might be management style (Čudanov, Jaško, &

Jevtić, 2009), control orientation (Čudanov & Jaško, 2010), the distribution of power in organization (Čudanov, 2007), or the size of company (Čudanov, Jaško, & Savoiu, 2010). It must be considered that the impact of the structure is achieved through growth, and that organizations are worried about keeping the flexibility of their structures. This can be solved by creating new business units which can be able to meet the new needs of the environment. The size of these new organizational units might be growing to such an extent that it does allow the efficient and effective operation. Usually, the core unit becomes a member with a coordinating role in particular business operation for these newly formed business units, as shown in the Figure 1. This mode of restructuring often leads to increasing number of the "outsourced" activities, which are sometimes seen as irrational or unreasonable (Stanimirović & Vintar, 2010).

Figure 1. Network model of responsive and agile organization (Hugos & Hulitzky, 2010)

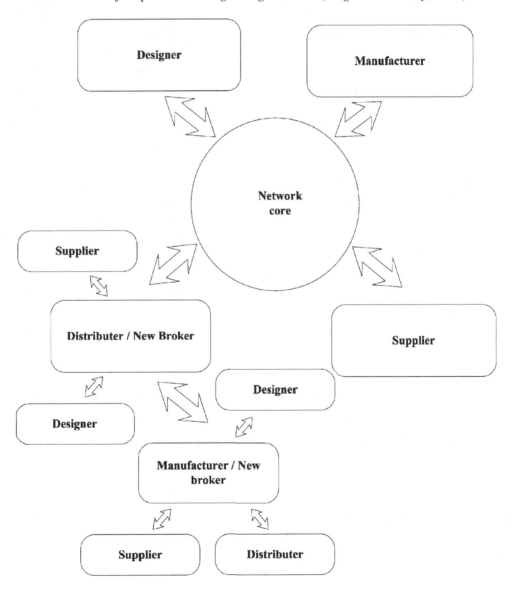

Introduction of network and virtual organizations opens space for organizational implementation of cloud computing concept in advanced fashion. Important issues for analysis are meta-system and coordination functions, since effective implementation depends strongly on efficiency of those functions. Migration of these functions on cloud makes it easier for the network core to build a firm ICT platform, establish and maintain a dynamic network structure (Jaško, Jaško, & Čudanov, 2010). Diverse intelligent and simulation systems allow for the relevant data to become easily accessible to the companies – network participants without significant costs. Emphasizing search for a high quality of coordination and communication, they are therefore in a position to get an insight into the status of the operations under way at any moment in the network.

In order to achieve those goals, various Business Intelligence (hereinafter: BI) and Business Process Management (BPM) methods are used. On one hand, they allow for the data transparency and visibility, however, they also control thc data and information that circulate through and between companies (Čudanov, Krivokapić, & Krunić, 2011). BI and BPM can offer the opportunity of tracking the status for every task or goal in the real time. To achieve higher quality performance companies can also employ the Complex Event Processing systems (hereinafter: CEP), which select especially significant and critical information. It should be noticed from technical perspective that cloud-based systems are characterised by well defined Application Program Interfaces (hereinafter: API), which allow for implementing a Service-Oriented Architecture (SOA), for the purpose of developing the network and implementing the best practices. All these are reflected in creating efficient organizational networks, and they in turn offer broad opportunities to the participant companies, since their implementation can result in considerable savings due to the realization of the economy of scope and increased collaboration (Figure 2).

IMPACT OF CLOUD COMPUTING ON ORGANIZATIONAL PERFORMANCE

Among important influences of the cloud computing concept on the organization, one of the crucial is impact on organizational performance by reducing operating costs. Companies can improve their business by meeting three standards of operation (Hugos & Hulitzky, 2010): variable operating costs, low capital costs, and scalable computer platform. It is important to realize that these impacts are important both for companies where ICT is used as a back-up for most of the key activities, and for those companies that mainly use ICT in supporting and auxiliary activities. Some operations can be left beside for all organizations that may be necessary for ICT resources (Jinhui, Shiping, Chen, David, & Zic, 2010) with variable costs. However, the financial crisis on business since 2009 influenced reduction of major capital investments. The request to provide the infrastructure that will be adjustable to these special needs to such an extent that the fixed costs of its development become virtually variable can be fulfilled by usage of "cloud computing" concept, as shown in Figure 3.

In the practical example given later in text, genomic research needs significant investment in ICT infrastructure due to large demand for computing power in analysis of sequenced DNA data. Risk of substantial fixed investment in infrastructure is particularly present in the field of ICT, because technological change makes technology obsolete much faster than in any other industries. The change from investing in their own infrastructure to new business areas is potentially smart move for the company due to the fact that services are charged based on consumption. This paying model is commonly known as "pay for drinks model" (Schwan, 2009). However, in the traditional model of IT costs in Figure 3, the cost of IT capacity, presented as a step-like dash-dot line, is fixed. It significantly deviates from the actual demand for IT resources, which is marked by a full line. It is not rare situation to have surplus of

Figure 2. Cloud concept-based business structure represented through network of different organizations (Hugos & Hulitzky, 2010)

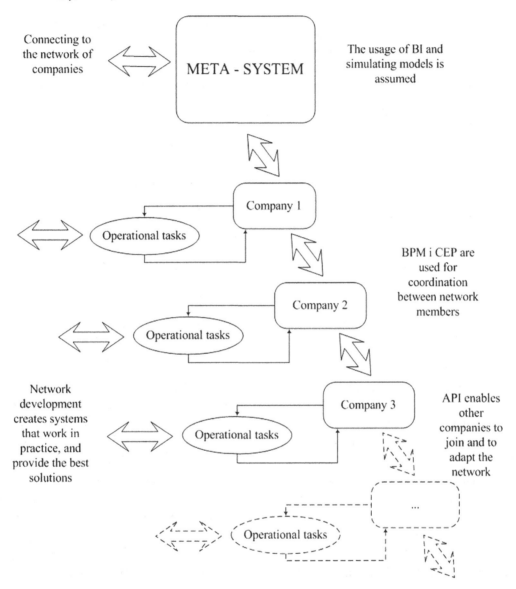

funds in terms of demand (marked as +). On the other hand, sometimes available capacity is not sufficient to meet current needs for IT resources. Such situation is often seen in usage of local computer cluster networks for analysis of scientific data. They are often adjusted and designed to answer for demand spikes, or period of time when their utilization is needed, while full capacities are used 10% of their potential most of the time.

Total deviations from lines presented in the figure might show potential loss. This loss could come from idle capital investments, but it can cause some larger business losses. Additional expenses which do not affect the functionality of the ICT infrastructure directly are presented as ΔC. These costs are caused by complexity of transactions or by their increased number, but also can be consequence of migration actions or

Figure 3. Traditional model of fixed costs in the context of IT demand oscilation (Hugos & Hulitzky, 2010)

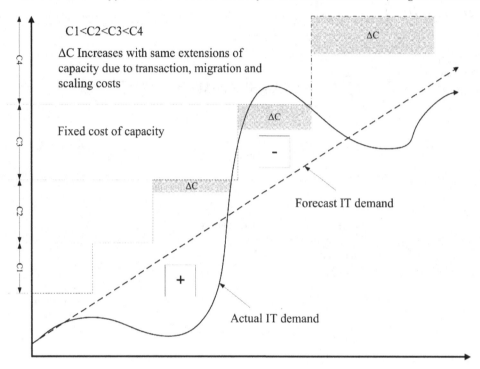

system scaling or growth scaling at the same ICT infrastructure capacity.

One of the main characteristics of businesses supported by cloud computing concept is that costs and offers are adjusted in very flexible manner. It might be compared with possibility to hire a taxi instead of buying a car, or to release some services (i.e. delivery services) to the others instead of buying equipment for own people that could do it. It is clear that in the case of ICT service delivery marginal costs of delivering one more service or digital delivery of contents to one more user are extremely low, practically equal zero value (Osterwalder & Pigneur, 2010), so it is possible to develop a model of free offer of contents. This model might be financed by charging the consumers of advanced, premium service. There are some examples of this kind of services in Google (Google calendar, Google docs, Google mail).

Thanks to that, the user doesn't have to consider the choice between different specialized software because he can get what he needs at no cost (An-

derson, 2009) whether it includes advanced services at variable prices or it is in the form of subscription which is many times reduced in comparison with fixed investments. This enables development of new business functions. Our practical example of Seven Bridges Genomics which will be presented in later text has exactly the same point. For another shorter example, implementation of distant learning programmes at a higher education organization becomes possible without employing large fixed investments (Vujin, 2010), and that provides both organizational benefits and benefits in performances. For small firms (which do not have big budgets) this might be the opportunity to use high class ICT services, and to pay only marginal costs of usage, increased for the commission for provider (Lagar-Cavilla, Whitney, Scannell, Patchin, Rumble, de Lara, Brudno, & Satyanarayanan, 2009). Service providers, on the other hand, have benefits by reaching the economy of scope (Iosup, Ostermann, Yigitbasi, Prodan, Fahringer, & Epema, 2011) and the economy of scale if they are able to implement one same platform in order to provide a variety of diverse services.

Company which chooses cloud computing approach to provide the required ICT resources is aware that infrastructure required for the ICT resources is much easier to follow the real needs. The variable costs model, which is shown in the example of the Amazon cloud service, is more appropriate for the turbulent market conditions, because it ensures availability of sufficient resources at any time, in order to meet the current demand. This means that the costs are higher only if the demand is higher, and, logically, smaller if the demand is lower. That concept is in perfect accordance with the efficiency of the company's business.

As it is shown in Figure 1, the difference between the real demand and the capacity consumption really is considerably smaller. Thanks to the flexible nature of the cloud computing concept of resource usage, the real demand does not exceed the capacities. The efficiency of busi-

ness operations is also significantly improved, since there is no failure while trying to satisfy the clients' needs, nor losses as consequences of inadequate estimates. It further means that there is no longer need for long-term planning of ICT capacities. Since the focus is upon customers themselves, the invested capital is employed in a considerably better way. It is much easier to meet customers' needs and requirements while the errors are being minimized simultaneously. On the other side, cloud computing is answering current need for "green" computing, if the off-site computing is located near sources of renewable energy, which does not create technical problems. Furthermore, as computing resources require energy consumption even when unused in a local data centre, low underutilization of computing resources through frequent usage by others increases the efficiency of energy usage. Capacity in comparison to implementation ratio for Amazon Web service documentation is shown in Figure 4 (Skilton, 2010).

Figure 4. Capacity in comparison to implementation ratio - Amazon Web service documentation

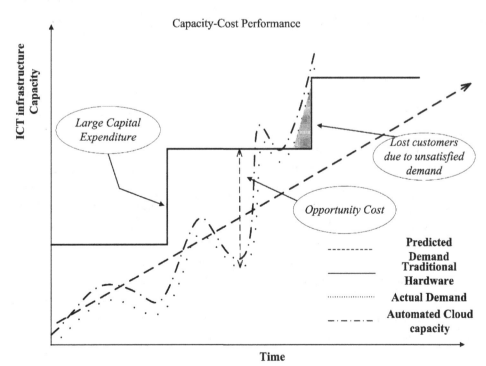

SEVEN BRIDGES GENOMICS: BUSINESS MODEL OF CLOUD COMPUTING APPLICATION IN SCIENCE

This case presents Seven Bridges Genomics (in further text SBG), a bio-informatics start-up based in Boston and Belgrade. Case study is mainly focused on business model of SBG and other organizational, financial and management aspects. Company is set to offer DNA processing as a service to research labs (Čudanov, Savoiu, & Jaško, 2012). Founded by four inspired entrepreneurs and funded by respectable team of angel investors, company is in a rapid growth phase. Current engineering efforts are directed towards launching and improving private beta version of the platform. The case is presented in order to illustrate theoretical outline on business model, organizational changes and financial benefits of using Cloud Computing in research, not as illustration of effective or ineffective business practices.

The service which SBG intends to offer is directed at institutions performing academic research, industry research and development in biotechnology and bioengineering, pharmaceuticals and other forms of research related to the field of genomics. Genomics, a discipline in genetics concerning the study of the genomes of organisms is a very prosperous field, with various applications. In the field of academic core research, popular genetic studies of human ancestry shed new light on paths of human prehistoric migrations (Moreno, 2011). Advances in the field of industrial R&D can be illustrated by analyzing genomes of species needed for efficient biofuel production. Analysis of 12 feedstock models, 25 Biomass degraders and 8 fuel producing organisms were either in draft, in progress phases or complete even during the year of 2008 (Rubin, 2010). Industry is very interested in developing approach to produce liquid fuel based on lignocellulosic biomass, due to various economic and environmental reasons like ability to cultivate plants in marginal soil that is not normally used in agriculture. Process includes cultivation of plants, physical, chemical and enzyme pre-treatment, conversion to sugars and later conversion of sugars to biofuel. Genomics is helping to facilitate three crucial steps in that process. Also, research performed on individual level is growing, and 38 companies offered direct-to-consumer genetic ancestry testing (Royal, Novembre, Fullerton, Goldstein, Long, Bamshad, & Clark, 2010). Having in mind distinguishing human curiosity and wide range of application in paternal, sibling and forensic context, it could be perceived as nucleus of future industry. Also there is wide healthcare application, where e.g. parallel sequencing can lead to identification of mutations causing rare diseases, like Miller syndrome, Metachondromatosis, Schinzel–Giedion syndrome, Fowler syndrome, Kabuki syndrome or Joubert syndrome (Ng, Nickerson, Bamshad, & Shendure, 2010). Concrete customer needs that SBG will answer can be illustrated with medical doctors who might want to know which illnesses patient could be pre-disposed to and thus come to a better diagnosis and treatment, or researchers with raw data could find the gene responsible for the surveyed condition (Čudanov, Savoiu, & Jaško, 2012). With all this in mind, genomic research can be regarded as explosively growing field, with numerous lucrative applications that will further propel the growth. Speed of growth in DNA sequencing can be illustrated by National Human Genome Research Institute chart, representing decline in costs per megabase (million base pairs) sequencing, compared with Moore's law which influences advancement in information and communication technologies. Costs per Megabase of DNA Sequence (National Human Genome Research Institute, 2013) are shown in Figure 5.

Prerequisite technology for genetic sequencing, as set of methods and technologies that are used for determining the order of the nucleotide bases—adenine, guanine, cytosine, and thymine in a molecule of DNA is exponentially growing. Ge-

Figure 5. Costs per megabase of DNA sequence

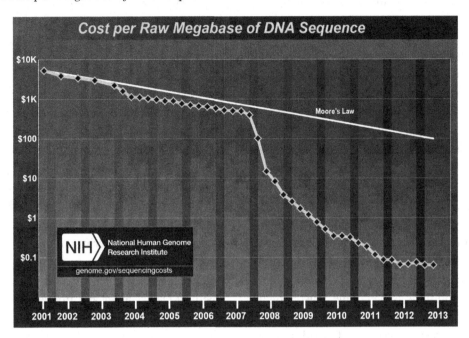

netic sequencing is becoming resource affordable for almost all standard laboratories with the advancement of benchtop sequencing machines for medium-size sequencing projects (Rusk, 2011). Very fast growing market of DNA decoders is dominated by players such as Illumina, Life Technologies, Complete Genomics, Pacific Biosciences, Oxford Nanopore, Roche and IBM (Herper, 2011). On the lower end of the spectrum, Personal Genome Machine (PGM) developed by the Jonathan Rothberg has cut the price to 50.000 USD per unit. That is particularly interesting, because in such case sequencing equipment is costing less than average computing resources needed to analyses sequenced DNA data, roughly estimated at 130.000 USD (Dudley, Pouliot, Chen, Morgan, & Butte, 2010). Even though accuracy of Personal Genome Machine may not fit advanced research requirements, it is still high and has application in research and practice. Such and similar devices could trigger revolution, where DNA sequencing would become usual procedure performed by trained medical personnel, just like radiology today.

Currently, costs of DNA sequencing are falling rapidly in a fashion similar, but now faster than Moore's law for computing costs. According to the research performed by Stein (2010) in the year of 2010 costs were on the level of 100.000.000 base pairs of sequenced DNA per US dollar, while in the year of 1990 not even a single base pair could be sequenced for US dollar. Until the year of 2004, advancement in genomic sequencing was in slower than advancement in the IT industry needed for analysis of that sequenced data, like costs of hard disk storage and processing. Until the year of 2004 in average, number of base pairs that could be sequenced for one US dollar doubled every 19 months. After the year of 2004 and introduction of next generation sequencing, trend has completely reversed, and currently doubling time for number of base pairs that can be sequenced for one US dollar is 5 months, creating a bottleneck e.g. in available hard disk space which is doubling every 14 months. (Stein, 2010)

While decentralization of DNA sequencing into independent laboratories and medical facilities is aided by this technology, sequencing itself does not bear benefits without further analysis. Suddenly increased output of sequenced data caused demand for bioinformation processing, thus creating a bottleneck represented by existing processing infrastructure. Computing resources needed for bioinformatics are substantial (Kim, Hou, & Cho, 2011), whatever the manner of the execution is. Problem with classic, server based data centers used for computing DNA sequenced information is that they are engineered to provide peak information process capacity.

However, demand for information processing varies greatly, and fixed investments in development of hardware infrastructure are not justified by usage in substantial periods where demand for processing is very low or none. For such reasons, even institutions as Wellcome Trust Sanger Institute, one of the leaders in Human Genome Project, and perhaps among best funded institutions in the industry are considering replacing their processing resources infrastructure with cloud computing approach (Čudanov, Savoiu, & Jaško, 2012). Motivation is found in elastic, pay-as-you-go nature of cloud services such as Amazon publicly hosted datasets meaning lower infrastructure overheads, as only in-use compute and storage is charged (Bateman & Wood, 2009). Among other benefits, Bateman and Wood state transfer of large datasets. As an alternative to shipping the data for others to analyze, cloud approaches allow the computing resources to remain close to the data, because allowing others to access your compute infrastructure may be preferable to distributing large datasets Bateman & Wood, 2009).

SBG BUSINESS MODEL

Among important reasons fostering development of Seven Bridges Genomics cloud computing supported business model is lack of available funds needed by research and medical institutions to develop platforms on their own. As one of the

Seven Bridges Genomics founders has observed, budget cuts prompted by the economic crisis tightened up budgets substantially, especially for capital investments (Čudanov, Savoiu, & Jaško, 2012). Research in the field support such claims, stating that budget cuts in medical research will make addressing the elements of an innovation framework more difficult (Smaglik, 2011).

Since few institutions today own computing resources needed for efficient processing of sequenced genome, and even those owning infrastructure doubt economic benefits of such approach, SBG has open space for developing a business model for offering an entirely cloud-based computing service. This model will be simplified and presented in business model canvas, developed by Osterwalder and Pigneur (2010). Main components of their canvas are:

- Customer Segments
- Value Propositions
- Channels
- Customer Relationships
- Revenue Streams
- Key Resources
- Key Activities
- Key Partnerships
- Cost Structure

Customer Segments

Customer Segments represent different groups of people that enterprise aim to reach and serve. In the case of Seven Bridges genomics, main customer segments are research institutions performing academic research, and commercial companies performing research and development in biotechnology, bioengineering, pharmaceuticals and other related fields. Common characteristic for both is lack of resources needed to develop processing infrastructure needed for analysis of sequenced DNA data or acceptance of economic incentive to use less costly cloud computing approach. According to PriceWaterhouseCoopers, at the beginning of 2011 medical gene tests and other molecular diagnostics generated 2.6 billion USD, while DNA sequencing hardware generated 1.5 billion of USD. It is generated mostly by customer segments targeted by Seven Bridges Genomics. According to Forbes article, this industry could grow to 100 billion USD in the near future (Herper, 2011) and generators of that value would be hospitals and research laboratories.

Value Propositions

Value propositions in the model of Osterwalder and Pigneur represent bundle of products that create value for specific customer segment. In this case, main value propositions of Seven Bridges Genomics are substantial cost reduction, increased collaboration, accessibility, usability and performance in this novel industry. Cost reduction is relative term, but recent research has proven that in general, local cluster setups and cloud computing services are best compared when taking into account average utilization rates and expectations on process runtimes. On-demand model of the cloud makes it most attractive when compared to a local, often under-utilized cluster, since paying for idle cycles is avoided using cloud (Angiuoli, White, Matalka, White, & Fricke, 2011) . In such case costs could be significantly reduced in comparison with developing alternative infrastructure for processing amount of sequenced data. Most analysis observed in previously cited article is performed in less than 24 hours for the cost below 100 USD. On the other hand, different set of authors estimated costs of setting up a local computer cluster consisting of 240 CPUs to roughly 130.000 USD on annual basis (Dudley, Pouliot, Chen, Morgan, & Butte, 2010).

Next part of value proposition consists of research software that is planned to be developed by third parties in a model similar to App Store (Sheffield, 2011). Instead of "reinventing the wheel" by developing genome analysis tools that grow obsolete in approximately six months, Seven

Bridges Genomics will focus on development of the platform that will use standard open-source software tools on the cloud (Sheffield, 2011). It has double benefits for the business model – one is value generation for the users, who gain access to standardized tools from different branches of genomics analysis. Analysis tools and algorithms standardized on one platform would relieve users from version control, updates, installation, program parameters and compatibility. Second benefit is cutting development costs of these tools, important issue in this stage of company. Such costs can additionally burden company in initial phases of development, where Seven Bridges Genomics is now. Those costs can be transferred to third parties that may have strong economic or non-economic incentives (such as research grant goals or comparison of different methods in analysis same data) to develop useful algorithms and tools. It is one of basic presumptions of network organization explained in theoretical part of this article. Anand and Daft also describe such organizational structure as modular, describing how such companies are able to share development costs with its partners, slash the cycle time required to launch a new product, and enter the market at a price point that was far beyond competitors, which was about $3 million less than nearest competitor in the case of Bombardier's Continental business jet described in their article (Anand & Daft, 2007).

Another plaguing issue in genomic analysis is usage of scripts necessary to use software for analysis. That requires engagement of script programmer (Tata, Patel, Friedman, & Swaroop, 2005; Kirsten & Rahm, 2006), which is in practice usually a dedicated position. Script programmer position in such case is bottleneck in spikes of frequent analysis, and underused when there is no need for performing the analysis. Since each step in the analysis process, like data conversion, assembly/alignment, variant calling or filtering and annotation is handled by a different tool (which is often produced by a different research institution) (Sheffield, 2011), scripts can be confusing and non-intuitive. User-friendly workflow editor enables graphical representation of every step of the analysis, precluding need for developed IT skills, installation and management of software and version control of software and data. Workflow editor in its beta version is presented in Figure 6, by courtesy of Seven Bridges Genomics.

As another value proposition, all researchers with Internet access and a computer, or practically all interested researchers can collaborate freely using same tools, same project workflows and same datasets. Such collaboration is very beneficial ground for generating new insights and ideas, therefore improving research process. Regarding levels of collaborator engagement, classes such as private, read-only and execute are defined as part of collaboration platform (Sheffield, 2011) Collaboration can be significant boost to creativity in research environment (Laudel, 2001) and researchers in genomics and related areas form a "small world network" that boost creativity up to a certain level (Milgram, 1967) even in different fields of collaboration, such as artistic expression Uzzi, & Spiro, 2005).

Channels

Osterwalder and Pigneur describe channels as a mean for company to communicate with and reach to customer segments, to which company plans to deliver value propositions. In the case of Seven Bridges Genomics, Web sales are the obvious solution. Since service itself is customized, other means of channels between company and customers would be below needed effectiveness and efficiency. Also, the very nature of the platform allows little space for other channels of value distribution to customers, or discussion on that topic.

Customer Relationships

Customer Relationships are regarded as set activities aimed at establishing relations with customers, with intention of customer acquisition, retention and boosting sales. Osterwalder and Pigneur categorize customer relations into personal assistance (general or dedicated), self service, automated services, communities and co-creation. Since

Figure 6. Workflow editor

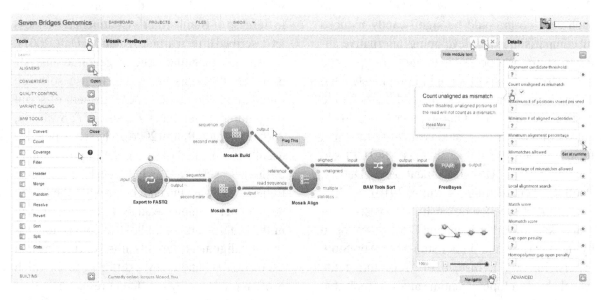

this part of business model is not yet extensively elaborated in Seven Bridges Genomics formal documents, we will suggest it in context of other business model segments. Customer relationships need to be a dynamic function of the company, which will differ in early and adolescent/prime/ stable stages of company development.

During early phases, dedicated personal assistance is an expensive, but strategically useful approach. Cooperation between customers who will use first software versions and dedicated company representatives usually yields positive "mouth-to-mouth" advertising and also forms a knowledge base that will enable development of automated customer support system.

According to other components of the business model, later stages of company development will need to have system customized to preferences of the individual users that will support their interaction with Seven Bridges Genomics platform.

Open nature of value creation also suggests development of networks that will support user communities. Interaction tools such as social networks, forums etc. can serve as a mean of communication between researchers and solve specific genomics issues better than company representatives would.

Revenue Streams

Revenue Streams segment is not disclosed in detail for the purpose of this case by Seven Bridges Genomics. Currently, company plans to implement pay-as-you-go model that will charge usage of SBG platform as a service and is still collecting data and designing appropriate software solutions for pricing in order to:

- Correctly incorporate usage of computing, storage, bandwidth and other costs, and
- Optimize mutual benefit of company and customers.

Since top management also leaves open space for innovation and improvement in that segment, we have proposed our opinions on approaches to revenue streams. According to that, we have taken care to fit other segments of Seven Bridges Genomics business and user needs. One important part of the context, from the perspective of the user, is a sum of costs of the analysis related to adding value after the process of genome sequencing. For the reference, costs of reliable sequencing are expected to fall below 1000$. In example shown by Sboner et al. these costs were at around 6500$ using Illumina HiSeq 2000 machine, while RNA sequencing would cost around 3500$, with data management and reduction costs included (Sboner, Mu, Greenbaum, Auerbach, & Gerstein, 2011) That analysis is using prices from July 2011. Afterwards user has option to perform calculation in own local computer cluster, paying relatively fixed price for its development, maintenance, upgrading, software licensing and personnel costs and relatively variable price for electricity and other similar costs, or to perform calculations using virtual machines on cloud service providers.

Following the sequencing, analysis would be performed on virtual machines that Seven Bridges Genomics platform can create via cloud services provider. Amazon Web Services (AWS) elastic compute cloud is suggested as a possible solution due to ability to quickly scale capacity according to computing requirements and other benefits such as existing databases of sequenced genetic data. Main revenues are expected from charging services performed by those virtual machines to customers via Seven Bridges Genomics software platform. There are two possible approaches of charging those services. First idea is to directly relate revenues to costs of cloud computing service, augmented by Seven Bridges Genomics platform fee. Second option is to use reversed approach, and to charge the fees according to perceived user benefits from performed analysis. Alternatives can be developed into these options:

- Cost related usage fee:
  - Pre-service price estimation,
  - Post service calculation.
- Service value based usage fees.

In first case, which includes *cost related usage fee*, user would perform calculations on a virtual machine costing e.g. 100$, which would be paid to Seven Bridges Genomics in amount of 100$*x%, where x depends on their pricing policies and strategies. This approach has its weak side since costs associated with usage of cloud computing resources cannot be exactly predicted. Most providers develop dynamic market based on system where customers place bids on free cloud resources and utilize instances for as long as the bid exceeds the current price. Since that mechanism introduces dynamic demand / supply environment that changes on hourly base, it makes this pricing method difficult to plan. Although prices of computing resources are steadily falling, it is indicative to analyse range of those prices, which was averaged $0.26 compared to an on-demand price of $0.68 per hour for c1.xlarge instance on Amazon Web Services (AWS) elastic compute cloud. C1.xlarge provided 8 virtual CPU cores, 8 GB RAM per instance, and 400 GB of local temporary disk storage (Angiuoli, White, Matalka, White, & Fricke, 2011) Therefore, there is possibility to perform same calculation for approximately third of the costs, if it is acceptable to wait and perform calculations when resources are low-priced. Such environment suggests following options:

Pre-service price estimation option would mean that Seven Bridges Genomics would use statistical approach to estimate highest cost level with acceptable reliability and charge that amount as exact costs before the resources needed for performing the operation are engaged. Strengths of that approach are that customers would not be burdened by complicated procedure and would be charged by intuitive "pay-per-drink" concept, and that company will have a solid base for further

development of a system that will offer more affordable pricing to users, related to the time they are agreed to wait for analysis results. Weaknesses are that company needs to develop and maintain modules for estimating costs of resource engagement, which is expensive, complicated and prone to change, and that estimations can be wrong and even lead to incurring greater costs for Seven Bridges Genomics than the amount customer is charged.

Second option *post service calculation* is similar to pre-paid service of mobile operators. User would need to open an account at Seven Bridges Genomics and pay initial amount of money that would be used for cloud resources engaging. Seven Bridges Genomics have to perform rough calculation, using peak demand prices to see if workflow designed by user would overcome available credit, and warn user that calculations might be stopped before they are finished. In case user has sufficient amount of money on his account, resources needed for the operation will be engaged, and service charged afterwards in exact amount of costs of cloud computing resources augmented by Seven Bridges Genomics fee, subtracting the calculated amount from available user credit. Pros of this approach are availability of cash that boosts liquidity of the company, elimination of risks that costs will not be adequately estimated and will overcome charged amount. Weaknesses are probability that users will be suspicious in placing initial credits before service proves as usable and company gains wide credibility, that approach still demands development of algorithms for estimation of analysis costs.

Second approach to revenue streams, *service value based usage fees*, is based on the idea that differences in speed of advancement of genome sequencing technology and information technology have open possibility that some of the research institutions can afford genome sequencing devices without being able to afford server farm with compatible computing power to analyse sequence data. Due to that, demand of such institutions for computing resources is currently very inelastic –

differences of few hundred USD in price is not too much important in case when research laboratories have to compare fixed costs of around several hundred thousand dollars with several hundred dollars of service. Therefore, perspective of pricing can be reversed, and Seven Bridges Genomics can calculate fee for its services on the basis of how much it is worth to the customer, estimating average budgets that research laboratories have for producing their results. Since every service is unique in nature, common unit will have to be found on base of classes of operations SBG will perform. For example SBG processor/hours for data conversion, assembly/alignment, variant calling or filtering and annotation could be priced, considering prices and taking care that they are not below cloud resource costs at peak demand level. Pros for this approach are that in the beginning, fees calculated on that way could be higher than cost-based calculations, it is more intuitive to determine price on the basis of user value and prices could have a better fit with user needs. Also, Seven Bridges Genomics has margin to refund back part of the money to the users if calculations are performed in times of less demand for cloud resources, which might cause positive reaction of customers. Weaknesses of this approach are that Seven Bridges Genomics will actively have to analyse its customers and values they create in order to estimate prices, and that such approach could strategically direct company toward profit maximisation instead of customer satisfaction maximization, hindering creation of fair long-term relationship with customers, leaving the company more vulnerable to competitors.

Targeted advertisements are possible revenue stream of lateral importance. Again, not disclosed by Seven Bridges Genomics, this decision is a mere author suggestion in context of other segments and environment. Industry worth tens of billions of dollars, with around thirty different genome sequencing companies have large rivalry, and targeted advertisements to companies who analyse sequenced data can be very valuable, therefore

giving Seven Bridges Genomics an opportunity to establish another lateral revenue stream. It is not imperative for Seven Bridges Genomics, and is depended on their policy of customer relationships. This revenue stream can be eliminated if such approach diminishes other advantages of the company.

Key Resources

Key Resources are defined as most important assets required for making a business model work (Osterwalder & Pigneur, 2010). Seven Bridges Genomics is mostly based on human resources that will develop and maintain their software platform, currently in beta testing version. So if we say that software platform is the heart of the system that will drive creation of value propositions, dedicated human resources who will further develop and maintain are its body and soul. Seven Bridges Genomics has already employed a team of about twenty software engineers and entrepreneurs, strengthened by external collaborators, which include key researchers, scholars or investors in growing genomics industry. Other important parts of key resources are numerous contacts Seven Bridges Genomics and external associates have in the field, and maybe most important long-term resource is trust that is currently building between the company and test users of beta version of the platform, and that could make basis of future strong SBG brand. Physical resources are not crucial for Seven Bridges Genomics for now, because lion's share of the computing power needed by the customers is currently outsourced to cloud service providers.

Key Activities

Key Activities are day-to-day tasks that need to be performed in order to create proposed values and achieve business goals. In the case of Seven Bridges Genomics, activities are mostly aimed to developing and maintaining complex software based platform. Important segments of platform are also third-party algorithm developers, customers, industry regulators, cutting-edge researcher and sequencing companies, whose interests and achievement will have to find delicate balance in the future of Seven Bridges Genomics Business, and it certainly will not be achieved by chance.

Key Partnerships

Key Partnerships are established at first with dedicated bioinformatics labs producing state of the art research software (Sheffield, 2011) compatible with and complimentary to Seven Bridges Genomics platform. These partnerships are necessary in order to outsource development of complimentary tools to parties that have better funding, motivation and knowledge to do it. Also, a long-term partnership with cloud service providers, currently Amazon, is important. Another set of key partnerships is formed with broad range of genomic concerns, like cancer genomic projects, DNA sequencing core laboratories and commercial sequencing facilities, basic academic researchers, agricultural genomics concerns, and at least one flagship National Genome Project (Sheffield, 2011) is needed as initial user of first software versions. Institutions funding research in genomics are also among key partners. Due to their primary goal of efficient and effective distribution of funds, they can be interested into development of platform that will relieve them from investing in expensive fixed assets. Also, companies producing sequencing equipment are important partner due to needed mutual adjustment in order to achieve compatibility. All those partnerships can be developed into strategic alliance, and maybe some of the large companies in sequencing industry might recognize interests of acquiring or merging with Seven Bridges Genomics in order to provide portfolio of hardware, full-service data and analysis power. There is also a possibility to extend partnership with genome research funding institutions. They might consider diverting some

funding to Seven Bridges Genomics and/or its future competitors who will provide services for researcher in return, instead of investing into costly and often redundant infrastructure.

Cost Structure

Cost Structure describes all costs incurred to operate business model (Osterwalder & Pigneur, 2010). Fixed costs are related to platform development and maintenance, mostly human resources and overhead costs. Variable costs are fees charged by cloud service providers. Due to the economies of scale, where costs per unit diminishes as output expands, and economies of scope, where large scope of different IT related operations is performed for less money, due to elimination of redundant support, cloud service providers can acquire hardware, software and other resources under better terms and transfer that discount to customers via Seven Bridges Genomics. Elaborate comparative analysis of cloud computing and classic local server centre costs is presented by Dudley et al. (2011), and it shows that direct costs of local centre were 0.06$ per CPU hour, in comparison with cloud resources used at total cost of 0.19$ per hour (Dudley, Pouliot, Chen, Morgan, & Butte, 2010). However, this analysis presumes that data centre is utilized with full capacity 100% of the time, which is totally unrealistic presumption. Since local server clusters are mostly designed to answer for peak demand spikes, it is not rare that utilization is around 10%. Also, price of 0.19$ per CPU hour does not include startup costs or losses in time needed for install, reconfigure and maintain local cluster. Therefore, Dudley et al. agree that cloud alternative is accommodating alternative considering cost and performance characteristics. Therefore, so far is expected that business model of the Seven Bridges Genomics will be based on using cloud computing storage service of other providers, probably Amazon, although in the future they can choose to perform it in-house.

In summary, business model of Seven Bridges genomics is presented in the following figure, according to the pattern developed by Osterwalder and Pigneur. Seven Bridges Genomics business model is shown in Figure 7.

CONCLUSION

This chapter argues organizational changes cloud computing paradigm is causing, in addition to technological change. There is a bulk of literature studying technological aspects of cloud computing, but its impact on organizational and business models is scarcely analyzed so far. Studies of technology influences on organizational structures have started as early as 1960s, with the pioneering works of Woodward and the ASTON group. Those authors have established the interdependence between technology and organizational structures, however, the papers that explore this interdependence in more detail are also still rare. This chapter has two main parts – theoretical analysis and practical example. A short theoretical

framework of the "cloud computing" approach and illustrations of its differences compared to the local approaches for providing ICT infrastructure is given at the beginning. Afterwards, we describe the impacts the concept has on structure of the organization. Description of platform for organizational networking through new functionalities this concept opens to the organizational network broker are described in theory, picturing the framework exactly as it has been implemented in the Seven Bridges Genomics case. Implementation of constant communication, coordination and control with key partners, as described both in theoretical part and later Seven Bridges genomics case, is necessary to facilitate a responsive rather than ad-hoc network expansion.

From a perspective of efficiency pressure on organizational structure, the impact upon organizational performances is analysed using a theoretical framework of variable and fixed ICT infrastructure costs as well as opportunity costs of business. Theoretical analysis suggests that implementation of cloud computing based business approach leads to better capital utilization, lower exposure

Figure 7. Seven Bridges Genomics business model

Key partners	Key activities	Value proposition	Customer relationships	Customer segments
Dedicated bioinformatics labs producing state of the art research software Cloud service providers Genomics concerns – first sofware users Seqence equipment producers Genomics research funding institutions	Platform maintenance and development Balancing stakeholder interests	Reduced costs in data processing Open platform standardized genome analysis tools Workflow instead of script approach Collaborative platform for boosting creativity	Dedicated personal collaboration (early stages) Automated customer support system User communities	Research institutions performing academic research, industry R&D in biotechnology and bioengineering, pharmaceuticals and other forms of research
	Key resources SBG software platform Human resources Contacts Trust		Channels Web sales	
Cost Structure Costs of platform maintenace and development Costs of computing resources used from the cloud		Revenue streams NOT DISCLOSED BY SBG, instead proposed: Pre/post calculated usage fee for virtual machine services Targeted advertizment		

to business risk, and therefore lowers transactional costs. Seven Bridges Genomics is later analysed as business according to understandable and broad but simple framework explained by Osterwalder and Pigneur (2010). Business model of Seven Bridges genomics fits into all important theoretical finding explained into first part, and leads into our most important conclusion. In the field of genomics, our conclusion fits into findings of Dudley et al. who find the most significant impediment facing biomedical researchers wishing to adopt cloud computing involves the software environment for designing the computing environment and running the experiments (Dudley, Pouliot, Chen, Morgan, & Butte, 2010). Seven Bridges Genomics develops exactly that kind of platform. However, we would like to extend our conclusions outside genomics environment, and suggest generalization of service-aggregative broker, such as

Seven Bridges Genomics is in genomics field as a centre of network that has better organizational structure, better divided work, better effectiveness and efficiency and better coordination and communication.

As our most important conclusion, we can suggest that cloud computing paradigm applied organizationally and by market means urges changes in the science research business model. Currently, and maybe most apparently in sciences like genomics, computing power, storage and other IT resources are needed for performing adequate science research. That leads us to sketching business model of a scientific research institution that generally has *two "businesses"*:

- Core, research performing business, and
- Research supporting business.

Figure 8. Improvement of science research business model influenced by cloud computing paradigm

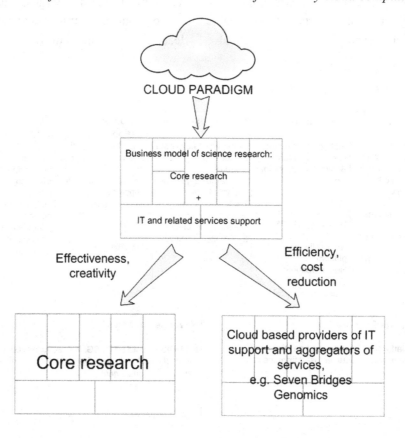

As partly can be seen in the description of Seven Bridges Genomics, those business are very different. First demands effectiveness and creativity, and second efficiency. It is organizational nightmare, and often unreachable goal to fulfil requirement of both businesses at the same time. Efficiency requires detailed plans of resources that need to be utilized in the future (e.g. server capacities) and strict schedules of its usage. All that order and rules help efficient utilization of resources, but strongly hinders creativity. On the other hand, performing creative and effective research hinders efficiency. E.g. good, but unorthodox idea might require one-time fixed investment of million US $ in particular ICT infrastructure to confirm it. If research institution performs both business functions without cloud computing concept of outsourcing, in each case something will suffer – either the idea will be suppressed on the grounds of non-existing funds, or the research institution will inefficiently spend fixed large amounts of money for what is in most cases unsuccessful shot in the dark. Also, key estimations needed for efficiently performing process supporting research often cannot be given by even most talented researches i.e. they cannot estimate how much support and what kind of support they will need. Here we give ourselves freedom to quote boldly formulated Albert Einstein sentence:

If we knew what it was we were doing, it would not be called research, would it?

Therefore, logical conclusion is that if research institution has to perform activities explained in the example of Seven Bridges Genomics in order to develop efficient support for core research, it is best to outsource it, if possible. That support is evidently necessary in some form for research, although specifically mostly needed in research requiring utilization of significant information and communication technology resources. Cloud computing paradigm has given solution in that outsourcing, dividing the business model of sci-

ence research in two without losing important aspects or increasing demand for coordination. In such way, both parties can focus on their goals and synergistically achieve better results. Main idea is presented in Figure 8.

In final conclusion, we can add that provider of support can develop large network core research institution it supports, as presented in Figure 2, and better utilize economy of scale. This model enables research institution to better focus upon the core research, rather than upon the activities of support and subsidiary activities which provider in IT will do better anyhow due to economy of scale, economy of scope and elastic engagement of resources in cloud computing. Such approach improves overall organizational performances of both partners, and we present it as one of the influences of cloud computing concept on business aspect of scientific research.

REFERENCES

Anand, N., & Daft, R. (2007). What is the right organization design? *Organizational Dynamics*, *36*(4), 329–344.

Anderson, C. (Ed.). (2009). *Free: The future of a radical price*. New York: Hyperion.

Angiuoli, S. V., White, J. R., Matalka, M., White, O., & Fricke, F. W. (2011). Resources and costs for microbial sequence analysis evaluated using virtual machines and cloud computing. *PLoS ONE*, *6*(10), 1–10. PMID:22028928

Bateman, A., & Wood, M. (2009). Cloud computing. *Bioinformatics (Oxford, England)*, *25*(12), 1475. PMID:19435745

Cowhey, P., & Aronson, J. (Eds.). (2009). *Transforming global information and communication markets*. Boston: MIT Press.

Čudanov, M. (Ed.). (2007). *Projektovanje organizacije i IKT*. Beograd: Zadužbina Andrejević.

Čudanov, M. (Ed.). (2011). *Organizacija i strateška primena informacionih i komunikacionih tehnologija*. Belgrade: Zadužbina Andrejević.

Čudanov, M., & Jaško, O. (2010). Adoption of information and communication technologies and dominant management orientation in organisations. *Behaviour & Information Technology*, *31*(5), 509–523.

Čudanov, M., Jaško, O., & Jevtić, M. (2009). Influence of information and communication technologies on decentralization of organizational structure. *Computer Science and Information Systems Journal*, *6*(1), 93–108.

Čudanov, M., Jaško, O., & Savoiu, G. (2010). Interrelationships of organization size and information and communication technology adoption. *Journal of Applied Quantitative Methods*, *5*(1), 29–40.

Čudanov, M., Krivokapić, J., & Krunić, J. (2011). The influence of cloud computing concept on organizational performance and structure. *Management – Journal for Management Theory and Practice*, *16*(60), 19-25.

Čudanov, M., Săvoiu, G., & Jaško, O. (2012). New link in bioinformatics services value chain: Position, organization and business model. *The Amfiteatru Economic Journal*, *14*(6), 680–697.

Dudley, J. T., Pouliot, Y., Chen, R., Morgan, A. A., & Butte, A. J. (2010). Translational bioinformatics in the cloud: An affordable alternative. *Genome Medicine*, *2*(51), 1–6. PMID:20193046

Henderson, J. C., & Venkatraman, V. N. (1993). Strategic alignment: Leveraging information technology for transforming organizations. *IBM Systems Journal*, *32*(1), 4–16.

Herper, M. (2011, January 17). Gene machine. *Forbes Magazine*. Retrieved September 15, 2013, from http://www.forbes.com/forbes/2011/0117/features-jonathan-rothberg-medicine-tech-gene-machine_1.html

Hugos, M., & Hulitzky, D. (Eds.). (2010). *Business in the cloud - What every business needs to know about cloud computing*. Hoboken, NJ: John Wiley & Sons.

Iosup, A., Ostermann, S., Yigitbasi, M. N., Prodan, R., Fahringer, T., & Epema, D. H. J. (2011). Performance analysis of cloud computing services for many-tasks scientic computing. *IEEE Transactions on Parallel and Distributed Systems*, *22*(6), 931–945.

Jaško, O., Čudanov, M., & Jevtić, M. (2009). Structure and functions of virtual organization as a framework for strategy design. *The IPSI BgD Transactions on Advanced Research*, *5*(2), 21–26.

Jaško, O., Jaško, A., & Čudanov, M. (2010). Impact of management upon organizational network effectiveness. *Management – Časopis za Teoriju i Praksu Menadžmenta*, *56*, 5-13.

Jinhui, Y., Shiping, C., Chen, W., David, L., & Zic, J. (2010). Accountability as a service for the cloud - From concept to implementation with BPEL. In *Proceedings of 2010 IEEE 6th World Congress on Services* (pp. 91-98). IEEE Computer Society.

Kim, T. K., Hou, B. K., & Cho, W. S. (2011). Private cloud computing techniques for interprocessing bioinformatics tools. In *Convergence and hybrid information technology (LNCS)* (Vol. 6935, pp. 298–305). Berlin: Springer.

Kirsten, T., & Rahm, E. (2006). BioFuice: Mapping-based data integration in bioinformatics. In *Proceedings of 3rd International Workshop on Data Integration in the Life Sciences* (LNCS), (Vol. 4075, pp. 124-135). Berlin: Springer.

Lagar-Cavilla, A. H., Whitney, J. A., Scannell, A., Patchin, P., Rumble, S. M., & de Lara, E. … Satyanarayanan, M. (2009). SnowFlock: Rapid virtual machine cloning for cloud computing. In Proceedings of Eurosys (pp. 1-12). ACM.

Laudel, G. (2001). Collaboration, creativity and rewards: Why and how scientists collaborate. *International Journal of Technology Management*, *22*(7-8), 762–781.

Mell, P., & Grance, T. (2009). *The NIST definition of cloud computing*. National Institute of Standards and Technology. Retrieved September 15, 2013, from http://pre-developer.att.com/home/learn/enablingtechnologies/The_NIST_Definition_of_Cloud_Computing.pdf

Milgram, S. (1967). The small world problem. *Psychology Today*, *1*(1), 61–67.

Moreno, E. (2011). The society of our out of Africa ancestors (I), the migrant warriors that colonized the world. *Communicative & Integrative Biology*, *4*(2), 163–170. PMID:21655430

National Human Genome Research Institute. (2013). *DNA sequencing costs - Data from the NHGRI genome sequencing program (GSP)*. Retrieved September 15, 2013, from http://www.genome.gov/sequencingcosts/

Ng, S. B., Nickerson, D. A., Bamshad, M. J., & Shendure, J. (2010). Massively parallel sequencing and rare disease. *Human Molecular Genetics*, *19*(2), 119–124. PMID:20846941

Nolan, R., & McFarlan, W. F. (2005). Information technology and the board of directors. *Harvard Business Review*, *83*(10), 96–106. PMID:16250628

Osterwalder, A., & Pigneur, Y. (Eds.). (2010). *Business model generation*. Hoboken, NJ: John Wiley & Sons.

Royal, C. D., Novembre, J., Fullerton, S. M., Goldstein, D. B., Long, J. C., Bamshad, M. J., & Clark, A. G. (2010). The inferring genetic ancestry: Opportunities, challenges, and implications. *American Journal of Human Genetics*, *86*(5), 661–673. PMID:20466090

Rubin, E. M. (2010). Genomics of cellulosic biofuels. *Nature*, *454*, 841–845. PMID:18704079

Rusk, N. (2011). Torrents of sequence. *Nature Methods*, *8*, 44.

Sboner, A., Mu, X. J., Greenbaum, D., Auerbach, R. K., & Gerstein, M. B. (2011). The real cost of sequencing: Higher than you think! *Genome Biology*, *12*(8), 1–12. PMID:21867570

Schwan, J. (2009). Open source software, cloud computing can save government money. *Government Technology*. Retrieved September 15, 2013, from http://www.govtech.com/pcio/Open-Source-Software-Cloud.html

Skilton, M. (2010). Building return on investment from cloud computing. *The Open Group*. Retrieved September 15, 2013, from http://www.opengroup.org/cloud/whitepapers/ccroi/intro.htm

Smaglik, P. (2011). Minnesota: Medicine and materials. *Nature*, *475*(7356), 413–414. PMID:21786466

Stanimirović, D., & Vintar, M. (2010). Decision making criteria for outsourcing or onsourcing of IT service provision in public sector. *Management – Časopis za Teoriju i Praksu Menadžmenta*, *58*, 65-69.

Stein, L. D. (2010). The case for cloud computing in genome informatics. *Genome Biology*, *11*(5), 1–7. PMID:20441614

Tata, S., Patel, J. M., Friedman, J. S., & Swaroop, A. (2005). *Towards declarative querying for biological sequences* (Technical Report CSE-TR-508-05). Ann Arbor, MI: University of Michigan.

Uzzi, B., & Spiro, J. (2005). Collaboration and creativity: The small world problem. *American Journal of Sociology*, *111*(2), 447–504. doi: doi:10.1086/432782

Vujin, V. (2010). Cloud computing in science and higher education. *Management – Časopis za Teoriju i Praksu Menadžmenta, 59*, 65-69.

Ward, J., & Peppard, J. (Eds.). (2009). *Strategic planning for information systems*. Chichester, UK: John Wiley & Sons.

ADDITIONAL READING

Angiuoli, S. V., White, J. R., Matalka, M., White, O., & Fricke, F. W. (2011). Resources and Costs for Microbial Sequence Analysis Evaluated Using Virtual Machines and Cloud Computing. *PLoS ONE, 6*(10), 1–10. PMID:22028928

Bateman, A., & Wood, M. (2009). Cloud computing. *Bioinformatics (Oxford, England), 25*(12), 1475. PMID:19435745

Bhattacharya, I. (2012). Healthcare Data Analytics on the Cloud. *Online Journal of Health and Allied Sciences, 11*(1), 1–4.

Brousseau, E., & Penard, T. (2007). The economics of digital business models: a framework for analyzing the economics of platforms. *Review of Network Economics, 6*(2).

Check, H. E. (2013). Gene-analysis firms reach for the cloud. *Nature, 495*, 293. PMID:23518540

Chesbrough, H. (2010). Business model innovation: opportunities and barriers. *Long Range Planning, 43*(2), 354–363.

Daft, R. (2004). *Organization Theory and Design* (8th ed.). Mason, USA: Thomson South-Western.

Jaško, O., Čudanov, M., Jevtić, M., & Krivokapić, J. (2013). Osnovi organizacije i menadžmenta. Belgrade, Serbia: Faculty of Organizational Sciences.

Jevtić, M., Čudanov, M., & Krivokapić, J. (2012). The impact of business strategy on organizational structure. *Strategic Management, 17*(1), 3–12.

Kim, T. K., Hou, B. K., & Cho, W. S. (2011). Private cloud computing techniques for inter-processing bioinformatics tools. In *Convergence and Hybrid Information Technology* (pp. 298–305). Berlin: Springer Berlin Heidelberg.

Krampis, K., Booth, T., Chapman, B., Tiwari, B., Bicak, M., Field, D., & Nelson, K. E. (2012). Cloud BioLinux: pre-configured and on-demand bioinformatics computing for the genomics community. *BMC Bioinformatics, 13*(1), 42. PMID:22429538

Lawler, J., Howell-Barber, H., Yalamanchi, R., & Joseph, A. (2011). Determinants of an effective cloud computing strategy. In *Proceedings of the Information Systems Educators Conference* (ISECON) (pp. 3-6).

Miles, R. E., & Snow, C. C. (1995). The new network firm: A spherical structure built on a human investment philosophy. *Organizational Dynamics, 23*(4), 5–18.

Miles, R. E., Snow, C. C., Meyer, A. D., & Coleman, H. J. (1978). Organizational strategy, structure, and process. *Academy of Management Review, 3*(3), 546–562. PMID:10238389

Ojala, A. (2012). Benefits of Software Renting in Cloud Business. In *Software Business* (pp. 304–309). Springer Berlin Heidelberg.

Ojala, A. (2012). Software renting in the era of cloud computing. In *IEEE 5th International Conference of Cloud Computing (CLOUD)* (pp. 662-669). IEEE.

Osterwalder, A., & Pigneur, Y. (2002). An e-business model ontology for modeling e-business. In *15th Bled Electronic Commerce Conference* (pp. 17-19). Bled.

Osterwalder, A., & Pigneur, Y. (2003). Modeling value propositions in e-Business. In *Proceedings of the 5th international conference on Electronic commerce* (pp. 429-436). ACM.

Porter, M. E., & Kramer, M. R. (2006). Strategy and society. *Harvard Business Review*, *84*(12), 78–92. PMID:17183795

Rusk, N. (2011). Torrents of sequence. *Nature Methods*, *8*, 44.

Ruthkoski, T. L. (2010). Exploratory project: State of the cloud, from University of Michigan and beyond. In *IEEE Second International Conference on Cloud Computing Technology and Science* (pp. 427-432). New York: IEEE.

Sboner, A., Mu, X. J., Greenbaum, D., Auerbach, R. K., & Gerstein, M. B. (2011). The real cost of sequencing: higher than you think! *Genome Biology*, *12*(8), 1–12. PMID:21867570

Shanker, A. (2012). Genome research in the cloud. *OMICS: A Journal of Integrative Biology*, *16*(7-8), 422–428. PMID:22734722

Skilton, M. (2010). Building Return On Investment From Cloud Computing. *The Open Group,* Retrieved September 15, 2013, from http://www.opengroup.org/cloud/whitepapers/ccroi/intro.htm

Snow, C. C. (1997). Twenty-first-century organizations: implications for a new marketing paradigm. *Journal of the Academy of Marketing Science*, *25*(1), 72–74.

Stein, L. D. (2010). The case for cloud computing in genome informatics. *Genome Biology*, *11*(5), 1–7. PMID:20441614

Wall, D. P., Kudtarkar, P., Fusaro, V. A., Pivovarov, R., Patil, P., & Tonellato, P. J. (2010). Cloud computing for comparative genomics. *BMC Bioinformatics*, *11*(1), 259. PMID:20482786

Ward, J., & Peppard, J. (Eds.). (2009). *Strategic Planning for Information Systems*. Chichester: John Wiley & Sons.

Wernicke, S., & Brubaker, K. (2013). The IGOR Cloud Platform: Collaborative, Scalable, and Peer-Reviewed NGS Data Analysis. *Journal of Biomolecular Techniques: JBT*, *24*(Suppl), S34.

Zott, C., Amit, R., & Massa, L. (2011). The business model: recent developments and future research. *Journal of Management*, *37*(4), 1019–1042.

KEY TERMS AND DEFINITIONS

Bioinformatics: Intersection of biology and information science, aimed at collection and analysis of complex and large sets of biology related data.

Business Model: General design of utilization of organizational resources for value creation, along with financial and market aspects of that process.

Cloud Computing: An approach that ensures access to the shared set of computer resources like networks, servers, computer memory, applications or data processing services. It can be configured, promptly protected and used with a minimum effort by the organizational management or interaction with the entity providing the services.

Management: The art of planning, organizing, leading, coordinating and controlling resources of the organization toward accomplishment of common goal.

Organization: System of social elements and relations among them.

Organizational Network: A set of legally independent organizational entities interacting toward accomplishment of common goal.

Organizational Structure: Formalized system of task and authority distribution, coordination of activities and procedures for usage of organizational resources.

Virtual Organization: A network of independent firms most often connected by information and communication technology tools joined together for delivering specific service or product, which creates external impression and effect as a major monolithically organized corporation.

Chapter 3
Digital Identity Management in Cloud

Vladimir Vujin
University of Belgrade, Serbia

Konstantin Simić
University of Belgrade, Serbia

Borko Kovačević
Microsoft, Serbia

ABSTRACT

Existing approaches for management of digital identities within e-learning ecosystems imply defining different access parameters for each service or application. However, this can reduce system security and lead to insufficient usage of the services by end-users. This chapter investigates various approaches for identity management, particulary in a cloud computing environment. Several complex issues are discussed, such as cross-domain authentication, provisioning, multi-tenancy, delegation, and security. The main goal of the research is to provide a highly effective, scalable identity management for end-users in an educational private cloud. A federated identity concept was introduced as a solution that enables organizations to implement secure identity management and to share information on the identities of users in the cloud environment. As a proof of concept, the identity management system was implemented in the e-learning system of Faculty of Organizational Sciences, University of Belgrade.

INTRODUCTION

The growing complexity of modern educational ecosystems requires new approaches in access control (Dong, Zheng, Yang, Haifei, & Qiao, 2009). Cloud computing environments are multi domain environments in which each domain can use different security, privacy, and trust requirements and potentially employ various mechanisms, interfaces, and semantics. Such domains could represent individually enabled services or other infrastructural or application components (Takabi, Joshi, & Ahn, 2010). In order to provide seamless user experience, technologies such as: cloud-based services, social Web, and rapidly expanding mobile platforms will depend on identity management.

DOI: 10.4018/978-1-4666-5784-7.ch003

Development and exploitation of the applications in cloud computing environment, both private and public, requires defining and implementation of efficient strategy and tools for user's identities management. Identity Management (hereinafter: IDM) is key issue for cloud privacy and security. IDM in educational cloud is more complex than in traditional Web-based systems since the users hold multiple accounts with different educational services. The traditional model of application-centric access control, where each application keeps track of its collection of users and manages them, is not acceptable in educational cloud-based architectures.

This chapter describes existing open standards, such as: SAML2, OpenID, OAuth authentication and authorization, SCIM and XACML. These standards aim to solve problems related to maintaining interoperability and enabling easy identity management in cloud environment. Several complex questions, such as: cross-domain authentication, provisioning, multi-tenancy, delegation and security are discussed as well.

The main goal of the research is to provide a highly effective, scalable identity management for end-users in an educational private cloud. The research context of this chapter is focused on the e-learning processes in the private cloud within the Laboratory for e-business at Faculty of Organizational Sciences, University of Belgrade.

THEORETICAL BACKGROUND

Digital Identities

Issue of digital identities is presented since the beginning of the world wide using of the Internet. Problem has appeared because of the initial architecture of Internet. Namely, identity layer didn't exist and access to Web resources was not clearly defined. Therefore, each user has multiple differ-

ent digital identities. Accordingly, managing these types of digital identities is fairly complex task.

In development of e-education system, problem of digital identity of users become significantly important. Concepts of anonymity and privacy are in confrontation with processes that require assessment, communication and access to services for learning, where exposure of information about identities is necessary. Digital identity can be observed from the different points of view. One perspective analyzes software solutions for digital identities management. Another one discusses organizations that implement these solutions. Third perspective is related to persons whose digital identities are managed.

Term digital identity refers to aspect of digital technology that deals with relations between human of identity and identity of other people and things. In the context of ICT, a digital identity is digital set of asserts a subject has about itself and other subjects. Identity is tightly coupled with terms of security and privacy. Information security is an area that deals with protecting integrity, privacy and confidentiality of information. Privacy refers to protection of attributes, affinities and characteristics of entities.

An identity is unique set of characteristics that uniquely identify a person or service. There are many different forms of personal identification in modern society. These forms of identification usually contain information that are unique, as well as information about authority that has issued the identification. Although, the term identity is well understood in physical world, defining digital identity is quite complex issue. An identity is set of data that describes attributes, characteristics and properties of a subject. Digital identity presents a set of information about particular entity. A subject or entity is person, group of people, organization, software tool or service that requires access to particular resource.

A digital identity is described through following elements:

- **Identifier:** Data that uniquely identifies subject of the identity within the specific context.
- **Identification Data:** Private or public data that can be used as a proof of identity's authenticity. This mechanism works properly because only user and system for authentification management know users' password. Identification data are proofs that particular subject correspondes to the particular identity.
- **Essential Attributes:** Data that describe basic characteristics of an identity. They can be used by numerous business applications.
- **Additional Attributes:** Data that help in describing identity. These types of attributes bring additional information about identity. They are primary related to the specific context in which the identity is used.

Identity management systems are IT infrastructures designed to facilitate the management of user identity, authentication and authorization data (Mueller, Park, Lee, & Kim, 2006). Digital identity is the fundamental of a person in an IDM system. A digital identifier is any piece of information (usually an alphanumeric character string, but potentially a biometric such as a fingerprint, voiceprint or retinal scan) that uniquely identifies an account at a networked service (Mueller, Park, Lee, & Kim, 2006). Attribute, identity and entity are three different representations of the characteristic of a person (or an organization) in identity management. Attribute is the fundamental element to describe a person. An identity is a set of attributes that describes the characteristic properties and identifies a person uniquely or an organization. An entity contains many identities and it is an overall profile of a person or an organization (Jin, Jian, Ming, & Ning, 2010). Figure 1 presents common student identities in an IDM

Figure 1. Student identities in e-learning ecosystem

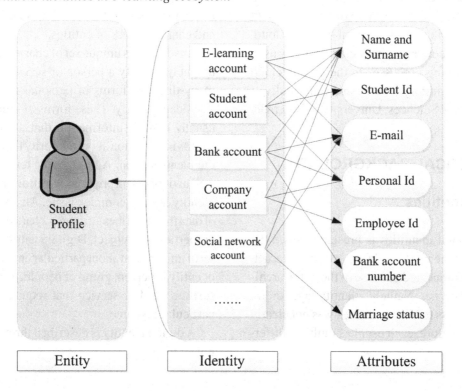

system integrated with e-learning ecosystem. Student can have a variety of identities related to specific area of interest: E-learning account, Student account, Social network account, Bank account, Company account, etc. Each of these entities uses different set of attributes.

A virtual identity of a user is a special kind of digital identity built up as the aggregation of attributes and credentials from different sources (providers). The virtual identity does not contain the actual aggregated data, but instead, it contains references to the information on its original source. Each virtual is identified by a unique virtual identifier (Pérez, López, Cánovas, & Gómez-Skarmeta, 2011).

As virtual identities are used to access different services, end users only need to remember the credentials that have been aggregated into the generated virtual identity. Additionally, as information is referred on virtual identities instead of copied, if an attribute value is modified or deleted on its original source, it has an immediate effect on the services accessed using a virtual identity (Pérez, López, Cánovas, & Gómez-Skarmeta, 2011).

Digital Identity in Cloud Computing Environment

Privacy and the interoperability of identities are among main challenges in the field of identity management in cloud computing environment. Digital identity management has to deal up with numerous different users and services and establish user their identity each time they use a new cloud service. Rather than investing heavily in identity when developing or using an application, it makes more sense for an educational institution to utilize a service for its identity needs. Identity as a service presents an on-demand model that delivers the right amount of capability at the right time (Olden, 2011). Therefore, the development of digital identity management systems suitable for cloud computing is crucial (Bertino, Paci, Ferrini, & Shang, 2009).

Development and usage of cloud computing services leads to a fact that boundary of trust and security in organizations become dynamic. Due to the sensitivity and privacy of information, identity and access management in the cloud has become a critical point of security within IT systems of an organization. It is necessary for the organization to expand the limits of control over the network, system and application resources in the cloud domain.

The first and most simple model is the use of the system for managing digital identities built-in applications which are set in the public cloud. In this approach, every cloud has its own application specific identities. The good side of this approach is the simplicity of applications. Compromised identity will not endanger more than one cloud provider. Nowadays this is one of the most common approaches. The downside of this approach is existence of many multiple identities in the cloud applications.

The second model synchronizes identities in the cloud with a system for managing the organization's identity. According to this approach, cloud services have separate and distinct identities, but centrally managed and delivered to the various services. This model allows organizations to use the well-known procedures and processes for identity management as well as existence a single point of administration identity. Disadvantages of this approach are reflected in the fact that:

- A single point of administration at the same time is a single point of failure, and
- The complexity of creating connectors between systems for identity management organizations and cloud service.

The third model describes creation of the federation credentials using an external directory. The model provides credentials to available service outside the organization firewall. Technology that is commonly used for the implementation of this approach is the Security Assertion Markup

Language (hereinafter: SAML) and the OpenID protocol. This model ensures scalable approach that can respond to organization needs for managing and provides a platform for a single sign on. The drawbacks of this approach are complex management models and complex support for SAML and OpenID protocols.

In the fourth model, the organization transfers the responsibility for identity management system to third parties and uses such a system as a service (IdaaS).

Administration of identity management is performed through IDaaS service, which serves as an interface for adding, deleting and editing. IDaaS service is used as a layer for integration with cloud applications. IDaaS is the most flexible approach for the implementation of identity management in the cloud from all four approaches. The drawback of this approach is the same as for all cloud services: if identity management system becomes inaccessible, the organization and its users have no way to access organizational system.

In the implementation of the system for identity management that uses parts or any or all of these four models, it is necessary to take into account:

- The number of public cloud applications that are used;
- Availability by the number of resources and capabilities of development resources;
- The single sign on service, etc.

In addition it is possible to develop applications that are based on a private cloud. Integration of applications in the private cloud is much simpler because of possible easier and faster integration with the local infrastructure and applications. In addition, the level of trust is inherently higher because the IT sector of organizations is responsible for infrastructure, applications and networks through which the access to the applications performs. Process of identity management in private cloud is presented in Figure 2.

Figure 2. Digital identity in private cloud

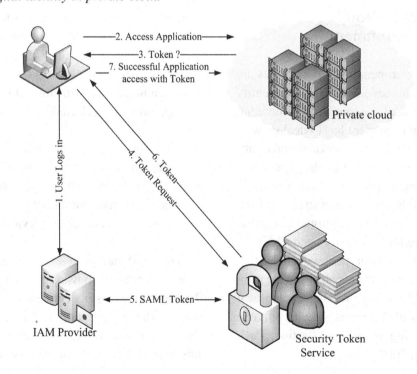

Identity Management Technologies

Although there are a few slightly different taxonomies related to requirements of an IDM system, main components and features of an IDM are presented in Figure 3.

Identity management component is implemented through following processes: account provisioning and deprovisioning, role management, users' registration and account credentials synchronization. Provisioning enables establishing effective connection between users' accounts and existing services and application within cloud. After registration system automatically get accounts for the applications. Role management provides user grouping by function, or role, enabling role-based permissions and access authorization.

The basis of an IDM is identities directory. The directory component stores identity and resource information, policies, and user credentials. It provides a logical architecture to define schemas and namespaces. It protects the confidentiality, integrity, and consistency of identity data as well as provides for monitoring and auditing of its data. LDAP is the emerging directory standard. Using the LDAP protocol, any application running on any platform can query and access data stored in the LDAP directory via TCP/IP.

Access management includes: authorization, authentication, single sign-on feature and federation. When a user initiates a request for access to an application or resource, the identity management first authenticates the user by asking for credentials, which may be in the form of a username and password, digital certificate, smart card, or biometric data. After the user successfully authenticates, the identity management system authorizes the appropriate amount of access based on the user's identity and attributes. However, as the number of different services increase, the number of credentials for each user increases and thereby possibility of losing or forgetting them also increases.

Federated Identity Management in Cloud Environment

Identity federation enables organizations to implement secure identity management and to share information on the identities of users in the cloud environment. Using this model the organization enhances control over the access rights to resources, regardless of where those resources are

Figure 3. Main components of an IDM

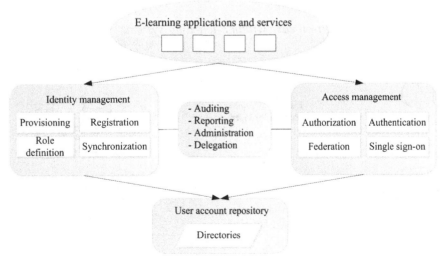

located. Federated identity management allows communication between systems and applications that are outside the organization.

Identity Federation can be implemented in a variety of ways using formal Internet standards such as SAML, Information Cards, and OpenID etc. Identity Federation has following solution areas:

- Single Sign-On;
- Application based Web Services Security;
- Identity Lifecycle.

Single Sign-On concept can be used to solve many problems related to multiple credentials for different applications. Single sign-on (hereinafter: SSO) is a mechanism that uses a single action of authentication to permit an authorized user to access all related, but independent software systems or applications without being prompted to log in again at each of them during a particular session. The Single Sign-on model is based on user/password authentication scheme. This system is achieved by maintaining a centralized server for user authentication processes. The client needs to provide his credentials for authentication. The authentication service verifies those credentials from credentials database and generates a service token for the entire client session. The service token is used for authentication purposes.

There are three main actors of a single sign-on system. An "Identity Provider" (hereinafter: IdP) and "Service Provider" (hereinafter: SP) and a user. SP relies on IdP(s) to authenticate user credentials. SSO approach outsources the responsibility of user authentication from service providers to IdPs (Suriadi, Foo, & Jøsang, 2009). Figure 4 describes an example of single sign-on case within e-learning system.

When a student accesses to e-learning course Web page (SP) they are being transferred to home page of the e-learning portal (IdP) that requires authentication. The student fills their credentials in login form. E-learning portal component for identity management checks credentials and send message to learning management system (Moodle LMS). The student gains access to the e-learning resources that are available to their permissions within the course.

SSO helps to improve user and developer productivity by avoiding the user to remember multiple passwords and also reduce the amount of time the user spends on typing various passwords to login. SSO also simplifies the administration by managing single credentials instead of multiple credentials.

A federated single sign-on (hereinafter: FSSO) system is an identity management system (hereinafter: IMS) that allows the use of the same user's

Figure 4. An example of single sign-on case within e-learning system

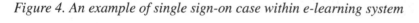
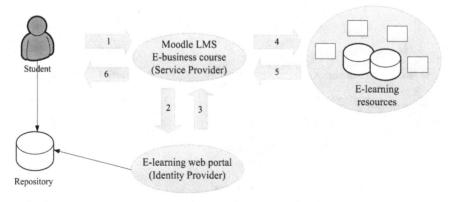

personal identification information (PII) across multiple organizations within a federation. In essence, this allows users to access services from different organizations but they are only required to provide their authentication data once. An FSSO system is made up of a group of identity providers (IdPs) and service providers (SPs).

There are several technologies and standards used for managing distributed identities. The most mature and widely deployed solutions for federated identity are the SAML and Liberty Alliance standards. SAML (Lewis & Lewis, 2009), developed by OASIS, is an XML-based framework for communicating user authentication, authorization and attribute information. SAML provides XML formats and protocols for encoding and exchanging identity information

SAML is an XML-based open standard for exchanging authentication and authorization data between security domains, i.e., an identity provider and a service provider. Using SAML, an online service provider contacts an online identity provider which authenticates users who are trying to access secure content. SAML doesn't specify how to authenticate a user, rather it defines a way how to exchange the authentication and authorization data once the user is authenticated.

OpenID is a decentralized framework for digital identity (Sun, Hawkey, & Beznosov, 2012). The underlying idea is that users can identify themselves on the Web like Websites do with URIs. OpenID allows a username/password login. The username is the personal URI and the password is safely stored on the OpenID Provider. To login to an OpenID-enabled Website, the user is required the OpenID URI and then gets redirected to the OpenID Provider to authenticate. OpenID Connect is essentially the third version of OpenID. It is a complete rewrite of the protocol and is not compatible with previous versions. It is an HTTP-based protocol that allows applications to authenticate users in foreign security realms. In this way, it provides SSO. Unlike other protocols

like SAML and WS-Federation that solve the same problem, OpenID Connect provides the following unique benefits and features:

- Built atop OAuth 2 which is much simpler to implement than prior versions of that specification;
- Designed with native mobile and HTML 5 Web applications in mind;
- Designed to achieve higher Levels of Assurance (LoA);
- RESTful in nature, providing all the benefits of that modern design paradigm;
- Low tech barrier that requires little more than HTTP and JSON support.

SAML and WS-Federation are flexible business-oriented specifications. They give implementers many options f or customized deployments. On the other hand, OpenID is a user-centric, lightweight protocol. OpenID does not abstract away any details from its specification, but offers a direct solution to the Web SSO problem.

Model proposed and implemented within this chapter is based on SAML protocol. Shibboleth presents one of the most used implementation of SAML protocol. The primary function of the Shibboleth system (Morgan, Cantor, Carmody, Hoehn, & Klingenstein, 2004) is to support identity federation between multiple sites using the SAML protocol standard. Shibboleth is an authentication and authorization architecture. From authorization perspective, Shibboleth is an attribute based mechanism and it supports federation wide sharing and access of resources based on users' attribute.

Although, numerous researches deal with identity management, the authors of this chapter couldn't find any concrete full implementation of the IDM features within e-learning system. For example, Eduroam (EDUcationROAMing) is the AAA-based roaming infrastructure used by the international research and education community to allow users to access a wireless network at a visited institution that is also connected to Eduroam using the same authentication credentials (e.g., username and password) as the users would use if they were at their home institution (Marin-Lopez, Pereñiguez-Garcia, Ohba, Bernal-Hidalgo, & Gomez, 2010). The AAA infrastructure in Eduroam facilitates mobility of students, lecturers and researchers around different institutions within the Eduroam network. Another example is Eduserv Athens (Lang, 2010), the de facto standard for secure access management to Web-based services for the UK education and health sectors. In (Jie, Arshad, & Ekin, 2009) The Athens Access Management System is presented as an advanced authentication infrastructure that has been developed for UK higher education to govern controlled access to a wide range of digital resources using a secure Single Sign-On process. Athens facilitates an organization to allow a single username to access all the subscribed Athens protected resources, but it has certain limitations.

The challenge in this area is that there are considerable efforts towards outsourcing the IDM that gave birth to the concept of identity as a service (IaaS) (Eludiora et al., 2011). An IDM in cloud has to manage - control points, dynamic composite/decommissioned machines, virtual device or service identities, etc. The background for this research can be found in works that explain the benefits of cloud computing and discuss theoretical and practical issues related to identity management within cloud computing environment.

Adoption of IDM in cloud computing environments imposes challenges (Zissis & Lekkas, 2012). In (Lang, 2010) author presented the concept of moving security and compliance policy automation for Cloud applications and mashups into the Cloud, to protect Cloud applications and mashups more seamlessly within the Cloud computing paradigm, and to improve and simplify the secure software development lifecycle for Cloud applications. Further, in (Vossen, & Westerkamp, 2006) the author proposed a protocol for IDM in cloud computing environment - U-IDM. They consid-

ered authentication, authorization and accounting (AAA) in developing this protocol. Concept of identity management of interconnected global "cloud of clouds" is discussed in (Núñez, Agudo, Drogkaris, & Gritzalis, 2011).

System for Cross-Domain Identity Management

Very often companies use products and services from multiple cloud providers in order to achieve variety of business requirements. Therefore, the approach that was based on maintainig user identities only in corporate LDAP is not suitable any more. At the same time, majority of SaaS providers also require specific user accounts to be created for the cloud service users. Consequently, problem of developing identity provisioning mechanisms become more urgent and complex.

Considering the fact that different cloud providers expose non-standard provisioning APIs, enterprises are having a huge problem during the implementation and maintaining of proprietary connectors for integration with multiple SaaS providers. SCIM is an open standard that defines a comprehensive REST API along with a platform neutral schema and a SAML binding to empower the user management operations across SaaS applications. SCIM focuses on simplicity and interoperability as well. Previously, SCIM was abbreviation for "Simple Cloud Identity Management" ("LDAP in the cloud," "Cloud Directory") but currently it denotes "System for Cross-domain Identity Management." SCIM provisioning is presented in Figure 5. Main goal of The System for Cross-domain Identity Management (SCIM) specification is to foster management of user identities in cloud-based applications and services. Further, this specification aims to reduce the cost and complexity of user management operations by providing a common user schema and extension model, as well as binding documents to provide patterns for exchanging this schema using standard protocols. SCIM should provide a common

Figure 5. SCIM provisioning

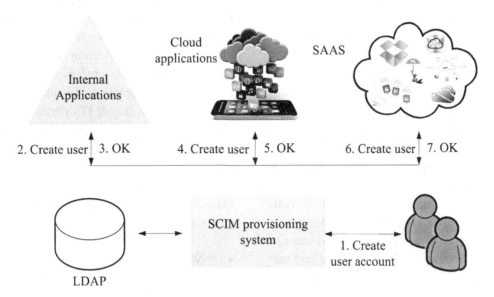

RESTful API for cloud SaaS providers that can be used by enterprises in order to provision accounts. Implementing previous approach an enterprise had to provision users to various cloud vendors using different APIs. However, SCIM enable a simple provisioning API that all application service providers could support. SCIM's deployment architecture model could be described as simple hub-and-spoke model where the enterprise IDM system presents "hub" and each cloud service presents spoke. Following the concept SCIM, each spoke is enabled by a standardized "connector" using a standardized SCIM RESTful API (Ping Identity, 2011).

SCIM includes following features:

- Clearly defined user attributes that enable to achieve interoperability.
- Easy updates for synchronization and ingest.
- Almost no technology limitations. Only knowledge of JavaScript or CURL technologies are needed.
- A provisioning API to manage users and groups.

- Federation for Just-in-Time (JIT) provisioning via OpenID, SAML, Connect, and other Web SSO protocols.
- Providing API security with OAuth 2 or other HTTP authentication schemes.

DIGITAL IDENTITY MANAGEMENT

The rapid development of information technology has led to the emergence of a large number of services, without the possibility of communication between them. Each of these services is specifically responsible for the authentication process. The attributes required for authorization and settings are stored and used in its own database. Functionality and security of such a system decreases with the addition of new services to the system.

Faced with the problem of integration of services in information systems, organizations had developed several new approaches for information exchanging between applications and services of information system. In aim of supporting strategic goals, data integration in organizations has several advantages in terms of resource optimization and improving access to shared information. The integration of data and services requires the integration of identity management systems to ensure efficient and safer way for managing the access to data and services.

System for identity and access management has to ensure the right of access to information and services to users. In the past, this system was implemented as a system with two identities that are distributed throughout the system. Adding of new services in this information infrastructure caused some problems related to the safe management of double identities. The solution of this problem was to establish a unified identity management system for all applications and services. Model of identity and access management system integrates all data sources with systems and services, which enable that all policies and procedures can be applicable to the one central place. The application of this model simplifies the management and access, while at the same time increasing the security of identity management processes.

The first step in building infrastructure of system for identity and access management is the collection of customers' data across distributed systems around the world. This is followed by making a decision about the importance of data, collecting and storing information about each user of the system in one record which presents a unique user identity. After consolidation of data related to user's identity, it is possible to use the tools that establish user roles and add user to an existing group where they can access to resources. Owners of resources can define specific interactions of these resources. In the past, the user membership was not coordinated in the services and during the every change of members' login, in each application or service, it must been changed. Consolidation of groups and privileges enable to groups, with only one change in the system for managing identities and rights, to have access to all applications and services.

With the consolidation of information on the identities, the management system becomes more efficient, because the system infrastructure for identity management becomes a link between the processes and institutional owners of resources and technology operations. Identity management system allows scaling of IT operations which results with the requirement for the development of processes and services, and concomitant changes that occur in only one place.

The usual requirements for centralized identity management and centralized management of user rights are:

- Management of the central database of certified licenses which are authentic and can be controlled and revised;
- Certificate of the compliance with regulative;
- Defined processes for access requests and approvals;
- Support for managing working functions;
- Automated creation of users' accounts and assigning rights;
- Automated shutdown of users' rights at the end of the study or employment;
- Establishment of the management system for easier administration;
- Establishment of clearly defined and transparent process;
- Establishment of a uniform system of identification for all applications in the field of organization.

Management from one point provides consolidated logging and consistent view of the access rights and needs of individuals and systems. This approach enables transparent way of using, monitoring and implementation of policies and decisions through technology infrastructure. It also provides the ability to track the history of activities that describe whom and what are being granted access, and a single place for auditing, reporting and monitoring of security events.

With the implemented system for identity management in the organization it is possible to use the key benefits such as improved safety, reduce of administration costs and improve of user productivity.

Benefits of the identity management system derive from the centralized administration of users. Allowing administrators to assign, forbid and handle access to resources for all users from a central location, it provides instantaneous and uniform distribution of current policies by all departments and locations within the organization. At the same time applying the rules to all users can reduce the possibility of human error and thus be protected from the consequences that may occur due to the granting of access to critical application to unauthorized users or improper banning of access to any resource. Centralized identity management system allows creation and implementation of policies, granting rights to ultimate users such as the right to change their own passwords by themselves and giving rights to themselves over resources that are not of great security importance. According to various studies, personal services through which users manage their own passwords can reduce the number of support calls by 40% to 60%.

Centralized identity management system allows users to post requests for different resources when the system can automatically give the right based on the rules and roles of the user or use the mechanism for seeking approval from the responsible party. Some systems allow users to keep their personal information such as phone number, home address, etc. Digital identity management is a set of processes that enable organizations to manage user identities more effectively. Solutions based on identity management also provide organizations complete security infrastructure.

Appointed requirements and limitations of the development of network information systems have led to solutions based on the identity management through an integrated, efficient and centralized infrastructure. This concept of integration of network services, policies and technologies provides:

- Secure access to all resources;
- More effective control of the access to resources;
- Faster changing of relations between identity and resources;
- Protection of confidential information from unauthorized access.

When defining the architecture of the system for managing digital identities, it identifies the following requirements:

- Integration and appropriate access to information and services requires much broader approach to identity management than the traditional approach;
- A comprehensive methodology for verifying the identity of an individual in an electronic environment;
- Linking of authentic identities with predetermined policies, which are provided access to network services and resources.

Without a system for managing digital identities each resource where users want to access requires the use of a new user name and password. The problems are obvious:

- The user needs to remember a large number of user names and passwords;
- For each resource administrator must register and provide access to the user.

A system for managing digital identities simplifies the process for users:

- The user can register only once.
- Identity check is always performed by the user's institution. The institution can also provide additional information about the user upon resource request and user's approval. This procedure enables the user to access all resources with a single set of credentials.

- Access privileges are determined according to user's information.

- Digital identities management is a process of using existing technologies for managing an entity's digital identity information and resource access control. The goals of digital identities management are: increasing the efficiency level, security level, as well as decreasing expenses for managing entities and their digital identities.

- The main task of digital identities management is using the identity in the appropriate context and in right time. When it comes to digital identities, identities management systems are usually considered as concepts for:
  ○ Defining the entity's identity;
  ○ Securely storing relevant information about the entity, while maintaining flexibility;
  ○ Enabling information access using a defined interface;
  ○ Ensuring a flexible, distributed and high quality infrastructure for managing identities;
  ○ Managing identities using a system that encompasses three key components:
    ▪ Managing identity's lifecycle;
    ▪ Managing access;
    ▪ Directory service.

The goal of digital identities management is creating the link between various service identifiers, so that the user information can be integrated with the service identifiers. This enables the identity management system to link business processes, security policies and technologies that aid in digital identities management, as well as resources access control. The function of the identity management system is to enable usage of singular user information to various services. Elementary identity management system use cases include creating, storing and accessing identities.

Therefore, these use cases represent the first requirements that need to be implemented. Privacy is reflected in two aspects. The first aspect of privacy implies that entity's identity is not available to other entities, unless the owner of the identity specifically allowed it. The second aspect of privacy is the provision of data available to a third person about a certain entity, to the entity itself. The data is provided with particular control level.

The advantages of digital identity management system introduction are:

- Decrease in expenses when introducing new systems;
- Decrease in number of human resources needed;
- Business process optimization;
- Improvement in quality of services for users; ensuring control and privacy;
- Decrease in time needed to gain access to demanded resources;
- Decrease in risk related to inaccurate information possession;
- Decrease in risk related to former employees.

The main shortcoming of digital identity management systems is incompatibility with various technologies for managing identities.

Directory Service

Directory service represents a core of the identity management system. The directory is a central place for saving and storing logical data and identities. Access to directory and information is restricted by applying security policy which is a part of the directory service. Globally, directory represents a set or a list of data. In information technologies, a directory permits structured data storage and it also permits easy accessing its objects. Directory Service is based on LDAP protocol.

Directory service is the main component of each identity management system as it represents a central repository for identities and resources which contains information about users' profiles. The great majority of directories are built on LDAP protocol which extends functionalities of centralized storage and efficient managing of identities. In order to provide a centralized management in heterogeneous and complex environments, where more than one directory is needed, it is important that there is only one entry point for all of the existing directories. A starting point for application of security standards is the creation of a global review of identity information that will allow decision making and implementation of the best directory technology.

Managing Lifecycle of Digital Identities

Lifecycle of a digital identity can be divided into stages that mimic the lifecycle of living creatures: creation, life and termination. Each phase of the identity's lifecycle has certain activities that are suitable for automatic management. All of the activities that make up a life cycle of a digital identity need to be safe, efficient and carefully managed.

Activities of identity lifecycle management can be split into several levels. Data types that need to be managed are shown on the "identity data" level. Based on the definition of digital identity, credentials contains relevant data - passwords, certificates and user attributes like names, addresses and phone numbers. Other than credentials and attributes, user rights need to be managed too. The term "rights" encompasses rights and privileges related to the identity. On the next level - data operations - specified activities reflect the kinds of operations that can be executed on the identities. Create, Read, Update, and Delete are primitive data operations and are used because they provide a convenient way to classify types of operations in identity management. The next

level shows two models of lifecycle management: personal and delegated model. In a traditional IT organization, administrative tasks are performed by a group of system administrators. However, organizations realized that there were economic and business reasons for introduction of different models of administration. For instance, it is often more economical and efficient for both administrators and user to have a possibility to change some of his own attributes, like address and phone number. Personal model allows this kind of management. The model of delegated administration is positioned between the personal model and the model of centralized administration. In the delegated model, responsibility of administering identity lifecycle is shared between the decentralized groups of administrators. Criteria that determine the scope of the delegation are the organizational structure and administrative roles.

Access Control

Access control supervises the process of control and provision of access to resources in real time based on the existing identities and assigned access rights. The key requirement of these services is the rapid access to a wide array of resource types. This process is carried out through the activities of identity verification, authorization and audit procedures. Identity verification is a process that proves identity of a party. A system for management of digital identities can be built inside of an educational institution in such a way to centralize the process of registration of users, and to have the information necessary for the authorization of users in a database. Processes of authentication and authorization (hereinafter: AA) are then carried out between the users, resources and the educational institution's authorization and authentication systems. A problem arises when it comes to authentication and authorization of users coming from different organizations. In that case users from one institution need to access and use resources belonging to another educational institution and when an institution wants to allow the use of its resources to users from another institution (Lenggenhager & Schnellmann, 2012). The solution of problems is the implementation of an infrastructure model for authentication and authorization (hereinafter: AAI). The foundations of AAI are three basic activities that take place between the user, its parent educational institution and resources. AA process consists of:

- Authentication of user performed by their parent educational institution;
- Transfer of user's authorization attributes from his parent institution to the owner of resources;
- Resources owner making a decision about access to the resource in question.

Use of AAI concept solves problems of accessing:

- Networks by individual users (modem, wireless, wired);
- Computer resources;
- Basic network services (ssh/telnet, e-mail, ftp);
- Web resources;

- Network applications (online databases, distance learning...).

Identity federation is a process that allows distribution of identification, authentication and authorization across the institution's borders and different platforms. Identity federation can be achieved between two organizations that have established a relationship based on trust. Based on this trust, organizations define sets of resources that can be accessed by other organizations and processes that allow such actions. Federation can be viewed as a circle of trust where all subjects that trust in the quality and reliability accept digital identities that are issued by parent institutions. In order to preserve the trust that was established, it is necessary that all subjects adhere to the relevant norms.

When the user is authenticated to the SSO system, an application informs the user access to Web browsers on the need to check user authentication. Web browser redirects the user to a page for user authentication. Page SSO authentication system verifies if the user has been already authenticated and if the user is authenticated, it redirects back to the application that requested authentication check (Figure 6).

Figure 6. AAI SSO

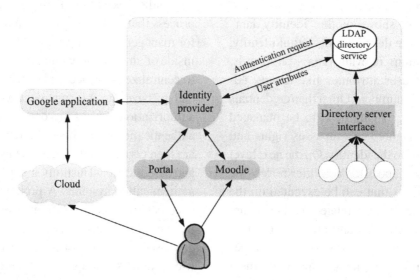

The main task of the parent institution is to ensure reliability and completeness of digital identity records it issued. The information issued by a parent institution related to a certain physical person can be required by some of the service providers in the process of authorization later on. However, this does not mean the parent institution can, or even should always have all of this information at its disposal. In order to solve this problem, a concept of additional repositories of attributes attached to digital identities was developed. These attributes need to be unambiguously connected with the core record about digital identity. An example of a case, when the use of such an extended AAI model is desirable, is the situation where one or more services target a group of individuals that are interconnected in some way, e.g. by working on a joint project or by membership in an organization. Such a group can encompass members from different institutions, regions or countries. This concept is titled "virtual organization" (VO) (Figure 7).

Implementations of VO concept depend on the technology and implementation of AAI in which the VO is implemented. VO systems can differ not only by the information model used, but also by applied technological solutions. Implementation that was realized in Swiss AII (Switch-AAI) is based on the Shibboleth technology, while the implementation of VO in the Norwegian AII (FEIDE) relies on the simple SAMLphp application (Vujin, 2012).

MODEL OF IDENTITY MANAGEMENT IN EDUCATIONAL CLOUD

Model of Identity as a Service in an Educational Institution

Nowadays, in an educational institution, there are numerous services that can be provided to students through Internet. Some of the most commonly used educational services are: system for e-education,

Figure 7. Model of virtual organization

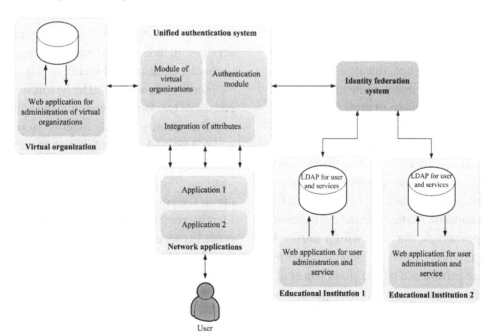

identity management, e-mail, ftp, customer relationship management (CRM), portal services, services for communication and collaboration, document management system, decision support system, services for scientific research, services for teaching support, administrative services, etc. Collaborative services for example enable various functionalities related to collaboration of users: information on the various activities and events, information management, project management, user groups, workshops, calendar, discussion forums, team work and so on. Document management system is system used to track and store electronic documents and/or images of paper documents. In the case of educational institution, CRM is a coherent and complete set of processes and technologies for managing relationships with current and potential students and associates of the educational institution. It represents the systematic care of a relationship between the university and students, where service quality is becoming an ever more interesting question (Vulić, 2013).

However, recent researches in e-learning focused on the reuse of learning material, but not on services and applications. With the increase in the number of services and users in educational system required processing power also increases. The best solution that information technologies could provide to users at higher education institutions and to their computer centers is the infrastructure model based on the cloud computing concept. The cloud computing infrastructure for educational institutions allows for an efficient usage of existing resources and gives a new perspective to scalability and reliability of educational services, software and a system for e-education (Jin et al., 2010). Researches and case studies pointed out the most common approaches, not only within universities, but in the other fields of cloud computing solutions, are private and public cloud (Jin et al., 2010). Public clouds are owned and operated by third parties, i.e. cloud service providers. Opposite the public cloud model, a private cloud model enables educational institutions to have com-

plete control of identity management, services, data security, applications and resources that are provided to their users. Recently, the number of private cloud based solutions within e-learning systems has been significantly increased (Liang & Yang, 2011). Managing identities and access control for e-learning applications remains one of the emerging challenges facing IT today. Further this problem became more complex in e-learning systems, where different resources and educational services are deployed through private cloud.

In an educational institution, it is possible to build a system for digital identity management by centralizing the process of user registration. All information needed for authorization process is stored in a database. Authentication and authorization processes are performed between users, resources and educational institution's system for authentication and authorization. Adding the on-premises capability of securely managing identities in educational cloud requires setting up and managing an Internet single sign-on federation solution. One of the larger tasks in running own federation solution is managing the relationships of the increasing number of services in educational cloud. The management of identity as a service includes creating customized connections for services in educational cloud, managing user accounts, auditing, and identity-related services.

Identity as a service (IDaaS) solutions usually consist of two key components: the identity store and the identity portal. Identity store contains a synchronized set of identities from an Active Directory, LDAP, relational databases and other sources. These identities are then provisioned out to the educational applications in the cloud. Identity portal is where users log on, and are then provided access to the educational cloud services for which they've been authorized (Figure 8).

Main functionalities of identity portal include: SSO, User management and Reporting. SSO system relies on a central database, and a Web portal used for login. Web applications use unique and standardized authentication method and sys-

Figure 8. Model of identity as a service in educational cloud

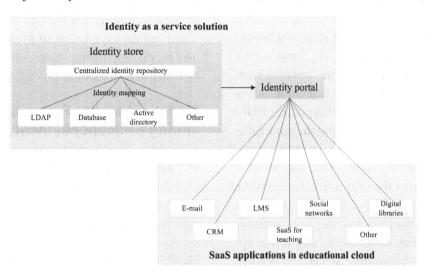

tem detects applications which are used by the user and it permits logging out from particular applications or services in the system. It is possible to implement SSO system via programming support of simpleSAMLphp with the support for SAML protocol, version 1.1 and 2.0. SimpleSAMLphp is a set of simple PHP scripts which enable data interchange via SAML protocol and simple embedding into other PHP applications. Because of using the standard SAML protocol, other non-PHP applications can be customized to use SSO

system as well. The IDaaS method of user authentication is fairly secure because passwords do not travel outside the educational institution. SSO capability means there will be little to no need to manage duplicate accounts at SaaS applications that don't support federation. The simple scenario of SSO using SAML is shown in Figure 9.

In order to manage access to cloud services and other federated applications, centralized policies can be defined in XACML. This can be

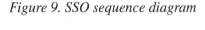

Figure 9. SSO sequence diagram

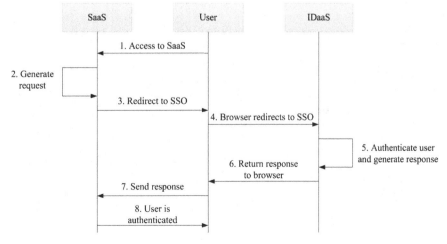

done by combining XACML with a federation protocol (e.g., SAML, OpenID Connect, etc.). Federation server has a central role, as it should create a security token which the Service Provider (SP) will use to identify the incoming user. Before creating this token, the federation server can call out to an authorization server (the PDP) to check these centralized rules. At the same time, the SP can also use XACML to control access. PDP checks digital signature of the token and, if valid, it can extract the user attributes from the message. Consequently, the SP posses high degree of confidence about the asserted user attribute without embedding entitlement rules in the application or the federation. SCIM and XAML could work together if provision entitlements policies were associated with users and groups to other domains. In this way, companies could extend their on-premises authorization solutions to the cloud, with some changes to SCIM.

Currently, there are various methods for user management. Although a few standards have been defined, very little adoption has occurred. IDaaS solution could be extended with a module for user management that provides a broadest set of user and group management capabilities: automatic import of users, provisioning and update of new accounts, user accounts deactivation and support for password synchronization.

IDaaS services for reporting enable auditing usage of SaaS application. Information and traffic that goes to the educational cloud services have to pass through an agent or through the IDaaS portal. These are data on user activity, user activation, user access, application usage, user provisioning, and user deprovisioning.

Model of Identity Federation among Educational Institutions

The next step in IDaaS development is creating identity federations among educational institution. Federation provides identities with some attributes presented as claims to a service provider. The service provider automatically manages these identities as a mirror of their original status. If an account authorized for federation has its authorization revoked or disabled, this revocation is immediately mirrored to the service provider.

It is relatively easy to develop a system for integrated identity management within one educational institution, where the described principles and guidelines are applied. However, the problem of developing identity management system across multiple institutions, where users from one institution require access to resources of another institution is more complex. The solution of this problem is an implementation of infrastructure for authentication and authorization. Basic components of this infrastructure (Figure 10) are users, institutions and resources, and the process flows through the following steps:

Figure 10. AAI infrastructure

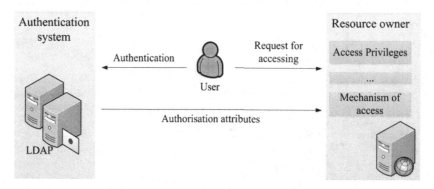

- Authentication of users performed by their parent institution;
- Transfer of user's authorization attributes from parent institution to the resource owner;
- Resource owner grants or denies access to the resource (authorization).

The main task of home institution is to provide reliability and integrity of issued records of digital identities. However, it does not mean that the home institution can always own all data related to a physical person who issued digital certificate and which can possible be needed by a service provider during the user authorization process. Solution for this problem could be adding new repositories of attributes which are connected to digital identities and uniquely connected with the main record of digital identity. Example where is advised to use this extended AAI model is related to situation where one or more services are dedicated to people's groups which are connected in some ways (e.g. working on the same project or organization membership). Such group can include members from several different organizations, regions or countries.

Through AAI, it is possible to manage the access to different resources and system components, such as: network for individual users (modem, wireless, etc.), computer resources (grid, network drives, etc.), network services (ssh, telnet, email, ftp, etc.), Web resources, network applications, etc.

Identity federation (Figure 11) is a process that enables distribution of identification, authentication and authorization outside the boundaries of an organization. It can be realized between organizations that share a certain level of trust. These organizations have to define resources that can be accessed by users from other organizations and implement enabling process.

Prototype as a Proof of Concept

As a proof of concept, one part of the model described in this chapter is deployed in the Laboratory for e-business at the Faculty of Organizational Sciences in Belgrade. Consolidation of computing resources for e-learning is realized using the model of private clouds. This approach has been chosen because it enables better usage of existing e-learning infrastructure and the model can subsequently be expanded into a hybrid or

Figure 11. Identity federation

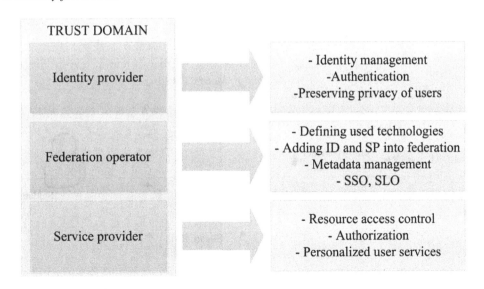

public cloud (Sotomayor, Montero, Llorente, & Foster, 2009). The aim of the implementation of the private cloud is to provide users run virtualized infrastructure, environment and service. The system for managing virtual infrastructure will automate, coordinate and integrate the existing solutions for: networking, storage, virtualization, monitoring and management of users. In this way, students and teachers are provided with tools for quick and easy access to the necessary educational and scientific services and resources.

The implemented private cloud consists of a server that hosts all described software tools and physical computers (nodes) and their recourses. The server serves for the management of: cluster of physical machines, individual machines, nodes, i.e. virtual machines set up on the nodes, memory resources, and system and network users. A solution for the management and fine tuning of the virtual infrastructure has been implemented in order to achieve better scalability and stability. This solution enables the real time management of the complete system infrastructure.

One of the core components of the model is the directory for identity management. It is a centralized repository for logical data and identities in the whole system. All components in the system communicate with the LDAP server when authenticating and authorizing users through IDaaS. All parts of the system communicate with the server for identity management during the authentication and authorization. Privileges are defined for the environment and for the available services. Each user in the model has a set of privileges for a specific environment and services within them. Users do not have the right of access to services that do not belong to an environment.

User data are stored in an LDAP repository and provided to applications in educational cloud as a Web service. Applications using this service include: Moodle learning management system, Webmail, customer relationship management application deployed in SugarCRM, and an application for managing and reserving cloud computing resources for teaching and learning purposes. The graphical representation is presented in the Figure 12.

A representative SaaS in the deployed cloud infrastructure is ELABCloud application which allows students to reserve any of the enabled VMs for the Moodle course for which they are registered. After a successful login through IDaaS, the student is shown a list of available VMs, depending on the Moodle courses they are enrolled in. The student can make a reservation for a VM, and choose the date and time when the VM will be used (Figure 13).

Figure 12. Model for identity management

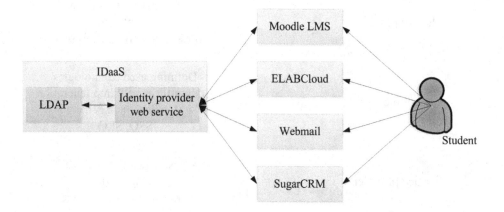

Figure 13. ELABCloud: Virtual machine reservation

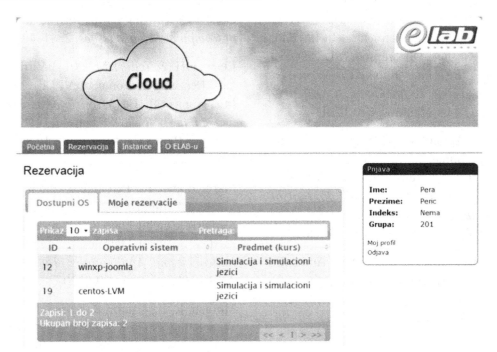

CONCLUSION

Issues associated with SaaS applications in educational clouds have been gaining wider attention over the last months, which have been fueling decision makers' interest in IDaaS. They're becoming increasingly aware that the IDaaS technology can solve many identity management problems.

Single sign on undoubtedly makes it easier and safer by reducing to only one account per user for all services, number of passwords, and central management of roles to define resources access control. It can be very beneficial to end-users, administrators and help desk. SSO can gain much more importance with the emerging cloud computing technology providing ICT services and also it reduces the chances of phishing attacks but as single sign on gives access with one login, it should be implemented in a secure way.

This chapter presented a model for digital identity management in the educational cloud. It can also be used in other types of institutions as well. To evaluate the proposed model, a part of the system for e-learning within Laboratory for e-business has been migrated to cloud, and identity management has been implemented. Further research is necessary to acquire quantitative and qualitative data for evaluation of the system performance.

Finally, we acknowledge the limitations of the described approach concerning the complexity and difficulty for setting and maintaining on-premise identity management. For many educational institutions, outsourcing the identity management could be simpler and less expensive solution. However, the described method provides higher level of security management comparing to any outsourced solution.

REFERENCES

Bertino, E., Paci, F., Ferrini, R., & Shang, N. (2009). Privacy-preserving digital identity management for cloud computing. *IEEE Data Eng. Bull.*, *32*(1), 21–27.

Dong, B., Qinghua, Z., Yang, J., Haifei, L., & Qiao, M. (2009). An e-learning ecosystem based on cloud computing infrastructure. In I. Aedo, N-S. Chen, Kinshuk, D. Sampson, & L. Zaitseva (Eds.), *Ninth IEEE International Conference on Advanced Learning Technologies, ICALT 2009* (pp. 125-127). Los Alamitos, CA: IEEE.

Eludiora, S., Abiona, O., Oluwatope, A., Oluwaranti, A., Onime, C., & Kehinde, L. (2011). A user identity management protocol for cloud computing paradigm. *International Journal of Communications. Network and System Sciences*, *4*(3), 152–163. doi:10.4236/ijcns.2011.43019

Jie, W., Arshad, J., & Ekin, P. (2009). Authentication and authorization infrastructure for grids - Issues, technologies, trends and experiences. *The Journal of Supercomputing*, *52*(1), 82–96. doi:10.1007/s11227-009-0267-8

Jin, H., Ibrahim, S., Bell, T., Gao, W., Huang, D., & Wu, S. (2010). Cloud types and services. In B. Furht & A. Escalante (Eds.), Handbook of cloud computing (pp. 335-355). Berlin: Springer Science+Business Media.

Jin, Z. P., Jian, X., Ming, X., & Ning, Z. (2010). An attribute-oriented model for identity management. In *Proceedings of International Conference on e-Education, e-Business, e-Management and e-Learning* (pp. 440-444). Los Alamitos, CA: IEEE Computer Society.

Lang, U. (2010). OpenPMF SCaaS: Authorization as a service for cloud & SOA applications. In J. Qiu, G. Zhao, & C. Rong (Eds.), *2010 IEEE Second International Conference on Cloud Computing Technology and Science (CloudCom)* (pp. 634-643). Los Alamitos, CA: IEEE Computer Society.

Lenggenhager, T., & Schnellmann, P. (2012). AAI - Authentication and authorization infrastructure. *SWITCHaai Attribute Specification*, 1-46. Retrieved September 1, 2013, from https://www.switch.ch/aai/docs/AAI_Attr_Specs.pdf

Lewis, K., & Lewis, J. (2009). Web single sign-on authentication using SAML. *International Journal of Computer Science Issues*, *2*, 41–48.

Liang, P. H., & Yang, J. M. (2011). Virtual personalized learning environment (VPLE) on the cloud. In Z. Gong et al. (Eds.), *Web information systems and mining* (Vol. 6988, pp. 403–411). Berlin: Springer Berlin Heidelberg. doi:10.1007/978-3-642-23982-3_49

Marin-Lopez, R., Pereñiguez-Garcia, F., Ohba, Y., Bernal-Hidalgo, F., & Gomez, A. (2010). A Kerberized architecture for fast re-authentication in heterogeneous wireless networks. *Mobile Networks and Applications*, *15*(3), 392–412. doi:10.1007/s11036-009-0220-3

Morgan, R. L., Cantor, S., Carmody, S., Hoehn, W., & Klingenstein, K. (2004). Federated security: The shibboleth approach. *Educause Quarterly*, 1-6. Retrieved September 1, 2013, from http://net.educause.edu/ir/library/pdf/EQM0442.pdf

Mueller, M., Park, Y., Lee, J., & Kim, T.-Y. (2006). Digital identity: How users value the attributes of online identifiers. *Information Economics and Policy*, *18*(4), 405–422. doi:10.1016/j.infoecopol.2006.04.002

Núñez, D., Agudo, I., Drogkaris, P., & Gritzalis, S. (2011). Identity management challenges for intercloud applications. *Communications in Computer and Information Science*, *187*, 198–204. doi:10.1007/978-3-642-22365-5_24

Olden, E. (2011). Architecting a cloud-scale identity fabric. *Computer*, *44*(3), 52–59. doi:10.1109/MC.2011.60

Pérez, A., López, G., Cánovas, O., & Gómez-Skarmeta, A. (2011). Formal description of the SWIFT identity management framework. *Future Generation Computer Systems*, *27*(8), 1113–1123. doi:10.1016/j.future.2011.04.003

Ping Identity. (2011). *Simple cloud identity management (SCIM)*. Retrieved September 1, 2013, from http://www.enterprisemanagement360.com/wp-content/files_mf/white_paper/simple-cloud-identity-management-scim.pdf

Sotomayor, B., Montero, R., Llorente, I., & Foster, I. (2009). Virtual infrastructure management in private and hybrid clouds. *IEEE Internet Computing*, *13*(5), 14–22. doi:10.1109/MIC.2009.119

Sun, S., Hawkey, K., & Beznosov, K. (2012). Systematically breaking and fixing OpenID security: Formal analysis, semi-automated empirical evaluation, and practical countermeasures. *Computers & Security*, *31*(4), 465–483. doi:10.1016/j.cose.2012.02.005

Suriadi, S., Foo, E., & Jøsang, A. (2009). A user-centric federated single sign-on system. *Journal of Network and Computer Applications*, *32*(2), 388–401. doi:10.1016/j.jnca.2008.02.016

Takabi, H., Joshi, J., & Ahn, G. (2010). Security and privacy challenges in cloud computing environments. *IEEE Security & Privacy*, *8*(6), 24–31. doi:10.1109/MSP.2010.186

Vossen, G., & Westerkamp, P. (2006). Secure identity management in a service-based e-learning environment. *International Journal of Intelligent Information Technologies*, *2*(4), 57–76. doi:10.4018/jiit.2006100104

Vujin, V. (2012). *IT infrastructure model for e-learning*. (Doctoral dissertation). University of Belgrade, Belgrade, Serbia.

Vulić, M. (2013). *Student relationship management model in e-education*. (Doctoral dissertation). University of Belgrade, Belgrade, Serbia.

Zissis, D., & Lekkas, D. (2012). Addressing cloud computing security issues. *Future Generation Computer Systems*, *28*(3), 583–592. doi:10.1016/j.future.2010.12.006

ADDITIONAL READING

Bakhshi, R., & Deepak, J. (2009). Cloud Computing - Transforming the IT Ecosystem. *SETLabs Briefings InfoSys*, *7*(7), 3–10.

Catteddu, D. (2010). Cloud Computing - Benefits, risks and recommendations for information security. *Communications in Computer and Information Science*, *72*(1), 17. doi:10.1007/978-3-642-16120-9_9

Costanzo, A., Assuncao, M. D., & Buyya, R. (2009). Harnessing Cloud Technologies for a Virtualized Distributed Computing Infrastructure. *IEEE Internet Computing*, *13*(5), 24–33. doi:10.1109/MIC.2009.108

De Alfonso, C., Caballer, M., Alvarruiz, F., Molto, G., & Hernandez, V. (2011). Infrastructure Deployment over the Cloud. In B. Werner (Ed.), *Third IEEE International Conference on Coud Computing Technology and Science* (pp. 517-521). Los Alamitos: IEEE Computer Society.

Doddavula, S., & Gawande, A. (2009). Adopting Cloud Computing Enterprise Private Clouds. *SetLabs Briefings Infosys*, *7*(7), 11–18.

Doelitzscher, F., Sulistio, A., Reich, C., Kuijs, H., & Wolf, D. (2011). Private cloud for collaboration and e-Learning services: from IaaS to SaaS. *Computing*, *91*(1), 23–42. doi:10.1007/s00607-010-0106-z

Giannoni, D., & Tesone, D. (2003). What academic administrators should know to attract senior level faculty members to online learning environments. *Online Journal of Distance Learning Administration, 6(1)*. Retrieved September 1, 2013, from http://www.westga.edu/~distance/ojdla/spring61/giannoni61.htm

Gopalakrishnan, A. (2009). Cloud Computing Identity Management. *SETLabs Briefings*, *7*(7), 45–54.

Hai, J., Shadi, I., Tim, B., Wai, G., Dachuan, H., & Song, W. (2010). Cloud Types and Services. In B. Furht, & A. Escalante (Eds.), *Handbook of Cloud Computing* (pp. 335–355). US: Springer.

He, W., Cernusca, D., & Abdous, M. (2011). Exploring Cloud Computing for Distance Learning. *Online Journal of Distance Learning Administration, 14(3)*, Retrieved September 1, 2013, from http://www.westga.edu/~distance/ojdla/fall143/he_cernusca_abdous143.html

Iosup, A., Ostermann, S., Yigitbasi, N., Prodan, R., Fahringer, T., & Epema, D. (2011). Performance Analysis of Cloud Computing Services for Many-Tasks Scientific Computing. *IEEE Transactions on Parallel and Distributed Systems, 22*(6), 931–945. doi:10.1109/TPDS.2011.66

Kogan, M. (2000). Higher Education Communities and Academic Identity. *Higher Education Quarterly, 54*(3), 207–216. doi:10.1111/1468-2273.00156

Milić, A., Barać, D., Jovanić, B., Paunović, L., & Radenković, B. (2011). Cloud computing in e-education. In V. Žuborova, D. Camelia Iancu, & U. Pinterič (Eds.), *Social responsibility in 21st century* (pp. 473–488). Ljubljana: Založba Vega.

Moore, M. G. (1989). Three types of interaction. *American Journal of Distance Education, 3*(2), 1–6. doi:10.1080/08923648909526659

Parameswaran, V., & Chaddha, A. (2009). Cloud Interoperability and Standardization. *SetLabs Briefings Infosys, 7*(7), 19–26.

Simić, K. (2011). *Usage of mobile technologies in the development of application for cloud computing infrastructure in e-education.* Master thesis, University of Belgrade, Serbia.

Singhal, M., Chandrasekhar, S., Tingjian, G., Sandhu, R., Krishnan, R., Gail-Joon, A., & Bertino, E. (2013). Collaboration in multicloud computing environments: Framework and security issues. *Computer, 46*(2), 76–84. doi:10.1109/MC.2013.46

Smoot, S., & Nam, T. (Eds.). (2012). *Private Cloud Computing: Consolidation, Virtualization, and Service-Oriented Infrastructure.* USA: Elsevier.

Srinivasa, R. V., Nageswara, R. N. K., & Kumari, E. K. (2009). Cloud Computing: An overview. *Journal of Theoretical and applied Information Technology, 9(1)*, 71-76.

Tian, W., Su, S., & Lu, G. (2010). Framework for Implementing and Managing Platform as a Service in a Virtual Cloud Computing Lab. In Z. Hu, Z. Ye (Eds.), *The Second International Workshop on Education Technology and Computer Science.* Los Alamitos: IEEE Computer Society.

Vaidya, J. (2009). Infrastructure Management and Monitoring. In S. Padmanabhuni (Ed.), SetLabs Briefings Infosys, 7(7), 79-88.

Vujin, V., Radenković, B., Milić, A., & Despotović-Zrakić, M. (2011). Model IT infrastrukture visokoškolske ustanove zasnovan na cloud computing-u. In XXXVIII Simpozijum o operacionim istraživanjima - SYM-OP-IS 2011 (pp. 117-120). Belgrade: Centar za izdavačku delatnost Ekonomskog fakulteta u Beogradu.

Zhang, Y., & Chen, J.-L. (2010). Universal Identity Management Model Based on Anonymous Credentials. In L. O'Conner (Ed.), *2010 IEEE International Conference on Services Computing.* (pp. 305-312). Miami: IEEE, Inc.

Zhang, Y., & Chen, J.-L. (2011). A Delegation Solution for Universal Identity Management in SOA. *IEEE Transactions on Services Computing, 4*(1), 70–81. doi:10.1109/TSC.2010.9

KEY TERMS AND DEFINITIONS

Authentication: Is a process of proving the identity of a previously registered end user.

Authorization: Is a process of granting or denying access rights for a resource to an authenticated end user.

Federated Identity Management (Identity Federation): Enables enterprises to exchange identity information securely across domains, providing browser-based Single sign-on.

Identity as a Service (IDaaS): Refers to the management of identities in the cloud, apart from the applications and providers that use them and represents an extremely broad term that includes services for software, platform and infrastructure services in both the private and public cloud.

Identity Management (IDM): Describes the management of individual principals, their authentication, authorization, and privileges within or across system and enterprise boundaries with the goal of increasing security and productivity while decreasing cost, downtime and repetitive tasks.

IDentity Provider (IDP): Is the application that takes authentication information (commonly a username and password) and translates that into identity information (name, email, affiliations, etc) which it provides to Service Providers based on defined policies.

Security Assertion Markup Language (SAML): Is an XML standard that allows secure Web domains to exchange user authentication and authorization data.

Service Provider (SP): Is the software that provides some access control and communicates with the IDentity Provider for identity information.

Single Sign-On (SSO): Is a process whereby credentials are entered only once and allow access to many separate systems without having to re-authenticate for the duration of the session.

System for Cross-Domain Identity Management (SCIM): Is a new standard that reduces the complexity of user management operations by providing REST-based protocol for carrying out cross-domain identity management operations. SCIM enables provisioning and deprovisioning between identity providers and service providers. This keeps users in sync and reduces administrative burdens.

Chapter 4
From Software Specification to Cloud Model

Dušan Savić
University of Belgrade, Serbia

Siniša Vlajić
University of Belgrade, Serbia

Marijana Despotović-Zrakić
University of Belgrade, Serbia

ABSTRACT

Applications are often multi-tier and require application servers, workflow engines, and database management systems. Cloud computing is a computing paradigm wherein the resources such as processors, storage, and software applications are provided as services via the Internet. Moving an enterprise application to the cloud can be a challenge. This application needs to be split into the components that then automatically deploy on the cloud. In this chapter, the authors introduce a way to automatically derivate the main architecture components from the software requirements that can serve as a basis for an architecture diagram in the MOCCA method. The proposed approach is model and use case driven.

1. INTRODUCTION

Applications today are often composite, multi-tier applications, consisting of application components such as UIs, services, workflows and databases as well as middleware components such as application servers, workflow engines and database management systems (Mietzner, Unger, & Leymann, 2009). When moving such a composite application into the cloud, decisions must be made about putting which tier and even which component of such an application to which cloud (Leymann, Fehling, Mietzner, Nowak, & Dustdar, 2011; Andrikopoulos, Binz, Leymann, & Strauch, 2013; Cardoso, Binz, Breitenbücher, Kopp, & Leymann, 2013; Demont, Breitenbücher, Kopp, Leymann, & Wettinger, 2013).

The authors (Leymann, Fehling, Mietzner, Nowak, & Dustdar, 2011) defined Move-to-Cloud problem as a two main problems:

DOI: 10.4018/978-1-4666-5784-7.ch004

1. How to rearrange the components of a multi-tier, multi-component application into disjoint groups of components, and
2. How each group can be provisioned separately to different clouds.

They describe methodology that allows application developers and architects to model their application components and properties and is named as MOCCA method.

We have developed Silab approach whose the main goal was to enable automated analysis and processing of software requirements in order to achieve automatic generation of different parts of a software system. Silab approach has been used for the Kostmod 4.0 project (Kostmod 4.0, 2009), which was implemented for the needs of the Royal Norwegian Ministry of Defense.

In this chapter we have introduced a way how Silab approach can be integrated with MOCCA approach. Therefore, we have defined transformation which automatically generates an architecture model for MOCCA method form software requirements.

This chapter is organized as follows. In the next section it gives an overview of the cloud computing. Section 3 introduces model and use case development (Jacobson, Christerson, Jonsson, & Overgaard, 1993; Cockburn, 2000), and Section 4 describes Silab approach. Finally, Section 5 presents integrated Silab and MOCCA approach and Section 6 concludes the chapter and outlines some future works.

2. CLOUD COMPUTING

The term cloud was first used at the end of the last century to refer to large ATM networks. At the beginning of this century, with the advent of Amazon's Web Services (Maggiani, 2009) the term cloud computing begins to be widely used (Leymann, 2009; Leimeister, Böhm, Riedl, & Krcmar, 2010; Talukder, Zimmerman, & Prahalad,

2010). Eric Schmidt (Aymerich, Fenu, & Surcis, 2008) was one of the pioneers and promoter of cloud computing. Cloud computing has emerged from grid computing and it is related with technologies and concepts such as: Simple Object Access Protocol (SOAP), Service Oriented Architecture (SOA), Web services, Software-as-a-Services (SaaS) (Janssen & Joha, 2011).

Cloud computing has evolved from Grid computing. The idea of grid computing is a generalization of the Web. Web is primarily a service that allows the presentation of information and exchange data via the Internet. GRID is a service primarily for the sharing of processing power and memory of computers on the network allowing local or global network turns into a huge computer resource.

The main characteristics of Grid Computing (Foster, Kesselman, & Tuecke, 2001) are:

1. Decentralized resource control,
2. Standardization, i.e. open and common protocols and interfaces are used in Grid middleware, and
3. Not-trivial qualities of services.

Grid application requires a middleware to enable communication via open and standardized protocols. All middleware attempts to apply the standards defined by the OGF community (OGF, 2013).

The large computing and storage capacity offered by grid technology has led to the development of another category of services that later came to be identified as cloud services (Aymerich, Fenu, & Surcis, 2008). There are many definition of the cloud computing. For Boss et al. (2007) a Cloud is a pool of virtualized computer resources, complement to Grid environment by supporting the management of Grid resources. Cloud computing implies component-based application construction (Skillicorn, 2002), based on existing technologies but integrated these technologies different from Grid, especially the combination with Utility Computing and data centers (Aaron, 2007).

In order to achieve a better understating and a common conceptualization Cloud computing the authors (Weinhardt et al., 2009) have developed Cloud Business Model Framework. The identified three layers similarly to the technical layers in Cloud realizations:

1. The infrastructure layer,
2. The platform-as-service layer, and
3. The application layer.

To make difference between two categories of infrastructure business model:

1. The provision of storage capabilities (Amazon) and
2. Provisioning of computer power (Sun).

The platform layer provides value-added services from a technical and business perspective. The authors emphasize two types of platform in the cloud:

1. Development platform such as Google App Engine and
2. Business platform such as Salesforce.

The application layer represents the actual interface for the customer (Software-as-a-Services or Web services on-demand).

3. MODEL AND USE CASE DRIVEN DEVELOPMENT

MDD process proposes using models in all phases of software development. In the initial phase (the phase of determining user requirements) requirements are usually described in text form, so transformation from the requirements to the different analysis model is difficult to perform on the automated or semi-automated way, primarily because the requirements are usually text document (Silva, Saraiva, Ferreira, Silva, & Videira,

2007; Saraiva & Silva, 2010). Different methods are based on MDA principles (definition and transformation models) mainly put emphasis on:

- Transformation of PIM models to PSM model and
- Transformation of PSM model to source code.

Defining the appropriate CIM models (the requirements model) and its transformation into the corresponding PIM model is generally not considered as part of the overall software development process. On the other hand, there are individual attempts to transform requirement model into analysis model, but there is no well-defined guidance how to apply that entire solution in the software development process (Li & Wei, 2008).

The requirements are usually described into textual form and because that the following problems occur:

- Requirements are not consistent among each other,
- Requirements are not complete;
- Requirements are not clear;
- Requirements are not suitable for transformation into various models of analysis,
- It is difficult to establish requirements traceability through all phases of software development.

If requirements described in text form authors (Loniewski, Armesto, & Insfran, 2011) propose to use Abbott (Abbott, 1983) heuristics, where the requirements are manually are translated into the appropriate analysis model (Bernd & Allen, 2004; Larman, 2004). In research (Loniewski, Armesto, & Insfran, 2011) the authors emphasize that due to the unclear definition of CIM and PIM models is very hard to apply the full MDA approach to software development that just starts with defining the CIM model. Although most attention in the MDA approach is focused on the PIM to PSM model transformation, especially transformation from PSM to source code, there are attempts to transform CIM into PIM model (Li & Wei, 2008; Kherraf, Lefebvre, & Suryn, 2008; Jamshidi et al., 2009).

Model-Driven Architecture (MDA) is the most famous implementation of this approach. MDA distinguishes three types of models: Computation Independent Model (CIM), Platform Independent Model (PIM), and Platform Specific Model (PSM). Each of these models can contain one or more models to specify the structural, functional and behavior aspect of the software system. The key to the success of MDA lies in automating the model2model and model2code transformations. A transformation is a process of the automatic generation of a target model from a source model. A source model is generated according to transformation rules which describe how one or more constructs in the source model can be transformed into one or more construct in the target model.

On the other hand, use case development considers use cases as the basis for the software development. While this sounds good in theory, practice has shown otherwise. Use cases are mainly used only in the initial stages of software development, while the later stages of development of software systems generally have no direct connection with the use case. The biggest problem in this development is the traceability of the software or the ability to create links between requirements and appropriate models of analysis, design, and even source code that implements these requirements. The literature cannot find a larger number of studies that suggest the generation of other artifacts from use case such as:

- The prototype of user interface or complete user interface applications (Miguel & Faria, 2009),
- Domain model (Elbendak, Vickers, & Rossiter, 2011) or
- Automatic tests (test cases).

4. OVERVIEW OF SILAB APPROACH

Silab Project (Savić, Simić, & Vlajić, 2010; Antović, Vlajić, Savić, Milić, & Stanojević, 2012; Savić et al., 2012) was initiated in Software Engineering Laboratory at Faculty of Organizational Sciences, University of Belgrade, in 2007. The main goal of this project was to enable automated analysis and processing of software requirements in order to achieve automatic generation of different parts of a software system.

At first project has been divided in two main subprojects SilabReq (Savić, Vlajić, Antović, Stanojević, & Milić, 2011) and SilabUI projects that were being developing separately. SilabReq project considered formalization of user requirements and transformations to different UML models in order to facilitate the analyses process and to assure the validity and consistency of software requirements. On the other hand, SilabUI project considered impacts of particular elements of software requirements and data models on resulting user interface in order to develop a software tool that enables automatic generation of user interface based on the use case specification and the domain model.

When both subprojects reach desired level of maturity, they were integrated in a way that some results of SilabReq project can be used as input for SilabUI project. As a proof of concept, Silab project has been used for the Kostmod 4.0 project, which was implemented for the needs of the Royal Norwegian Ministry of Defense.

The SilabReq project includes SilabReq Language, SilabReq Transformation and SilabReq Visualization components. These components are shown in Figure 1.

The SilabReq language component presents our SilabReq DSL for use case specification.

The SilabReq transformation component is responsible for transformation software requirements into different models. Currently, we have developed transformations that transform SilabReq model into an appropriate UML model. All

Figure 1. Main components of the SilabReq project

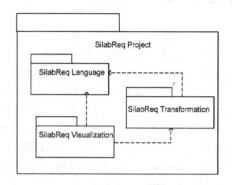

these transformations are defined through Kermeta language for meta-modeling (Kermeta, 2013).

The SilabReq visualization component is responsible for visual presentation of the specified software requirements. Currently, we have developed only UML presentation of these requirements. So, we can present SilabReq use

cases specification through UML use case, UML sequence, UML activity or UML state-machine diagram. Silab approach is shown in Figure 2.

Use Case Identification

Silab approach starts with identification of the use cases. The result of this activity is identified use cases that specified in User Requirements specification document, in the Use Case declaration section. Along with the identification of use cases, the users of the system are identified, that is declared in the declaration section of the Actor in User Requirements specification document (Figure 3).

Specification of use cases is provided via a text editor that recognizes the SilabReq language syntax. Declaration of use cases is done by specifying

Figure 2. The Silab approach

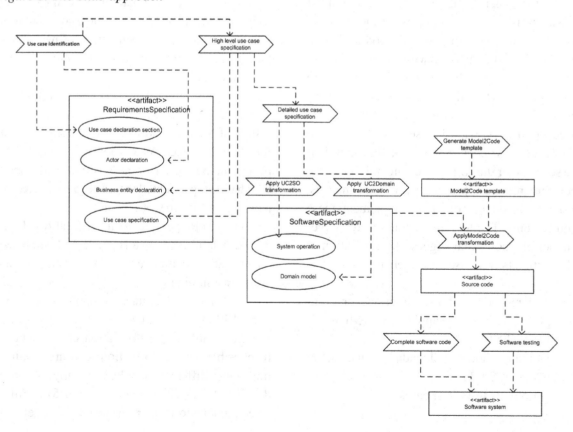

Figure 3. The User Requirements specification document

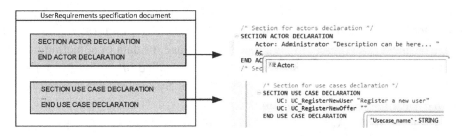

- Unique use case identifier (UC_RegisterNewUser) and
- The name of the use case (Register a new user).

Along with the declaration of use cases, actors are declared. The Actor of the system is declared by specifying a unique identifier which describe actor's role. Text description of the actors of the system is optional.

High Level of Use Case Specification

Following the identification of use cases (label 1 in Figure 4) use cases are specified at a high level abstraction. At this level of use case specification is necessary specified:

1. Actors who can participate in use cases (label 2 in Figure 4);
2. Business entity over which the use case is executed (label 3 in Figure 4);

Figure 4. High level use case specification

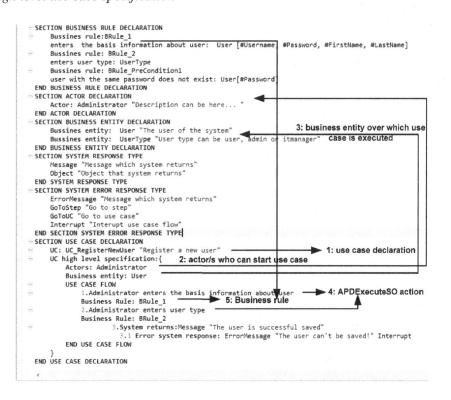

3. Specification of the actions Actor Prepare Data to execute System Operation (APDExecuteSO) (label 4 in Figure 4) with appropriate business rules (label 5 in Figure 4).

Rules describe what user enters information (puts / chooses / selects) in the APDExecuteSO action. User enters some value that can be:

*   Attribute of a business entity (BRule_1 in Figure 4) or
*   A business entity (BRule_2 in Figure 4).

Figure 4 describes a high level specification of the "Register a new user" use case.

At this level, use case specification (Register a new user) is done as follows:

*   First the use case is associated with one (or a more) actors who perform use case (Figure 5).
*   Actor has previously declared in the section actor declaration (Figure 6).
*   After, the use case is associated with an entity that stands as a base-use-case business entity over which use case is executed. A certain use case manipulated with this base-use-case business entity and other business entities that are related with it (Figure 7.).
*   Before the use case is associated with a specific business entity, it is declared in the section Business entity declaration of the User Requirements specification document (Figure 8).
*   After that, use case actions are specified. At this use case specification level it is possible to specify two types of use case actions: (1) APDExecuteSO, and (2) System replies and returns the Result of the System Operation execution (SRExecutionSO). The result of execution of the system operation can be successful (statement System

returns) or unsuccessful (statement Error System response). The type of the result that system returns to the use can be message, or data or something else and can be specified in section (System response type or System error response type).

Detailed Use Case Specification

Detailed use case specification extends high level use case specification and enriches it. At this level two types of use case action are introduced:

1. Actor Calls System to execute System Operation (ACSExecuteSO) and,

Figure 5. Associated actor with use case

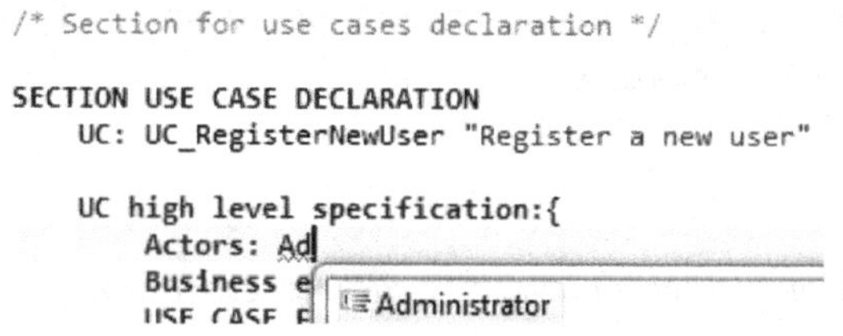

Figure 6. Actor declaration

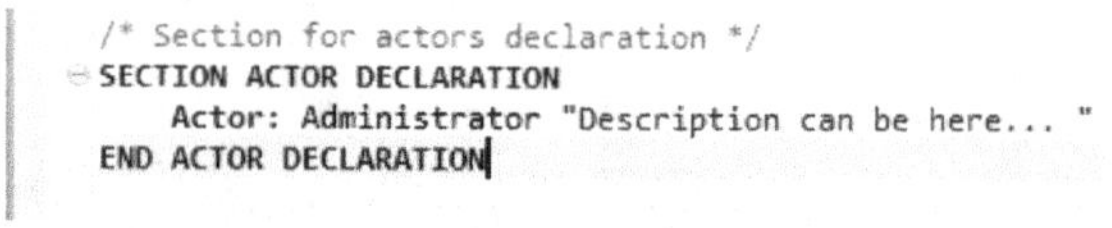

Figure 7. Associated business entity with use case

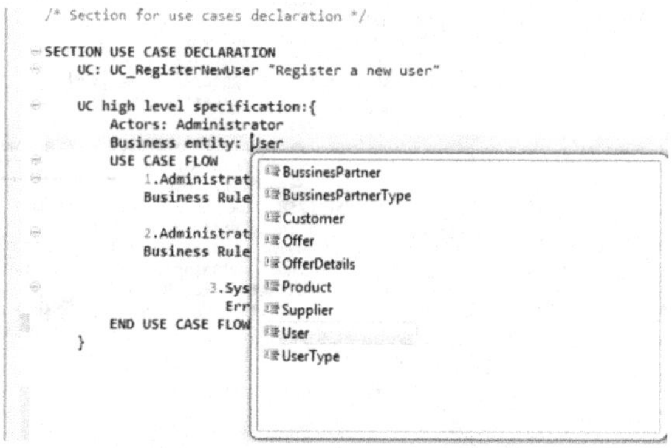

Figure 8. Business entity declaration

```
/* Section for business entities declaration */
SECTION BUSINESS ENTITY DECLARATION
    Bussines entity:  User "The user of the system"
    Bussines entity:  UserType "User type can be user, admin or itmanager"
END BUSINESS ENTITY DECLARATION
```

2. System executes System Operation (SExecuteSO).

At this level system operation is specified detailed:

1. Precondition is defined,
2. System operation name is defined and,
3. The result of system operation execution is.

Figure 9 describes detailed use case specification for the "Register a new user" use case.

At this level, use case specification of "Register a new user" use case is done as follows:

1. Firstly, the use case actions at high-level use case specification are automatically import;

2. Use case actions types ACSExecuteSO (action 3 in Figure 9) and SExecuteSO (action 4 on the Figure 9) are specified.

Transformations is Silab Approach

There are two key transformations in Silab approach that need to be executed before generating code:

- Apply UC2Domain Transformation, used to automatically identified or verified domain model, and
- Apply UC2SO Transformation, used to generate system operations.

Figure 9. Detailed use case specification

```
/* Section for use cases declaration */
SECTION USE CASE DECLARATION
    UC: UC_RegisterNewUser "Register a new user"
    UC detailed specification level:{
        SECTION system operation DECLARATION
            precondidtion
                BRule_PreCondition1
            end precondition
            registerNewUser "Register new user in system"
            postcondidtion
                User "The user is successful saved"
            end postcondition
            response successful:
                Message "The user is successful saved"
                savedUser :: User
            response error:
                ErrorMessage "The user can't be saved"
        END system operation DECLARATION

        Actors: Administrator
        Business entity: User

        USE CASE FLOW
            1.Administrator enters the basis information about user
            Business Rule: BRule_1
            2.Administrator enters user type
            Business Rule: BRule_2
            3.Administrator calls system to execute system operation #registerNewUser
            4.System execute system operation #registerNewUser
        END USE CASE FLOW
    }
END USE CASE DECLARATION
```

A prerequisite for the execution of these transformations is detailed specified use cases. Figures 10 and 11 show a way for generation domain model (Figure 10) and system operation (Figure 11).

Apply Model2Code Transformation is initiated after the identification of system operations that should be designed. Before generating source code it is necessary to select an appropriate template according to which the source code will be generated. Currently, we have integrated in the Silab approach template that for each system operation generates the appropriate class which is responsible its execution. Generating source code is based on the GRSAP Low Coupling and High Cohesion patterns and GoF Template Method pattern (Figure 12).

Software testing can be performed after automatically generated source code or/and after complete finished source code.

5. INTEGRATED APPROACH

The MOCCA method (Leymann, Fehling, Mietzner, Nowak, & Dustdar, 2011) proposes three main artifacts that should be provided:

1. An architecture model of application,
2. A deployment model of the application, and
3. Implementation artifacts.

The architecture model describes architectural components of the software system and relations among them. The model suggests that the granularity of the components in the architectural model has an impact on the flexibility and quality of the split of the application into groups that are provisioned in the different clouds. The deployment model specifies the runtime containers. Within these containers the components from architecture

Figure 10. UC2Domain transformation

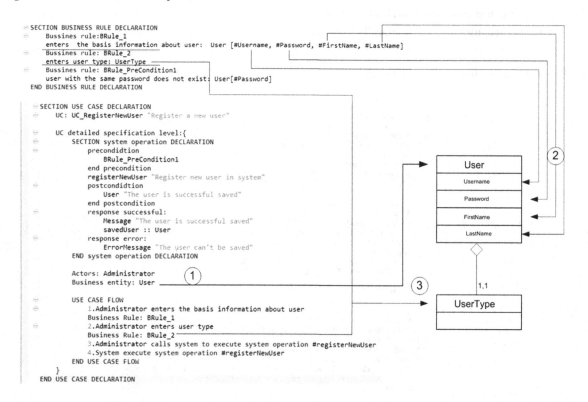

Figure 11. UC2SO transformation

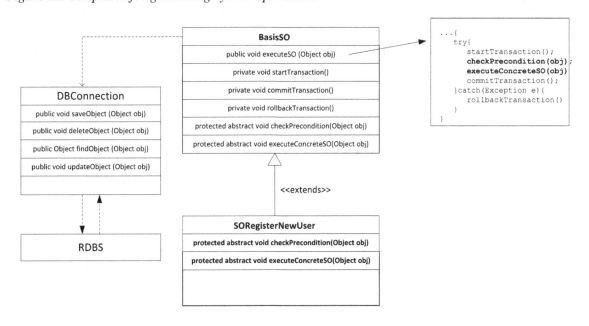

```
SECTION BUSINESS RULE DECLARATION
    Bussines rule:BRule_1
    enters  the basis information about user:  User [#Username, #Password, #FirstName, #LastName]
    Bussines rule: BRule_2
    enters user type: UserType
    Bussines rule: BRule_PreCondition1
    user with the same password does not exist: User[#Password]
END BUSINESS RULE DECLARATION

    UC detailed specification level:{
        SECTION system operation DECLARATION
            precondidtion
                BRule_PreCondition1
            end precondition
            registerNewUser "Register new user in system"
            postcondidtion
                User "The user is successful saved"
            end postcondition
            response successful:
                Message "The user is successful saved"
                savedUser :: User
            response error:
                ErrorMessage "The user can't be saved"
            END system operation DECLARATION

        Actors: Administrator
        Business entity: User

        USE CASE FLOW
            1.Administrator enters the basis information about user
            Business Rule: BRule_1
            2.Administrator enters user type
            Business Rule: BRule_2
            3.Administrator calls system to execute system operation #registerNewUser
            4.System execute system operation #registerNewUser
        END USE CASE FLOW
    }
END USE CASE DECLARATION
```

Figure 12. Templates for generating system operations

model are hosted. The Implementation artifacts of the application encompass installable units of the application.

The main idea behind the MOCCA method is that an architecture model of the application is enriched by additional information and that this enriched model becomes the basis for automatically rearranging the application and provisioning the rearranged application in different clouds. The MOCCA method consists of the following major steps (Leymann, Fehling, Mietzner, Nowak, & Dustdar, 2011):

1. As the basis, an architecture model of the application to be moved to the cloud has to be provided.
2. Furthermore, a deployment model of the application is required.
3. Also, the architecture model is rearranged into groups of components that belong into the same cloud. The creation of the cloud distribution and the deployment model can be performed in any order, even in parallel.
4. To support automatic provisioning, all implementation units must be provided that are required to actually run the application.
5. Finally, the cloud distribution and the combined architecture/deployment model annotated with the required implementation

units are combined into a provision cluster. The provision cluster represents all the information needed to provision the rearranged application into its target clouds.

The MOCCA method begins with a task that provides an architectural model. This chapter introduces a way to automatically produce an architectural model from specification of the application. The specification of application contains detailed use case specified using SilabReq DSL(Savić, Vlajić, Antović, Stanojević, & Milić, 2011; Savić et al., 2012).

SilabReq Meta-Model Overview

The SilabReq Language component is the base component for the SilabReq project as well as the whole Silab project. Its main part is SilabReq language. The aim of this language is to be used for functional specification of the software requirements in use case form. The longer version of SilabReq language is given in (Savić, Vlajić, Antović, Stanojević, & Milić, 2011). The abstract syntax of the SilabReq language is defined by meta-model, while SilabReq grammar is used to define concrete syntax of the language. Some part of SilabReq meta-model is presented in Figure 13. Software requirements for particular software

Figure 13.The SilabReqUseCaseModel meta-model

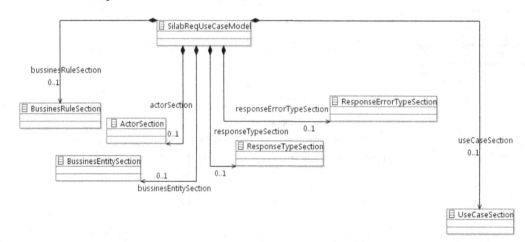

system are represented by an instance of the entity type SilabReqUseCaseModel.

Such SilabReqUseCaseModel entity is associated with an appropriate entity for business rule description (BussinesRuleSection entity), actor declaration (ActorSection entity), business entity declaration (BussinesEntitySection entity), description of successful (ResponseTypeSection entity) and error system operation response (ResponseErorTypeSection entity) as well as section for use case specification (UseCaseSection entity).

Business rule section in Silab requirements specification document is used to specify APDExecuteSO action. In SilabReq DSL meta-model this section is described as instance of BussinessRuleSection enity class (Figure 14). A BussinessRuleSection consists of zero ore more BusinessRuleEnters entity class which present entity rule that actor uses when prepare data for system operation execution. User can enter either some attributes of the business entity (BussinessEntityProperty entity) or particularly business

Figure 14. The BussinesRuleSection meta-model

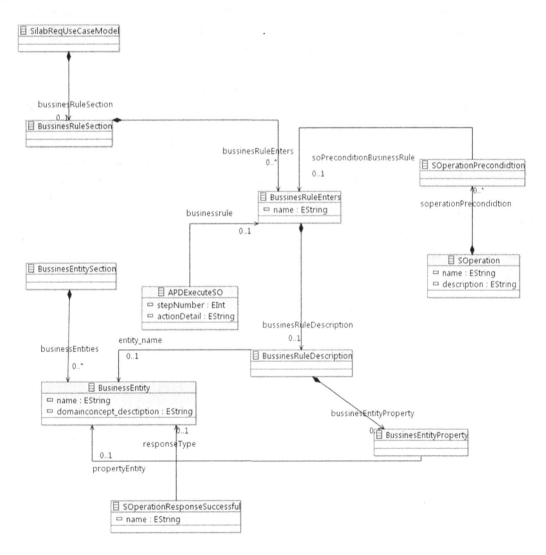

entity (BussinessEntity entity). Business rules are used to specify data that user enters in APDExecuteSO action, as well as to describe precondition for use case operation (SOperationPrecondidtion and SOperation entity) The most important attribute of the SOperation entity is name that define the system operation name.

The use case section for particular specification of the application contains zero or more use cases which are in SilabReq DSL meta-model are presented as instance of UseCaseDeclaration entity type (Figure 15). Each use case contains unique name (name) and short use case name (usecase_name). Detailed use case specification contains zero or more system operation that are executed entire use case. Furthermore, each use case is associated with actors who can execute use case (Actor entity) well as business entity over which use case is executed (BussinesEntity entity). The use case flow in SilabReq DSL meta-model is presented as instance of UseCaseFlowDetailed entity type.

MOCCA Meta-Model Overview

The MOCCA method can be used for solving the move2cloud problem. This method contains the various steps that need to be performed and

artifact to be created in order to move an application to the cloud. The meta-model that formally describes these artifacts and their relationship is presented in Figure 16.

The application which is customized is represented by an instance of the entity type Application Template. This entity contains one or more instances of the Component entity type. A component is composite entity the can contain other component. The component is source of as well as target of zero or more Component Relation entities. The key attribute of Component Relation entity is Type attribute that contains the semantics of the relation between two related components. Each Component Relation has zero or more Labels, specified as a pair of a Name and a Value attribute. Each Component is realized by exactly one Implementation. The manner used to realize the Implementation is specified in the Type attribute. The implementation contains zero ore more Artifacts. Artifact is generalization of different kinds of artifact like BPEL files, WSDL files and so on.

Components and Component Relations of the meta-model are used to describe elements of the architectural diagram of an application. Labels associated with the Component or with Component Relation on the architectural diagram are used to automatically propose cloud distribution. The

Figure 15. The UseCaseSection meta-model

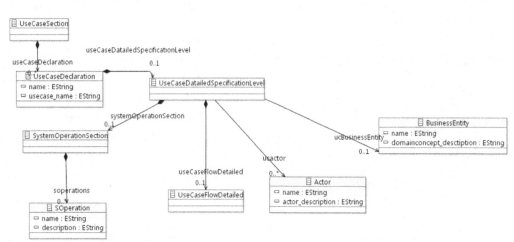

Figure 16. The MOCCA meta-model

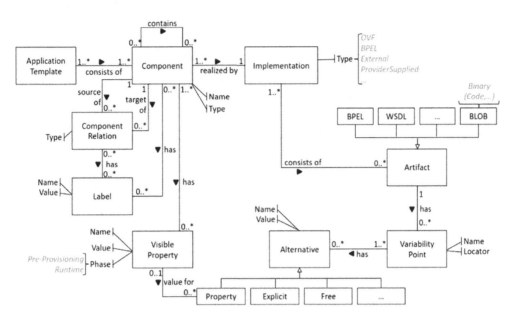

Implementation and Artifact of a component is used to support automatically installation of an application.

Example: Move2Cloud Application

The application to be moved into the cloud is a simple order system; it is a simple application, but it shows all the major relevant aspects relevant to see how our approach can be used integrated with MOCCA method. This example presents the specification of the order system using approach, as well as transformation that can be occurred to generate an architecture model for application that will be moved to the cloud.

The specification of order system is presented in Figure17 and Figure18. Before actor (ITManager) register new offer, he need to:

1. Enter the basis information about the offer (action 1, business rule BRule_3),
2. Find and select an appropriate business partner for offer (call included use case UC_SelectBussinesPartner),

3. Enter offer details (action 3 which can be executed several times, business rule BRule_4) and,
4. Call system to save new offer in the system.

After, the use case specification using Silab approach we generate an appropriate architecture model of the application. Use case (UC_RegisterNewOffer) is transformed into the two components (Offer Register Entry) (label 1 in Figure 19) which is used to enter basic information about the new offer. The execution of use case UC_RegisterNewOffer in action 2 includes the execution of use cases UC_SelectBusinessPartner. Because that we generate an appropriate component for searching business partners (Entry select business partner) (label 2 in Figure 19), and between these two components (Entry Offer Register Entry and select business partner) establish the association (label 3 in Figure 19).

During the use case execution one or more of system operations can be occurred. Thus, system operation "find business partner" is performed during the UC_SelectBusinessPartner use case execution, while in the use case UC_RegisterNe-

Figure 17. The specification of use case Register new offer (UC_RegisterNewOffer)

Figure 18. The specification of use case Select business partner (UC_SelectBusinessPartner)

wOffer system operation "save new offer" is performed. During the transformation of use case specification into an application architecture model, each system operation is transformed into a separate component that is responsible for its execution. Thus, in the use case UC_RegisterNe-

wOffer system operation "save new offer" is transformed into Order process component (label 4 in Figure 19), while in the use case UC_Select-BusinessPartner system operation "find business partner" is transformed into "Process business partner" component (label 5 in Figure 19).

Figure 19. Move2Cloud transformation

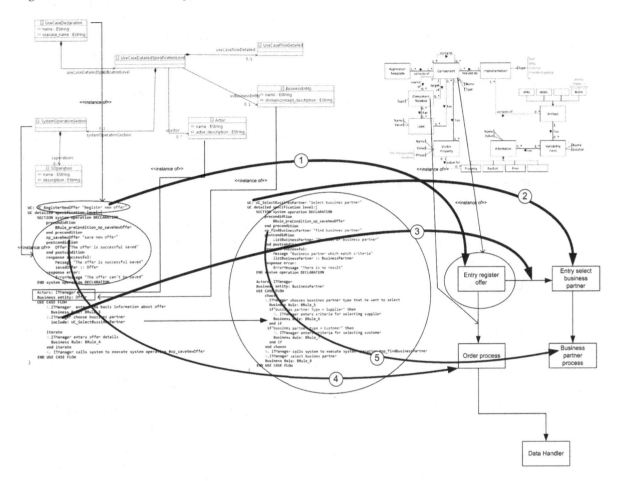

In general, for each use case our transformation generates special component responsible to receive the actor request, while for each system operation it generates a separate component that is responsible for its execution. The corresponding generated architecture model from use case specification for Offer system example is presented in the Figure 19.

6. CONCLUSION

In this chapter, we introduce a way how automatically to derivate the main architecture components that is used in MOCCA method to solve Move-to-Cloud problem. This method has been described using various steps to be performed and artefact

to be created in order to move an application to the cloud. The move2cloud problem emphasises the problem of rearranging the components of an application into groups that might be provisioned into different clouds. The architecture model describes architectural components of the application and it is initial model in MOCCA method. In this chapter, we have introduced a transformation that can be used to automatically derive architectural model from software requirements specification which is specified using Silab approach. Silab approach is model and use case driven. The future work will be directed on an appropriate tool which will integrate developed transformation. Also, we will consider a way how we can derivate another artifact especially for implementation model.

REFERENCES

Aaron, W. (2007). Computing in the cloud. *netWorker, 11*(4), 16–25. doi:10.1145/1327512.1327513

Abbott, R. (1983). Program design by informal English descriptions. *Communications of the ACM, 26*(11), 882–894. doi:10.1145/182.358441

Andrikopoulos, V., Binz, T., Leymann, F., & Strauch, S. (2013). How to adapt applications for the cloud environment - Challenges and solutions in migrating applications to the cloud. *Computing, 95*(6), 493–535. doi:10.1007/s00607-012-0248-2

Antović, I., Vlajić, S., Savić, D., Milić, M., & Stanojević, V. (2012). Model and software tool for automatic generation of user interface based on use case and data model. *IET Software, 6*(6), 559–573. doi:10.1049/iet-sen.2011.0060

Aymerich, F. M., Fenu, G., & Surcis, S. (2008). An approach to a cloud computing network. In *Applications of digital information and web technologies* (pp. 113–118). IEEE. doi:10.1109/ICADIWT.2008.4664329

Bernd, B., & Allen, D. (2004). *Object-oriented software engineering using UML, patterns, and Java* (2nd ed.). Upper Saddle River, NJ: Prentice Hall.

Boss, G., Malladi, P., Quan, S., Legregni, L., & Hall, H. (2007). *Cloud computing (Technical Report, IBM high performance on demand solutions, version 1.0a)*. IBM.

Cardoso, J., Binz, T., Breitenbücher, U., Kopp, O., & Leymann, F. (2013). Cloud computing automation: Integrating USDL and TOSCA. [CAiSE.]. *Proceedings of CAiSE, 2013*, 1–16.

Cockburn, A. (Ed.). (2000). *Writing effective use cases*. New York: Addison-Wesley.

Demont, C., Breitenbücher, U., Kopp, O., Leymann, F., & Wettinger, J. (2013). Towards integrating TOSCA and ITIL. In O. Kopp & N. Lohmann (Eds.), *Proceedings of the 5th Central-European Workshop on Services and their Composition (ZEUS 2013)* (pp. 28-31). ZEUS.

Elbendak, M., Vickers, P., & Rossiter, N. (2011). Parsed use case descriptions as a basis for object-oriented class model generation. *Journal of Systems and Software, 84*(7), 1209–1223. doi:10.1016/j.jss.2011.02.025

Foster, I., Kesselman, C., & Tuecke, S. (2001). The anatomy of the grid – Enabling scalable virtual organizations. *International Journal of High Performance Computing Applications, 15*(3), 200–222. doi:10.1177/109434200101500302

Jacobson, I., Christerson, M., Jonsson, P., & Overgaard, G. (1993). *Objectoriented software engineering – A use case driven approach*. Boston: Addison Wesley Longman Publishing Co. Inc.

Jamshidi, P., Khoshnevis, S., Teimourzadegan, R., Nikravesh, A., Khoshkbarforoushha, A., & Shams, F. (2009). ASSM: Toward an automated method for service specification. In *Proceedings of IEEE Asia-Pacific Services Computing Conference, APSCC 2009* (pp. 451-456). IEEE.

Janssen, M., & Joha, A. (2011). Challenges for adopting cloud-based software as a service (SaaS) in the public sector. In *Proceedings of ECIS 2011*. ECIS.

Kermeta. (2013). *Kermeta - Breathe life into your metamodels*. Retrieved April 11, 2013 from http://www.kermeta.org/

Kherraf, S., Lefebvre, E., & Suryn, W. (2008). Transformation from CIM to PIM using patterns and archetypes. In *Proceedings of 19th Australian Conference on Software Engineering* (pp. 338-346). Academic Press.

Larman, C. (Ed.). (2004). *Applying UML and patterns: An introduction to object-oriented analysis and design and iterative development* (3rd ed.). Upper Saddle River, NJ: Prentice Hall.

Leimeister, S., Böhm, M., Riedl, C., & Krcmar, H. (2010). The business perspective of cloud computing: Actors, roles, and value networks. In *Proceedings of 18th European Conference on Information Systems ECIS*. ECIS.

Leymann, F. (2009). Cloud computing: The next revolution in IT. In *Proceedings of the 52th Photogrammetric Week* (pp. 3-12). Stuttgart, Germany: Photogrammetric Week.

Leymann, F., Fehling, C., Mietzner, R., Nowak, A., & Dustdar, S. (2011). Moving applications to the cloud: An approach based on application model enrichment. *International Journal of Cooperative Information Systems*, *20*(3), 307–356. doi:10.1142/S0218843011002250

Li, Z., & Wei, J. (2008). Transforming business requirements into BPEL: A MDA-based approach to web application development. In *Proceedings of WSCS'08: IEEE Int. Workshop on Semantic Computing and Systems* (pp. 61-66). IEEE.

Loniewski, G., Armesto, A., & Insfran, E. (2011). Incorporating model-driven techniques into requirements engineering for the service-oriented development process. In *Proceedings of ME'11: Proceedings of the 2011 Conference on Method Engineering,* (vol. 351, pp. 102-107). Boston: Springer.

Maggiani, R. (2009). Cloud computing is changing how we communicate. In *Proceedings of IEEE International Professional Communication Conference, IPCC 2009* (pp.1-4). IEEE.

Mietzner, R., Unger, T., & Leymann, F. (2009). Cafe: A generic configurable customizable composite cloud application framework. *Lecture Notes in Computer Science*, *5870*, 357–364. doi:10.1007/978-3-642-05148-7_24

Miguel, A. R. D., & Faria, J. P. (2009). Automatic generation of user interface models and prototypes from domain and use case models. In *Proceedings of the International Conference on Software Engineering and Data Technologies,* (pp. 169-176). Academic Press.

Saraiva, J., & Silva, A. R. D. (2010). A reference model for the analysis and comparison of MDE approaches for web-application development. *Journal of Software Engineering and Applications*, *3*, 419–425. doi:10.4236/jsea.2010.35047

Savić, D., Silva, A. R. D., Vlajić, S., Lazarević, S., Stanojević, V., Antović, I., & Milić, M. (2012). Use case specification at different levels of abstraction. In *Proceedings of Eighth International Conference on the Quality of Information and Communications Technology (QUATIC '12)* (pp. 187-192). Washington, DC: IEEE.

Savić, D., Simić, D., & Vlajić, S. (2010). Extended software architecture based on security patterns. *Informatica*, *21*(2), 229–246.

Savić, D., Vlajić, S., Antović, I., Stanojević, V., & Milić, M. (2012). Language for use case specification. In *Proceedings of 34th Annual IEEE Software Engineering Workshop*. Limerick, Ireland: IEEE.

Silva, A. R. D., Saraiva, J., Ferreira, D., Silva, R., & Videira, C. (2007). Integration of RE and MDE paradigms: The ProjectIT approach and tools. *IET Software*, *1*(6), 294–314. doi:10.1049/iet-sen:20070012

Skillicorn, D. (2002). The case for datacentric grids. In *Proceedings of the International Parallel and Distributed Processing Symposium*. Washington, DC: IEEE Computer Society.

Talukder, A. K., Zimmerman, L., & Prahalad, H. A. (2010). Cloud economics: Principles, costs, and benefits. In N. Antonopoulos, & L. Gillam (Eds.), *Cloud computing: Principles, systems and applications* (pp. 343–360). London: Springer-Verlag. doi:10.1007/978-1-84996-241-4_20

Weinhardt, C., Arun, A., Benjamin, B., Nikolay, B., Thomas, M., Wibke, M., & Jochen, S. (2009). Cloud computing – A classification, business models, and research directions. *Business Information Systems Engineering, 1*(5), 391–399. doi:10.1007/s12599-009-0071-2

ADDITIONAL READING

Barham, P., Dragovic, B., Fraser, K., Hand, S., Harris, T. L., Ho, A., et al. (2003). Xen and the art of virtualization. *In Proceedings of the 19th ACM Symposium on Operating Systems Principles (pp.* 164-177). New York.

Breitenbücher, U., Binz, T., Kopp, O., Leymann, F., & Schumm, D. (2012). Vino4TOSCA: A Visual Notation for Application Topologies Based on TOSCA. *Lecture Notes in Computer Science, 7565,* 416–424. doi:10.1007/978-3-642-33606-5_25

El Maghraoui, K., Meghranjani, A., Eilam, T., Kalantar, M. H., & Konstantinou, A. V. (2006). Model driven provisioning, bridging the gap between declarative object models and procedural provisioning tools. In *Proc. of the 7th Intl. Middleware Conference* (pp. 404-423). New York: Springer-Verlag.

Fatolahi, A., Some´, S. S., & Lethbridge, T. C. (2008).Towards a semi-automated model-driven method for the generation of web-based applications from use cases. In *Proc. Fourth Model-Driven Web Engineering Workshop (pp.* 31-45). Toulouse.

Fehling, C., Ewald, T., Leymann, F., Pauly, M., Rütschlin, J., & Schumm, D. (2012). Capturing Cloud Computing Knowledge and Experience in Patterns. In *IEEE 5th International Conference on Cloud Computing* (pp. 726-733). IEEE, Inc.

Ferreira, D., & Silva, A. R. D. (2009). A Controlled Natural Language Approach for Integrating Requirements and Model-Driven Engineering. In ICSEA 2009 (pp. 518-523). IEEE, Inc.

Ferreira, D., & Silva, A. R. D. (2010). Survey on System Behavior Specification for Extending ProjectIT-RSL. In *Seventh International Conference on the Quality of Information and Communications Technology* (pp. 210-215). IEEE, Inc.

Glinz, M. (2000). Problems and Deficiencies of UML as a Requirements Specification Language. In *IWSSD '00: Proceedings of the 10th International Workshop on Software Specification and Design (pp.* 11-22). Washington: IEEE Computer Society.

Görlach, K., & Leymann, F. (2012). Dynamic Service Provisioning for the Cloud. In *Proceedings of the 9th IEEE International Conference on Services Computing (pp.* 555-561). Germany: IEEE Computer Society.

Grance, T., & Mell, P. (2009). The NIST definition of Cloud Computing. *National Institute of Standards and Technology,* 1-3. Retrieved September 13, 2013, from http://csrc.nist.gov/publications/nistpubs/800-145/SP800-145.pdf

Herman, K., & Svetinovic, D. (2010). On confusion between requirements and their representation. *Requirements Engineering, 15*(3), 307–311. doi:10.1007/s00766-009-0095-7

Hoffmann, V., Lichter, H., Nyßen, A., & Walter, A. (2009). Towards the Integration of UML- and textual Use Case Modeling. *Journal of Object Technology, 8*(3), 85–100. doi:10.5381/jot.2009.8.3.a2

IEEE Computer Society Professional Practices Committee. (2010). *SWEBOK®, Guide to the Software Engineering Body of Knowledge.* The Institute of Electrical and Electronics Engineers, Inc.

Jacobson, I., Booch, G., & Rumbaugh, J. (Eds.). (1998). *The Unified Software Development Process.* New York: Addison-Wesley.

Jha, S., Merzky, A., & Fox, G. (2009). Using clouds to provide grids higher-levels of abstraction and explicit support for usage modes. *Journal Concurrency and Computation: Practice & Experience - A Special Issue from the Open Grid Forum, 21(8),* 1087-1108.

Koehler, P., Anandasivam, A., Dan, M. A., & Weinhardt, C. (2010). Customer heterogeneity and tariffs biases in Cloud Computing. In *Proceedings of the International Conference on Information Systems (ICIS).*

Kotonya, G., & Sommerville, I. (Eds.). (1998). *Requirements Engineering Processes and Techniques.* John Wiley and Sons.

Loniewski, G., Insfran, E., & Abrahao, S. (2010). A Systematic Review of the Use of Requirements Engineering Techniques in Model-Driven Development. In Petriu, D.C., Rouquette, N., Haugen (Eds.), MoDELS. Lecture Notes in Computer Science, vol. 6395 (pp. 213-227). Springer.

Martens, B., Teuteberg, F., & Gräuler, M. (2011). Design and Implementation of a Community Platform for the Evaluation and Selection of Cloud Computing Services: A Market Analysis. In *Proceedings of the 19th European Conference on Information Systems*, Helsinki.

Nguyen, P., & Chun, R. (2006). Model Driven Development with Interactive Use Cases and UML Models. *Software Engineering Research and Practice.*534-540.

Peng, J., Zhang, X., Lei, Z., Zhang, B., Zhang, W., & Li, Q. (2009).Comparison of Several Cloud Computing Platforms. *Second International Symposium on Information Science and Engineering (pp.* 23-27). IEEE.

Pfleeger, S. L., & Atlee, J. M. (Eds.). (2006). *Software engineering theory and practice.* Prentice-Hall.

Schleicher, D., Grohe, S., Leymann, F., Schneider, P., Schumm, D., & Wolf, T. (2011). An approach to combine data-related and control-flow-related compliance rules. In *Proceedings of the 2011 IEEE International Conference on Service-Oriented Computing and Applications (pp.* 1-8). Washington: IEEE Computer Society.

Silva, R. d., Saraiva, J., Ferreira, D., Silva, R., & Videira, C. (2007). Integration of RE and MDE Paradigms: The ProjectIT Approach and Tools, *IET Software: On the Interplay of. NET and Contemporary Development Techniques, 1*(6), 294–314.

Siqueira, F.L., & Silva, P.S.M. (2011). An Essential Textual Use Case Meta-model Based on an Analysis of Existing proposals, *WER 2011.*

Smialek, M., Nowakowski, W., Jarzebowski, N., & Ambroziewicz, A. (2012). From use cases and their relationships to code. *MoDRE, 2012,* 9–18.

Somé, S. (2009). A Meta-model for Textaul Use Case Description. *Journal of Object Techology, 8*(7), 87–106. doi:10.5381/jot.2009.8.7.a2

Tran, H., Zdun, U., & Dustdar, S. (2007). View-based and model-driven approach for reducing the development complexity in process-driven SOA. In *Proc. of the Intl. Conf. on Business Processes and Services Computing, vol. 116 (pp.* 105-124). Leipzig.

Valderas, P., & Pelechano, V. (2011). A Survey of Requirements Specification in Model-Driven Development of Web Applications, *Journal ACM Transactions on the Web, 5(2),* 10:1-10:51.

Videira, C., Ferreira, D., & Silva, A. R. D. (2006). A linguistic patterns approach for requirements specification. In *Proc. 32nd EUROMICRO Conf. Software Engineering and Advanced Applications (EUROMICRO'06)* (pp. 302–309). Washington: IEEE Computer Society.

Wang, L., & Laszewski, G. v. (2008). Scientific Cloud Computing: Early Definition and Experience. In *IEEE International Conference on High Performance Computing and Communications* (pp. 825-830). Dalian.

Whittle, J., & Jayaraman, P. K. (2006). Generating Hierarchical State Machines from Use Case Charts. In *RE '06: Proceedings of the 14th IEEE International Requirements Engineering Conference (RE'06) (pp.* 16-25). Washington: IEEE Computer Society.

Wiegers, K. E. (Ed.). (2006). *More about software requirements: thorny issues and practical advice.* Microsoft Press.

KEY TERMS AND DEFINITIONS

Cloud Model: Is a model of components that communicate among each other to provide infrastructure for different type of clients.

Cloud Platform: Is a combination of software and hardware platform that provides functionality for developers to develop and end users to use it as a service.

Model Driven Software Development: Is an approach to software development in which model is a communication tool between different software development phases.

Platform: A platform represents a subsystem or a set of subsystems that provide certain functionality.

Software Architecture Model: Is a model of software components and relations among them.

Software Specification: Is a model of a software system which contains enough unambiguous information to be implemented.

Use Case Driven Development: Is an approach to software development in which use case is a loadstar for requirements and software specification as well as its validation and verification.

Section 2
Cloud Computing in Education

Chapter 5
Model of E-Education Infrastructure based on Cloud Computing

Zorica Bogdanović
University of Belgrade, Serbia

Aleksandar Milić
University of Belgrade, Serbia

Aleksandra Labus
University of Belgrade, Serbia

ABSTRACT

With rapid increase in the number of users, services, educational content, and required resources, educational institutions face new challenges in design and deployment of IT infrastructure for e-education. This chapter deals with defining and developing a model of IT infrastructure for e-learning by using cloud computing concept. The first challenge is adoption and implementation of digital identity management systems and the second is providing support for a system that would be able to use all advantages of federation systems for digital identities management. The experimental part of the chapter consists of a study directed towards the validation of the proposed IT infrastructure model for e-learning. Research was conducted in the Laboratory for E-Business at the Faculty of Organizational Sciences. The results of the research show that the implemented model of IT infrastructure enables the system of e-learning to be more efficient, flexible, and more economical.

INTRODUCTION

Modern information and communication technologies are used on a daily basis for communication, collaboration, retrieving information and other services. Development, availability and accessibility of these technologies lead to new paradigms in teaching and learning processes. Nowadays, many universities in the world organize courses and trainings via distance learning systems. The number of users and the quantity of content within these systems grows rapidly. Therefore, the design and implementation of these systems become more complex. With a huge growth in the number of

DOI: 10.4018/978-1-4666-5784-7.ch005

users, services, education contents and resources, e-learning systems become more and more large-scale. One of the basic problems in developing a model of infrastructure for e-education is how to provide scalability and reliability of educational applications and services.

This chapter discusses one possible approach for providing reliability and scalability of an e-education system for a higher education institution. The developed model for e-learning is based on cloud computing infrastructure. The model includes all services necessary for the implementation of activities in educational institutions and services for scientific research. The rest of the chapter is organized as follows: in the second chapter, a theoretical background on application of cloud computing as infrastructure for e-learning has been given; the third chapter describes the proposed model for implementing e-learning infrastructure through cloud computing; chapter four gives details on the realization of the proposed model within the e-learning system of Laboratory for e-business at University of Belgrade; in chapter five results on evaluation of the implemented infrastructure are presented. Finally, concluding remarks are given.

The main objective of this chapter is to provide a preview of development and realization of model for e-learning which is based on cloud computing infrastructure in a higher education institution. Proposed model is developed in aim to provide scalability and reliability of educational applications and services.

THEORETICAL BACKGROUND

Talking about application of cloud computing infrastructure in higher education, three basic approaches can be noticed. First approach is complete outsourcing of e-education infrastructure (Sultan, 2010) which educational institutions provide to their users (teaching staff, administrative staff, researchers, students, etc.) with services such as

e-mail, digital libraries, etc., through the leased infrastructure of a cloud provider. Second approach is cloud within the private infrastructure (Caron, Desprez, Loureiro, & Muresan, 2009) that requires highly skilled cloud administrators and appropriate hardware and software resources within the educational institution. Third approach represents combination of previous two approaches (Costanzo, Assuncao, & Buyya, 2009). The educational institution can develop and deploy its own cloud infrastructure. If the infrastructure becomes overloaded, a third party cloud services can be leased in the periods of increased demand.

In the previous years, there has been much research in the field of cloud computing. However, only a few dealt with the problem of developing and deploying models for e-learning infrastructure using cloud computing. Main research directions important for the problems considered in this chapter include: identity management within cloud computing environment, modelling the cloud computing infrastructure, analyzing performances of the cloud computing, and resource management in e-learning systems.

The problem of identity has been present from the beginning of the mass use of the Internet. Nowadays, every user has multiple different digital identities, so that in the today's modern and quite scattered systems, the activity of authentication and authorization when accessing services is a problem for both users and system administrators. This problem also reflects in e-learning systems in higher education institutions, where different resources and services are often deployed through heterogeneous systems. Much research has proved that security, digital identity and access management are essential for successful deployment of infrastructure for e-learning (Zhang & Chen, 2010; Zhang & Chen, 2011). The aim of identity management systems is to establish a connection between identifiers of different services, so that information about the user associated with the identifier can be integrated. In this way, the system connects identity management business processes, security policies and technologies to help higher education institution in the management of identity and control to the access to resources. Specific problems arise in identity management in the cloud environment (Takabi, Joshi, & Ahn, 2010). The model presented in (Danfeng, Fangchun, & Yeap, 2011) uses dynamic control policies to support the multiple roles and flexible authority. However, most of these researches present theoretical models for identity management in the cloud that cannot easily be applied in e-education environments.

Cloud computing (hereinafter: CC) can be applied in educational institutions using different deployment and technology models. The problem of modelling infrastructure is specific in term of resource provisioning and how to deploy virtualized services (Sotomayor, Montero, Llorente, & Foster, 2009). In (Ercan, 2010) author gives a review on how higher education institutions can benefit from CC infrastructure. Main areas of application include: students and administrative personnel have the opportunity to quickly and economically access various application platforms and resources through the Web pages on-demand, cost of organizational expenses are reduced and more powerful functional capabilities can be offered. There have been several successful implementation of CC in higher education institutions (Khmelevsky & Voytenko, 2010; Bogdanovic, Jovanic, Barac, Milic, & Despotovic-Zrakic, 2011). One of the most successful implementations has been developed at the Hochschule Furtwangen University, where a specific solution for private cloud has been developed (Doelitzscher, Sulistio, Reich, Kuijs, & Wolf, 2011).

Within the cloud computing infrastructure, resources are managed using specific set of tools (Nathani, Chaudharya, & Somani, 2012). Some authors focus on resource management frameworks for automatic runtime set-up (Gallard et al., 2012), while others focus on algorithms for resource scheduling (Chang & Tang, 2011).

For measuring the performance of deployed CC infrastructure a specific set of measurements has to be used. Some authors evaluate CC infrastructure using performance indicators such as I/O performance, CPU performance and network transfer rate (Baun & Kunze, 2009). However, there are no standardized methods for CC performance analysis, and different authors use different metrics to evaluate their cloud computing infrastructure (Iosup et al., 2011).

Within the private cloud infrastructure there are demands for centralised system that enables different services for his users. Digital identity management is defined as the process by which the existing technologies are used to manage digital identity information entities as well as to control access to resources (Takabi, Joshi, & Ahn, 2010). The digital identities management objective is to improve the productivity and security while reducing costs associated with managing entities and their digital identities.

MODEL OF IT INFRASTRUCTURE FOR E-EDUCATION

Main goal of developing a model of IT infrastructure for e-education is to create a framework, standrads and techniches that will lead to higher quality of the overall education process. Key principles in designing the model include:

- **Scalability:** Design of the system should enable reaching strategic goals in the ever changing environment.
- **Availability:** Services and information need to be available to user anytime and anyplace.
- **Security:** Only authorized users can access resources; centralized identity management is performed.
- **Open Standards:** Adaptability of the system and interoperability of the system components can easily be achieved through application of open standards.

- **Modularity:** Functionality of the system is based on the integration of smaller modules and components.
- **Adaptive Interface:** Services are designed not to support fixed input or output interfaces, but can be adapted according to various criteria.

The model for IT infrastructure is shown in Figure 1. The model contains four main components: physical infrastructure, private cloud, e-learning services, and security services. All components are in details described in the text that follows.

Physical Infrastructure

The physical IT infrastructure for e-learning should set a base for a system with high level of availability, scalability and security. It should be flexible, so to support requirement for services and resources in realtime. The physical infrastructure needs to be dynamically scaled, by adding new servers and clusters. The system should support centralized identity management, with distributed virtual and physical infrastructure.

The architecture of the physical IT infrastructure for e-learning should include heterogenuous resources available to different departments and users. Consolideation of servers will lead toward lower number of physical servers, lower space for datacenter and lower administration requirments. The infrastructure should provide federations of private and public clouds and eliminate unnecessary hardware procurement (Katz, 2008).

An end user should be provided with fast access to all required services. Services and applications with different requirements should be provided with an environment where all of them can be deployed. An e-learnig system should be flexible and integrate all available services and

Figure 1. The structure of the model

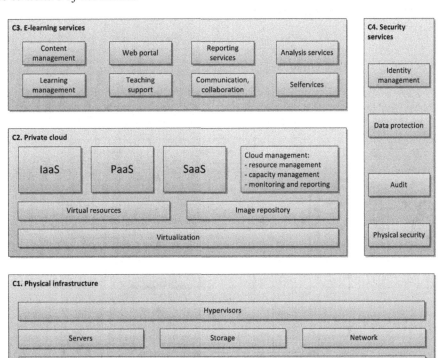

components of the existing infrastructure within an education institution (De Alfonso, Caballer, Alvarruiz, Molto, & Hernandez, 2011).

Private Cloud

The arhitecture of the private cloud is based on flexible federations of servers, storages and networking (Cerbelaud, Garg, & Huylebroeck, 2009). Virtualization provides efficient resource usage through separation of abstract platform from IT infrastructure. Model of a private cloud enables a large number of users to share resources and leads to higher level of resource usage and cost effectivness. Within an e-education system, this approach leads to a perception of limitless IT capacities, where services can be used according to users' needs. Architecture of a private cloud enables active planning and monitoring capacities in real time, so that infrastructure can dynamically be scaled to support high loads of users' requests. In this way, a balance between the need for agility and costs of unused capacities is easily achieved. The model of IT infrastructure enables continu-

ous availability of e-learning services, even in cases of interruptions within the infrastructure itself. Permanent availability is achieved through architecture of redundant IT infrastructure and application of standardized procedures for automated management. E-learning services are provided with the same level of quality independently of when or from where they are accessed to. High level of quality and functionality is chieved by standardization of system components, including physical servers, network devices, storage devices, resources, etc. In order to provide high scalability of an e-education system, a model for IT infrastructure of an educational institution has to be based on a private cloud. Physical infrastructure should be owned by the educational institution and located on premisses. Model should also contain an interface toward public clouds (Dong, Zheng, Qiao, Shu, & Yang, 2009), so that e-learning infrastructure can be expanded when it is needed (Velte, Velte, & Elsenpeter, 2010). Figure 2 depicts the architecture of a private cloud for an educational institution.

Figure 2. Architecture of a private cloud

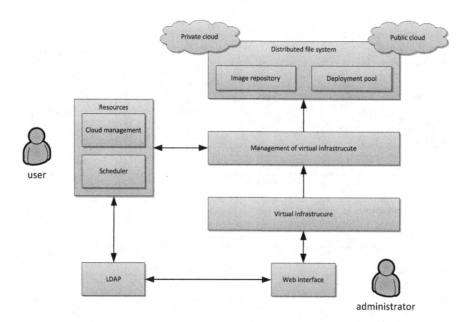

Main components a private cloud include resource pool: servers, storage, and network. Server pools include physical resources, such as CPU, memory, network interfaces, graphycal adapters, and storage units, which are all building blocks of virtual machines (Qian, Luo, Du, & Guo, 2009). Network pool includes address services amd package delivery between physical infrastructure and virtual machines. This component includes physical and virtual swithes, routers, firewalls and virtual private networks. Storage resource pool referrs to data stored in a private cloud. Storage resources need to be connected in a network in order to support migration of virtual machines across servers. Virtual hardware is presented to virtual machine's operating system by hypervizor (Raichura & Agarwal, 2009). Hypervizor controls communication amang virtual machines and resources such as memory or hard drives.

Primary goal of a private cloud is to decrease time and money necessary for deploying new hardware and software. In this way, new services can be deployed more quickly (Dong, Zheng, Yang, Li, & Qiao, 2009). Private cloud can provide its' users with infrastructure as a service (IaaS), platform as a service (PaaS) and software as a service (SaaS).

A model of IaaS through a private cloud enables high level of mobility and availability of infrastructure and services, thus creating an environment where applications can easily be moved from development to production (Figure 3). Afterwards, these applications can be stored in image repositories. Students can be given an enviroment where they can reserve and use resources of virtual infrastructure, while the same resources can be used by other users in different periods of time.

Model of PaaS through a private cloud also provides possibility to delover platform as a service to end users. Platform as a service includes operation system, middlware, and development tools. On virtualized servers, users can run their applications, or develop new applications, but they cannot manage or configure operation systems, hardware or other infrastructure resources (Tian, Su, & Lu, 2010). Platform as a service gives an educational institution an opportunity to provide each student with a virtual computer that they can use during the course of study (Schaffer, Averitt, & Hoit, 2009). Through Web interface, a student can manage virtual resources from the repository of platforms and choose a platform they want (Figure 4). After starting the image of a platform, a student can use all resources supported within that platform. After the platform is shut down, the image of the platform is stored in the repository and the student can use it later. It is also possible to create repository of platforms for each subject, where students who study this subject can start the platform and use tools and applications related to that course. After a class, images may or may not be saved, depending on the concept of the course.

Figure 3. Infrastructure as a service in e-learning

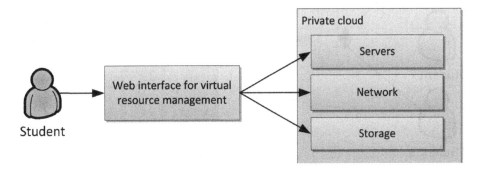

Figure 4. Platform as a service in e-learning

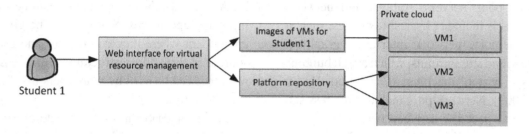

Finally, the model of a private cloud gives possibility to deliver software as a service (Figure 5). Unlike traditional application that needs to be installed on a user's computer, SaaS presents one instance of the software that can be used by multiple users (Vouk, Sills, & Dreher, 2010).

By consuming services of big cloud, users acquire perception of seamless cloud capacities, where limits are defined by providers' rules or contracts. However, there are no real limitless capacities, only an illusion created through optimized and efficient usage resources (Buyya, 2009). Educational institutions usually own less IT capacities comparing to cloud provides, therefore it is not always possible to provide all users with requested resources anytime. Therefore, requests need to be prioritized, and users need to be provided with possibility to reserve resources for

specific period of time. Model of a private cloud must also provide a sophisticated system for resource scheduling (Figure 6) (Rittinghouse & Ransome, 2009).

Digital Identity Management

Fast development of ICT and its application for learning, research and management in educational institutions resulted in a large number of services. Each service usually implements its own authentication and authorization functionalities, which leads to lower performance of the overall system and lower security.

Educational institutions that faced this problem have developed several approaches for integration of information and services. Integration on the data level is suitable for optimazing the access

Figure 5. Software as a service in e-education

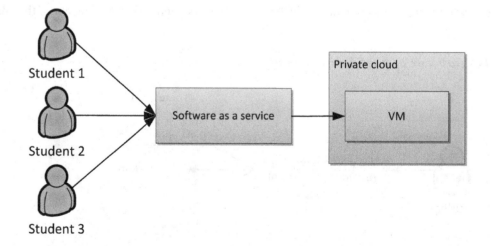

Figure 6. Reserving and scheduling resources within a private cloud

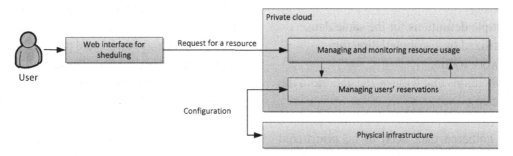

and usage of resources. Integration on the level of services requires efficient digital identity management system and secure access to services. Model of a digital identity management system should integrate all data sources and services, where all policies and procedures are stored and applied centrally (Figure 7).

The first step in developing the infrastructure for centralized identity management in an educa-

tional institution is to gather data on all users. When gathering data from the existing applications within an educational institution, aspects that should be considered include:

- Data sources within the system;
- Data access;
- Structured data;

Figure 7. Model of a system for digital identity management

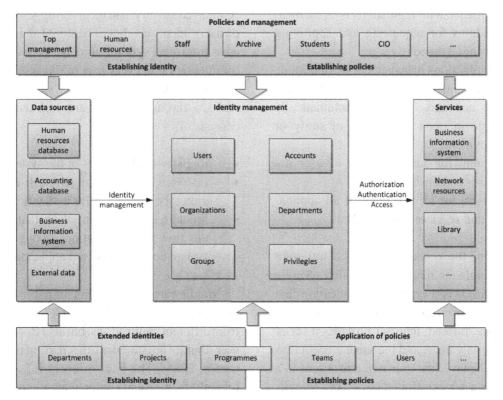

- Sources used for updating the data in the directory;
- Multiple definitions for the same data;
- Centrlized or distributed directory;
- Network traffic;
- Applications that will use the data from the directory.

Then, gathered data need to be prioritized and stored. A single record shoud be created for each user. After consolidating the data on users, it is possible to develop tools for managing roles and access rights. Owner of a reasource within the system can define rules for interaction with these resources. A system for managing digital identities enables scaling IT operations where privileges for new resources and service are assigned or updated at one place.

Centralized identity management system is characterized by the following:

- Privileged in the centralized database can be checked and revised;
- Compliance with regulations is confirmed;
- Procedures for requesting and approving access are defined;
- Work functions management is supported;
- User accounts can be created automatically;
- User accounts can be automatically shut down upon completion of study or employment;
- A system for administration of user accounts is established;
- A system for identification of all applications and services is established.

Managing the system from one central point enables single sign on functionality. Single Sign-On (SSO) is a type of authentication that prevents users from multiple loggings to different applications. Instead, the user provides a set of credentials only once, and the same credentailas are used whenever the user requests access to a resource or a service (Radenković, Despotović,

& Bogdanović, 2006). SSO system relies on a central database, and a Web portal used for login (Tilborg & Jajodia, 2005). History on users' activity can also be monitored, and potentials misuses and irregularities detected. Through this system, educational institutions can benefit from improved security, lower administration costs, and higher productivity of users.

Main advantages of introducing the described system are dereived from centralized user management. Administrators can grant or deny users cetrain resources through a single management console. Access rules can easily be distributed and applied accross the whole system of educational institution. At the same time, when applying the centralized set of access rules for all users, the possibility of human error is reduced. Also, users can request access to certain resources, and the system can automatically grant or deny access with respect to user's role and defined policies. It is also possible to allow user to manage some of their personal data, such as addresses, phone numbers or passwords. The described model for centralized identity management suggests that data on users' identities should be stored and managed apart from other system components, but available for integration in every part of the system.

The identity management system is usually realized through middleware architecture that consists of:

- Registry of all entities in the system;
- Interface for applications, such as LDAP directory or a server for authentication;
- Metadirectory infrastructure that controls the flow of information among records, system components, and applications.

Middleware is just a mean for publishing data in a simple and accessible way. It integrates data from different applications, but also stores data on users that are not stored in other parts of the system (Jones, 2005). The base of every infrastructure for authorisation and authentication is a clear and well defined system for identity management. For implementation of such a system it is important to define a scheme, i.e. a set of attributes with the proper definitions, syntax and semantics. These data are stored in the directory, which can be implemented as an LDAP directory. The access to the directory is defined through system security policies, which are also stored in the directory. System administrators, as well as applications that access or change the contents of the directory must follow these policies.

Defining the policies of using directory schemes in LDAP hierarchy is not mandaroty. Rules are only used as a representaion of relationships between objects. The scheme defines which data and in what form will be stored in the directory. The data that are stored for every user in the system include (Simić, 2011):

- Personal data: name, surname, date of birth, ID number, phone number, email, address, etc.

- Institutional data: name of institution, role, status, address, etc.
- Account data: username, password, roles, etc.

An example of LDAP hierarchy is shown in Figure 8.

Rules that need to be abided when creating the hierarchy scheme are following (Simić, 2011):

- There can be only one record of personal data for one user;
- The account is identified by using the username;
- One user can belong to multiple roles within the same organization;
- Data should be stored for the orgaizations that are related to existing users in the system;
- An account is assosiated to one password, but multiple password for the same account can be implemented as well;

Figure 8. Example of an LDAP directory

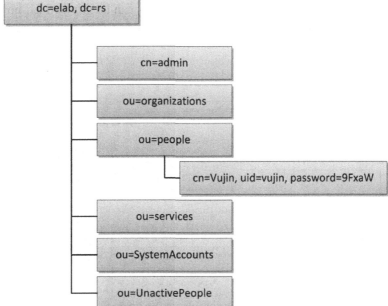

- Accounts are associated with services and groups of services, and on this level thay have to be unique;
- Data about who and how manages with the LDAP directory are stored in the LDAP directory.

It is relatively easy to develop a system for integrated identity management within one educational institution, where the described principles and guidelines are applied. However, the problem of developing identity management system across multiple institutions, where users from one institution require access to resources of another institution is more complex. The solution of this problem is an implementation of infrastructure for authentication and authorization (AAI). Basic components of this infrastructure are users, institutions and resources, and the process flows through the following steps (Figure 9) (Devetaković, Gajin, & Mitrović, 2010):

- Authentication of users performed by their parent institution;
- Transfer of user's authorization attributes from parent institution to the resource owner;
- Resource owner grants or denies access to the resource (authorization).

Through AAI, it is possible to manage the access to different resources and system components, such as: network for individual users (modem, wireless, etc.), computer resources (grid, network drives, etc.), network services (ssh, telnet, email, ftp, etc.), Web resources, network applications, etc.

Identity federation is a process that enables distribution of identification, authentication and authorization outside the boundaries of an organization. It can be realized between organizations that share a certain level of trust. These organizations have to define resources that can be accessed by users from other organizations and implement enabling process.

E-Learning Services

An important component of e-learning infrastructure is a learning management system (LMS). All students' activities are stored within this system. LMSs provide students and teachers with functionalities for managing courses, communication, collaboration, etc. When integrating LMS into Web portal, it is necessary to integrate all e-learning services with Web portal and other applications (Radenković, Despotović, & Bogdanović, 2006; Despotović, Savić, & Bogdanović, 2006). LMS services can be grouped as shown in Figure 10.

Figure 9. AAI model

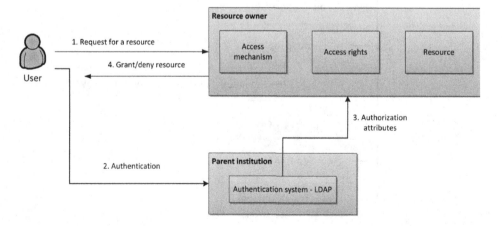

Figure 10. E-learning services

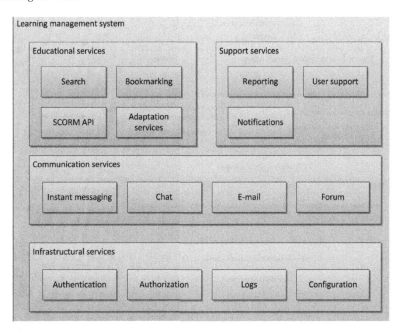

Infrastructural services provide common interface to other applications and services within Web portal. Communication services provide integration of applications for communication and collaboration (Despotović, Savić, & Bogdanović, 2006).

Integration

The development of a typical system for e-learning includes: the implementation of LMS, the integration of Internet services in a network of educational institutions and a business information system. The integration of components of the system is realized using multiple layers (Sempolinski & Thain, 2010):

- **Human Resource Integration:** Students, teachers and other participants in the learning process can access the system and can communicate from any location. Each participant can access the personalized set of services according to their system role.

- **Information Integration:** The system enables gathering heterogeneous, unstructured data, while users can access structured data. Different kinds of reports, analysis, data interpretations etc. can be shown to users.
- **Process Integration:** Adaptive e-learning processes are integrated using Web services.
- **Application Integration:** The integration is realized at the application level on CC infrastructure.

The method of integration of e-learning services with the cloud computing infrastructure is shown in Figure 11.

There are five phases in the proposed model. In the first phase, the user accounts are created. The user accounts are stored on LDAP server. The LDAP server is integrated with the user directory of the educational institution where the student accounts are located. In the second phase, the courses are created in the Moodle LMS. Teach-

Figure 11. Designing web services for integration of components

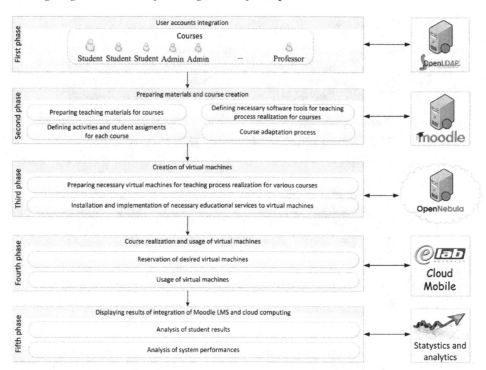

ing materials are prepared, the activities and the assignments are defined. The necessary software tools for teaching process realization are chosen. The course adaptation process is performed. In the third phase, the virtual machines with necessary operating systems and software are prepared. Each VM is adapted to students' learning styles and needs at a specific course. Afterwards, the prepared VMs are stored into the CC infrastructure. In the fourth phase, students use the ELABCloud application for VM reservation and its deployment. The application allows students to reserve any of the provided VMs for the Moodle course to which they are enrolled. Students can perform the reservation using either a Web or a mobile application. In the fifth and the final phase, teachers and administrators of the system can view and analyze students' results and the performance of the system.

IMPLEMENTATION OF THE PROPOSED MODEL

Physical Implementation of the Private Cloud

In order to achieve higher scalability of the system, as well as possibility to introduce new services for students, E-business Lab at Faculty of Organizational Sciences has introduced CC infrastructure. Software used for managing this infrastructure is OpenNebula, and runs under CentOS 6.2 operating system. This infrastructure, shown in Figure 12, uses two network interfaces, one external, and one internal, so to support fast data flow between nodes. Extern network interface uses range of public IP addresses (147.91.130.0/24), while internal network interface uses range of private IP addresses (10.20.30.0/24). At the moment of

Figure 12. Scheme of cloud infrastructure

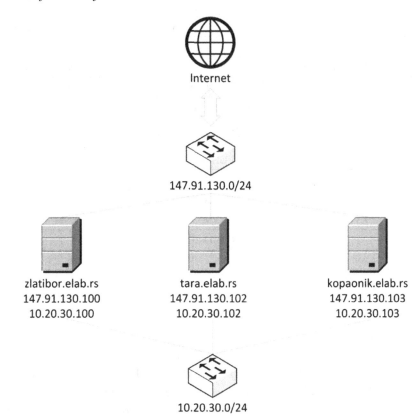

writing this chapter, the CC infrastructure consists of three nodes used for deploying VMs, and one cloud front end, installed on the same hardware as one of the nodes.

Technical specification of the infrastructure is shown in Table 1.

There are two roles used for accessing the cloud computing infrastructure. The first role is system administrator (root), who can configure the operation system. This role is applicable for all computers within the infrastructure. System administrator accesses remotely, using the SSH connection. The second role is cloud administrator. Cloud administrator can manage virtual machines available for users, but cannot perform any changes in operating systems. This role is applicable only for cloud front-end. The access is realized through a Web application.

Managing the Private Cloud

Management of the implemented cloud computing infrastructure is realized through OpenNebula software. It is a software tool for virtualization of computer centres. It implements high number of functionalities and solutions for managing the cloud platform. OpenNebula is designed with respect to the following principles (Cardos, 2011; Srinivasa, Nageswara, & Kumari, 2009):

- Open architecture, and open source code;
- Adapable for managing all types of hardware and software;
- Intagration with other cloud platforms and services;
- Interoperability;
- Stability;

Table 1. Technical specification of the infrastructure

	Computer 1	Computer 2	Computer 3
Network configuration			
Public IP	147.91.130.100	147.91.130.102	147.91.130.103
Private IP	10.20.30.100	10.20.30.102	10.20.30.103
Hostname	zlatibor.elab.rs	tara.elab.rs	kopaonik.elab.rs
Hardware specification and configuration			
Processor	Intel Core i7-2600K @3.40 GHz	Intel Core2Duo-E6550 @2.33 GHz	Intel Core2Duo-E6550 @2.33 GHz
Memory	16 GB	8 GB	8 GB
Operation system	CentOS 6.2	CentOS 6.2	CentOS 6.2
Virtualization	KVM	KVM	KVM
Role in CC infrastructure			
Cloud Frontend	yes	no	no
Cloud Node	yes	yes	yes

- Scalability;
- Standardization.

The infrastructure and service layers are shown in Figure 13.

OpenNebula is based on clusterized architecture with front-end server and a set of node servers connected with at least one physical network (Figure 14) (Cardos, 2011). OpenNebula is used for managing storage, network, virtualization, monitoring and dynamically grouping virtual machines. Through this architecture it is possible to enable instant response of infrastructure to business needs, because new resources can dynamically be added to the infrastructure. Management of the physical and virtual infrastructure is performed centrally.

Figure 13. Infrastructure and service layers

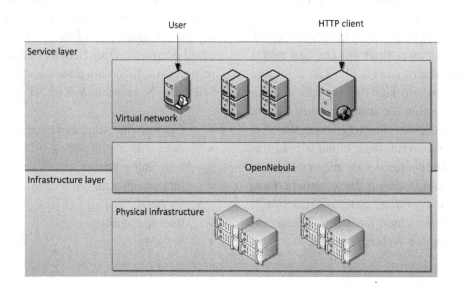

Figure 14. Clusterized architecture of the private cloud

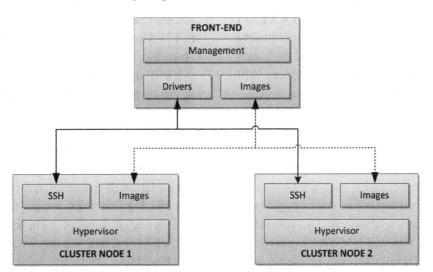

OpenNebula includes the following services: image management, image storage and transfer management, hypervisor management, scheduling, monitoring, user management, Web access, API. All these components communicate via XML-RPC and can be installed on separate servers. Detailed structure of OpenNebula is shown in Figure 15. Users of a private cloud access, use and manage resources through Web interface of EC2 or OCCI server.

Figure 15. Detalied structure of OpenNebula

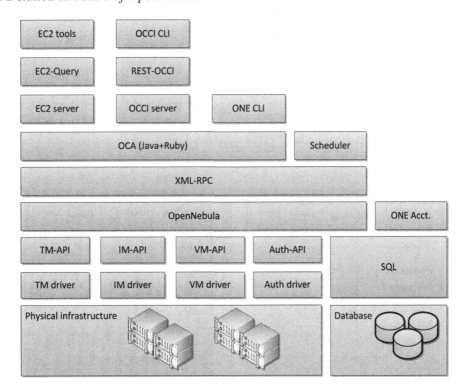

OpenNebula OCCI API is a service based on REST architecture. It is based on OGF OCCI API specification and it can be used for monitoring and control of cloud resources. Cloud resources can also be managed through EC2 Query API which provides the same functionalities as Amazon EC2: image upload, registration of images, monitoring and shuting down instances, etc. Common users can manage their resources through a simple Web interface that relies on OpenNebula OCCI server.

OpenNebula communicates with hypervisor through virtualization subsystem. This subsystem support XEN, KVM, and VMWare hypervisors. KVM hypervisor is installed on every cluster node in the E-business Lab. KVM enables full virtualization, so that every virtual machine has its own virtualized hardware. In KVM, a virtual machine is implemented as a Linux process, so all Linux kernel functionalities can be used. Virtualization in OpenNebula is shown in Figure 16.

When a user starts a virtual machine through Web interface, OpenNebula connects the network interface defined in NIC section of virtul machine template, with bridge or physical interface defined in configuration of virtual network. In this way,

virtual machines can be connected with different computer networks, both private and public (Figure 17). The realization of the CC network in the E-business Lab is shown in Figure 18.

KVM supports the following options for defining virtual networks in OpenNebula:

- **Basic:** Default driver which is not related to any specific network option.
- **Firewall:** Firewall rules are applied, but isolation of computer network is ignored.
- **802.1Q:** Network access through VLAN routing is limited; switches that support VLAN markup are required.
- **Ebtables:** Network access is limited through ebtables rules.
- **Open vSwitch:** Network access is limited through Open vSwitch Virtual Switch.

Information about private cloud in OpenNebula is stored in MySQL database. It is also necessary to provide storage space for images and virtual machines. The architecture of the image management subsystem is shown in Figure 19. For storing images in the repository, image driver is used.

Figure 16. Virtualization in OpenNebula

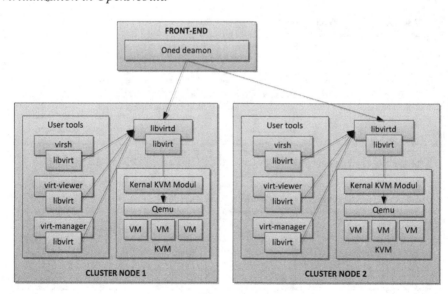

Figure 17. Model of network infrastructure

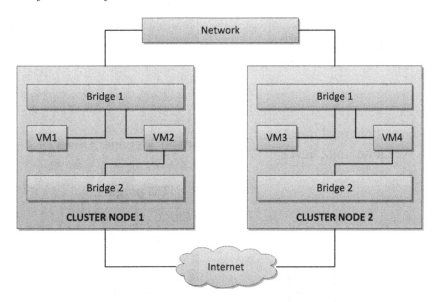

Main operations for image management include:

- Copying image into the repository;
- Creating and initialization of a new image;
- Putting image into the repository;
- Deleting image from the repository.

Transfer manager is used for moving images as well as for operations with cluster nodes. Transfer manager driver performs the following operations:

- Copying image;
- Creating symbolic links;
- Generation swap file;
- Creating disk image;

Figure 18. Realization of network infrastructure

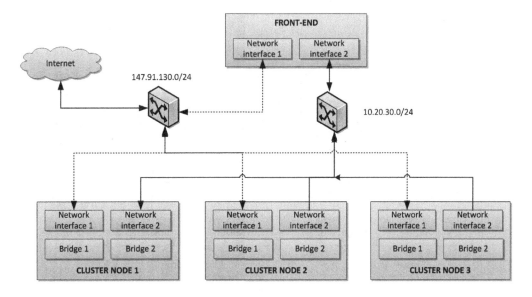

Figure 19. Image management in OpenNebula

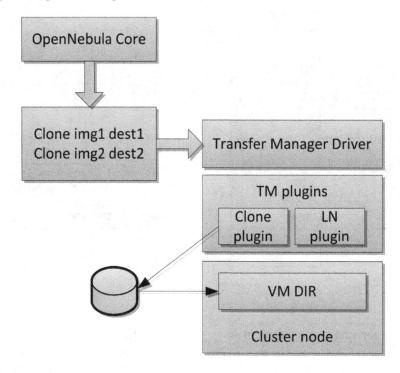

- Deleting file or directory;
- Moving images.

For implementation of storage subsystem of a private cloud a shared file system has been chosen. This model requires front end and cluster nodes to share the VM directory and image repository (Figure 20). Model of shared storage reduces the time needed to start the VM and provides a function of migration in real-time, as well as transfer of VM from one cluster node to another without stopping the VM. Most hypervisor requires running VM on a shared file system to facilitate the migration of functions in real time. The limitation

Figure 20. Image repository

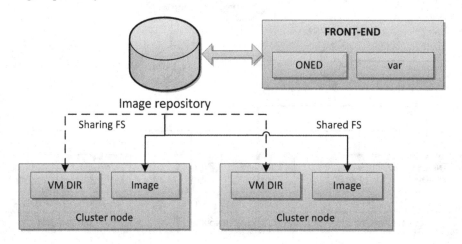

of this model is a degradation of VM performance in cases when virtualized services require intensive work with hard drives. These insufficiencies are usually overcome with local caching of VM image or improved file system.

In the CC infrastructure of the E-business Lab, MooseFS has been chosen as a distributed file system. This system allows data storage on multiple physical servers, while that user gains perception of one resource. Architecture of MooseFS consists of four components:

- **Management Server-Master Server:** Manages the entire system, stores the metadata for each file.
- **Information Servers-Chunk Servers:** Servers on which data are placed and which performs the synchronization.
- **Metadata Backup Server-Metaloger Server:** Serves as a backup server of metadata in case of failure of the master server.
- **Client File Access:** Access and data management is provided through mfsmount process.

OpenNebula includes a complete system for managing users and users' groups. There are four basic types of users:

- **Administrator:** Belongs to the administrators' group and can perform all operations.
- **Regular User:** Can access most functions.
- **Public User:** Can perform only basic operations.
- **Service User:** The user type who uses the OpenNebula services.

Resources managed by the OpenNebula associated permissions that define access rules and management. Rules related to the owner, groups or other rules and can have the following values:

- **Use:** Operations that do not change a resource, such as a review of the available resources.
- **Manage:** Operations that modify resources, such as stopping the VM or modify values of attribute of image.
- **Admin:** Special operations whose use is restricted only to administrators, such as updating information about hosts or delete users' group.

OpenNebula includes a module for the allocation and assignment of VM to available hosts. The aim of this module is establishing a priority of the resources that are characteristically the most suitable for starting VM. Deployment of VM is based on the match making algorithm as follows (Figure 21):

1. Reject all hosts that don't meet the requirements of VM and who don't have enough resources.
2. Calculate rank based on information collected through monitoring.
3. Resources with the highest rank are first used for allocation of VM.

Figure 22 shows OpenNebula network interfaces of a virtual machine.

The image repository is OpenNebula's component responsible for storing the created VM images. The image repository must be accessible through the front-end using appropriate technologies such as NAS, SAN or through directly connected storage system. The images must be transferred to the nodes in order to be used by VM. OpenNebula supports different models of image storage. Figure 23 shows a model of shared storage, implemented using any shared file system. This way of storing images makes it possible to exploit all the possibilities of hypervisor and achieve shorter time for deploying VMs.

Figure 21. Realization of process for reserving and scheduling

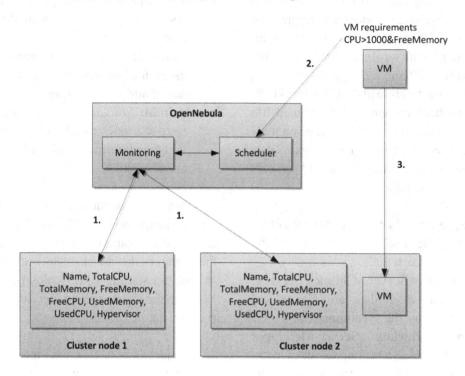

Figure 22. OpenNebula: Network interfaces of a virtual machine

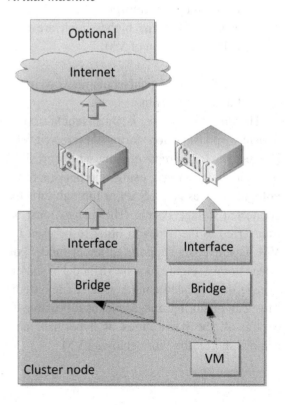

OpenNebula Sunstone represents a Web interface which enables configuring the cloud environment. It is a part of OpenNebula software. Sunstone enables configuring hosts where virtual machines are executed, changing settings and features for different virtual machines, viewing status of running virtual machines and defining user permissions. After a successful login, OpenNebula administrators are able to view a dashboard, which informs them about current state of the system. Dashboard contains data related to running virtual machines and basic resource consumation. Dashboard is shown in Figure 24.

SunStone enables configuration of hosts which serve for running virtual machines. A list of enabled hosts is displayed in Figure 25.

The main part of SunStone interface is configuring image repository. Administrators are able to define which images are going to be running in the private cloud. The list of prepared images is displayed in Figure 26.

Figure 23. OpenNebula image repository

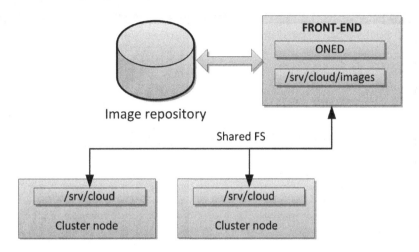

Figure 24. OpenNebula SunStone dashboard

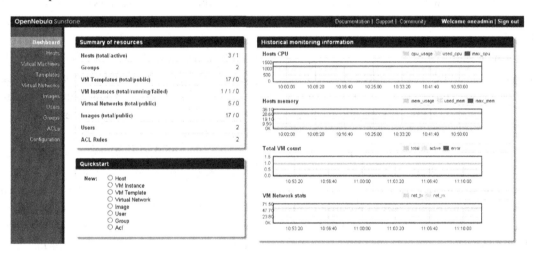

Figure 25. Hosts configured for OpenNebula

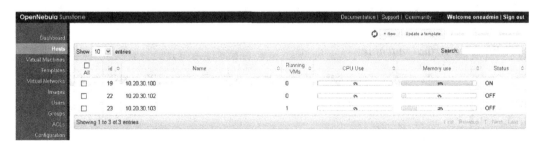

Figure 26. Predefined images

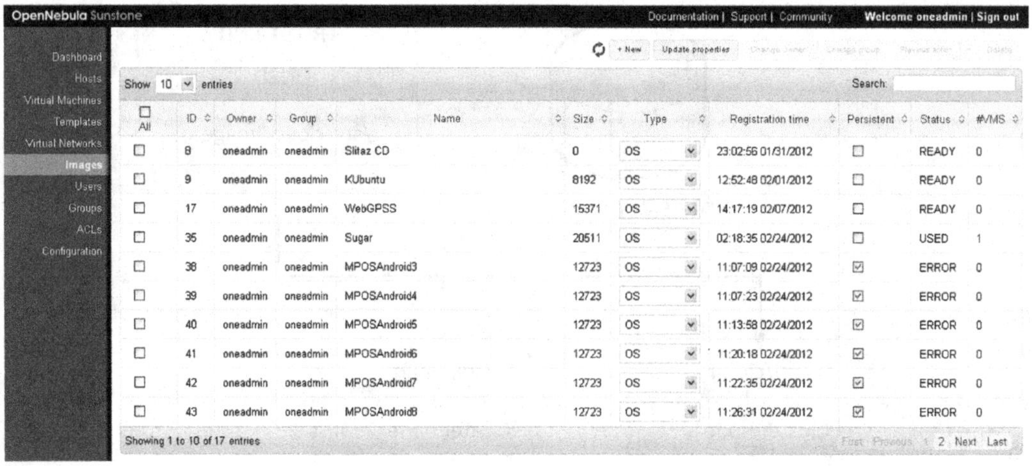

Figure 27 shows which virtual machines are running on OpenNebula's nodes. This part of SunStone also tracks statuses of all virtual machines in the cloud.

Ganglia is a scalable distributed monitoring system for high-performance computing systems such as clusters and Grids. It is based on a hierarchical design targeted at federations of clusters. It leverages widely used technologies such as XML for data representation, XDR for compact, portable data transport, and RRD tool for data storage and visualization. It uses carefully engineered data structures and algorithms to achieve very low per-node overheads and high concurrency. The implementation is robust, has been ported to an extensive set of operating systems and processor architectures, and is currently in use on thousands of clusters around the world. It has been used to link clusters across university campuses and around the world and can scale to handle clusters with 2000 nodes (ENISA, 2010). Ganglia can be used for monitoring the CC infrastructure. In Figure 28, Ganglia home page is displayed. It shows CPU and memory usage for the last hour.

Ganglia enables displaying of nodes' system data, which are shown in Figure 29.

Ganglia supports tracking of different metrics, including CPU usage, memory usage, disk space usage and network usage, for different periods (i.e. last hour, last day, last week or last month). In Figure 30, graphs which track some metrics for the period of last week are shown.

Figure 27. Running virtual machines

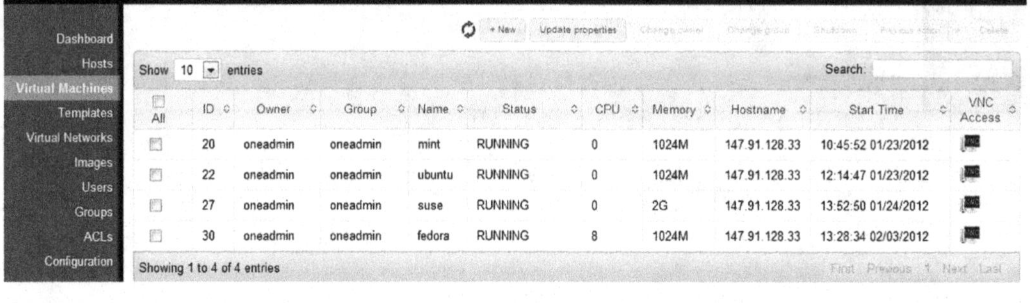

Figure 28. Ganglia home page

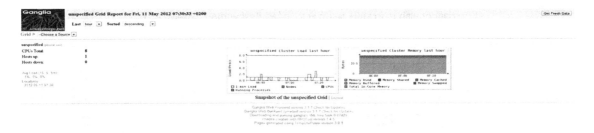

Figure 29. System data acquired by Ganglia

Application for Managing Resources and Integration with Learning Management System

One possibility for improving the existing e-learning system which provides the private cloud environment is integration of the private cloud with Moodle LMS. This integration which uses Web service approach enables displaying virtual machines available to users. LDAP protocol is used for the user authentication. User accounts are located on the OpenLDAP server. LDAP authentication enables using of a unique username-password combination, which can be used for access to multiple services. Thus, the same login data can be used for Moodle LMS login, private cloud applications, Webmail, and all future services provided by the E-business Lab.

Process of accessing and starting a virtual machine by using the Moodle interface (Figure 31):

1. Student 1 accesses the Moodle LMS login page using a Web browser and enters username and password.
2. Moodle LMS is configured to use LDAP authentication.
3. LDAP server returns the result of authentication.
4. After successful login to Moodle, student accesses the image repository where chooses a desired image.
5. Availability of images for students is checked in LDAP server.
6. LDAP server returns the response.
7. A new window in browser for accessing the virtual machine is opened to the student.

Figure 30. Tracking different metrics

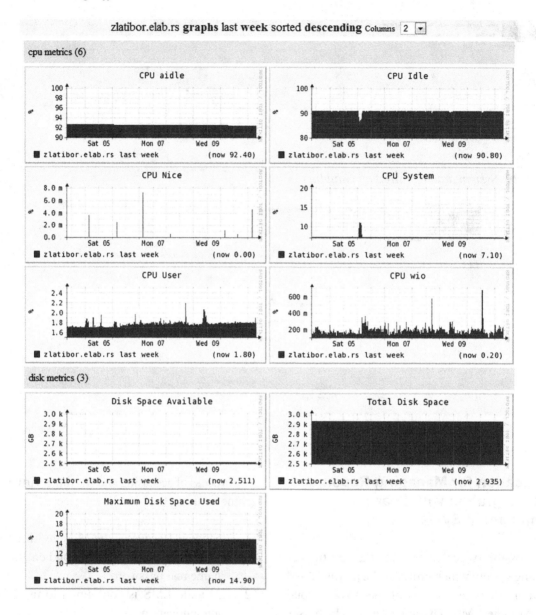

8. Image is moved to an available cluster and it is started.
9. Student uses all disponsible virtual machine resources.
10. If the student wants to save the status of the VM for later work, he/she gives a name to the image which will be created according to the current state of the virtual machine.

Among current components for CC resource management, a module which enables resource management from a Web application has been developed (Simić, 2011). This module uses existing CC infrastructure and it is integrated with the user directory which contains student accounts. The users of the application are primarily students of the Faculty of Organizational Sciences. The

Figure 31. Integration of Moodle and a private cloud

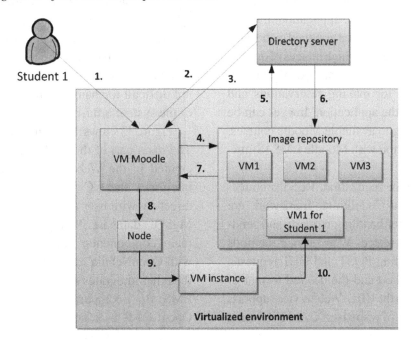

students are able to make reservations and to run predefined images with installed operating systems and application software which are used during the teaching process.

The application is based on the service-oriented architecture, which allows parallel development of Web and mobile applications. This approach of software development enables later creation of different applications and integration with the existing system. The system architecture is shown in Figure 32. Web service is the main part of the application logic and the integration of system components. It integrates the CC infrastructure, OpenLDAP directory with user accounts, Moodle LMS and MySQL database. Web service represents the application logic of the application. End-user can access the application by using either Web or mobile application. In the future, other application can be developed as well (Uden, Wangsa, & Damiani, 2007; Vaidya, 2009).

Figure 32. Architecture of application for resource management within a private cloud

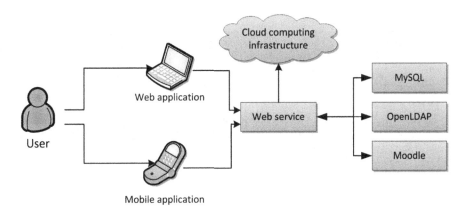

Web application is used for system administration. For administrating the application, the role of the administratior has to be assigned to the user. Administrator can define which images of operating systems stored at the private cloud are available to end-users for making reservations and running by using the application. Images can be grupped according to available Moodle courses, due to the integration with Moodle LMS (Simić, 2011).

For Web service realization, REST architectural principle and CodeIgniter framework are used. A protocol for handling requests and sending responses is created. Web service methods are called by sending POST and GET requests. The name of method and the desired format of response are sent in the URL. Web service supports following formats of response: XML, JSON and JSON which is customized for displaying tables in the Web application. Web service is integrated with Moodle LMS and OpenLDAP directory. Integration with these two platforms is realized by calling their external Web services.

For the implementation of the application CodeIgniter PHP framework has been used. CodeIgniter configuration files are used to define main configuration settings, such as the path to Open-Nebula frontend, enable or disable the integration with Moodle, path to Moodle, LDAP parameters etc. The main benefit of using configuration files is easy maintenance of the application. Since all parameters are locating at the same place, it is not difficult to change them in case of a change of the system inftastructure.

Figure 33 shows the architecture of the system. The main part of the application logic is impelemnted in the Web service. The Web service integrates the CC infrastructure, OpenLDAP directory with user accounts, Moodle LMS and MySQL database. Web service consists of two main components: one integrates the system with OpenNebula's external Web service, while the other integrates the application with Moodle LMS. Both components are integrated with the OpenLDAP user accounts directory and with MySQL database (Despotovic-Zrakić, Marković, Bogdanović, Barać, & Krčo, 2012).

The main Web service integrates the system with OpenNebula. OpenNebula has its own API which enables CC infrastructure management. This Web service is based on the XML-RPC protocol. The service communicates with Open-Nebula and returns all available images and running instances on the cloud.

Figure 33. Architecture of ELABCloud application

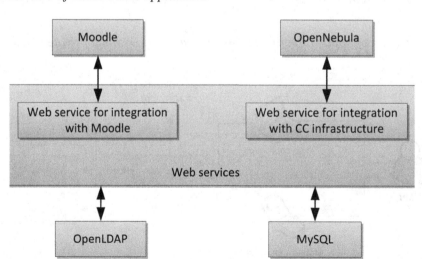

The other Web service integrates the system with Moodle LMS. It returns all Moodle courses where the user is enrolled in. Moodle LMS has a support for external Web services. All modern architectures and protocols are supported (XML-RPC, SOAP, and REST). Web service for the integration with Moodle LMS calls Moodle services' methods and returns its responses.

User authentication is implemented using the LDAP protocol. All user accounts are stored at the OpenLDAP server. LDAP authentication enables single sign-on for all services available at the E-business Lab. In other words, students can use the same username-password combination for accessing the private cloud application, Moodle LMS and other services.

Database is required for Web services. Database stores all data related to the reservation of virtual machines. The database model is shown in Figure 34.

One table stores data related to virtual machine reservations performed by system users. Other two table stores data about virtual machines enabled by the system administrator in the case of enabled and disabled integration with Moodle LMS. Database tables are connected with Open-Nebula and Moodle Web services through the

application logic tier. Web service acquires data realated to the virtual machine title and other properties, as well as data related to Moodle courses with the specific identification.

There are two user roles in the Web application: user and administrator. After the analysis of user's requirements, the use cases shown in Figure 35 have been identified.

Different technologies are used for the realization of Web application. For presentation, HTML5 and CSS are used. For the realization of the application logic tier, PHP and CodeIgniter framework are used. For the realization of the database tier, MySQL server is used.

The home page of ELABCloud application is shown in Figure 36. For accessing the application, a user must be logged into the system. The system checks the privileges of the user and displays the appropriate options, depending on the assigned privileges. If the user does not have a role of the administrator, he is only able to make a reservation of the desired virtual machine and choose the date and time when the virtual machine will be available. When the user logs into the application at the time assigned upon the reservation, they can access the previously reserved virtual machine. The VNC (Virtual Network Computing) protocol is used for

Figure 34. Data model of ELABCloud application

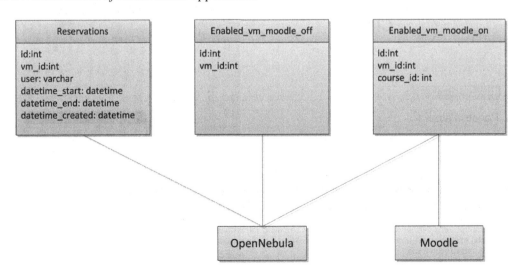

Figure 35. Use case diagram

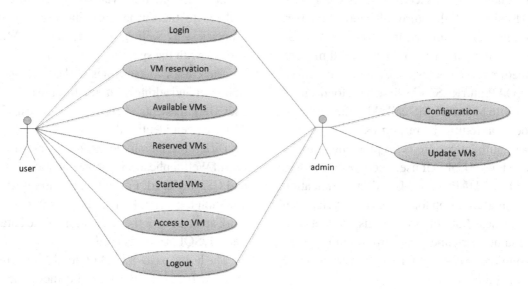

VM access. Web application is integrated with the TightVNC program which enables remote access to the virtual machine from a Web browser. This integration is realized by dynamical generating of a JAVA Webstart file based on XML standard from the ELABCloud application.

Web application administrator is able to review the settings that are defined in the application configuration files (Figure 37). For safety reasons, it is not possible to edit configuration files from the application interface. That is only possible by directly modifying the text configuration file. In

Figure 36. Homepage of ELABCloud application

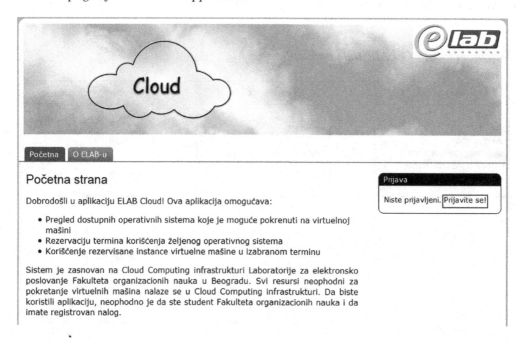

Figure 37. System settings

Pregled glavnih podešavanja

LDAP server:	localhost
Cloud kontroler:	147.91.130.106
Moodle integracija:	uključena
Moodle webservis:	http://147.91.130.198/moodle_servis/
Adresa Moodle instalacije:	http://147.91.130.198/moodle/

Figure 38. A list of Moodle courses

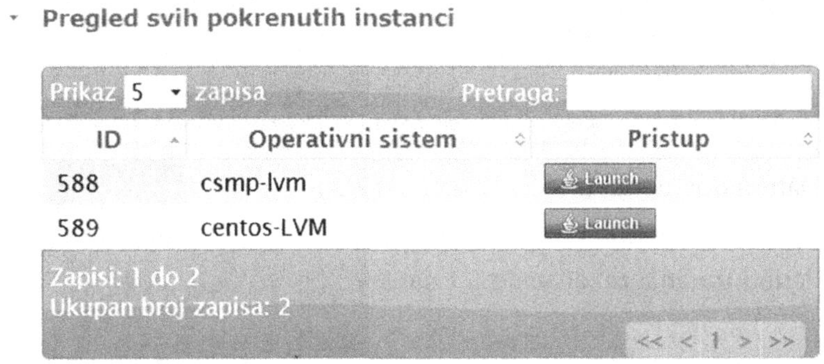

Pregled svih pokrenutih instanci

Prikaz 5 ▾ zapisa		Pretraga:
ID ⌃	**Operativni sistem** ⌄	**Pristup** ⌄
588	csmp-lvm	🔥 Launch
589	centos-LVM	🔥 Launch

Zapisi: 1 do 2
Ukupan broj zapisa: 2

<< < 1 > >>

these settings, the address of the server of the OpenNebula's frontend and the port where the XML-RPC interface of OpenNebula is started are defined. The address of the Moodle LMS installation is also defined, as well as the address of the host where the OpenLDAP server is installed.

Other features related to administrator include displaying all running instances of virtual ma-

chines and displaying and modifying virtual machines. Administrators make a choice which course they want to change available virtual machines for (Figure 38).

System displays a form for modification of enabled virtual machines for selected course (Figure 39). Administrator chooses which virtual

Figure 39. Enabled virtual machines

Dostupne VM (uključena integracija sa Moodle-om)

Prikaz 5 ▾ zapisa		Pretraga:
ID ⌃	**Kratki naziv** ⌄	**Naziv kursa** ⌄
1	moodletest	Moodle test
2	iteh	Internet tehnologije
3	ssj	Simulacija i simulacioni jezici
4	epos	Elektronsko poslovanje

Zapisi: 1 do 4
Ukupan broj zapisa: 4

<< < 1 > >>

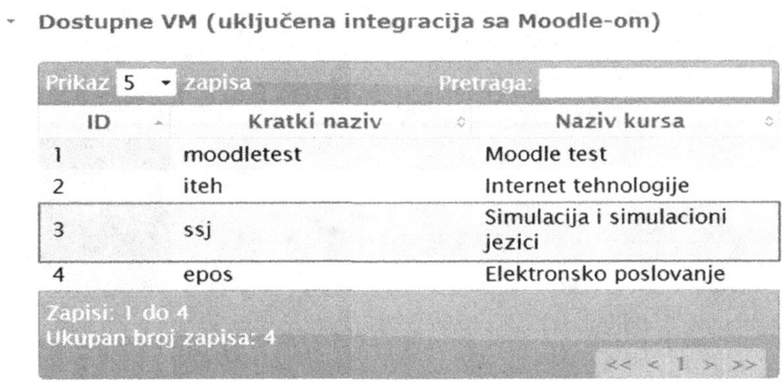

machines are going to be available for desired course and confirms the entry.

System informs the administrator about the change.

Similarly, if students are logged in, they can choose an option for making a reservation for a virtual machine. After choosing a desired virtual machine, they should choose a date and time when they want to use virtual machine and a period of duration in hours (Figure 40).

Finally, if a student is logged into the application at the time defined for a previously made reservation, it is possible to invoke a remote access to a virtual machine choosing an appropriate option (Figure 41).

Mobile ELABCloud is developed for Android platform 2.2 or later. Using the mobile ELABCloud application, student can make a reservation of any available virtual machine and it is also possible to view previously made reservations. This ap-

Figure 40. A form for making a reservation of a virtual machine

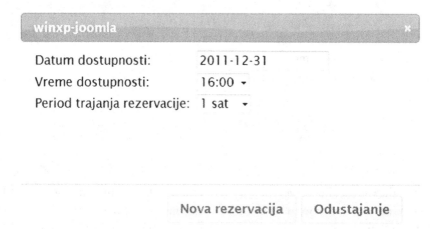

Figure 41. Remote access to a running virtual machine

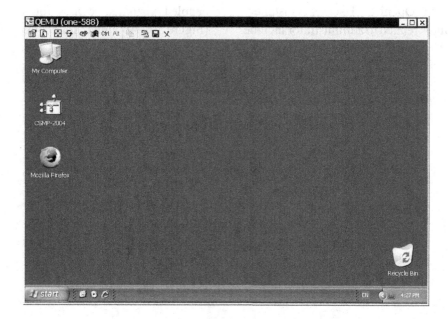

plication uses same Web services as the Web application, thus the integration with Moodle LMS platform is supported as well. Currently, it is not supported to invoke remote access to a virtual machine by using a mobile device.

The procedure of making a reservation is very similar to the Web application's procedure. After a successful login, the student needs to select an appropriate option from the main menu and then it is needed to select a virtual machine, date and time of availability and duration. The system then informs the student about a successful reservation.

EVALUATION

The E-business Lab, University of Belgrade, organizes e-learning courses using a ubiquitous learning concept (Massie, Chun, & Culler, 2004). More than 1000 students are engaged in over 20 undergraduate and postgraduate studies. The e-learning system is based on the Moodle learning management system (LMS).

Most e-learning resources are deployed and assigned for some specific assignment, and physical machines are usually stacked simply and exclusively. When receiving high workloads, an e-learning system commonly deals with them by using new resources. With the growth of resources, the overhead of resource management becomes a key issue. E-learning systems often engage resources in as much the same way as when they are at their peak hours, even when some of them are idle. Meanwhile, educational contents are various and grow rapidly in amount, requiring scalable storage capacity. Specifically, the requests to education contents follow a highly dynamic rule. These issues affect resource utilization to a great extent. During the learning process a large amount of teaching material is generated, which further aggravates the available resources. One of the biggest problems in the implementation of IT infrastructure is a competitive access to the shared resources in the higher education institution.

In addition to scalability, the efficiency of the existing resources represents another problem. The E-business Lab owns a computer centre which was designed and built specifically for its own use. Its capacity has gradually become inadequate to meet the demands of scientific research and educational activities, while at the same time it has become expensive to maintain. In each semester students mostly require the most modern hardware with specific software requirements for their laboratory exercises and practical projects. Low utilization of available resources requires a different approach to the implementation of infrastructure systems for e-learning.

The three courses that enroll the highest number of students are E-business, Internet technologies and Simulation and simulation languages. The E-business course is organized at the third year, while Internet technologies and Simulation and simulation languages are at the fourth year of study.

E-business is a course that deals with key concepts in the designing and implementation of e-business projects. In the scope of their activities within the course, students create Web presentations and e-commerce Web sites, they learn how to use and customize customer relationship management solutions, and learn about social computing service in e-business. All these activities require appropriate platforms to be installed, as well as Web hosting services. Students should be provided with virtual machines created in accordance with their needs.

The basic idea of the course Internet technologies is to learn key concepts in development of Web applications. Students have to create advanced Web applications enriched with JavaScript, JQuery, XML technologies. Further, students learn about service oriented architecture and develop their own Web services in PHP, Java or Microsoft technologies. In order to implement their projects, it is necessary to provide different operating systems (Linux, Windows), development platforms (NetBeans, Eclipse, Dreamweaver, Aptana, Visual Studio), software tools, database management tools (SQL server, MySQL), Web servers (Apache, IIS), applications servers (PHP, Biztalk, WebSphere), all modern browsers, etc. Therefore, various combinations of these technologies and platforms should be available to students on virtual machines.

The main goal of the course Simulation and simulation languages is to teach students the basic and advanced concepts of computer simulation. The course includes three areas: continuous simulation, discrete simulation and 3D modelling. According to this, students need different software solutions: CSMP, FONWebGPSS and 3ds Max. CSMP and 3ds Max are desktop applications running on Windows operating system. FONWebGPSS is a Web application running on Windows Server 2003, and it requires a set of specific Web services for building a simulation model, executing the simulation and visualizing the results of the simulation.

Participants and Design

In order to evaluate developed infrastructure for e-learning based on CC, a research has been conducted. Main goal of the research was to gain answers to three questions:

- In what extent e-learning based on implemented CC infrastructure influences the results that students achieve on final exams?
- Are teachers satisfied with implemented CC infrastructure for e-learning?
- Is performance of implemented CC infrastructure satisfactory?

In order to determine in what extent CC infrastructure for e-learning contributes to students' results, we have compared results of students who learned within the implemented CC infrastructure for e-learning and results of those who learned within previously used infrastructure for e-learning, where CC services were not available.

For experimental group (EG), we have selected students who attended courses E-business, Internet technologies and Simulation and simulation languages in winter semester of the school year 2011/12. Students in EG attended the appropriate e-learning course, where some resources were provided in the form of VMs. In the end of the course, they took the final exam.

For control group (CG), we have selected students who attended same courses in school year 2010/11. These students have learned on e-learning infrastructure bases only on Moodle LMS, where neither resources nor services were provided through CC.

In order to test equivalence of the EG and CG, we have used the average grades that students of both generations achieved in their previous course of study. Data was gathered within the business information system of Faculty of Organizational Sciences. Average grades for both EG and CG are shown in Table 2, for students of all three considered e-learning courses. Since Sig>0.05, we can conclude that there is no significant statistical difference of average grades for students in EG and CG.

For determining teachers' attitudes toward teaching in the implemented CC environment for e-learning, we have created a survey. Survey was

Table 2. Statistical equivalence of average grades in EG and CG

Course	EG (2011/12)		CG (2010/11)		F	Sig.
	N	Mean	N	Mean		
E-business	461	8.01	470	7.97	0.352	0.553
Internet technologies	256	8.07	228	8.03	0.283	0.595
Simulation and simulation languages	176	8.11	171	8.05	0.285	0.594

distributed to all teachers who taught the three considered courses in the school year 2011/12. Teachers completed the survey at the end of the semester. Total 26 teachers participated: 11 teaching E-business course, 8 teaching Internet technologies course and 7 teaching Simulation and simulation languages course.

In order to evaluate the performance of implemented infrastructure for e-learning based on CC, we have used a software tool Ganglia. Ganglia is a tool for collecting and displaying server performance metrics on pools of VMs (Massie, Chun, & Culler, 2004). This software tool enabled analysis of the performance attributes such as stability of the system, availability, speed, and CPU performance.

Instruments

Experiment has been conducted using the following instruments:

- A survey for examining teachers' attitudes toward e-learning infrastructure on CC,
- Knowledge test for measuring students results in the course E-business,
- Knowledge test for measuring students results in the course Internet technologies,
- Knowledge test for measuring students results in the course Simulation and simulation languages.

The survey for examining teachers' attitudes toward e-learning infrastructure on CC included total 5 questions. The questionnaire has been validated using Cronbach's alpha coefficient, which is 0.814.

Questions were formed in order to determine: productivity of teachers while preparing the course on CC infrastructure, productivity of teachers in realization of the course, satisfaction with technical support, satisfaction with e-learning analytics, and overall opinion on suitability of developed infrastructure for e-learning. All questions were

assigned with a Likert five point scale. Questions can be seen in Table 4, further in the text.

Knowledge test was taken by all students in both EG and CG. Knowledge tests contained questions on the matter studied within the attended course. Knowledge test was used to determine if there is statistically significant difference between results achieved by student in EG and CG. A specific knowledge test was created for each considered course (E-business, Internet technologies, Simulation and simulation languages). Cronbachs' alpha coefficients are 0.910, 0.875, and 0.890, respectively. The same tests are used during the previous five years in the considered courses.

Procedure

The procedure of integration of e-learning services with the CC and conducting e-learning courses is shown in the Figure 42. The courses are created in Moodle LMS by a professor or a course creator. Then, teaching materials are prepared, as well as the activities and the assignments for each e-course. Also, specific software tools necessary for learning are chosen. The student accounts in Moodle LMS are created and stored on LDAP server integrated with the user directory of the educational institution where the student accounts are located. After that, the virtual machines with necessary operating systems and software are prepared. The prepared virtual machines are stored into the clod computing infrastructure. Students use a specific Web interface to reserve any of the provided virtual machines for the Moodle LMS course they are enrolled in. Finally, professors and administrators of the system can view and analyze students' results and the performance of the system.

Results on Knowledge Tests

Table 3 shows means and standard deviations for students' grades achived on knowledge tests.

Figure 42. Process of integration of e-learning services with cloud

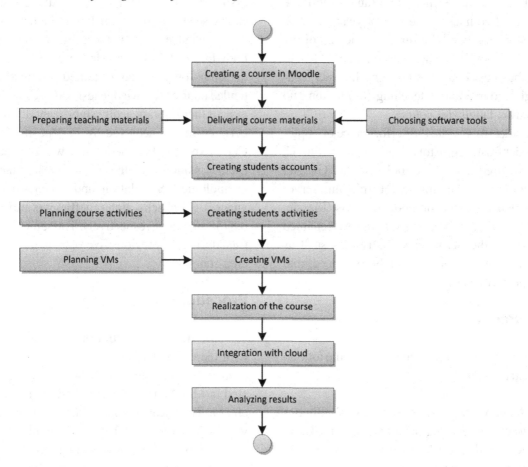

Table 3. Students' grades on knowledge tests

Course	N	Mean	Std. Deviation
E-Business			
EG	461	7.98	0.961
CG	470	7.72	0.949
Internet Technologies			
EG	256	8.09	1.032
CG	228	7.88	1.262
Simulation and Simulation Languages			
EG	176	8.22	1.059
CG	171	7.98	0.994

For testing if there are statistically significant differences between results achieved by students in EG and CG, we have used analysis of variance (ANOVA). Results show that there are statistically significant differences between results achieved by students in EG and CG for all three considered subject:

- **E-Business:** $F(1,929)=16.648$ ($p<0.05$).
- **Internet Technologies:** $F(1,482)=4.130$ ($p<0.05$).
- **Simulation and Simulation Languages:** $F(1,345)=4.930$ ($p<0.05$).

Results on Teachers' Satisfaction

Data collected by surveying teachers are shown in Table 4.

Analyzing data gathered through the questionnaire for teachers, we can conclude the following:

- Most of the teachers agreed or strongly agreed that CC infrastructure contributes to higher productivity in preparing e-courses. However, there were few teachers that disagreed on this. These were mainly teachers responsible for specific course topics that require more effort for preparing virtual machines.
- Considering applicability of CC infrastructure for realization of e-courses, most of teachers agreed or strongly agreed that CC infrastructure contributes to higher productivity in realization of e-learning courses.
- Technical support for using CC infrastructure is on adequate level for most of teachers. However, there were several teachers who were not satisfied with the quality of technical support.
- E-learning analytics is on adequate level for most of teachers. However, there is a significant number of teachers who do not have opinion on e-learning analytics. These are mainly teachers who did not need to use analytics services.
- Finally, there were no teachers who thought that implemented CC infrastructure is not suitable for e-learning process. Most of the teachers strongly agreed that the infrastructure is suitable for e-learning process.
- Teachers are satisfied with the quality of identity management system. Most teachers agree or strongly agree that all necessary resources can easily be accessed through integrated identity management system.

Table 4. The results of the questionnaire for teachers

Score:	5	4	3	2	1
Q1: Working on e-learning infrastructure based on CC contributes to higher productivity in the process of course preparation					
E-business	3	3	3	2	0
Internet technologies	2	2	1	3	0
Simulation and simulation languages	3	2	0	2	0
Q2: Working on e-learning infrastructure based on CC contributes to higher productivity in realization of courses					
E-business	5	4	2	0	0
Internet technologies	5	1	2	0	0
Simulation and simulation languages	5	2	0	0	0
Q3: Technical support is on adequate level					
E-business	3	4	2	1	1
Internet technologies	2	3	2	1	0
Simulation and simulation languages	2	3	2	1	1
Q4: E-learning analytics is on adequate level					
E-business	2	3	5	1	0
Internet technologies	0	5	3	0	0
Simulation and simulation languages	0	4	2	1	0
Q5: In my opinion, developed infrastructure based on CC is suitable for e-learning process					
E-business	5	4	2	0	0
Internet technologies	6	1	1	0	0
Simulation and simulation languages	4	2	1	0	0
Q6: Identity management system is efficient and provides single sign on for all necessary resources					
E-business	4	5	2	0	0
Internet technologies	4	3	1	0	0
Simulation and simulation languages	5	1	1	0	0

Scores: 5-strongly agree; 4-agree; 3-neither agree nor disagree; 2-disagree; 1-strongly disagree

Results on Performance of Infrastructure

Table 5 shows values for each considered performance indicator. All indicators are shown for winter semester of the school year 2011/12, including exams. Upon results shown in Table 5, we can conclude that all considered indicators are on satisfactory level.

Parameters were measured during the period of the highest system load (peak hours) and during the period of normal system load (off-peak hours). Peak hours include performing exams and performing the teaching process. During off-peak hours students can access the system from their homes.

The measured parameters include the maximal number of students which access the system simultaneously (number of access), the number of system failures (stability), system availability in percents, system response rate in milliseconds (speed) and average CPU performance in percents. System availability can be computed using the following formula:

$$AV = \frac{NA - ST}{NA} * 100[\%]$$

where:

AV = availability
NA = number of access
ST = stability

In peak hours, during the teaching process or during exams, 80 students averagely accessed the system in the period of 2 hours without interruption. During lab exercises, there was only one system failure when one student wasn't able to access his virtual machine. Availability was 98.75% during peak hours. Response rate (speed) of the system is measured using the ping command. It was 15 ms during the peak hours and 7 ms during off-peak hours. Finally, CPU performance wasn't

Table 5. Performance indicators

	Peak Hours	Off-Peak Hours
Max. number of concurrent access	80	32
Stability (number of system failures)	1	0
Availability (in percents)	98.75%	100%
Speed (response rate in milliseconds)	15 ms	7 ms
CPU performance (average CPU performance in %)	65%	22%

greater than 65% in any moment. Thanks to these parameters, we conclude that the system is stable. Figure 43 shows CPU performance during the period of the highest load.

CONCLUSION

Numerous studies have pointed out that cloud computing can provide support and empower e-learning services. The benefits of using CC in e-learning are reflected in: effective usage of resources, improved scalability, integration of different e-learning services, etc. The work presented in this chapter demonstrates a measurable improvement of the e-learning system by developing infrastructure for e-learning through CC. The significance of the research context is reflected in the integration and synchronization of information, processes, applications and human resources in an adaptive e-learning system.

Most of the studies within the area of using cloud computing concept in e-learning deals with theoretical aspects and models (Dong, Zheng, Qiao, Shu, & Yang, 2009), but only few of them include implementation in real e-learning environment (Doelitzscher, Sulistio, Reich, Kuijs, & Wolf, 2011; Vouk, Sills, & Dreher, 2010). A majority of the existing solutions for e-learning based on cloud computing implement some of the cloud service models without sophisticated mechanisms for user and resource management. This study is oriented towards making an impact in practice.

Figure 43. CPU performance during the period of the highest load

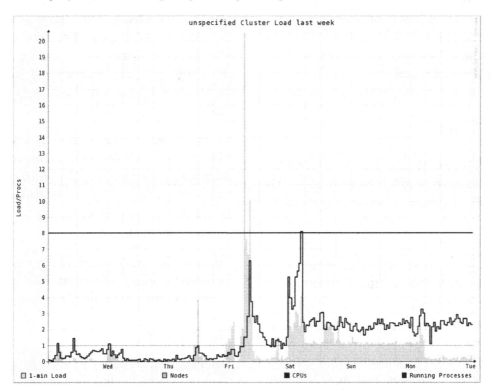

The approach in this research can be used in any Moodle-centric environment. In addition, the students are enabled to manage available VMs via both Web and mobile applications.

The approach proposed in this chapter mainly conforms to the one used in the CloudIA project (Doelitzscher, Sulistio, Reich, Kuijs, & Wolf, 2011), where the e-learning system is based on private cloud that delivers all three cloud service models (IaaS, PaaS, SaaS). Both solutions include features such as: authentication, resource management, collaboration services, customized on-demand VMs, etc. However, while the CloudIA project mainly focuses on collaboration, the approach proposed in this chapter supports other learning activities as well.

Another benefit of applying the described model can be related to cost effectiveness of the private cloud. The proposed solution is related to a more efficient usage of the existing IT resources within educational institutions, and therefore can be economically more acceptable in comparison with using cloud providers' services.

The results obtained in the experimental part of the chapter suggest that students achieve best results when they both learn and take the exam in the cloud environment. However, since the students in CG1 achieved better results than the students in CG2, we can conclude that even if there are no conditions in an educational institution to organize a complete teaching and learning process in the cloud environment, providing some learning resources through cloud computing can also have a favorable influence upon the students' knowledge.

Future research is oriented towards improving the integration with the Moodle LMS, in terms of running virtual machines directly from a Moodle course. The system for analytics should be improved to provide reports and analyses of the students' results through both Moodle and ELABCloud applications. It is also necessary to achieve a better integration with the OpenLDAP server, allowing an LDAP authentication of instances in the cloud. Mobile applications for all mobile operating systems (Windows Phone, IOS, etc.) should be developed.

REFERENCES

Baun, C., & Kunze, M. (2009). Performance measurement of a private cloud in the opencirrus (TM) testbed. In H.-X. Lin, M. Alexander, M. Forsell, A. Knüpfer, R. Prodan, L. Sousa, & A. Streit (Eds.), *Euro-Par 2009 - Parallel Processing Workshops* (pp. 434–443). Berlin: Springer-Verlag.

Bogdanovic, Z., Jovanic, B., Barac, D., Milic, A., & Despotovic-Zrakic, M. (2011). An application of cloud computing as infrastructure for Eeducation. In L. Gómez Chova, D. Martí Belenguer, & A. López Martínez (Ed.), *Edulearn11 International Conference on Education and new Learning Technologies* (pp. 4699-4707). International Association of Technology, Education and Development (IATED).

Buyya, R. (2009). Market-oriented cloud computing: Vision, hype, and reality of delivering computing as the 5th utility. In F. Cappello, C.-L. Wang, & R. Buyya (Eds.), *10th IEEE International Conference on High Performance Computing and Communications* (pp. 1-1). Los Alamitos, CA: IEEE Computer Society.

Cardos, N. (2011). *Virtual clusters sustained by cloud computing infrastructures.* (Master Thesis). Faculdade De Engenharia Da Universidade Do Porto.

Caron, E., Desprez, F., Loureiro, D., & Muresan, A. (2009). Cloud computing resource management through a grid middleware: A case study with DIET and eucalyptus. In J. E. Guerrero (Ed.), *2009 IEEE International Conference on Cloud Computing* (pp. 151-154). Los Alamitos, CA: IEEE Computer Society.

Cerbelaud, D., Garg, S., & Huylebroeck, J. (2009). Opening the clouds: Qualitative overview of the state-of-the-art open source Vmbased cloud management platforms. In *Proceedings of the 10th ACM/IFIP/USENIX International Conference on Middleware*, (pp. 1-8). New York: Springer-Verlag.

Chang, H., & Tang, X. (2011). A load-balance based resource-scheduling algorithm under cloud computing environment. In *New Horizons in Web-Based Learning - ICWL 2010 Workshops* (pp. 85–90). Berlin: Springer-Verlag. doi:10.1007/978-3-642-20539-2_10

Costanzo, A., Assuncao, M., & Buyya, R. (2009). Harnessing cloud technologies for a virtualized distributed computing infrastructure. *IEEE Internet Computing, 13*(5), 24–33. doi:10.1109/MIC.2009.108

Danfeng, Y., Fangchun, Y., & Yeap, T. (2011). Service security architecture and access control model for cloud computing. *China Communication, 8*(6), 44–50.

De Alfonso, C., Caballer, M., Alvarruiz, F., Molto, G., & Hernandez, V. (2011). Infrastructure deployment over the cloud. In B. Werner (Ed.), *Third IEEE International Conference on Coud Computing Technology and Science* (pp. 517-521). Los Alamitos, CA: IEEE Computer Society.

Despotović, M., Savić, A., & Bogdanović, Z. (2006). System components' integration within the portal for postgraduate distance education. [SymOrg.]. *Proceedings of SymOrg, 2006,* 1–9.

Despotovic-Zrakić, M., Marković, A., Bogdanović, Z., Barać, D., & Krčo, S. (2012). Providing adaptivity in moodle LMS courses. *Journal of Educational Technology & Society, 15*(1), 326–338.

Devetaković, M., Gajin, S., & Mitrović, B. (2010). Amres e-learning portal. [YuInfo.]. *Proceedings of YuInfo, 2010,* 1–6.

Doelitzscher, F., Sulistio, A., Reich, C., Kuijs, H., & Wolf, D. (2011). Private cloud for collaboration and e-learning services: From IaaS to SaaS. *Computing, 91*(1), 23–42. doi:10.1007/s00607-010-0106-z

Dong, B., Zheng, Q., Qiao, M., Shu, J., & Yang, J. (2009). BlueSky cloud framework: An e-learning framework embracing cloud computing. In M. G. Jaatun, G. Zhao, & C. Rong (Eds.), *The 1st International Conference on Cloud Computing (CloudCom 2009)* (pp. 577-582). Berlin: Springer.

Dong, B., Zheng, Q., Yang, J., Li, H., & Qiao, M. (2009). Jampots: A mashup system towards an e-learning ecosystem. In L. O'Conner (Ed.), *Fifth International Joint Conference on INC, IMS and IDC* (pp. 200-205). Los Alamitos, CA: IEEE Computer Society.

Ercan, T. (2010). Effective use of cloud computing in educational institutions. *Procedia - Social and Behavioral Sciences, 2*(2), 938-942.

European Network and Information Security Agency (ENISA). (2010). *Cloud computing: Benefits, risks and recommendations for information security*. Retrieved September 1, 2013, from http://www.coe.int/t/dghl/cooperation/economiccrime/cybercrime/cy-activity-interface-2010/presentations/Outlook/Udo%20Helmbrecht_ENISA_Cloud%20Computing_Outlook.pdf

Gallard, J., Lèbre, A., Morina, C., Naughton, T., Scott, S. L., & Vallée, G. (2012). Architecture for the next generation system management tools. *Future Generation Computer Systems, 28*(1), 136–146. doi:10.1016/j.future.2011.06.003

Iosup, A., Ostermann, S., Yigitbasi, N., Prodan, R., Fahringer, T., & Epema, D. (2011). Performance analysis of cloud computing services for many-tasks scientific computing. *IEEE Transactions on Parallel and Distributed Systems, 22*(6), 931–945. doi:10.1109/TPDS.2011.66

Jones, R. (Ed.). (2005). *Internet forensics using digital evidence to solve computer crime*. Farnham, MA: O'Reilly.

Katz, R. (Ed.). (2008). *The tower and the cloud*. New York: EDUCAUSE.

Khmelevsky, Y., & Voytenko, V. (2010). Cloud computing infrastructure prototype for university education and research. In *Proceedings of 15th Western Canadian Conference on Computing Education* (pp. 1-5). New York: ACM.

Massie, M., Chun, B., & Culler, D. (2004). The ganglia distributed monitoring system: Design, implementation, and experience. *Parallel Computing, 30*(7), 817–840. doi:10.1016/j.parco.2004.04.001

Nathani, A., Chaudharya, S., & Somani, G. (2012). Policy based resource allocation in IaaS cloud. *Future Generation Computer Systems, 28*(1), 94–103. doi:10.1016/j.future.2011.05.016

Qian, L., Luo, Z., Du, Y., & Guo, L. (2009). Cloud computing: An overview. *Lecture Notes in Computer Science, 5931*, 626–631. doi:10.1007/978-3-642-10665-1_63

Radenković, B., Despotović, M., & Bogdanović, Z. (2006). Web portal for postgraduate e-education. [SymOpis.]. *Proceedings of SymOpis, 2006*, 1–4.

Raichura, B., & Agarwal, A. (2009). Service exchange @ cloud. *SetLabs Briefings Infosys, 7*(7), 55–60.

Rittinghouse, J., & Ransome, R. (Eds.). (2009). *Cloud computing implementation, management, and security*. Boca Raton, FL: CRC Press.

Schaffer, H. E., Averitt, S. F., & Hoit, I. M. (2009). NCSU's virtual computing lab: A cloud computing solution. *IEEE Computer, 42*(7), 94–97. doi:10.1109/MC.2009.230

Sempolinski, P., & Thain, D. (2010). A comparison and critique of eucalyptus, OpenNebula and nimbus. In J. Qiu, G. Zhao, & C.G. Rong (Eds.), *2nd IEEE International Conference on Cloud Computing Technology and Science* (pp. 1-10). Los Alamitos, CA: IEEE Computer Society.

Simić, K. (2011). *Usage of mobile technologies in the development of application for cloud computing infrastructure in e-education.* (Master Thesis). University of Belgrade, Belgrade, Serbia.

Sotomayor, B., Montero, R., Llorente, I., & Foster, I. (2009). Virtual infrastructure management in private and hybrid clouds. *IEEE Internet Computing, 13*(5), 14–22. doi:10.1109/MIC.2009.119

Srinivasa, R. V., Nageswara, R. N. K., & Kumari, E. K. (2009). Cloud computing: An overview. *Journal of Theoretical and Applied Information Technology, 9*(1), 71–76.

Sultan, N. (2010). Cloud computing for education: A new dawn? *International Journal of Information Management, 30*(2), 101–182. doi:10.1016/j.ijinfomgt.2009.09.004

Takabi, H., Joshi, J. B. D., & Ahn, G. (2010). Security and privacy challenges in cloud computing environments. *IEEE Security Privacy, 8*(6), 24–31. doi:10.1109/MSP.2010.186

Tian, W., Su, S., & Lu, G. (2010). Framework for implementing and managing platform as a service in a virtual cloud computing lab. In Z. Hu & Z. Ye (Eds.), *The Second International Workshop on Education Technology and Computer Science.* Los Alamitos, CA: IEEE Computer Society.

Tilborg, H. C. A., & Jajodia, S. (Eds.). (2005). *Encyclopedia of cryptography and security.* Berlin: Springer. doi:10.1007/0-387-23483-7

Uden, L., Wangsa, T., & Damiani, E. (2007). The future of e-learning: E-learning ecosystem. In E. Chang, & K. Hussain (Eds.), *Digital EcoSystems and Technologies Conference, DEST '07: Inaugural IEEE-IES* (pp. 113–117). IEEE.

Vaidya, J. (2009). Infrastructure management and monitoring. *SetLabs Briefings Infosys, 7*(7), 79–88.

Velte, T., Velte, A., & Elsenpeter, R. (Eds.). (2010). *Cloud computing: A practical approach.* New York: The McGraw-Hill Companies.

Vouk, M. A., Sills, E., & Dreher, P. (2010). Integration of high-performance computing into cloud computing services. In B. Furht, & A. Escalante (Eds.), *Handbook of cloud computing* (pp. 255–276). Berlin: Springer. doi:10.1007/978-1-4419-6524-0_11

Zhang, Y., & Chen, J.-L. (2010). Universal identity management model based on anonymous credentials. In L. O'Conner (Ed.), *2010 IEEE International Conference on Services Computing* (pp. 305-312). Miami, FL: IEEE, Inc.

Zhang, Y., & Chen, J.-L. (2011). A delegation solution for universal identity management in SOA. *IEEE Transactions on Services Computing, 4*(1), 70–81. doi:10.1109/TSC.2010.9

ADDITIONAL READING

Barać, D., Bogdanović, Z., & Damjanović, S. (2008). Implementacija personalizovanog sistema elektronskog učenja. In *Telfor2008* (pp. 862–865). Belgrade: Telecommunications Society and Academic Mind.

Barać, D., Milić, A., & Dadić, J. (2012). Tailoring E-learning Courses Using Mechanisms for Adaptation. In *XIII International symposium SymOrg 2012* (pp. 592-600). Belgrade: Faculty of Organizational Sciences.

Bertino, E., Paci, F., & Ferrini, R. (2009). Privacy-preserving Digital Identity Management for Cloud Computing. *A Quarterly Bulletin of the Computer Society of the IEEE Technical Committee on Data Engineering, 32*(1), 21–27.

Bogdanović, Z., Despotović, M., & Radenković, B. (2007). Data mining in e-education system. *InfoM*, *6*(21), 269–34.

Catteddu, D. (2010). Cloud Computing - Benefits, risks and recommendations for information security. *Communications in Computer and Information Science*, *72*(1), 17.

Despotović, M., Bogdanović, Z., & Barać, D. (2008). Analyzing risks in exploitation of an e-learning system. In Information and Communication Technologies: from Modern to Information Society. (pp. 343-359).

Despotović, M., Savić, A., & Bogdanović, Z. (2006). Content management in E-Education. *Journal for Management Theory and Practice*, *11*(42), 55–61.

Despotović-Zrakić, M., Barać, D., Bogdanović, Z., Radenković, B., & Savić, A. (2011). *FONWebG-PSS aplikacija za simulaciju diskretnih događaja* (Vol. 10, pp. 788–792). Infoteh.

Despotović-Zrakić, M., Bogdanović, Z., Barać, D., Labus, A., & Milić, A. (2010). A Model for Infrastructure of E-Education System Based on Cloud Computing. *InfoM*, *9*(35), 23–28.

Despotović-Zrakić, M., Milić, A., Radenković, B., & Labus, A. (2010). Infrastruktura sistema za e-obrazovanje zasnovana na cloud comput-ing-u. In XXXVII Simpozijum o operacionim istraživanjima SYMOPIS 2010 (pp. 111-114). Belgrade: Visoka građevinsko-geodetska škola.

Despotovic-Zrakic, M., Simic, K., Bogdanovic, Z., Milic, A., & Vujin, V. (2012). An Application for Integrated Resource Management in Educational Cloud. In L. Gomez Chova, A. Lopez Martinez, I. Candel Torres (eds.) *6th International Technology, Education and Development Conference (INTED 2012)* (pp. 1089-1097). Spain: INTED.

Gopalakrishnan, A. (2009). Cloud Computing Identity Management. *SETLabs Briefings*, *7*(7), 45–54.

Graf, S. (2007). *Adaptivity in Learning Management Systems Focusing on Learning Styles*. PhD Thesis, Vienna University of Technology, Austria.

Hai, J., Shadi, I., Tim, B., Wai, G., Dachuan, H., & Song, W. (2010). Cloud Types and Services. In B. Furht, & A. Escalante (Eds.), *Handbook of Cloud Computing* (pp. 335–355). US: Springer.

He, W., Cernusca, D., & Abdous, M. (2011). Exploring Cloud Computing for Distance Learning. *Online Journal of Distance Learning Administration*, *14(3)*, Retrieved September 1, 2013, from http://www.westga.edu/~distance/ojdla/fall143/he_cernusca_abdous143.html.

Hignite, K., Katz, R. N., & Yanosky, R. (2010). Shaping the Higher Education Cloud. Retrieved September 1, 2013, from http://net.educause.edu/ir/library/pdf/pub9009.pdf

Marks, E., & Lozano, B. (Eds.). (2010). *Executive's Guide to Cloud Computing*. New Jersey: John Wiley & Sons, Inc.

Milić, A., Barać, D., Jovanić, B., Paunović, L., & Radenković, B. (2011). Cloud computing in e-education. In V. Žuborova, D. Camelia Iancu, & U. Pinterič (Eds.), *Social responsibility in 21st century* (pp. 473–488). Ljubljana: Založba Vega.

Milić, A., Despotović-Zrakić, M., & Barać, D. (2010). Cloud computing as infrastructure for distance education. In *XII International symposium SymOrg 2010* (pp. 1-8). Belgrade: Faculty of Organizational Sciences.

Milić, A., Simić, K., & Labus, A. (2012). *Servisi za upravljanje cloud computing infrastrukturom u e-obrazovanju* (Vol. 11, pp. 961–965). Infoteh.

Parameswaran, V., & Chaddha, A. (2009). Cloud Interoperability and Standardization. *SetLabs Briefings Infosys*, 7(7), 19–26.

Radenković, B., Despotović-Zrakić, M., Vujin, V., Bogdanović, Z., & Barać, D. (2012). Identity as a service in educational cloud. In SED 2012, 5th International Confrence Science and Higher Education in Function of Sustainble Development (pp. 1-6). Užice: Visoka poslovno-tehnička škola strukovnih studija.

Simić, K., Bogdanović, Z., & Labus, A. (2012). Mobile Application for Educational Cloud Management. In *XIII International symposium SymOrg 2012* (pp. 608-615). Belgrade: Faculty of Organizational Sciences.

Simić, K., Vulić, M., Labus, A., & Barać, D. (2012). Developing service-oriented application for the educational cloud. In U. Lechner, D. Lux Wigand, A. Pucihar (Eds.), The 25th Bled eConference eDependability: Reliable and Trustworthy eStructures, eProcesses, eOperations and eServices for the Future (pp. 324-332). Kranj: Moderna organizacija.

Vujin, V., Milić, A., Despotović-Zrakić, M., Jovanić, B., & Radenković, B. (2012). Development and implementation of e-education model in a higher education institution. *Scientific Research and Essays*, 7(13), 1432–1443.

Vujin, V., Radenković, B., Milić, A., & Despotović-Zrakić, M. (2011). Model IT infrastructure visokoškolske ustanove zasnovan na cloud computing-u. In XXXVIII Simpozijum o operacionim istraživanjima - SYM-OP-IS 2011 (pp. 117-120). Belgrade: Centar za izdavačku delatnost Ekonomskog fakulteta u Beogradu.

Vujin, V., Simić, K., Despotović-Zrakić, M., & Radenković, B. (2012). Federation of Digital Identities in E-education. In G. Ćirović (Ed.), XXXIX Simpozijum o operacionim istraživanjim SYMOPIS 2012 (pp. 1-4). Belgrade: Visoka građevinsko-geodetska škola.

Vujin, V., Simić, K., & Milić, A. (2012). Management of Cloud Computing Infrastructure for E-learning. In XIII *International symposium SymOrg 2012* (pp. 981-988). Belgrade: Faculty of Organizational Sciences.

KEY TERMS AND DEFINITIONS

Cloud Computing (CC): Is a model for enabling convenient, on-demand network access to a shared pool of configurable computing resources.

E-Education: Refers to use of information and communication technologies in education.

Identity Management Systems (IDM): Represent an IT infrastructure that is used to manage users' identities and authentication and authorization data.

Infrastructure as a Service (IaaS): Provides the consumer with the capability to provision processing, storage, networks, and other fundamental computing resources, and allows the consumer to deploy and run arbitrary software, which can include operating systems and applications.

Learning Management Systems (LMS): Are powerful integrated systems that support a number of activities performed by teachers and students during the e-learning process.

Platform as a Service (PaaS): Provides the consumer with the capability to deploy consumer-created or acquired applications, which are produced using programming languages and tools supported by the provider, onto the cloud infrastructure.

Private Cloud: Is an infrastructure operated for a private organization that may be managed by the organization or a third party, and may exist on premise or off premise.

Software as a Service (SaaS): Provides the consumer with the capability to use the provider's applications running on a cloud infrastructure.

Virtualization: Is one of prerequisites for the realization of cloud computing and enables an efficient usage of resources, because several virtual machines can operate on one physical machine.

Chapter 6
Mobile Learning Services on Cloud

Dušan Barać
University of Belgrade, Serbia

Miloš Radenković
Union University, Serbia

Branislav Jovanić
University of Belgrade, Serbia

ABSTRACT

This chapter discusses providing mobile learning services on cloud. Mobile cloud computing brings numerous benefits and enables overcoming technical constraints of mobile learning. The main techniques and approaches in mobile cloud computing are analyzed. A model for mobile learning services delivering through cloud computing is proposed. Several examples of mobile learning services implementations on cloud are presented: Android native application that provides Moodle learning management system features and a SMS service and mobile application for managing the infrastructure of e-learning system.

INTRODUCTION

Rapid advancement and ubiquity of mobile tehnologies has significantly increased interest in mobile learning. Main idea of mobile learning paradigm is to enable anyone to access information and learning materials from anywhere and at anytime, using a mobile device (Ally, 2009; Chen, Chang, & Wang, 2008).

Mobility is seen by researchers and pedagogues as a new opportunity for education since it provides more chances for learners to personalize their learning process, enhance social interactions, learn more effectively and more autonomously, and collaborate with other peers and teachers at anytime and from anywhere, inside and outside the formal collaborative learning context (El-hussein & Cronje, 2010; Laouris & Eteokleous, 2005; Martin, Diaz, Sancristobal, Gil, Castro, & Peire, 2011).

In (Chen, Kao, & Sheu, 2003) the authors describe five main characteristics of mobile learning:

- Urgency of learning need;
- Initiative of knowledge acquisition;
- Mobility of learning setting;

DOI: 10.4018/978-1-4666-5784-7.ch006

- Interactivity of learning process;
- Integration of instructional content.

Ubiquitous learning environments overcome the restrictions of classroom or workplace-restricted learning and extend e-learning by bringing the concepts of anytime and anywhere to reality, aiming at providing people with better educational experience in their daily living environments (Graf, 2008). In a ubiquitous computing environment, many small computers are embedded in daily life objects, enabling these objects to support and assist people in tasks about work, education, and daily life. Such environments allow students to learn at any time and any place, encouraging them to more experiential learning (Lay, 2007) such as learning by doing, interacting and sharing, and facilitate on-demand learning, hands on or minds-on learning and authentic learning (Graf, 2008). Ubiquitous learning combines mobile and pervasive learning and assumes that computers are embedded in everyday objects. A ubiquitous learning system (ULS) supports learners through embedded and invisible computers in everyday life (Ogata & Yano, 2003).

Simultaneously, with wide range of features and technologies used in the context of mobile learning, complex requirements are to appear in projecting and implementation of ubiquitous e-learning environment. Main problems are related to: device interoperability, technical issues (i.e. battery consumption, screen size, limited computational resources), costs, etc. These constraints have lead to finding new innovative approaches in order to enhance m-learning. In this chapter, we propose introducing mobile cloud computing for educational services in order to overcome these obstacles. Currently, mobile cloud computing application in mobile learning services is emerging area (Ouf, Nasr, & Helmy, 2010; Shuqiang & Hongkuan, 2012).

Primary goal of this chapter is to investigate possibilities for delivering mobile learning services through cloud computing. We analyze the need and requirements for implementing m-learning services on cloud. Different approaches and techniques of mobile cloud computing in learning are discussed. Main issue in this chaper is mobile cloud computing in e-learning. Several examples of mobile services provided on cloud are presented in this work: ELAB Android native application that provides Moodle LMS fetaures, SMS service, and mobile application for managing infrastructure of e-learning system.

MOBILE LEARNING SERVICES

Mobile learning systems include set of complex processes, various components, services and user roles. In order to develop effective environment for m-learning, it is necessary to determine the characteristics the users, and then use the information obtained for the creation and implementation of educational processes. Model of m-learning could be expressed through the following function:

$$MLearn = f\{t, s, LE, c, IT, MM, m\}$$

t=time
s=space
LE=learning environment
c=content
IT=technologies
MM=mental model
m=method

In the literature, there are a few definitions of what constitutes a mobile application. An application is mobile if it runs on a mobile device, namely a mobile phone, and is either always or occasionally connected to a network. A mobile application may include data storage, data processing or viewing or transmission to another application or server (Vazquez-Briseno, Vincent, Nieto-Hipólito, & Sánchez-López, 2012). The definition of mobile services that is used in this work - a mobile service is an electronic service that consists of three main components: a mobile application as a client, wireless networking and server implementation that provides the needed functionality or information (Content) to the user (Vazquez-Briseno, Vincent, Nieto-Hipólito, & Sánchez-López, 2012). In other words, application is a more technical term referring to the solution itself, whereas service is better associated with some 3rd parties (e.g., content provider or network based server) who provide some value added product to the end customer (Vazquez-Briseno, Vincent, Nieto-Hipólito, & Sánchez-López, 2012).

The previous research in the field of mobile education mainly refer to m-learning theory and pedagogical models, preconditions for mainstreaming mobile learning (Doering, 2007), methodology for developing educational applications for mobile devices. Several researchers studied developing alternative interfaces, psycological factors of m-learning, adaptive mobile learning and application of specific mobile services in specific field of learning. More details on these researches can be found in (Doering, 2007; Chen & Huang, 2010; Chu, Hwang, Tsai, & Tseng, 2010; Churchill & Hedberg, 2008; Clough, Jones, McAndrew, & Scanlon, 2007; Coulby, Hennessey, Davies, & Fuller, 2011; Hwang & Tsai, 2011; Mahamad, Ibrahim, & Taib, 2010; Martin, Diaz, Sancristobal, Gil, Castro, & Peire, 2011; Romero, Ventura, & De Bra, 2009; Sánchez & Olivares, 2011; Sharples, 2000; Uzunboylu & Ozdamli, 2011). Currently, there have been a lot of researches related to mobile learning application in learning (Hwang & Tsai, 2011). Several researchers studied the development of alternative interfaces, psycological factors, adaptive mobile learning and application of mobile services in a specific field of learning. Chu et al. (2010) employed the Radio Frequency Identification (RFID) technology to conduct a ubiquitous learning activity for a natural science course, in which individual students were equipped with a mobile device that guided them to observe the features of plants in the school campus (Chu, Hwang, Tsai, & Tseng, 2010).

They also investigated the network conditions and learners' diverse preferences in order to efficiently provide a properly personalized learning content in mobile learning environments. Ideas of using mobile serious games in problem based learning are implemented in (Churchill & Hedberg, 2008). The importance of providing adaptivity within mobile learning environments was discussed in (Graf, 2008; Su, Tseng, Lin, & Chen, 2011). They proposed a personalized learning content adaptation mechanism to meet diverse user needs in mobile learning environments. In (Su, Tseng, Lin, & Chen, 2011) the authors provide a framework for adaptation of the Moodle content on different types of devices. Further, they consider different approaches for the implementation of the user interface on mobile devices.

Mobile learning services categories are presented in Figure 1.

Advanced services such as those from categories of social networking, multimedia, edutainment, context-aware services require integrations of different technologies and strong hardware support. Although, nowadays smartphones show a huge improvement considering hardware and software performances, several obstacles are not overcome yet.

Mobile Learning Services Constraints

Today, the popularity of smart devices and mobile networks has substantially changed the way people access computers and network services. However, majority of the listed researches are experimental within smaller group of students, focused on the advantages of m-learning and do not involve e-learning systems with huge number of users. Many mobile devices have significant constraints imposed upon them because of the importance and desirability of smaller sizes, lower weights, longer battery life and other features.

Main problems in using mobile application are related to:

Figure 1. Mobile learning services

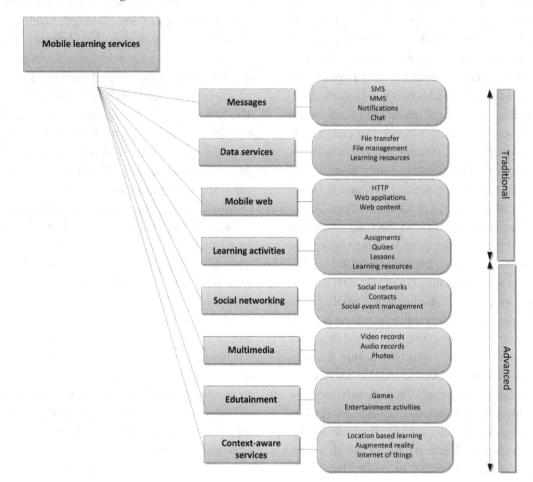

- **Processing Power:** Many of the services provided over the Internet, such as gaming, music, and video, requires faster machines and higher memory levels.
- Small display screens
- Limited memory and storage
- **Compute Power Limitations:** Each advance mobile learning application or service demands highly intensive computational operations.
- **Battery Life:** Batteries are important for the mobility and portability of mobile devices. Batteries run out quickly in most handheld devices. This is especially true if the user is on the move and has no time to charge the battery. There is an ongoing ef-

fort to reduce consumption of power and increase battery life for mobile devices. Some of these efforts include new battery technologies, like the fuel cell.
- **Flaky Connections:** For many users on the move, connectivity is very important. In order to maintain connectivity and minimize dropouts, mobile devices should have the ability to save and minimize the loss of data, while conducting transactions.
- Availability, scalability, reliability
- **Mobile Services Integration:** Mobile learning services are developed for different types of devices, mobile operating systems, mobile browsers, etc. When it comes

to integration of the services a lot of problems are to appear.

- **Standards:** Mobile devices are being produced by various producers. Each of them follows its own standards. Although there are some initiatives directed toward developing standards in this area, problems of standardization should be taking into account when providing mobile services

- **Costs:** Modern smart phones have fairly impressive performances, but prices are still quite high, particularly for students

MOBILE CLOUD COMPUTING

Mobile phone applications are exploding in popularity, and can strongly benefit from services and resources offered by cloud computing. Mobile cloud computing (MCC) refers to an infrastructure where data storage and data processing happen outside of the mobile device enabling a new class of applications previously not possible, e.g. context-aware mobile social networks. MCC integrates the cloud computing into the mobile environment and overcomes obstacles related to the performance (e.g., battery life, storage, and bandwidth), environment (e.g., heterogeneity, scalability, and availability), and security (e.g., reliability and privacy) discussed in mobile computing (Dinh, Lee, Niyato, & Wang, 2011).

The full potential of mobile cloud applications can only be unleashed, if computation and storage is offloaded into the cloud, but without hurting user interactivity, introducing latency or limiting application possibilities. The applications should benefit from the rich built-in sensors which open new doorways to more smart mobile applications. As the mobile environments change, the application has to shift computation between device and cloud without operation interruptions, considering many external and internal parameters (Kovachev, Cao, & Klamma, 2011).

The Mobile Cloud Computing Forum defines MCC as follows (Giurgiu, Riva, Juric, Krivulev, & Alonso, 2009): "Mobile Cloud Computing at its simplest refers to an infrastructure where both the data storage and the data processing happen outside of the mobile device. Mobile cloud applications move the computing power and data storage away from mobile phones and into the cloud, bringing applications and mobile computing to not just smart phone users but a much broader range of mobile subscribers."

Cloud computing for mobile devices has a major benefit in that it enables running applications between resource-constrained devices and Internet based clouds. Moreover, these devices can outsource computation/communication/resource intensive operations to the cloud.

The combination of cloud computing, wireless communication infrastructure, portable computing devices, location-based services, mobile Web, etc., has laid the foundation for a novel computing model, called mobile cloud computing, which allows users an online access to unlimited computing power and storage space. Taking the cloud computing features in the mobile domain, following is defined: "Mobile cloud computing is a model for transparent elastic augmentation of mobile device capabilities via ubiquitous wireless access to cloud storage and computing resources, with context-aware dynamic adjusting of offloading in respect to change in operating conditions, while preserving available sensing and interactivity capabilities of mobile devices." (Kovachev, Cao, & Klamma, 2011).

Mobile cloud computing could be described as the availability of cloud computing services in a mobile ecosystem, i.e. worldwide distributed storage system, exceed traditional mobile device capabilities, and offload processing, storage and security (Kovachev, Cao, & Klamma, 2011). MCC is simply cloud computing in which at least some of the devices involved are mobile. Model of the mobile cloud computing architecture is shown in Figure 2.

Figure 2. Mobile cloud computing architecture

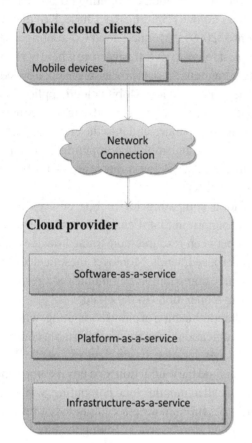

MCC Technologies and Techniques

Two main directions could be noticed in the mobile cloud computing (Shanklin, n.d.). First group are techniques that aim to develope general systems for using cloud to foster mobile phone performance. These techniques are referred to as general-purpose mobile cloud computing (GPMCC). Second, many individual applications used today with mobile devices such as smart phones employ cloud computing to a greater or lesser extent. There are multiple methods used and proposed by which the cloud can be leveraged. This can be referred to as application-specific cloud computing (ASMCC). (Shanklin, n.d.).

General Purpose MCC

However, there is also the possibility of a more general-purpose use of these resources in order to help alleviate the limited computational power of mobile devices. It is feasible to develop systems in which tasks that are usually performed locally on the mobile device are outsourced to the cloud as they happen. This can leverage the computing resources of remote computers seamlessly without requiring applications specifically developed for that purpose (Shanklin).

Researchers from Berkeley have considered the possibility of increasing the performance of hardware-limited smartphones using cloud computing (Chun & Maniatis, 2009).Their main method involves creating virtual clones of smart-phone execution environments on non-mobile computers and pushing task execution to these virtual devices. Because non-mobile devices often have significantly more computational power, this enables much better performance from smart-phones. This could enable a broader spectrum of applications and could ease the burden of software developers to create ultra-efficient software for a more limited platform.

Augmented execution is performed in four steps:

1. Initially, a clone of the smartphone is created within the cloud (laptop, desktop, or server nodes);
2. The state of the primary (phone) and the clone is periodically or on-demand synchronized;
3. Application augmentations (whole applications or augmented pieces of applications) are executed in the clone, automatically or upon request; and
4. Results from clone execution are re-integrated back into the smartphone state (Chun & Maniatis, 2009).

Five different types of augmentation they believe could be performed (Chun & Maniatis, 2009). First, there is primary functionality outsourcing. This takes intensive tasks like speech recognition or video indexing and ports them to the cloud while allowing less intensive tasks to still be executed on the phone itself. Second there is background augmentation. This type of augmentation takes tasks that do not need to be performed immediately, such as virus checking or indexing files and moves them to the cloud. Mainline augmentation allows users to specifically pick an application to be run in an augmented fashion. This preserves the workings of the program but changes the method by which it is executed. Hardware augmentation modifies the virtual clone of the smartphone to modify low level system software. For example, modifying garbage collection to be less aggressive (since less aggressiveness is needed on the clone which has more memory) can speed up execution significantly. Finally, augmentation through multiplicity uses multiple clones of the device to speed up execution. This can help applications which require a great deal of parallel processing.

Many other examples where the cloud can augment mobile devices can be envisioned, e.g. virus scan, mobile file system indexing, augmented reality applications.

Application-Specific MCC Solutions

In contrast to GPMCC, application-specific MCC involves developing specific applications for mobile devices which use cloud computing. While both can potentially allow a mobile device to perform more intensive operations than it could use only local execution, ASMCC has the added benefit that it allows for uses of cloud computing which require more than simply increased computational power. For example, chat or e-mail clients require ASMCC because the Internet is used as a communication resource and not simply for storage or additional computational power (although such applications may leverage these resources as well).

Several methods and systems have been proposed which aim to specifically facilitate mobile cloud computing for applications (MapReduce, Mobile cloud service (Shanklin, n.d.; Samimi, Mckinley, & Sadjadi, 2006), RESTful Web services (Christensen, 2009), Weblets (Zhang, Schiffman, Gibbs, Kunjithapatham, & Jeong, 2009; Chun & Patti, 2011). In (Ally, 2009) the authors combine the context that can be ascertained from the sensors on the smart mobile device with the ability to offload processing capabilities, storage, and security to cloud computing over any one of the available network modes via RESTful Web-services. Mobile cloud services model presented in (Samimi, Mckinley, & Sadjadi, 2006) enables dynamic instantiation, composition, configuration, and reconfiguration of services on an overlay network to support mobile computing.

Implemented prototype of this model was applied to the problem of dynamically instantiating and migrating proxy services for mobile hosts. In the following section elastic Web application are described in details, as this technique was used in providing mobile learning services within our laboratory.

Weblets

A concept of elastic applications was described in (Zhang, Schiffman, Gibbs, Kunjithapatham, & Jeong, 2009). These applications can run efficiently on resource constrained devices, by seamlessly and transparently making use of cloud resources whenever needed. Giurgiu et al. (2009) develop an application middleware that can automatically distribute different layers of an application between the device and the server while optimizing several parameters such as latency, data transfer, cost, etc. The application is split down to a UI component, Weblets, and a manifest describing the application (Figure 3). Weblets are autonomous functional software entities that run on the device or cloud, performing computing, storing and network tasks (Giurgiu, Riva, Juric, Krivulev, & Alonso, 2009).

Each of the Weblets can be launched on a device or cloud, and can be migrated between them according to dynamic changes of the computing environment or user preferences on the device. When the application is launched an elasticity manager running on the device monitors the resource requirements of the Weblets of the application and makes decisions where they should be launched. Computation or communication intensive Weblets such as image and video processing usually strain the processors of mobile devices, therefore they can be launched on one or more platforms in the cloud; while user interface components (UI) or those needing extensive access to local data may be launched on the device. If one Weblet should be launched on the cloud, the elasticity manager talks to an elasticity service residing on the cloud, which arranges the execution resources of the Weblet, e.g., on which cloud node it should be launched, and how much storage should be allocated. The service also returns some information after successfully launching the Weblet, such as its endpoint URL. A Weblet can be platform independent such as using Java or .Net bytecode or Python script or

platform dependent, using a native code. In some situations, even with heavy computational tasks, there may be times when running on the device is preferred. When, for example, the device is offline, or the media is small in size or number, or fast response is not a requirement, then it is certainly possible to consider running on the device. The mobile device and the elasticity service can work together to decide where and how the tasks can be executed. The elasticity service organizes cloud resources and delegates application requirements from mobile devices (Zhang, Schiffman, Gibbs, Kunjithapatham, & Jeong, 2009; Chun & Patti, 2011).

One possible scenario of using Weblet concept in u-learning is shown in Figure 4. An application for u-learning enable student to capture a building or monument and get information about it. Learning application sends both captured image and location information to Web service. The Web service for image processing is hosted on the cloud. It uses computational resources of the cloud and sends information back to the mobile learners' device.

Figure 3. Weblets concept

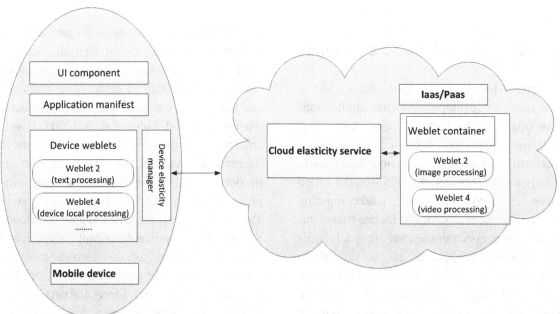

Figure 4. An Weblet scenario in ubiquitous learning

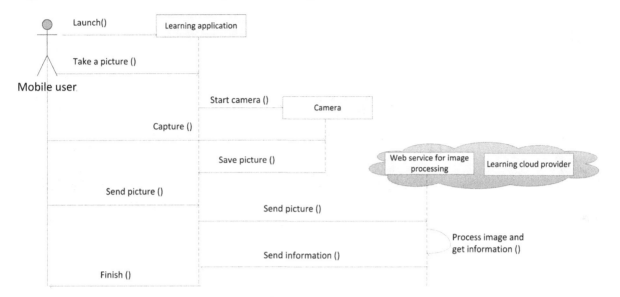

Cloudlets

Instead of connecting on a distant "cloud," the resource poverty of a mobile device can be addressed by using a nearby resource-rich cloudlet. The need for real-time interactive response can be met by low latency, one-hop, and high-bandwidth wireless access to the cloudlet. In this cloudlet concept a mobile user exploits virtual machine (VM) technology to rapidly instantiate customized service software on a nearby cloudlet, and then uses that service over a wireless LAN. The mobile device typically functions as a thin client with respect to the service. A cloudlet is a trusted, resource-rich computer or cluster of computers that is well-connected to the Internet and is available for use by nearby mobile devices (Satyanarayanan, Bahl, Caceres, & Davies, 2009).

Physical proximity of the cloudlet is essential: the end-to-end response time of applications executing in the cloudlet needs to be fast (few milliseconds) and predictable. If no cloudlet is available nearby, the mobile device can gracefully degrade to a fallback mode that involves a distant cloud or, in the worst case, solely its own resources. Full functionality and performance can

return later, when a nearby cloudlet is discovered (Satyanarayanan, Bahl, Caceres, & Davies, 2009).

Cloudlet tends to be (Loke, 2012):

- Transient,
- Localized to the current environment of the mobile user (which could even be a business premise or coffee shop), as opposed to some air-conditioned machine room,
- Ownership is decentralized (e.g., owned by local business or current site such as a museum), rather than centralized ownership by a large provider,
- Network is via LAN and WLAN instead of Internet scale, and
- There are fewer users at a time, instead of thousands.

At the same time sensor or context cloudlet makes use of a relatively small set of (typically local) sensors, context servers, or context-aware systems, compared to the large (Internet-scale) set of resources as typical in a cloud model.

Figure 5 illustrates cloudlets concept. A cloudlet resembles a data center in a box; it is self-managing and requires little more than power,

Figure 5. Cloudlets concept

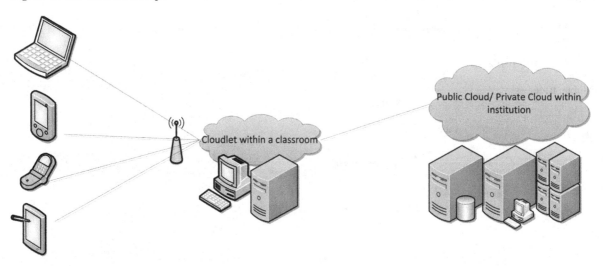

Internet connectivity, and access control for setup. Such simplicity of management is similar to an appliance model of computing resources and makes cloudlets simple to deploy in a business premises. Internally, a cloudlet resembles a cluster of multicore computers, with gigabit internal connectivity and high-bandwidth wireless LAN (Dinh, Lee, Niyato, & Wang, 2011).

The mobile client acts as thin client, with all significant computation occurring in a nearby cloudlet. This approach relies on technique called dynamic VM synthesis. A mobile device delivers small VMs overlay to the cloudlet infrastructure that already owns the base VM from which this overlay was derived.

MOBILE CLOUD COMPUTING IN E-LEARNING

Combination of m-learning and cloud computing enhances the communication quality between students and teachers (Dinh, Lee, Niyato, & Wang, 2011). Cloud computing is the promising infrastructure which can provide tremendous values to m-learning system, due to its abilities of delivering computation and storage resources as services. Cloud provides QoS-guaranteed in-

frastructures, the support of varies of applications and the automatic resource management which make m-learning system reliable, flexible, cost efficient, self-regulated, and QoS-guaranteed.

Utilizing a cloud with the large storage capacity and powerful processing ability, the applications provide learners with much richer services in terms of data (information) size, faster processing speed, and longer battery life. The architecture of mobile cloud computing infrastructure in an educational institution is presented in Figure 6. Cloud services and resources can be delivered to end users through any of the delivery models (SaaS, PaaS, IaaS), but considering the typical usage scenarios for handheld devices, SaaS is the most suitable approach.

There have been several examples of integrating mobile cloud service in educational institutions. For example, (Zhao, Sun, & Dai, 2010) describes a smartphone software based on the open source JavaME UI framework and Jaber for clients. Through a Web site built on Google Apps Engine, students communicate with their teachers at anytime. Also, the teachers can obtain the information about student's knowledge level of the course and can answer students' questions in a timely manner.

Figure 6. Mobile cloud computing architecture within educational institution

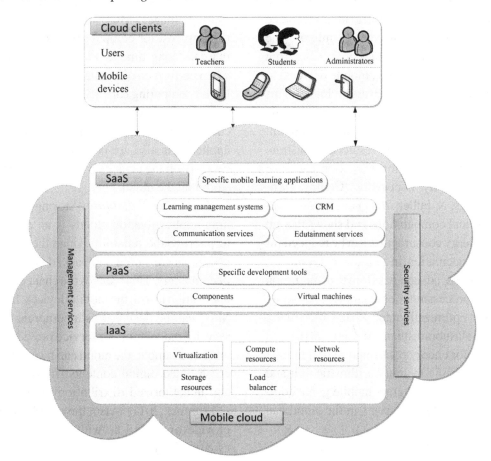

In (Yin, David, & Chalon, 2009), a contextual m-learning system based on IMERA platform shows that a cloud-based m-learning system helps learners access learning resources remotely.

Another example of MCC applications in learning is "Cornucopia" implemented for researches of undergraduate genetics students and "Plantations Pathfinder" designed to supply information and provide a collaboration space for visitors when they visit the gardens (Yin, David, & Chalon, 2009). The purpose of the deployment of these applications is to help the students enhance their understanding about the appropriate design of mobile cloud computing in supporting field experiences.

In (Ferzli & Khalife, 2011), an education tool based on cloud computing is developed to create a course about image/video processing. Through mobile phones, learners can understand and compare different algorithms used in mobile applications (e.g., de-blurring, de-noising, face detection, and image enhancement).

The mobile cloud can be used to overcome obstacles in mobile learning, emphasizing the main benefits of the educational cloud.

Extending Battery Lifetime: Battery is one of the main constraints of mobile devices. Several solutions have been proposed to enhance the CPU performance (Dinh, Lee, Niyato, & Wang, 2011; Shanklin, n.d.) and to manage the disk and screen in an intelligent manner to reduce power consumption. However, these solutions require changes in the structure of mobile devices, or they require a new hardware that results in an increase of cost and may not be feasible for all mobile devices. Computation offloading technique is proposed with the objective to migrate the large computations and complex processing from resource-limited devices (i.e., mobile devices) to resourceful machines (i.e., servers in clouds). This avoids taking a long application execution time on mobile devices which results in large amount of power consumption. The results demonstrate that the remote application execution can save energy significantly. Especially, (Coulby, Hennessey, Davies, & Fuller, 2011) evaluates large-scale numerical computations and shows that up to 45% of energy consumption can be reduced for large matrix calculation. In addition, many mobile applications take advantages from task migration and remote processing. For example, offloading a compiler optimization for image processing (Cuervo, Balasubramanian, & Cho, 2010) can reduce 41% for energy consumption of a mobile device. Also, using memory arithmetic unit and interface (MAUI) to migrate mobile game components (Gad, 2011) to servers in the cloud can save 27% of energy consumption.

Improving Data Storage Capacity and Processing Power: Storage capacity is also a constraint for mobile devices. MCC is developed to enable mobile users to store and access the large data on the cloud through wireless networks. First example is the Amazon Simple Storage Service (Amazon S3) (Dinh, Lee, Niyato, & Wang, 2011) which supports file storage service. Another example is Image Exchange which utilizes the large storage space in clouds for mobile users (Shanklin). This mobile photo sharing service enables mobile users to upload images to the clouds immediately after capturing. Users may access all images from any devices. With cloud, the users can save considerable amount of energy and storage space on their mobile devices since all images are sent and processed on the clouds. Flickr and ShoZu are also the successful mobile photo sharing applications based on MCC. Facebook is the most successful social network application today, and

it is also a typical example of using cloud in sharing images. MCC also helps reducing the running cost for compute-intensive applications that take long time and large amount of energy when performed on the limited-resource devices. Cloud computing can efficiently support various tasks for data warehousing, managing and synchronizing multiple documents online. Mobile applications also are not constrained by storage capacity on the devices because their data now is stored on the cloud.

Improving Reliability: Storing data or running applications on clouds is an effective way to improve the reliability since the data and applications are stored and backed up on a number of computers. This reduces the chance of data and application lost on the mobile devices. In addition, MCC can be designed as a comprehensive data security model for both service providers and users. For example, the cloud can be used to protect copyrighted digital contents from being abused and unauthorized distribution (Kovachev, Cao, & Klamma, 2011). Also, the cloud can remotely provide to mobile users with security services such as virus scanning, malicious code detection, and authentication (Giurgiu, Riva, Juric, Krivulev, & Alonso, 2009). Also, such cloud-based security services can make efficient use of the collected record from different users to improve the effectiveness of the services (Gad, 2011; Zhang & Chen, 2011).

Social Networking: All personal information, different social networking accounts, pictures, videos, articles, blogs, messages, micro blogs, tweets, and other content can be managed on the cloud and with real time faster access and almost at no cost.

Games: The biggest and most popular use case are games with no need to install it on the phone and the processing done by clouds at a higher speed enabling a breathtaking gaming experience without any glitches or interruptions or processing power limitations.

More examples of cloud computing application in m-learning can be seen in (Bai, 2010; Barbosa, Hahn, Barbosa, & Geyer, 2008; Hsu, Hsieh, Lo, Hsu, Cheng, Chen, & Lai, 2011; Shuai, 2011; Fogel, 2010; Chao, 2012; Angin & Bhargava, 2011; Shuai & Ming-quan, 2011; Vouk, Sills, & Dreher, 2010; Fan, Cao, & Mao, 2011).

The biggest challenges in embracing cloud computing in education are:

- The cloud computing is still considered as a less mature solution at this point of time
- Low confidence in cloud computing current data security, privacy, authentication and authorization scenarios
- For device manufacturers to achieve the ROI from their previous and existing investments in the hardware and software design and development infrastructure is the primary reason to avoid cloud computing
- API standardization is a major hurdle from application development point of view.
- Lack of Internet access everywhere (e.g. at countryside) and intermittent connectivity
- Not yet efficient mobile protocols (high data throughput with variable connectivity quality)
- Lack of standard interfaces and communication protocols for interoperability with different clouds

MODEL FOR DELIVERING MOBILE LEARNING SERVICES THROUGH CLOUD COMPUTING

Model for delivering mobile learning services through cloud computing is presented in Figure 7. The model contains four main layers.

User Layer: In the e-learning ecosystem, three user roles can be noticed: student, teacher and educational institution staff. When implementing cloud computing services it is important to clearly define scope of each user role in terms of access rights and set of available features.

Device Layer: As described in section 1, currently a variety of mobile devices types is available on the market. Nowadays, the most used devices for mobile learning are: smart phones, tablets and laptops. In addition, context-aware and ubiquitous learning introduce using sophisticated devices, such as: different types of sensors, RFID tags, GPS receivers, NFC devices, smart devices, etc. When implementing mobile applications hosted on cloud computing, technical characteristics and capabilities of the mobile devices should be thoroughly analyzed.

Connection Layer: In order to use cloud computing services, a device has to ensure secure and reliable network connection. Considering availability, GSM networks are the most often used network connection technology (GPRS, HSDPA, 3G). In terms of reliability, network bandwidth and latency for mobile device connection to Internet, best way is using WiFi or WiMax connection. In context-aware learning environments, group of RFID tags or sensors are connected to appropriate reader or other device, that connects to cloud via LAN or WAN. Cloudlet concept can be used as well. Mobile device connects to a trusted, resource-rich computer or cluster of computers that is well-connected to the Internet (for instance group of computers in the classroom or within campus).

Cloud Layer: Cloud that hosts mobile learning services can be implemented in according any of deployment models of cloud computing: private cloud, public cloud, hybrid cloud or community cloud. More details about these models can be found in Vouk, Sills, and Dreher (2010). In this research, cloud is implemented as private cloud. Considering service models of cloud computing, SaaS is the most appropriate. Mobile learning applications are provided to the users of mobile learning ecosystem on demand as service. First approach implies services delivering through Web

Figure 7. Model for delivering mobile learning services through cloud computing

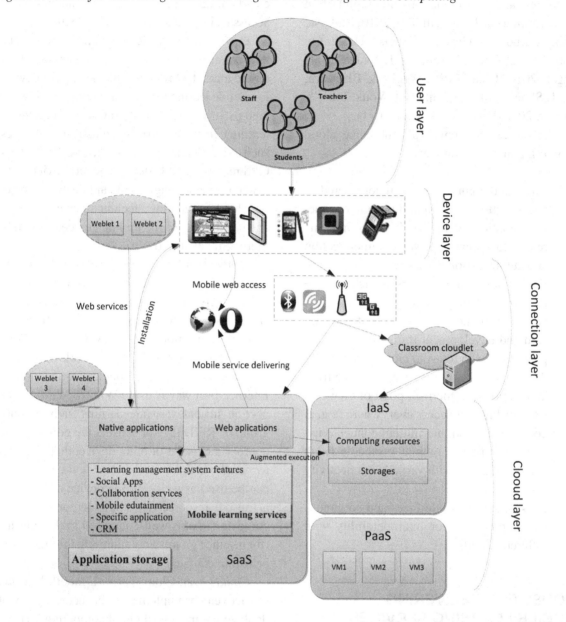

application. Users access to cloud via mobile Web browser. Execution of the application tasks is completely performed on cloud infrastructure. The mobile learning application provider has to optimize application interface to work properly in different mobile browsers. Second approach implies providing services by delivering native mobile applications. The applications are installed on the users' mobile device. Tasks that are not intensive in terms of energy consumption and computation are performed on the mobile user's device. Weblet concept can be used to create elastic applications. Augmented execution approach can be used for performing particular operation on cloud infrastructure. The provider has to take into account various characteristics of devices and operating systems. List of suitable mobile learning services on cloud include following, but not limited to: learning management systems features, mobile edutainment, social networking, CRM, collaboration services. When delivering mobile learning services on cloud, IaaS is not directly accessed or used, bud SaaS services are hosted on the underlying infrastructure. PaaS enable using prepared virtual machines with appropriate development and testing tools.

However, not all mobile learning services should be delivered on cloud. Attributes, such as compute intensity, network bandwidth, network latency and required memory should be taken into account. Applications that provide features, such as: Webmail, social networking, Web browsing very often could be completely performed on the mobile devices, without need to apply any of the mobile cloud computing techniques. On the other hand, learning services that include: gaming, augmented reality, face recognition, language translation, video streaming, etc., require high computational power of mobile devices and should be provided on cloud.

PROTOTYPE DEVELOPMENT AS A PROOF OF CONCEPT

In the following section we provide description of mobile learning services and application that were implemented within ELAB private cloud in E-business Lab, University of Belgrade.

ELAB Android Application on Cloud

Moodle LMS is one of the most frequent used learning management systems in the e-learning environments. This solution has been used within our lab for more than twelve years (Despotovic-Zrakić, Marković, Bogdanović, Barać, & Krčo, 2012). The idea of ELAB Android application was to provide native mobile application that can be used by students anytime and anywhere. Main goal was to foster learning processes within our courses from the area of e-business, Internet

technologies, mobile business, simulation, etc. The application provides students with common Moodle learning activities and resources. The synchronization between the application and the Moodle LMS is implemented with respect to three aspects: user accounts, processes and learning resources (Figure 8). The integration of user accounts is based on the LDAP (Lightweight Directory Access Protocol). Both Moodle and ELAB Android app use same database. Therefore, when exploring the application, students and teachers can use the same credentials as in Moodle. Further, they can perform activities, such as: forum, lesson preview, take a quiz, etc in the mobile application. The application logic is divided into three components-Weblets. Tasks that include simple operations, for instance lesson or forum preview, are executed on the user device. Weblet 2 is called by Web service, when mobile user requires recording data in the database. Weblet 3 is responsible for managing files that the mobile application users upload to the cloud.

Figures 9 and 10 present ELAB Android app modules for students and teachers.

ELAB Cloud Administration via Mobile Application

The mobile application is developed for the Android platform. All phones with installed version of Android 2.2 operating system or later are supported. The main menu of the mobile applications is displayed after the user successfully logs onto the system (Figure 11). Using this application, the user can make a reservation for the available virtual machines, and also to view his reservations. The integration with Moodle LMS is also fully supported. Currently, the VNC access from mobile devices is not supported.

The ELABCloud mobile application is developed for the Android operating system. It provides students with the following operations: view of all available VMs, making a reservation of a particular VM and viewing the reservations they

Figure 8. ELAB Android app for Moodle LMS

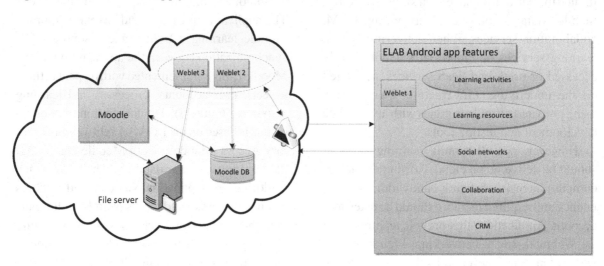

Figure 9. ELAB Android app for Moodle: Student module

Figure 10. ELAB Android app for Moodle: Teacher module

previously made. This application currently does not permit a remote access to a running VM. After a successful login, the user can choose one of the three options available: VM reservation, Review of the reserved VMs and Logout. If the user chooses a reservation option, they can choose the virtual machine they want to reserve (Figure 12a). The students then choose the date and time when they will be using the VM (Figure 12b and 12c). The users can also see the reservations they had previously made.

SMS Services on Cloud

For enabling certain services for students, Ozeki SMS Gateway was installed. It is software which is able to send and receive SMS messages by using SIM card of the mobile device that is connected with computer. This software enables defining an action in the case of receiving a SMS. This feature enables development of SMS services. The main benefit of using the SMS technology is that the content is available to larger number of mobile users (students) than in the case of using a mobile application for a specific platform. All mobile devices, including the oldest ones, are equipped with SMS service. The main con of this approach

Figure 11. Main menu in the application

is not-so-rich content. SMS services enable sending and receiving only textual contents.

In the Figure 13, the infrastructure of the educational system in scope of the Laboratory for E-business is shown.

The main system components are in the cloud computing infrastructure. Moodle and Ozeki are integrated by using a Web service. For sending and receiving SMS, it is needed to connect a mobile device with the server. Beside the mobile device, it is needed to have a connection cable, as well.

Description of Realized Mobile Services

According to analyses of students' needs, Laboratory for E-business introduced two mobile services. One service enables sending a reminder about dates and times of exams and another one enables sending results and grades from courses to students. Both services are realized by using the SMS technology and they support two ways of access. Students can receive a message on demand or they can opt-in for automatic notifications.

In Figure 14 the chart which describes how on-demand SMS services work is shown.

Web service integrates Moodle LMS's database with Ozeki SMS Gateway. During the reception of an SMS from user, SMS Gateway processes the message contents (key words) and it sends a request to the Web service which requests data from the database. Database returns the results to the Web service which forwards them to the SMS gateway. SMS gateway generates a new SMS and it sends it to the user's mobile phone number.

SMS Service for Sending the Calendar

Moodle supports working with calendar. It provides a simple interface for users. Moodle's

Figure 12. ELABCloud: Making a VM reservation using the mobile application

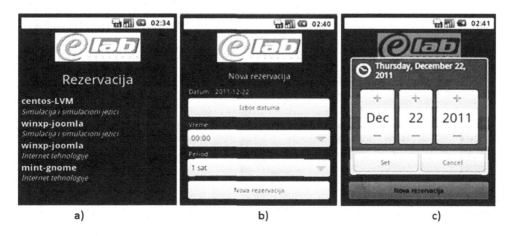

a)   b)   c)

Figure 13. Infrastructure of the educational system of the laboratory for e-business

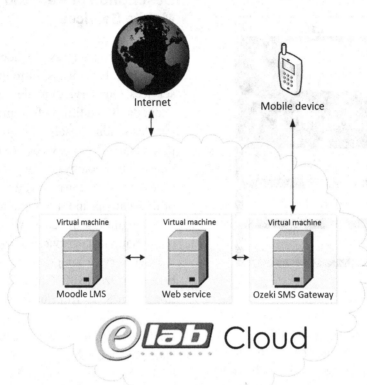

Figure 14. SMS service

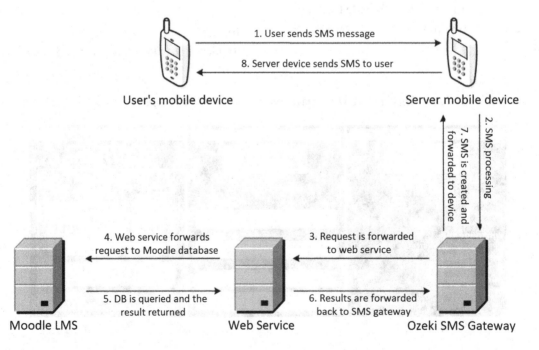

calendar can be system-wide, course-wide and group-wide. Course-wide calendar displays all assignment activities and all notifications posted by teachers or system administrators. Moodle supports exporting the calendar in ics format, which is compatible with a great number of mobile devices and it can be sent via SMS.

Ozeki SMS Gateway can define different actions which depend of the content of a SMS which is sent to the unique mobile phone number of the connected SIM card. For example, if a user sends a SMS with contents "KAL EPOS," he/she will get another message with the calendar for the course E-business. If students want to use this service, they have to assign their mobile phone numbers to their Moodle profiles.

Identification of students is provided by using Web services which are activated by Ozeki SMS gateway during the reception of a SMS message. This Web service use following parameters: the mobile phone number of SIM card where the message was sent from and the content of the message (e.g. KAL EPOS). The system checks the number of SIM card, it finds the corresponding Moodle user and it compares the SMS contents and student's privileges. If everything is fine, Moodle LMS forwards corresponding calendar in ics format to Ozeki SMS Gateway, which sends the SMS to user. If an error occurs, the user is informed.

This service enables automatic sending of SMSs as reminders, as well. Students need to check a field in their profiles if they want to register for the reception of SMS reminders. System sends SMSs with calendar automatically to all registered users 48 hours before any event in the course.

SMS Service for Notification about the Grades

Another Web service enables sending notifications to students about their grades. Moodle tracks results at each course. System administrator or course creator defines grading scale and points for each activity at course. Using Moodle LMS, students can see their grades for any course at any moment. Moodle also can compute the finale course grade according to grades for activities.

By sending the SMS with the key word "GRADE" and the parameter "the name of course," students receive callback information with their grades. For example, if a student sends a message with contents "GRADE EPOS" to the number of Ozeki SMS Gateway, he/she will get a response with their grades for the course E-business. If a user has following grades for corresponding activities: 10,8, 10 and 9, respectively, he/she will get a response: "EPOS, z1:10, z2:8, z3:10, z4:9."

If students want to get automatic SMS notifications about their grades, they need to check a corresponding field in their profiles. In that case, students will get a SMS about a grade for activity at the same moment when a teacher reviews that activity.

CONCLUSION

Numerous studies emphasized that cloud computing as emerging paradigm brings numerous benefits and enable overcoming technical constraints of mobile learning (Dinh, Lee, Niyato, & Wang, 2011; Shanklin, n.d.; Chun & Maniatis, 2009; Bai, 2010; Barbosa, Hahn, Barbosa, & Geyer, 2008; Hsu, Hsieh, Lo, Hsu, Cheng, Chen, & Lai, 2011; Shuai, 2011; Fogel, 2010; Chao, 2012). Cloud computing service models: IaaS, PaaS and particularly SaaS provide flexible and efficient ways to augment computing, storage and communication capabilities of mobile learning services and application. This chapter investigated possibilities for delivering mobile learning services through cloud computing. A model for mobile learning services delivering through cloud computing was proposed. Different approaches and techniques of mobile cloud computing in learning were discussed.

Several examples of mobile services provided on cloud are presented in this work: ELAB Android native application that provides Moodle LMS fetaures, SMS service, and mobile application for managing infrastructure of e-learning system.

Future researches are directed toward testing proposed model in real e-learning ecosystem. Further, in order to use all features and benefits of ubiquitous learning new mobile learning services should be developed and integrated on cloud infrastructure.

REFERENCES

Ally, M. (2009). *Mobile learning: Transforming the delivery of education and training.* Retrieved from http://www.aupress.ca/books/120155/ebook/99Z_Mohamed_Ally_2009-MobileLearning.pdf

Angin, P., & Bhargava, B. K. (2011). Real-time mobile-cloud computing for context-aware blind navigation. *International Journal of Next Generation Computing, 2*(2).

Bai, X. B. X. (2010). Affordance of ubiquitous learning through cloud computing. In *Proceedings of Frontier of Computer Science and Technology FCST 2010 Fifth International Conference on.* IEEE Computer Society.

Barbosa, J., Hahn, R., Barbosa, D. N. F., & Geyer, C. F. R. (2008). Learning in small and large ubiquitous computing environments. In *Proceedings of 2008 IEEEIFIP International Conference on Embedded and Ubiquitous Computing.* IEEE. Retrieved from http://ieeexplore.ieee.org/lpdocs/epic03/wrapper.htm?arnumber=4756367

Chao, L. (2012). *Cloud computing for teaching and learning: Strategies for design and implementation.* Hershey, PA: IGI Global. doi:10.4018/978-1-4666-0957-0

Chen, G. D., Chang, C. K., & Wang, C. Y. (2008). Ubiquitous learning website: Scaffold learners by mobile devices with information-aware techniques. *Computers & Education, 50*(1), 77–90. doi:10.1016/j.compedu.2006.03.004

Chen, H., & Huang, H. (2010). User acceptance of mobile knowledge management learning system: Design and analysis. *Journal of Educational Technology & Society, 13*(3), 70–77.

Chen, Y. S., Kao, T. C., & Sheu, J. P. (2003). A mobile learning system for scaffolding bird watching learning. *Journal of Computer Assisted Learning, 19*(3), 347–359. doi:10.1046/j.0266-4909.2003.00036.x

Christensen, J. H. (2009). Using RESTful web-services and cloud computing to create next generation mobile applications. In *Proceeding of the 24th ACM SIGPLAN Conference Companion on Object Oriented Programming Systems Languages and Applications OOPSLA 09.* ACM Press. Retrieved from http://portal.acm.org/citation.cfm?doid=1639950.1639958

Chu, H.-C., Hwang, G.-J., Tsai, C.-C., & Tseng, J. C. R. (2010). A two-tier test approach to developing location-aware mobile learning systems for natural science courses. *Computers & Education, 55*(4), 1618–1627. doi:10.1016/j.compedu.2010.07.004

Chun, B., & Maniatis, P. (2009). Augmented smartphone applications through clone cloud execution. *Heart (British Cardiac Society), 43*(5), 8.

Chun, B., & Patti, A. (2011). CloneCloud: Elastic execution between mobile device and cloud. *Most, 17,* 301–314.

Churchill, D., & Hedberg, J. (2008). Learning object design considerations for small-screen handheld devices. *Computers & Education, 50*(3), 881–893. doi:10.1016/j.compedu.2006.09.004

Clough, G., Jones, A. C., McAndrew, P., & Scanlon, E. (2007). Informal learning with PDAs and smartphones. *Journal of Computer Assisted Learning, 24*(5), 359–371. doi:10.1111/j.1365-2729.2007.00268.x

Coulby, C., Hennessey, S., Davies, N., & Fuller, R. (2011). The use of mobile technology for work-based assessment: The student experience. *British Journal of Educational Technology, 42*(2), 251–265. doi:10.1111/j.1467-8535.2009.01022.x

Cuervo, E., Balasubramanian, A., & Cho, D. (2010). MAUI: Making smartphones last longer with code offload. *Energy, 17*(1), 49–62.

Despotovic-Zrakić, M., Marković, A., Bogdanović, Z., Barać, D., & Krčo, S. (2012). Providing adaptivity in moodle LMS courses. *Journal of Educational Technology & Society, 15*(1), 326–338.

Dinh, H. T., Lee, C., Niyato, D., & Wang, P. (2011). A survey of mobile cloud computing: Architecture, applications, and approaches. *Computer*, 1–38. Retrieved from http://onlinelibrary.wiley.com/doi/10.1002/wcm.1203/full

Doering, N. M. (2007). The mainstreaming of mobile learning at a German university. In *Proceedings of Proceedings of the Fifth IEEE International Conference on Pervasive Computing and Communications Workshops* (pp. 159-164). IEEE. doi: 10.1109/PERCOMW.2007.114

El-Hussein, M. O. M., & Cronje, J. C. (2010). Defining mobile learning in the higher education landscape research method. *Higher Education, 13*(3), 12–21.

Fan, X., Cao, J., & Mao, H. (2011). *A survey of mobile cloud computing.* ZTE Corporation.

Ferzli, R., & Khalife, I. (2011). Mobile cloud computing educational tool for image/video processing algorithms. In *Proceedings of 2011 Digital Signal Processing and Signal Processing Education Meeting DSPSPE.* IEEE.

Fogel, R. (2010). *The education cloud: Delivering education as a service.* Intel Corporation.

Gad, S. H. (2011). Cloud computing and MapReduce for reliability and scalability of ubiquitous learning systems. In *Proceedings of the Compilation of the Colocated*, (pp. 273-277). ACM. Retrieved from http://dl.acm.org/citation.cfm?id=2095096

Giurgiu, I., Riva, O., Juric, D., Krivulev, I., & Alonso, G. (2009). Calling the cloud: enabling mobile phones as interfaces to cloud applications. In *Proceedings of the 10th ACMIFIPUSENIX International Conference on Middleware.* Springer-Verlag. Retrieved from http://portal.acm.org/citation.cfm?id=1656987

Graf, S. (2008). Adaptivity and personalization in ubiquitous learning systems. In *HCI and usability for education and work* (LNCS), (vol. 5298, pp. 331-338). Berlin: Springer. Retrieved from http://www.scopus.com/inward/record.url?eid=2-s2.0-70350656112&partnerID=40&md5=19c6ab266a19c8a127a145354ad8fab0

Hsu, J.-T., Hsieh, S.-H., Lo, C.-C., Hsu, C.-H., Cheng, P.-H., Chen, S.-J., & Lai, F.-P. (2011). Ubiquitous mobile personal health system based on cloud computing. In *Proceedings of TENCON 2011 2011 IEEE Region 10 Conference.* IEEE. Retrieved from http://ieeexplore.ieee.org/lpdocs/epic03/wrapper.htm?arnumber=6129036

Hwang, G.-J., & Tsai, C.-C. (2011). Research trends in mobile and ubiquitous learning: A review of publications in selected journals from 2001 to 2010. *British Journal of Educational Technology.* Wiley-Blackwell Publishing Ltd. Retrieved from http://ovidsp.ovid.com/ovidweb.cgi?T=JS&PAGE=reference&D=psyc7&NEWS=N&AN=2011-12000-017

Kovachev, D., Cao, Y., & Klamma, R. (2011). Mobile cloud computing: A comparison of application models. *Information Systems Journal*, (4): 14–23. Retrieved from http://arxiv.org/abs/1107.4940

Laouris, Y., & Eteokleous, N. (2005). We need an educationally relevant definition of mobile. In *Proceedings of mLearn*. Cyprus Neuroscience & Technology Institute. Retrieved from http://citeseerx.ist.psu.edu/viewdoc/download?doi=10.1.1.106.9650&rep=rep1&type=pdf

Ley, D. (2007). *Ubiquitous computing*. Retrieved from http://dera.ioe.ac.uk/1502/2/becta_2007_emergingtechnologies_vol2_report.pdf

Loke, S. W. (2012). Supporting ubiquitous sensor-cloudlets and context-cloudlets: Programming compositions of context-aware systems for mobile users. *Future Generation Computer Systems*, 28(4), 619–632. doi:10.1016/j.future.2011.09.004

Mahamad, S., Ibrahim, M. N., & Taib, S. M. (2010). *M-learning: A new paradigm of learning mathematics in Malaysia*. Retrieved from http://arxiv.org/abs/1009.1170

Martin, S., Diaz, G., Sancristobal, E., Gil, R., Castro, M., & Peire, J. (2011). New technology trends in education: Seven years of forecasts and convergence. *Computers & Education*, 57(3), 1893–1906. doi:10.1016/j.compedu.2011.04.003

Ogata, H., & Yano, Y. (2003). *How ubiquitous computing can support language learning 2*. Retrieved from http://citeseerx.ist.psu.edu/viewdoc/download?doi=10.1.1.77.6786&rep=rep1&type=pdf

Ouf, S., Nasr, M., & Helmy, Y. (2010). An enhanced e-learning ecosystem based on an integration between cloud computing and web 2.0. In *Proceedings of Signal Processing and Information Technology ISSPIT 2010 IEEE International Symposium on*. IEEE. Retrieved from http://ieeexplore.ieee.org/stamp/stamp.jsp?tp=&arnumber=5711721

Romero, C., Ventura, S., & De Bra, P. (2009). Using mobile and web-based computerized tests to evaluate university students. *Computer Applications in Engineering Education*, 17(4), 435–447. doi:10.1002/cae.20242

Samimi, F. A., Mckinley, P. K., & Sadjadi, S. M. (2006). Mobile service clouds: A self-managing infrastructure for autonomic mobile computing services. *Science*, 3996, 130–141.

Sánchez, J., & Olivares, R. (2011). Problem solving and collaboration using mobile serious games. *Computers & Education*, 57(3), 1943–1952. doi:10.1016/j.compedu.2011.04.012

Satyanarayanan, M., Bahl, V., Caceres, R., & Davies, N. (2009). The case for VM-based cloudlets in mobile computing. *IEEE Pervasive Computing / IEEE Computer Society [and] IEEE Communications Society*, 8(4), 14–23. doi:10.1109/MPRV.2009.82

Shanklin, M. (n.d.). *Mobile cloud computing*. Retrieved from: http://www.cse.wustl.edu/~jain/cse574-10/ftp/cloud/index.html

Sharples, M. (2000). The design of personal mobile technologies for lifelong learning. *Computers & Education*, 34(3-4), 177–193. doi:10.1016/S0360-1315(99)00044-5

Shuai, Q. (2011). What will cloud computing provide for Chinese m-learning? In *Proceeding of the International Conference on eEducation Entertainment and eManagement*. IEEE.

Shuai, Q., & Ming-Quan, Z. (2011). Cloud computing promotes the progress of m-learning. In *Proceedings of 2011 International Conference on Uncertainty Reasoning and Knowledge Engineering*. IEEE.

Shuqiang, H., & Hongkuan, Y. (2012). A new mobile learning platform based on mobile cloud computing. *Advances in Intelligent and Soft Computing*, 159, 393–398. doi:10.1007/978-3-642-29387-0_59

Su, J.-M., Tseng, S.-S., Lin, H.-Y., & Chen, C.-H. (2011). A personalized learning content adaptation mechanism to meet diverse user needs in mobile learning environments. *User Modeling and User-Adapted Interaction, 21*(1-2), 5–49. doi:10.1007/s11257-010-9094-0

Uzunboylu, H., & Ozdamli, F. (2011). Teacher perception for m-learning: Scale development and teachers' perceptions. *Journal of Computer Assisted Learning, 27*(6), 544–556. doi:10.1111/j.1365-2729.2011.00415.x

Vazquez-Briseno, M., Vincent, P., Nieto-Hipólito, J. I., & Sánchez-López, J. D. D. (2012). Applying a modular framework to develop mobile applications and services. *Journal of Universal Computer Science, 18*(5), 704–727.

Vouk, M. A., Sills, E., & Dreher, P. (2010). Integration of high-performance computing into cloud computing services. In B. Furht & A. Escalante (Eds.), *Handbook of cloud computing* (pp. 255-276). New York: Springer. Retrieved from http://www.springerlink.com/index/10.1007/978-1-4419-6524-0

Walczak, K., Chmielewski, J., Wiza, W., Rumiński, D., & Skibiński, G. (2011). Adaptable mobile user interfaces for e-learning repositories. In *Proceedings of IADIS International Conference on Mobile Learning* (pp. 10-12). IADIS.

Yin, C. Y. C., David, B., & Chalon, R. (2009). Use your mobile computing devices to learn - Contextual mobile learning system design and case studies. In *Proceedings of 2009 2nd IEEE International Conference on Computer Science and Information Technology*. IEEE. Retrieved from http://ieeexplore.ieee.org/lpdocs/epic03/wrapper.htm?arnumber=5234816

Zhang, X., Schiffman, J., Gibbs, S., Kunjithapatham, A., & Jeong, S. (2009). Securing elastic applications on mobile devices for cloud computing. In *Proceedings of the 2009 ACM Workshop on Cloud Computing Security CCSW 09*. ACM Press. Retrieved from http://portal.acm.org/citation.cfm?doid=1655008.1655026

Zhang, Y., & Chen, J.-L. (2011). A delegation solution for universal identity management in SOA. *IEEE Transactions on Services Computing*. Retrieved from http://ieeexplore.ieee.org/lpdocs/epic03/wrapper.htm?arnumber=5440168

Zhao, W. Z. W., Sun, Y. S. Y., & Dai, L. D. L. (2010). Improving computer basis teaching through mobile communication and cloud computing technology. In *Proceedings of Advanced Computer Theory and Engineering ICACTE 2010 3rd International Conference*. IEEE. Retrieved from http://ieeexplore.ieee.org/xpls/abs_all.jsp?arnumber=5578977

ADDITIONAL READING

Alizadeh, M., & Haslina Hassan, W. (2013). *Challenges and Opportunities of Mobile Cloud Computing*. Challenges and Opportunities of Mobile Cloud Computing. doi:10.1109/IWCMC.2013.6583636

Alzaza, N. S., & Yaakub, A. R. (2011). Students' Awareness and Requirements of Mobile Learning Services in the Higher Education Environment. *American Journal of Economics Business Administration, 3*(1), 95-100. Science Publications. Retrieved from http://search.ebscohost.com/login.aspx?direct=true&db=bth&AN=71490893&site=ehost-live

Chandrasekaran, I. (2011). Mobile Computing with Cloud. In D. Nagamalai, E. Renault, & M. Dhanuskodi (Eds.), *Advances in Parallel Distributed Computing* (Vol. 203, pp. 513–522). Springer Berlin Heidelberg. Retrieved from. doi:10.1007/978-3-642-24037-9_51

Chen, G. C. G., Lu, J. L. J., Huang, J. H. J., & Wu, Z. W. Z. (2010). SaaAS - The mobile agent based service for cloud computing in internet environment.*Natural Computation ICNC 2010 Sixth International Conference on.* IEEE. Retrieved from http://ieeexplore.ieee.org/ielx5/5564900/5582333/05582438.pdf?tp=&arnumber=5582438&isnumber=5582333

Chen, S., Lin, M., & Zhang, H. (2011). Research of mobile learning system based on cloud computing. *Proceeding of the International Conference on eEducation Entertainment and eManagement.* IEEE.

Choi, M., Park, J., & Jeong, Y.-S. (2011). Mobile cloud computing framework for a pervasive and ubiquitous environment. *The Journal of Supercomputing*, 1–26. Retrieved from http://www.springerlink.com/index/10.1007/s11227-011-0681-6

Deepak, G., & Pradeep, B. S. (2012). Challenging Issues and Limitations of Mobile Computing. *Computing, 3*(1), 177–181. Retrieved from http://ijcta.com/documents/volumes/vol3issue1/ijcta2012030132.pdf

Fernandez-Llatas, C., Ibañez, G., Sala, P., Pileggi, S. F., & Naranjo, J. C. (2011). Mobile cloud computing architecture for ubiquitous empowering of people with disabilities. *6th International Conference on Software and Database Technologies ICSOFT 201* (Vol. 1, pp. 377-382). Retrieved from http://www.scopus.com/inward/record.url?eid=2-s2.0-80052572436&partnerID=40&md5=8a86fef3ad016f6e10e579581e155724

Fernando, N., Loke, S. W., & Rahayu, W. (2013). Mobile cloud computing: A survey. *Future Generation Computer Systems, 29*(1), 84-106. Elsevier B.V. Retrieved from http://linkinghub.elsevier.com/retrieve/pii/S0167739X12001318

Georgieva, E. S., Smrikarov, A. S., & Georgiev, T. S. (2011). Evaluation of mobile learning system. *Procedia Computer Science, 3*, 632-637. Elsevier. Retrieved from http://linkinghub.elsevier.com/retrieve/pii/S1877050910004813

Guan, L., Ke, X., Song, M., & Song, J. (2011). A Survey of Research on Mobile Cloud Computing. *2011 10th IEEEACIS International Conference on Computer and Information Science, 48*(1), 387-392. Ieee. Retrieved from http://ieeexplore.ieee.org/lpdocs/epic03/wrapper.htm?arnumber=6086500

Kim, S., Yoon, Y., In, M., Lee, K., & Lee, S. (2011). The evolution of standardization for mobile cloud. *ICTC 2011*. IEEE. Retrieved from http://ieeexplore.ieee.org/xpls/abs_all.jsp?arnumber=6082667

Ma, R. K. K., Lam, K. T., & Wang, C.-L. (2011). eXCloud: Transparent runtime support for scaling mobile applications in cloud. *2011 International Conference on Cloud and Service Computing.* IEEE. Retrieved from http://ieeexplore.ieee.org/lpdocs/epic03/wrapper.htm?arnumber=6138505

Mishra, J., Dash, S. K., & Dash, S. (2012). Mobile-Cloud: A Framework of Cloud Computing for Mobile Application. [). Springer Berlin Heidelberg.]. *Engineering, 86*, 347–356.

Necat, B. (2007). Distance learning for mobile internet users. *The Turkish Online Journal of Distance Education, 8*(2), 1–11.

Nkosi, M. T., & Mekuria, F. (2010). Cloud Computing for Enhanced Mobile Health Applications. *Cloud Computing Technology and Science CloudCom 2010 IEEE Second International Conference on.* IEEE. Retrieved from http://ieeexplore.ieee.org/lpdocs/epic03/wrapper.htm?arnumber=5708511

Paverd, A. J., Inggs, M. R., & Winberg, S. L. (2010). Towards a Framework for Enhanced Mobile Computing Using Cloud Resources. *satnacorgza.* Retrieved from http://www.satnac.org.za/proceedings/2011/papers/Work_In_Progress/Internet_Services_and_Applications/230.pdf

Pu, H., Lin, J., Song, Y., & Liu, F. (2011). Adaptive device context based mobile learning systems. *International Journal of Distance Education Technologies.* IGI Global. Retrieved from http://ovidsp.ovid.com/ovidweb.cgi?T=JS&PAGE=reference&D=psyc7&NEWS=N&AN=2011-10062-003

Qi, H., & Gani, A. (2012). Research on mobile cloud computing: Review, trend and perspectives. *2012 Second International Conference on Digital Information and Communication Technology and its Applications DICTAP,* 195-202. Ieee. Retrieved from http://ieeexplore.ieee.org/lpdocs/epic03/wrapper.htm?arnumber=6215350

Qureshi, S. S., Ahmad, T., Rafique, K., & Shuja-ul-islam. (2011). Mobile cloud computing as future for mobile applications Implementatio methods and challenging issues. *2011 IEEE International Conference on Cloud Computing and Intelligence Systems.* IEEE.

Rongbutsri, N. (2011). Mobile learning for Higher Education in Problem-Based Learning Environment. *Proceedings of the 19th International Conference on Computers in Education ICCE 2011* (pp. 32-35). Retrieved from https://www.scopus.com/inward/record.url?eid=2-s2.0-84860477436&partnerID=40&md5=6b5f5e1d7e9e1244d60e863bd8619d90

Song, W., & Su, X. (2011). Review of Mobile cloud computing 1: Hardware of handheld equipment and independence Virtual layer. *City,* 1-4. Retrieved from http://www.computer.org/portal/web/csdl/doi/10.1109/MC.2010.89

Wang, Q. A. (2011). Mobile Cloud Computing. *Strategies, 31*(6), 624-628. Springer Berlin Heidelberg. Retrieved from http://www.springerlink.com/index/Q4234HM67730023T.pdf

Yang, S. J. H., & Chen, I. Y. L. (2006). Providing Context Aware Learning Services to Learners with Portable Devices. *Sixth IEEE International Conference on Advanced Learning Technologies ICALT06.*

Zhang, X., Kunjithapatham, A., Jeong, S., & Gibbs, S. (2011). Towards an Elastic Application Model for Augmenting the Computing Capabilities of Mobile Devices with Cloud Computing. *Mobile Networks and Applications, 16*(3), 270-284. Springer Netherlands. Retrieved from http://www.springerlink.com/index/10.1007/s11036-011-0305-7

Zimmermann, M. (2011). Adaption of multimedia E-Learning services to mobile environments. *2011 IEEE Global Engineering Education Conference EDUCON.* IEEE. Retrieved from http://ieeexplore.ieee.org/lpdocs/epic03/wrapper.htm?arnumber=5773211

KEY TERMS AND DEFINITIONS

Cloud Computing Application: Is an application program that functions in the cloud, with some characteristics of a pure desktop app and some characteristics of a pure Web application.

Cloud Services: Are designed to provide easy, scalable access to applications, resources and services, and are fully managed by a cloud services provider.

Mobile Cloud Application: Run on servers external to the mobile device and require the use of a browser on the mobile device to display and then use the app user interface.

Mobile Cloud Computing Infrastructure: Can be viewed as a cloud infrastructure enhanced to provide a mobile ecosystem for mobile apps and to allow access to business apps.

Mobile Learning: Is considered to be the ability to use mobile devices to support teaching and learning.

Ubiquitous Computing: Is computing concept which can occur using any device and where computing can appear everywhere and anywhere.

Ubiquitous Learning: May use more context awareness then eLearning to provide most adaptive contents for learners.

Chapter 7
Student Relationship Management Using Social Clouds

Marko Vulić
University of Belgrade, Serbia

Ivanka Kovačević
CT Computers, Serbia

Pavle Petrović
University of Belgrade, Serbia

Vanjica Ratković Živanović
Radio Television Serbia (RTS), Serbia

ABSTRACT

A new vision of higher education systems, in which the student is the central subject of the teaching process, opens up new learning opportunities that include customization of teaching methods to the students' needs, and new modes of communication both between teachers and students and among students themselves. The main subject of this chapter is the implementation and improvement of the Student Relationship Management (SRM) concept as a cloud service in an e-education system by using social media. The experimental part of the chapter presents the design and implementation of an e-education model based on cloud computing. The proposed model is implemented at the Faculty of Organizational Sciences, University of Belgrade, by using the existing cloud computing infrastructure of the Laboratory for E-Business.

INTRODUCTION

Nowadays, concept Customer Relationship Management (hereinafter: CRM) becomes very important for an educational institution that aims to manage with relationships between students, teachers and administrators. Educational institution needs to identify the problems of students and to enhance the cohesion in relationships with them. A good customer relationship is the key to success. The use of customer relationship management systems in education is becoming significantly important for increasing student life time value. Student Relationship Management concept (hereinafter: SRM) is used to present the systematic care of a business relationship between the university and students, where the students are the central subject (Vulić, Barać, & Bogdanović, 2011).

DOI: 10.4018/978-1-4666-5784-7.ch007

Given the possibility of dissemination of information to many users, social computing can play important role in improving the educational process. Many social networks formed groups for educational purposes. This chapter discusses possible solutions for improving relations between students and educational institutions in the process of e-learning through social media. The main focus is on the development of social media metrics that can be applied in e-education. The metrics should be defined with respect to processes in e-education, on strategic and operative levels, and synchronized with the strategy of educational institution. This chapter also deals with metrics that consider the quality of teaching and learning process and learning outcomes.

LITERATURE REVIEW

Customer Relationship Management

Customer relationship management has been defined as a management approach that involves identifying, attracting, developing and maintaining successful customer relationships over time in order to increase the retention of profitable customers. CRM is a coherent and complete set of processes and technologies for managing relationships with current and potential customers and associates of the company, using the marketing, sales and service departments, regardless of the channel of communication (Chen & Popovich, 2003). Presents a highly fragmented environment and has different meanings for different people (Sohrabi, Haghighi, & Khanlari, 2010). CRM is endorsed to generate and administer bonds with clients more efficiently through the itemized and precise analysis of customer information utilizing distinctive information technologies (Peppers & Rogers, 2011). To assess future customer behavior and offer the best possible care, it is necessary to exploit, evaluate and regularly update the company's knowledge about the customer

(Wilde, 2011). CRM is therefore understood as a customer-oriented management approach where information systems provide information to support operational, analytical and collaborative CRM processes and thus contribute to customer profitability and retention (King & Burgess, 2008).

Student Relationship Management

Educational institutions are becoming aware that education belongs to the service industry and students' demands and desires have to be met. Independent learning and teaching is an educational system and consists of sub-systems: a learner, a teacher and a method of communication (Moore, 1973). Blended learning represents a fundamental reconceptualization and reorganization of the teaching and dynamic learning, starting with various specific contextual needs and contingencies (Garrison, & Kanuka, 2004).

The introduction of CRM into e-learning is a long and demanding process, because students' demands are increasing parallel with the growth of technology capability. The steps of the CRM implementation in the field of e-education are the following (Vulić, 2013):

- Defining the CRM goal and strategies, and
- Adaptation and implementation.

From the perspective of the educational institutions, the CRM business strategy provides a clear and complete picture of each individual and all the activities pertaining to the individual. On the other hand, from the perspective of the student, the CRM strategy allows interaction with the educational institutions from a single entity that has a complete understanding of their unique status.

Student Relationship Management is the systematic care of a business relationship between the university and students, where service quality is becoming an ever more interesting question (Vulić, Barać, & Bogdanović, 2011). In this way, student's satisfaction can be increased. Furthermore, the mutual trust can stay intense, even after graduation. Figure 1 shows the life cycle of a SRM concept applied in an educational institution.

In the first phase, trough better presentation of their program, an educational institution wants to attract attention of prospective students. The main aim, of an educational institution, is to influence on the students' final choice for enrolment on their studies. In this period, risk of institution refers to loss of applicants and revenue from scholarship. The next phase begins with the prospective students' decision about the choice of educational institution in which they wish to continue education. In this phase, potential risk of an educational institution is related to potential loss of students and revenue from registration. After enrolment of students, educational institutions' activities are focused on establishing solid relationships with students. The output from this phase includes the enlargement of educational personnel. If an educational institution, during the studies, doesn't pay enough attention to the students' needs and neglects the comments and suggestions, the result of this will be students' dissatisfaction.

Students' dissatisfaction can result with decision about abandoning the studies. In that case, an educational institution will be faced with financial losses. After the completion of undergraduate studies, in case the students decide not to continue their further education, for an educational institution, this can be manifested as loss opportunities for fundraising. The CRM concept has found its application in different areas. Based on the analysis and on the viewpoint of various authors, the theoretical CRM model consists of the following phases and elements shown in Figure 2 (Urbanskienė, Žostautienė, & Chreptavičienė, 2008).

Social CRM

Social CRM is a philosophy and a business strategy, supported by a system and a technology. It's designed to engage the customer in a collaborative interaction that provides mutually beneficial value in a trusted and transparent business environment. Social CRM can provide the tools and strategies for meaningful and accurate insight in customers. It can change the face and nature of gathered information from customers' records. Companies

Figure 1. Lifetime SRM

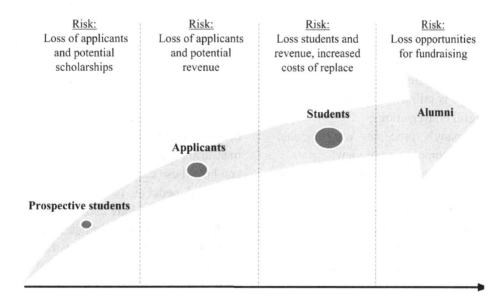

Figure 2. Theoretical CRM model

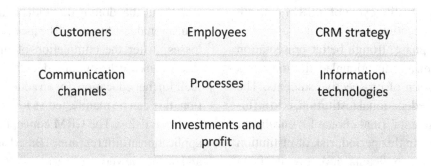

can learn from that information and figure how to apply them. The information includes the nature of conversations about the company by an individual customer, customers associated with an account, or discussions going on in the general population about a company (Greenberg, 2010). Social CRM is based on the ability of a company to meet the personal agendas of their customers, while at the same time meets the objectives of their own business plan. The aim is directed on customer's engagement rather than customer management (Garcia-Crespo, Colomo-Palacios, Gomez-Berbis, & Ruiz-Mezcua, 2010).

The characteristics of Social CRM are (Greenberg, 2010):

- Fully integrated into an enterprise value chain and includes the customer as part of it;
- Customer interactions are encouraged through authenticity and transparency;
- Knowledge is utilized in context to create meaningful conversations;
- The company's processes are modeled from the customer point of view;
- Both information-seeking and information-contributing behavior are encompassed into the customer business ecosystem;
- Resides in a customer ecosystem;
- Creating conversation with customer - engaging customer in activity and discussion - observing and redirecting conversations

among customers are activities done in the marketing frontline;

- Business is an aggregator of experiences, products, services, tools and knowledge for the customer;
- The intellectual property, that is created with the customer, partner, supplier and problem solver, is in together ownership;
- The business is focused on environments and experiences that engage the customer;
- Focus of technology is on both, operational and social/collaborative areas and customer is integrated into the value chain.

Social CRM strategies often involve an integration of new tools with traditional measures. In social-communicative context social networking means the initiation of connection, mostly between strangers. Besides the cultural, media and social contexts, social networks are aimed at interaction as one of the most important communication practices. Social networks typically deal with measuring and quantifying the relationships between individuals in a group. The focus is on measuring interaction of the structural patterns and how these can explain outcomes.

Social media are two-way media. In the most cases, the interactions and dialogues on social media sites have been initiated and conducted by private individuals, rather than company's representatives or officials. Social media can serve as a resource for understanding customers' expressions about the brand (Peppers & Rogers, 2011). Furthermore, social media can be defined as a type of Web page through which the connection of modern Internet technology and interaction is easily enabled (DeAndrea, Ellison, LaRose, Steinfield, & Fiore, 2012). Social media add a level of qualitative information to the quantitative data that are available through Web analytics. The most popular social media applications/services are blogs, wikis, social network sites and micro-blogging (Stuart, 2009).

In terms of social media metrics, blogs have the big advantage of allowing the use of traditional Web analytics. Wiki software can be used for the collaborative creation of Web pages. The success of a wiki may be quantitatively measured in several different ways: number of pages created, number of editors and the amount of edits. Social network site metrics are heavily dependent on the information that a site shares. This can vary considerably not only from site to site but also according to a user's type of account (Stuart, 2009). Social network sites have been defined as Web services that allow individuals to construct public or semi-public profiles, articulate a list of other users with whom they are connected, and view and traverse connections made by others (Boyd & Ellison, 2007). They are usually based on the Internet or mobile technologies. Professional title for social Web services is the Social Network Services (hereinafter: SNS). SNS allow the user to create and maintain personal or business contacts through a network with close friends or business partners (Radovanović, 2010). Represent one of the most popular forms of online communication. They enable the exchange and review of large amounts of multimedia content, finding persons of the same interests, exchange of knowledge and experiences. SNS are primarily focused on creating a community of the like-minded or on connecting a particular group of people primarily through the Internet.

Social CRM in E-Education

Educational institutions are becoming aware that education belongs to the service industry. Students' demands and desires have to be met. Independent learning and teaching is an educational system and consists of sub-systems: a learner, a teacher and a method of communication (Moore, 1973). Nowadays, the use of social media represents a trend in scope of educational institutions. Within them, social media are used among employees and between employees and students. Often employees go outside of the institution to participate in environments as Facebook, or use software as a service (SaaS) in the cloud, where they create their own social environments. Possible problems are that employees expose the organization to potential risk, and the organization misses an opportunity to make community collaboration a valuable corporate competence (Bradley & McDonald, 2011).

Setting a vision for community collaboration is the first step in gaining control. A vision tells people which community collaboration is valued and will be actively pursued. Building the strategy involves two main activities (Bradley & McDonald, 2011):

- Establishing the resources for intelligent selection from multitude of community collaboration possibilities;
- Determining where and when to invest, or continue investing, in specific collaborative communities.

Strategy always begins with purpose. Purpose drives all other strategy considerations. Social organizations must understand the central role of purpose. Determination of the power and potential value of purpose can be done by assessing it against the following characteristics (Bradley & McDonald, 2011):

- **Magnetic:** The purpose should naturally draw people to participate.
- **Business-Aligned:** The purpose should have a clear alignment with business goals.
- **Low Community Risk:** The purpose, especially early in an organization's use of community collaboration, should not run against the grain of the current culture in the community or the institution.
- **Measurable:** Institution should be able to measure the success of a good purpose.
- **Facilitates Evolution:** Select purposes that you and the community can build on.

The CRM integration into e-learning is a long and demanding process because students' demands simultaneously increase with the growth of technology capability. Defining the CRM goal and strategies, adaptation and implementation, represents the steps of the CRM implementation in e-learning field. From the students' perspective, the CRM strategy allows interaction with the educational institutions from a single entity that has a complete understanding of their unique status. On the other hand, from the perspective of the educational institutions, the CRM business strategy provides a clear and complete picture of each individual and all the activities pertaining to the individual.

SRM is a new vision of higher education system in which the student is the central subject of the teaching process. It opens up learning opportunities that include customization to the student and teaching methods, modes of communication, both between teachers and students and among students themselves (Kumar, 2008). Data related to students' characteristics and interaction are substantial for SRM. Collected data should be acquired, stored, analyzed, distributed and applied throughout the educational institution in a timely manner. Educational institutions need to consider which data about students are required for supporting analytics and operational processes.

SRM technologies are fundamental part of any educational institution's application portfolio and architecture. Requirements of SRM application should be considered as providing of integrated functionality that supports seamless student-centric processes across all areas of the learning.

Performance measurement is one of the key aspects of managing the SRM system. It's very hard to effectively manage SRM system, if educational institutions don't have insight in functionality of the system. Well defined SRM system metrics increases chances for success through synchronization of processes in an educational institution. This affects on increase of quality of the educational process. The absence of appropriate SRM metrics has bad influence on students' results, communication and satisfaction of their demands.

Techniques of performance measurement and system metrics put focus on key performance indicators. Bigger part of literature focuses on analysis and classification of system for performance management, and smaller part to SRM metrics. SRM must be observed as one entity and system for performance measurement must have global character. Goal is development of system metrics that enables identification of fields for improvement SRM system performance. In this way, educational institution can focus their efforts and achieve better performance.

With considering all specificity of SRM system, system metrics should satisfy following criteria:

- Metrics are based on processes;
- Metrics are defined on all levels (strategic, operative);
- Metrics are synchronized with the strategy of educational institutions;
- Metrics cover all relevant processes.

Standard definitions, quality description, formulas for calculation and relations between metrics on different levels, provide standard and consistent performance measurement of SRM system on global level, and in internal and collaborative processes. Important element of system metrics are descriptions and instructions for collecting data that are necessary for defining metrics.

SRM MODEL IN E-EDUCATION

The advantages of modern information and communication technologies allow to connect students with teachers, as well as students and colleagues in many manners: from communicating via electronic mail (e-mail), talking over the Internet (chat), maintenance of electronic conferences (forum), teaching in an electronic classroom (e-classroom).

Figure 3 shows the influence of CRM in an educational institution (Beyou, 2005).

Figure 3 shows significance of good communication between educational institution and teaching staff with students. Positive or negative influence between elements of educational CRM model is presented with "+" and "-" symbols. Node of communication processes, in an educational institution, represents a portal which enables access for teachers, students, and other users. Students' satisfaction with educational system of the institution where they study, positively affect on their attitude toward the same. Students' loyalty toward educational institution decreases/ disappears if they decide not to continue their further education at the institution (postgraduate

Figure 3. Influence of CRM in an educational institution

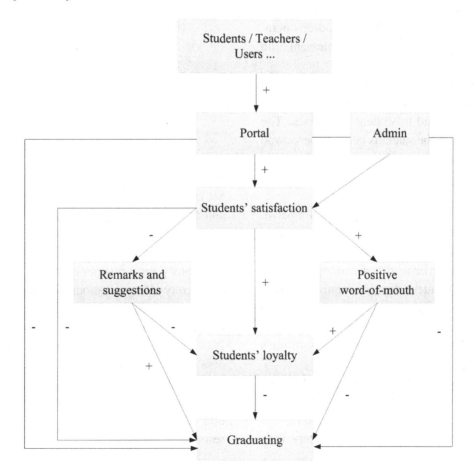

studies). If the teaching staff and the management of educational institutions do not consider students' suggestions and opinions on possible improvements related to the educational process, their dissatisfaction and lack of loyalty toward educational institution may arise.

SRM Metrics in E-Education

Figure 4 shows building blocks for successful SRM projects (Vulić, 2012). The framework can be used for internal learning and debate in developing the SRM vision and SRM strategies.

The educational institution must take proactive approach in creating a student relationship management. The SRM vision should be used as a guide to the creation of a SRM strategy. The strategy refers to build and develop a valuable asset - database with students' information. It must set objectives and metrics for attaining that goal. It directs the objectives of other operational strategies and the SRM implementation strategy.

The student experience must be designed in line with the SRM vision and must be constantly updated with regard to students' feedback. The relationship with the students needs to be viewed and managed in terms of the student's life cycle. Formalized processes must exist for managing this life cycle.

Data about students present the key for SRM. It must be acquired, stored, analyzed, distributed and applied throughout the educational institution in a timely manner. Educational institutions should consider what student data are required to support the desired insight (analytics) and interaction (operational) processes. SRM technologies form a fundamental part of any educational institution's application portfolio and architecture.

SRM metrics not only gauge the level of success, but also provide the feedback mechanism for continuous development of strategy and tactics. They must follow and measure the enterprise's

Figure 4. SRM building blocks

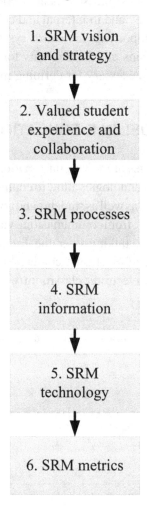

SRM strategy. A hierarchy of metrics is necessary and depends on their purpose and who using them.

In this chapter, teaching and learning processes for graduate master studies are considered in the Laboratory for e-business (hereinafter: Elab) at the Faculty of Organizational Sciences, University of Belgrade. These processes are realized using blended learning concept (Garrison & Kanuka, 2004). E-learning courses deal with area of business information systems, Internet technologies and Internet marketing. Moodle LMS (Learning Management System) is used for realization of common e-learning activities (learning resources, assignments, communication, etc.)

and system administration (course management, students' enrolment, etc.). CRM activities are implemented through SugarCRM. This software solution provides variety of features that enables implementation of CRM activities in e-learning, such as collaboration and communication among teachers and students. It provides students with appropriate information about course schedule, course promotions, users' roles and management, analytics of students' activities.

The following processes are identified as important for this study:

- Promotion of studies,
- Admission of new students,
- Realization of studies,
- Master thesis defense.

A promotion of studies is one of the most important SRM processes. Features of SugarCRM solution, faculty Website and social networks are tools used for promotion. Following activities are performed within processes, such as: e-mail marketing, forum, Elab Facebook page, YouTube channel, Android application, etc. Table 1 provides description of metrics for studies promotion.

Figure 5 presents sequence diagram for process of student admission.

Elab's SRM features are implemented in accordance to the activities related to the student admission. After available initial information via faculty's Web site and social networks about student's admission, Elab's collects information about students that intend to study their master studies within the Laboratory.

Data are stored through CRM module "Leads." After entrance examination, the students who passed the test receive new roles. They become Contacts in Elab's SRM. Furthermore, students are automatically enrolled in appropriate Moodle LMS course (Figure 6).

Based on information about number of students and teachers on a particular course, CRM activity schedule is created. Students from the Moodle's course get information via e-mail. Teachers can classify students into the groups. At the same time, schedule is available on Moodle LMS course, as well as on the official Elab Facebook page (Figure 7). Page contains basic information about a course and gives students an opportunity to get more familiar with the course subject.

Detailed description of the metrics related to process of admission of new students is presented in Table 2.

Realization of the course is the most complex process within an e-learning system. Figure 8 shows main activities within this process. Main SRM activities performed during the course realization are: statistic analysis about students' interaction with the e-learning system, fostering collaboration and communication among e-learning system users, announcements, publishing information related to lectures, labs and examination.

Table 1. Metrics for process of studies promotion

Attribute of Performance	Definition	SRM Metrics
The number of social media interactions	Conversation is related to the number of blog posts, forum discussions, tweets on the social network site. Volume is a strong metric when is measured over time.	Conversation volume
The details of online customers	Social tools for listening customers can collect data location, gender, and age of customers.	Demographic metrics
The number of total impressions in an online and offline discussion	Measured by the number of different sources covering a topic and each source potential official site views.	Message reach
The number of students' discussions around educational institution	Frequency and qualitative analysis related to discussions about an educational institution brand.	Topic frequency

Figure 5. Student admission

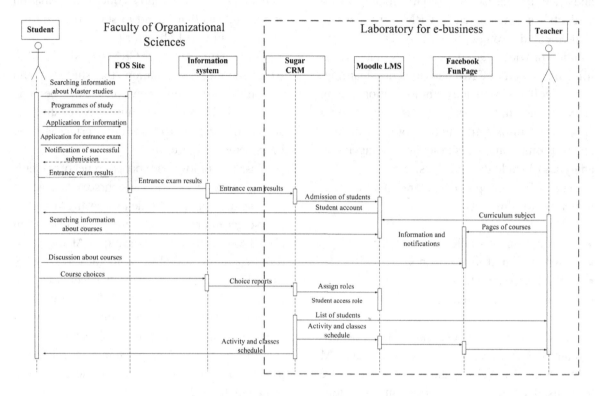

Figure 6. SRM portal of the Elab

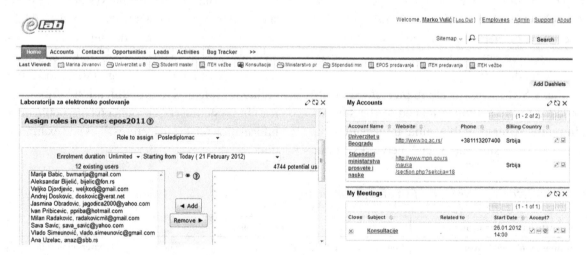

Figure 9 shows one of the Elab's courses in Moodle LMS.

Table 3 provides description of metrics for realization of the studies.

Figure 10 presents the process of Master thesis defence.

Table 4 presents main identified metrics for process of Master thesis defence.

Figure 7. Elab Facebook page

Table 2. Metrics for process of admission of new students

Attribute of Performance	Definition	SRM Metrics
The attitudes of students	Non-adequate analysis of the students' needs and neglecting comments and suggestions that can be made by educational institutions during the studies can result with dissatisfaction and a large negative impact on the students and future prospective candidates.	Sentiment Type
Financial position	University provides financial benefits for some students.	Student equity
The number of company partners	The number of enterprises that signed contracts with the university.	Practice work
Distance and speed of spreading information	Measured by number of different entries around the same topic within a certain time period.	Viral propagation

Figure 8. Activities of course realization in e-learning process

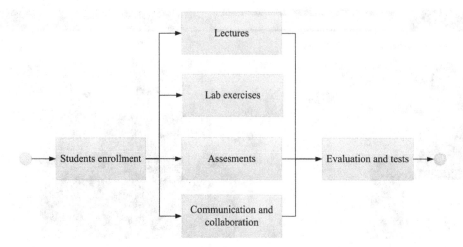

Figure 9. Moodle LMS: E-business course

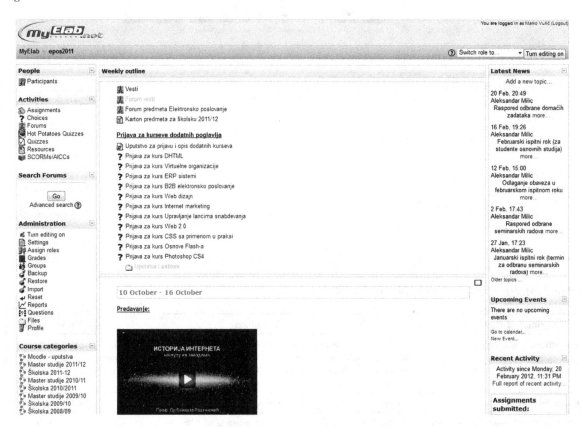

Table 3. Metrics for process of the studies realization

Attribute of Performance	Definition	SRM Metrics
The number of access to LMS	Automatically collected data from Web server logs. These are rich collections of data related to specific Web pages.	The intensity of the use of LMS
The number of posts on forum	Interactivity between students and teachers in the Moodle LMS system is measured through the amount of comments, which clearly shows the interest of both sides for good communication and obtains the necessary information.	The intensity of the interaction trough Moodle LMS
The number of group members	Interactivity between students and teachers in social networks is measured trough the number of posts. Significant indicator of student's interest for the Elab's Web site is the number of Web site views.	The intensity of the interaction on social networks
The average score	The sum of scores that students' achieved on assignments and tests that are available in the Elab courses.	Students' results
The number of students who pass the exam	The number of students who pass the exam in each test period.	Time of examination
Percent of students who pass the exam	Passed/Failed	The passing rate on the exam

Figure 10. Process of master thesis defence

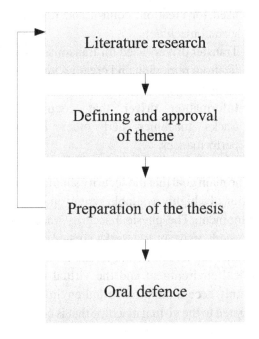

IMPLEMENTATION OF SRM THROUGH CLOUD COMPUTING

Cloud computing refers to providing and using computational resources via the Internet (Sultan, 2010). It enables the access to technology in the form of service on demand. Services and data coexist in shared and dynamically scaled set of resources (Jin et al., 2010). The concept of cloud computing is based on technology of virtualization (Costanzo, Assuncao, & Buyya, 2009). It enables resources to be used when they are necessary. Virtualization provides logical instead of physical computing resources. Depending on the type of infrastructure ownership and physical resources, the following models of cloud computing can be developed (Jin et al., 2010): private cloud, public

Table 4. Metrics for process of Master thesis defense

Attribute of Performance	Definition	SRM Metrics
The number of student referrals	The number of students who have previously finished final paper with the teachers or listened courses in his department.	Good reputation of educational process
Satisfaction with the professor's work	Availability of teachers for consultation and help, as well as recommendations for practice and work.	Expertise and availability of teacher
The number of open opportunities	Percentage of students who were employed in the profession after graduation.	Employed students

cloud, hybrid cloud and community cloud. There are three ways of access to cloud services (Costanzo, Assuncao, & Buyya, 2009): infrastructure (IaaS), platform (PaaS) and application (SaaS).

Applying cloud computing in higher education institutions improves the efficiency of existing resources usage, as well as the reliability and scalability of software tools and applications for e-learning. When the system becomes busy and overloaded, the problem of scalability could be solved by adding new physical resources. Introducing new resources implies a significant increase in costs. According to that fact, it is necessary to find other ways of solving the problem of scalability and usage of resources. A simultaneous access to common resources is one of the most important problems in using the IT infrastructure. When it is talk about cloud computing application in the realization of a higher education IT infrastructure, three basic approaches can be noticed: full outsourcing of infrastructure, cloud in private and combination of two previous approaches.

The basic components of the faculty SRM model in e-learning are:

- Services for e-learning (identity management system, e-mail, LMS, document management system, CRM, portal services, business intelligence, etc.);
- Software components: MS SharePoint Server 2010, Moodle, IIS, Apache, MySql, etc.;
- Network and hardware infrastructure;
- Users (students, non-teaching staff, etc.).

The first phase in the development and implementation of the private cloud model is the consolidation of computer resources of a higher education institution. The requirements that private cloud model should fulfill are following: security, credentials and distributed file system (DFS). Virtual machine system management enables users to choose, start and turn off virtual machine image via Web interface.

The primary goal of a private cloud implementation is to provide users with the run of virtualized infrastructure, environment and services. The virtual infrastructure management system automates, coordinates and integrates the existing solutions for: networking, storage, virtualization, and monitoring and user management. The key components of implemented private cloud enable an efficient work with the virtual machine. Virtual machines are put on the image repository and can be moved and run on users' demands. The system component for virtual machine management allows achieving of scalability and reliability of implemented services on the virtual machine. The private cloud layer (Driver) that enables access by using virtualized infrastructure includes:

- Virtual Machine Manager (VMM) driver used for creation, control and tracking of virtual machine;
- Transfer drivers used for transmission, replication, removing and creating virtual machine images;
- Information driver that controls and tracks machines and other hardware performances.

The main goal that the security should fulfill is creation of a highly available system and a secure environment. The physical security, that makes the system resistant to attacks created at virtual machine, requires a strict separation between the physical environment and the virtual machine. The only access point to virtual environment is delegated to the virtual machine that is connected to the physical network interface. By using a firewall, the system is protected from unauthorized access to virtual networks and to the system itself. The firewall disables the communication between virtual machines in configured virtual networks.

In the scope of private cloud development, the following software tools were implemented: Operating system - Centos 5.6 64 bit, Xen - hypervisor, OpenNebula 3.0 - virtual infrastructure management system, MooseFS - distributed file system, Moodle 1.9 LMS and Sugar CRM. By using the implemented model (Figure 11) the system achieves better agility, because now it is possible to transfer the virtual machine to any other hardware and get better performances and response time from the operating system and application. All these improvements do not have an interference impact on the users that are connected to the particular virtual machine at that moment.

SRM as SaaS on Cloud Computing Infrastructure for E-Learning

The developed cloud computing infrastructure is used in the realization of the whole teaching and scientific process at the Faculty of Organizational Sciences, University of Belgrade. The cloud computing infrastructure enables the realization/

hosting of all services and additional tools with the best possible performances.

All courses organized within e-Lab are realized via the learning portal (Despotovic-Zrakić, Marković, Bogdanović, Barać, & Krčo, 2012). Web portals are complex sites that combine different information from multiple sources and provide access to numerous applications. The learning Web portal is a single access point to all relevant information, resources and applications in the learning process. Main requirements that learning Web portal should fulfill are:

- Ensure students with an easy access of useful information and learning services;
- Open lines of interaction among the community users;
- Allow both students and teachers to share information for common class activities;

Figure 11. E-education model based on cloud computing

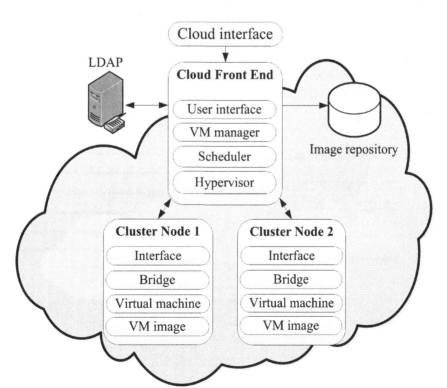

- Provide a tool for faculties and universities to innovate teaching and a tool for students to experience alternative forms of learning;
- Use a single consistent Web-based front end or interface to present information from a variety of resources.

The primary role of the learning Web portal, in this research, is the integration of e-learning system components. The existing Moodle LMS for e-learning is enriched with additional services for managing communication and interaction. Figure 12 shows homepage of SRM portal.

In order to overcome these problems and improve the system performances, Elab has implemented a cloud computing infrastructure. The implemented infrastructure based on cloud computing enables an efficient and scalable work of teachers and students. For the purposes of the teaching process, the virtual machine is deployed and the required services and work environment are installed.

Within the portal following features are provided: information management, filtering, as well as services for notifications, report creating and presentation to users. In this way the portal provides single access point to various personalized services and shared information. Single sign on feature enables users to authentication themselves once and access all relevant data. This option differ portal from Web services, where users have to log in each time they use different functionality. The portal has aggregator and integrator role, as it make connection with all activity and resources that are available locally and as distributed applications. One of the Web services that are integrated in the portal is SMS service.

Mobile service (Ozeki Message Server), as integrated part of portal, provides possibility for sending notifications when particularly requirement is fulfilled (Figure 13 and Figure 14) (Vulić, Labus, & Milić, 2011). By using this service teachers can send notifications to different users

Figure 12. SRM portal homepage

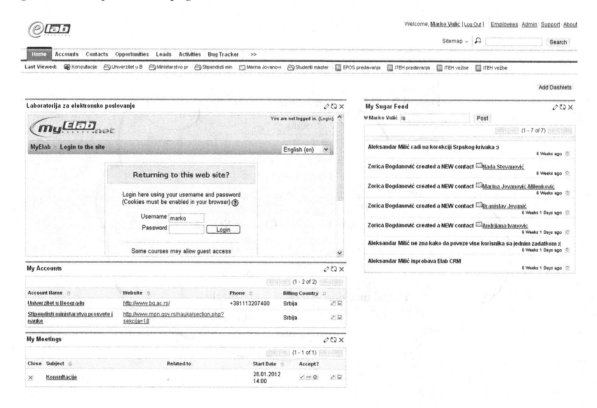

Figure 13. Sequence diagram for sending SMS

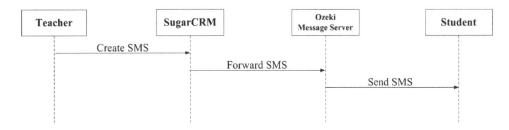

Figure 14. Message sending form

via SMS. Integration between the portal and SMS server enables sending automatic and personalized information about learning activities.

Figure 15 shows notification from teacher to student via short message.

Figures 16 through 18 show schedule of classes for students of master studies in Elab (Figure 16), detailed view of teachers who are in charge for teaching for specified day (Figure 17) and daily list of teacher engagement in class (Figure 18).

CONCLUSION

This chapter provides a description of social media metrics and the possibilities of their use in e-education. For educational institutions, concept of CRM presents a tool for more effective management of communication. The educational institutions that use the CRM are able to automate activities such as generating and sending e-mails,

Figure 15. Received SMS notification

Figure 16. Schedule of classes for master studies

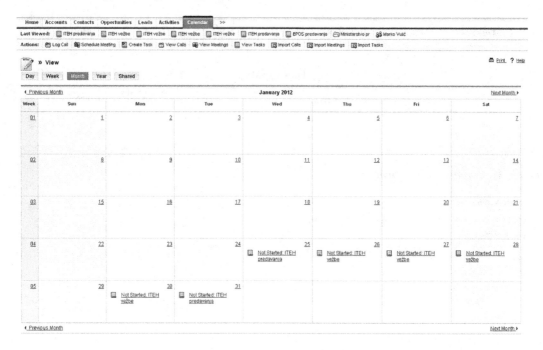

Figure 17. Schedule of classes for master studies with name of teachers

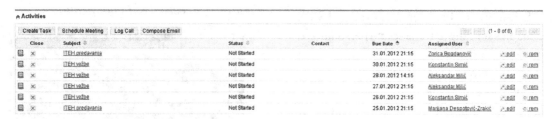

Figure 18. Teacher's daily activity

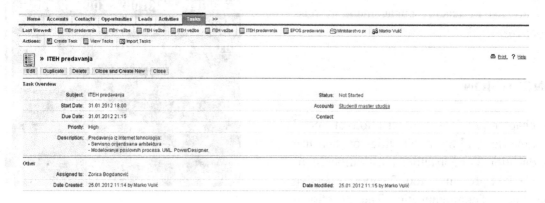

responding to student requests for a particular type of information, etc. The system based on maintaining relationships with students, the prospective students and the graduates represents the imperatives of competitiveness.

Customer interactions, conversations, and relationships transform CRM into social CRM. CRM metrics not only gauge the level of success, but also provide the feedback mechanism for continuous development of strategy and tactics. CRM metrics must follow and measure the enterprise's CRM strategy. A hierarchy of metrics is required and depends on their purpose and who using them.

The future research directions include the improving of social media model, more detailed consideration of the indicators in the field of e-education and highlighting the significance of social media in all areas of education and educational institutions.

REFERENCES

Beyou, D. (2005, March/April). Treating students like customers. *BizEd Magazine*, 44-47.

Boyd, D. M., & Ellison, N. B. (2007). Social network sites: Definition, history, and scholarship. *Journal of Computer-Mediated Communication*, *13*(1), 210–230. doi:10.1111/j.1083-6101.2007.00393.x

Bradley, A. J., & McDonald, M. P. (Eds.). (2011). *The social organization: How to use social media to tap the collective genius of your customers and employees*. Boston: Harvard Business Review Press.

Chen, I. J., & Popovich, K. (2003). Understanding customer relationship management (CRM), people, process and technology. *Business Process Management Journal*, *9*(5), 672–688. doi:10.1108/14637150310496758

Costanzo, A. D., Assuncao, M. D. D., & Buyya, R. (2009). Harnessing cloud technologies for a virtualized distributed computing infrastructure. *IEEE Internet Computing*, *13*(5), 24–33. doi:10.1109/MIC.2009.108

DeAndrea, D. C., Ellison, N. B., LaRose, R., Steinfield, C., & Fiore, A. (2012). Serious social media: On the use of social media for improving students' adjustment to college. *The Internet and Higher Education*, *15*(1), 15–23. doi:10.1016/j.iheduc.2011.05.009

Despotovic-Zrakić, M., Marković, A., Bogdanović, Z., Barać, D., & Krčo, S. (2012). Providing adaptivity in moodle LMS courses. *Journal of Educational Technology & Society*, *15*(1), 326–338.

Garcia-Crespo, A., Colomo-Palacios, R., Gomez-Berbis, J. M., & Ruiz-Mezcua, B. (2010). SEMO: A framework for customer social networks analysis based on semantics. *Journal of Information Technology*, *25*(2), 178–188. doi:10.1057/jit.2010.1

Garrison, D. R., & Kanuka, H. A. (2004). Blended learning: Uncovering its transformative potential in higher education. *The Internet and Higher Education*, *7*(2), 95–105. doi:10.1016/j.iheduc.2004.02.001

Greenberg, P. (2010). The impact of CRM 2.0 on customer insight. *Journal of Business and Industrial Marketing*, *25*(6), 410–419. doi:10.1108/08858621011066008

Greenberg, P. (Ed.). (2010). *CRM at the speed of light: Social CRM strategies, tools, and techniques for engaging your customers* (4th ed.). New York: McGraw-Hill Companies, Inc.

Jin, H., Ibrahim, S., Bell, T., Gao, W., Huang, D., & Wu, S. (2010). Cloud types and services. In B. Furht & A. Escalante (Eds.), Handbook of cloud computing (pp. 335-355). New York: Springer Science+Business Media.

King, S. F., & Burgess, T. F. (2008). Understanding success and failure in customer relationship management. *Industrial Marketing Management*, *37*(4), 421–431. doi:10.1016/j.indmarman.2007.02.005

Kumar, M. (2008). *Customer relationship management in services, focus: Educational institutions. New Delhi*. Hyderabad: ICFAI Business School.

Moore, M. G. (1973). Grahame toward a theory of independent learning and teaching. *The Journal of Higher Education*, *44*(9), 661–679. doi:10.2307/1980599

Peppers, D., & Rogers, M. (Eds.). (2011). *Managing customer relationships: A strategic framework* (2nd ed.). Hoboken, NJ: John Wiley & Sons, Inc.

Radenković, B., Despotović-Zrakić, M., Labus, A., & Vulić, M. (2011). Enhancing e-education process with social networking. In *Proceedings of SED 2011, 4th International Conference Science and Higher Education in Function of Sustainble Development* (pp. 1-7). Užice: Visoka poslovnotehnička škola strukovnih studija.

Radovanović, D. (2010). Internet paradigma, struktura i dinamika onlajn društvenih mreža: Fejsbuk i mladi u Srbiji. In *Proceedings of International Interdisciplinary Conference Problems of Adolescence,* (pp. 20-26). Serbia: Pančevačko čitalište.

Sohrabi, B., Haghighi, M., & Khanlari, A. (2010). Customer relationship management maturity model (CRM3): A model for stepwise implementation. *International Journal of Human Sciences*, *7*(1), 1–20.

Stuart, D. (2009). Social media metrics. *Online*, *33*(6), 22–24.

Sultan, N. (2010). Cloud computing for education: A new dawn? *International Journal of Information Management*, *30*(2), 101–182. doi:10.1016/j.ijinfomgt.2009.09.004

Urbanskienė, R., Žostautienė, D., & Chreptavičienė, V. (2008). The model of creation of customer relationship management (CRM) system. *The Engineering Economist*, *3*(3), 51–59.

Vulić, M. (2013). *Student relationship management model in e-education*. (Doctoral dissertation). University of Belgrade, Belgrade, Serbia.

Vulić, M., Barać, D., & Bogdanović, Z. (2011). CRM as a cloud service in e-education. In *Proceedings of 19th Telecommunications Forum (TELFOR)* (pp. 1470-1473). Belgrade: Telecommunications Society and Academic Mind.

Vulić, M., Labus, A., & Milić, A. (2011). Application of mobile services for improving CRM concept in e-education. *InfoM*, *10*(39), 55–60.

Wilde, S. (Ed.). (2011). *Customer knowledge management: Improving customer relationship through knowledge application*. Berlin: Springer Verlag. doi:10.1007/978-3-642-16475-0

ADDITIONAL READING

Baird, C. H., & Parasnis, G. (2011). From social media to social CRM - What customers want. *IBM Global Business Services Executive Report,* 1-20. Retrieved September 1, 2013, from http://public.dhe.ibm.com/common/ssi/ecm/en/gbe03391usen/GBE03391USEN.PDF

Band, W., & Petouhoff, N. (2010). *Topic Overview: Social CRM Goes Mainstream*. Cambridge: Forrester Research Inc.

Bejou, D. (2005). Treating students like customers. *BizEd Magazine, March/April*, 44–47.

Bogdanovic, Z., Barac, D., Labus, A., Simic, K., & Vulic, M. (2012). Student relationship management in the cloud. In L. Gomez Chova, A. Lopez Martinez, I. Candel Torres (Eds.), *Proceedings of 6th International Technology, Education and Development Conference (INTED 2012)* (pp. 1079–1088). Valencia: INTED2012 Organising Committee.

Bogdanovic, Z., Jovanic, B., Barac, D., Milic, A., & Despotovic-Zrakic, M. (2011). An application of cloud computing as infrastructure for Eeducation. In *L. Gómez Chova, D. Martí Belenguer*. A. López.

Chard, K., Caton, S., Rana, O., & Bubendorfer, K. (2010). Social cloud: Cloud computing in social networks. In *IEEE 3rd International Conference on Cloud Computing (CLOUD)* (pp. 99-106). Miami: IEEE, Inc.

Cheung, C. M. K., Chiu, P.-Y., & Lee, M. K. O. (2011). Online social networks: Why do students use Facebook? *Computers in Human Behavior, 27*(4), 1337–1343. doi:10.1016/j.chb.2010.07.028

Chine, K. (2009). Scientific computing environments in the age of virtualization toward a universal platform for the cloud. In B. G. Hu, X.Y. Xie, C. Saguez, C. Gomez (Eds.), *2009 IEEE International Workshop on Open-Source Software for Scientific Computation* (pp. 44-48). USA: IEEE.

Elnaffar, S., Maamar, Z., & Sheng, Q. Z. (2013). When clouds start socializing: The sky model. [IJEBR]. *International Journal of E-Business Research, 9*(2), 1–7. doi:10.4018/jebr.2013040101

Ercan T. (2010). Effective use of cloud computing in educational institutions. *Procedia - Social and Behavioral Sciences, 2(2)*, 938-942.

Falasi, A. A., Serhani, M. A., & Elnaffar, S. (2013). The sky: A social approach to clouds federation. *Procedia Computer Science, 19*(0), 131–138. doi:10.1016/j.procs.2013.06.022

Grant, G. B., & Anderson, G. (2002). Customer relationship management: A vision for higher education. In Richard N. Katz & Associates (Eds.), Web Portals and Higher Education: Technologies to Make IT Personal (pp. 23-32). San Francisco: Jossey-Bass a Wiley Company.

Greenberg, P. (2010). The impact of CRM 2.0 on customer insight. *Journal of Business and Industrial Marketing, 25*(6), 410–419. doi:10.1108/08858621011066008

Greenberg, P. (Ed.). (2010). *CRM at the speed of light: Social CRM strategies, tools, and techniques for engaging your customers (fourth.)*. USA: The McGraw-Hill Companies.

Krishnakumar, K., & Jayakumar, A. (2009). CRM in education. Retrieved September 1, 2013, from http://www.articlesbase.com/college-and-university-articles/crm-in-education-1033696.html

Labus, A., Bogdanović, Z., Vulić, M., Radenković, B., & Despotović-Zrakić, M. (2011). Application of social networks in education. In V. Žuborova, D. Camelia Iancu, U. Pinterič (Eds.), *International Scientific Conference: Digitalisation of Cultural and Scientific Heritage, University Repositories and Distance Learning* (pp. 423-442). Fiesa: Založba Vega, Ljubljana.

Labus, A., Simić, K., Vulić, M., Despotović-Zrakić, M., & Bogdanović, Z. (2012). An application of social media in eLearning 2.0. In U. Lechner, D. Lux Wigand, A. Pucihar (Eds.), The 25th Bled eConference eDependability: Reliable and Trustworthy eStructures, eProcesses, eOperations and eServices for the Future (pp. 557-572). Kranj: Moderna organizacija.

Mahmood, Z., & Hill, R. (Eds.). (2011). *Cloud computing for enterprise architectures*. London: Springer Verlag. doi:10.1007/978-1-4471-2236-4

Martínez (Ed.). (n.d.). *Edulearn11 International Conference on Education and new Learning Technologies*. (pp. 4699-4707). Spain: International Association of Technology, Education and Development (IATED).

Naismith, L. (2007). Using text messaging to support administrative communication in higher education. *Active Learning in Higher Education, 8*(2), 155–171. doi:10.1177/1469787407078000

Piedade, M. B., & Santos, M. Y. (2008). Student relationship management: Concept, practice and technological support. In *IEEE International Engineering Management Conference (IEMC Europe) 2008*. (pp. 1-5). IEEE, Inc.

Praveena, K., & Betsy, T. (2009). Application of cloud computing in academia. *The IUP Journal of Systems Management, 7*(3), 50–54.

Reinhold, O., & Alt, R. (2011). Analytical social CRM: Concept and tool support. In 24th Bled eConference eFuture: Creating Solutions for the Individual, Organisations and Society (pp. 226–241). Kranj: Moderna organizacija.

Reinhold, O., & Alt, R. (2012). Social customer relationship management: State of the art and leanings from current projects. In U. Lechner, D. Lux Wigand, A. Pucihar (Eds.), 25th Bled eConference eDependability: Reliable and Trustworthy eStructures, eProcesses, eOperations and eServices for the Future (pp. 155–169). Kranj: Moderna organizacija.

Trainor, K. J., Andzulis, J. M., Rapp, A., & Agnihotri, R. (2013). Social media technology usage and customer relationship performance: A capabilities-based examination of social CRM. *Journal of Business Research, 2013*. doi: doi:10.1016/j.jbusres.2013.05.002

KEY TERMS AND DEFINITIONS

Cloud Computing (CC): An infrastructure that brings a new value to an e-learning system, because provides suitable environment for ubiquitous learning activities that can be delivered in a reliable and efficient way.

Customer Relationship Management (CRM): The management approach that involves identifying, attracting, developing and maintaining successful customer relationships over time in order to increase the retention of profitable customers.

E-Learning: Represents all forms of electronically supported learning and teaching which have aim to effect on the construction of knowledge of the learners.

Social Computing (SoC): An interactive and collaborative behavior between computer users, where the Internet allows them to interact through social media tools, such as: social networks, blogs, microblogging services, multiplayer games, wikis and instant messages.

Social CRM: A philosophy and a business strategy, supported by a system and a technology, designed to engage the customer in a collaborative interaction that provides mutually beneficial value in a trusted and transparent business environment.

Social Media: Term is related to use of the technology and platforms that enable collaboration among participants through the creation and exchange of interactive content on Web.

Student Relationship Management (SRM): A specialized CRM concept applied to academic institutions, which involves automating and synchronizing a number of different processes such as academic advising and counseling, in aim to improve the student experience, reduce dropout rates, and improve organizational efficiency.

Student Relationship Management Metrics: Represent measures of success and feedback mechanism for continuous development of strategies and tactics of an educational institution.

Chapter 8
Ontology-Based Multimodal Language Learning

Miloš Milutinović
University of Belgrade, Serbia

Vukašin Stojiljković
Institute for the Serbian Language of the Serbian Academy of Sciences and Arts, Serbia

Saša Lazarević
University of Belgrade, Serbia

ABSTRACT

L2 language learning is an activity that is becoming increasingly ubiquitous and learner-centric in order to support lifelong learning. Applications for learning are constrained by multiple technical and educational requirements and should support multiple platforms and multiple approaches to learning. This chapter investigates the possibility of applying ontology-based, dynamically generated learning objects implemented on a cloud computing infrastructure in order to satisfy these requirements. Previous work on using mobile learning objects is used as a starting point in an attempt to design a system that will preserve all of the advantages of utilizing learning objects, while eliminating any flaws and maximizing compatibility with existing systems. A model of a highly modular, flexible, multiplatform language learning system is presented along with some implementation remarks and advices for future implementation.

INTRODUCTION

Modern society is constantly in a state of flux, and changing lifestyles impose the development of new paradigms in the field of education. Language learning is an especially vibrant area, since learners are not limited by previous education, age, or profession. Mobile technologies are only the latest ingredient in a dynamic socio-technological landscape, allowing learners to control the preferred pace and the location of learning. This is a large step towards achieving omnipresent learning or "learning at any place, any time" (Holzinger, Nischelwitzer, Friedl, & Hu, 2010). With learning often being performed on the move, the challenge is to integrate learning processes across all environments in order to provide a true ubiquitous learning experience.

DOI: 10.4018/978-1-4666-5784-7.ch008

Language learning applications can appear in several forms - as desktop, mobile, and Web applications. Although many such applications are designed for a single platform, there is a tendency of convergence towards Web-centric solutions accessible from all platforms and devices. This underlines the problem of adaptation of learning processes and educational materials for a specific platform. Language learning applications should attempt to provide seamless integration across all domains, preferably by operating on an established core of common principles.

Designers of language learning applications need to adjust the learning environment and the presentation of educational content in order to find an optimal model of interaction with the users. Richer forms of content (images, audio, video) can enable multimodal learning and are especially helpful to less motivated learners. Methods of delivery, storage and presentation need to be adjusted to the capabilities of specific platforms and devices, as well as the cognitive capacity of learners, which might be limited in some contexts. Learning objects are a suitable concept for encapsulation and delivery of independent, reusable educational resources with a specific educational goal (McGreal, 2004). Learning objects are somewhat flexible since they can be aggregated into larger educational units, but are still strictly limited by their data model and by various technical constraints inherent to their design. In order to support a truly multimodal, multiplatform, ubiquitous learning experience, additional flexibility is required at all levels of design and implementation.

Rigid models designed for a specific purpose or platform can be replaced with a richer description of the language learning domain using ontologies. An ontology represents an open vocabulary, a model to describe the world using types, attributes, and relations, at any level of detail desired. The downside of using ontologies is the increased complexity of both the design and the implementation. A more complex model will produce more complex information resources, requiring an appropriate storage system and access methods in order to satisfy client applications. A cloud-based infrastructure presents itself as an appropriate solution for a Web based, interconnected, ontology application that caters to different client applications and provides a multitude of services that operate on common data standards.

This chapter explores the possibility of using an expandable, evolving ontology of language concepts in order to describe the language-learning domain and provide a basis for generation of learning objects and provision of language learning services. The main aim was to design a model for a language learning system that can satisfy several key requirements - to be usable on various platforms, to provide for different learning processes, and to allow unlimited expansion according to developing needs. The resulting model relies on several established theoretical concepts and practical technologies, including learning objects, ontologies, cloud computing, and Web services.

LITERATURE REVIEW

Modern computing devices vary both in size and hardware characteristics, as well as in platform architectures utilized. Most of these devices are capable of supporting various applications and processes, with even the smallest devices being capable of accessing the Internet and utilizing remote resources or processing power. This has also influenced the development of software, bringing about a diversification and specialization of applications for certain platforms, as well as the opposite process of unification through Web-based services and interfaces.

New possibilities such as seamless and ubiquitous language learning are being made possible thanks to the improved power and connectivity of modern mobile platforms (Ogata & Yano, 2003).

Learning is being pushed closer to the learners using nonstandard devices, while mobile devices are taking over the role of creating seamlessly connected learning experiences and making a pedagogical shift to a participatory student-centered learning (Looi et al., 2010). Specific hardware elements like built-in GPS, cameras, sensors, accelerometers, and compasses can be introduced into the learning process as valuable sources of context information (Godwin-Jones, 2011). Learner motivation and the ability to control the process of learning are strongly tied in to the mobile learning experience, which places the learners' personal factors and behavioral patterns in an important position (Sha, Looi, Chen, & Zhang, 2012). Well designed mobile applications exert a motivating effect on language learners and generally offer enough studying opportunities in order to create a positive impact on the learning process (Wang, Shen, Novak, & Pan, 2009). A three year research has shown a growing popularity of mobile devices in vocabulary learning, with some learners showing patterns of interchangeable use of both desktop and mobile platforms (Stockwell, 2010). When considering all the possibilities and modalities of use introduced to language learning by mobile devices, it is clear that learning applications can benefit from supporting a wide array of different platforms, and for the best outcome should attempt to integrate desktop and mobile learning into a single process.

Several important questions arise when considering such a generic language learning system. The first question is how the educational materials will be structured. The same structure is not appropriate for use on both the desktop and the mobile devices. Learning materials for desktop devices should feature longer, richer lessons, while the constraints of the mobile environment impose the use of smaller, highly granulated and more focused educational units. However, developing two sets of educational resources in advance is wasteful and introduces discrepancies that com-plicate any integration effort. A solution would be to structure the knowledge into small, discrete, reusable units that can be aggregated into larger ones as needed. Since the need for reusable learning materials is not new, a concept that satisfies stated requirements already exists in the area of e-education under the name of learning objects.

Learning Objects and Reuse across Platforms

Learning objects are often described inconsistently by different authors, with some describing them as any entities that can be used for learning, education and training (IEEE Learning Technology Standards Committee, 2002), and others requiring the existence of some specific elements like having a goal and a method of assessment beforehand (L'Allier, 1997). Most, however, put the emphasis on their characteristics: smaller scope, reusability, relative independence, and the possibility of aggregation. Another consistent point is that their capabilities generally stem from their heavy reliance on metadata. Metadata can describe the learning object content in several ways, comprising both the technical and the educational descriptive data. Using metadata, better, more efficient information use can be facilitated, providing higher quality search results to human users, and allowing machines to use the strictly defined relationships between information objects to apply higher-level logic in their processing.

Different metadata models and standards for learning objects have been developed, IEEE Learning Object Metadata (LOM) being among the most prominent. Another, more general metadata vocabulary is Dublin Core that defines a set of 15 core properties applicable to information resources. Both standards provide for flexibility – IEEE LOM allows the definition of application profiles, modifications for a specific application, while the simpler Dublin Core was intended to be a core element set that can be further augmented with new elements or refined using qualifiers (Weibel, 2005). They also contain provisions for describing content of different formats, and IEEE LOM can even describe specific technical requirements for learning object use. With flexible metadata, the problem is often the format of the actual educational content.

Some popular and well supported standards for learning objects and their content are the IMS Content Packaging (CP) (IMS Global Learning Consortium, 2007) and the Sharable Content Object Reference Model (SCORM) that further expands on the IMS CP (Advanced Distributed Learning, 2009). Both standards use content packages with the content being mostly comprised from browser-openable files, typically in the HTML format. All content is packed inside a single file, as a structure of files and folders, with a special "manifest" file and a number of XML and DTD schemas. These files are mostly used as transport packages to ensure interoperability between different LMS systems. Learners access this content in the form of HTML pages, mixed with markup and style data, using a Web browser. In order to display SCORM objects on mobile devices, their content usually needs to be manually repurposed. Most SCORM implementations use frames or popup windows that are not consistently supported by mobile browsers and potentially offer a poor user experience. Native mobile applications for SCORM playback behave as replacements for Web browsers modified to satisfy SCORM requirements; mobile application developers must adapt to a technology that is not designed to be used on their platforms.

Specialized mobile learning objects are not as popular as more established standards like SCORM, but some existing research papers provide an interesting insight. In (Bradley, Haynes, Cook, Boyle, & Smith, 2008), authors develop cohesive (with a single learning objective) and decoupled (no external links, all content encapsulated) learning objects, starting from already existing desktop learning objects. By using the Flash Lite technology, the authors' resulting objects contain presentation and content intermingled together, and there is a risk of objects created by different individuals looking and behaving differently. Some authors describe design principles for mobile learning objects and give advice concerning educational content granulation, interface organization, and multimedia adjustment for small screens. Churchill gives a set of recommendations for presentation on small screens of mobile devices, mainly about different ways of displaying and repeating the content on a limited surface while avoiding complexity of user interface (Churchill & Hedberg, 2008). Such recommendations also imply that the developer of educational content should also design the user interface and presentation of content.

In order to develop a truly flexible set of learning resources, a clear separation of concern is needed. If educational content is rid of extraneous detail, it will inherently be much more reusable. Presentation details can be added later by services that operate on educational content or by actual platform-native applications that are best aware of their own presentation capabilities. Even without presentation, the educational content itself still might need to be adjusted in volume and complexity according to the device capabilities. This can be achieved using some form of device based reasoning (Chorfi, Sevkli, & Bousbahi, 2012), but the content model and its metamodel need to be rich and flexible enough to support some higher level logic that would perform needed adjustments. Learning objects can be used as bricks to produce larger, aggregated objects, but the quality of the result will depend on the size and flexibility of individual units. The smaller the learning objects are, the easier it will be to mix them as needed, but they will contain less learning context in return. An ideal solution would be to have the smallest possible and preferably atomic content units that would still retain some semantic links to various levels of context information.

Ontologies and Wordnets for Language Learning

Ontologies can be used to produce a rich model of a language learning domain in line with the previously outlined requirements. A short, concise definition of ontologies states that they are a "formal, explicit specification of a shared conceptualization" (Gruber, 1993). Ontologies can be said to be similar to meta-models or class diagrams in software engineering, since they use types, attributes and relations to describe some domain of the world. Relationships in ontologies are strongly typed, so any actual form of relationship existing between two concepts can be expressed in detail. Ontologies allow their creators to define them at will and to make them as powerful as needed. If designed properly, ontologies can accurately describe any domain, but caution needs to be exercised. The ontology designer needs to balance the expressiveness of the designed ontology with its complexity.

When developing a new ontology, two different approaches can be undertaken. The first is to analyze the domain of interest and to define only the relevant concepts, resulting in a simple, specialized ontology. The other approach is to analyze and reuse other existing domain ontologies or, if none are available, use generic upper and mid level ontologies as a general concept/relation vocabulary upon which a new, specific domain ontology will be designed. Both approaches have some merit; the first simplifies the resulting ontology, while the second simplifies the design process and maximizes interoperability. A combined approach is also valid, and any ontology development effort should first start by exploring similar developments (Noy & McGuinness, 2001).

Ontologies can be found in several domains relevant to language learning. A starting point for language learning is often the vocabulary, and several machine readable vocabularies, "wordnets," exist, defining concepts, words and their relations in different languages. The original wordnet was developed by Princeton for English language and is described by its authors as a lexical database (Miller, 1995). Other authors often refer to it as an ontology and it has been linked to formal ontologies like SUMO upper ontology (Fellbaum, 2010). Similar projects in different languages have been modeled after the WordNet, one of them being the EuroWordNet that encompasses eight languages. This wordnet is especially interesting for language learning since words in different languages are interconnected with interlingual links stored in a Interlingual Index (ILI) (Vossen, 2002). A similar project is BabelNet, which integrates lexicographic and encyclopedic knowledge from WordNet and Wikipedia and boasts coverage of 50 languages (Navigli & Ponzetto, 2012).

Vocabulary learning is specific in the level of granularity of content that can be achieved. Other aspects of language learning might require more content in order to be comprehensible (e.g. grammar lesson that explains rules and provides examples) and some general cases of ontology application in e-learning are highly relevant. A learning object repository can be combined with an ontology of relationships between objects, providing a basis for serving content adjusted to learner and device models (Basaeed, Berri, Zemerly, & Benlamri, 2007). The use of ontologies can facilitate adaptivity by describing both the specific educational domain, and the more general domain of learning and learning context. The Loco-cite ontology framework (Jovanović, Gašević, Knight, & Richards, 2007) utilizes several ontologies to this end: content structure ontology, content type ontology, topic/relation ontology, learning design ontology, user model ontology, and the learning object context ontology. Semantically described learning resources can be used in curriculum sequencing to produce personalized learning paths for each learner (C.M. Chen, 2009).

A MODEL FOR ONTOLOGY BASED LANGUAGE LEARNING

In order to design a learning system that will support various learning processes on different devices and future evolvability, all components must be selected appropriately. In this section we outline a model for language learning that will utilize the following components:

- An ontology as a flexible, detailed data model, and a knowledge base containing ontology-compliant instances of concepts;
- Learning objects for delivery of educational content to learners and institutions;

- Web services as a platform-neutral, developer-friendly interface for accessing system functions;
- Cloud computing infrastructure for scalability support.

We base our suggestions on previous experiences in related areas, and especially on our previous work on designing a mobile language learning system based on lightweight learning objects (Milutinović, Labus, Stojiljković, Bogdanović, & Despotović-Zrakić, 2013). The comparison of the developed J-GO learning objects and the IMS-CP based packages (e.g. SCORM) outlined in this chapter is a valid starting point for further consideration and is given in Figure 1.

Figure 1. Comparison of IMS CP-based packages and lightweight J-GO XML files (Milutinović et al., 2013)

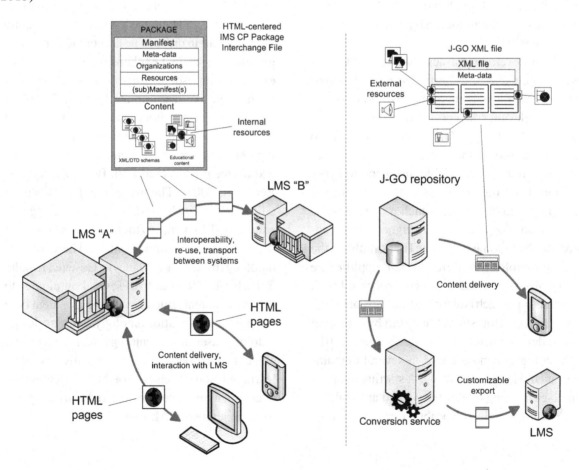

IMS-CP based learning objects are often used for achieving interoperability, re-use and transport between learning management systems. The main method of accessing such learning objects is through an LMS, using a Web browser. Alternatives do exist, and some special mobile clients behave as "playback devices," locally mimicking the required environment and interacting with an LMS in background. J-GO objects were designed with different priorities, as lightweight objects that can directly be delivered to the mobile learners. The principle of separation of concerns was applied, so the J-GO objects themselves do not contain any presentation elements and are platform-independent. For even better reusability, use of conversion services to produce custom format objects was envisioned as a simple future expansion.

Both types of learning objects have a strictly defined structure and format, and introducing any changes not predicted by the content model will break their compatibility to client applications. The model presented in this chapter (Figure 2) was developed in response to this issue, with a more elementary set of learning resources being placed at the core of the system instead of the pre-formed learning objects. The formatting and

Figure 2. The proposed model for cloud & ontology based language learning

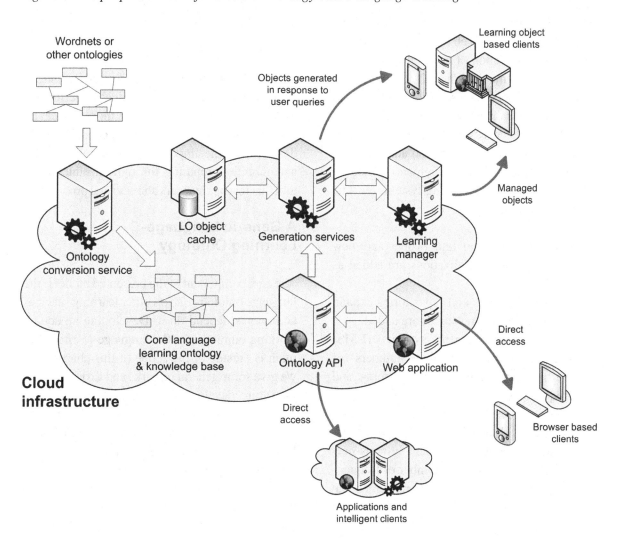

structuring of learning objects were considered as separate, higher level problems, allowing the independent development of various services that can operate on a core set of elements to produce any desired output.

Cloud Infrastructure in Language Learning

The use of ontologies provides many possibilities, with some added complexity. The designed learning system should be completely transparent for the users and they should be shielded from any added complexity. For a Web-centric learning system this can be achieved by providing access to core concepts through Web services (Kreger, 2003) operating with standard interchange format like XML and JSON. Web services allow easier sharing and integration of components between educational systems (W. Chen, 2002). Some examples of Web services used for e-learning can be found in (Kocabicak & Dural, 2012; Peredo, Canales, Menchaca, & Peredo, 2011).

Learning systems must expand and evolve in order to adapt to changing requirements. Ontology and Web-service based learning systems must be scalable in several aspects:

- Ontologies expand and evolve and new concepts and specializations are added as needed.
- Knowledge bases and repositories expand as more learning resources are added.
- Learning management systems (LMS) need to support varying numbers of learners, with different use patterns and frequencies.
- Web services inherently support communication with any system that operates on standard data formats. Client systems may independently grow in number of frequency of use. Service-provided resources can often be utilized in ways not predictable at design time.

In order to support high flexibility and scalability of the entire system, the implementation can be placed on a cloud computing infrastructure. Cloud computing is a set of disciplines, technologies, and business models for delivery of hardware, platforms, and software as a scalable, on-demand, elastic service (Blakley & Reeves, 2010). Educational institutions can utilize their computing resources to develop private cloud infrastructures and decrease expenses for deployment of new equipment and services. An overview of benefits stemming from cloud computing application in educational institutions is given in (Ercan, 2010). An example of a successful implementation of a private cloud in an educational institution, covering all three levels of cloud service models can be found in (Doelitzscher, Sulistio, Reich, Kuijs, & Wolf, 2010).

Mobile learning can especially benefit from cloud computing since processing, storage, and adaptation of educational resources can be performed using cloud resources instead of those on heavily constrained devices. (Ferzli & Khalife, 2011) demonstrate the importance of coupling cloud and mobile computing through an educational tool that teaches learners about visual processing.

A Generic Language-Learning Ontology

The core component of the presented model is the language ontology and all other learning services and clients depend on it. Developing an actual, working ontology for the language-learning domain is outside of the scope of this chapter, but we give some general remarks and a rough model for future development. When defining a new ontology, the first step is to define its domain and scope (Noy & McGuinness, 2001). The language learning domain will likely require concepts of varying complexity to be described – starting from simple "words" and "concepts" described by words, to larger units like grammar rules, typical sentences, or even entire units, lessons and courses.

The ontology development process is iterative, and starting constraints can be revised later, and new concepts added if necessary.

When developing an ontology, any existing similar ontologies should be analyzed and reused, if possible. We suggest using one or more of existing wordnets to describe core vocabulary concepts in the system. The original, English wordnet, defines several relations, including synonymy, antonymy, hyponymy, meronymy, troponomy, and entailment (Miller, 1995). These relations connect both the concepts (e.g. jet plane is a type of plane, toe is a part of foot), and the words (e.g. interrogate, interrogator, interrogation), providing rich semantics that can be utilized for generation of tailored learning resources. Other wordnets follow similar principles, but our proposal for ontology structure attempts to remain somewhat more generic in order to remain flexible implementation-wise. Some wordnets differ slightly, with most adopting some of the fundamental design changes introduced by EuroWordNet (Fellbaum, 2010). Not all wordnets are available for free use and may require compliance with different licences. Combining any two separate wordnets to make them usable for language learning will also require some adjustments according to the degree of their similarity. Combinations of wordnets with other resources like BabelNet (Navigli & Ponzetto, 2012) can also

be cleverly utilized to acquire advanced textual and multimedia descriptions for concepts/words, allowing the creation of richer learning objects. Because of all the variables in selecting and using a wordnet, only the generic multilayer ontology structure is given (Figure 3) for a wordnet-based or similar system.

The concept layer and the word layer correspond to any single wordnet. Concept layer should contain a set of describable concepts that exist in any of the languages for which the system is being developed. Relations between concepts should describe actual, real-world relations that can be later used by learners to navigate the domain (e.g. "generate a learning object about car parts"). The words should be defined in a word layer, and every word should be connected to concept it describes. The relations between these two layers will then represent a core vocabulary in a single language. In order to enable language learning, more than one language should be present in this layer, with all languages referencing the same set of core concepts. Such construction can provide translations between words groups (sets of synonyms – synsets) through common connections to core concepts, but in order to provide best translations for individual words, an additional translation layer should be added. This layer should address which synonyms from two languages best

Figure 3. The generic structure of the language learning ontology

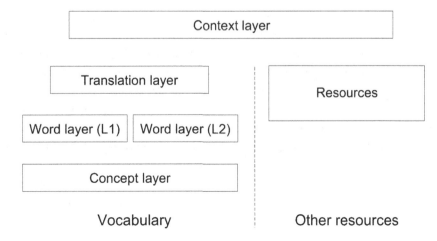

correspond to each other, especially considering the context of their use.

Taken together, the concept, word, and translation layers result in useable vocabulary learning units. For other, non-word types of learning resources, their relations and structure should be provided as separate components. This will include somewhat larger units like grammar rules and reading lessons, as well as the external, reused resources that cannot be restructured easily. If an existing learning object repository is being integrated into a new ontology-based system, such objects might be numerous, and their metadata should be extracted and inserted into the ontology, with any relations between units also being described there. A similar approach with already existing learning objects combined with an ontology can be found at (Basaeed et al., 2007). For increased richness, these resources can reference concepts in the vocabulary section, but these relations should be considered non-essential.

If all vocabulary units and other resources are annotated adequately, they can be used by some higher-level logic to generate learning objects of specified complexity, content type, and topic. However, learning objects tend to contain minimal context in order to maximize reusability, and this is especially likely to be true for learning objects composed out of even smaller learning units. In order to provide additional context when needed, a final layer should stand at the top of the ontology, with concepts to describe larger learning units like lessons, and non-reusable or partially reusable "glue" units that tie other elements together and infuse them with context (McKinney, 2003). The concepts at this layer can be used by teachers to create sets of lessons or courses according to some preconception.

The proposed ontology provides a basis for generation of custom learning objects and general properties of such objects need to be considered. The main trait of learning objects is their reusability, which is achieved by concentrating on a single educational goal and removing unnecessary context. Reusability is often inversely proportional to the amount of context infused in the learning objects, and larger objects will inherently contain more context. Similar conclusions and a model of multilevel content hierarchy are given by Hodgins (Hodgins, 2004). In our previous work on mobile learning objects, we have developed a comparable hierarchy with more bias towards smaller objects better suited for mobile devices (Milutinović et al., 2013). The use of the ontology at the core of the system provides a basis for generation of objects at all levels of hierarchy, and a comparison with Hodgins's and our own hierarchy is shown in Figure 4.

The lowest level of the hierarchy are the "raw" elements, in this case the atomic instances defined by the ontology - words, concepts, grammar rules, other language learning units, and semantic relations between them. The next level is that of an information object that describes a single concept, and is represented by a single concept and its main relations (e.g. a word and its translation, explanation, example, synonyms). Above that are actual learning objects, which contain several concepts connected by relations of a different "mid-range" type, with each concept bringing its own main relations to the mix. An example would be a learning object about "car parts" with several words and their translations. There is no limit to how many concepts and relations can be included in the learning object, and in an extreme case, the entire ontology can be considered as a single learning object. In practice, it is up to the implementation of the system to decide the size of generated learning objects and the higher levels of content hierarchy can be emulated by increasing the size and the complexity of automatically generated learning objects. In order to increase the quality of larger educational units (lessons, courses) we propose the manual or semi-manual injection of context elements defined at the context level of the ontology to serve as a "glue" for other materials, per requirements of teachers using the system.

Figure 4. The comparison of content hierarchy described by Hodgins and by Milutinović (Hodgins, 2004; Milutinović et al., 2013) with the ontology-based hierarchy

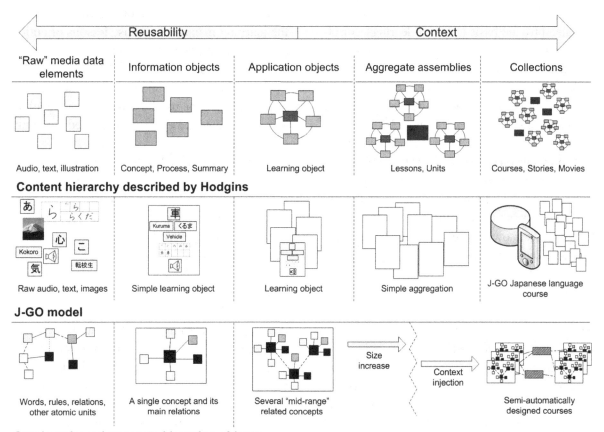

Content hierarchy described by Hodgins

J-GO model

Ontology-based generated learning objects

Cloud-Based Web Services for Language Learning

After a core ontology is defined and appropriate wordnets or other sources are selected, a transformation from external sources into a usable language learning ontology needs to be defined. Depending on the similarity of sources to the designed ontology, this process might require the input of human users and might need to be performed gradually. The source also might be incomplete and still in development, or only a partial version might be available for free. In that case, a permanent conversion service could be developed, potentially keeping the developed ontology up-to-date with any changes the original

developers make. All automatically transferred and unverified concepts and relations can be marked accordingly and made invisible to learners, allowing utilization of a partially populated system.

All access to the core ontology should be performed through a Web service offering a consistent API to both internal and external clients. Using APIs internally will promote modularity and eliminate duplication of code for common ontology operations. This creates another point of separation of concerns, with internal functioning of the system being free to change as long as the API remains constant. The API serves two main purposes internally. The first, necessary addition to the model is a management interface that will be used by system administrators and teachers to administrate and review the educational content and its semantic relations. This interface can be developed in the form of a Web application, and can also provide basic access to learners, for elementary browsing of words and other concepts. The other purpose is to provide services to some higher level logic that will generate learning objects according to external requirements. External clients of this service represent applications, intelligent clients, and systems of other institutions that cooperate on the project. The highly granular nature of learning resources in the ontology makes it less useful directly for learning purposes and any clients using the ontology API are expected to apply their own logic before presenting the results to learners.

A well developed, consistent API can provide for any number of services and applications, including an important component of the model, the generation services. These services are tasked with generating usable learning materials in the form of learning objects or other standard forms (e.g. Web pages, word documents) according to user or application queries. The generation services can again be accessed through an internal or external Web interface or a client application that uses any of supported, generated formats.

Generation services should accept a number of parameters that will determine the final form of the generated objects. With richly annotated educational materials, complex search queries can be defined by the users or their client applications, and the services can automatically recognize client device types, or accept such information as additional query parameters. Parameter combinations can result in many learning objects of different structure and format that might need to be generated. In order to offload some work from the ontology API, we suggest that often generated objects be cached and delivered as needed, similar to a regular learning object repository.

Generation services respond to requests and generate appropriate learning objects, but do not concern themselves with the actual learning pro-

cess. This role should be placed a level above and entrusted to a separate learning manager service. Teachers can use a Web interface built on top of the learning manager to devise lessons or entire courses, and add context information to the ontology. The learning manager can be expanded to track learner progress and form a learner model, which can then be used to direct the generation services and to produce personalized learning objects and lessons.

The outlined model relies on a number of Web services, Web interfaces, and clients as elements for provision of a language learning process on various devices and platforms. Services and interfaces at all levels of hierarchy (ontology API, generation service, learning manager) can be offered to external clients. With multiple options, both thin and fat clients can use the learning system, as well as the existing learning applications that use supported learning object formats. Depending on the amount and type of clients, service utilization patterns might be unpredictable. Dynamic provisioning of cloud resources can be utilized to provide automatic scaling of offered services. The modular, Web service based architecture envisioned in the presented model allows easy separation of all services to independent virtual machines in the cloud. Most cloud infrastructures provide several types of performance tracking, and services that exhibit spikes in resource consumption can get additional resources allotted or new VM instances added.

FUTURE RESEARCH DIRECTIONS

The presented model is designed as a first step towards an actual implementation and therefore provides a number of points for future research. The modularity of the model and the strict separation of concerns help us to analyze different problems independently. A detailed analysis of existing wordnets and their cross-compatibility should be performed to determine the best candidates for inclusion in a language learning system. Other sources of both semantic and non-semantic data should also be taken into consideration, including regular vocabularies and encyclopedias, and other ontologies that can be incorporated into, or used along with the ontology developed for language learning.

When describing a model of the proposed ontology in this chapter, we have mainly concentrated on its vocabulary aspect, where the highest level of granulation of concepts and richness of semantic relations can be achieved. Future works should also attempt to deconstruct other types of language resources to a similar extent.

Higher level components of the presented model, like the learning object generation services should be developed on a small set of manually prepared learning resources. The generated objects should be presented to actual learners in order to ascertain the type and the extent of the semantic relations that contribute most to the quality of the result.

Finally, the model presented in this chapter does not represent a learning management system, but mainly an educational resource repository and a delivery system. The proposed services could be utilized to introduce LMS capabilities to the system on top of the existing model and infrastructure. Another approach would be to explore more substantial methods of integration with various existing LMSs, although a certain level of interoperability can already be achieved through standard learning object formats.

CONCLUSION

In this chapter we have presented a model for a cloud and ontology-based multiplatform language learning system. The ontology at the core of the system was envisioned to describe atomic language learning resources and numerous semantic relations between them, with a special accent on vocabulary learning. The core resources can then be utilized to produce learning objects or resources of any desired format, using a higher-level logic that can base its decisions on external parameters like the device and learner model.

The price of increased flexibility of learning resources is the increased complexity of establishing and maintaining an ontology. The rest of the model attempts to offset this increase in complexity in several ways. First, we considered the reuse of external ontologies and resources like wordnets that define useful relations between words and concepts. Second, we proposed the development of a hierarchy of Web services on top of the ontology in order to hide the complexity of the underlying system using strictly defined interfaces. By envisioning a hierarchy of Web services, problems in the domain were also cleanly separated into several parts - knowledge base, data access, learning object generation, and learning management. Finally, the cloud infrastructure was proposed as a method of simplifying management and providing scalability of various Web services. The use of cloud infrastructure also supports future expansion, integration and cooperation with other systems and institutions.

Future research will mainly concentrate on implementing the core ontology and producing a sufficient volume of language learning resources in order to test higher level logic for generation of learning objects. Another important point that needs to be considered is the integration with existing LMSs and generation of user models that would be utilized in combination with the device models to produce both technically and pedagogically adjusted learning objects for each learner.

REFERENCES

Advanced Distributed Learning. (2009). *SCORM 2004 content aggregation model* [CAM]. 4th ed.). Alexandria, VA: ADL Initiative.

Basaeed, E., Berri, J., Zemerly, M. J., & Benlamri, R. (2007). Learner-centric context-aware mobile learning. *IEEE Multidisciplinary Engineering Education Magazine, 2*(2), 30–33.

Blakley, B., & Reeves, D. (Eds.). (2010). *Defining cloud computing*. Stamford, CT: Gartner Inc.

Bradley, C., Haynes, R., Cook, J., Boyle, T., & Smith, C. (2008). Design and development of multimedia learning objects for mobile phones. In M. Ally (Ed.), *Mobile learning in education and training* (pp. 158–181). Edmonton, Canada: AU Press.

Chen, C.-M. (2009). Ontology-based concept map for planning a personalised learning path. *British Journal of Educational Technology, 40*(6), 1028–1058. doi:10.1111/j.1467-8535.2008.00892.x

Chen, W. (2002). Web services - What do they mean to web-based education? In *Proceedings of International Conference on Computers in Education* (vol. 1, pp. 707-708). Washington, DC: IEEE Computer. Society Press.

Chorfi, H. O., Sevkli, A. Z., & Bousbahi, F. (2012). Mobile learning adaption through a device based reasoning. *Procedia - Social and Behavioral Sciences, 47*, 1707-1712.

Churchill, D., & Hedberg, J. (2008). Learning object design considerations for small-screen handheld devices. *Computers & Education, 50*(3), 881–893. doi:10.1016/j.compedu.2006.09.004

Doelitzscher, F., Sulistio, A., Reich, C., Kuijs, H., & Wolf, D. (2010). Private cloud for collaboration and e-Learning services: From IaaS to SaaS. *Computing, 91*(1), 23–42. doi:10.1007/s00607-010-0106-z

Ercan, T. (2010). Effective use of cloud computing in educational institutions. *Procedia - Social and Behavioral Sciences, 2*(2), 938-942.

Fellbaum, C. (2010). WordNet. In R. Poli, M. Healy, & A. Kameas (Eds.), *Theory and applications of ontology: Computer applications* (pp. 231–243). Dordrecht, The Netherlands: Springer. doi:10.1007/978-90-481-8847-5_10

Ferzli, R., & Khalife, I. (2011). Mobile cloud computing educational tool for image/video processing algorithms. In *Proceedings of 2011 Digital Signal Processing and Signal Processing Education Meeting (DSP/SPE)* (pp. 529-533). Piscataway, NJ: IEEE Signal Processing Society.

Godwin-Jones, R. (2011). Emerging technologies: Mobile apps for language learning. *Language Learning & Technology, 15*(2), 2–11.

Gruber, T. R. (1993). A translation approach to portable ontology specifications. *Knowledge Acquisition, 5*(2), 199–220. doi:10.1006/knac.1993.1008

Hodgins, H. (2004). The future of learning objects. In *Proceedings of 2002 ECI Conference on e-Technologies in Engineering Education: Learning Outcomes Providing Future Possibilities*. ECI.

Holzinger, A., Nischelwitzer, A., Friedl, S., & Hu, B. (2010). Towards life long learning: Three models for ubiquitous applications. *Wireless Communications and Mobile Computing, 10*(10), 1350–1365. doi:10.1002/wcm.715

IEEE Learning Technology Standards Committee. (2002). *Draft standard for learning object metadata*. Institute of Electrical and Electronics Engineers, Inc. Retrieved from http://ltsc.ieee.org/wg12/files/LOM_1484_12_1_v1_Final_Draft.pdf

IMS Global Learning Consortium. (2007). *IMS content packaging specification primer*. Retrieved from http://www.imsglobal.org/content/packaging/cpv1p2pd2/imscp_primerv1p2pd2.html

Jovanović, J., Gašević, D., Knight, C., & Richards, G. (2007). Ontologies for effective use of context in e-learning settings. *Journal of Educational Technology & Society, 10*(3), 47–59.

Kocabicak, U., & Dural, D. (2012). Secure and interoperable e-learning platforms based on web services. *Procedia - Social and Behavioral Sciences, 55*, 1265-1271.

Kreger, H. (2003). Fulfilling the web services promise. *Communications of the ACM, 46*(6), 29. doi:10.1145/777313.777334

L'Allier, J. J. (1997). *Frame of reference: NETg's map to the products, their structure and core beliefs.* Retrieved October 13, 2013, from http://journals.tdl.org/jodi/index.php/jodi/article/viewArticle/89/88

Looi, C.-K., Seow, P., Zhang, B., So, H.-J., Chen, W., & Wong, L.-H. (2010). Leveraging mobile technology for sustainable seamless learning: A research agenda. *British Journal of Educational Technology, 41*(2), 154–169. doi:10.1111/j.1467-8535.2008.00912.x

McGreal, R. (2004). Learning objects: A practical definition. *The Internatonal Journal of Instruction Technology & Distance Learning, 1*(9), 21–32.

McKinney, J. (2003). Shareable content objects (SCORM), whole course design and implementation issues. *Learning Solutions Magazine.* Retrieved October 13, 2013, from http://www.learningsolutionsmag.com/articles/319/shareable-content-objects-scorm-whole-course-design-and-implementation-issues

Miller, G. A. (1995). WordNet: A lexical database for English. *Communications of the ACM, 38*(11), 39–41. doi:10.1145/219717.219748

Milutinović, M., Labus, A., Stojiljković, V., Bogdanović, Z., & Despotović-Zrakić, M. (2013). Designing a mobile language learning system based on lightweight learning objects. *Multimedia Tools and Applications.* doi:10.1007/s11042-013-1704-5

Navigli, R., & Ponzetto, S. P. (2012). BabelNet: The automatic construction, evaluation and application of a wide-coverage multilingual semantic network. *Artificial Intelligence, 193*, 217–250. doi:10.1016/j.artint.2012.07.001

Noy, N. F., & McGuinness, D. L. (2001). *Ontology development 101: A guide to creating your first ontology.* Academic Press.

Ogata, H., & Yano, Y. (2003). How ubiquitous computing can support language learning. In *Proceedings of KEST* (pp. 1-6). Retrieved October 13, 2013, from http://www-b4.is.tokushima-u.ac.jp/ogata/pdf/KEST2003ogata.pdf

Peredo, R., Canales, A., Menchaca, A., & Peredo, I. (2011). Intelligent web-based education system for adaptive learning. *Expert Systems with Applications, 38*(12), 14690–14702. doi:10.1016/j.eswa.2011.05.013

Sha, L., Looi, C.-K., Chen, W., & Zhang, B. H. (2012). Understanding mobile learning from the perspective of self-regulated learning. *Journal of Computer Assisted Learning, 28*(4), 366–378. doi:10.1111/j.1365-2729.2011.00461.x

Stockwell, G. (2010). Using mobile phones for vocabulary activities: Examining the effect of the platform. *Language Learning & Technology, 14*(2), 95–110.

Vossen, P. (2002). *EuroWordNet general document.* Retrieved October 13, 2013, from http://vossen.info/docs/2002/EWNGeneral.pdf

Wang, M., Shen, R., Novak, D., & Pan, X. (2009). The impact of mobile learning on students' learning behaviours and performance: Report from a large blended classroom. *British Journal of Educational Technology*, *40*(4), 673–695. doi:10.1111/j.1467-8535.2008.00846.x

Weibel, S. (2005). The state of the Dublin core metadata initiative: April 1999. *Bulletin of the American Society for Information Science and Technology*, *25*(5), 18–22. doi:10.1002/bult.127

ADDITIONAL READING

Adzic, V., Kalva, H., & Furht, B. (2011). A survey of multimedia content adaptation for mobile devices. *Multimedia Tools and Applications*, *51*(1), 379–396. doi:10.1007/s11042-010-0669-x

Bilgin, O., Cetinoglu, O., & Oflazer, K. (2004). Building a Wordnet for Turkish. *Romanian Journal of Information Science and Technology*, *7*(1-2), 163–172.

Bogdanović, Z., Barać, D., Jovanić, B., Popović, S., & Radenković, B. (2013). Evaluation of mobile assessment in a learning management system. *British Journal of Educational Technology*. doi:10.1111/bjet.12015

Cameron, T., & Bennett, S. (2010). Learning objects in practice: The integration of reusable learning objects in primary education. *British Journal of Educational Technology*, *41*(6), 897–908. doi:10.1111/j.1467-8535.2010.01133.x

Cheng, S.-C., Hwang, W.-Y., Wu, S.-Y., Shadiev, R., & Xie, C.-H. (2010). A mobile device and online system with contextual familiarity and its effects on English learning on campus. *Journal of Educational Technology & Society*, *13*(3), 93–109.

Collins, a., & Halverson, R. (2010). The second educational revolution: rethinking education in the age of technology. *Journal of Computer Assisted Learning, 26(1)*, 18-27.

Colomb, R. M. (2002). Use of Upper Ontologies for Interoperation of Information Systems: A Tutorial (pp. 1-42). Padova, Italy.

De Jong, T., Specht, M., & Koper, R. (2009). A study of contextualised mobile information delivery for language learning. *Journal of Educational Technology & Society*, *13*(3), 110–125.

Dinh, H. T., Lee, C., Niyato, D., & Wang, P. (2011). *A survey of mobile cloud computing: architecture, applications, and approaches*. Wireless Communications and Mobile Computing.

Fallahkhair, S., Pemberton, L., & Griffiths, R. (2007). Development of a cross-platform ubiquitous language learning service via mobile phone and interactive television. *Journal of Computer Assisted Learning*, *23*(4), 312–325. doi:10.1111/j.1365-2729.2007.00236.x

Fellbaum, C. (Ed.). (1998). *WordNet: An Electronic Lexical Database* (p. 423). Cambridge, MA, USA: MIT Press.

Fellbaum, C., & Vossen, P. (2007). Connecting the Universal to the Specific: Towards the Global Grid. In T. Ishida, R. S. Fussell, & P. T. J. M. Vossen (Eds.), *Intercultural Collaboration: First International Workshop* (pp. 1-16). Springer, Berlin, Heidelberg: Springer-Verlag.

Godwin-Jones, R. (2011). Emerging technologies: Mobile apps for language learning. *Language Learning & Technology*, *15*(2), 2–11.

Henze, N., Dolog, P., & Nejdl, W. (2004). Reasoning and Ontologies for Personalized E-Learning in the Semantic Web. *Journal of Educational Technology & Society*, *7*(4), 82–97.

Hsu, C.-C., & Ho, C.-C. (2012). The design and implementation of a competency-based intelligent mobile learning system. *Expert Systems with Applications*, *39*(9), 8030–8043. doi:10.1016/j.eswa.2012.01.130

Kim, D., & Kim, D.-J. (2012). Effect of screen size on multimedia vocabulary learning. *British Journal of Educational Technology, 43*(1), 62–70. doi:10.1111/j.1467-8535.2010.01145.x

Klemke, R., Ternier, S., Kalz, M., & Specht, M. (2010). Implementing infrastructures for managing learning objects. *British Journal of Educational Technology, 41*(6), 873–882. doi:10.1111/j.1467-8535.2010.01127.x

Legg, C. (2007). Ontologies on the Semantic Web. *Annual Review of Information Science & Technology, 41*(1), 407–451. doi:10.1002/aris.2007.1440410116

Martin, S., Diaz, G., Sancristobal, E., Gil, R., Castro, M., & Peire, J. (2011). New technology trends in education: Seven years of forecasts and convergence. *Computers & Education, 57*(3), 1893–1906. doi:10.1016/j.compedu.2011.04.003

Minović, M., Milovanović, M., & Starčević, D. (2011). Learning object repurposing for various multimedia platforms. *Multimedia Tools and Applications, 63*(3), 927–946. doi:10.1007/s11042-011-0964-1

Ouf, S., Nasr, M., & Helmy, Y. (2010). An enhanced e-learning ecosystem based on an integration between cloud computing and Web2.0. *The 10th IEEE International Symposium on Signal Processing and Information Technology,* 48-55. Piscataway, N.J.: IEEE Signal Processing Society.

Parsons, D., & Cranshaw, M. (2006). A Study of Design Requirements for Mobile Learning Environments. In *Sixth IEEE International Conference on Advanced Learning Technologies (ICALT'06)* (pp. 96-100). Washington, DC: IEEE Computer Society Press.

Shamsi, K. N., & Khan, Z. I. (2012). Development of an E-Learning System Incorporating Semantic Web. *International Journal of Research in Computer Science, 2*(5), 11–14. doi:10.7815/ijorcs.25.2012.042

Vossen, P. (2004). EuroWordNet: A Multilingual Database of Autonomous and Language-Specific Wordnets Connected via an Inter-Lingual Index. *International Journal of Lexicography, 17*(2), 161–173. doi:10.1093/ijl/17.2.161

Wong, S. H. S., & Pala, K. (2001). Chinese Radicals and Top Ontology in EuroWordNet. In *Text, Speech and Dialogue: 4th International Conference* (Vol. 2166). Berlin Heidelberg: Springer Verlag.

Yin, C., David, B., & Chalon, R. (2009). Use your mobile computing devices to learn - Contextual mobile learning system design and case studies. In *Computer Science and Information Technology, 2009. ICCSIT 2009. 2nd IEEE International Conference on* (pp. 440-444). Beijing, China.

Zhao, W. Z. W., Sun, Y. S. Y., & Dai, L. D. L. (2010). Improving computer basis teaching through mobile communication and cloud computing technology. In *2010 3rd International Conference on Advanced Computer Theory and Engineering(ICACTE)* (Vol. 1, pp. V1–452-V1–454). Chengdu: IEEE.

KEY TERMS AND DEFINITIONS

Domain Ontology: An ontology that describes all of the relevant concepts in a single domain of interest.

Learning Management System (LMS): An application, often Web-based, that allows teachers and administrators to deliver learning materials and services to learners, and perform tracking and assessment of their learning progress.

Learning Object: A package containing educational resources on a single topic, described by a set of metadata.

Learning Object Repository: A type of a digital library for sharing, management, and retrieval of learning resources. Often involves both the resources and their metadata.

Metadata: Data that describes other data; can be used by data users, managers, software agents and other entities to provide various services including data management, browsing, searching, restructuring, analysis, distribution, aggregation, and adaptation.

Ontology: A formal, explicit model describing concepts in the real world using classes, relations, and attributes.

System Scalability: The ability of a system to adapt to changing, typically growing amounts of work.

Wordnet: Name used for lexical databases derived from the original Princeton WordNet; they group words into synonym sets and interlink them using lexical and conceptual-semantic relations. Used for computational linguistics and natural language processing.

Web Service: A software functionality available remotely (on the Internet or in the cloud) to any client that will conform to its typically platform-independent interface.

Section 3
High Performance and Cloud Computing in Scientific Research

Chapter 9

High Performance and Grid Computing Developments and Applications in Condensed Matter Physics

Aleksandar Belić
University of Belgrade, Serbia

ABSTRACT

This chapter introduces applications of High Performance Computing (HPC), Grid computing, and development of electronic infrastructures in Serbia, in the South Eastern Europe region, and in Europe as a whole. Grid computing represents one of the key enablers of scientific progress in many areas of research. Main HPC and Grid infrastructures, initiatives, projects and programs in Europe, Partnership for Advanced Computing in Europe (PRACE) and European Grid Initiative (EGI) associations, as well as Academic and Educational Grid Initiative of Serbia (AEGIS) are presented. Further, the chapter describes some of the applications related to the condensed matter physics, developed at the Scientific Computing Laboratory of the Institute of Physics, University of Belgrade.

INTRODUCTION

Electronic Infrastructures (hereinafter: eInfrastructures) represent key enablers of modern scientific research and development of information society. eInfrastructures effectively consist of underlying computer networks and Distributed Computing Infrastructures (DCIs). Enabling large-scale innovative research, conducted through collaboration of distributed teams of scientist across the European Research Area (ERA), paves the way towards a long-term vision of a sustainable, transparent, ubiquitous electronic infrastructure open to a wide range of scientific user communities.

Numerical simulations in all fields of science are now necessary ingredient in research and development, offering the possibility of virtual, or in silico experiments, which become as important as

DOI: 10.4018/978-1-4666-5784-7.ch009

the real experiments. On the other hand, theoretical models of most of complex systems studied today usually require sophisticated numerical simulations in order to compare their predictions with the experimental data. Therefore, computational science (not to be confused with computer science, which deals with algorithms, programming, and architecture of computer systems) that designates research related to numerical simulations and in silico, virtual experiments, is now well-established approach to research, at the equal footing to theory and experiment.

Detailed modelling and testing of realistic theories, as well as processing of huge amounts of data produced in large-scale experiments or derived from complex systems in nature or from social systems present a standing challenge for many decades. The almost exponential development of computer systems, in particular computer power of modern CPUs, had allowed computational science to become a reliable and favoured approach for research and development, now able to tackle realistic systems and to provide critical information in many industrial applications. However, to achieve this, supercomputers or large high performance computing systems are necessary, which can execute highly parallel algorithms, in which case we refer to High Performance Computing (HPC), or provide capacity of simultaneous calculation of huge numbers of independent tasks, in which case we speak about Grid computing. In this chapter we will briefly introduce these topics and describe in more details one application relevant to condensed matter physics.

HIGH PERFORMANCE COMPUTING: SUPERCOMPUTING

A supercomputer (Hoffman & Traub, 1989) is a computer at the frontline of current data processing capacity, particularly related to the speed of calculation. Supercomputers were introduced in the 1960s and at that time were designed primar-

ily by Seymour Cray at Control Data Corporation (CDC), and later at Cray Research. While the supercomputers of the 1970s used only a few processors, in the 1990s, machines with thousands of processors began to appear and by the end of the 20th century, massively parallel supercomputers with tens of thousands of "off-the-shelf" processors were the norm.

Systems with a massive number of processors generally take one of two paths: in one approach, e.g. in Grid computing (Foster & Kesselman, 2004), the processing power of a large number of computers in distributed, diverse administrative domains, is opportunistically used whenever a computer is available. In another approach, a large number of processors are used in close proximity to each other, e.g. in a computer cluster. The use of multi-core processors combined with centralization is an emerging direction. Currently, Japan's K computer is the fastest in the world.

Supercomputers are used for compute-intensive tasks such as problems including quantum physics, weather forecasting, climate research, oil and gas exploration, molecular modelling (computing the structures and properties of chemical compounds, biological macromolecules, polymers, and crystals), and physical simulations (such as simulation of airplanes in wind tunnels, simulation of the detonation of nuclear weapons, and research into nuclear fusion).

Approaches to supercomputer architecture (Hill, Jouppi, & Sohi, 2000) have taken dramatic turns since the earliest systems were introduced in the 1960s. Early supercomputer architectures pioneered by Seymour Cray relied on compact innovative designs and local parallelism to achieve superior computational peak performance. However, in time the demand for increased computational power ushered in the age of massively parallel systems.

Supercomputers of the 21st century usually comprise of over 100,000 processors (some being general purpose graphical processing units) connected by fast computer networks. In such centralized massively parallel systems, the speed and flexibility of the interconnection becomes very important and modern supercomputers have used various approaches ranging from enhanced Infiniband systems to three-dimensional tori interconnects. The use of multi-core processors combined with centralization is an emerging direction, e.g. as in the Cyclops64 (Tan, Sreedhar, & Gao, 2011) system.

As the price-per-performance of general-purpose graphical processing units (GPGPUs) has improved, a number of petaflops supercomputers such as Tianhe-I and Nebulae have started to rely on them. However, other systems, i.e., K computer, continue to use conventional processors such as SPARC-based designs and the overall applicability of GPGPUs in general purpose high performance computing applications has been the subject of debate, in that while a GPGPU maybe tuned to score well on specific benchmarks its overall applicability to everyday algorithms may be limited unless significant effort is spent to tune the application towards it. However, GPUs are gaining

ground and in 2012 the Jaguar supercomputer was transformed into Titan by accompanying CPUs with GPUs.

A number of "special-purpose" systems have been designed dedicated to a single problem. This allows the use of specially programmed FPGA chips or even custom VLSI chips, allowing higher price/performance ratios by sacrificing generality. Examples of special-purpose supercomputers include Belle, Deep Blue, and Hydra, for playing chess, Gravity Pipe for astrophysics, MDGRAPE-3 for protein structure computation molecular dynamics and Deep Crack, for breaking the DES cipher.

Since 1993, the fastest supercomputers have been ranked on the TOP500 list (Figure 1) according to their LINPACK [5] benchmark results. The list does not claim to be unbiased or definitive, but it is a widely cited current definition of the "fastest" supercomputer available at any given time. Today, the K computer is the world's fastest supercomputer at 10.51 petaflops. It consists of 88,000 SPARC64 VIIIfx CPUs, and spans 864 server racks.

Figure 1. Countries share of Top 500 supercomputers (as of June 2010)

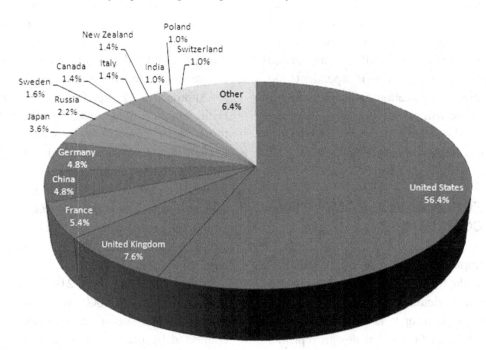

HIGH PERFORMANCE COMPUTING PROJECTS

The pan-European HPC activities over the past years have evolved through two specific paths. DEISA (Lederer, 2011) was linking national HPC centers (Tier-1), while PRACE as an ESFRI initiative has already started the implementation of a large Tier-0 facility in Europe. The next few years will see the merging of the two infrastructures into a pan-European HPC facility, ran by a central PRACE (PRACE, 2012) office requiring substantial financial contributions by members, and open to European researchers through a high standard peer-review process.

At the regional level, HP-SEE (HP-SEE, 2013) aspires to contribute to stabilization and development of South-East Europe, by overcoming fragmentation in Europe and stimulating eInfrastructure development and adoption by new virtual research communities, thus enabling collaborative high-quality research across a spectrum of scientific fields. The scientific computing ecosystem can be described by the pyramid that is presented in Figure 2.

On the top level of the pyramid there a few top capability HPC systems, which are operated by PRACE (Tier-0). The Tier-0 systems can provide (at the time of writing of this document) capabilities, which are beyond the Petaflops level. PRACE is responsible for the provision and operation of Tier-0 resources.

On the second level there are the Tier-1 systems, which belong to national or regional centres and have a lower capability than the Tier-0 systems. Tier-1 systems can be also used as a step for the applications towards using Tier-0 resources. On the pan European level, integration of the Tier-1 HPC systems was operated by the DEISA projects, while recently the management of the pan European integrated Tier-1 service is managed by the PRACE implementation projects. Tier-1 capacity systems as well as Tier-2 systems are managed by EGI.

Figure 2. Computing performance pyramid

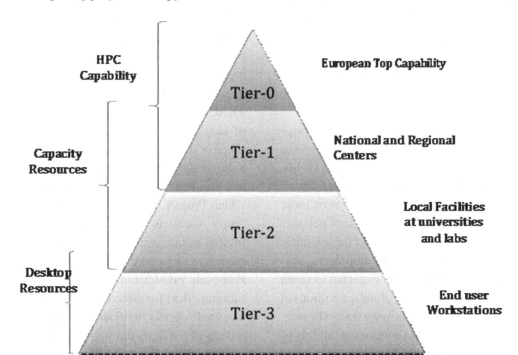

On the third level of the pyramid Tier-2 systems, are systems that belong and are operated by universities, research centres and other individual institutions. Finally, Tier-3 resources consist of workstations or desktop computers that belong to the individual researches.

PRACE Programme

Partnership for Advanced Computing in Europe (hereinafter: PRACE) created a persistent pan-European Research Infrastructure (RI) providing leading High Performance Computing services (PRACE, 2012). PRACE enables world-class science and engineering for European academia and industry. The PRACE RI is operated in collaboration with national and regional HPC centres and governed by representatives of partner governments. Access to the PRACE services is open to all European researchers affiliated with recognized European academic institutions and industries. The Scientific Steering Committee composed of Europe's leading scientists and engineers selects project proposals and grants access to resources. Twenty-four countries are currently members of the PRACE-RI: Austria, Bulgaria, Cyprus, Czech Republic, Denmark, Finland, France, Germany, Greece, Hungary, Ireland, Israel, Italy, Norway, the Netherlands, Poland, Portugal, Serbia, Slovenia, Spain, Sweden, Switzerland, Turkey and the United Kingdom.

PRACE provides a pan-European HPC service with world-class systems (Tier-0) well integrated into the European HPC ecosystem (Tier-1). Initial PRACE Tier-0 systems have a capability to carry out computations at a rate of one or more Petaflops/s (one quadrillion operations per second). To keep pace with the needs of the scientific communities and technical developments, systems deployed by PRACE are expected to reach capabilities of one Exaflops/s (one quintillion) in less than a decade. Four European states (France, Germany, Italy, and Spain) committed funding of €400M for the initial PRACE systems. Access to

PRACE Tier-0 and Tier-1 resources is granted to European researchers and their collaborators through a single European peer-review process overseen by the PRACE Scientific Steering Committee. Leading scientists evaluate the proposals submitted in response to the bi-annual calls. The PRACE Tier-0 systems are presently:

- JUGENE, IBM BlueGene/P, 1 Petaflop/s, hosted by GCS/FZJ;
- CURIE, Bull Bullx cluster, 1.6 Petaflop/s, hosted by GENCI/CEA;
- Hermit, Cray, 5 Petaflop/s, hosted by GCS/HLRS.

GCS/LRZ (Germany) has committed to host an additional Tier-0 system in 2012, and CINECA (Italy) and BSC (Spain) have committed to host two additional Tier-0 systems in 2013.

The PRACE-RI offers three different forms of access: Project Access, Programme Access and Preparatory Access. Project Access is the normal form of access for individual researchers and research groups. It is open to European researchers and their collaborators from recognized European academic institutions and industry for projects deemed to have significant European and International impact. Calls for Proposals are issued twice a year and are evaluated by leading scientists and engineers in a peer-review process governed by a PRACE Scientific Steering Committee comprised of leading European researchers from a broad range of disciplines. Programme Access is available to major European projects or infrastructures that can benefit from PRACE resources and for which Project Access is not appropriate. Preparatory Access is a simplified form of access for limited resources for the preparation of resource requests in response to Project Access Calls for Proposals. PRACE has an extensive education and training effort for effective use of the RI through seasonal schools, workshops and scientific and industrial seminars throughout Europe. Seasonal Schools target broad HPC audiences, whereas workshops are focused on particular technologies, tools or disciplines or research areas. Education and training material and documents related to the RI are available on the PRACE website as is schedule of events.

The European Commission supports PRACE through a series of projects to accelerate the implementation of the PRACE Research Infrastructure. The Preparatory Phase Project has successfully concluded, leading into the First Implementation Phase Project (PRACE-1IP, 2010– 2012). The project is in full swing, having picked up the DEISA project, which is now winding down. PRACE-1IP is granting access to Tier-0 systems across Europe. The second Implementation Phase Project (PRACE-2IP, 2011–2013) has started integration of Tier-1 services and extending scientific and industrial community relations and support. The Third Implementation Phase Project (PRACE-3IP) is being planned presently for 2012–2014. This phase has a focus on the scaling of applications, joint pre-commercial procurement pilot, training and outreach. The total European funding is expected to be €70M and complements the consortium budget of over €60M.

HP-SEE Programme

HP-SEE (HP-SEE, 2013), High-Performance Computing Infrastructure for South East Europe's Research Communities will link existing and upcoming HPC facilities in South East Europe in a common infrastructure, and it will provide operational solutions for it. As a complementary action, the project will establish and maintain a GÉANT link for Southern Caucasus. The initiative will open the South East European HPC infrastructure to a wide range of new user communities, including those of less-resourced countries, fostering collaboration and providing advanced capabilities to researchers, with an emphasis on strategic groups in computational physics, computational chemistry and life sciences. HP-

SEE receives EC support through FP7 under the "Research Infrastructures" action.

The HP-SEE initiative builds on the lasting cooperation in the SEE region embodied in a number of eInfrastructure EC-funded initiatives, aiming at equal participation of less-resourced countries of the region in European trends. The SEEREN initiative established a regional network and the SEE-GRID initiative the regional Grid, while BSI project has established GÉANT link to Caucasus. The SEE-LIGHT project is working towards establishing a dark-fibre backbone that will interconnect most National Research and Education Networks in the Balkan region.

HP-SEE aspires to contribute to the stabilization and development of South-East Europe, by overcoming fragmentation in Europe and stimulating eInfrastructure development and adoption by new virtual research communities, thus enabling collaborative high-quality research across a spectrum of scientific fields.

In the field of High Performance Computing, the region is still lagging behind the European developments. Only few HPC installations are available – one large supercomputing top500 installation in Bulgaria and some smaller HPC ones in couple of other countries, and these are not open to cross-border research. The user communities using HPC are limited. Similarly, the less-resources countries have no mechanism established for interfacing to PRACE, DEISA, or any related initiatives. Currently only Greece, Bulgaria, Serbia, Hungary and Turkey are affiliated to PRACE.

Moreover, for a number of user communities the resources provided by high-throughput cluster-based Grid infrastructures are not suitable due to one or more of the following reasons: the available computing/storage resources are not sufficient; the available interconnect (Gigabit Ethernet) makes application less efficient to run on the Grid or even individual Linux cluster; the access to the storage requires high bandwidth, and input/output files are of TB size or larger; the application requires shared-memory system; the application requires large amount of scratch space, or a large high-throughput shared file-system. Finally, there are access problems with Grid-based solutions in terms of availability. Thus, regional eInfrastructure must be expanded to address these specific needs of scientific and engineering communities in the region.

The regional vision of establishing an eInfrastructure compatible with European developments, and empowering the scientists in the region in equal participation in the use of pan-European infrastructures, requires a set of coordinated actions in the area of HPC and application fields making use of HPC initiatives. Moreover, the regional scientists and engineers must be provided with access to capability computers of leadership-class to remain competitive and the European and international level, thus overcoming fragmentation in Europe.

Figure 3 depicts the multi-dimensional regional eInfrastructure in South-East Europe, where HP-SEE effectively adds the new Research Infrastructure: HPC infrastructure and knowledge/user layer, on top of the existing network plane, and parallel to the existing Grid plane, thus optimizing all RI layers and further enabling a wide range of new cross-border eScience applications to be deployed over the regional eInfrastructure. This approach effectively creates an integrated eInfrastructure for new virtual research communities, and provides a platform for collaboration between ICT engineers and computational scientists dealing with the infrastructure on one hand, and on the other the scientists from diverse scientific communities in the region.

The HP-SEE project works across several strategic lines of action. First, it will link the existing HPC facilities in the region into a common infrastructure, and provide operational and management solutions for it. Second, it will open this infrastructure to a wide range of new user communities, including those of non-resourced countries, fostering collaboration and providing

advanced capabilities to more researchers, with an emphasis on strategic groups in computational physics, computational chemistry and life sciences. Finally, it will act as a catalyst for establishment of national HPC initiatives, and will act as a SEE bridge for PRACE. Also in this context, the project will aim to attract political and financial support for materializing the eInfrastructure vision.

The work of the HP-SEE project will also be strongly supported by the current SEERA-EI project (3 years, started in April 2009), who's consortium consists of policy makers – programme managers from 10 countries in the region. The project aims to establish a communication platform between programme managers, pave the way towards common eInfrastructure strategy and vision, including HPC and implement concrete actions for common funding of electronic infrastructures.

Serbian National Supercomputing Centre

Designated by the Ministry of Science and Technological Development of the Republic of Serbia in 2008, Institute of Physics Belgrade is

Figure 3. SEE eInfrastructure with HPC, and new user communities

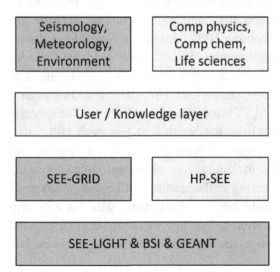

coordinating institution for all HPC activities and development at the national level. It is actively working towards establishment of the National Supercomputing and Data Storage Facility Blue Danube. The principle aim of the project is to set up the new HPC facility as a national and regional focal point for development and application of High Performance Computing, and to procure and install the Blue Danube supercomputer as the centrepiece of the new infrastructure. The project has been designated a priority by the country's Science and Technological Development Strategy.

The field of ICT represents one of the priority areas of modern R&D, and a key step for building a knowledge economy and bridging the intra-European developmental gap (digital divide). The successes of the Institute of Physics Belgrade in European ICT projects have shown that Serbia has a realistic chance to become competitive in this field.

In addition to the procurement and installation of the Blue Danube supercomputer, main aims of the project can be summarized as:

- Training for users, developers, and administrators.
- Development and implementation of user support services for accessing Serbia's HPC infrastructure.
- Comprehensive integration of national supercomputer facility into European Union supercomputing and Grid eInfrastructures.
- Growth of national supercomputer facility into a regional hub for development and application of High Performance Computing.
- Development of key partnerships with technological leaders in the field.

GRID COMPUTING PROJECTS

Computing resources and services able to support needs of modern scientific work are available at different layers: local computing centres, national and regional computing centres, and European supercomputing centres. The gap between needs of various user communities and computing resources able to satisfy their requirements is addressed by introduction of Grid technology on the top of pan-European academic network.

Computing Grids (Figure 4) are conceptually not unlike electrical grids. In an electrical grid, the wall outlets allow us to link to and use an infrastructure of resources, which generate, distribute, and bill for electrical power. When we connect to the electrical grid, we do not need to know details on the power plant currently generating the electricity we use. In the same way Grid technology uses middleware layer to coordinate and organize into one logical resource a set of available distributed computing and storage resources across a network, allowing users to access them in a unified fashion. The computing Grids, like electrical grids, aim to provide users with easy access to all the resources they need, whenever they need them, regardless of the underlying physical topology and management model of individual clusters.

Grids address two distinct but related goals: providing remote access to information technology (IT) assets, and aggregating processing and storage power. The most obvious resources included in Grids are processors (CPUs), but Grids also can encompass various sensors, data-storage systems, applications, and other types of resources. One of the first commonly known Grid initiatives was the SETI@HOME project (Anderson, Cobb, Korpela, Lebofsky, & Werthimer, 2002), which solicited several millions of volunteers to download a screensaver, which was able to use idle processor time to analyze the astronomical data in the search for extraterrestrial life.

Europe has played a leading role in Grid technology development, starting with the EU DataGrid (Wilson, 2001) project and related efforts under the Framework Programme 5. After this proof of concept, demonstrating the potential impact of Grid technologies on European science and industry, a first large scale production Grid

Figure 4. Screenshot of the 3D real time monitor of computational grid activity

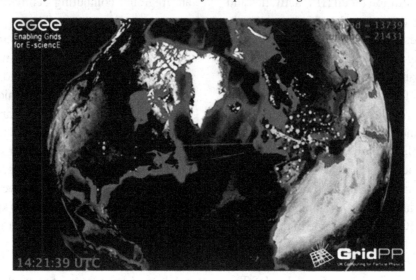

infrastructure was deployed by the Enabling Grids for E-SciencE (Jones, 2009) project (EGEE), and its operation was further consolidated in its second (EGEE-II) and third phase (EGEE-III). Following a decade of successful research in using Grid technologies to provide Distributed Computing Infrastructures (DCIs), today the EGI-InSPIRE (Girone, 2011) consortium consolidates its experiences to deliver a sustainable high-quality infrastructure for the European Research Area (ERA) along with those support services necessary for its exploitation by the European research and scientific community.

In the past the European Commission has funded through a number of targeted initiatives activating of new user communities and enabling collaborative research across a number of fields in order to close existing technological and scientific gaps, and thus bridging the digital divide, stimulating research and consequently alleviating the brain drain in the less-developed regions of Europe. This was especially successful in the South-East Europe (SEE), where a number of such initiatives show excellent results. The SEEREN (SEE Research and Education Networking initiative) project (Rusu, 2004), through its two phases, established the SEE segment of the pan-European GÉANT network and successfully connected the scientific communities in the region. The SEE-LIGHT project aimed towards establishing a dark-fibre backbone that will interconnect most national research and education networks in the region. Currently, the South-East European eInfrastructure initiatives aim to ensure equal participation of the region in European networking and Grid computing trends. SEERA-EI capitalizes on this momentum and link national-level programme managers and provide an open forum for information exchange, in order to enable coordination of national programmes in eInfrastructures, and set the framework for a common regional agenda. The SEERA-EI project gather and exchange information regarding current programmes and carry out a state-of-the-art analysis; produce set of best practices and guidelines for national eInfrastructure programmes; and identify areas for joint regional activities, ranging from short-term soft actions, mid-term policy-level actions, to preparatory activities for long-term actions. In the Grid arena, the SEE-GRID (South-East European GRid eInfrastructure Development) project (Balaž et al., 2011), similarly through its two phases, has established a strong human network in the area of scientific computing and has set up a powerful regional

Grid infrastructure, attracting large number of applications from diverse fields from countries throughout the South-East Europe. The third phase of SEE-GRID programme (SEE-GRID-SCI) aimed to have a catalytic and structuring effect on a number of SEE user groups, with a strong focus on the key seismological, meteorological, and environmental communities.

In line with the European and regional vision of paving the way towards a long-term sustainable European Grid Initiative, Academic and Educational Grid Initiative of Serbia (Vudragović, Balaž, Slavnić, & Belić, 2009) (AEGIS) is bringing together under one umbrella at the national level all interested parties involved in provisioning and using of Serbian research computing infrastructure. Institute of Physics Belgrade (IPB) coordinates AEGIS initiative through its Scientific Computing Laboratory (SCL). IPB represents Serbia in EGI, and is a member of its Council. It currently participates in EGI-InSPIRE service Grid project, after a successful participation in two of EGEE series of projects (EGEE-II and EGEE-III), and three of SEE-GRID series of projects (SEE-GRID, SEE-GRID-2, and SEE-GRID-SCI).

EGI-InSPIRE Programme

As the next generation of DCI technologies (e.g. desktop grids and clouds) matures the EGI-InSPIRE (Girone, 2011) consortium is ideally placed to help accelerate the evolution of these technologies to a production status, and rapidly deploy these new innovative technologies to benefit the European Research Area. EGI-InSPIRE provides a structure that can assess the maturity of these new technologies in a production environment and providing relevant feedback to the developers. Desktop grids, clouds and virtualization are all very different technologies maturing at very different rates and their suitability and applicability to the needs of the European Research Area needs to be continually assessed. An important lesson learned from the experiences in adopting

the current generation of DCI technologies is the importance in establishing standard interfaces and recognized operating models so that the infrastructure is not dependent in the long-term on a single software provider. The EGI model provides the central coordination necessary to deploy a new technology in over 35 separate organizations across Europe (the NGIs and EIROs) and still ensure that this technology can be seen as an integrated whole by its pan-European user community.

The coordination effort necessary to integrate and harmonize access to various distributed computing resources balancing the individual constraints and requirements of different resource providers and user communities, is undertaken by a new dedicated organization, EGI.eu. This coordination activity encompasses the operation of the core services needed to provide an integrated European infrastructure and the interface into national services; coordination of user support working with national, generic and domain specific support teams; and the specification, integration and deployment of middleware from external software providers to provide an integrated secure infrastructure to support the user communities. EGI.eu is the main partner in the EGI-InSPIRE project, which supports the establishment of this organization, and the continued transition to a sustainable a pan-European production infrastructure. The focus of the EGI-InSPIRE project is an Integrated Sustainable Pan-European Infrastructure for Researchers in Europe. This will be achieved through:

- The continued operation and expansion of today's production infrastructure by transitioning to a governance model and operational infrastructure that will be increasingly sustained beyond specific project funding.
- The continued support for researchers within Europe and their international collaborators that are using the current production infrastructure.

- The support for current heavy users of the infrastructure in Earth Science, Astronomy & Astrophysics, Fusion research, Computational Chemistry and Materials Science, Life Sciences and High Energy Physics as they move to sustainable support models for their own communities.
- Interfaces that expand access to new user communities including new potential heavy users of the infrastructure from the ESFRI projects.
- Mechanisms to integrate existing infrastructure providers in Europe and around the world into the production infrastructure so as to provide transparent access to all authorised users.
- Establishment of processes and procedures to allow the inclusion of new DCI technologies and resources (e.g. Cloud infrastructures, volunteer desktop grids, etc.) into the production infrastructure as they mature and demonstrate value to the European community.

The EGI-InSPIRE consortium has 50 partners, which includes 37 NGIs, 2 EIRO members, the European Organization for Nuclear Research (CERN) and the European Molecular Biology (EMBL), and partners from the Asia Pacific region is in a strong position to deliver this new sustainable model of service provision as they have built up a globally unique experience in the field of delivering such services to national and discipline-specific research communities. The consortium has unparalleled experience in operating production-quality distributed computing resources, an in depth knowledge of the current middleware and operational software needed for production infrastructures, and nearly a decade of experience in working together in different collaborations.

Local, regional, national and international users increasingly expect a consistent set of services to access the resources that they have authorized access to. The EGI provides benefits at the European level that filter down through the NGIs to local campus (or equivalent) resources. In this way EGI's coordinating function drives the definition of clear operational interfaces and procedures that encompass different resource types and technologies. This will certainly benefit the heavy multinational users of federated distributed computing infrastructures, but also those users that wish to use resources outside of their own organization, but still within their national borders.

Both of these user groups certainly expect capabilities beyond a set of reliable site-based services discovered through a central information service. They also expect higher-level services and applications that enable coordinated access to site services, such as workload-management services, file-transfer services, meta-data catalogues, replica services, etc. Both these higher-level and the site-based services are critical to all user communities. The rapid investigation and resolution of critical issues found during their deployment and in production use within EGI needs to be assured at the European level through EGI and at the national level through the NGI.

AEGIS Programme

Academic and Educational Grid Initiative of Serbia (Vudragović, Balaž, Slavnić, & Belić, 2009) (AEGIS) was established in 2005 to coordinate efforts on developing academic and educational high performance computing facilities (e.g. computers, storage, networks, instruments, and visualization resources) in Serbia, and help to integrate them in the AEGIS infrastructure. One of the major AEGIS tasks is dissemination and training activities organization, and help to Serbian research communities in developing and production use of applications on the AEGIS eInfrastructure.

AEGIS is also focal point in Serbia for facilitation of wider participation of AEGIS members in Framework Programme 7 and other international

Grid projects, coordination of fund raising efforts to improve AEGIS infrastructure and human resources, creation of national Grid development policy, and lobbying for its position within an overall research agenda.

AEGIS Grid eInfrastructure provides more than 1000 CPUs and 50 TB of data storage to all user communities through a distributed set of Grid sites hosted by major research institutes and universities. This eInfrastructure is fully utilized by a number of scientific high-performance applications, developed Serbian researchers and adapted for optimal use on the Grid with the support of the Scientific Computing Laboratory of the Institute of Physics Belgrade. Such support

is provided either directly for specific applications or through advanced training activities for application developers.

The Serbian Grid infrastructure consists of 11 Grid sites (Figure 5), comprising from tens to hundreds of computing nodes and disk-based storage elements ranging from several hard disks to tens of terabytes. Apart from computing and storage resources, core Grid services which enable seamless access to all resources are provided to national users. AEGIS sites are running Scientific Linux operating system and the latest version of the EMI gLite middleware. Beside standard serial tasks, sites are optimized and heavily tested for parallel processing mode using MPICH framework.

Figure 5. Overview of the Serbian grid infrastructure

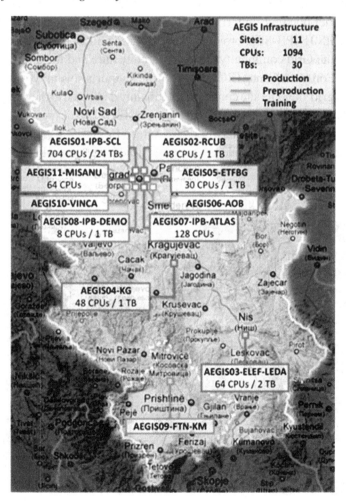

The resources are fully dedicated to national and international Grid communities within AEGIS and EGI-InSPIRE projects.

The first Grid site in Serbia AEGIS01-IPB-SCL (Figure 6) is installed at the Scientific Computing Laboratory of the Institute of Physics Belgrade. This Grid site is a set of 89 worker nodes (2 x quad core Xeon E5345 on 2.33 GHz with 8GB of RAM) and 15 service nodes (Xeon based nodes). AEGIS01-IPB-SCL, as the largest, is the Tier-0 site in the Serbian Grid infrastructure, providing all core services and managing national AEGIS Virtual Organization. All computing and core services nodes at AEGIS01-IPB-SCL Grid site are interconnected by the star topology Gigabit Ethernet network through three stacked high- throughput Layer 3 switches, each node being connected to the switch by two Gigabit Ethernet cables in channel bonding. In terms of storage resources, AEGIS01-IPB-SCL provides 24 TB of disk space to the Grid community.

Belgrade University Computer Centre (RCUB) hosts AEGIS02-RCUB grid site. The site consists of 14 nodes with 2.0 GHz AMD Sempron CPUs with 1GB of RAM. The Storage Area Network (SAN) cluster is connected to the storage element via NFS. The Laboratory for Electronic Design Automation (LEDA) of the Faculty of Electronic Engineering, University of Nis has deployed AEGIS03-ELEF-LEDA site. The site capacity is currently being extended to 64 CPUs (Intel Xeon Quad-core 2.4GHz, with 12MB L2 cache and 4GB RAM per node), and the site storage capacity is 2TB.

The site AEGIS04-KG is installed at the Bio-engineering Research and Development Center of the University of Kragujevac since June 2006. It consists of 42 CPU cores with the total RAM of 40GB. The School of Electrical Engineering of the University of Belgrade hosts AEGIS05-ETFBG Grid site. It consists of 30 nodes (AMD 2600+ Sempron CPUs), with 1GB RAM and 80 GB of disk space at the storage element.

AEGIS07-IPB-ATLAS (Figure 7) is the second site hosted by the Institute of Physics Belgrade, and is based on 128 Intel Xeon processors with 32-bit architecture and the total of 96GB of RAM. The site supports several virtual organizations, but is mainly dedicated to the ATLAS VO community of the CERN LHC experiment. Another site at Institute of Physics Belgrade, AEGIS08-IPB-DEMO, is used purely for educational/training purposes.

Figure 6. AEGIS01-IPB-SCL grid site

Figure 7. AEGIS07-IPB-ATLAS grid site

It is based on Xen virtual machines deployed on a single node with two Intel Xeon Quad-core CPUs with 16 GB of RAM. It is used in various training events for demonstration of installation and configuration of different Grid services.

With the support of the GRINKO project, AEGIS09-FTN-KM Grid site has been established in Kosovska Mitrovica at the Faculty of Technical Sciences of the University of Pristina. This site consists of four quad-core CPU computing nodes.

SPEEDUP: HPC AND GRID APPLICATION

The presented HPC and Grid computing resources supported and maintained by pan-European, regional, and national projects and programs are used by many user communities and research groups. Condensed matter physics community is by far the largest user of computing resources in Serbia, and many applications are deployed at

clusters through the infrastructure. Here we describe SPEEDUP application, which is deployed at AEGIS01-IPB-SCL, AEGIS07-IPB-ATLAS, and several other clusters in the region of South-East Europe.

Problem Specification and Effective Action Approach

Exact solution of a given many-body model in non-relativistic quantum theory is usually expressed in terms of eigenvalues and eigenfunctions of the corresponding Hamiltonian

$$\hat{H} = \sum_{i=1}^{M} \frac{\hat{p}_i^2}{2m_i} + \hat{V}(\hat{q}_1,...,\hat{q}_M), \qquad (1)$$

where M represents the number of particles. The complete analytic solution of the model can be also expressed in terms of general transition amplitudes

$$A(\mathbf{a},\mathbf{b};T) = \langle \mathbf{b} \mid e^{-iT\hat{H}/\hbar} \mid \mathbf{a} \rangle$$

from the initial state $|\mathbf{a}\rangle$ to the final state $|\mathbf{b}\rangle$ during the time of propagation T. However, exact solutions can be found only in a very limited number of cases. Therefore, use of various analytic approximation techniques or numerical treatment is necessary for detailed understanding of the behaviour of almost all models of interest.

Recently introduced effective action approach (Bogojević, Balaž, & Belić, 2005a, 2005b, 2005c, 2005d; Balaž, Bogojević, Vidanović, & Pelster, 2009) provides an ideal framework for exact numerical calculation of such quantum amplitudes. It gives systematic short-time expansion of transition amplitudes for a general potential, thus allowing accurate calculation of relevant short-time properties of quantum systems directly, as has been demonstrated in (Vidanović, Bogojević, & Belić, 2009; Balaž, Vidanović, Bogojević, & Pelster, 2010). For numerical calculations that require long times of propagation to be considered, relying on the use of Monte Carlo method, the effective action approach provides improved discretized actions leading to the speedup in the convergence of numerically calculated discretized quantities to their exact continuum values. This has been demonstrated not only for the amplitudes, but also in Monte Carlo calculations of energy expectation values using the improved energy estimators (Grujić, Bogojević, & Balaž, 2006; Bogojević, Vidanović, Balaž, & Belić, 2008).

From inception of the path integral formalism, expansion of short-time amplitudes in the time of propagation was used for the definition of path integrals through the time-discretization procedure (Feynman & Hibbs, 1965; Kleinert, 2009). This is also straightforwardly implemented in the Path Integral Monte Carlo approaches (Ceperley, 1995), where one usually relies on the naive discretization of the action. Several improved discretized actions, mainly based on the Trotter formula and its generalizations, were developed and used in the past (Takahashi & Imada, 1984; Li & Broughton, 1987).

The effective action approach is based on the concept of ideal discretization. It was introduced first for single-particle 1D models and later extended to general many-body systems in arbitrary number of spatial dimensions. This approach allows systematic derivation of higher-order terms to a chosen order p in the short time of propagation. Recursive method for deriving the discretized effective actions, established in (Balaž, Bogojević, Vidanović, & Pelster, 2009), is based on solving the underlying Schrödinger equation for the amplitude. It represents the most efficient tool to analytically calculate higher-order effective actions.

We will illustrate this approach on the example of one-dimensional quantum theory. In this case, the transition amplitudes are expressed in terms of the ideal discretized action S^* in the form

$$A(\mathrm{a},\mathrm{b};\mathrm{T}) = \frac{1}{\sqrt{2\pi T}}\, e^{-S^*(\mathrm{a},\mathrm{b};\mathrm{T})}, \qquad (2)$$

which can be also seen as a definition of the ideal action (De Raedt, & De Raedt, 1983). Therefore, by definition, the above expression is correct not only for short times of propagation, but also for arbitrary large T. The ideal effective potential W is introduced by

$$S^*(\mathrm{a},\mathrm{b};\mathrm{T}) = T\left[\frac{1}{2}\left(\frac{b-a}{T}\right)^2 + W\right], \qquad (3)$$

as a reminiscent of the naive discretized action, with the arguments usually written in the form

$$W\left(\frac{a+b}{2}, \frac{b-a}{2}; \mathrm{T}\right),$$

to emphasize that we will be using the mid-point prescription. As was shown earlier, the effective potential is symmetric in its second argument, and allows systematic and hierarchic double expansion in the form

$$W(\mathrm{x},\overline{\mathrm{x}};\varepsilon) = \sum_{m=0}^{\infty}\sum_{k=0}^{m} c_{m,k}(x)\varepsilon^{m-k}\,\overline{\mathrm{x}}^{2k} \qquad (4)$$

If we restrict the above sum over m to p-1, the obtained truncated level p effective potential $W_p(\mathrm{x},\overline{\mathrm{x}};\varepsilon)$ gives the expansion of the effective action S_p^* to order ε^p, and hence the level designation p for both the effective action and the corresponding potential W_p.

As shown previously (Bogojević, Balaž, & Belić, 2005a, 2005b, 2005c), when used in Path Integral Monte Carlo simulations for calculation of long time amplitudes, the use of level p effective action leads to the convergence of discretized amplitudes proportional to ε^p, i.e. as $\dfrac{1}{N^p}$, where N is the number of time steps $\varepsilon = T/N$ used in the discretization. This was implemented in the SPEEDUP code (Balaz et al., 2012). and used in several numerical studies (Vidanović, Bogojević, & Belić, 2009; Balaž, Vidanović, Bogojević, & Pelster, 2010).

QSPEEDUP code, which implement the effective action approach using the SPEEDUP algorithm, and quasi-Monte Carlo method to efficiently generate relevant trajectories. We verify the correctness of the new code by comparison with the standard SPEEDUP MC implementation and study in detail the performance and behaviour or errors of quasi-MC algorithm. In the following sections we first give brief overview of the algorithm used in the SPEEDUP and QSPEEDUP codes, introduce quasi-MC method and low-discrepancy sequences, and tests the performance of this method on simple but instructive examples of low-dimensional integrals of the Gaussian type. We will describe details of quasi-MC implementation of the SPEEDUP code and present numerical results obtained for several one-dimensional quantum models.

SPEEDUP Algorithm Description

In the standard Path Integral Monte Carlo approach based on the use of effective actions, the time of propagation T is divided into N time steps, such that $\varepsilon = T/N$ is sufficiently small and that the effective potential (which has the finite radius of convergence) can be used. This applies to the original Feynman's definition of path integrals, which corresponds to $p=1$, as well as to the higher-order effective actions. The discretization of the propagation time leads to the following expression for the discretized amplitude

$$A_N^{(p)}\left(a, b; T\right) = \int \frac{dq_1 ... dq_{N-1}}{\left(2\pi\varepsilon\right)^{N/2}} \exp\left(-S_N^{(p)}\right), \quad (5)$$

where $S_N^{(p)}$ stands for the discretized level p effective action,

$$S_N^{(p)} = \sum_{k=0}^{N-1}\left[\frac{\left(q_{k+1} - q_k\right)^2}{2\varepsilon} + \varepsilon W_p\left(x_k, \bar{x}_k; \varepsilon\right)\right], \quad (6)$$

and we have used the abbreviations $q_0 = a$, $q_N = b$, $x_k = (q_{k+1} + q_k)/2$, $\bar{x}_k = \left(q_{k+1} - q_k\right)/2$.

The trajectory of q's is constructed using the bisection method. The procedure starts from bisection level $n=0$, where we only have initial and final position of the particle (i.e. the trajectory consists of only these two points). At the next bisection level $n=1$, the propagation is divided into two time-steps, and we have to generate a coordinate q of the particle at the moment $T/2$, thus constructing the piecewise trajectory connecting points a at the time $t=0$, q at $t=T/2$, and b at $t=T$. The coordinate q is generated from the Gaussian probability density function centred at the mid-point $(a+b)/2$, with the width $\sigma_1 = \sqrt{T/2}$. The procedure continues iteratively, and each time a set of points is added to the piecewise trajectory. At each bisection level n the coordinates are generated from the Gaussian centred at mid-points of coordinates generated at previous level n-1, with the width $\sigma_n = \sqrt{T/2^n}$. To generate numbers η from the Gaussian centered at zero we use the standard Box-Müller method,

$$\eta = \sqrt{-2\sigma_n^2 \ln \xi_1} \cos 2\pi\xi_2, \quad (7)$$

where numbers ξ_1 and ξ_2 are generated from the uniform distribution on the interval [0,1], using the SPRNG library. If the target (maximal) bisection level is s, then at bisection level $n \leq s$ we have to generate 2^{n-1} numbers from the Gaussian distribution using the above formula, and to construct the new trajectory by adding to already existing points the new ones, according to

$$q\left[\left(1+2i\right)\cdot 2^{s-n}\right] = \eta_i$$
$$+\frac{1}{2}\left(q\left[i\cdot 2^{s-n+1}\right] + q\left[\left(i+1\right)\cdot 2^{s-n+1}\right]\right),$$ (8)

where i runs from 0 to $2^{n-1}-1$. This ensures that at bisection level s we get trajectory with $N=2^s$ time-steps, consisting of $N+1$ points, with boundary conditions $q[0]=a$ and $q[N]=b$. At each lower bisection level n, the trajectory consists of 2^n+1 points obtained from the maximal one (level s trajectory) as a subset of points $q[i\cdot2^{s-n}]$ for $i=0,1,...,2^n$.

Figure 8 illustrates the typical results obtained from the SPEEDUP code on the example of 1D-MPT theory. In this figure we can see the convergence of numerically calculated amplitudes with the number of time-steps N time to the exact continuum value, obtained in the limit $N\to\infty$. Such convergence is obtained for each level p of the effective action used. However, the convergence

is much faster when higher-order effective action is used. Note that all results corresponding to the one value of level p on the graph are obtained from a single run of the SPEEDUP code with the maximal bisection level s=10. The simplest way to estimate the continuum value of the amplitude is to fit numerical results from single run of the code to the appropriate level p fitting function:

$$A_N^{(p)} = A^{(p)} + \frac{B^{(p)}}{N^p} + \frac{C^{(p+1)}}{N^{p+1}} + \cdots.$$ (9)

The constant term obtained by fitting corresponds to the best estimate of the exact amplitude, which can be found from the available numerical results.

The effective action approach can be used for accurate calculation of a large number of energy eigenstates and eigenvalues by diagonalization of the space-discretized matrix of transition am-

Figure 8. Convergence of SPEEDUP Monte-Carlo results for the transition amplitude $A_N^{(p)}\left(-0.5, 0.5; 1\right)$ of 1D-MPT potential as a function of the number of time steps N, calculated with level p=1,2,10 effective action. The full lines give the fitted functions (9), where the constant term A_p corresponds to the continuum-theory amplitude A(-0,5,0.5,1). The number of Monte-Carlo samples was $N_{MC}=10^6$.

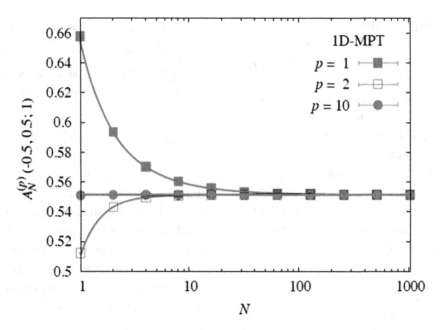

plitudes (Vidanović, Bogojević, & Belić, 2009; Vidanović, Bogojević, Balaž, & Belić, 2009; Balaž, Vidanović, Bogojević, & Pelster, 2010). Figure 9 illustrates this for the case of an anharmonic and double-well potential. The graph on the left gives several eigenvalues and eigenstates for 1D-AHO potential with A=1 and quartic anharmonicity g=48, while the graph on the right gives low-lying spectrum and eigenfunctions of the doublewell potential, obtained for A=-10, with the moderate anharmonicity g=12. More details on this approach, including study of all errors associated with the discretization process, can be found in (Vidanović, Bogojević, & Belić, 2009; Vidanović, Bogojević, Balaž, & Belić, 2009).

Low-Dimensional Quasi-MC

In this section we will first introduce low-discrepancy sequences and then apply quasi-Monte Carlo method for calculation of low-dimensional integrals of the Gaussian type. Since the SPEEDUP code requires calculation of high-dimensional integrals of the similar type, this preliminary study

is done to verify the quasi-MC algorithm to be implemented in the QSPEEDUP code. It is also used to determine the appropriate distribution of deviations from the exact result on an ensemble of independent quasi-MC runs, which then could be instrumental in estimating errors of quasi-MC results. In addition to this, such study can be used to estimate the expected improvement in the performance of the SPEEDUP code when quasi-MC is implemented.

The usual implementation of the Monte Carlo method uses pseudo-random numbers for calculation of the integrals. In the simplest case, if we are calculating d-dimensional integral on a unit cube U^d, and if ξ is a sequence of pseudo-random d-dimensional points in U^d, then the MC estimate of the integral of the function $f(x)$ is given by the average of the function f evaluated at the MC sample of points ξ_i. According to the central limit theorem, such estimate converges to the exact value of the integral when the number of MC samples N_{MC} goes to infinity. Furthermore, central limit theorem states that the statistical distribution of numerical results obtained using large number of

Figure 9. Left: The anharmonic potential 1D-AHO, its energy eigenvalues (horizontal lines) and eigenfunctions, obtained by direct diagonalization of the space-discretized matrix of the evolution operator with level p=21 effective action and parameters A=1, g=48. Right: Results for the double-well potential, A=-10, g=12. On both graphs, left y-axis corresponds to V(x) and energy eigenvalues, while scale on the right y-axis corresponds to values of eigenfunctions, each vertically shifted to level with the appropriate eigenvalue.

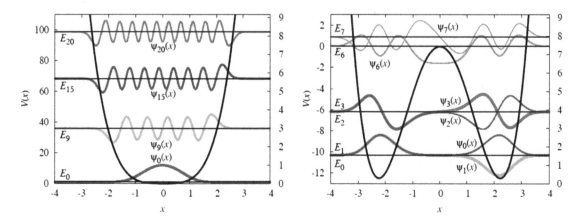

independent MC samples is a Gaussian, centred at the exact value of the integral, with the variance $\sigma^2(f)/N_{MC}$, where $\sigma^2(f)$ is given by the analytic formula

$$\sigma^2 \left(f \right) = \int_{U^d} f^2 \left(x \right) dx - \left(\int_{U^d} f \left(x \right) dx \right)^2 , \qquad (10)$$

and can be estimated as well from a single MC run. This gives clear statistical interpretation of errors when MC method is used: the distribution of deviations

$$\Delta = \int_{U^d} f \left(x \right) dx - \frac{1}{N_{MC}} \sum_{i=1}^{N_{MC}} f \left(\xi_i \right) , \qquad (11)$$

is a Gaussian with the expected standard deviation

$$E \left(\Delta \right) = \sqrt{\frac{\sigma^2 \left(f \right)}{N_{MC}}} . \qquad (12)$$

This shows the familiar convergence rate of $N_{MC}^{-1/2}$ associated with MC pseudo-random methods, and its main advantage: we can decrease the deviation of numerical results (i.e. increase the accuracy of results) by simply increasing N_{MC}, the number of MC samples.

The key property of (pseudo-)random sequences is their uniformity, so that any contiguous subsequence is well spread throughout the domain of integration. This idea has lead to the suggestion that using other sequences, which are more uniformly distributed than a random sequence, may produce even better results. Such sequences are called quasi-random or low-discrepancy sequences (Atanassov, Dimov, & Durchova, 2004).

Initially it may appear that a simple d-dimensional grid would provide optimal uniformity. However, grids suffer from several difficulties. First, the number of points required to create even a coarse mesh grows exponentially with the number of dimensions. Also, grids tend to have rather high discrepancy, a quantity measuring the deviation from the uniformity of a set of points. Finally, the size of the grid cannot be increased incrementally. The only obvious method for increasing the size of a uniform grid is to halve the mesh size, which requires addition of 2^d times the current number of points. Even such an exponential increase in the number of points would only yield a polynomial (depending on the discretization approach) increase in the accuracy.

Solution to this problem is to use infinite sequences of points such that for every N, the first N terms of a sequence are uniformly distributed throughout the cube. In order to quantify this, we introduce the discrepancy D_N of the sequence ξ_i of N points, defined as

$$D_N = \sup_{Q \in U^d} \left| \frac{\text{number of points in } Q}{N} - m \left(Q \right) \right| , \qquad (13)$$

where Q is any d-dimensional rectangle contained within U^d, with surfaces parallel to coordinate axes, and $m(Q)$ is its volume. By the law of the iterated logarithm, the expectation of the discrepancy of a random sequence is bounded by $(\log \log N) N^{-1/2}$.

There are many known quasi-random sequences (Sobol', 1967; Faure, 1992) for which the discrepancy is bounded by $(\log N)^d / N$, which suggests greater uniformity than a (pseudo-)random sequence. In this chapter we will use Sobol's sequence (Sobol', 1967) for implementation of the quasi-MC algorithm within the existing SPEEDUP code, as well as for a comparison with the earlier developed MC algorithm.

In order to verify the quasi-MC algorithm, which will be later used in the improved version of the SPEEDUP code, we have considered calculation of the Gaussian-type integrals

$$I = \int_{U^d} \exp \left(-\sum_{i=1}^{d} x_i^2 \right) dx , \qquad (14)$$

where d is the number of dimensions. In order to verify the expected approximate $1/N_{QMC}$ scaling of deviations from the exact value of the integral, we have performed the numerical calculation using the large number of independent QMC samples for different values of dimensionality d. The first important observation is that the obtained distribution of numerical estimates for the value of the integral was always found to be a Gaussian, whose parameters can be found by fitting. The obtained distributions were centred on the exact values of integrals (14) within the errors estimated by the fitted widths of Gaussians. The typical deviations of quasi-MC results are shown in Figure 10 as a function of the size of a quasi-random sample N_{QMC}. As can be seen from this log-log graph, the deviations are proportional to N_{QMC}^{-1}.

Quasi-MC Implementation of the SPEEDUP Code

In this section we present application of the quasi-MC method for calculation of quantum mechani-cal transition amplitudes, based on the modified version of the SPEEDUP code. We also study the statistical distribution of the obtained results on a large ensemble of samples, identify the appropriate estimate of deviations from the exact amplitudes and their dependence on the size of the sample, and assess the performance of the code. This will be done on a simple model of a quartic anharmonic oscillator, which however exhibits all features relevant for the proper assessment of the method and improved implementation of the algorithm.

QSPEEDUP, the modified version of the code, uses Sobol's set of low-discrepancy quasi-random numbers, instead of the pseudo-random numbers generated by the SPRNG library in the original SPEEDUP code. In the previous Section we presented results for the case of low-dimensional integrals of the Gaussian type. This allowed us to determine that the distribution of numerical results obtained by the quasi-MC algorithm is also of the Gaussian type. Although calculation of general transition amplitudes assumes calculation of discretized path integrals of much higher dimen-

Figure 10. Deviations of numerically calculated values of the integral (14) from the corresponding exact values, as a function of the number of quasi-random numbers NQMC for different dimensionalities d of the integral. Sobol' set in the appropriate number of dimensions was used.

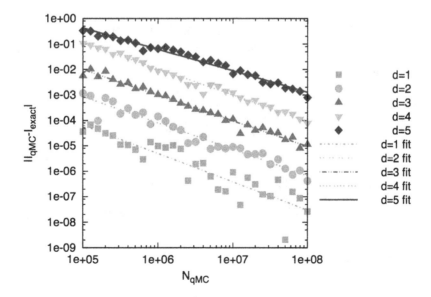

sionality and of a more complex type, depending on the potential, the dominant behaviour is still mostly given by the Gaussian integrals stemming from the kinetic part of the Hamiltonian.

The only modification in the code was related to the use of quasi-random instead of pseudo-random numbers. The implementation of Sobol's sequence we used allows generation of quasi-random numbers in a large number of dimensions, which were used in the Box-Müller method to obtain the trajectories according to the bisection algorithm. QSPEEDUP code is tested on the example of calculation of the transition amplitudes $A(0,1;1)$ for the anharmonic potential

$$V(x) = \frac{1}{2} m\omega^2 x^2 + \frac{1}{24} gx^4, \qquad (15)$$

for the values of parameters $m=1$, $g=1$, with the level $p=4$ effective action, and using the target bisection level $s=8$, corresponding to 255-dimensional integrals. For such a physical system we have first considered a distribution the ensemble

of 10^3 independently calculated transition amplitudes, each obtained from the sample of $N_{QMC}=10^8$ trajectories. The distribution is shown in Figure 11.

As expected from the results of previous Section, the observed distribution of transition amplitudes is again Gaussian. If we fit these numerical results to a Gaussian function, for the mean value and the associated error we get the estimate

$$\left\langle A_{QMC}^{p=4}\left(0,1;1\right)\right\rangle = 0.187029267\left(3\right),$$

while for the standard deviation the fitting gives $\sigma_{\left\langle A_{QMC}^{p=4}\right\rangle} = 5.6\left(2\right)\times 10^{-9}$. If the standard Monte Carlo method is used, for the same size of the sample we would get the standard deviation of around 3×10^{-6}, which is substantially higher than the standard deviation of quasi-MC results presented in Figure 11. Since the generation of quasi-random numbers has very similar complexity to the generation of pseudo-random numbers using the SPRNG library, the obtained increase

Figure 11. Distribution of numerically calculated transition amplitudes for anharmonic potential (15) for the parameters given in the text using the QSPEEDUP code. Each amplitude is obtained using the sample of NQMC=10⁸. The histogram is obtained from the ensemble of 10³ samples.

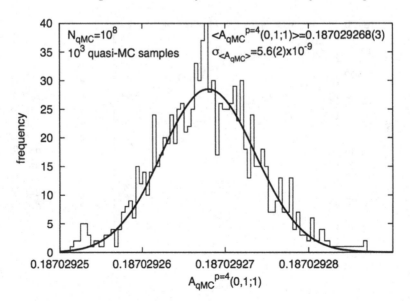

in the accuracy directly translates to the increase in the performance of the QSPEEDUP code.

In order to assess the obtained estimate for the amplitude (mean value of the Gaussian) is correct, i.e. if it is consistent with the exact value of the amplitude, we have used the MC SPEEDUP code with the exceedingly large number of samples $N_{MC}=10^{12}$. With such a sample we achieved the comparable precision for the amplitude, $A_{exact}^{p=4} = 0.18702926(3)$, which is used as our estimate for the exact value in further calculation of deviations of numerical results obtained from the QSPEEDUP code. As we see, this value is in excellent agreement with the mean value of the distribution from Figure 12 (i.e. the deployed quasi-MC algorithm is found to give the correct value of the amplitude).

Since the standard deviation of quasi-MC results cannot be estimated using the MC approach, where one simply calculates the standard deviation of the sample according to Equation (12), we have next studied the dependence of the deviation from the exact value of the amplitude as a function of the size of the sample N_{QMC}. Another approach would be to always study the distribution as in Figure 12 and estimate the standard deviation from an ensemble of samples. However, this takes a considerable amount of time, which is not justified if there are other means to reliably estimate the deviation. Here we use the exact value of the amplitude obtained by the MC algorithm, and therefore simplify the numerical analysis considerably. The results are given in Figure 12. As we see, the earlier observed approximate N_{QMC}^{-1} scaling of deviations is present for all values of the target bisection level.

Such scaling leads to the improved performance of quasi-MC algorithm compared to the standard MC method. As explained earlier, generation of pseudo-random and quasi-random numbers is of similar complexity, and therefore the fact that one needs much smaller size of quasi-MC sample in order to obtain the same accuracy as when MC algorithm is used presents a significant advantage.

Figure 12. Deviations of transition amplitudes calculated using the QSPEEDUP code from the exact value as a function of the quasi-MC sample NQMC. The results are shown for different values of the target bisection level s, corresponding to the discretization with 2s-1 time steps.

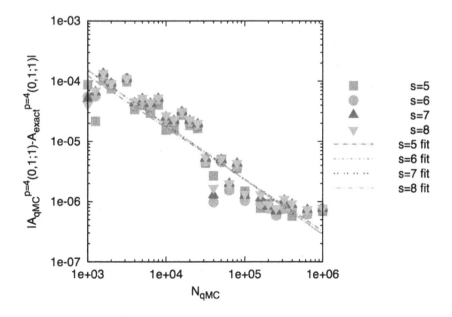

This is illustrated in Figure 13, where we plot the speedup, i.e. the ratio of required CPU time for the execution of MC and quasi-MC code in order to achieve the same deviation from the exact value of the amplitude. As we can see, even for a moderate value of the precision Δ, one obtains improvement of many orders of magnitude, approximately proportional to $1/\Delta$.

PORTING OF (Q) SPEEDUP CODES TO HPC INFRASTRUCTURE

Porting of (Q) SPEEDUP code to new HPC architectures enables its use on a broader set of clusters and supercomputer facilities. The purpose of the code optimization is to fully utilize available computing resources, eliminating bottlenecks that may be located in different parts of the code, depending on the details of hardware implementation and architecture of the CPU. In some situations even compiling, linking or choosing more appropri-

ate (optimized) libraries can lead to significant reduction in program execution times. However, the optimization must be performed carefully and the new code has to be verified after each change by comparison of its numerical results with the correct reference values.

In addition to obtaining highly optimized code, the above procedure can be also used to benchmark different hardware platforms and to compare their performance on a specific application/code. Such application-specific benchmarking, based on the assessment of hardware performance for the chosen set of applications, can be also used for the proper planning of hardware upgrades of computing centres supporting several user communities.

Here we describe the performed optimization and the obtained benchmarking results. In all benchmarks in this chapter we have executed the code with $N_{MC} = 5120000$ *MC* samples for the quantum-mechanical amplitude of the quartic anharmonic oscillator with the boundary conditions

Figure 13. The speedup in the calculation of transition amplitudes at the given precision using the QSPEEDUP CODE, compared with the required CPU time for the calculation using MC algorithm implemented in the SPEEDUP code

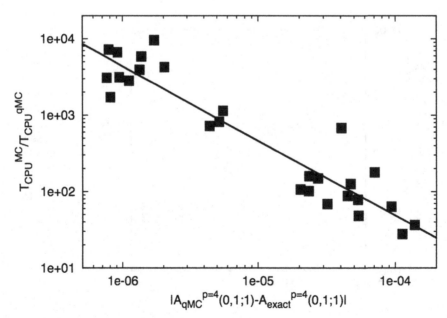

$q(t=0)=0, q(t=T=1)=1$, with zero anharmonicity and with level $p=9$ effective action.

The hardware platform used for the testing reported here was IBM BladeCenter with three kinds of servers within the H-type chassis commonly used in high performance computing and a separate 1U server based on latest Intel Nehalem Xeon processors:

- HX21XM blade Server based on Intel Xeon technology. It features two Intel Xeon E5405 processors that run on 2.0 GHz with front side bus of 1333MHz and level two cache (L2) of 12MB with support for Intel SSE2, SSE3, SSE4.1 extensions.
- The BladeCenter JS22 server is a single-wide, 4-core, 2-socket with two cores per socket, 4.0 GHz POWER6 SCM processors. Each processor includes 64 KB I-cache and 32 KB D-cache L1 cache per core with 4 MB L2 cache per core.
- Intel Server System SR1625UR based on latest Intel Xeon processors with Nehalem micro-architecture. Two quad-core Xeon X5570 processors are present within the system. These CPUs run on 2.93GHz with triple channel DDR3 memory subsystem with support of latest SSE4.2 extensions. They are equipped with 256 Kb of Mid-Level cache per core and 8MB of cache shared between cores (L3).

This chapter gives results for a serial (Q) SPEEDUP code on each platform with different compilers. These results are later used as a reference in benchmarking and in verification of the optimized code. Furthermore, chapter gives results for (Q) SPEEDUP MPI code tested on Intel platform, and presents the threaded (Q) SPEEDUP code and results obtained with Intel and POWER architectures.

SERIAL (Q) SPEEDUP CODE

For Intel Xeon 5405 Blade server we compiled the serial code with GCC C compiler using optimization flag –O1, which turns to give the best performance. Along with GCC, we also used ICC compiler with optimization flag –fast, equivalent to the combination –O3 –xHOST –ipo –no-prec-div –static. Intel Nehalem platform shows best results with GCC flags –O1 –funroll-loops (loop unrolling), and with the –fast flag for Intel's ICC. On POWER6 the code was compiled with both GCC and IBM XLC compiler. On POWER6 Blade –q64 –O5 –qaltivec –qenablevmx flags were used with XLC and –O3 –funroll-loops with GCC. Results for the serial program benchmarking are presented in Table 1.

Table 1 demonstrates the significant increase in the speed of the execution of the code when platform-specific compiler is used. New Nehalem platform in conjunction with ICC compiler gives the best performance compared to all other platforms.

MPI (Q) SPEEDUP Code

On the Intel Blade Xeon 5405 and Intel Nehalem platform, we tested the performance of the (Q) SPEEDUP code with MPI implementation, compiled by the ICC compiler with –fast flag. Also we tested the behaviour of Nehalem CPUs with Hyper-Threading feature enabled and disabled. The results are shown in Figure 14.

Table 1. Average times of execution of a serial (Q) SPEEDUP code on all tested platforms with different compilers. The flags used are given in the text.

Platform/Compiler	GCC [s]	ICC [s]	XLC [s]
Intel Xeon 5405	6280±20	1600±20	-
Intel Nehalem	3520±10	920±10	-
POWER6	8980±10	-	1830±10

Figure 14. Average times of execution of the MPI (Q) SPEEDUP code on Intel Xeon 5405 and Intel Nehalem platforms compiled with ICC (-fast flag)

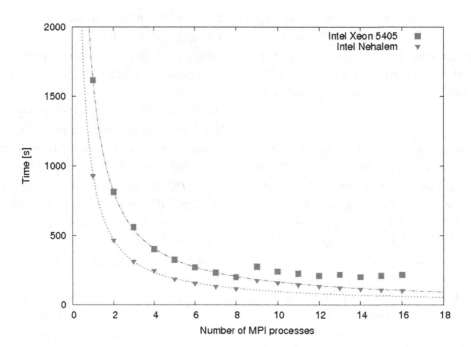

As we can see, the MPI version of the code shows excellent scalability with the number of MPI processes. When the number of MPI processes exceeds the number of physical cores in the system (eight), the operating system is trying to distribute the load among already fully loaded cores, which creates additional overhead. This is less pronounced at the Nehalem platform, with the Hyper-Threading enabled. In that case, as shown in Figure 15, slightly better results are achieved when the numbers of MPI instances exceeds the number of physical cores. Below this threshold the results are identical.

MPI implementation gives minimal execution time of around 100s for Nehalem platform and around 200s for Intel Xeon 5405.

Modified (Q) SPEEDUP Code

To fully optimize the parallel (Q) SPEEDUP code, instead of using MPI API, we implemented its threaded version using the POSIX threads (pthreads). Each thread calculates N_{MC}/N_{TH} of Monte Carlo samples, where N_{TH} represents the number of initiated threads. Also, some minor additional modifications of the code were performed, focusing on specific improvements for $p=9$ effective action. The Intel version of the code was compiled with ICC, while the POWER version was compiled with XLC. The obtained numerical results are summarized in Figure 16.

With the threaded code we obtained non-negligible increase in the speed of the code compared to previous implementations. Again, Intel Nehalem with the ICC compiler was much faster than all other platforms. If we compare the increase in the speed gained by implementing the threaded code, the POWER6 platform shows a 12% performance gain (threaded vs. the serial code), and we get around 6% gain for Intel platforms (threaded vs. MPI code).

The minimal execution time with the threaded code was 190s on Intel Xeon 5405 Blade, 95s on Intel Nehalem and 235s on the POWER Blade.

Figure 15. Average times of execution of the MPI (Q)SPEEDUP code on Intel Nehalem platform compiled with ICC (fast flag) with hyper-threading technology enabled (HT on) and disabled (HT off)

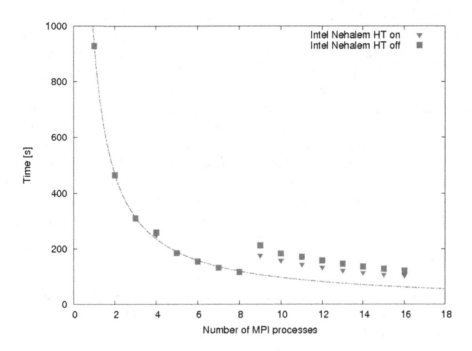

Figure 16. Average times of execution of the threaded (Q) SPEEDUP code on Intel and POWER6 platforms

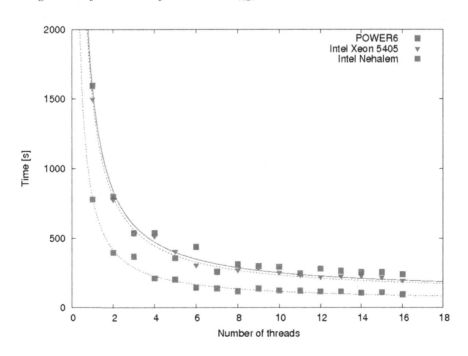

Again, we can see a small impact on the execution speed when Hyper-Threading technology is enabled on the Intel Nehalem CPUs.

We have also observed an interesting behaviour on Intel platforms, which is presented in Figure 17. Although the threaded code gives better performance when compiled with ICC compared to the code compiled with GCC, the times of execution of the ICC-complied code for the same parameters and the same number of threads differ significantly for several consecutive runs. Such relatively large scattering of execution times around the average might be accredited to the low-level hardware implementation details of Intel CPUs, as well as to the aggressive optimization techniques used by the –fast flag. On the other hand, the execution of the same code compiled with GCC did not exhibit such behaviour. This might point to the load-balancing issues when aggressive optimization is used with ICC, while GCC is not able to achieve such level of optimization and thus is not affected. The similar behaviour was also observed on Intel Xeon 5405 platform.

CONCLUSION

We have presented the high performance computing and Grid computing approaches to computational science, which now represents one of the key enablers of scientific progress in many areas of research. Each of these approaches is well suited for a particular set of challenges lying ahead of different research groups. Grid computing is designed and optimized for large-scale distributed computing ideally supporting execution of enormous numbers of independent tasks (Monte Carlo simulations, search of large, multidimensional parameter spaces). On the other hand, HPC is ideally suited for capability computing, when solving of challenging problems requires highly parallel and scalable systems, able to support simultaneous execution of thousands or tens of thousands parallel processes.

It should be noted that problems and applications ported to Grid infrastructures could be easily deployed to HPC resources, and take advantage of various types of computing infrastructures. The

Figure 17. Times of execution of the threaded (Q) SPEEDUP code on Intel Nehalem platform with ICC and GCC compiler

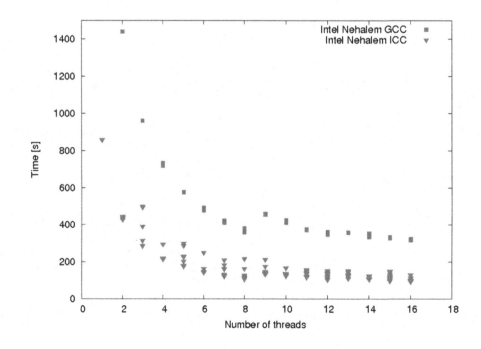

presented (Q) SPEEDUP application is precisely one of such use-cases, and it can be successfully used in the Grid framework, as well as in the HPC setup.

Future development of distributed computing infrastructures will include many different directions currently being investigated. Prototypes of new ICT technologies are being built and tested by many stakeholders. For instance, PRACE research infrastructure is investing a significant fund in exploring energy efficient solutions for HPC, new technologies for parallel I/O, large SMP prototypes and new types of interconnect. The challenge of constructing, managing, and effectively using next-generation Exaflops supercomputers is an active area of research from hardware point of view, but also from the application point of view. The scalability of many applications critically depends on interconnect technology and communication protocols, and in that regard important new developments are present in China, whose new series of supercomputers is based on the self-developed interconnect solutions. Combining many-core CPUs, each of which now practically becomes a small SMP cluster, with GPGPUs is also a critical task. Development of libraries, frameworks and standards that enable efficient programming of applications for such systems is another challenge that represents active area of research.

ACKNOWLEDGMENT

This work was supported in part by the Ministry of Education and Science of the Republic of Serbia, under project No. ON171017 and project No. III43007, and the Swiss National Science Foundation, through the SCOPES grant IZ73Z0-128169. Numerical simulations were run on the AEGIS e-Infrastructure, supported in part by FP7 projects PRACE-1IP, PRACE-2IP, HP-SEE, and EGI-InSPIRE.

REFERENCES

Anderson, D. P., Cobb, J., Korpela, E., Lebofsky, M., & Werthimer, D. (2002). SETI@home: An experiment in public-resource computing. *Communications of the ACM, 45*(11), 56–61. doi:10.1145/581571.581573 PMID:12238525

Atanassov, E. I., Dimov, I. T., & Durchova, M. K. (2004). A new quasi-Monte Carlo algorithm for numerical integration of smooth functions. *Lecture Notes in Computer Science, 2907*, 128–135. doi:10.1007/978-3-540-24588-9_13

Balaž, A., Bogojević, A., Vidanović, I., & Pelster, A. (2009). Recursive Schroedinger equation approach to faster converging path integrals. *Physical Review E: Statistical, Nonlinear, and Soft Matter Physics, 79*, 036701. doi:10.1103/PhysRevE.79.036701

Balaž, A., Prnjat, O., Vudragović, D., Slavnic, V., Liabotis, I., & Atanassov, E. etal. (2011). Development of grid e-infrastructure in South-Eastern Europe. *Journal of Grid Computing, 9*(2), 135–154. doi:10.1007/s10723-011-9185-0

Balaž, A., Vidanović, I., Bogojević, A., & Pelster, A. (2010). Ultra-fast converging path-integral approach for rotating ideal Bose-Einstein condensates. *Physics Letters. [Part A], 374*(13-14), 1539–1549. doi:10.1016/j.physleta.2010.01.034

Balaž, A., Vidanović, I., Stojiljković, D., Vudragović, D., Belić, A., & Bogojević, A. (2012). SPEEDUP code for calculation of transition amplitudes via the effective action approach. *Computer Physics Communications, 11*(3), 739–755.

Bogojević, A., Balaž, A., & Belić, A. (2005a). Systematically accelerated convergence of path integrals. *Physical Review Letters, 94*(18), 180403–180407. doi:10.1103/PhysRevLett.94.180403 PMID:15904348

Bogojević, A., Balaž, A., & Belić, A. (2005b). Systematic speedup of path integrals of a generic n-fold discretized theory. *Physical Review Letters, B 72*, 064302:1-8.

Bogojević, A., Balaž, A., & Belić, A. (2005c). Generalization of Euler's summation formula to path integrals. *Physics Letters. [Part A], 344*, 84–90. doi:10.1016/j.physleta.2005.06.053

Bogojević, A., Balaž, A., & Belić, A. (2005d). Asymptotic properties of path integral ideals. *Physical Review E: Statistical, Nonlinear, and Soft Matter Physics, 72*(036128), 1–4.

Bogojević, A., Vidanović, I., Balaž, A., & Belić, A. (2008). Fast convergence of path integrals for many-body systems. *Physics Letters. [Part A], 372*(19), 3341–3349. doi:10.1016/j.physleta.2008.01.079

Ceperley, D. M. (1995). Path integrals in the theory of condensed helium. *Reviews of Modern Physics, 67*(2), 279–355. doi:10.1103/RevModPhys.67.279

De Raedt, H., & De Raedt, B. (1983). Applications of the generalized Trotter formula. *Physical Review A., 28*(6), 3575–3580. doi:10.1103/PhysRevA.28.3575

Dongarra, J. J., Luszczek, P., & Petitet, A. (2003). The LINPACK benchmark: Past, present and future. *Concurrency and Computation, 15*, 803–820. doi:10.1002/cpe.728

Faure, H. (1992). Good permutations for extreme discrepancy. *Journal of Number Theory, 42*(1), 47–56. doi:10.1016/0022-314X(92)90107-Z

Feynman, R. P., & Hibbs, A. R. (Eds.). (1965). *Quantum mechanics and path integrals*. New York: McGraw-Hill.

Foster, I., & Kesselman, C. (2004). *The grid 2: Blueprint for a new computing infrastructure* (2nd ed.). San Francisco, CA: Morgan Kaufmann.

Girone, M. (2011). *EGI-InSPIRE current requirements & outlook*. Retrieved September 11, 2013, from http://storageconference.org/2011/Presentations/MSST/15.Girone.pdf

Grujić, J., Bogojević, A., & Balaž, A. (2006). Energy estimators and calculation of energy expectation values in the path integral formalism. *Physics Letters. [Part A], 360*(2), 217–223. doi:10.1016/j.physleta.2006.08.044

Hill, M. D., Jouppi, N. P., & Sohi, G. S. (2000). *Readings in computer architecture*. San Francisco: Morgan Kaufmann Publishers.

Hoffman, A. R., & Traub, J. F. (Eds.). (1989). *Supercomputers: Directions in technology and applications*. Washington, DC: National Academy Press.

HP-SEE. (2013). *High-performance computing infrastructure for South East Europe's research communities*. Retrieved September 11, 2013, from http://www.hp-see.eu/

Jones, B. (2009). *Enabling grids for e-science*. Retrieved September 11, 2013, from http://ec.europa.eu/research/conferences/2009/rtd-2009/presentations/infrastructures/robert_jones_-_egee_enabling_grids_for_e-science.pdf

Kleinert, H. (Ed.). (2009). *Path integrals in quantum mechanics, statistics, polymer physics, and financial markets* (5th ed.). Singapore: World Scientific Publishing Co. Pte. Ltd. doi:10.1142/9789814273572

Lederer, H. (2011). *DEISA: Six years of extreme computing*. Retrieved September 11, 2013, from http://www.deisa.eu/

Li, X. P., & Broughton, J. Q. (1987). High-order correction to the Trotter expansion for use in computer simulation. *The Journal of Chemical Physics, 86*(9), 5094. doi:10.1063/1.452653

PRACE. (2012). *PRACE – The scientific case for HPC in Europe*. Retrieved September 11, 2013, from http://www.prace-ri.eu/

Rusu, O. (Ed.). (2004). *Information societies technology (IST) programme: South Eastern European research & education networking*. Retrieved September 11, 2013, from http://www.seera-ei.eu/images/stories/seeren/SEEREN-WP4-RoEduNet-006-D14bConfAndPerf-b-2004-10-09.pdf

Sobol', I. M. (1967). On the distribution of points in a cube and the approximate evaluation of integrals. *U.S.S.R Comput. Maths. Math. Phys*, *7*(4), 784–802.

Takahashi, M., & Imada, M. (1984). Quantum Monte Carlo simulation of a two-dimensional electron system – Melting of Wigner crystal. *Journal of the Physical Society of Japan*, *53*(11), 3765–3769. doi:10.1143/JPSJ.53.3765

Tan, G., Sreedhar, V. C., & Gao, G. R. (2011). Analysis and performance results of computing betweenness centrality on IBM Cyclops64. *The Journal of Supercomputing*, *56*(1), 1–24. doi:10.1007/s11227-009-0339-9

Vidanović, I., Bogojević, A., Balaž, A., & Belić, A. (2009). Properties of quantum systems via diagonalization of transition amplitudes: II: Systematic improvements of short-time propagation. *Physical Review E: Statistical, Nonlinear, and Soft Matter Physics*, *80*, 066706. doi:10.1103/PhysRevE.80.066706 PMID:20365301

Vidanović, I., Bogojević, A., & Belić, A. (2009). Properties of quantum systems via diagonalization of transition amplitudes: I: Discretization effects. *Physical Review E: Statistical, Nonlinear, and Soft Matter Physics*, *80*, 066705. doi:10.1103/PhysRevE.80.066705 PMID:20365300

Vudragović, D., Balaž, A., Slavnić, V., & Belić, A. (2009). Serbian participation in grid computing projects. In *Proceedings of the XXII International Symposium on Nuclear Electronics & Computing* (pp. 286-293). Academic Press.

Wilson, R. J. (2001). *The European DataGrid project*. Retrieved September 11, 2013, from http://www.snowmass2001.org/e7/papers/wilson.pdf

ADDITIONAL READING

Anderson, P. W. (Ed.). (1984). *Basic Notions of Condensed Matter Physics*. London: Benjamin/Cummings.

Ashcroft, N. W., & Mermin, N. D. (Eds.). (1976). *Solid State Physics*. New York: Holt, Rinehart, and Winston.

Berry, M. W., Gallivan, K. A., Gallopoulos, E., Grama, A., Philippe, B., Saad, Y., & Saied, F. (Eds.). (2012). *High-Performance Scientific Computing: Algorithms and Applications*. New York: Springer. doi:10.1007/978-1-4471-2437-5

Chaikin, P. M., & Libensky, T. C. (Eds.). (2000). *Principles of Condensed Matter Physics*. Cambridge, UK: Cambridge University Press.

Cheptsov, A., Brinkmann, S., Gracia, J., Resch, M. M., & Nagel, W. E. (Eds.). (2013). *Tools for High Performance Computing 2012*. Heidelberg: Springer. doi:10.1007/978-3-642-37349-7

Erl, T., Puttini, R., & Mahmood, Z. (2013). *Cloud Computing: Concepts, Technology & Architecture*. Upper Saddle River, NJ: Prentice Hall.

Foster, I., Gentzsch, W., Grandinetti, L., & Joubert, G. R. (Eds.). (2011). *High Performance Computing: From Grids and Clouds to Exascale*. Amsterdam: IOS Press.

Fradkin, E. (Ed.). (1991). *Field Theories of Condensed Matter Systems*. Redwood City, CA: Addison-Wesley.

Grandinetti, L. (Ed.). (2008). *High Performance Computing and Grids in Action*. Amsterdam: IOS Press.

Guo, Y., & Grossman, R. L. (Eds.). (1999). *High Performance Data Mining: Scaling Algorithms, Applications and Systems*. New York: Springer.

Hager, G., & Wellein, G. (2011). *Introduction to High Performance Computing for Scientists and Engineer, Chapman & Hall/CRC Computational Science Series*. Boca Raton, FL: Taylor & Francis.

Hwang, K., Dongarra, J., & Fox, G. C. (Eds.). (2011). *Distributed and Cloud Computing: From Parallel Processing to the Internet of Things*. Burlington, MA: Morgan Kaufmann Publishers.

Jamsa, K. (Ed.). (2013). *Cloud Computing*. Burlington, MA: Jones & Bartlett Learning.

Khaitan, S. K., & Gupta, A. (Eds.). (2013). *High Performance Computing in Power and Energy Systems*. Heidelberg: Springer. doi:10.1007/978-3-642-32683-7

Levesque, J., & Wagenbreth, G. (2011). *High Performance Computing: Programming and Applications, Chapman & Hall/CRC Computational Science Series*. Boca Raton, FL: Taylor & Francis.

Lin, S. C., & Yen, E. (Eds.). (2011). *Data Driven e-Science*. New York: Springer. doi:10.1007/978-1-4419-8014-4

Nagaosa, N. (Ed.). (1999). *Quantum Field Theory in Condensed Matter*. Berlin: Springer. doi:10.1007/978-3-662-03774-4

Pethick, C. J., & Smith, H. (2008). *Bose-Einstein Condensation in Dilute Gases*. Cambridge, UK: Cambridge University Press. doi:10.1017/CBO9780511802850

Pitaevskii, L., & Stringari, S. (Eds.). (2003). *Bose-Einstein Condensation*. Oxford, UK: Oxford University Press.

Preve, N. P. (Ed.). (2012). *Computational and Data Grids: Principles, Applications, and Design*. Hershey: IGI Global.

Reese, G. (Ed.). (2009). *Cloud Application Architectures: Building Applications and Infrastructure in the Cloud*. Sebastopol, CA: O'Reilly Media.

Sloan, J. D. (Ed.). (2005). *High Performance Linux Clusters with OSCAR, Rocks, OpenMosix, and MPI*. Sebastopol, CA: O'Reilly Media.

Taniar, D., Leung, C. H. C., Rahayu, W., & Goel, S. (2008). *High Performance Parallel Database Processing and Grid Databases, Wiley Series on Parallel and Distributed Computing*. Hoboken, NJ: John Wiley & Sons. doi:10.1002/9780470391365

Udoh, E. (Ed.). (2011). *Cloud, Grid and High Performance Computing: Emerging Applications*. Hershey: IGI Global. doi:10.4018/978-1-60960-603-9

Vanderbauwhede, W., & Benkrid, K. (Eds.). (2013). *High-Performance Computing Using FPGAs*. New York: Springer. doi:10.1007/978-1-4614-1791-0

Vetter, J. S. (Ed.). (2013). *Contemporary High Performance Computing: From Petascale toward Exascale, Chapman & Hall/CRC Computational Science Series*. Boca Raton, FL: Taylor & Francis.

Yang, L. T., & Guo, M. (Eds.). (2006). *High-Performance Computing: Paradigm and Infrastructure*. Hoboken, NJ: John Wiley & Sons.

KEY TERMS AND DEFINITIONS

Cloud Computing: Is a term that represents use of computer resources, including computing and data storage services, which are served over the real-time network, usually in a virtualized environment. The cloud provider manages large number of computers, and services are offered through virtualization of hardware, i.e. users deploy virtual machines on provider's hardware, thus instantiating the desired services. This model is known as Infrastructure as a Service (IaaS). In the model of Platform as a Service (PaaS), the provider offers a computing platform (operating system, compilers, databases, web server). Also widely use in business applications is Software as a Service (Saas), where the emphasis is on providing specific software and databases. Network as a Service (NaaS) is also offered for users requiring network connectivity services (including inter-cloud connectivity).

Condensed Matter Physics: Is a branch of physics studying many-body systems in the condensed phase of matter, i.e. liquids (including quantum liquids) and solids (including crystallography and magnetism). The methods used include experiment, theory, and numerical simulations. Condensed matter physics applies ideas of quantum mechanics, quantum field theory, and statistical mechanics, and widely overlaps with materials science, nanotechnology, and chemistry.

Grid Computing: Is distributed computer systems, comprising of many geographically scattered computer resources, which are connected by high-speed network, and logically organized into a single system by a software layer, usually designated as middleware. Typical examples of Grids include large networks of computer clusters distributed over many institutions contributing computer resources. Most notable are the Grids operated by EGI (European Grid Infrastructure) and OSG (Open Science Grid in USA), used for scientific computing by researchers (primarily for particle physics applications, but the number of fields of science and user groups relying on these Grids is significantly increasing over the years).

High Performance Computing: Is use of large-scale computer clusters and supercomputers for numerical simulations that require significant computer resources for execution. Typically, this involves massively parallel numerical simulations, running on thousands of processors, and large amounts of memory available in a shared fashion (typical for mainframe supercomputers)

or distributed among the computing nodes (typical for computer clusters).

Numerical Simulation: The detailed description of various physical, social, etc. systems is usually done by developing sophisticated models, which are then implemented through computer algorithms and (serial or parallel) programs. Execution of such programs on computers, with the aim of simulating real systems, is usually designated as numerical simulation.

Parallel Programming: The serial programming paradigm involves a single processor that executes a program, a set of instructions defined by a programmer, in a serial fashion, one by one. Parallel programming paradigm is developed for a multi-processor computer (either multi-core single-physical processor, or massively parallel system with many processors), and assumes that a given problem can be divided into sub-tasks, which can then be executed in parallel, concurrently, with possible exchange of data during the execution. The programming that enables such type of parallel execution of instructions is usually called parallel programming.

Supercomputer: Is a computer system capable of executing large number of operations, comprising a massive number of processors and large shared or distributed memory. The processors are running in parallel and are able to exchange the data, thus making possible to achieve high computing power, which is usually measured in the number of floating point operations being executed in one second. The required computer power for a system to be designated as a supercomputer is time-dependent, and is usually defined through a list of most powerful systems in the world, such as Top500 (top500.org), where only a limited number of systems (e.g. first 500) at any given time are considered to be supercomputers. As of 2013, petaflops-capable systems are classified as supercomputers, and in the coming years this will shift towards exaflop-capable systems.

Chapter 10
Exploiting Spatial and Temporal Patterns in a High-Performance CPU

Goran Rakočević
Serbian Academy of Sciences and Arts, Serbia

Veljko Milutinović
Univeristy of Belgrade, Serbia

ABSTRACT

In modern computer systems, the effect known as the memory gap has become a serious bottleneck. It is becoming increasingly difficult to bridge this gap with traditional solutions, and much effort is put into developing new and more effective solutions to this problem. An earlier design, the Dual Data Cache (DDC), is a cache design that implies separation of data into two different cache subsystems so as to increase effectiveness of the cache. Data are separated accordingly to their predominant type of locality. The modified DDC, described here, introduces different internal organizations of the temporal and spatial parts, for better utilization of data characteristics. Conducted simulations show substantial improvements over traditional cache systems, with little increase in surface area and power consumption.

INTRODUCTION

With the development of the technology, the amount of comuptation that can be done in a unit of time within a microprocessor chip has grown dramatically. On the other hand, the speed at which data can be reterived from the main memory was not able to keep up. The result is a situation where microprocessor hardware remains underutilized, as it has to wait for inputs from the main memory, effictly making the memory a major system bottleneck. This phenomenon is known as the memory wall (McKee, 2004).

Memory wall has been a major target of research for decades (Wulf, 1995; McKee, 2004; Xie, 2013). The most effective way of allivating this problem has been the utilizations of cache mechanisams (Smith, 1987; Baer, 1988). A small,

DOI: 10.4018/978-1-4666-5784-7.ch010

very fast piece of memory is placed between the microprocessor chip and the main memory. This cache holds some of the data and respondes to requests form the CPU, while the main memory is accessed only when the data is not available in the cache. Cache memories soon became integrated with the microprocessor chips, enableing for very fast access times.

Further developments went in the direction of building data predictors – logic that could predict what data will be needed next, and than bring that data into the cache ahead of time (Lipasti & Shen, 1996). Unlike control flow (i.e. branch) predcitors, data predictors proved effective in only a small subset of cases, with relatively regular access patterns (Daly, 2013). An alternative solution was to offer pre-fetching primitieves, allowing the programmers to do this manulay, or thorugh compler support (Koufaty, 1998).

A number of approaches followed a different directon: to make the structure of the cache different and optimized to the data at hand. One such approach is presented here.

Problem Statement

Traditional cache memory architectures are based on the locality property of common memory reference patterns. This means that a part of the contents of the main memory is replicated in smaller and faster memories closer to processor. The processor can then access these data in the nearby fast cache, without suffering the long penalties of waiting for a main memory access.

Increasing the performance of a cache system is typically done by enlarging the cache. This has led to caches that consume an ever-growing part of modern microprocessor chips. However, bigger caches induce longer latencies, so making a cache larger, beyond a certain point, becomes counter-productive. At this point, a further increasing of the performance of the cache represents a difficult problem.

EXISTING SOLUTIONS

Most common solution to the above stated problem is the introduction of multiple level cache hierarchies, where the problem of speed is solved with fast and small lower level caches closer to the processor, while the problems of capacity and hit ratio are solved with slower and much larger higher level caches closer to the memory (Milutinovic, 1996). These high level caches occupy large portions of the chip, and induce high latencies in the system.

A number of attempts have been made towards developing mechanisms that improve performance of the cache by adding some logic to caching, rather than by increasing the cache size. Some of these mechanisms have focused on examining (physical) properties of cache memories and suggested solutions based on combing two or more cache memories of different characteristics on the same level (i.e. the Victim (Jouppi, 1990) and the Assist (Etsion, 2012) cache). These solutions mostly deal with increasing associativity of very fast direct-mapped cache memories, without incurring long latencies of highly associative caches. Others have looked at patterns of data accesses in order to build a cache system that suits the characteristics of data better (i.e. the Dual Data Cache, Split Temporal/Spatial cache, etc.).

These solutions mostly deal with increasing hit ratio, or decreasing complexity (allow for smaller sized caches) without compromising hit ratio. A detailed taxonomy can be found in (Gašić, 2007).

The modified Dual Data Cache (modified DDC) falls in to the second category, as some of the concepts used in this chapter are taken from the Dual Data Cache (DDC), which was first introduced in a series of papers in the 1990' (González, 1995; Milutinovic, 1996; Milutinovic, 1996). However, the system also utilizes two cache memories of different characteristics on the same level, as the solutions in the first category.

Finally, the major goal of the modified DDC system is to decrease the overall access latency of the system. A certain improvement in hit ratio might be inherited from the original DDC system, but as this is not of primary interest, hit ratio will not be examined in detail.

The major idea behind DDC is that two different types of locality (spatial and temporal) in data access patterns can be observed, and that data exhibiting predominantly one of these types of localities should be treated differently than the data that exhibit the other (González, 1995). "Data exhibiting predominantly" spatial locality would mean that, after a given address is accessed, there is a relatively high probability that a neighboring address will be accessed, too. These data should thus be fetched in larger blocks. This, however, means that some of the unnecessary data will also be brought into the cache, so a larger (and thus slower) cache is in order (Kumar, 2012). "Data exhibiting temporal locality" implies a relatively high probability of referencing a certain address again in the near future. These data are better suited to smaller block sizes (i.e. one word block size). Consequently, only the (frequently) used data are fetched. This means that a smaller and a faster cache can be used.

DETAILS OF THE PROPOSED APPROACH

In this section we will discuss the basic design behind the approach and analyze the major source of improvements introduced by a modified DDC system. We then go on to examine some further issues concerning any DDC system.

Basic Design

Solution basis is splitting the cache into two parts dedicated for data exhibiting temporal and spatial locality (Figure 1). Each part has a different

organization and data handling, according to the characteristics of the data, which are stored in it.

The spatial part is a larger cache with the usual block size. This part is accessed with latencies usual for similarly sized traditional caches. The temporal part is organized as a small and fast direct mapped cache with one-word block size. Smaller size and direct mapping should mean that this cache can be accessed with lower latencies when compared to the spatial part (Resnick, 2012).

For determination of data locality (spatial or temporal), each memory word is augmented with one bit tag. A single tag can be used for an entire spatial block. Those tags can be initially set at compile time and later changed at profile and run time. The system can also be used with legacy software compiled without DDC support. In this case, a default locality can be assumed (it will later become clear that default locality type should be set to spatial). As tags are changed in

Figure 1. Organization of the DDC cache. Legend: MM = main memory; CPU = central processing unit; SC = spatial part; TC = temporal part. Description: The novel cache organization – DDC cache consists of two parts: the temporal and the spatial part. Temporal part is organized as a small and fast direct mapped cache with one-word block size. Spatial part is a larger cache with the usual block size.

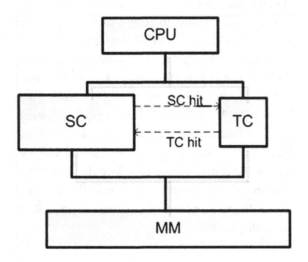

run time and data evicted and later refetched, the system will begin to function properly.

Memory reference request from the processor is simultaneously sent to the both DDC cache modules. When a hit in one part of the DDC (temporal or spatial) is detected, a signal is sent to the other part of the DDC to prevent its request to the main memory.

If requested data are not found in any of the DDC modules, a memory fetch will be initiated. Memory returns the block of appropriate length depending upon its current locality tag. This tag determines whether the block to be placed either into spatial or into temporal DDC part. The appropriate part responds by receiving the data and responding to the CPU, while the other part cancels the request received from the CPU. If a writeback is generated the cache should also send the information back to the memory on whether the data have been retagged. For this purpose the bus is augmented with one bit showing the type of locality of the data that are currently being transported.

The main memory is assumed to respond to requests in a critical-word-first manner, therefore the miss penalty should be the same for both the temporal and the spatial misses. If data are retagged, they are not evicted immediately, but are only marked as retagged. The new locality setting is taken into account only after the data have been evicted and fetched again.

Expected Improvement Analysis

The main source of performance improvements generated by a modified DDC system is the short access latency of the temporal part of the cache. This latency directly affects the average memory access latency of the whole system.

In a traditional cache system the average memory access latency (t) is:

$$t = p * tc + (1-p)*tm$$

where p stands for the probability of a cache hit, tc is the cache access latency, and tm is the cache miss latency.

In a modified system the average memory access latency (t) would be:

$$t = ps * ts + pt * tt + (1-(ps + pt))*tm$$

where ps and pt stand for the probabilities of hits in the spatial and temporal part of the cache, ts and tt stand for access latencies of the spatial and the temporal parts of the cache, and tm is the cache miss latency.

As the hit probability of a modified DDC system equals the sum of probabilities in both its parts, it is easily shown that the overall average memory access latency is shorter for a modified DDC system (assuming same hit probabilities for the whole modified DDC system and the traditional cache system, which will be discussed shortly):

$$ps * ts + pt * tt < ps * ts + pt * ts = (ps + pt) * ts = p * tc$$

The modified DDC system should also show an improvement in hit ratio (thus an improvement in hit probabilty) over a traditional cahe system of a similar size. The data with poor spatial (and high temporal) locality go to the temporal cache leading to a better cache utilization because the data from the same spatial block as the temporal data being accessd are not fetched and thus do not casue eviction of potentionaly usefull data. This also means less contention on the bus, as less useless data is transfered.

Locality Resolving

Mechanisms for resolving the data locality are basically the same as described in (González, 1995) for the original DDC system. Determining the locality of the data can be done at compile-time, profile-time, run-time, or, preferably as a combinations of these methods.

Compile-Time Resolution

The simplest compile-time algorithm for the initial allocation implies that the simple variables and constants are labeled as T (temporal) and the elements of complex data structures are labeled as S (spatial). More sophisticated algorithms are also possible. However, it should be noted that proper labeling is vastly dependant on the (spatial) block size, as well as the size of both parts of the cache.

With larger blocks stronger spatial locality is needed to justify transfer of the whole blocks and the space they occupy in the spatial cache. Thus, with large spatial blocks more data should be mark as temporal. With smaller spatial blocks less bus occupancy is generated and less useless data is fetched, so the temporal cache is best reserved for only the data exhibiting the highest temporal locality.

As for the cache size, larger cache means that a fetched data resides longer in the cache (on average), so data that exhibit no spatial or temporal locality in a small cache might start to exhibit it in a larger cache. This means that it would be difficult to perform a fine compile-time locality resolution, unless only a specific system with known block and cache size is targeted.

It should also be noted that the profile- and run- time mechanisms (which will be described in the following sections) can only change the locality from spatial to temporal. Therefore, when compile-time resolution is used in combination with another method, it is best to mark more data as spatial. Only the data for which high temporal and low spatial locality is anticipated with a high degree of certainty should be marked as temporal.

Profile-Time Resolution

All data blocks are initially regarded as spatial. Then, a profile time algorithm (depicted in Figure 2) is used for detected and retagging to temporal those blocks that are found to exhibit temporal locality.

Profile time mechanism associated each block with two counters (Xcount and Ycount). The Xcount value for a particular data block (initially zero) is incremented on each access to the upper half of the block, decremented on the access to the lower half of the block, and reset on the replacement of the block. When the Xcount value reaches upper (x) or lower limit (-x), further counting is disabled. The Xcount value is checked periodically (because the density of accesses in a unit of time determines the degree of temporal locality). Period of Xcount checking is controlled by Ycount which counts overall number of accesses to this block. When this counter reaches some pre-specified value (y), the value of corresponding Xcount is checked. If either limit (x or -x) is reached, the block is tagged as "temporal," otherwise, it is tagged as "spatial." The block once tagged as temporal, cannot later be retagged to spatial (as it can be in the run time algorithm).

The profile-time mechanism should give a better assessment of which data should be marked as

Figure 2. The simple profile time algorithm for tagging of data blocks against their locality. Legend: Xcount and Ycount = counters; X and Y = limits for Xcount and Ycount, respectively; Hi = flag which indicates hit in an upper half of block. Description: The two counters are associated with each block in the data memory.

```
if(hit.in.block)
  if(Tag=Spatial){
     if(-X<Xcount<X)
          if(Hi) Xcount=Xcount+1;
          else   Xcount=Xcount-1;
     if(Ycount<Y) Ycount=Ycount+1;
       else{
          if(-X<Xcount<X) Tag=Spatial;
          else Tag=Temporal;
             Xcount=0;
             Ycount=0;
          }

    }
```

spatial, and which as temporal, than the proposed compile-time mechanism (at the cost of running the profiler). However, the problem with the temporal and spatial locality being relative to a block and cache size remains the same.

Run-Time Resolution

The algorithm very similar to the profile time algorithm can be easily implemented in hardware for run time tagging/retagging of data according to dynamically observed changing access pattern (Figure 3). It works very similarly to the profile time algorithm, with two counters being and the appropriate control logic being implemented in hardware and attaché to each block in the spatial part of the cache.

The run-time algorithm is implemented as a hardware part of the system. Therefore, the criteria for tagging can be adjusted to the parameters of the specific system. However, if only a run-time system is used, there will be a cold-start period during which all the data are marked spatial. Therefore, it is best to use a conservative compile- or profile time assessment to alleviate the cold-start and use the run-time mechanism for maximizing the performance.

Figure 3. The simple run time logic for dynamic tagging/retagging of data blocks against their locality. Description: The two-counter logic is associated with each block in data cache.

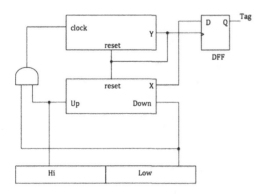

Modifed DDC in a Multicore System

In a multicore chip a problem of manitinig consitancy within a chip that utilizes a Modified DDC system might arise (Hechtman, 2013). There are several possible solutions for this problem.

One way to go would be to put an inclusive, non-shared L2 cache that would contain copies full 64 Byte blocks of all the data in the L1 cache (regardless of whether a block is tagged as spatial or temporal). This L2 cache could then implement any of consitancy protocols used eith regular caches (such as *Modified, Exclusive, Shared, Invalid* - MESI; *Modified, Owned, Exclusive, Shared, Invalid* - MOESI; etc.). However, this solution would eliminate any benefits that a Modifed DDC might have in terms of reducing traffic on the memory bus, as whole block would be fetched form the memory, regardless of whether a block is tagged as spatial or temporal.

A second solution migth be to have both parts of the system snoop the bus independly and act as two separate caches (Flanders, 2013). This approach might have an additional benefit in the form of reducing false-sharing, as two or more temporal data from what would be the same sptial block might find themselves simultaniosly in caches of different CPUs. This solution, as well as the whole topic of using the Modified DDC in a mulicore system requires some further tougth and is likely to be a topic of future research.

CONDITIONS AND ASSUMPTIONS

In this section we introduce the conditions and the assumptions for the simulation to follow.

All caches in the cache subsystem employ write-back policy. The block size is eight 64-bit words for conventional hierarchy and for the spatial part in the DDC variants and one word for the temporal hierarchy in the DDC. Organizational parameters of the cache memory are: 4-way set associatively, and the *Least Recently Used* (LRU) replacement algorithm (Kampe, 2004).

The latency of conventional cache and the spatial part of the DDC was 3 cycles, and the latency of the temporal part was 30% less than that (2 cycles). Only the run-time mechanism for determining data locality was used, so a worst case scenario (when there is no compile-time support and no profiling) was examined. Cache memories were non-blocking, data bus was 32 bits wide. Simulated system had 512 MB of ram and a 2 GHz CPU based on Alpha ISA.

SIMULATION ANALYSES

The simulation of the DDC was done with the M5 Simulator System modified to work with DDC. For reference, the same simulations were run under the standard M5, representing a traditional cache system. M5 is a modular platform for computer system architecture research, encompassing system-level architecture as well as processor micro architecture. For further information regarding the M5 simulator please see (Binkert, 2006). M5 was chosen over specialized memory-oriented simulators, such as (Schintke, 2001) due to its ability to execute full-system simulations.

All of the simulations were done under the syscall emulation mode. A SimpleTiming model of the CPU was used. Simulations were done using the Radix application with 262144 keys and a 1024 radix. Power consumption of the system was estimated using CACTI 4.2 (Tarjan, 2006).

Compared to a conventional cache system of a similar size, modified DDC system shows shorter average memory access latency. Also, in some configuration the modified DDC manages to outperform substantially larger traditional cache systems.

OVERALL PERFORMANCE

Effects of the Temporal Latency

The latency of the temporal part of the cache is an important parameter of a modified DDC system. Several simulations were done in order to get a clear view of how much this latency impacts the overall performance of the system.

Figure 4 shows the improvement in overall memory access latency against a traditional system, for a modified DDC system with the same amount of cache, but different temporal latencies.

Figure 4. Normalized memory reference latency for the Radix application for different setups (lower is better). Description: Modified DDC system shows an improvement over the traditional system of a similar size.

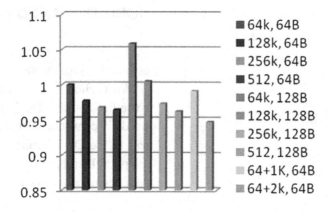

For 3-cycle latency of the temporal part of the cache, which was the same as the spatial part (and the reference traditional system), modified DDC performs worse than the traditional system. As this latency is decreased the performances improve, up to 7% for a single cycle temporal latency (Figure 5).

Simulations were also done with the latency of the spatial part (and the reference cache) set to 4 cycles.

Again, a similar pattern can be observed, with the performances being worse than the reference system for the 4 cycle temporal latency (same as the spatial part and the reference traditional system), and a linear improvement as the temporal part is decreased, up to a 10% improvement for a single cycle latency of the temporal part of the cache (Figure 6).

Effects of the Temporal Cache Associativity

Low latency of the temporal part of the cache is instrumental to the performance of an modified DDC system. However, at a certain point it becomes difficult (if not impossible) to further

decrease this latency. At this point it might be possible to increase the associativety without hurting the latency. In order to understand possible benefits of an increased associativity we conducted several simulations. An LRU replacement policy was assumed.

From Figure 7 it is obvious that there is a significant improvement when going from a direct-mapped to a 2-way associative temporal part of the cache. Increasing associativity beyond this point brings less of an improvement.

The X Limit Parameter

The X limit parameter determines the "strictness" of the criteria data have to meet in order to be marked as temporal.

For lower values of the X limit more data are marked as temporal, so if this value was set too low there would be too much temporal data, leading to a decrease in performance due to trashing. Higher values of X limit mean less temporal data. If X limit is set too high little or no data will be marked as temporal, leading to temporal part of the cache not being used. X limit must be no less than a half of block size (in words) in order for

Figure 5. Effects of the temporal cache part latency on the performance of a modified DDC system (lower is better). Description: Temporal cache part latency has a large effect on the performance of the system.

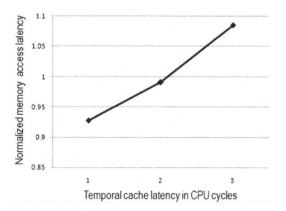

Figure 6. Effects of the temporal cache part latency on the performance of a modified DDC system (lower is better). Description: Temporal cache part latency has a large effect on the performance of the system.

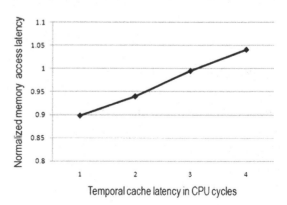

Figure 7. Effects of the temporal cache part associativety on the performance of a modified DDC system (lower is better). Description: Increasing the temporal cache associativity from direct-mapped to 2-way associative generates a substantial improvement in performances. Further increases in the associativity create a much lesser improvements.

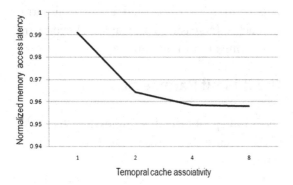

Figure 8. Effects of the X limit parameter on the performance of a modified DDC system (lower is better). Description: With 1KB of temporal, and 64KB of spatial cache and a block size of 8 64bit words a modified DDC system shows maximum performance for the X limit set to 33. Form smaller values of X limit the temporal cache are overburdened, and for higher values it is underutilized.

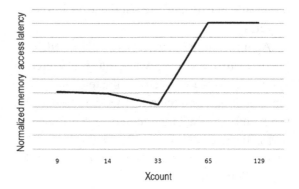

the system to function properly (otherwise all data might end up marked as temporal).

The results show (Figure 8) a maximum improvement in performances for the X limit assuming the value of 33. It should be noted that the optimal value of the X limit parameter will vary with the access patterns in the software, as well as the size of the temporal part of the cache.

It should also be noted that to small values of the X limit hurt the performances less than the too large ones. This is due to the very limited amount of the data that can meet even the relaxed criteria for strong temporal locality. On the other hand, with too large X limit no data meet the criteria, so the low latency temporal cache remains unused.

Power Consumption

The power conuption of the system was estimated using CACTI.4.2. The results, along with some reference values, are shown in the Figure 9. The modified DDC system discipates around 10% more power than the traditional cache system used for referance.

CACTI tool was also used to verify that the assumption that temporal cache latency could be at least 30% shorter than that of the spatial cache. The result showed an estimated access latency of 0.96 (ns) for the 64K spatial part of the cache, and 0.631 and 0.64 (ns) for 1K and 2K direct caches (which would be used for the temporal cache part) respectively.

Figure 9. Power consumption of modified DDC systems. Description: The modified DDC systems discipate around 10% more power than the traditional cache system used for referance.

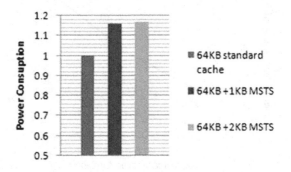

CONCLUSION

The DDC approach manages to outperform traditional cache systems of the similar size, and, in many cases, matches the performance of substantially lager traditional caches. Therefore, by implementing DDC, better returns from invested transistors can be achieved, as well as a reduction of the transistor count consumed by the cache.

Furthermore, since the increase in cache size leads to an increase in latency, it might be possible to improve performances beyond those that can be achieved by a traditional single-level hierarchy, regardless of the size.

It is important to point out that the implementation of the DDC doesn't affect possible higher level caches, so it is still possible to add a traditional level to cache to the system, in order to further increase the performance, much like in the traditional cache. The results of the simulations are based on a system with only a run-time locality resolution. Further improvements can be expected if a compile- or profile-time support is added.

Finally, in the simulations we concentrated on the average memory access latency as the important parameter for performance evaluation. A modified DDC system should also bring improvements in terms of reducing bus contention, as the unnecessary data are not fetched (the data that would be in the same block with some temporal data that are being fetched).

ACKNOWLEDGMENT

The author would like to thank Dragiša Janković for his input and assistance throughout this research.

REFERENCES

Baer, J. L., & Wang, W. H. (1988). On the inclusion properties for multi-level cache hierarchies: Vol. 16. *No. 2* (pp. 73–80). IEEE Computer Society Press.

Binkert, N. L., Dreslinski, R. G., Hsu, L. R., Lim, K. T., Saidi, A. G., & Reinhardt, S. K. (2006). The M5 simulator: Modeling networked systems. *IEEE Micro*, *26*(4), 52–60. doi:10.1109/MM.2006.82

Daly, D. M., Goodman, B. L., Powell, S. J., Sawdey, A. C., & Stuecheli, J. A. (2013). *U.S. patent no. 20,130,151,780*. Washington, DC: U.S. Patent and Trademark Office.

Etsion, Y., & Feitelson, D. (2012). *Exploiting core working sets to filter the L1 cache with random sampling*.

Flanders, W. H., & Khosa, V. (2013). *U.S. patent no. 20,130,024,629*. Washington, DC: U.S. Patent and Trademark Office.

Gašić, M. (2007) A survey of split data caches [PowerPoint slides]. Belgrade, Serbia: University of Belgrade.

González, A., Aliagas, C., & Valero, M. (1995). A data cache with multiple caching strategies tuned to different types of locality. In *Proceedings of the ACM 1995 International Conference on Supercomputing* (pp. 338-347). ACM. Retrieved from http://portal.acm.org/citation.cfm?id=224622

Hechtman, B. A., & Sorin, D. J. (2013). Evaluating cache coherent shared virtual memory for heterogeneous multicore chips. In *Proceedings of the IEEE International Symposium on Performance Analysis of Systems and Software*. IEEE.

Jouppi, N. P. (1990, May). Improving direct-mapped cache performance by the addition of a small fully-associative cache and prefetch buffers. In *Proceedings of Computer Architecture* (pp. 364–373). IEEE. doi:10.1109/ISCA.1990.134547

Kampe, M., Stenstrom, P., & Dubois, M. (2004). Self-correcting LRU replacement policies. In *Proceedings of the 1st Conference on Computing Frontiers* (pp. 181-191). ACM.

Koufaty, D., & Torrellas, J. (1998). Comparing data forwarding and prefetching for communication-induced misses in shared-memory MPs. In *Proceedings of the 12th International Conference on Supercomputing* (pp. 53-60). ACM.

Kumar, S., Zhao, H., Shriraman, A., Matthews, E., Dwarkadas, S., & Shannon, L. (2012). Amoeba-cache: Adaptive blocks for eliminating waste in the memory hierarchy. In *Proceedings of the 2012 45th Annual IEEE/ACM International Symposium on Microarchitecture* (pp. 376-388). IEEE Computer Society.

Lipasti, M. H., & Shen, J. P. (1996). Exceeding the dataflow limit via value prediction. In *Proceedings of the 29th Annual ACM/IEEE International Symposium on Microarchitecture* (pp. 226-237). IEEE Computer Society.

McKee, S. A. (2004). Reflections on the memory wall. In *Proceedings of the First Conference on Computing Frontiers CF04*. ACM Press. Retrieved from http://portal.acm.org/citation.cfm?doid=977091.977115

Milutinovic, V., Markovic, B., Tomasevic, M., & Tremblay, M. (1996). The split temporal/spatial cache: A complexity analysis. In *Proceedings of the SCIzzL-6*. Santa Clara, CA: ACM.

Milutinovic, V., Tomasevic, M., Markovic, B., & Tremblay, M. (1996). A new cache architecture concept: The split temporal/spatial cache. In *Proceedings of 8th Mediterranean Electrotechnical Conference on Industrial Applications in Power Systems Computer Science and Telecommunications MELECON 96*. MELECON.

Resnick, D. (2012). Ideas for future high performance CPU and system architectures (No. SAND2012-1717C). Albuquerque, NM: Sandia National Laboratories (SNL-NM).

Schintke, F., Simon, J., & Reinefeld, A. (2001). A cache simulator for shared memory systems. In V. Alexandrov, J. Dongarra, B. Juliano, R. Renner, & K. Tan (Eds.), *Computational science - ICCS 2001 (LNCS)* (Vol. 2074, pp. 569–578). Berlin, Germany: Springer-Verlag. doi:10.1007/3-540-45718-6_62

Smith, A. J. (1987). Line (block) size choice for CPU cache memories. *IEEE Transactions on Computers*, *100*(9), 1063–1075. doi:10.1109/TC.1987.5009537

Tarjan, D., Thoziyoor, S., & Jouppi, N. P. (2006). *CACTI 4.0*. HP laboratories. Retrieved from http://www.hpl.hp.com/techreports/2006/HPL-2006-86.pdf

Wulf, W. A., & McKee, S. A. (1995). Hitting the memory wall: Implications of the obvious. *ACM SIGARCH Computer Architecture News*, *23*(1), 20–24. doi:10.1145/216585.216588

Xie, Y. (2013). Future memory and interconnect technologies. In Proceedings of Design, Automation & Test in Europe Conference & Exhibition (DATE), 2013 (pp. 964-969). IEEE.

ADDITIONAL READING

Adler, M., Fleming, K. E., Parashar, A., Pellauer, M., & Emer, J. (2011, February). Leap scratchpads: automatic memory and cache management for reconfigurable logic. In *Proceedings of the 19th ACM/SIGDA international symposium on Field programmable gate arrays* (pp. 25-28). ACM.

Borkar, S., & Chien, A. A. (2011). The future of microprocessors. *Communications of the ACM*, *54*(5), 67–77. doi:10.1145/1941487.1941507

Chen, J., & John, L. K. (2009, July). Efficient program scheduling for heterogeneous multi-core processors. In *Proceedings of the 46th Annual Design Automation Conference* (pp. 927-930). ACM.

Christen, M., Schenk, O., Neufeld, E., Messmer, P., & Burkhart, H. (2009, May). Parallel data-locality aware stencil computations on modern micro-architectures. In *Parallel & Distributed Processing, 2009. IPDPS 2009. IEEE International Symposium on* (pp. 1-10). IEEE.

Conway, P., Kalyanasundharam, N., Donley, G., Lepak, K., & Hughes, B. (2010). Cache hierarchy and memory subsystem of the AMD Opteron processor. *Micro, IEEE*, *30*(2), 16–29. doi:10.1109/MM.2010.31

Dall'Osso, M., Biccari, G., Giovannini, L., Bertozzi, D., & Benini, L. (2012, September). Xpipes: a latency insensitive parameterized network-on-chip architecture for multi-processor SoCs. In *Computer Design (ICCD), 2012 IEEE 30th International Conference on* (pp. 45-48). IEEE.

Ding, W., Srinivas, J., Kandemir, M., & Karakoy, M. (2011, October). Compiler Directed Data Locality Optimization for Multicore Architectures. In *Parallel Architectures and Compilation Techniques (PACT), 2011 International Conference on* (pp. 171-172). IEEE.

Ekanayake, J., & Fox, G. (2010). High performance parallel computing with clouds and cloud technologies. In *Cloud Computing* (pp. 20–38). Springer Berlin Heidelberg. doi:10.1007/978-3-642-12636-9_2

Gordon-Ross, A., Vahid, F., & Dutt, N. D. (2009). Fast configurable-cache tuning with a unified second-level cache. *Very Large Scale Integration (VLSI) Systems. IEEE Transactions on*, *17*(1), 80–91.

Howard, J., Dighe, S., Vangal, S. R., Ruhl, G., Borkar, N., Jain, S., & Van Der Wijngaart, R. (2011). A 48-core IA-32 processor in 45 nm CMOS using on-die message-passing and DVFS for performance and power scaling. *Solid-State Circuits. IEEE Journal of*, *46*(1), 173–183.

Jacob, B., Ng, S., & Wang, D. (2010). *Memory systems: cache, DRAM, disk*. Morgan Kaufmann.

Jiang, Y., Zhang, E. Z., Tian, K., & Shen, X. (2010, January). Is reuse distance applicable to data locality analysis on chip multiprocessors? In Compiler Construction (pp. 264–282). Springer Berlin Heidelberg. doi:doi:10.1007/978-3-642-11970-5_15 doi:10.1007/978-3-642-11970-5_15

Kalla, R., Sinharoy, B., Starke, W. J., & Floyd, M. (2010). Power7: IBM's next-generation server processor. *Micro, IEEE*, *30*(2), 7–15. doi:10.1109/MM.2010.38

Liu, J., Zhang, Y., Ding, W., & Kandemir, M. (2011, April). On-chip cache hierarchy-aware tile scheduling for multicore machines. In *Code Generation and Optimization (CGO), 2011 9th Annual IEEE/ACM International Symposium on* (pp. 161-170). IEEE.

Liu, X., & Mellor-Crummey, J. (2011, April). Pinpointing data locality problems using data-centric analysis. In *Code Generation and Optimization (CGO), 2011 9th Annual IEEE/ACM International Symposium on* (pp. 171-180). IEEE.

López, S., Garnica, Ó., Albonesi, D. H., Dropsho, S., Lanchares, J., & Hidalgo, J. I. (2011). A phase adaptive cache hierarchy for SMT processors. *Microprocessors and Microsystems*, *35*(8), 683–694. doi:10.1016/j.micpro.2011.08.008

Madan, N., Zhao, L., Muralimanohar, N., Udipi, A., Balasubramonian, R., Iyer, R., & Newell, D. (2009, February). Optimizing communication and capacity in a 3D stacked reconfigurable cache hierarchy. In *High Performance Computer Architecture, 2009. HPCA 2009. IEEE 15th International Symposium on* (pp. 262-274). IEEE.

Majo, Z., & Gross, T. R. (2011, June). Memory management in NUMA multicore systems: trapped between cache contention and interconnect overhead. In ACM SIGPLAN Notices (Vol. 46, No. 11, pp. 11-20). ACM.

Martin, M. M., Hill, M. D., & Sorin, D. J. (2012). Why on-chip cache coherence is here to stay. *Communications of the ACM*, *55*(7), 78–89. doi:10.1145/2209249.2209269

Park, J., Chaudhari, A., & Abraham, J. A. (2013, March). Non-speculative double-sampling technique to increase energy-efficiency in a high-performance processor. In Design, Automation & Test in Europe Conference & Exhibition (DATE), 2013 (pp. 254-257). IEEE.

Park, J., Yoo, R. M., Khudia, D. S., Hughes, C. J., & Kim, D. (2013). Location-Aware Cache Management for Many-Core Processors with Deep Cache Hierarchy.

Pelley, P. H., & McShane, M. B. (2010). *U.S. Patent No. 7,777,330*. Washington, DC: U.S. Patent and Trademark Office.

Pesterev, A., Zeldovich, N., & Morris, R. T. (2010, April). Locating cache performance bottlenecks using data profiling. In *Proceedings of the 5th European conference on Computer systems* (pp. 335-348). ACM.

Prieto, P., Puente, V., & Gregorio, J. A. (2011). Multilevel Cache Modeling for Chip-Multiprocessor Systems. *Computer Architecture Letters*, *10*(2), 49–52. doi:10.1109/L-CA.2011.20

Rusu, S., Tam, S., Muljono, H., Stinson, J., Ayers, D., Chang, J., & Vora, S. (2010). A 45 nm 8-core enterprise Xeon processor. *Solid-State Circuits. IEEE Journal of*, *45*(1), 7–14.

Schroeder, B., & Gibson, G. A. (2010). A large-scale study of failures in high-performance computing systems. *Dependable and Secure Computing. IEEE Transactions on*, *7*(4), 337–350.

Shrestha, S. (2013, June). Using platform-independent data locality analysis to predict cache performance on abstract hardware platforms. In *Proceedings of the 27th international ACM conference on International conference on supercomputing* (pp. 487-488). ACM.

Sudan, K., Chatterjee, N., Nellans, D., Awasthi, M., Balasubramonian, R., & Davis, A. (2010). Micropages: increasing DRAM efficiency with locality-aware data placement. *ACM Sigplan Notices*, *45*(3), 219–230. doi:10.1145/1735971.1736045

Wang, M., Bodin, F., & Matz, S. (2010). Automatic data distribution for improving data locality on the Cell BE Architecture. In *Languages and Compilers for Parallel Computing* (pp. 247–262). Springer Berlin Heidelberg. doi:10.1007/978-3-642-13374-9_17

Yavits, L., Morad, A., & Ginosar, R. (2013). Cache Hierarchy Optimization.

Zia, A., Jacob, P., Kim, J. W., Chu, M., Kraft, R. P., & McDonald, J. F. (2010). A 3-D cache with ultra-wide data bus for 3-D processor-memory integration. *Very Large Scale Integration (VLSI) Systems. IEEE Transactions on*, *18*(6), 967–977.

KEY TERMS AND DEFINITIONS

Caching Block Size: The amount of data brough together from the main memory to the cache.

Caching Hierarchy: Organization of a cache with multiple levels.

Caching Strategy: Mechanisam of cache function.

Data Locality: Patterns of access to different segments of data during program execution.

High Performce Processor: A central processing unit designed for high performance systems.

Processor Cache: Small, fast memories placed between the CPU and the main memory.

Split Data Cache: A cache that consists of several subsections.

Chapter 11
Designing Parallel Meta-Heuristic Methods

Teodor Gabriel Crainic
Département de Management et Technologie, Université du Québec à Montréal, CIRRELT, Canada

Tatjana Davidović
Mathematical Institute, Serbian Academy of Science and Arts, Serbia

Dušan Ramljak
Center for Data Analytics and Biomedical Informatics, Temple University, USA

ABSTRACT

Meta-heuristics represent powerful tools for addressing hard combinatorial optimization problems. However, real life instances usually cannot be treated efficiently in "reasonable" computing times. Moreover, a major issue in meta-heuristic design and calibration is to provide high performance solutions for a variety of problems. Parallel meta-heuristics aim to address both issues. The objective of this chapter is to present a state-of-the-art survey of the main parallelization ideas and strategies, and to discuss general design principles applicable to all meta-heuristic classes. To achieve this goal, the authors explain various paradigms related to parallel meta-heuristic development, where communications, synchronization, and control aspects are the most relevant. They also discuss implementation issues pointing out the characteristics of shared and distributed memory multiprocessors as target architectures. All these topics are illustrated by the examples from recent literature related to the parallelization of various meta-heuristic methods. Here, the authors focus on Variable Neighborhood Search and Bee Colony Optimization.

INTRODUCTION

Meta-heuristic methods are widely used for solving various combinatorial optimization problems. Computing optimal solutions is intractable for many important industrial and scientific optimization problems. Therefore, meta-heuristic

algorithms are used for practical applications, since, in the majority of cases, they provide high quality solutions within reasonable CPU times. However, as the problem size increases, the execution time required by a meta-heuristic to find a high quality solution may become unreasonably long. Parallelization has proven to be an efficient method for overcoming this problem.

DOI: 10.4018/978-1-4666-5784-7.ch011

Since meta-heuristics usually represent stochastic search processes, it is important to properly define measures to evaluate the performance of their parallelized versions, as we cannot use the standard performance measures (speedup and efficiency) for the evaluation of parallel meta-heuristics. Actually, parallelization changes the original algorithm, and consequently, the evaluation of both *the execution time* and *the quality of the final solution* is needed. Indeed, for the majority of parallelization strategies, the sequential and parallel versions of heuristic methods yield solutions that differ in value, composition, or both. Thus, an important objective when parallel heuristics are considered is to design methods that outperform their sequential counterparts in terms of solution quality and, ideally, computational efficiency. More precisely, the parallel method should not require a higher overall computation effort than the sequential method, or should justify the effort by a higher quality of the final solutions. Consequently, we select the execution time and the quality of the final solution as our performance measures.

A significant amount of work has been performed in defining, implementing, and analyzing parallelization strategies for meta-heuristics. According to the survey papers (Verhoeven & Aarts, 1995; Cung, Martins, Ribeiro, & Roucairol, 2002; Crainic & Toulouse, 2010), several main ideas related to the parallelization of meta-heuristic methods can be recognized: starting from the low level parallelization realized by distributing neighborhoods among processors, up to the cooperative multi-thread parallel search (Crainic & Hail, 2005; Crainic & Toulouse, 2010). Many parallelization strategies dealing with various meta-heuristic methods have been proposed in recent literature (Verhoeven & Aarts, 1995; Toulouse, Crainic, & Gendreau, 1996; Ferreira & Morvan, 1997; Cung, Martins, Ribeiro, & Roucairol, 2002; Crainic & Hail, 2005; Crainic & Toulouse, 2010). The rich collection of papers on parallel meta-heuristics (Alba, 2005) is devoted to both theoretical and

practical aspects of this topic. Here, we briefly recall important issues, and then focus on two main classes of meta-heuristics: neighborhood-based and population-based methods. We select a representative for each class and give a survey of the existing approaches to their parallelization. As the representative for neighborhood-based meta-heuristic methods we select Variable Neighborhood Search (hereinafter: VNS) because of its numerous successful sequential and parallel applications. Parallelization of population-based methods is illustrated on Bee Colony Optimization (hereinafter: BCO), the nature-inspired meta-heuristic recently on the rise.

The rest of this chapter is organized as follows. The next section contains a brief overview of meta-heuristic methods. Review of recent literature addressing the parallelization strategies for various meta-heuristic methods is presented in Section 3. The parallelization strategies proposed in recent literature for VNS are described in Section 4, while Section 5 contains the review of the parallel BCO method. Section 6 concludes the chapter.

META-HEURISTICS

Combinatorial optimization problems involve the selection of the best among (finitely many) feasible solutions. Each problem is defined by a set of objects, with associated contributions; an objective function computing the value of a particular subset or order of objects; and the feasibility rules specifying how subsets/orderings may be built. The best solution is the one satisfying feasibility rules and yielding the value of the objective function which is the highest/lowest among all possible combinations. This solution is called *the optimal solution (optimum)*. For a more formal definition, let us assume that one desires to minimize an objective function $f(x)$, linear or not, subject to $x \in X \subseteq \mathbb{R}^n$. The set X collects constraints on the decision variables x and defines the feasible domain. Decision variables are generally non-negative and some or all of them usually take discrete values. A globally optimal solution $x^* \in X$ is the one for which holds the relation $f(x^*) \leq f(x)$ for all $x \in X$.

The main difficulty in solving combinatorial optimization problems is that the number of feasible solutions usually grows exponentially with the number of objects in the initial set. Therefore, meta-heuristics represent the only practical tools in addressing these problems in real-life dimensions. Meta-heuristics are computational methods that optimize a problem by iteratively trying to generate a new or to improve an existing solution with respect to a given objective. Meta-heuristics are general methods, in the sense that they do not use *a priori* knowledge about the problem to be optimized. They usually apply some form of stochastic search. However, when using meta-heuristics, it is hard to guarantee the quality of the final solution: how far it is from the optimal one or if it is at all possible to reach the optimal solution by the application of meta-heuristic rules. Nonetheless, to obtain any feasible solution in the majority of the real-life applications, meta-heuristics are the only possible choice.

Meta-heuristics represent general approximate algorithms applicable to a large variety of optimization problems (Talbi, 2009), but should be tailored for each particular optimization problem. They deal with instances of problems that are believed to be hard in general by efficiently exploring suitably limited sub-spaces of their large solution search space. Meta-heuristics serve three main purposes: solving problems faster, solving large problems, and obtaining robust algorithms. Moreover, they are very flexible, and simple for designing and implementing.

Numerous meta-heuristics have been developed in the past twenty years to solve complex optimization problems. Many of them are inspired by natural metaphors (e.g., evolution of species, annealing process, insect colony behavior, particle swarms, immune systems, etc.). Others are based on mathematical search principles. They include

the definition of some metric to measure the distance between solutions, the neighborhoods to distinguish solutions that are close to each other, and local search principles which enable efficient searches of the solution space. Examples of these methods are Tabu Search (Glover & Laguna, 1997; Gendreau & Potvin, 2010) and Variable Neighborhood Search (Mladenović & Hansen, 1997; Hansen, Mladenović, Brimberg, & Moreno-Pérez, 2010). Another classification of meta-heuristics is based on the number of solutions used during the search: we distinguish single solution methods and population-based ones. Meta-heuristics are also classified as constructive (if they build new and better solutions during their execution), or based on improvement (in the case when they transform a given solution in order to obtain an improved ancestor). Constructive meta-heuristics include Greedy Randomized Adaptive Search Procedure (Feo & Resende, 1995; Resende & Ribeiro, 2010), Ant Colony Optimization (Dorigo & Stützle, 2010) and Bee Colony Optimization (Lučić & Teodorović, 2001, 2003a, 2003b), while Genetic Algorithms (Goldberg, 1989; Reeves, 2010), Simulated Annealing (Kirkpatrick, Gelatt, & Vecchi, 1983; Nikolaev & Jacobson, 2010), and Variable Neighborhood Search represent methods based on the improvement of given initial solutions. All relevant details about the design and implementation of meta-heuristic methods can be found in (Talbi, 2009).

Variable Neighborhood Search

Variable Neighborhood Search meta-heuristic was proposed in (Mladenović & Hansen, 1997). It is a simple and effective optimization method widely used for dealing with combinatorial and global optimization problems (Hansen, Mladenović, Brimberg, & Moreno-Pérez, 2010). The basic idea behind VNS is a systematic change of neighborhoods within a descent phase to find a local optimum, as well as within a perturbation phase to get out of the corresponding valley. VNS is a single-solution neighborhood-based method whose basic building block is a Local Search (hereinafter: LS) procedure. It uses multiple neighborhoods in order to increase the efficiency of the search. VNS is based on three simple facts (Hansen & Mladenović, 2003):

- **Fact 1:** A local optimum with respect to one neighborhood structure is not necessarily an optimum for another;
- **Fact 2:** A global optimum is a local optimum with respect to all possible neighborhood structures;
- **Fact 3:** For many problems, local optima with respect to one or several neighborhoods are relatively close to each other.

To describe VNS, we first introduce the following notation. For a given optimization problem, e.g., the one defined as $\min f(x)$, the set of *solutions S* and the set of *feasible solutions* $X \subseteq S$ are defined. Let $x \in X$ be an arbitrary solution, we define the neighborhood of $x (\mathcal{N}(x))$ as the set of all solutions obtained from x by the application of a predefined elementary transformation. Let, $\mathcal{N}_k$, $(k = 1, ..., k_{max})$, be a finite set of pre-selected neighborhood structures. Then, $\mathcal{N}_k(x)$ is the set of solutions in the k-th neighborhood of x, i.e., the set of solutions obtained from x by the application of k elementary transformations. Steps in the basic VNS are illustrated in Figure 1.

Usually, the initial solution is determined by some constructive scheduling heuristic and then improved by LS before the beginning of actual VNS procedure. The role of a *shake* procedure is to prevent trapping in a local minimum. Intensification of the search is realized by the *improvement* step involving the selected LS procedure to improve the current solution. The whole VNS procedure is concentrated around the current global best solution, and therefore, the *move* step has to ensure that this solution is always updated as soon as possible.

As a meta-heuristics, VNS runs until some predefined stopping criterion is met. The possible stopping criteria can include the maximum total number of iterations, the maximum total number of iterations without improvement of the objective function, or the maximum allowed CPU time. Once the stopping criterion is met, the global best solution is reported.

VNS has a unique parameter k_{max}, the maximum number of neighborhoods. Sometimes, but not necessarily, successive neighborhoods are nested.

Figure 1. Pseudocode of the VNS algorithm

```
Initialization. Find an initial solution x ∈ X;
                improve it with the local search; choose stopping criterion; STOP = 0.
Repeat
    1. Set k = 1.
    2. Repeat
        (a) Shake. Generate a random point x'
            in the k^th neighborhood of x, (x' ∈ N_k(x)).
        (b) Improve. Apply some LS method with x' as initial solution;
            denote with x" the obtained local optimum.
        (c) Move. If this local optimum is better than the
            current incumbent,
                then move there (x=x"), and continue search within N_1 (k=1);
                otherwise move to the next neighborhood (k = k+1).
        (d) Stopping criterion. If the stopping condition is met,
                then set STOP = 1.
        until k == k_max.
    until STOP == 1.
```

There are several variations and modifications of this basic VNS scheme, as well as many successful applications. Readers are referred to (Hansen & Mladenović, 2005; Hansen, Mladenović, Brimberg, & Moreno-Pérez, 2010) for more details.

Bee Colony Optimization

Lučić and Teodorović (2001, 2003a, 2003b) were among the first to use the basic principles of collective bee intelligence in solving combinatorial optimization problems. BCO is a meta-heuristic method in which a population of *artificial bees* (consisting of B individuals) searches for the optimal solution. Every artificial bee generates a solution to the problem through a sequence of construction steps. This is done over multiple iterations, until some predefined stopping criterion is met. Each step of the BCO algorithm is composed of two alternating phases named the *forward pass* and the *backward pass*. These phases are repeated until all solutions (one for each bee) are completed. The best among them is used to update the global best solution, and an iteration of BCO is completed. The number of forward/backward passes (NC), as well as the number of bees (B), are the parameters of the BCO algorithm, and should be given before its execution starts. The pseudocode of the BCO algorithm is given in Figure 2.

During the forward pass, every bee adds new components to its partial solution. The number of components is calculated in such a way that a single iteration of BCO completes after NC forward/backward passes. At the end of the forward pass, the new (partial or complete) solution is generated for each bee.

The bees start the second phase, the so-called backward pass by sharing the information about their solutions. In nature, bees perform a dancing ritual, to inform other bees about the amount of food they have found, and the proximity of

Figure 2. Pseudocode of the BCO algorithm

Initialization: Read problem data, parameter values and
stopping criterion.
Do
  (1) Assign an empty solution to each bee.
  (2) **For** ($i=0$; $i<NC$; i++) // *forward pass*
    (i) **For** ($b=0$; $b<B$; b++)
      For ($s=0$; $s<f(NC)$; s++) //count moves
        (a) Evaluate all possible moves;
        (b) Choose one move using the roulette wheel;
    // *backward pass*
    (ii) **For** ($b=0$; $b<B$; b++)
      Evaluate the (partial/complete) solution of bee b;
    (iii) **For** ($b=0$; $b<B$; b++)
      Loyalty decision using the roulette wheel for bee b;
    (iv) **For** ($b=0$; $b<B$; b++)
      If (b is uncommitted), choose a recruiter using the
      roulette wheel.
  (3) Evaluate all solutions and find the best one.
while stopping criteria is not satisfied.

the patch to the hive. In the optimization search algorithm, the values of the objective functions are compared. Each artificial bee decides, with a certain probability, whether it will stay *loyal* to its solution or not. The bees with better solutions have higher chances of keeping and advertising them. The bees that are loyal to their partial solutions are called *recruiters*. Once a solution is abandoned, the bee becomes *uncommitted* and has to select one of the advertised solutions. This decision is made probabilistically, in such a way that better advertised solutions have higher chances to be chosen for further exploration. This way, within each backward pass, all bees are divided into two groups (R recruiters, and the remaining B-R uncommitted bees). Values for R and B-R vary from one backward pass to another.

Here, we presented a brief description of the basic form for the BCO algorithm. Some variations and applications are surveyed in (Teodorović, 2009).

META-HEURISTICS AND PARALLELISM

The main goal of traditional parallelization is to speed up the computations needed to solve a particular problem by engaging several processors and dividing the total amount of work between them. For stochastic algorithms, meta-heuristics in particular, several goals may be achieved (Talbi, 2009): speeding up the search (i.e., reducing the search time); improving the quality of the obtained solutions (by enabling searching through different parts of the solution space); improving the robustness (in terms of solving different optimization problems and different instances of a given problem in an effective manner; robustness may also be measured in terms of the sensitivity of the meta-heuristic to its parameters); and solving large-scale problems (i.e., solving very large instances that cannot be solved by a sequential machine). A combination of gains may also be

obtained: parallel execution can enable an efficient search through different regions of the solution space, yielding an improvement of the quality of the final solution within a smaller amount of execution time.

A significant amount of work concerning the parallelization of meta-heuristics already exists. The approach can be twofold: considering theoretical aspects of parallelization, or developing practical applications of parallel meta-heuristics for different optimization problems. The survey articles (Verhoeven & Aarts, 1995; Cung, Martins, Ribeiro, & Roucairol, 2002; Crainic & Hail, 2005; Alba, 2005; Crainic & Toulouse, 2010) summarize these works and propose adequate classifications.

One of the first papers introducing classification of parallelization strategies is (Verhoeven & Aarts, 1995). This classification, based on the control of the search process, resulted in two main groups of parallelization strategies: single walk and multiple walks parallelism. To refine the classification of parallelization strategies, communication aspects (synchronous or asynchronous) and search parameters (same or different initial point and/or same or different search strategies) have to be considered. The resulting classification is described in details in (Crainic & Hail, 2005), and we briefly recall it here in order to be able to adequately classify our parallelization strategies for VNS and BCO.

The classification from (Crainic & Hail, 2005) takes three main aspects of parallel execution into account: search control, communication control, and search differentiation. Such an approach resulted in the 3D-Taxonomy $X \,/\, Y \,/\, Z$. Here, X is used to denote *search control cardinality*, which could take centralized (hereinafter: 1C) or distributed (hereinafter: pC) values. Y deals with two aspects of *communication control*, synchronization and type of data to be exchanged. The four possibilities for Y are Rigid Synchronous (hereinafter: RS), Knowledge Synchronous (hereinafter: KS), Collegial Asynchronous (hereinafter: C), and Knowledge Collegial (hereinafter: KC).

Search differentiation Z specifies the part of the search executed by each of the parallel processes. The difference is characterized by the initial point and by the search strategy. Each process can start from the same or different initial point, and it can perform the same or different search procedure. Therefore, there exist four combinations for Z: Same initial Point-Same search Strategy (hereinafter: SPSS), Same initial Point-Different search Strategies (hereinafter: SPDS), Multiple initial Points-Same search Strategy (hereinafter: MPSS), Multiple initial Points-Different search Strategies (hereinafter: MPDS). The particular implementation of each of the described strategies may vary, depending on the given multiprocessor architecture and the characteristics of the problem at hand.

Considering implementation issues, we have to take care of the target architecture for parallel execution of meta-heuristics. When shared memory multiprocessor systems are used, the synchronization of execution steps represents the main difficulty. Namely, since all processors have access to a common (shared) memory, it is important to ensure that the relevant information is treated correctly. More precisely, it is important that no data is read before being stored to a given location, as well as that it is not overwritten before accessed by all processors. Barriers and semaphores are common control variables used for the synchronization of processors. Software resources supporting shared memory parallel

implementations include openMP (Dagum & Menon, 1998) and POSIX threads (Butenhof, 1997), with directives and library routines available for various programming languages.

In the case of distributed memory multiprocessor systems, the main problem is information exchange between various processors. Each processor needs a copy of the data relevant for its own processes to be stored in its local memory. Therefore, the physical data transfer has to be performed, causing communication delays that may significantly deteriorate the performance of parallel execution. Besides minimizing the amount and/or frequency of data exchanges, selecting of the proper multiprocessor interconnection topology can yield the minimization of communication delays. The most commonly used multiprocessor systems are illustrated in Figure 3.

The completely connected architecture in Figure 3(a) provides the minimal communication delay since each processor can directly exchange data with any other processor. On the other hand, it becomes hard for implementation when the number of processors increases. Star architecture in Figure 3(b) is the easiest for implementation, and the communication delay is not too large since the distance between any two processors is at most two. It is used to implement centrally coordinated parallel applications or asynchronous cooperative methods that require global memory. However, this architecture is highly fault sensitive: if the

Figure 3. (a) Complete interconnection network of 5 processors; (b) star architecture; (c) unidirectional processor ring

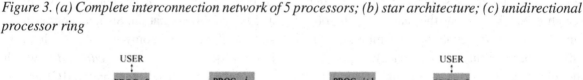

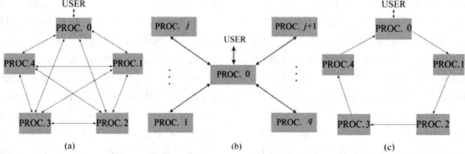

central processor crashes, the resulting system becomes unconnected. Processor rings in Figure 3(c) are also quite popular and easy for implementation. They provide platforms suitable for autonomous, non-centrally coordinated parallel applications. Basic advantages and disadvantages of various multiprocessor topologies are analyzed in (Cvetković & Davidović, 2011) using the theory of graph spectra.

Usual way to realize distributive memory parallel applications is to use Message Passing Interface (hereinafter: MPI) communication protocol (library for C, FORTAN, JAVA, and some other programming languages) (Gropp, Lusk, & Skjellum, 1994; Gropp & Lusk, 1996). As we could notice, distributed memory implementations dominate in recent literature, probably due to the available hardware resources and/or straightforward application of the MPI routines. The implementations described in this chapter are also based on the distributed memory multiprocessor systems.

PARALLELIZATION OF VARIABLE NEIGHBORHOOD SEARCH

The first parallelization strategies for VNS were tested with benchmark instances of the *p*-Median Problem in (García-López, Melión-Batista, Moreno-Pérez, & Moreno-Vega, 2002). These authors proposed and compared three strategies. The first approach involved low-level parallelism, and may be classified as 1C/RS/SPSS: it attempted to cut computation time by parallelizing the local search phase within a sequential VNS. The second one implemented an independent search strategy that ran a sequential VNS procedure on each processor, the best solution being collected at the end. We can classify it as pC/RS/MPSS. The third method applied a synchronous cooperation mechanism through a classical master-slave approach. The master processor ran a sequential VNS. The cur-

rent best solution was sent to each slave processor that had to shake it to obtain an initial solution from which a local search would be started. The solutions were passed on to the master to select the best among them and continue the algorithm. The authors tested their methods using the tsplib problem instances with 1400 customers. Not surprisingly, the last two strategies found better solutions compared to the first one. In addition, the third (1C/KS/SPSS) approach used marginally less iterations than the second one.

The *p*-Median Problem has also been used in (Crainic, Gendreau, Hansen, & Mladenović, 2004) for the evaluation of the proposed parallelized VNS algorithms. Besides the independent run from (García-López, Melión-Batista, Moreno-Pérez, & Moreno-Vega, 2002), an asynchronous centrally coordinated parallelization strategy (classified as pC/C/MPSS) has been proposed. It was implemented on master-slave multiprocessor topology, with the master processor playing the role of central (globally accessible) memory, and the slaves performing basic VNS steps (shake and local search, SH+LS) in parallel. The proposed parallel VNS has been extensively tested on *p*-median benchmark problem instances of up to 1000 medians and 11948 customers. The results of comparison between parallel and sequential VNS indicated that the cooperative strategy yields significant gains in terms of computation time without losing solution quality. The results also showed that, for a given time limit, the cooperative parallel method was able to find better solutions than the sequential strategy. The parallel VNS allowed solving large-scale problem instances, and the quality of the obtained solutions was comparable to the quality of the best results in literature (when available).

Parallel VNS algorithms for Job Shop Scheduling problems were proposed in (Sevkli & Aydin, 2007). Four parallelization strategies were taken into account:

1. Synchronized cooperative strategy proposed in (García-López, Melión-Batista, Moreno-Pérez, & Moreno-Vega, 2002);
2. Asynchronous centrally coordinated method from (Crainic, Gendreau, Hansen, & Mladenović, 2004);
3. Non-centralized parallelism via unidirectional-ring topology;
4. Non-centralized parallelism via bidirectional-ring topology.

The last two strategies were applied to VNS for the first time in (Sevkli & Aydin, 2007). *Non-centralized parallelism via unidirectional-ring topology* can be classified as pC/C/MPSS. It implies that the processors are organized in a unidirectional-ring topology, in which the processors with succeeding indices are adjacent to each other and the first processor is adopted to be the adjacent to the last one. The idea in (Sevkli & Aydin, 2007) was to feed a particular processor for the next generation with the outcome of the previous processor while the first processor was fed by the last processor. A particular processor was executing a single set of basic VNS steps (SH+LS), sending the obtained result to the succeeding one, and collecting the result generated by the preceding processor. The newly arrived solution became an initial point for the next execution cycle. This method provided a number of different ongoing runs with different initial solutions and diversifying with exchanging intermediate states. The authors proposed another peer-to-peer organization of processors: *non-centralized parallelism via mesh (bidirectional-ring) topology*. Each particular processor considered three different solutions: one obtained by the processor itself, and the other two received from the previous and the next adjacent processors. The processor selected the best of these solutions for the next execution cycle. The experimental investigation revealed that central coordination was less efficient than non-central coordination. Since the synchronous policy offers a rigorous simultaneous search

within a particular region of the space, the weakest performance occurred within this approach. On the other hand, unidirectional-ring topology proposed a concurrent search in various regions of the space and outperformed the others with respect to the solution quality. The comparison between parallel and sequential VNS implementation was performed in (Aydin & Sevkli, 2008).

Two cooperation schemes, based on a central memory mechanism, for parallelization of VNS were proposed in (Polacek, Benkner, Doerner, & Hartl, 2008). They were tested on the Multi Depot Vehicle Routing Problem with Time Windows. The used parallelization strategy was an extension of the one implemented in (Crainic, Gendreau, Hansen, & Mladenović, 2004). Each worker had to search through a certain number of neighborhoods. In the fine-grained cooperation scheme (pC/C/MPSS), the search in a single cycle did not necessarily include the whole set of neighborhoods. In the coarse-grained cooperation scheme, however, the number of iterations performed by each worker before the information exchange was significantly higher than the number of neighborhoods. This resulted in a more independent search of the individual processes. The authors proposed making the cooperative scheme adaptive by adjusting search parameters during the execution. This adjustment resulted in a pC/KC/MPSS classification of the coarse-grained cooperation scheme. For the experimental evaluation cooperative execution with up to 32 search threads was compared to the sequential procedure, and to 32 independent runs. The fine-grained cooperation scheme performed better for cases where the characteristics of the problem instances were known in advance and the appropriate parameter settings could be made. Both cooperation schemes showed high efficiency, resulting in excellent runtime scalability.

Parallel VNS for the Car Sequencing Problem was developed in (Knausz, 2008). Using Time Restricted LS (hereinafter: TRLS), in which the local search procedure was allowed to run until a predefined amount of CPU time, was proposed.

TRLS was incorporated into Randomized Variable Neighborhood Descent (hereinafter: VND), where "randomized" means that the order of neighborhoods is not fixed. Several iterations of TRLS in different neighborhoods were performed in parallel, the processes were synchronized, and the best solution identified and propagated to the next TRLS phase. The described parallel VNS falls into the 1C/KS/SPDS class. Computational tests were twofold: identifying the most appropriate order of neighborhoods and increasing the efficiency by parallelization. It was shown that a substantial reduction of the computation time is possible. Further, the tests revealed that no "perfect" neighborhood ordering could be identified, which implies that such a parallel self-adaptive approach is valuable and necessary for obtaining solutions of good qualities.

Several VNS instances running on different processors and exchanging the best solution after several iterations have been used in (Pirkwieser & Raidl, 2009) for tackling the Periodic Vehicle Routing Problem with Time Windows. The number of iterations between two communications was determined with respect to the number of VNS instances, i.e., the number of available processors. The main aim of implementing this pC/KS/MPDS parallel VNS was to increase the quality of the final solution within the same amount of CPU time as required by the sequential VNS. In the second version of parallel VNS, the authors combined a heuristic search with an Integer Linear Programming solver used to improve the best solution after communication. The experimental results showed that the hybrid version yielded an improvement in the quality of the final solution for 80% of used test instances.

Multiple independent runs of various VNS algorithms were used in (Yazdani, Amiri, & Zandieh, 2010) in order to increase exploration of the search space for the Flexible Job-Shop Problem (hereinafter: FJSP). The main part of the proposed algorithm was comprised of internal and external loops. The internal loop was responsible for searching the solution space, whereas the external loop controlled the stopping condition of the algorithm. A number of processors in the internal loop were used in the search process to perform a single run of shake and local search procedures, independently, in parallel. These procedures used different neighborhood structures, and this strategy is therefore classified as 1C/RS/SPDS. Shaking was always applied to the current best solution. The performance of the presented algorithm was evaluated on 181 benchmark problems of FJSP. The computational results showed that the proposed algorithm was competitive to similar methods from relevant literature.

Six strategies for the parallelization of VNS applied to the multiprocessor scheduling problem with communication delays were considered in (Davidović & Crainic, 2013a). The first strategy involved independent execution of various (different) VNS algorithms. It was named IVNS, classified as pC/RS/MPDS, and used as a referent sequential execution result: parallel executions were compared to the best sequential one (the best among all independent executions) within the same amount of CPU time. In (Davidović & Crainic, 2013b) the parallelization of LS procedure was considered. The best-performing parallel LS procedure was incorporated into VNS. The reported experimental evaluation of such a fine-grained parallel VNS showed that both, the quality of final solution and the running time were improved when parallel LS was executed on a modest number of processors (up to 10). The resulting parallel VNS, named PVNSPLS, was the second strategy used in (Davidović & Crainic, 2013a). It was classified as 1C/C/SPSS, as it represented the sequential VNS speeded up by parallelizing the most computationally intensive part, namely the local search procedure. The third strategy was distributive VNS (hereinafter: DVNS), classified as 1C/C/MPSS, based on the main idea to explore different neighborhoods in parallel. This was realized by performing basic VNS steps (SH+LS) on different processors at the same time. This strategy is similar to the one proposed in (Crainic, Gendreau, Hansen, & Mladenović, 2004), but it performs search in more systematic way. Centralized, medium-grained asynchronous cooperation of different VNS algorithms represented the fourth strategy proposed in (Davidović & Crainic, 2013a). It was implemented on star multiprocessor architecture with the central processor playing the role of global memory and the others executing various VNS algorithms. The central processor was updating the current global best solution and sending it to the others upon request. Each out the remaining processors executed basic VNS steps (SH+LS) and referred to the global memory. The resulting solution was sent to the central processor who replied with the actual global best solution. The better among these two solutions served as the new reference point for further search. This strategy was named CVNSall and classified as pC/C/SPDS, as well as the fifth one, coarse-grained centralized asynchronous cooperation named CVNSkkALL. The main difference between these two was in the amount of work performed between two communications with the global memory. In the latter case each processor performed the whole VNS iteration (until $k = k_{max}$) before referring to the global memory. As the last strategy, the medium-grained non-centralized asynchronous cooperation on unidirectional processor ring (pC/C/MPDS) was implemented and named CVNSring. The main difference between this and the corresponding strategy proposed in (Sevkli & Aydin, 2007) was that CVNSring always took the better solution as the new reference point. The experimental evaluation reported in (Davidović & Crainic, 2013a) showed that CVNSring was the best performing parallel VNS. Moreover, all parallel methods (except DVNS) outperformed sequential VNS within the same amount of wall clock time.

We summarize the characteristics of the described methods in Table 1. As can be seen from this table, both synchronous and asynchronous strategies have been used. However, in the ma-jority of papers better performance of the asynchronous parallelization has been reported. On the other hand, cooperative execution dominates centrally coordinated not only with respect to the performance but also regarding the frequency of the usage.

PARALLELIZATION OF BEE COLONY OPTIMIZATION

The BCO algorithm is created as a multi-agent system which inherently provides a good basis for parallelization on different levels. High-level parallelization assumes a coarse granulation of tasks, and can be applied to the iterations of BCO. Smaller parts of the BCO algorithm (the forward and backward passes within a single iteration) are suitable for low-level parallelization because they contain a lot of independent executions. To the best of the authors' knowledge, parallel execution of BCO was treated only in (Davidović, Ramljak, Šclmić, & Teodorović, 2011; Davidović, Jakšić, Ramljak, Šelmić, & Teodorović, 2013). However, there are some papers in recent literature describing parallelization techniques for another bees-inspired meta-heuristic, the Artificial Bee Colony (hereinafter, ABC) method (Karaboga, 2005; Karaboga, Akay, & Ozturk, 2007). In this survey, we cover both ABC and BCO meta-heuristics.

The parallelization of BCO reported in (Davidović, Ramljak, Šelmić, & Teodorović, 2011) considered independent multiple executions of different BCO algorithms using distributed memory processors. The authors reported a significant speedup, while preserving solution quality. They also evaluated fine-grained (low-level) parallelization and showed that it was not suitable for these multiprocessor systems. On the other hand, in (Subotić, Tuba, & Stanarević, 2011) it was shown that this strategy was hard to implement efficiently for ABC even on shared-memory multiprocessor systems. The conclusion was that the portion of work is too small, and thus

Table 1. Summary of the parallelization strategies for VNS

Reference	Strategies	Classification	Details
García-López, Melión-Batista, Moreno-Pérez, & Moreno-Vega, 2002	PLS in seq. VNS	1C/RS/SPSS	Low level
	IVNS	pC/RS/MPSS	independent execution
	SH+LS in parallel	1C/KS/SPSS	same k synchronous
Crainic, Gendreau, Hansen, & Mladenović, 2004	IVNS	pC/RS/MPSS	independent execution
	SH+LS in parallel	pC/KS/MPSS	random k asynchronous
Sevkli, & Aydin, 2007	SH+LS in parallel	1C/KS/SPSS	same k synchronous
	SH+LS in parallel	pC/C/MPSS	random k asynchronous
	SH+LS ring	pC/C/MPSS	systematic asynchronous
	SH+LS mesh	pC/C/MPSS	systematic asynchronous
Polacek, Benkner, Doerner, & Hartl, 2008	SH+VND in parallel	pC/C/MPSS	fine grained cooperation
	multiple SH+VND	pC/KC/MPSS	coarse grained cooperation
Knausz, 2008	SH+RVND in parallel	1C/KS/SPDS	random neighborhood subset
Pirkwieser, & Raidl, 2009	several VNS in parallel	pC/KS/MPDS	synchronous VNS multi-search
Yazdani, Amiri, & Zandieh, 2010	SH+LS in parallel	1C/RS/SPDS	different neighborhoods for LS
Davidović, & Crainic, 2013a	IVNS (different VNS)	pC/RS/MPDS	independent execution
	PLS in seq. VNS	1C/C/SPSS	low level
	SH+LS in parallel	1C/C/MPSS	different k-same LS
	SH+LS in parallel	pC/C/SPDS	different k and different LS
	VNS iteration in parallel	pC/C/SPDS	coarse centralized asynchronous
	SH+LS in parallel	pC/C/MPDS	different k-different LS, non-centralized

the extensive use of CPU time for creating threads and their synchronization outweighs the benefits of parallel execution.

Various coarse grain strategies for the parallelization of BCO using distributed memory multiprocessor systems were considered in (Davidović, Jakšić, Ramljak, Šelmić, & Teodorović, 2013). These included two synchronous strategies, distributed BCO (hereinafter: DBCO) and cooperative BCO (hereinafter: CBCO), and an asynchronous strategy named general BCO (hereinafter: GBCO). DBCO assumed that the total amount of computation was (equally) distributed among available processors. CBCO involved a knowledge exchange between various BCO algorithms executed on different processors. GBCO implemented asynchronous cooperation of various BCO

algorithms as the most general parallelization concept. All strategies were implemented in several different ways, and compared with each other and with the sequential BCO execution. Scheduling of independent tasks to identical machines was used as test problem. Here, we present some details about these strategies, and point out the analogy with the corresponding parallelization of ABC when applicable.

The independent execution of all necessary computations on different processors represents the simplest form of coarse-grained parallelization strategies. For BCO it was implemented in three different ways (Davidović, Jakšić, Ramljak, Šelmić, & Teodorović, 2013). All the calculations were equally distributed among the available processors by reducing the stopping criterion

(DBCO), the number of bees (hereinafter, BBCO), or both (hereinafter, MBCO). In all cases, each processor independently performed a sequential variant of BCO, with a different seed or different parameter values.

The main aim of the DBCO approach was to speed up the execution of BCO by dividing the total workload among several processors, and therefore it could be classified as pC/RS/MPSS. DBCO is similar to the second approach proposed in (Parpinelli, Benitez, & Lopes, 2011) for the ABC algorithm, while for BCO was proposed for the first time in (Davidović, Ramljak, Šelmić, & Teodorović, 2011). BBCO is similar to the first approach proposed for ABC in (Subotić, Tuba, & Stanarević, 2011). It was assumed that the BCO parameters (the number of bees B and the number of forward/backward passes NC) were the same for all BCO processes executing on different processors, in order to ensure load balancing between all processors. Therefore, this approach was also classified as pC/RS/MPSS.

Combining these two approaches, it was possible to vary the values of the BCO parameters and change the stopping criterion at the same time. This approach was referred to as MBCO (Multiple BCO) and classified as pC/RS/MPDS. It had the best performance among the independent executions since it introduced more diversification into the search process.

A more sophisticated way to achieve coarse-grained parallelization in (Davidović, Jakšić, Ramljak, Šelmić, & Teodorović, 2013) was through cooperative execution of several BCO processes. At certain predefined execution points, all processes were exchanging the relevant data (usually the current best solutions). These data were used to guide further searches. The synchronous cooperative strategy, named CBCO, was classified as pC/KS/MPSS if all BCO processes had the same values of the parameters B and NC or as pC/KS/MPDS otherwise. Similar approaches were used for the parallelization of the ABC meta-heuristic in (Narasimhan, 2009; Banharnsakun, Achalakul, & Sirinaovakul, 2010; Subotić, Tuba, & Stanarević, 2011).

The communication points in CBCO were determined in two different ways: fixed and processor-dependent. In the first case, the best solution was exchanged 10 times during the parallel BCO execution, regardless of the number of processors engaged. The processor-dependent communication frequency was defined using the following rule: the current global best solution was exchanged each *runtime*/(10*q) iterations where *runtime* represented the maximum allowed CPU time.

The experimental results were performed on completely connected multiprocessor architectures consisting of 2 to 20 processors. The authors showed that in both cases the quality of the final solution obtained by CBCO was either improved, or at least preserved, for a modest number of processors ($q \leq 12$), with respect to the sequential execution of the best performing BCO. At the same time, in the majority of cases, the CPU time was reduced. The CBCO variant with less frequent communications showed a slightly better performance with respect to both solution quality and minimum CPU time.

To decrease the communication and synchronization overhead during the cooperative execution of different BCO algorithms, the asynchronous execution strategy was proposed as the third approach in (Davidović, Jakšić, Ramljak, Šelmić, & Teodorović, 2013). This strategy was named GBCO and was implemented in two different ways. The first implementation involved a centrally coordinated knowledge exchange, while the second one utilized non-centralized parallelism. Each processor executed a particular sequential variant of BCO until some predefined communication condition was satisfied. It then informed others about its search status, collected the current global best, and continued its execution. As its main characteristic, this strategy did not require all of the processors to participate in the communication at the same time. Each processor would send its results, and collect the results from other processors, when it reached its own communication condition.

The first implementation of GBCO assumed the existence of a central blackboard (a global memory) (Crainic & Toulouse, 2010) to which each processor had access to. The communication condition was defined as the improvement of the current best solution or the execution of five iterations without improvement. Each improvement of the current best solution was immediately noted on the blackboard. On the other hand, if improvement did not occur after 5 iterations, the corresponding processor referred to the blackboard for the improvements generated by other processors. If some other processor reported an improved solution, that new solution was used as the reference point for further search. When an improvement had not been announced by others, the execution continued with the previous best as the reference point. This strategy was classified as pC/C/MPSS when the BCO parameters were the same on all processors (only the seed differs), and as pC/C/MPDS otherwise. The implementation used the master-slave multiprocessor system, with the master processor playing a role of central blackboard and slaves executing the cooperating BCO algorithms.

Non-centralized GBCO execution was implemented on a unidirectional ring of processors. Each processor was communicating only with its neighbors. More precisely, the processor was allowed to write (put new best solutions) to the blackboard of its predecessor and to read from the blackboard associated to its successor. The communications were performed after a single iteration of the corresponding BCO was completed. This strategy was also classified as pC/C/MPSS or pC/C/MPDS, depending on the search parameters. Analysis of the computational results showed that non-centralized asynchronous execution outperformed all other parallel variants in the majority of the cases, with respect to both the solution quality and the running time. The strategies proposed in (Davidović, Jakšić, Ramljak, Šelmić, & Teodorović, 2013) are summarized in Table 2.

CONCLUSION

Parallel meta-heuristics represent powerful tools for dealing with hard combinatorial optimization problems, especially for large size real-life instances. Therefore, a systematic approach to the design and implementation of parallel meta-heuristic methods is of great importance. The main objective of this chapter was to present a state-of-the-art survey of the ideas and strategies for parallel meta-heuristic, and to discuss general design and implementation principles applicable to all meta-heuristic classes, neighborhood- and population-based, in particular. We explained various paradigms related to the parallel meta-heuristic development. We recalled the corresponding taxonomy and used it for the

Table 2. Summary of the parallelization strategies for BCO

Name	Description	Classification	Details
DBCO	same BCO, different seed	pC/RS/MPSS	reduced stopping criteria
BBCO	same BCO, different seed	pC/RS/MPSS	reduced number of bees
MBCO	different BCO, independent	pC/RS/MPDS	different B and NC
CBCO1	cooperative synchronous	pC/KS/MPDS	fixed number of communications
CBCO2	cooperative synchronous	pC/KS/MPDS	variable number of communications
GBCO1	cooperative asynchronous	pC/C/MPDS	centralized communications
GBCO2	cooperative asynchronous	pC/C/MPDS	non-centralized communications

classification of the described strategies. We also discussed implementation issues, namely the influence of the target architecture on parallel execution of meta-heuristics. The characteristics of shared and distributed memory multiprocessor systems were pointed out. These topics were illustrated through examples from recent literature. These examples are related to the parallelization of two meta-heuristic methods, population-based Bee Colony Optimization and neighborhood-based Variable Neighborhood Search. The common conclusion for both methods is that non-centralized asynchronous parallelization performs the best. The extensive literature and practical experience provided in this overview should help researchers in designing efficient parallel optimization algorithms.

ACKNOWLEDGMENT

This work has been partially supported by the Serbian Ministry of Science, Grant nos. 174010 and 174033. Partial funding for this work has also been provided by the Natural Sciences and Engineering Research Council of Canada, the Canada Foundation for Innovation, and the Quebec Ministry of Education. The authors would also like to thank Mrs. Branka Mladenović and Mr. Alexey Uversky for the proofreading efforts.

REFERENCES

Alba, E. (Ed.). (2005). *Parallel metaheuristics: A new class of algorithms*. Hoboken, NJ: John Wiley & Sons. doi:10.1002/0471739383

Aydin, M., & Sevkli, M. (2008). Sequential and parallel variable neighborhood search algorithms for job shop scheduling. In F. Xhafa, & A. Abraham (Eds.), *Metaheuristics for scheduling in industrial and manufacturing applications* (Vol. 128, pp. 125–144). Berlin: Springer. doi:10.1007/978-3-540-78985-7_6

Banharnsakun, A., Achalakul, T., & Sirinaovakul, B. (2010). Artificial bee colony algorithm on distributed environments. In H. Takagi, A. Abraham, M. Koppen, K. Yoshida, & A. C. P. L. F. de Carvalho (Eds.), *Second world congress on nature and biologically inspired computing (NaBIC'10)* (pp. 13-18). The Institute of Electrical and Electronics Engineers, Inc.

Butenhof, D. R. (Ed.). (1997). *Programming with POSIX threads*. Reading, MA: Addison-Wesley Professional.

Crainic, T. G., Gendreau, M., Hansen, P., & Mladenović, N. (2004). Cooperative parallel variable neighborhood search for the p-median. *Journal of Heuristics*, *10*(3), 293–314. doi:10.1023/B:HEUR.0000026897.40171.1a

Crainic, T. G., & Hail, N. (2005). Parallel meta-heuristics applications. In E. Alba (Ed.), *Parallel metaheuristics: A new class of algorithms* (pp. 447–494). Hoboken, NJ: John Wiley & Sons. doi:10.1002/0471739383.ch19

Crainic, T. G., & Toulouse, M. (2010). Parallel meta-heuristics. In M. Gendreau & J.Y. Potvin (Eds.), Handbook of metaheuristics (pp. 497-541). New York: Springer Science+Business Media.

Cung, V.-D., Martins, S. L., Ribeiro, C. C., & Roucairol, C. (2002). Strategies for the parallel implementations of metaheuristics. In C. C. Ribeiro, & P. Hansen (Eds.), *Essays and surveys in metaheuristics* (pp. 263–308). Norwell, MA: Kluwer Academic Publishers. doi:10.1007/978-1-4615-1507-4_13

Cvetković, D., & Davidović, T. (2011). Multiprocessor interconnection networks. In D. Cvetković & I. Gutman (Eds.), Selected topics on applications of graph spectra (pp. 35-62). Serbia: Mathematical Institute SANU.

Dagum, L., & Menon, R. (1998). OpenMP: An industry standard api for shared-memory programming. *IEEE Computational Science & Engineering*, *5*(1), 46–55. doi:10.1109/99.660313

Davidović, T., & Crainic, T. G. (2013a). *Parallelization strategies for variable neighborhood search, CIRRELT-2013-47*. Retrieved September 10, 2013, from https://www.cirrelt.ca/DocumentsTravail/CIRRELT-2013-47.pdf

Davidović, T., & Crainic, T. G. (2013b). Parallel local search to schedule communicating tasks on identical processors. *CIRRELT-2013-54*. Retrieved September 10, 2013, from https://www.cirrelt.ca/DocumentsTravail/CIRRELT-2013-54.pdf

Davidović, T., Jakšić, T., Ramljak, D., Šelmić, M., & Teodorović, D. (2013). Parallelization strategies for bee colony optimization based on message passing communication protocol. *Optimization: A Journal of Mathematical Programming and Operations Research, 62*(8), 1113-1142.

Davidović, T., Ramljak, D., Šelmić, M., & Teodorović, D. (2011). MPI parallelization of bee colony optimization. In *Proceedings of 1st International Symposium & 10th Balkan Conference on Operational Research,* (vol. 2, pp. 193-200). Thessaloniki, Greece: University of Macedonia, Economic and Social Sciences.

Dorigo, M., & Stützle, T. (2010). Ant colony optimization: Overview and recent advances. In M. Gendreau & J-Y. Potvin (Eds.), Handbook of metaheuristics (2nd ed.), (pp. 227-263). New York: Springer Science+Business Media.

Feo, T. A., & Resende, M. G. C. (1995). Greedy randomized adaptive search procedures. *Journal of Global Optimization, 6*(2), 109–133. doi:10.1007/BF01096763

Ferreira, A., & Morvan, M. (1997). Models for parallel algorithm design: An introduction. In A. Migdalas, P. Pardalos, & S. Storøy (Eds.), *Parallel computing in optimization* (pp. 1–26). Dordrecht, The Netherlands: Kluwer Academic Publishers. doi:10.1007/978-1-4613-3400-2_1

García-López, F., Melión-Batista, B., Moreno-Pérez, J. A., & Moreno-Vega, J. M. (2002). The parallel variable neighborhood search for the p-median problem. *Journal of Heuristics, 8*(3), 375–388. doi:10.1023/A:1015013919497

Gendreau, M., & Potvin, J.-Y. (2010). Tabu search. In M. Gendreau & J-Y. Potvin (Eds.), Handbook of metaheuristics (2nd ed.), (pp. 41-59). New York: Springer Science+Business Media.

Glover, F., & Laguna, M. (Eds.). (1997). *Tabu search*. Boston: Kluwer Academic Publishers. doi:10.1007/978-1-4615-6089-0

Goldberg, D. E. (Ed.). (1989). *Genetic algorithms in search, optimization, and machine learning*. Reading, MA: Addison-Wesley Longman Publishing Co., Inc.

Gropp, W., & Lusk, E. (1996). *Users guide for mpich a portable implementation of MPI*. New York: Mathematics and Computer Science Division. doi:10.2172/378910

Gropp, W., Lusk, E., & Skjellum, A. (Eds.). (1994). Using MPI: Portable parallel programming with themessage-passing interface. Cambridge, MA: The MIT Press.

Hansen, P., & Mladenović, N. (2003). Variable neighbourhood search. In F. Glover, & G. Kochenagen (Eds.), *Handbook of metaheuristics* (pp. 145–184). Boston: Kluwer Academic Publishers.

Hansen, P., & Mladenović, N. (2005). Variable neighbourhood search. In E. K. Burke & G. Kendall (Eds.), Search methodologies: Introductory tutorials in optimization and decision support techniques (pp. 211-238). New York: Springer Science+Business Media.

Hansen, P., Mladenović, N., Brimberg, J., & Moreno-Pérez, J. A. (2010). Variable neighbourhood search. In M. Gendreau & J-Y. Potvin (Eds.), Handbook of metaheuristics (2nd ed.), (pp. 61-86). New York: Springer Science+Business Media.

Karaboga, D. (2005). *An idea based on honey bee swarm for numerical optimization* (Technical report-TR06). Retrieved September 10, 2013, from http://mf.erciyes.edu.tr/abc/pub/tr06_2005.pdf

Karaboga, D., Akay, B., & Ozturk, C. (2007). Artificial bee colony (ABC) optimization algorithm for training feed-forward neural networks. In V. Torra, Y. Narukawa, & Y. Yoshida (Eds.), *Modeling decisions for artificial intelligence* (Vol. 4617, pp. 318–319). Berlin: Springer. doi:10.1007/978-3-540-73729-2_30

Kirkpatrick, S., Gelatt, C. D., & Vecchi, M. P. (1983). Optimization by simulated annealing. *Science*, 220(4598), 671–680. doi:10.1126/science.220.4598.671 PMID:17813860

Knausz, M. (2008). *Parallel variable neighbourhood search for the car sequencing problem. Diplomarbeit zur Erlangung des akademischen Grades*. Fakultät für Informatik der Technischen Universität Wien.

Lučić, P., & Teodorović, D. (2001). Bee system: Modeling combinatorial optimization transportation engineering problems by swarm intelligence. In *Preprints of the TRISTAN IV Triennial Symposium on Transportation Analysis* (pp. 441-445). Sao Miguel, Azores Islands.

Lučić, P., & Teodorović, D. (2003a). Computing with bees: attacking complex transportation engineering problems. *International Journal of Artificial Intelligence Tools*, 12(3), 375–394. doi:10.1142/S0218213003001289

Lučić, P., & Teodorović, D. (2003b). Vehicle routing problem with uncertain demand at nodes: The bee system and fuzzy logic approach. In J. L. Verdegay (Ed.), *Fuzzy sets based heuristics for optimization* (pp. 67–82). Berlin: Springer-Verlag. doi:10.1007/978-3-540-36461-0_5

Mladenović, N., & Hansen, P. (1997). Variable neighborhood search. *Computers & Operations Research*, 24(11), 1097–1100. doi:10.1016/S0305-0548(97)00031-2

Narasimhan, H. (2009). Parallel artificial bee colony (PABC) algorithm. In A. Abraham, A. Carvalho, F. Herrera, & V. Pai (Eds.), *VIII International Conference on Computer Information Systems and Industrial Management (CISIM, 2009), World Congress on Nature and Biologically Inspired Computing (NaBIC'09)* (pp. 306-311). IEEE.

Nikolaev, A. G., & Jacobson, S. H. (2010). Simulated annealing. In M. Gendreau & J-Y. Potvin (Eds.), Handbook of metaheuristics (2nd ed.), (pp. 1-39). New York: Springer Science+Business Media.

Parpinelli, R. S., Benitez, C. M. V., & Lopes, H. S. (2011). Parallel approaches for the artificial bee colony algorithm. In B. K. Panigrahi, Y. Shi, & M.-H. Lim (Eds.), *Handbook of swarm intelligence: Concepts, principles and applications* (Vol. 8, pp. 329–346). Berlin: Springer. doi:10.1007/978-3-642-17390-5_14

Pirkwieser, S., & Raidl, G. (2009). Multiple variable neighborhood search enriched with ilp techniques for the periodic vehicle routing problem with time windows. In M. J. Blesa, C. Blum, L. Gaspero, A. Roli, M. Sampels, & A. Schaerf (Eds.), *Hybrid metaheuristics* (pp. 45–59). Berlin: Springer. doi:10.1007/978-3-642-04918-7_4

Polacek, M., Benkner, S., Doerner, K. F., & Hartl, R. F. (2008). A cooperative and adaptive variable neighborhood search for the multi depot vehicle routing problem with time windows. *Business Research*, 1(2), 1–12.

Reeves, C. R. (2010). Genetic algorithms. In M. Gendreau & J-Y. Potvin (Eds.), Handbook of metaheuristics (2nd ed.), (pp. 109-139). New York: Springer Science+Business Media.

Resende, M. G. C., & Ribeiro, C. C. (2010). Greedy randomized adaptive search procedures: Advances, hybridizations, and applications. In M. Gendreau & J-Y. Potvin (Eds.), Handbook of metaheuristics (2nd ed.), (pp. 283-319). New York: Springer Science+Business Media.

Sevkli, M., & Aydin, M. E. (2007). Parallel variable neighbourhood search algorithms for job shop scheduling problems. *IMA Journal of Management Mathematics*, *18*(2), 117–133. doi:10.1093/imaman/dpm009

Subotić, M., Tuba, M., & Stanarević, N. (2011). Different approaches in parallelization of the artificial bee colony algorithm. *International Journal of Mathematical Models and Methods in Applied Sciences*, *5*(4), 755–762.

Talbi, E.-G. (Ed.). (2009). *Metaheuristics: From design to implementation*. Hoboken, NJ: John Wiley & Sons, Inc. doi:10.1002/9780470496916

Teodorović, D. (2009). Bee colony optimization (BCO). In C. P. Lim, L. C. Jain, & S. Dehuri (Eds.), *Innovations in swarm intelligence* (pp. 39–60). Berlin: Springer-Verlag. doi:10.1007/978-3-642-04225-6_3

Toulouse, M., Crainic, T. G., & Gendreau, M. (1996). Communication issues in designing cooperative multi thread parallel searches. In I. H. Osman, & J. P. Kelly (Eds.), *Meta-heuristics: Theory & applications* (pp. 501–522). Boston: Kluwer Academic Publishers. doi:10.1007/978-1-4613-1361-8_30

Verhoeven, M. G. A., & Aarts, E. H. L. (1995). Parallel local search. *Journal of Heuristics*, *1*(1), 43–65. doi:10.1007/BF02430365

Yazdani, M., Amiri, M., & Zandieh, M. (2010). Flexible job-shop scheduling with parallel variable neighborhood search algorithm. *Expert Systems with Applications*, *37*(1), 678–687. doi:10.1016/j.eswa.2009.06.007

ADDITIONAL READING

Alba, E., Luque, G., & Nesmachnow, S. (2013). Parallel metaheuristics: recent advances and new trends. *International Transactions in Operational Research*, *20*(1), 1–48. doi:10.1111/j.1475-3995.2012.00862.x

Błażewicz, J., Drozdowski, M., & Ecker, K. (2000). Management of resources in parallel systems. In *Handbook on Parallel and Distributed Processing* (pp. 263–341). Springer Berlin Heidelberg. doi:10.1007/978-3-662-04303-5_6

Bozejko, W., & Wodecki, M. (2004, September). Parallel tabu search method approach for very difficult permutation scheduling problems. In *Parallel Computing in Electrical Engineering, 2004. PARELEC 2004. International Conference on* (pp. 156-161). IEEE.

Brucker, P. (Ed.). (2007). *Scheduling algorithms*. Springer.

Corrêa, R., Dutra, I., Fiallos, M., & Gomez, F. (2002). *Models for Parallel and Distributed Computation: Theory, Algorithmic Techniques and Applications*. Kluwer Academic Publishers. doi:10.1007/978-1-4757-3609-0

Crainic, T. G. (2005). Parallel computation, co-operation, tabu search. In C. Rego and B. Alidaee (Eds.) Metaheuristic Optimization Via Memory and Evolution: Tabu Search and Scatter Search (pp. 283-302). Springer US.

Crainic, T. G. (2008). Parallel Solution Methods for Vehicle Routing Problems. In B. Golden, S. Raghavan, & E. Wasil (Eds.), *The Vehicle Routing Problem: Latest Advances and New Challenges* (pp. 171–198). New York: Springer. doi:10.1007/978-0-387-77778-8_8

Crainic, T. G., Di Chiara, B., Nonato, M., & Tarricone, L. (2006). Tackling Electrosmog in Completely Configured 3G Networks by Parallel Cooperative Meta-Heuristics. *IEEE Wireless Communications, 13*(6), 34–41. doi:10.1109/MWC.2006.275196

Crainic, T. G., Li, Y., & Toulouse, M. (2006). A First Multilevel Cooperative Algorithm for the Capacitated Multicommodity Network Design. *Computers & Operations Research, 33*(9), 2602–2622. doi:10.1016/j.cor.2005.07.015

Davidović, T., & Crainic, T. G. (2012). MPI Parallelization of Variable Neighborhood Search. *Electronic Notes in Discrete Mathematics, 39,* 241–248. doi:10.1016/j.endm.2012.10.032

Davidović, T., Ramljak, D., Šelmić, M., & Teodorović, D. (2011). Bee colony optimization for the p-center problem. *Computers & Operations Research, 38*(10), 1367–1376. doi:10.1016/j.cor.2010.12.002

Davidović, T., Šelmić, M., Teodorović, D., & Ramljak, D. (2012). Bee colony optimization for scheduling independent tasks to identical processors. *Journal of Heuristics, 18*(4), 549–569. doi:10.1007/s10732-012-9197-3

Delévacq, A., Delisle, P., Gravel, M., & Krajecki, M. (2013). Parallel ant colony optimization on graphics processing units. *Journal of Parallel and Distributed Computing, 73*(1), 52–61. doi:10.1016/j.jpdc.2012.01.003

Garey, M. R., & Johnson, D. S. (1979). *Computers and Intractability: A guide to the theory of NP-completeness.* San Francisco: WH Freeman & Co.

Gendreau, M., & Potvin, J. Y. (Eds.). (2010). *Handbook of metaheuristics* (Vol. 146). Springer. doi:10.1007/978-1-4419-1665-5

Jin, H., Jespersen, D., Mehrotra, P., Biswas, R., Huang, L., & Chapman, B. (2011). High performance computing using MPI and OpenMP on multi-core parallel systems. *Parallel Computing, 37*(9), 562–575. doi:10.1016/j.parco.2011.02.002

Jin, J., Crainic, T. G., & Lokketangen, A. (2012). A Cooperative Parallel Metaheuristic for the Capacitated Vehicle Routing Problem. *CIRRELT-2012-46* (1-23) Retrieved September 30, 2013, from https://www.cirrelt.ca/DocumentsTravail/CIRRELT-2012-46.pdf.

Jin, J., Crainic, T. G., & Løkketangen, A. (2012). A parallel multi-neighborhood cooperative tabu search for capacitated vehicle routing problems. *European Journal of Operational Research, 222*(3), 441–451. doi:10.1016/j.ejor.2012.05.025

Kwok, Y. K., & Ahmad, I. (1997). Efficient scheduling of arbitrary task graphs to multiprocessors using a parallel genetic algorithm. *Journal of Parallel and Distributed Computing, 47*(1), 58–77. doi:10.1006/jpdc.1997.1395

Le Bouthillier, A., & Crainic, T. G. (2005). A Cooperative Parallel Meta-Heuristic for the Vehicle Routing Problem with Time Windows. *Computers & Operations Research, 32*(7), 1685–1708. doi:10.1016/j.cor.2003.11.023

Luong, T., Melab, N., & Talbi, E. (2013). GPU computing for parallel local search metaheuristic algorithms. *IEEE Transactions on Computers, 62*(1), 173–185. doi:10.1109/TC.2011.206

Mahmood, Z. (2013). *Cloud Computing: Methods and Practical Approaches.* Springer. doi:10.1007/978-1-4471-5107-4

Maniezzo, V., Stèutzle, T., & Voss, S. (Eds.). (2009). *Matheuristics: hybridizing metaheuristics and mathematical programming* (Vol. 10). Springer.

Melab, N., Luong, T. V., Boufaras, K., & Talbi, E. G. (2011). Towards paradisEO-MO-GPU: a framework for GPU-based local search metaheuristics. In *Advances in Computational Intelligence* (pp. 401–408). Springer Berlin Heidelberg. doi:10.1007/978-3-642-21501-8_50

Moreno Pérez, J. A., Hansen, P., & Mladenović, N. (2005). Parallel variableneighborhood search. In E. Alba (Ed.), *Parallel Metaheuristics* (pp. 247–266). Hoboken, NJ: John Wiley & Sons. doi:10.1002/0471739383.ch11

Pedemonte, M., Nesmachnow, S., & Cancela, H. (2011). A survey on parallel ant colony optimization. *Applied Soft Computing*, *11*(8), 5181–5197. doi:10.1016/j.asoc.2011.05.042

Porto, S. C., & Ribeiro, C. C. (1996). Parallel tabu search message-passing synchronous strategies for task scheduling under precedence constraints. *Journal of Heuristics*, *1*(2), 207–223. doi:10.1007/BF00127078

Raynal, M. (2012). *Concurrent programming: algorithms, principles, and foundations*. Springer Publishing Company, Incorporated.

Ribeiro, C., & Hansen, P. (Eds.). (2002). *Essays and surveys in metaheuristics*. Kluwer Academic Publishers. doi:10.1007/978-1-4615-1507-4

Rothlauf, F. (2011). *Design of Modern Heuristics: Principles and Application*. Springer. doi:10.1007/978-3-540-72962-4

Rozenberg, G., Bäck, T., & Kok, J. N. (Eds.). (2012). *Handbook of natural computing*. Springer Publishing Company, Incorporated. doi:10.1007/978-3-540-92910-9

Shankar, A. U. (2012). *Distributed Programming: Theory and Practice*. Springer.

Subramanian, A., Drummond, L. M. D. A., Bentes, C., Ochi, L. S., & Farias, R. (2010). A parallel heuristic for the vehicle routing problem with simultaneous pickup and delivery. *Computers & Operations Research*, *37*(11), 1899–1911. doi:10.1016/j.cor.2009.10.011

Taillard, E., Melab, N., & Talbi, E. G. (2012). Parallelization strategies for hybrid metaheuristics using a single GPU and multi-core resources. In *Parallel Problem Solving from Nature-PPSN XII* (pp. 368–377). Springer Berlin Heidelberg.

Talbi, E. G. (Ed.). (2006). *Parallel combinatorial optimization* (Vol. 58). John Wiley & Sons. doi:10.1002/0470053925

Teodorović, D. (2008). Swarm intelligence systems for transportation engineering: Principles and applications. *Transportation Research Part C, Emerging Technologies*, *16*(6), 651–667. doi:10.1016/j.trc.2008.03.002

Wodecki, M., & Bozejko, W. (2001). Solving the flow shop problem by parallel simulated annealing. *LNCS* 2328, 236-247, 2002.

Yeo, C. S., Li, E. W. K., & Foo, Y. S. (2011). Handling Large Datasets in Parallel Metaheuristics: A Spares Management and Optimization Case Study. In *Advanced Information Networking and Applications (WAINA), 2011 IEEE Workshops of International Conference on* (pp. 261-266). IEEE.

KEY TERMS AND DEFINITIONS

Combinatorial Optimization: Finding the optimal solution of a given problem, i.e., the one satisfying feasibility rules and yielding the extreme value of the objective function.

Communication: Data exchange between processing elements.

Meta-Heuristics: General computational algorithms using stochastic search processes applied to the various search and optimization problems.

Parallelization: Division of computational load between multiple processing elements.

Synchronization: Coordination of computations and communications.

Chapter 12
Application of Cloud–Based Simulation in Scientific Research

Mihailo Marinković
Telenor, Serbia

Sava Čavoški
MDS Information Engineering, Serbia

Aleksandar Marković
University of Belgrade, Serbia

ABSTRACT

This chapter is a review of the literature related to the use of cloud-based computer simulations in scientific research. The authors examine the types and good examples of cloud-based computer simulations, offering suggestions for the architecture, frameworks, and runtime infrastructures that support running simulations in cloud environment. Cloud computing has become the standard for providing hardware and software infrastructure. Using the possibilities offered by cloud computing platforms, researchers can efficiently use the already existing IT resources in solving computationally intensive scientific problems. Further on, the authors emphasize the possibilities of using the existing and already known simulation models and tools in the cloud computing environment. The cloud environment provides possibilities to execute all kinds of simulation experiments as in traditional environments. This way, models are accessible to a wider range of researchers and the analysis of data resulting from simulation experiments is significantly improved.

INTRODUCTION

In last couple of years, Cloud Computing has become a standard for delivering hardware and software infrastructure. It is based on a *pay-per-use* business model where resources are acquired only when really needed and customer pays only

for resources actually used. Cloud computing represents the mechanism for dealing with the use of external services as part of the computational foundation (Tor-Morten, 2012). It provides scalable, distributed computer services as needed. The aim of cloud computing is to present a service layer for its users where all detailed logic is made transparent and drawn upon as needed. In general, cloud computing is recognized as an

DOI: 10.4018/978-1-4666-5784-7.ch012

infrastructure where all underlying resources (storage, RAM, processors, load balancers etc.) are completely abstracted from the end user. This leads to the cloud provider/vendor to be in charge of performance, reliability and scalability. Gartner defines cloud computing as a style of computing in which scalable and elastic IT-enabled capabilities are delivered as a service using Internet technologies (Gartner, 2013). The National Institute of Standards and Technology (NIST) defines cloud computing as:

A model for enabling ubiquitous, convenient, on-demand network access to a shared pool of configurable computing resources (e.g., networks, servers, storage, applications, and services) that can be rapidly provisioned and released with minimal management effort or service provider interaction (Peter & Grance, 2011).

The same authors list three service models: Infrastructure as a Service (IaaS), Platform as a Service (PaaS) and Software as a Service (SaaS). The same source, and also other authors (Jeffery & Neidecker-Lutz, 2010) provide five essential characteristics (On-demand self-service, Broad network access, Resource pooling, Rapid elasticity and Measured Service), and four deployment models (Private, Community, Public and Hybrid cloud). The introduction of Cloud Computing had a significant impact on all segments of IT industry, including computer-based modeling and simulation.

Cloud Computing Expert Group (Jeffery & Neidecker-Lutz, 2010) provided an overview of all main aspects of Cloud Computing (Figure 1).

This chapter offers an overview of the existing cloud-based simulation software and explores the possibilities of using the existing simulation models and tools in this new environment. One of the

Figure 1. Main aspects of clouds (Adapted from [Jeffery & Neidecker-Lutz, 2010])

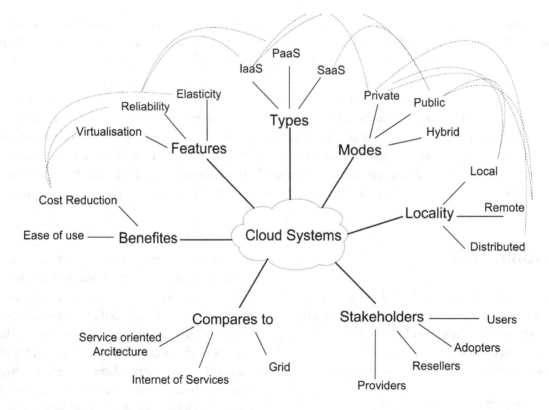

hypotheses is that it is possible to reuse existing models and tools in cloud environment and also to improve them. In Cloud environment it is possible to execute all kinds of simulations, which are used in traditional environment, while models availability and analysis of results of simulation experiments can be significantly improved.

Simulation, in this context, refers to the process of creating abstract models out of real existing or future systems and their use for performing experiments. When computers are used for performing simulation experiments, then we are talking about computer simulation (Radenković, Stanojević, & Marković, 2010). Computing infrastructure is the foundation for computer simulation and has a significant impact on simulation model development process and simulation experiment execution. Computer simulation dates back to mainframe systems period and has been continuously improved and developed along with the development of IT infrastructure, services and technologies. The development of Cloud infrastructure and services has also impacted on the development in the field of computer modeling and simulation, mostly in simulation experiment execution techniques and analysis of data resulting from these experiments.

WEB BASED SIMULATION

We may say that cloud computing is perceived as one of the most significant achievement for the entire IT industry. Cloud computing offers exactly this: the IT infrastructure and software as a service. The same applies to the simulation. The first step was the adjustment of the existing simulation tools for Internet use. Hence, in the following we will briefly address web-based simulations.

Web based simulation represents the integration of web and simulation methodologies. This discipline has been rapidly developed in the last 15 years. The first scholarly articles addressing this issue emerged at the Winter Simulation Conference in 1996 (Fishwick, 1996; Buss & Stork, 1996;

Nair, Miller, & Zhang, 1996). The first conference devoted specifically to this topic was held in 1998, where the main focus was the application of Java technology and CORBA architecture, which was most promising at the time.

We can define three approaches of the Web based simulation modeling. The first is the access to *Server-hosted simulation*, which enables the existing simulation tools to be hosted on the server and to be accessed through classic HTML web pages. The advantage of this approach lies in the use of the existing software tools and models. The main flaw of this approach is the fact that the user cannot follow the simulation experiment on the Internet. The tools are not adjusted for this purpose. This approach has thus been abandoned.

The second approach, known as *Client-side simulation*, enables the use of simulation tools as applets based application where everything happens on the client page. The performance results of this simulation depend on the local IT resources. Several Java based simulation packages and languages are developed: SimJava, API for discreet simulation models, JSIM, Java-based animation environment based on both the process interaction and event scheduling approaches to simulation etc.

The third approach is the *Hybrid client/server* simulation which combines the advantages of the two previous models. This simulation platform is based on the server, while Java, PHP, NET frameworks are used for visualization and animation at client computers. This is the most frequently used approach in relation to cloud environment which will be discussed later in the text.

The web based simulation has significant advantages if compared to classic simulation systems. Its main advantages are the following, (Byrne, Heavey, & Byrne, 2010):

- **Easy to use:** In classic simulation systems the creation of simulation models as well as the launching of the simulations experiments is very demanding both for the beginners and professionals. Web based simulation ensures the easy use of third party models as well as the easy distribution of simulation models which are often very expensive.

- **Collaboration and communication:** Communication and interaction are one of the main factors for the successful simulation project. Web based simulation ensures the easy communication between the participants in the project.
- **Licensing and model development:** This is especially useful for companies which are not developing simulation models on daily basis. Web-based simulation provides new business models for use of software on the principle of SaaS.
- **Model reuse:** Bearing in mind its distributive nature, the Internet supports the reuse of existing simulation models, their maintenance and easy research.
- **Ability to use it on all platforms and operating systems:** Web technologies enable the launching of applications on all operating systems and on all Web browsers.
- **Access control:** The access control is performed through the authentication of user name and password as well as the time limit to access the applications.
- **Wide access:** Web application and web simulation models may be accessed at any time and at any location.
- **Versioning, customization and maintenance:** The maintenance of web based system is reduced to the minimum. The new version of the program is centrally put on the server which enables the frequent change of versions and adjustment of the simulation models and experiments in the environment.
- **Integration and interoperability:** A Web-based tool can integrate and interoperate with both existing and future Web-based applications, as well as with Web-enabled desktop applications.

- Easy data collection which may be regarded as the access to the system.

Disadvantages of the web based simulation in comparison with the classic systems (Byrne, Heavey, & Byrne, 2010):

- **Slow implementation:** In certain circumstances it is possible to have a slower implementation of the simulation experiments in Web browsers.
- **Limitation in the graphical interface:** Desktop applications have more options in comparison to web application. However, the continuous development of the web programming tools, development of RIA applications as well as the speedy development of Web2.0 and HTML 5.0 technologies, are reducing this difference.
- **Application safety:** Web based applications are usually subject to malicious attacks. If the simulation software is used as a SaaS service, the problem is the fact that the confidential data are on the provider's server.

A Web based simulation may be used:

1. **In education:** As it is the case with other disciplines, the web is regarded as a main medium for distribution and exchange of all information used for modeling and simulation. There is also a need to promote the use of different technologies (virtual reality, video conferencing, multimedia content) which emphasize the educational aspect of materials facilitating the learning process.
2. **In simulation programs:** Thanks to the Internet, the software for simulation is more accessible since it can be launched from any location on the Internet. The special advantage is the launching of distributive simulation and the possibility of launching parallel simulations.

The architecture of the Web based simulation models is similar to all other web applications. All new web technologies may be used for the creation of simulation models.

The well known three-tier architecture presented in Figure 2 is mostly used in the creation of web based applications.

ARCHITECTURE FOR IMPLEMENTATION OF SIMULATION SYSTEMS IN CLOUD ENVIRONMENT

We demonstrated how the development of Internet and Internet technologies brought about changes in IT simulation. In the last few years the development of virtual platforms and virtual platforms hardware infrastructure modified the way in which the applications, services and hardware are used on Internet. Cloud computing represents a new way for using infrastructure, hardware and software resources. We may differentiate between private, public and hybrid clouds (Figure 3). The well known public ones are: Amazon, Google, Microsoft Azure and Salesforce. The private clouds are often developed within big companies, by using the virtual platforms (commercial: VMware, Citrix, or open source: Eucalyptus).

The use of cloud computing is inevitable in the majority of research institutions with the aim of solving the need for increased IT resources and data storing. The three factors which influence the expansion of cloud computing use are the following:

1. Constant increase of the price of hardware and the need for IT resources and data storing. The emergence of new multi core architectures and modern super computers with thousands of processors;

Figure 2. Architecture of the web-based simulation application (Adapted from [Byrne, Heavey, & Byrne, 2010])

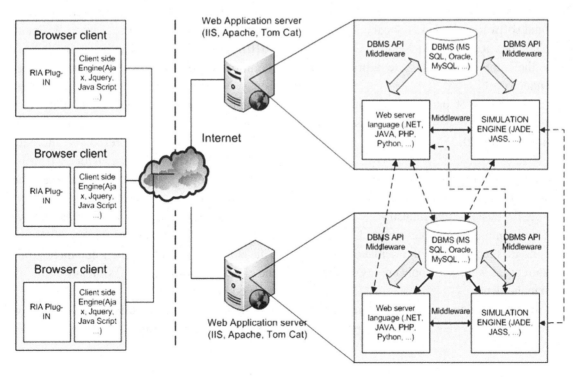

Figure 3. Types of clouds according to the development model (Adapted from [Slook, 2009])

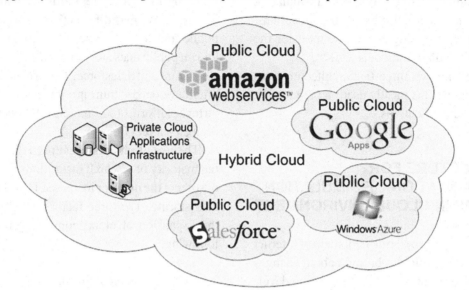

2. Exponential growth of data used in research;
3. Greater use of Service computing which use Web 2.0 applications.

Beside the application of the hardware Cloud infrastructure, the majority of universities and other research institutions are starting to replace the traditional software installed on local computers for applications accessible on the Internet, which reduces the complexity of IT system, prices and maintenance costs.

The advantages of using Cloud computing for educational and research institutions are the following (Kalim, 2013):

- Cloud computing makes research capacities of the research institutions more accessible for business and industry;
- Cloud computing enables research institutions to keep up with the demand for resources, as well as to apply energy efficient management;
- Cloud computing assists educational institutions to apply new and innovative ways in education;

- Cloud computing assists students and professors in using software without the need to be installed on the local computers, and also offers access to other research materials from any location on the Internet.

One of the best known clouds used for research in USA is NEBULA (Steven, Linton, & Spence, 2010). NEBULA.net project began in 2008 with the aim of consolidating NASA research resources. Today, NEBULA is an open-source cloud computing project whose services are used by NASA researchers and engineers in their research and development projects. It represents an alternative to data centers which are formed for each project. This cloud is open for all scientists and researchers who work on NASA projects (Figure 4).

We may conclude that Cloud infrastructure in research and educational purposes is widely used. This chapter will address the implementation of the cloud technologies in IT simulations, as well as in commercial use.

The application of simulation in cloud environment may be divided into two groups:

Figure 4. Architecture of NEBULA cloud (Adapted from [Steven, Linton, & Spence, 2010])

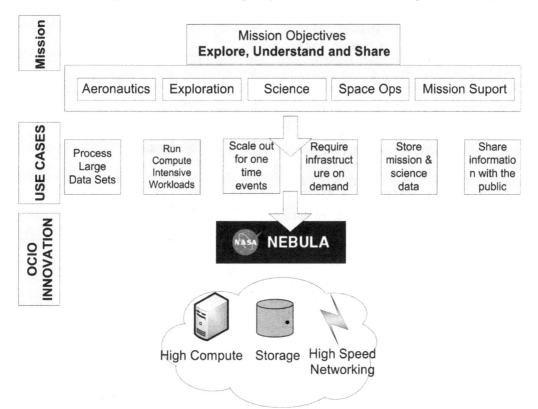

1. Lease of hardware infrastructure for simulation launching;
2. Use of simulation tools as service.

Lease of Hardware Infrastructure for Simulation Launching

Cloud computing is most frequently connected with the lease of resources in public clouds, IaaS and PaaS models. IaaS model entails the lease of virtual machines and data storage, while PaaS model lease systematic software (operating systems, DBMS, application server and development tools) (Figure 5).

The architecture of this system is standardized and the technical implementation depends on the vendor whose equipment is used for the implementation of the cloud. The general architecture of the cloud system is presented in Figure 6. Lease

of hardware resources for launching clouds for research and educational purposes may be implemented in the same way as any other resource within the cloud infrastructure.

Each cloud infrastructure has the following components:

1. **Hardware Layer:** Storage, IT and network infrastructure (EMC, IBM, CISCO, NetApp, HP, ...).
2. **Virtual Layer:** Application of virtual technologies: VMware, Citrix, Microsoft.
3. **Application Layer:** Applications which are offered to users.

In relation to the lease of hardware and virtual hardware infrastructure, there are three new aspects introduced by cloud computing (Armbrust et al., 2009):

Figure 5. Service models of cloud computing (Adapted from [Mell & Grance, 2009])

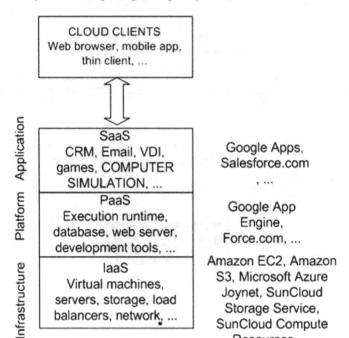

Figure 6. General architecture of the cloud system (Adapted from [Calsoft, 2013])

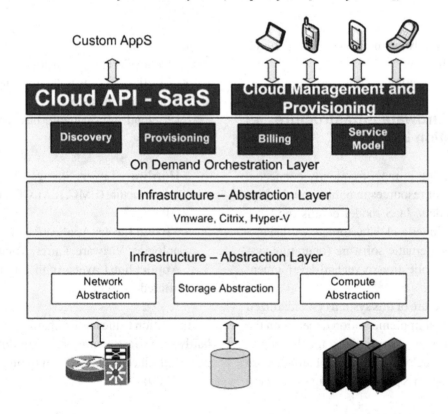

1. User's impression that the resources are unlimited, which implies that there is no need to plan for new resources;
2. The ability to extend resources at any time and according to current needs;
3. The ability to lease IT resources for a short period of time (for example processors for an hour, data storage for one day) and their abandonment when the activity ends.

The launching of simulation experiments with complex models has been always hardware demanding and time consuming. Besides, the required memory space in these instances is extensive. Usually, it is realized as big data bases which store numerous experiment results. Although they are usually structured, there is a great number of unstructured data output such as pictures, videos, etc. A special challenge is the use and processing of data resulting from the simulation experiments.

We may conclude that the IT infrastructure required for the implementation of the simulation experiment was one of the most expensive elements of the entire simulation projects. As a result of the lease of hardware infrastructure, cloud computing enables users to perform numerous experiments which may be executed at the same time, in parallel, without the need to have their own IT infrastructure. On the other hand, if there is a need to change the hardware infrastructure in the project implementation, it is possible to do it during the very experiment. There is a business community plan for the virtual infrastructure which means that the break-up of hardware does not influence the implementation of the simulation experiment.

Poole, Cornelius, Trapp and Langton provide good examples for the implementation of the simulation experiment (Poole, Cornelius, Trapp, & Langton, 2012), by using the Monte Carlo simulation. This type of simulation is common in financial simulations field, and it can be implemented even in spreadsheet (Marković & Čavoški, 2005; Marković, Barjaktarović-Rakočević,

& Čavoški, 2005; Barjaktarović-Rakočević, Marković, & Čavoški, 2006). The users of Cloud infrastructure have the possibility to multiply calculations in a short time period within the Monte Carlo simulation experiments, which is the basis of the Monte Carlo simulation (Marković, Barjaktarović-Rakočević, & Čavoški, 2005; Barjaktarović-Rakočević, Marković, & Čavoški, 2006; Marković & Čavoški, 2005; Mun, 2006). The classic infrastructure would require an expensive and specialized hardware. If it is not available it will be time consuming to perform calculations. The new infrastructure model ensures the repetition of a great number (tens of thousands) of experiments within a very short period of time.

The chapter mentioned before (Poole, Cornelius, Trapp, & Langton, 2012) analyzes the application of GEANT4 C++ tool for simulation of penetration of particles through geometrical shapes by using the Monte Carlo simulation. Flexible definition of geometry and adjustment of physical processes offer the user a high level of control and the ability to simulate a wide spectrum of radio therapy techniques with the aim of rapid and quality determination of therapy with cancer patients.

In carrying out this study researchers used Amazon EC2 as the computing platform and Amazon S3 as storage. By using the Amazon public cloud the Monte Carlo simulation was significantly speeded up by increasing the number of instances of simulation experiment. The results are shown in Figure 7.

Figure 7 presents results in two aspects. First one is (a) total simulation time in function of instance time. Stars indicate the total instance uptime, squares indicate the time to simulation completion and the dashed line indicates the predicted simulation completion time. The marker size indicates 2 standard deviations about the mean, R2 = 0.97. The second aspect is billable instance time (b) as a function of instance count where stars indicate the total compute required, triangles indicate the billable instance time, and the dashed line indicates

Figure 7. (a) Experiment duration as function of instances count. (b) Billable instance time as function of instances count. (Adapted from [Buss & Stork, 1996])

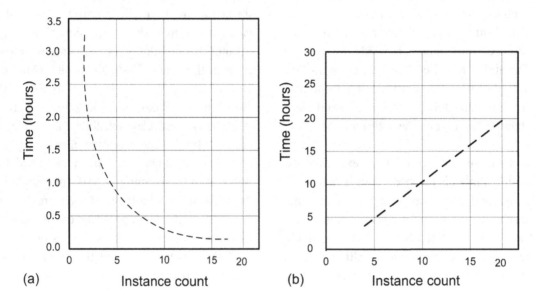

(a) Instance count   (b) Instance count

the predicted billable instance time. As Figure 7 shows, total time needed for simulation has decreased 1/n times, where n represents instances count, and costs are linearly increasing as number of instances grows. In cases where time is a critical factor, by increasing the number of instances it is possible to speed up the simulation experiment execution with linear cost increase.

This example shows that it is possible to speed up the simulation experiment execution and refine results by using public cloud in two ways, by horizontal (number of instances) and vertical (adding resources to each instance) scaling.

Simulation Software as Service in Cloud Environment

Resource demanding simulation software used to be available to researchers in big scientific centers and big companies which could afford expensive hardware for this purposes. Each researcher needed access to computer with software that is used for modeling and simulation execution and data analysis. Limited resources implied also limited

possibilities for performing experiments. Besides that, there were limitations in software infrastructure, especially in simulation experiments which included two or more linked simulations.

Traditional approach to computer simulation, together with hardware resources, usually requires intensive software development. As we have seen, Cloud computing offers virtually unlimited hardware infrastructure, so companies and researchers who are users of simulation platforms do not need to possess their own servers and other infrastructure. Today, leasing of simulation software as service (SaaS) offers notable advantages: scalability, configurability, significantly less time for simulation models and software development. The most common architecture used for development of Web oriented simulation software is service oriented architecture (SOA) (Tsai, Sun, & Balasooriya, 2010), as shown in Figure 8. This architecture is widely used for the development of software that uses Internet technologies. Anyway, any type of web oriented architecture can be used for the development of simulation software which can be used as service.

Figure 8. SOA architecture (Adapted from [Tsai, Sun, & Balasooriya, 2010])

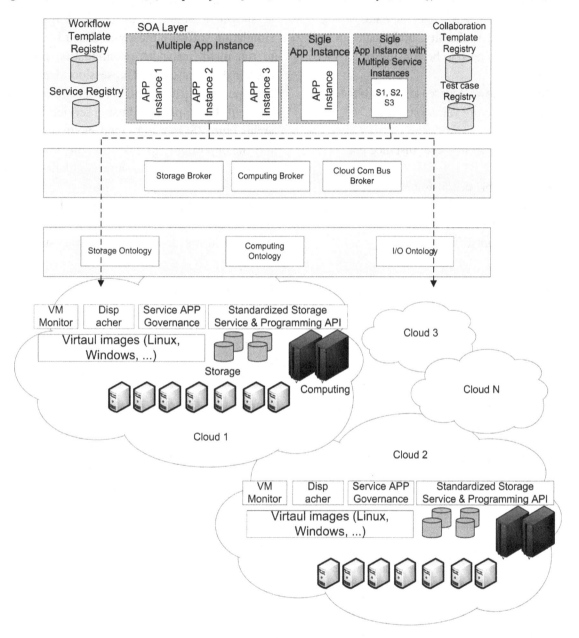

The benefits of executing simulation experiments in Cloud environment derive from the possibility of using many processors and simulation software in multi-tenancy (MTA) architecture (Tsai, Wu, Sarjoughian, & Qihong, 2011).

The architecture for providing software as service must have the following characteristics (Tsai, Wu, Sarjoughian, & Qihong, 2011):

- To support configurability at multi-layers, both simulation supporting framework and simulation models need to be included.
- To support MTA, the system should have the abilities to add/modify/delete the tenants, address the tenants' accessibility controls, distinguish tenants' simulation

interaction message during executions and isolate tenant's own specific data.

- To support scalability, both scale up and scale down need to be considered.

Figure 9 shows four cases of multi-tenant software architecture variations:

1. Ad-Hoc/Custom – One Instance per customer;
2. Configurable per customer;
3. Configurable & Multi-Tenant-Efficient;
4. Scalable, Configurable & Multi-Tenant-Efficient.

Simulation software exposed as service (SaaS), as shown in Figure 9, differs from traditional simulation software mostly in that it is possible to run many instances of simulation for each user or different users. The session identifier is an important attribute and it must be traceable at any step. The approach of using service oriented architecture (SOA) and cloud environment offers the opportunity to link different simulations or many instances of the same simulation in the workflow.

In traditional simulation approach, the user receives data at the end of the experiment execution. Now, users can monitor temporary states and

Figure 9. Multi-tenant architecture (Adapted from [Baker, 2009])

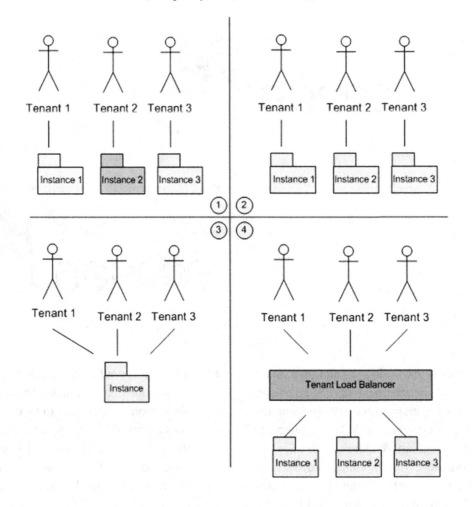

preview intermediate results during the experiment execution. This is enabled by event-driven communication, where the results are "pushed" or "published" to the user as soon as results become available. Users should be aware of the fact that intermediate results, presented at some moment, could change in the next moment during simulation execution, depending on the current state of simulated system instance. This architecture makes it possible to provide such intermediate results not only to end-users, but also to other simulation software (Guo, Bai, & Hu, 2011). In such a scenario, each instance depends on the output data from some other instance. Such data needs to be synchronized before next calculation.

Simulation software exposed as service can be conceived as a set of simulation services included in simulation experiment which can communicate with each other and exchange results. It can be conceived as a black box with common properties: inputs, outputs, starting state, data resource, execution control and model's configuration parameters. Just like a traditional simulation model, cloud based simulation has to go through all the steps of simulation process. The simulation process is related to the structure which defines simulation life cycle. The simulation process structure is not necessarily sequential, and it is possible to jump back to previous steps in the process, depending on the results calculated in different phases of the process (Radenković, Stanojević, & Marković, 2010). Number of phases and their execution order depends on the current simulation experiment. The basic steps of simulation process, according to (Law & Kelton, 1982) are:

1. **Defining Modeling Objectives:** Deciding the required outcome of modeling and which information the model should provide.
2. **System Identification:** Describing system components, their interaction, behavior, relations and formal description of the system.
3. **Data Collection and Analysis:** Collecting and measuring of data relevant to the system, data analysis using standard statistical procedures, such as distribution fitting.

4. **Simulation Model Development:** Creation of conceptual model that adequately describes the system and enables problem solving.
5. **Simulation Software Development:** Choosing programming language or package and building simulation program.
6. **Simulation Software Verification:** Testing of simulation program towards simulation model settings. If this step fails, step 5 has to be performed again.
7. **Validation of Simulation Model:** Testing if the simulation model adequately represents the real system (by comparing output from model and real system, analysis of results by an expert, using sensitivity analysis). If simulation model validation fails, step 4 has to be done again.
8. **Planning and Executing Simulation Experiments:** Planning of simulation experiments which are fulfilling the objectives of the study (plan of model parameters variation, experiment repetition because of impact analysis of random variables, etc.). Performing the simulation experiment according to accepted plan.
9. **Output Analysis:** Statistical analysis of simulation experiment results. During this phase it can be concluded that step 8 has to be supplemented by performing additional experiments.
10. **Conclusions and Recommendations:** Presentation of relevant results which can help in making decisions (choosing system configuration, system changes, etc.).

Simulation process flow diagram is shown in Figure 10.

The modeling phase usually starts from the mental model which is the base for building the logical model of the system. There are numerous tools (structural, graphical models) for the creation

Figure 10. Simulation process flow diagram

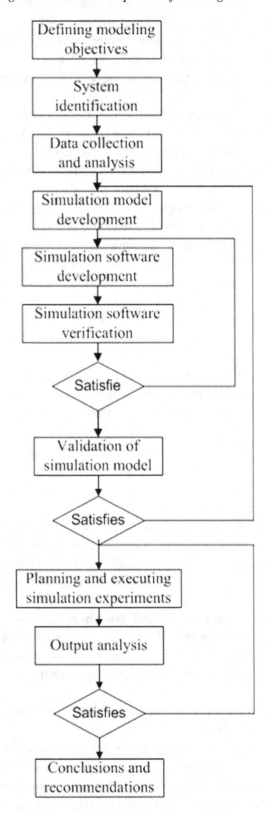

of the logical model of system, which usually shows the structure of the system. From the logical model, the researcher generates the mathematical model which represents all the components of the system using mathematical formalism. The final step in the modeling process is building the simulation model of the system, and there are specialized simulation tools and software for this purpose. The difference between the classical simulation process described before and cloud based simulation is that before running the simulation experiment, the simulation model has to be placed in the cloud repository. In the simulation experiment execution phase, in the same way as in classic simulation, it is necessary to define a scenario which sets how many times the experiment has to be repeated and variable values and model parameters which will be used during the experiment execution. Module for simulation execution takes model from repository and input data and then runs the experiment. Simulation results analysis can be done on-line, together with simulation execution, or off-line.

The system which exposes simulation software as service has to support all simulation process phases and provide three key services:

1. Modeling service (simulation model creation)
2. Simulation execution service
3. Simulation results analysis service

Services have to be designed in such a way that customers can lease them independently, so they can decide in which phase they want to use the service. These services are usually available as web services. An important characteristic of this kind of systems is that they are allowing the reuse of the existing simulation libraries and frameworks (Calheiros, Ranjan, De Rose, & Buyya, 2009).

One of the possible solutions for exposing simulation software as service is CSim platform (Liu, He, Qiu, Chen, & Huang, 2012), and its architecture is shown in Figure 11.

Figure 11.The architecture of the CSim (Adapted from [Liu, He, Qiu, Chen, & Huang, 2012])

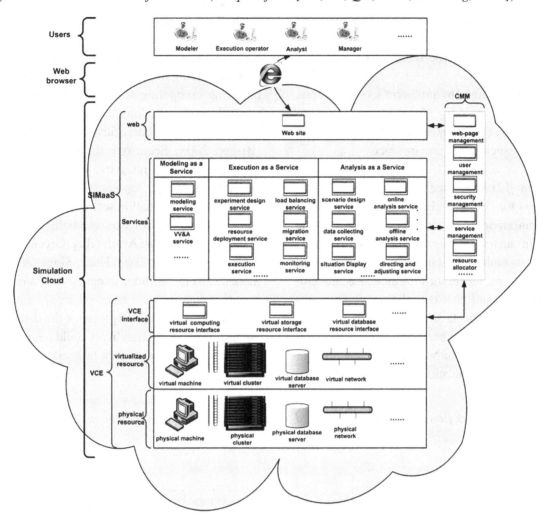

The author advocates that, CSim is a SaaS type cloud, which can also be called a SIMaaS (SIMulation as a service) in M&S field. SIMaaS Cloud provides the following services to end users: MaaS (Modeling as a Service), EaaS (Execution as a Service) and AaaS (Analysis as a Service). MaaS service also includes VV&A service (Verification, Validation and Accreditation).

The service for simulation experiment execution EaaS, besides its main functionality, can offer additional services: experiment design service, resource deployment service, simulation monitoring service, load balancing service (Liu, He, Qiu, Chen, & Huang, 2012).

The data analysis module AaaS provides possibilities for scenario creation and includes subsystems for data collection, data presentation, and on-line and off-line data analysis.

Efficient resources usage in SIMaaS cloud is achieved by using monitoring and scalability module. In cases of increased number of service requests and/or additional demand for computing resources, which are registered by the monitoring module, the information is sent to the scalability module which further reserves or releases resources.

All commercial and open source solutions for virtualization provide API, which is part of hypervisor, offering access to the virtual hardware infrastructure. Scalability module, by using API, can allocate/release resources even when the system is running, allowing on-line system optimization. The system scaling can be divided into two groups:

1. Scaling caused by number of service requests change
2. Scaling caused by resources utilization during execution of one instance

Figure 12 provides the algorithm which defines the steps for system scaling:

Cloud environment enables installing multiple nodes in cluster allowing dynamic system scaling. This way, multiple instances can be executed in the same time, where some of them execute temporary tasks and after completion are de-provisioned. Also, one task can be executed using multiple instances in parallel. Depending on the current needs, the hardware can be upgraded or changed during simulation experiment execution.

The Security of the Cloud Environment

Security is an important aspect of the computer system. Having in mind that cloud computing is based on computing resources utilization over network and/or the Internet, computer and network security, or cyber security, are critical issues (Bishop, 2003). Security is the key to protecting the confidentiality, integrity, and availability of computer systems, resources, and data. Core principles of information security are: Authentication, Access Control, Confidentiality, Integrity, Non-Repudiation and Availability (Greene, 2006; Stallings & Brown, 2008; Hada, Singh, & Manmohan, 2011). Without integrity we cannot be sure that data we have received are the same as the data that were initially sent, or the data were altered. Without availability it could happen that computing resources cannot be used.

Figure 12.The work flow of scalability (Adapted from [Liu, He, Qiu, Chen, & Huang, 2012])

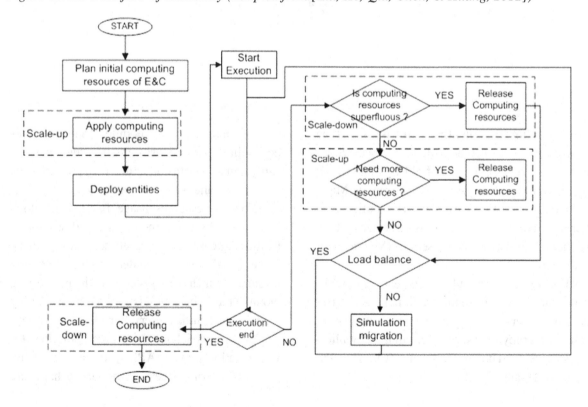

In cases when simulation is used in the process of new technologies research, modeling of new products or improving existing ones, there is a big probability that competitors or other parties would try to gain access to computer systems and data in order to steal important information or to perform sabotage. As well, malicious hackers could try to gain access to the system. It is important to perform all the necessary measures for preventing such scenarios. One of the essential measures is pre-scribing and implementing security procedures, regular control checks of procedure compliance and improvements, security assessments, security audits and penetration tests (Gollmann, 2010). It is common practice to engage external consulting companies which have computer security special-ists and experts for such purposes.

As the system intended to be used over the Internet is more accessible to third parties which otherwise would not have access to isolated system, locked in private secured data center, without link to global or local network, it is necessary to be aware of all kind of risks which appear in this case.

On the other hand, cloud service providers are serving lot of customers. This imposes the question as to whether they have taken all the necessary measures of protection and prevented possible cases where one customer could access data belonging to another customer or by exhaustive using of resources degrades resource performance to another customer.

System security in cloud environment is limited by the security provided by the cloud provider (Rittinghouse & Ransome, 2009). Also control panels offered by cloud providers for managing cloud resources (allocating additional resources, powering system on/off, dealocation and closing, setting public and private network parameters, payment of consumed resources) are, in most of the cases, protected only by username and pass-word (Carlin & Curran, 2011). Today, this type of protection cannot be considered sufficient and efficient, but rather a huge problem and threat (Mat, 2012). Cloud providers, in most of the cases, rely on encryption as way of protection and they are ensuring their customers that they are safe.

Many authors have offered different security models for the cloud architecture. Some of them (Dastjerdi, Bakar, & Tabatabaei, 2009; Hada, Singh, & Manmohan, 2011; Domenico, 2011), recommend using mobile agents for collecting information from virtual machines, and that information can be used by the cloud provider or cloud consumer for monitoring privacy and security of their data and virtual machines. These agents monitor the integrity and authenticity of virtual machines. Security agents can dynamically move through the network, copy themselves ac-cording to requests and perform virtual machines monitoring tasks.

Along with digital threats, physical threats should be also considered. It is important where the customer's data are located, in which part of the world, which country, what security measures are applied for protecting data center (physically-technical, biometrical, paired keys, digital cer-tificates…) and if there exists an independent and certified revision and consultancy company which is regularly reviewing security and if cloud provider has been issued and security certificate (for instance, Sarbanes-Oxley Act, 2002), the Gramm-Leach-Biley Act, 2000, and the Health Insurance Portability and Accountability Act, 1996 and others). Different countries have different law regulations in data privacy field, which applies both to cloud provider and cloud consumer, and regulations which are limiting cloud consumers on data that are allowed to be kept outside of home country.

THE ANALYSIS OF SOFTWARE SIMULATION SOLUTIONS IN CLOUD ENVIRONMENT

In this section we will present two representative simulation software solutions, realized on virtual-ized platforms in cloud environment.

Discrete Event System Simulation

Chungmanet et al. presented a possible solution for discrete events system simulation according to DEVS (Discrete Event System Specification) formalism (Zeigler, Kim, & Praehofer, 2000). The DEVS model can be an atomic model or a coupled model which is made up of component models and the coupling relations which establish the desired communication links.

The system is user friendly, and can be used for models development both by modeling professionals, so they can improve and speed up the development process, and also by people with basic knowledge in the modeling field (Figure 13). This environment helps faster development of new models and lowers time and costs of improvement of existing models through reusability and interoperability of software components. The system is based on SOA architecture. The DEVS simulation service interface can be classified into three categories: simulation protocol, messaging protocol and reporting service.

The system exposes three services: DEVS simulator for running simulation experiment, DEVS service for modeling, DEVS service for integration and end-user serving. DEVS simulation services consist of: protocol for simulation, message information and reporting. This architecture is fully compatible with the architecture model described in the previous chapter.

The aim of DEVS model provider service is registering of simulation model in simulation service. The service provider creates, modifies and tests DEVS models using DEVS model provider service, compiling and simulation tools. After

Figure 13. Overall architecture for model and simulation based data engineering methodology (Adapted from [Seo, Han, Lee, & Jung, 2010])

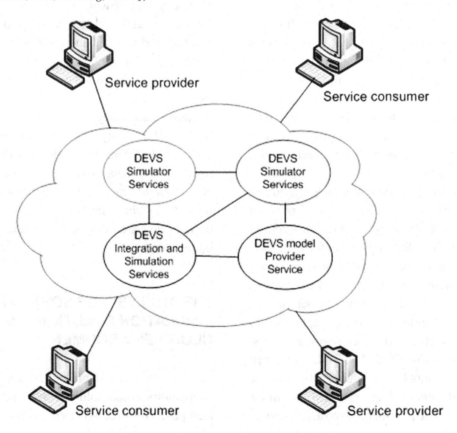

DEVS model testing is finished, service provider uploads it in the models repository. Messaging is implemented using standard XML messages exchange, as presented in Figure 14.

DEVS simulator service consists of modeling and simulation service (DEVS M&S), DEVS interface and web service. DEVS M&S is in charge of DEVS messages, and DEVS interface converts DEVS messages to XML format and delivers XML messages to web service which then generates SOAP messages. Together with this serialization process, the system implements deserialization, too. Users of this platform are able to integrate their models, or to use the existing ones relying on the services implemented in the cloud without expert knowledge of languages or platform used for DEVS services implementation.

mJADES

The main idea behind mJADES system is that it is possible to speed up the process of parallel executing of multiple simulation instances by using distributed hardware. mJADES relies on two emerging technologies: mOSAIC cloud middleware and JADE simulation library.

mJADES simulation manager does all the operations related to simulation experiment execution, manages the experiment and runs it concurrently in multiple instances. This process-oriented discrete events simulation engine is based on JADES platform. The data collected during experiment are transferred to the analysis module, and its task is to collect, calculate and generate reports for end-users.

In order to be able to get all the benefits from the cloud environment, and to be able to run the system dynamically on different cloud platforms delivered by different providers, mJADES relies on mOSAIC platform. mOSAIC is cloud middleware, which enables development in cloud environment. In fact, mJADES is developed as a module in mOSAIC platform, and easily communicates with other objects, and allows the creation of REST APIs and web interfaces, and also enables SLA management and monitoring.

mOSAIC is usually used in three scenarios, and mJDAES fits in the first two:

- When a developer wishes to develop an application not tied to a particular cloud provider;
- When an infrastructure provider aims at offering "enhanced" cloud services in the form of SaaS;
- When a final user (e.g., a scientist) wishes to execute his own application in the cloud because he needs processing power.

Sequential Java simulation engine JADES is a system for discrete systems simulations development and evaluation. It consists of a set of

Figure 14. Procedure of conversion of DEVS messages to XML messages (Adapted from [Seo, Han, Lee, & Jung, 2010])

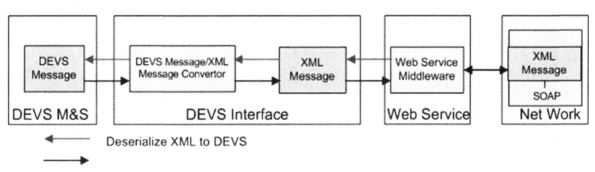

Java libraries, enabling the developer to describe whole simulation process. It contains an extensive set of building blocks which are used for models composition and it enables the user to create big, complex models and evaluate them quickly.

mJADES is composed of three cloudlets (Rak, Cuomo, & Villano, 2012):

1. mJADES Manager
2. mJADES Simulation Core
3. mJADES Simulation Analyzer

Architecture of mJADES is presented in Figure 15.

mJADES Manager coordinates the distributed execution of simulation. Request for simulation execution is received as a message, either from http interface or from other components. From these requests, component creates jobs, which receive unique global ID, so results, metadata and job status can be assigned to the job. All these conform to SaaS simulation software requirements described before.

mJADES Simulation Core realized using JADES (Java Discrete Event Simulator) environment. It executes tasks which are part of the simulation experiment and generates results of simulation experiment putting them in a queue for further processing. This module is realized on mOSAIC platform and thanks to this, launching of multiple simulation tasks is fully transparent to the end-user. New instances of cloudlets are automatically provisioned, according to a number of simulation tasks that must be executed, and all of this tasks are expected to be executed in parallel, so the best performance is achieved. According to the mOSAIC approach, where each component should be independent, this module has two links to the rest of the system, simulation requests queue and simulation results queue.

The third component of the system is *JADES Simulation Analyzer cloudlet*, which analyses simulation logs and simulation results. This module also receives analysis requests from mJADES Manager containing request ID. Then, it reads simulation task results of the job from the

Figure 15. mJADES architecture (Adapted from [Rak, Cuomo, & Villano, 2012])

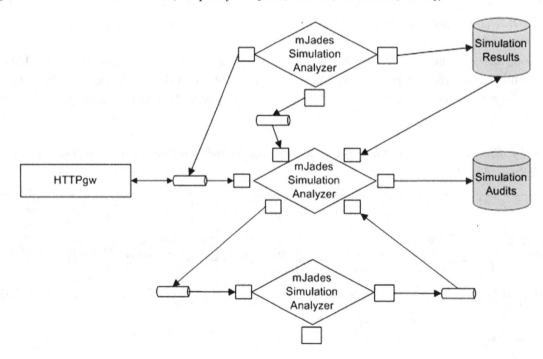

Simulation Results Key-Store and executes data analysis (e.g., statistical measurements, sensitivity analysis, and summary statistics), and stores the aggregated results back in the repository.

Having in mind all the previous features of mJADES system, we can conclude that it is a good example of deploying concurrent simulations in the cloud. The system can be used for simulation of complex systems, which require preferment and robust hardware and software infrastructure, especially in cases which require multiple simulation experiments, variation of some parameters or methods used for calculation.

Table 1. Advantages of cloud based simulation

Cloud Simulation	Traditional Simulation
Lower IT infrastructure costs.	Every researcher needs a high-powered and high-priced computer to run simulation experiment.
Reduced software costs	Every computer need licenced software
The computing resources are pooled to serve multiple consumers using a multi-tenant model, with different physical and virtual resources dynamically assigned and reassigned according to consumer demand. Cloud systems automatically control and optimize resource	There is no possibility to change hardware platform during the simulation experiments.
The system which exposes simulation software as service has to support all simulation process phases and provide three key services: • Modeling service • Simulation execution service • Simulation results analysis service	Different software for • Modeling, • Simulation execution service, • Simulation results analysis service
Simulation software exposed as service (SaaS), can run many instances of simulation for each user or different users, in parallel	Simulation software is expensive to: • purchase • difficult to install and maintain • complicated to run Every user can perform one instance of simulation experiment
It is possible to speed up the process of parallel executing of multiple simulation instances by using distributed hardware.	One instance for every simulation experiment
Users can monitor temporary states and preview intermediate results during the experiment execution.	In traditional simulation approach, the user receives data at the end of the experiment execution.
Cloud environment helps faster development of new models and lowers time and costs of improvement of existing models through reusability and interoperability of software components.	Modeling is a time consuming

Table 2. Disadvantages of cloud based simulation

Cloud Simulation	Traditional Simulation
As the system intended to be used over the Internet is more accessible to third parties. Implementing security procedures, regular control checks of procedure compliance and improvements, security assessments, security audits and penetration tests.	Details stored in isolated system, locked in private secured data center, without link to global or local network.
Adoption of new approach is slower within existing users of traditional software. New way of thinking has to be accepted.	Users are familiar with traditional simulation software
Internet access is necessary in order to use systems in cloud	Traditional software can be used offline

CONCLUSION

We have tried to present the application of cloud computing platforms in simulation modeling and simulation experiment execution. Earlier most of the simulation software's paradigm was that each software user has his software copy installed on his computer. There was a strong relation between user, software and computing resources and this approach lacked scalability. By introducing virtualization and cloud environment, the way software is being developed and used has changed significantly. There is no more need for having own computing infrastructure. Distributed computing is now performed using multiple virtual machines rented from one or more cloud providers.

Application of cloud computing, especially in research and education institutions and projects, started with infrastructure renting for storing data, hosting web, mail and database servers and other infrastructural resources. Today, more and more cloud services are used as software as a service, because it requires less effort for development, administration and is more cost efficient.

As many sources suggest (Armbrust et al., 2009; Marcos Dias, Di Costanzo, & Buyya, 2009; Etro, 2009; Derrick, Javadi, Malecot, Cappello, & Anderson, 2009; Grossman, 2009; Rolf & Yamartino, 2010; Andreas et al., 2010), the use of cloud computing brings a significant reduction of IT cost. This is more obvious in cases where the system is used from time to time, executing tasks which require intensive computing resources usage, and then powered off. In the same manner, universities and research centers can benefit from cloud computing use for simulation tasks and increase efficiency, reducing costs at the same time.

Cloud technologies have a great impact on simulation and modeling software architecture and encouraging cloud providers to offer simulation services as standards. This ways robust and advanced modeling and simulation software is made available to the wider public, researchers, scientists, commercial companies and students. These technologies have a bright future and we expect lot of effort invested in further development.

Tables 1 and 2 summarize the advantages and disadvantages of cloud based simulation.

REFERENCES

110. *Stat. 1936 - Health Insurance Portability and Accountability Act of 1996*. (1996). Retrieved October 10, 2013, from http://www.gpo.gov/fdsys/pkg/STATUTE-110/pdf/STATUTE-110-Pg1936.pdf

Andreas, B., Gelenbe, E., Di Girolamo, M., Giuliani, G., De Meer, H., Dang, M. Q., & Pentikousis, K. (2010). Energy-efficient cloud computing. *The Computer Journal, 53*(7), 1045–1051. doi:10.1093/comjnl/bxp080

Armbrust, M., Fox, A., Griffith, R., Joseph, A., Katz, R., & Konwinski, A. … Zaharia, M. (2009). *Above the clouds: A Berkeley view of cloud computing* (Technical Report No. UCB/EECS-2009-28). Berkeley, CA: University of California at Berkley.

Baker, M. (2009). *Cloud computing*. Retrieved October 10, 2013, from http://www.cse.unr.edu/~mgunes/cpe401/lect15_cloud.ppt

Barjaktarović-Rakočević, S., Marković, A., & Čavoški, S. (2006). Common stocks valuation using simulation models - Case of Serbian capital market. In Proceedings of International Scientific Days 2006, Competitivness in the EU - Challenge for the V4 Countries (pp. 1110-1116). Nitra: Faculty of Economic and Management SAU in Nitra.

Bishop, M. (2003). What is computer security? *IEEE Security & Privacy, 1*(1), 67–69. doi:10.1109/MSECP.2003.1176998

Buss, A. H., & Stork, K. A. (1996). Discrete-event simulation on the world wide web using Java. In *Proceedings of the 28th Conference on Winter Simulation* (pp. 780-785). Washington, DC: IEEE Computer Society.

Byrne, J., Heavey, C., & Byrne, P. J. (2010). A review of web-based simulation and supporting tools. *Simulation Modelling Practice and Theory*, *18*(3), 253–404. doi:10.1016/j.simpat.2009.09.013

Calheiros, R. N., Ranjan, R., De Rose, C. A. F., & Buyya, R. (2009). *CloudSim: A novel framework for modeling and simulation of cloud computing* (CoRR, abs/0903.2525). Retrieved October 10, 2013, from http://arxiv.org/abs/0903.2525

Calsoft. (2013). *Infrastructure-as-a-service*. Retrieved October 10, 2013, from http://www.calsoftinc.com/IaaS-new.aspx

Carlin, S., & Curran, K. (2011). Cloud computing security. *International Journal of Ambient Computing and Intelligence*, *3*(1), 14–19. doi:10.4018/jaci.2011010102

Dastjerdi, A. V., Bakar, K. A., & Tabatabaei, S. G. H. (2009). Distributed intrusion detection in clouds using mobile agents. In *Proceedings of Third International Conference on Advanced Engineering Computing and Applications in Sciences* (pp. 175-180). IEEE, Inc.

Derrick, K., Javadi, B., Malecot, P., Cappello, F., & Anderson, D. P. (2009). Cost-benefit analysis of cloud computing versus desktop grids. In *Proceedings of IPDPS 2009. IEEE International Symposium on Parallel & Distributed Processing* (pp. 1-12). IEEE.

Dias, M. De A., Di Costanzo, A., & Buyya, R. (2009). Evaluating the cost-benefit of using cloud computing to extend the capacity of clusters. In *Proceedings of the 18th ACM International Symposium on High Performance Distributed Computing* (pp. 141-150). New York: ACM.

Domenico, T. (2011). Cloud computing and software agents: Towards cloud intelligent services. In G. Fortino, A. Garro, L. Palopoli, W. Russo, & G. Spezzano (Eds.), WOA (pp. 2-6). CEUR-WS.org.

Etro, F. (2009). The economic impact of cloud computing on business creation, employment and output in Europe. *Review of Business and Economics*, *54*(2), 179–208.

Fishwick, P. A. (1996). Web-based simulation: Some personal observations. In *Proceedings of the 28th Conference on Winter Simulation* (pp. 772-779). Washington, DC: IEEE Computer Society.

Gartner. (2013). *Gartner IT glossary - Cloud computing*. Retrieved October 10, 2013, from http://www.gartner.com/it-glossary/cloud-computing/

Gollmann, D. (2010). *Computer security*. London: John Willey & Sons, Ltd.

Gramm-Leach-Bliley Act. (2000). *U.S. government printing office*. Retrieved October 10, 2013, from http://www.gpo.gov/fdsys/pkg/PLAW-106publ102/pdf/PLAW-106publ102.pdf

Greene, S. S. (Ed.). (2006). *Security policies and procedures*. Upper Saddle River, NJ: Prentice Hall.

Grossman, R. L. (2009). The case for cloud computing. *IT Professional*, *11*(2), 23–27. doi:10.1109/MITP.2009.40

Guo, S., Bai, F., & Hu, X. (2011). Simulation software as a service and service-oriented simulation experiment. In *Proceedings of 2011 IEEE International Conference on Information Reuse and Integration (IRI)* (pp. 113-116). IEEE Systems, Man, and Cybernetics Society (SMC).

Hada, P. S., Singh, R., & Manmohan, M. (2011). Security agents: A mobile agent based trust model for cloud computing. *International Journal of Computers and Applications*, *36*(12), 12–15.

Jeffery, K., & Neidecker-Lutz, B. (2010). *The future of cloud computing*. Retrieved October 10, 2013, from http://cordis.europa.eu/fp7/ict/ssai/docs/cloud-report-final.pdf

Kalim, A. (2013). Clouds on the academic horizon. *International Journal of Computer Science and Management Research, 2*(4), 2239–2243.

Law, A. M., & Kelton, W. D. (Eds.). (1982). *Simulation modeling and analysis*. New York: McGraw-Hill Book Co.

Liu, X., He, Q., Qiu, X., Chen, B., & Huang, K. (2012). Cloud-based computer simulation: Towards planting existing simulation software into the cloud. *Simulation Modelling Practice and Theory, 26*, 135–150. doi:10.1016/j.simpat.2012.05.001

Liu, X., He, Q., Qiu, X., Chen, B., & Huang, K. (2012). Cloud-based simulation: The state-of-the-art computer simulation paradigm. In *Proceedings of ACM/IEEE/SCS 26th Workshop on Principles of Advanced and Distributed Simulation (PADS)* (pp. 71-74). Washington, DC: IEEE Computer Society.

Marković, A., Barjaktarović-Rakočević, S., & Čavoški, S. (2005). Spreadsheet models in stock valuation. *Management – Časopis za Teoriju i Praksu Menadžmenta, 10*(38), 26-33.

Marković, A., & Čavoški, S. (2005). Primena ADD-in programa u finansijskoj spreadsheet simulaciji. *Info M, 4*(13), 32–37.

Mat, H. (2012). *Kill the password: Why a string of characters can't protect us anymore*. Conde Nast Digital, 13 Nov.2012 Web. 06 July 2013.

Mell, P., & Grance, T. (2009). *Effectively and securely using the cloud computing paradigm*. Retrieved October 10, 2013, from http://gat1.isoc.org.il/conf2010/handouts/Yesha_Sivan.pdf

Mun, J. (Ed.). (2006). *Modeling risk applying Monte Carlo simulation, real options analysis, forecasting and optimization techniques*. Hoboken, NJ: John Wiley & Sons, Inc.

Nair, R. S., Miller, J. A., & Zhang, Z. (1996). Java-based query driven simulation environment. In *Proceedings of the 28th Conference on Winter Simulation* (pp. 786-793). Washington, DC: IEEE Computer Society.

Peter, M., & Grance, T. (2011). *The NIST definition of cloud computing (NIST special publication 800-145: 7)*. Washington, DC: NIST.

Poole, C. M., Cornelius, I., Trapp, J. V., & Langton, C. M. (2012). Radiotherapy Monte Carlo simulation using cloud computing technology. *Australasian Physical & Engineering Sciences in Medicine, 35*(4), 497–502. doi:10.1007/s13246-012-0167-8 PMID:23188699

Radenković, B., Stanojević, M., & Marković, A. (Eds.). (2010). *Računarska simulacija*. Faculty of Organizational Sciences and FON and Faculty of Transport and Traffic Engineering.

Rak, M., Cuomo, A., & Villano, U. (2012). mJADES: Concurrent simulation in the cloud, complex. In *Proceedings of 2012 Sixth International Conference on Intelligent and Software Intensive Systems (CISIS)* (pp. 853-860). IEEE, Inc.

Rittinghouse, J., & Ransome, J. F. (Eds.). (2009). *Cloud computing: Implementation, management and security*. San Francisco: Taylor and Francis Group, LLC.

Rolf, H., & Yamartino, M. (2010). *The economics of the cloud* (Microsoft whitepaper). Retrieved October 10, 2013, from http://www.microsoft.com/en-us/news/presskits/cloud/docs/the-economics-of-the-cloud.pdf

Sarbanes-Oxley Act. (2002). Retrieved October 10, 2013, from http://www.sec.gov/about/laws/soa2002.pdf

Seo, C., Han, Y., Lee, H., & Jung, J. J. (2010). Implementation of cloud computing environment for discrete event system simulation using service oriented architecture. In *Proceedings of 2010 IEEE/IFIP 8th International Conference on Embedded and Ubiquitous Computing (EUC)* (pp. 359-362). IEEE, Inc.

Slook, B. (2009). *Cloud architecture and the need for an architectural perspective bobs technology briefs*. Retrieved October 10, 2013, from http://bslook.wordpress.com/2009/04/27/cloud-architecture-and-the-need-for-an-architecture-perspective/

Stallings, W., & Brown, L. V. (Eds.). (2008). *Computer security*. Upper Saddle River, NJ: Prentice-Hall.

Steven, H. R., Linton, M., & Spence, M. C. (2010). *Cloud computing architecture, IT security, & operational perspectives*. National Aeronautics and Space Administration. Retrieved October 10, 2013, from http://www.nasa.gov/ppt/482833main_2010_Tuesday_5_Hunt_Linton_ChweSpence.ppt

Tor-Morten, G. (2012). Cloud computing and context-awareness: A study of the adapted user experience. *Lecture Notes in Computer Science*, *6762*, 427–435.

Tsai, W.-T., Sun, X., & Balasooriya, J. (2010). Service-oriented cloud computing architecture. In *Proceedings of 2010 Seventh International Conference on Information Technology: New Generations (ITNG)* (pp. 684-689). The Institute of Electrical and Electronics Engineers, Inc.

Tsai, W.-T., Wu, L., Sarjoughian, H., & Qihong, S. (2011). SimSaaS: Simulation software-as-a-service. In *Proceedings of the 44th Annual Simulation Symposium* (pp. 77-86). San Diego, CA: Society for Computer Simulation International.

Zeigler, B. P., Kim, T. G., & Praehofer, H. (Eds.). (2000). *Theory of modeling and simulation* (2nd ed.). New York: Academic Press.

ADDITIONAL READING

Andrzejak, A., Kondo, D., & Anderson, D. P. (2010). Exploiting Non-Dedicated Resources for Cloud Computing. In *Network Operations and Management Symposium (NOMS), 2010 IEEE* (pp. 341-348). IEEE.

Buyya, R., Ranjan, R., & Calheiros, R. N. (2009). Modeling and Simulation of Scalable Cloud Computing Environments and the CloudSim Toolkit: Challenges and Opportunities. In *Proceedings of the 7th High Performance Computing and Simulation (HPCS 2009) Conference (pp.* 1-11). IEEE.

Byrne, J., Heavey, C., & Byrne, P. J. (2006). Simct: An application of web based simulation. *In the proceedings of the 2006 Operational Research Society (UK) 3rd Simulation Workshop (SW06)*, Retrieved October 10, 2013, from http://www.academia.edu/230163/SIMCT_AN_APPLICATION_OF_WEB_BASED_SIMULATION

Cayirci, E., & Rong, C. (2011). Intercloud for Simulation Federations. In *2011 International Conference on High Performance Computing and Simulation (HPCS)* (pp. 397-404). IEEE.

Chu, X., Nadiminti, K., Jin, C., Venugopal, S., & Buyya, R. (2007). Aneka: Next-Generation Enterprise Grid Platform for e-Science and e-Business Applications. In *Third IEEE International Conference on e-Science and Grid Computing (pp.* 151-159). IEEE.

D'Angelo, G. (2011). Parallel and Distributed Simulation from Many Cores to the Public Cloud. In *2011 International Conference on High Performance Computing and Simulation (HPCS)* (pp. 14-23). IEEE.

Dikaiakos, M. D., Katsaros, D., Mehra, P., & Pallis, G. (2009). Cloud Computing: Distributed Internet Computing for IT and Scientific Research. *Internet Computing, IEEE, 13*(5), 10–13. doi:10.1109/MIC.2009.103

Fox, A. (2011). Cloud Computing-What's in It for Me as a Scientist? *Science, 331*, 406–407. doi:10.1126/science.1198981 PMID:21273473

Garg, S. K., & Buyya, R. (2011). NetworkCloudSim: Modelling Parallel Applications in Cloud Simulations. In *2011 Fourth IEEE International Conference on Utility and Cloud Computing (UCC)* (pp. 105-113). IEEE.

Hoffa, C., Mehta, G., Freeman, T., & Deelman, E. (2008). On the Use of Cloud Computing for Scientific Workflows. In *IEEE Fourth International Conference on eScience, 2008 (pp.* 640-645).

Kajita, S. (2010). Academic Refactoring through realizing Academic Cloud. In TENCON 2010 - 2010 IEEE Region 10 Conference (pp. 1082-1087). IEEE.

Lindskog, E., Berglund, J., & Vallhagen, J. (2012). Combining point cloud technologies with discrete event simulation. In *Proceeding WSC '12 Proceedings of the Winter Simulation Conference Article No. 281 (pp.* 1-10). IEEE.

Malik, A. W., Park, A. J., & Fujimoto, R. M. (2010). An Optimistic Parallel Simulation Protocol for Cloud Computing Environments. *SCS M&S Magazine, 4*, 1-9.

Pratx, G., & Xing, L. (2011). Monte Carlo simulation of photon migration in a cloud computing environment with MapReduce. *Journal of Biomedical Optics, 16*(12), 125003. doi:10.1117/1.3656964 PMID:22191916

Rak, M., Cuomo, A., & Villano, U. (2012). Cloud-Based Concurrent Simulation at Work: Fast Performance Prediction of Parallel Programs, Enabling Technologies: Infrastructure for Collaborative Enterprises (WETICE). In *2012 IEEE 21st International Workshop (pp.* 137-142). IEEE.

Sethia, P., & Karlapalem, K. (2011). A multi-agent simulation framework on small Hadoop cluster. *Engineering Applications of Artificial Intelligence, 24*, 1120–1127. doi:10.1016/j.engappai.2011.06.009

Tsai, W. T., Fan, C., & Chen, Y. (2006). DDSOS: A Dynamic Distributed Service-Oriented Simulation Framework1. In *The 39th Annual Simulation Symposium (ANSS), Huntsville (pp.* 160-167). IEEE.

Vanmechelen, K., De Munck, S., & Broeckhove, J. (2012). Conservative Distributed Discrete Event Simulation on Amazon EC2. In *Proceedings of the 2012 12th IEEE/ACM International Symposium on Cluster, Cloud and Grid Computing (pp.* 853-860). IEEE.

Vouk, M. A. (2008). Cloud Computing - Issues, Research and Implementations. *Journal of Computing and Information Technology, 4*, 235–246.

Wang, H., Ma, Y., Pratx, G., & Xing, L. (2011). Toward real-time Monte Carlo simulation using a commercial cloud computing infrastructure, Retrieved October 10, 2013, from http://www.ncbi.nlm.nih.gov/pubmed/21841211

Xu, L.-j., & Wu, K.-j. (2012). On Cloud Computing Technology in the Construction of Digital Campus. In *International Conference on Innovation and Information Management (ICIIM 2012), Vol. 36 (pp.* 288-292). Singapore: IACSIT Press.

Yamazakia, T., Hirata, Y., Ikeno, H., Inagaki, K., Okumura, Y., & Ishihara, A. et al. (2011). Reprint of: Simulation Platform: A cloud-based online simulation environment. *Neural Networks, 24*, 927–932. doi:10.1016/j.neunet.2011.08.007 PMID:21944492

Zhang, Y., Wang, Z., Gao, B., Guo, C., Sun, W., & Li, X. (2010). An Effective Heuristic for On-line Tenant Placement Problem in SaaS. In *2010 IEEE International Conference on Web Services (pp.* 425-432).

Zhao, W., Peng, Y., Xie, F., & Dai, Z. (2012). Modeling and simulation of cloud computing: A review. In 2012 IEEE Asia Pacific Cloud Computing Congress (APCloudCC) (pp. 20-24). IEEE.

KEY TERMS AND DEFINITIONS

Cloud-Based Simulation: Is an approach that provides a new way to utilize computing resources in the simulation, which means infrastructure, platform, and software for researchers and scientists that they use as a service.

Discrete Event System Specification: A modular and hierarchical formalism for modeling and analyzing general systems that can be: discrete event systems, described by state transition tables, continuous state systems, described by differential equations, and hybrid continuous state and discrete event systems.

Multi-Tenant Architecture: Multi-tenancy refers to a principle in software architecture where a single instance of software runs on a server, serving multiple users (tenants).

Scientific Research: Entails the use of scientific methods and theories and their application to individual phenomenon.

Service-Oriented Simulation Experiment: Uses cloud infrastructure and simulation software as service. The cloud system can automatically control and optimize needed resources depending on demand of experiment.

Simulation Models: A special type of model implemented in one of the simulation languages suitable for performing experiments on their computers.

Simulation Software as a Service: Is a new way of using existing simulation tools in cloud environment. It involves a new emerging paradigm where simulation software and its associated data are hosted centrally in the cloud and researchers can use simulation software as "on-demand software."

Web-Based Simulation: Entails the integration of the Web technologies within the field of simulation in order to use simulation tools and perform simulation experiments on the Web.

Chapter 13
Grids, Clouds, and Massive Simulations

Levente Hajdu
Brookhaven National Laboratory, USA

Jérôme Lauret
Brookhaven National Laboratory, USA

Radomir A. Mihajlović
New York Institute of Technology, USA

ABSTRACT

In this chapter, the authors discuss issues surrounding High Performance Computing (HPC)-driven science on the example of Peta science Monte Carlo experiments conducted at the Brookhaven National Laboratory (BNL), one of the US Department of Energy (DOE) High Energy and Nuclear Physics (HENP) research sites. BNL, hosting the only remaining US-based HENP experiments and apparatus, seem appropriate to study the nature of the High-Throughput Computing (HTC) hungry experiments and short historical development of the HPC technology used in such experiments. The development of parallel processors, multiprocessor systems, custom clusters, supercomputers, networked super systems, and hierarchical parallelisms are presented in an evolutionary manner. Coarse grained, rigid Grid system parallelism is contrasted by cloud computing, which is classified within this chapter as flexible and fine grained soft system parallelism. In the process of evaluating various high performance computing options, a clear distinction between high availability-bound enterprise and high scalability-bound scientific computing is made. This distinction is used to further differentiate cloud from the pre-cloud computing technologies and fit cloud computing better into the scientific HPC.

INTRODUCTION

Modern science is hard to imagine without massive computing support. Almost all recent significant discoveries were in a way a consequence of great computation effort. Times of external wise Aristotelian observation and insightful scientific postulates, based on minimal measurements, are mostly a thing of the past. Scientific work and discoveries of Archimedes, Isaac Newton or Galileo, based on a few manual computations we may consider as legacy science.

DOI: 10.4018/978-1-4666-5784-7.ch013

Throughout the later history of science, computing and computing machines have gradually crept into the scientific process. For instance, early sixteenth century astronomer Nicolaus Copernicus, in search of heavenly body trajectories, or nineteenth century geneticist Gregor Mendel, who was crossbreeding pea plants and describing their inherited traits, used pen and paper and abacus' to perform numerical processing of their measurement data. The mechanical calculators of the day, more sophisticated than the abacus, have started to emerge as scientific tools about the time of European renaissance. The seventeenth century has brought mechanical computing devices such as: multiplying bones, John Napier's bones, the slide rule, Pascaline, and Leibniz stepped-drum (Redin, 2012). Charles Xavier Thomas's arithmometer J. H. Muller's difference engine, Charles Babbage's analytical engine, and Thomas Fowler's ternary calculator of 1875, have followed, with much higher calculating power and even rudimentary programmability. One hundred years later, James D. Watson and Francis Crick have discovered the structure of DNA, and in 1990 the Human Genome Project has started identifying and mapping the three billion chemical base pairs that make up human DNA. DNA and genomic research tasks would not have been conceivable without modern electronic computing technology.

Geneticists were fortunate in as much as the computing technology required for the field has become available before the need for it emerged, or maybe, the research necessity has caused the introduction of adequate electronic computing. One may state that geneticists with their marvelous discoveries are standing on the shoulders, not of great biologist of the past, but on the shoulder of Babbage, Turing, von Neumann, and all others that have made modern electronic computing possible. This statement applies to almost all modern scientific disciplines, as a sort of meta science, computing science serves as a driving force propelling modern science in general. Among all scientific fields, the most prominent one, the true field from which necessity has promoted the greatest computing discoveries, is physics, or more precisely, high energy and nuclear physics.

Working on the famous Manhattan Project (Manhattan Project Hall of Fame Directory, 2005), John von Neumann (in whose honor the Von Neumann computer architecture is named), Stanislaw Ulam, and others, faced the problem of how far a neutron would travel through a material before colliding with an atomic nucleus. The geometry was known along with all of the base data for the problem, however no deterministic mathematical solution could be found. Consequently, a quite unusual statistical technique was envisioned by Stan Ulam (Metropolis & Ulam, 1949). Since it required huge computational support, available only on electronic computers of that time, the implementation of the technique was delegated to Von Neumann. Due to the intense computations needed, one of the rare experts on electronic computing in the early 1940's, the key innovator in the field, John Von Neumann was invited to handle the problem. In March, 1945, at the Moore School of Electrical Engineering at the University of Pennsylvania, John von Neumann, nick named Johnny, also known as the first computer hacker ever (Myhrvold, 1999), professor of Mathematics at the Institute for Advanced Study and a consultant to Los Alamos Nuclear Center, with several associates, has initiated on the ENIAC machine, the first computer simulation project ever. The code name for the project was "Monte Carlo" (Metropolis, 1987). The method used in the project, also named "Monte Carlo" is still used today in a wide range of fields, from nuclear research, particle physics, modeling the flows of fluids, complex systems engineering to even finance and financial engineering.

This chapter is dedicated to the tight coupling relationship between high performance computing (HPC), massive computing simulations of the Monte Carlo type and high energy physics. By presenting an abbreviated historical background and some experience gained at Brookhaven National Laboratory, we illustrate the inseparable relationship between experimental physics and computing.

SIMULATION BASED PROBLEM SOLVING

Many quantitative problems are hard or even impossible to solve in the closed form by means of traditional mathematical analysis. For instance, stochastic process parameter determination is a problem that requires drawing a sample of the random variable measurements and calculation of the parameter value in a form of an estimate. Being directly related to the values of the observed random variable, an estimate value itself is a random variable too. Opposing these classes of problems are deterministic problems which can be solved by application of a simulation of certain relevant stochastic experiments that indirectly leads to the solution of the original problem. Such an approach may be classified into a group of Monte Carlo problem solving methods. Monte Carlo is a term used for computing simulation based methods which involve artificial generation of well-defined random processes that may be applicable to problems with no probabilistic content. It is important to note that the Monte Carlo methods may be also applied to problems that are inherently probabilistic. With wider availability of the low cost computation power, application of Monte Carlo algorithms to scientific problem solving has gained in value and has become more attractive.

The very name "Monte Carlo" for algorithm methods described above has been selected by the unknown author after the famous European gambling town of Monte Carlo situated in the Monaco principality. Name and the systematic development of Monte Carlo methods dates from about 1944 (Metropolis, 1987).

To highlight the meaning and to clarify the essence of the Monte Carlo method we shall

present one simple illustrative case. Probably the most elementary example of straightforward application of computation and simulation is the popular problem of computing approximates the value of irrational number π (Pi) by simulating random throwing of a dart at the circular target. This experimental approach to calculation of π value, assumes that a square target of size a=2r contains a circle of radius r, (See Figure 1). If the random shot is aimed at the square target, with the probability of missing the square being 0, probability of hitting the circular area Awc is equal to the ratio of the areas of the circle Awc and the square A:

$$p = A_{wc} / A = \pi r^2 / (2r)^2 = \pi/4 \qquad (1)$$

Obviously, by evaluating the probability p we may be able to calculate the value of π, as:

$$\pi = 4p \qquad (2)$$

If we conduct an experiment as a sequence of n random shots at the target shown in Figure 1, it is possible to estimate the probability p, i.e., it is possible to calculate an estimate πn of the value

Figure 1. Square target containing unit circle

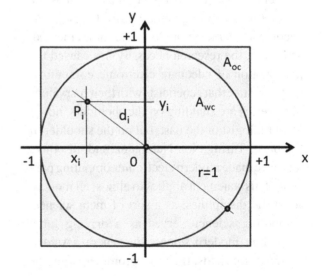

of π. With the circle radius value being r=1, simulated version of this experiment requires a random generation of a sequence of coordinate pairs (xi, yi), both having absolute values smaller than 1. The key step in the experiment would be to classify the hit points Pi, i.e., to count the number of hits nwc that fell within the unit circle area Awc, (having the Pi point distance from the center of the circle satisfy the condition $d_i \leq 1$). The number of shots that have missed the circle, falling in the area Aoc, with $d_i > 1$, would be noc where i=1,2,3,…, n, the sample size is n= nwc+noc and the distance of the hit point from the center of the target is $d_i = [x_i^2 + y_i^2]^{1/2}$.

Applying the area ratio of expression (1), we may rearrange expression (2) as:

$$\pi = 4p = 4A_{wc}/A \qquad (3)$$

Expression (3) can be further used to define an experimental value or the estimate of π as:

$$\pi_n = 4\,n_{wc}/n \qquad (4)$$

One run of the simulation experiment with two random number generators producing values xi and yi, with n=1,000 has produced n_{wc}=807 points P_i which landed inside the circle area A_{wc}.

$$\pi_n = 4(807/1000) = 3.228 \approx \pi, \text{ for n=1000} \qquad (5)$$

Since the known value of π is 3.141592653589793…, the estimate π1000= 3.228, obtained via the initial short simulations is quite close to the known value. Of course if finding π is our true objective we would use method whose efficiency is many orders of magnitude greater. By using a larger sample size n, with more randomly generated dots, the approximate value of πn approaches closer and closer to the known value of π. Table 1 shows the results of the simulation runs with different sample size values of n, with the estimation error defined as $\varepsilon = |\pi - \pi_n|$, and with the computation time consumed tn.

Apparently, it is not computationally costly to solve problems analytically and deterministically, using pen and paper. However, closed analytical solution is not always possible. For many problems in science the simulation approach may be the only possible way leading to the solution. In some cases of slow experiment convergence, a very large number of samples are required to provide data leading to error levels sufficiently low enough. To achieve acceptable results computational experiments may take a very long time. Yet in some other situations, with fast convergence experiments, the time required to process a single data sample could take several hours, resulting in long computation times too. Besides mathematical convergence evaluation, proper determination of the Monte Carlo experiment efficiency requires computation measurements on the system used. Although Monte Carlo has many different applications the method always follows general model shown in Figure 2.

The stochastic nature of the experiment originates from the random number generator that has to be design to produce as random as possible values. Most random number generation algorithms exhibit periodic repetition of the random sequence, i.e., the random number generator is in fact a pseudo random number generator. The pseudo randomness, hidden as a deep determinism in such Monte Carlo methods, is the most serious practical problem to deal with.

Input domain limiting and model blocks specify the semantics of the experiment and input summation performs integration of the experimental

Table 1. Parameter evaluation precision and simulation length relationship

n	π_n	ε	t_n (ms)
100	3.28	0.138407	9
1,000	3.228	0.086407	16
1,000,000	3.14062	0.000973	111
1,000,000,000	3.141586032	0.000007	91,225

Figure 2. The Monte Carlo method processing pipeline

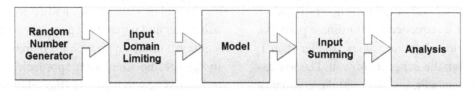

values. When dealing with the massive experiments, these two stages can be parallelized (Figure 3). In most Monte Carlo applications the input summing step and analysis are computationally inexpensive so that the output of each parallel process can be saved individually and combined later. If there is no need for different parallelized threads to communicate with each other in run time the workflow can be called "embarrassingly parallel." Embarrassingly parallel processing is always preferred, because it can be run on off-the-shelf hardware, or if needed on large parallel computing systems. With such processing, individual processes do not even need to run at the same point in time and advance resource allocation in real time is not required.

Solving deterministic problems by means of stochastic or statistical methods was an idea introduced right after the birth of the probability as mathematical discipline. In 1931, father of probability Kolmogorov, showed the relationship between Markov stochastic processes and certain integro-differential equations, (Kolmogoroff, 1931). Within 80 years of history, probability, statistics, stochastic processes and methods cov-

ered under the umbrella of Monte Carlo have evolved concurrently with the development of computing technology. These developments have reached the levels where almost miraculous achievements became possible. Examples such as, human genome and genetic engineering, dark matter and black holes research, or an array of newly discovered subatomic particles, would not be possible without massive computing support.

EVOLUTION OF SCIENTIFIC COMPUTING

Processor Speed Problems

In order to perform as many as possible scientific calculations, computing processors have to be as powerful as possible. For decades, successive generations of computing processors have been built to run ever faster. As their elementary building blocks, individual switching transistors were made ever smaller, the clock speeds pacing binary computing operations were allowed to increase. Basic electrical engineering wisdom states that smaller

Figure 3. Parallelized Monte Carlo method processing pipeline

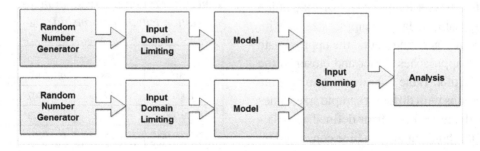

transistors will be able to switch faster. Physically smaller transistor switch is able to respond to the input control signal faster. Building smaller and faster switching semiconductor elements is limited by the existing microelectronics technology and material science problems. Inability to continuously reduce transistor size is the primary problem behind the limited maximal operating clock speeds of modern computing hardware. We refer to this limitation as semiconductor wall.

About five years ago, the top speed for most processors peaked when their clocks passed the boundary of 3GHz. The 3GHz boundary has been primarily conditioned by the size of the individual transistors themselves which were "walled" at roughly 50nm in diameter. The secondary cause of the maximal clock speed boundary originates, not from the transistor size, but from the design of basic switching elements that dissipate heat, mainly at a time of rapid switching, current spikes are generated due to parasitic capacitances with nonzero signal voltages. With increased frequency of switching between binary signal levels dissipation of heat increases. The heat and increased temperatures are threatening to initiate destructive chemical processes. Increasing the clocking speed for the many millions of switching elements found on a typical processor would, accumulate

significant thermal energy that would require processors to dissipate impractical amounts of heat, impractical in the sense of impossible heat sinking and processor cooling. Computer engineers refer to this design limitation as the power wall. Given the obstacles of the semiconductor and the power wall, it is quite clear that electronic computer engineers have been doing a great job. The ongoing success of processor designers is well described by the infamous Moore's law curve shown in Figure 4. In summary, Moore's law pictures a long-term trend in the history of computing hardware. According to this law the number of switching transistors that can be placed on an integrated circuit of a processor doubles approximately every two years, (Moore, 2006).

The two above mentioned limiting walls are the basic reasons why the slope of the exponential Moore's law curve has not been steeper.

With the wider availability and application of computing power, an interesting phenomena was taking place, phenomena that we refer to as computation or software pressure, abbreviated here as Sp factor. Like the Moore's curve, the Sp factor time curve is exponential too, but rising much faster. Typical user computing ambitions and demands of application software imposed upon processor power are, rapidly moving with time to the higher

Figure 4. Moore's Law curve of transistor count per processor vs. time

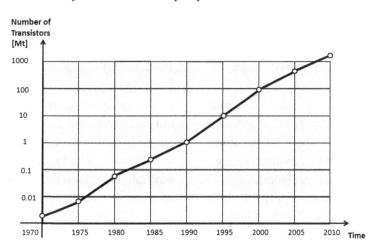

and higher levels. Users demand increasingly larger and faster running programs at lower cost. The pressure generated by the Sp phenomena is forcing processor designers to bypass the Moore's curve by looking for alternative computing models and architectures. On the quest for more of the computing power without increasing transistor density or area of the processor chips creative chip architectures or higher level designs are the way to accommodate the Sp. In the struggle with the Sp factor, processor and hardware system architects were forced to tightly couple their efforts with systems and even application software designers and jointly attempt to maximize the overall computing systems performance. Along these joint effort guidelines, hardware architectures and novel hardware aware software algorithms are being continuously introduced and perfected. To illustrate this trend, we shall describe some of the efforts that hardware architects have exercised.

Work against, or trying to "move," the above mentioned semiconductor and power walls appears to be excessively costly. Instead of pursuing technological solutions of "clocking" processors faster, and so make processors better and have processors "crunch" larger numbers of instructions per second, processor architects have offered less costly options to improve processor's performance. The main thrust of the processor improvement ideas were aimed at the parallelisms of various sorts. Parallelisms in question, aiming at processor improvements were:

- Bit-level parallelisms with wider processor datapaths or busses, starting with 8, 16, 32, 64 and more bits.
- Data-level or operand parallelisms with ability of a processor to fetch in a single word a small batch of operands, avoiding fetching each operand individually (e.g., SIMD, SLP or Vector processors).
- Instruction-level parallelism or ILP with an idea to fetch and process a batch of instructions of a given program at the same time,

(e.g., pipelining, superscalar, Very Long Instruction Word VLIW and Explicitly Parallel Instruction Computing EPIC processor architectures).

- Program level parallelism, better known as Simultaneous Multithreaded SMT architectures, where processor may fetch several threads or fibers of instructions and appear as executing within each clock interval multiple programs at the same time. This application driven parallelism requires co-operative effort on the software generation end. Software has to be designed and divided into distinct threads or fibers that can be serviced by the processor of the SMT kind, (Lo et al., 1997). Both, the instruction set used by the program and program's multi threaded structure have to be matched with the processor.

Since all of these parallelisms were bounded by the Moore's law, each and every idea could stretch only as far as the Moore's log-line would permit. Apparently, to accommodate increasingly aggressive Sp factor, processor and multithreaded application architects had to be joined by the hardware systems specialists and systems software developers.

Hardware System Computing Speed Problems

The previous section has discussed parallel processing methods that are transparent, invisible from the systems hardware systems point of view. Such covert parallelisms reside hidden inside the processor architecture, manifesting themselves only as increased processor performance on a single stream of instructions, (Single instruction stream may contain multiple threads fetched in a multiplexed manner). As mentioned, parallelisms of such sort are known as "pipelined," "super scalar," VLIW, SMT, etc.

To better quantify software pressure Sp factor, in the absence of a better idea, it is reasonable to select as a measure of such a pressure, popular benchmarking unit well known as "million floating point operations per second," Megaflop per second or Mflop/s. Mflop/s is commonly used for measurement of the rate of computing instruction execution in millions of 64-bit floating point addition or multiplication operations per second. Larger units Gflop/s refers to thousand, Tflop/s to million and Pflop/s refers to one billion of Mflop/s.

Modern science is driven, directly or indirectly by the massive number "crunching." Numerical processing used is orchestrated to directly support related experiments or indirectly, as a background computation, to be embedded in computerized scientific equipment and plants. Application of computing to scientific processes has escalated to very high levels. As some disciplines became so much computation hungry new distinct class of massive computation-bound science had to be differentiated as the so called petascale science, (Bader, 2007). At the top of the computation power consumption pyramid we find the extraordinary scientific experiments of petascale science, which are typically consuming (and/or producing) petabytes worth of data and petaflops of processor power. Subsequent sections will discuss examples of petascale science experiments as well as the high performance computing (HPC) infrastructure developments that were necessary for such experiments.

One of the major systems' architecture improvements is based on teaming up multiple processors into a batch of parallel or concurrent processors, appearing as one virtual super processor.

If parallel processing is not transparent, if it is visible to software developers and designers of compilers, extra effort is needed to parallelize low level software. To be executable on multi processors, application software has to be broken into parallel threads of instructions. Developing multi threaded programs and supervising such programs at run time adds to the complexity of using multiprocessors.

From the systems point of view, hardware systems based on multiplication of processors are known as parallel systems. A number of early parallel systems used processor replication not to improve performance but to overcome the reliability problems of the poor quality legacy hardware. Parallel processing for faster program execution, emerged in the late 1960s with the infamous ILLIAC IV project at the University of Illinois, (ILLIAC IV, 1974). ILLIAC IV presented a significant step forward in computing systems architecture offering greatly improved performances at lower switching clock speeds. Using an array of 64 processors, fantastic computing power for that time, of 200Mips (Mips stands for Mega instructions per second) was achieved. Instructions in question were not floating point instructions so that Mips as computing power measure remains a bit illusive. However, the I/O speed of 1Gbps was quite impressive back 40 years ago.

Cray Research, Inc. founded in 1972, has delivered in 1976, and celebrated Cray-1 supercomputer with the price tag of 8.8 million USD, (The Cary-1 computer system, 1977). Vector processing array with 12 functional reconfigurable computing units was capable of delivering 80Mflop/s of computing power. Special FORTRAN compiler was used to generate object code that could fully benefit from using this multiprocessor machine.

Starting in the late 1970s and early 1980s, hardware systems developers had noticed that low-cost microprocessors had better price/performance ratio than larger computers. In parallel, organized as Symmetrical Multi Processors or SMPs, microprocessors could significantly raise the total system performance at low cost. With emergence of the Internet, new commercial market for high end parallel processing enterprise servers has been created. Through the years of parallel server "evolution," two distinct systems levels of parallelism have evolved:

315

- Low level processor parallelism or multi-processing, and
- High level host parallelism or clustering.

On the lower levels of parallelism there are two general architectural approaches:

- Massive scale parallel architectures with low-power processors, and
- Small scale parallel architectures with higher-power processors.

The speed-up of a program on parallel processor architecture is limited by the program's nature, i.e., by how much of the given program can be parallelized. It is important to observe that some algorithms are parallel bound and some are not. This means that some algorithms may result in multiple threads of instructions that are easy to parallelize, while some algorithms result in programs that can barely be parallelized. For example, if 80% of the program can be parallelized, the theoretical maximum speed-up using parallel computing would be at most 5 fold no matter how many processors are used, (Hypothetical massive parallel systems could reduce 100% of the computing job to 20% of UN parallelizable making the execution time of the parallelizable 80% portion negligible). In the ideal case of the totally parallel bound algorithm, the speed-up from parallelization would be linear, where doubling the number of processors should double the execution speed, and doubling it further speed would continue to rise, (i.e., the run time should decrease towards the hardware bottom limit. However, very few parallel algorithms achieve such an optimal speed-up. Most of them have initially, a near-linear speed-up for small numbers of processors, which flattens out into a constant value after certain, relatively small number of processors. This rapid diminishing of parallelism benefits is well described by the celebrated Amdahl's law, (Amdahl, 1967). Gene Amdahl has stated that a small portion of the program which cannot be parallelized will limit

the overall speed-up offered by the ideal parallel processing system. If we assume that is the run time fraction of a sequential non-parallelizable program portion, then s=1/a is the theoretical maximum execution acceleration by means of parallelization. For example, regardless of how many processors are added, when the sequential, non-parallelizable, portion of a program accounts for 20% of the execution time, no more than a 5× acceleration is possible.

Amdahl's Law was used as an argument against massively parallel processing. Based on certain counter arguments, not discussed here, the so called Gustafson's law may be used to justify massively parallel processing systems (MPPs), (Gustafson, 1988). Gustafson's law states that special problems with large, repetitive data sets can be efficiently parallelized. It states that the speedup with N processors is:

$$S(N)=N - a(N-1) \qquad (6)$$

Gustafson revealed that it was indeed possible to achieve more than 1000 fold speedup using 1024 processors (Gustafson, 1988). In spite of seeming contradiction, both, the Amdahl's and the Gustafson's laws are in fact formulations of the same law, making their contradictory points on two different sets of algorithms and two different types of data sets, (Shi, 1996).

In high end scientific computing systems, behind the continuous increasee of systems memory and storage capacities, we find again the Sp factor. Memory and storage hungry modern science computing jobs may be using massive memory in storage in such an intensive way, so that high speed parallel processing may be forced to stall waiting for expanded memory and storage to deliver data. This abuse of the parallel systems by the larger and slower memory is known as the "memory wall." When intensive storage I/O activities become necessary, to load huge amounts of input data, parallelism power may be again wasted in a form of the so called Von Neuman

Bottleneck (VNB). Architectures such as MPPs or Processor-in-Memory (PIMs) (Sterling & Zima, 2002), aiming at Pflop/s powers, avoid the VNB observed in conventional systems, by using massive I/O parallelism and highly customized and optimized object code of application programs. Different programming paradigm from the one used in common symmetric SMP systems is used when developing software for MPP or PIM systems. In addition to these problems, custom hardware manufacturing procedures of MPP and PIM basic building blocks may drive the Total Cost of Ownership (TCO) figures too high, resulting in a low performance/price ratio.

Parallel System Architectures

The primary attributes of computing in science are:

- Sheer necessity,
- Availability on demand better known as scalability, and
- Affordable cost.

To accommodate high scalability, modern high end computers are based on parallelisms elevated above the level of building massively parallel virtual processors made up of MPPs or PIMs, to the levels of building virtual host machines and complete virtual super systems.

Massive parallelism of distinct processors implied significant departure from the ordinary technologies of hardware as well as software production. To avoid such a problem alternative solutions were considered. The solutions in question proposed higher levels of parallelism implementation based on small scale networks of powerful standard common off the shelf (COTS) computing units, in a form of clusters, (Buyya, 1999; Graham, Snir, & Patterson, 2005). Programming clusters, where each computing unit could be an SMP of multi core processors, appears as a far easier job than programming MPPs or PIMs.

To all that promote hierarchical parallelism, it appears that the most cost-effective solution would promote a mixture of the low level small scale multiprocessors and high level clustering of such multiprocessors (Pfister, 1998).

A cluster is a set of custom-networked complete computing host machines working together as a single super host system. The initial idea of clustering host machines was developed in the 1960s at IBM as a way of networking large mainframes to provide high computing power at low cost by means, what we call now, rough grain or coarse parallelism. IBM still supports clustering of mainframes through their Parallel Sysplex system, For instance, with IBM's Parallel Sysplex technology, users can harness the power of up to 32 z/OS mainframe class systems, yet make these systems behave like a single, logical computing facility. The underlying networked structure of the Parallel Sysplex remains transparent to user applications. Application execution is the same as it would be operating on monolithic system.

To accomplish clustered set of machines to appear as virtually monolithic machine, the z/OS Parallel Sysplex combines two critical capabilities:

- Parallel processing, and
- Enabling read/write data sharing across multiple systems with full data integrity.

This combination makes the z/OS Parallel Sysplex unique among other system solutions mentioned above so far. It results in a scalable growth path that may extend beyond Gflop/sec of computing power.

The unique high level parallel structure of clusters in general, gives users flexibility to resolve key operational issues such as:

- Reducing the overall cost of computing,
- Providing rapid, flexible responses as computing needs change,
- Ensuring the continuous availability, and

- Leveraging past investments by allowing execution of costly legacy software.

Cluster parallel hardware, customized operating system, glue type of systems software known as middleware, and system administration software, provides dramatic performance at reduced cost while permitting old machine users to continue to run their existing applications.

Continuous improving performance of processors and high-speed networks with matured and standardized software tools for high performance computing distribution has made cluster computing feasible. In addition, in the context of the rising Sp pressure and the steep TCO curve associated with custom made supercomputers, cluster computing has gained significant momentum. The recent advance in cluster technologies and low cost of making clusters of personal computers is an appealing idea how to make cost-effective high performance machines. Building block cluster elements are mostly inexpensive COTS products (COTS products are sold in large volumes and as such are mostly sold at reduced prices). The COTS nature of cluster building blocks is the key factor behind the reasonable cost of clusters used as enterprise systems.

Cluster based parallelization and integration benefits are accompanied by the pronounced presence and importance of the integration systems software layer. As designers move up along parallelization and integration hierarchy, compared to systems hardware problems become buried deeper into the systems software layers, whose problems and importance become dominant.

HIGH PERFORMANCE SCIENTIFIC COMPUTING

Availability and Scalability Issues

This chapter deals with the fundamental issues regarding meeting extremely demanding Peta scale scientific software needs and forms of massive hybrid parallel processing systems defined as supercomputers.

In general, by definition, high performance parallelized systems should have the following three primary attributes:

- High availability,
- High scalability, and
- User friendly or productive manageability.

Availability is of utmost importance to business mission critical operations, i.e., to the so called 24/7 or non-stop operations. Availability is defined as the time that a system is capable of providing service to its users (i.e. uptime). It is expressed as a percentage that represents the ratio of the time in which the system provides acceptable service versus the total time during which the system is expected to be operational. (For instance, uptime of 525,599 out of 525,600 minutes in a year represents 99.9999% of availability).

A simpler measurement of availability to system administrators is downtime. Downtime is the ratio between the times to repair a system outage versus the MTBF (Mean Time Between Failures) of such outages. Minimized downtime to less than a minute per year (0.0001%), by means of redundancy in a form of parallelism may be of great value to mission critical enterprise systems users but not of equal importance to scientific computing users. Though a bank can't afford to lose a few clients, bank balances losing a statistically insignificant fraction of a dataset is tolerable in scientific computing. Having a small fraction of downed worker nodes in a large processing facility is common.

Scalability as the number two criteria mentioned above, is an important issue in the environments with constantly fluctuating number of users, types of computing jobs, with both, seasonal and random extreme demand requirements that must be serviced effectively. System slow-downs are no less problematic than outages, and both must be minimized with the proper system design and maintenance. Prolonged slow-downs can be unacceptable in scientific computing, when results may be desirable to meet certain, mainly long term deadlines, such as scientific conference or budget related schedule results reporting.

Scalability is defined as the ability of a system to increase its computing power by adding additional processors or additional cluster node, with increased computing loads. The addition of computing nodes is typically not a linear function of computing load service effort. Extra system overhead is associated with all activities involving each cluster expansion.

Scalability is an issue that primarily affects the choice of preferable parallel system solution for high end scientific computing projects. In terms of clustering, the shared-nothing architectural option of loosely coupled cluster nodes provides the higher degree of linear scalability, while the more tightly coupled clusters would provide better performance, i.e., higher computing job throughput (Graham, Snir, & Patterson, 2005).

Scientific and Enterprise Computing

High end scientific computing jobs such as subatomic particle physics, financial market or climate process simulations are quite demanding. For instance, the amount of CPU time slices, network packets, memory frames and disk storage blocks requested at a starting time of high end scientific simulations drastically exceeds average systems load demands between the runs of such simulations. Figure 5 illustrates a hypothetical example of a standalone systems load surges during the simulations of enterprise and scientific systems. In case of scientific systems, prominent load peaks such as value CP_p outstand against the average base line load CP_a which may be observed most of the time on the standalone Peta scale scientific system.

Computation Power parameter of Figure 5 is assumed lumped all basic computation resources measured in relevant computation quanta such as processor time slice, memory frame and storage store block. Computation load pattern variations such as the one shown in Figure 5 can be serviced by the massive computing system at extreme procurement, maintenance and power consumption costs (Graham, Snir, & Patterson, 2005).

There is a great deal of difference between large footprint enterprise type of applications (web server, e-mail servers or database servers), and scientific applications. Enterprise application servers typically sit idle on the high power systems, until a service request is made. Hence the resource usage of these applications is fine grained, I/O bound and "spiky" in nature (Figure 5). It is in fact important that resources remain available, underutilized and

Figure 5. Typical high end enterprise and Peta science computing load variations

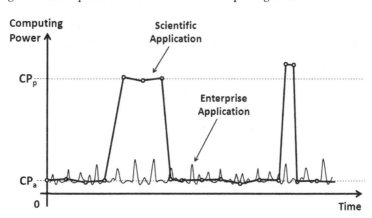

free because large delays could result in delays of business transactions, customer dissatisfaction and loss of revenue. The responsiveness, i.e. system availability, is crucial with enterprise systems. For instance, delays greater than one or two seconds are considered too long amounts of time to load a web page. In addition, the amount of data moving in and out of an enterprise system is relatively small, (on the order of kB per request).

Scientific applications involved in reconstruction and simulation are different in nature, in that they saturate resources for prolonged periods of time. Unlike enterprise applications, scientific simulations are predominantly processor power bound and not I/O bound (some experiments may be both processor and I/O bound). Scientific applications are mostly not interactive, (there is no need to wait for user actions). The only eventualities that can slow down processing are bottle necks in I/O (loading in input or storing, i.e. writing out output data). Reconstruction jobs require large input data volumes, typically of about 5GB per process with output sizes of about 1/5 the input size. Common simulations in HENP experiments have quite small input data files of a few kB and may have output files of hundreds of MB or even a few GB in size, (the size highly depends on the number of Monte Carlo events chosen to be run per job).

Supercomputing

Well funded organizations such as the University of Tokyo, PLA National Defense University of China, or US Department of Energy national laboratories (Strohmaier, 2011), are able to acquire and maintain supercomputers that are capable to scale up to the extreme peak computing loads of Peta science applications. Figure 6 illustrates exponential growth of super computing power and historic evolution of top performing supercomputers. Petaflop/s threshold has been reached recently and systems delivering well over 10Petaflop/s of computing power are in use (Table 2).

Most of the supercomputer architectures on the top500 list of www.top500.org are built as a hierarchy of clusters and SMPs. On the bottom of the hierarchy are blades as cluster units, each containing an SMP network of multi-core processors.

A multi-core processor is a single integrated device with two or more independent processors called "cores" capable of executing independent threads of object code instructions. Multi-core processors are commonly implemented as single chip multi-core-processors (CMPs), or hybrid circuit micro networks of multiple core chips (Hybrid circuits are made of several integrated

Figure 6. Historical progress of supercomputing power, (Adapted from [Foster & Kesselman, 1999])

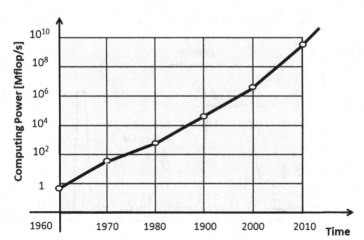

Table 2. Supercomputers at the top of the Top500 list (Adapted from top500.org)

Model	No of Cores	Power MW	Peak Performance Pflop/s	US Power Cost M$/year
Fujitsu/K-Computer	705024	12.65	11.280	11.08
Fujitsu/K-Computer	548352	9.80	8.770	8.58
NUDT/Ianhe-1A	186368	4.04	4.700	3.54
IBM/Roadrunner	129600	2.483	1.456	2.18

chips and a micro network on a common substrate). The maximal core count threshold on a CMP is roughly in the range of several tens of cores. To have a larger number of cores on CMP, special network on chip technology featuring custom core switches and an on-chip mesh network is used to reduce the signal propagation delays and data traffic congestion.

CMP designers may couple cores in a multi-core device tightly or loosely. For example, cores may or may not share caches, and they may implement message passing or shared memory inter-core communication methods. The common core interconnect topology is a two-dimensional mesh or crossbar. Homogeneous CMP includes only identical cores and heterogeneous CMP has cores which are not identical. Just as was the case with earlier mentioned single-processor chips, CMP cores may implement internal parallel architectures such as superscalar, Very Long Instruction Word (VLIW), vector processing, Single Instruction Multiple Data (SIMD), or Simultaneous Multithreading (SMT).

On the higher layers of supercomputing architectures are layers of clustered clusters interconnected with customized high speed data networks into a farm of systems. Supercomputer farm elements are subjected to the transparent systems computation distribution load balancing software.

It is interesting to observe that the supercomputer TOC figure contains as a significant portion, the cost of consumed electrical power. If we assume 24/7 operation and average 2011 commercial price of $100.00/MWh (Electric Power Monthly Report: DOE/EIA-0226 (2011/12), 2011), than

electricity bill for running the last system in Table 2, can easily mount to over 2 million USD per year.

Power dissipation is a problem at multiple levels of supercomputer architectures, from bottom chip level cooling to the top data center level with building cooling. Besides power used to run supercomputer additional power is needed to cool it. Thermal and power issues at the data center level contributes sizable amount to the cost of running supercomputers. At data center level, only half of electricity bill goes to systems, other half goes to air conditioning with the power budget of approximately 25 kW/rack.

With exorbitant TOC figures and frequent periods of low usage, organizations in control of supercomputing sites are forced to share unused capacity in any manner possible. By sharing their sites, desirable sharing of the TOC is accomplished. Two of the most celebrated methods of cost reducing technologies are Grid and Cloud computing.

GRID AND CLOUD COMPUTING

Grid Model

With the rapid development of infrastructure, using Internet to integrate remote autonomous computing systems was logical progression and naturally the next step to be taken on the way to achieve larger computing power (Mihajlovic, Palande, & Mihajlovic, 2006).

A grid is an embarrassingly parallel super system structured as a network of remote independent high power systems that are individually administered by different organizations. Grids permit access of heterogeneous resources, such as host machines, data sources, people and devices, all distributed geographically and organizationally. Grids benefit both, user and provider organizations. By permitting provider organizations to offer unused costly IT resources and so manage to reclaim otherwise wasted portions of TCO. Users manage to claim costly IT infrastructure at low "rental" prices bypassing the prohibitively high local TCO.

As much as it may sound absurd, Grid computing cannot be considered as distributed computing. The term "Distributed Computing" refers to the open technology used for distributing, not of the load, but of application modules and data of distributed application into two or more communicating processes. Industry standard distributed processing technologies such as DCE/RPC or CORBA/RMI are used as distributed application software engineering technologies. Grid computing is not software engineering but systems engineering technology.

The implementation models of computational grids are mostly in the systems software domain. As shown in Figure 7, a Grid consists of software services that run on top of native operating systems. These services provide functionality such as authentication, failure detection, object and process management, and remote I/O, and are accessed via Grid libraries. Typically, an application programmer will not access these libraries directly, but will use a programming library such as MPI (The Message Passing Interface (MPI) standard, 1995) or MPL (Grimshaw & Wulf, 1997), which in turn will call the underlying Grid libraries. The advantage of this layered model is that application programmers can use familiar programming tools and interfaces and are shielded from the complexity of accessing Grid services.

Grid as a distributed on-demand, data-intensive, collaborative and networked supercomputing is managed by gridware. Gridware can be viewed as a special type of middleware that handles sharing and managing Grid components based on user requirements and resource attributes.

As distributed super computing systems Grids combine multiple high-capacity resources into a single, virtual distributed supercomputer allowing solving problems that cannot be solved on a single component system or cluster. The Grids projects provide high throughput computing by the opportunistic usage of idle computing resources.

The scalability is why grids easily match and meet variable on demand computing needs of scientific computing experiments. Scientific computing jobs may use Grid capabilities to have satisfied short and medium-term requirements for resources that are not locally accessible, Grids are sometimes even able to respond in real-time to fluctuating computing demands.

Figure 7. Grid computing layered architecture (Adapted from [Foster & Kesselman, 1999])

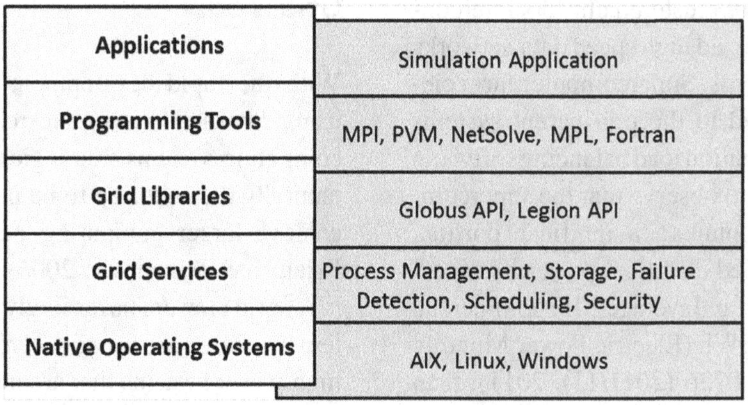

Applications	Simulation Application
Programming Tools	MPI, PVM, NetSolve, MPL, Fortran
Grid Libraries	Globus API, Legion API
Grid Services	Process Management, Storage, Failure Detection, Scheduling, Security
Native Operating Systems	AIX, Linux, Windows

With high throughput I/O and large storage capacities, Grid data intensive computing may focus on synthesizing new information from data that is maintained in geographically distributed repositories, in digital libraries, and databases, (e.g. massive distributed data mining application).

Grid applications are often structured in terms of a virtual shared space with possibility of global scheduling and optimization of data movement.

Some may treat Grid as an intelligent network which explicitly models storage resources in the network. By doing so, Grid becomes "logistical" network behaving as the systems of business warehouses, depots, and distribution channels.

Grid computing provides capability and capacity computing qualities which are of great importance in scientific computing. Capability computing is typically thought of as using the peak computing power to solve a large problem in the shortest amount of time. We may define capability computing to be new mechanism with which to conduct massive scientific computing experiments. Often a capability system is able to solve a problem of a size or complexity that no other computer can. Capacity computing in contrast implies using cost-effective computing power to solve large problems or to prepare for a run on a capability system. We define capacity computing loosely as the ability to conduct larger computational experiments either by expending more resources on a single problem or by doing the same in parts on multiple, independent problems.

By enabling computations on a large scale, grids support capacity computing. Depending upon software support grid's flexible and extensible object model may supports capability computing by permitting novel methods of computation.

The typical user of a Grid has a single login account to access all resources where resources may be owned by diverse organizations. This simple signing on user convenience is preceded by the establishment of the so called Grid virtual organization. Foster et al. (Foster & Kesselman, 1999) outlined that resource sharing among different administrative domains has to be governed by certain organizational structures and rules. Hence, participating computing sites are typically managed as virtual organization, where institutes agree on common sharing rules.

Cloud Computing

Grids have showed to provide a fairly good solution to integrate remote powerful supercomputing sites but failed, in spite of great expectations, to produce a satisfactory solutions for aggregating large number of smaller systems, to offer fast and fine-tuned distribution of computing power and offer truly seamless environment to their end-users (the heterogeneity of Grids, by nature of their constructs, implied a hidden large need for software support on a plethora of platform for the full exploitation of the available resources). Secure fine grain allocation of huge computing systems resources to the massive number of users could not be accomplished easily with grids either.

Following the migration of Virtual Machine technology from the arena of IBM mainframe technology to the domain of inexpensive servers, a new computing paradigm of Cloud Computing (CC) has emerged. This new technology appears to be the right systems solution for the mentioned problems of grids. The best illustration of the power of CC is large computing capacity users such as Google and Amazon, which have built enormous data centers for their own applications. Apparently, after paying first several electric power bills, they have realized that they could permit others to access their computing resources, hidden as "clouds" of computing power, at relatively affordable prices. By definition (IBM Virtual Machine Facility/370: Introduction, 1976) CC is one perfect vehicle to retail computing power in small packages.

The first version of a virtual machine released in 1972, was VM/370, or officially Virtual Machine Facility/370, (IBM Virtual Machine Facility/370: Introduction, 1976). The original concept of the

Virtual Machine or VM has been formulated by Popek and Goldberg in 1974 (Popek & Goldberg, 1974). A virtual machine is a virtual memory management based method of emulating processor in software supported by special purpose address translation processor known as Virtual Memory Management Unit (VMMU) and dedicated storage volume. VMMU was initially supposed to help enlarge memory by involving storage, but was later recognized as a perfect security tool for isolation of concurrently running programs, (Each of the isolated programs would use own, isolated and distinct virtual memory space). Systems designers have welcomed virtual memory management as a tool for flexible and safe "packetizing" of computing power. The packets in questions are known as VMs.

To many, cloud computing was and still is a vague term for a very vague utility computing "on a tap" in which computing would occur in a few remote locations, seamlessly without the need for very much human intervention. Cloud is assumed to provide "infinite" computing and storage resources available for any need at costs approaching zero, which certainly is still not true.

Besides VM migration to smaller processors, development of Storage Area Networks (SANs) and virtual storage volume management have played significant role in the evolution of cloud technology (Armbrust et al., 2009). By using VM technology, cloud computing enables dynamic scale-in and scale-out of applications by the provisioning and de-provisioning of resources. Clouds enable the monitoring of resource utilization to support accounting, dynamic load-balancing and re-allocations of resources.

The very essence of clouds in fine distribution of computing power comes at a cost of reduced performance. For small cloud users and for computing power retailers trying to cash on potentially wasted capacities, this is not critical. However, for HENP and Peta science cloud users that would hope for the largest possible performance during the experiments, more efficient grids may be bet-

ter option. In addition, predominantly interactive nature of small cloud user jobs is in sharp contrast with the scientific computing jobs that are mostly large and of the batch type.

The remainder of this chapter is dedicated to the practical illustration of Grid and cloud use in highly demanding scientific experiments conducted at Brookhaven National Laboratory, indicated as BNL in Figure 8.

STAR EXPERIMENT AND HPC

STAR Experiment at RHIC

The Solenoidal Tracker at Relativistic Heavy Ion Collider (RHIC) or STAR experiment (Figures 8 and 9) is one of the largest US-based high energy and nuclear physics experiments which make use of HTC (Thomas, 2005) for data mining STAR is one of the detectors of the RHIC located on Long Island off the coast of New York State. RHIC collides two beams of ions (atoms which have had their outer cloud of electrons stripped off) travelling at nearly the speed of light (relativistic speeds). The beams travel in opposite directions around RHIC's 2.4-mile, two beam lines. At intersections, the beams moving in opposite directions are push together so they can collide. This produces temperatures and pressures more extreme than exist now even in the cores of the hottest stars. The collisions last a few billionths of a second. From the protons and neutrons of the atom, quarks and gluons are liberated and thousands more particles form as the system condenses (The Physics of RHIC).

STAR weighs 1,200 tons (1,200,000kg) and is as large as a three story building. The STAR detector is wrapped around the beam line where the particles collide. With each collision the subatomic particles fly through the detector and register as hits. Each time particles move through the detector it is digitally read out by analog to digital converters and digitally recorded as an

Figure 8. RHC computing facility and STAR location (satelite view of the site)

Figure 9. RHC computing facility and STAR location (aerial view of the site)

event. One file stores many events. So far STAR has collected over 4PB of event data.

The STAR experiment involves mainly four kinds of computing:

- **Data Reconstruction:** The raw data composed of particle hit traces, deposited energies in calorimeters or time of flight information are analyzed and the information correlated. Hits are connected together to form tracks, each of them corresponding to the passage of a particle throughout the detector systems. Energy and time of flight provide further information on their properties and allow refining their identi-

fication. A vertex, or the position at which particles were created, is also determined (it is noteworthy to mention that many vertices are available in one event, making the reconstruction process even more so complex). The final particles species are determined by their properties (mass, momentum, energy deposited, and whether they came from the primary vertex or not).

- **Simulation:** This process involves running Monte Carlo models describing the collision at RHIC. Collection of the simulated data is followed by a simulation of the detector responses to include the geometrical acceptance of the apparatus (particles falling within a region of space not covered by active detectors may be lost). Produced simulated data that can be compared with real data and the resulting output can be used to measure the geometrical acceptance of the detector, the systematic uncertainties in data or even to evaluate the efficiency of the reconstruction algorithm.

- **Embedding:** This involves taking tracks (real or simulated) and mixing them (embedding) into other events. This process is primarily used to make accurate estimates of the environmental contribution of track reconstruction efficiencies.

- **Analysis:** This is a broader range of computing that involves searching the data and making measurements for the purpose of doing pure science.

We will limit our conversation to reconstruction and simulation.

The Pre-Grid Era

STAR needs to use embarrassingly parallel computing to process, simulate, and analyze the incredible amount of data it generates. STAR's processing needs can change from week to week based on incoming datasets, new analyses starting, and the need to double check data before publishing papers and so on. The local batch system provides 5,500 computing CPU cores, with each core able to hold one batch slot or job. The batch system has a queue when the slots are saturated jobs idles inside the queue waiting for a free slot. The allocation of slots is based on resource matching and policy weighted fair-share algorithms. Because of batch system inefficiencies, saturation typically occurs between 70%~90% of farm occupancy. Before the Grid era, if resources were not available, users had to submit their jobs, and wait in the long term queue for their jobs to go into run mode. Waiting in the long term queue could take days if a "perfect storm" of resource usage occurs.

The Promise of the Grid Era

With numerous experiments and many sites within one organization there became a great desire to opportunistically use resources (slots and storage) on other sites. In other words, when site X has free unused slots and site Y's queue is full, site Y can run some of their jobs on site X's batch system. The idea of using idling sites computing power is the idea behind the Grid system that was discussed earlier. However, to make Grid based sharing work, there were many systems problems to overcome.

Grid software used with the STAR experiment, most notably the Globus Toolkit, has been applied as the low level underlying framework across all Grid member sites. Globus Toolkit resolves such problems as user authentication on remote sites, mapping of users from one site to another, (one Grid identify can be mapped to any account at any site, allowing for user account to be diverse), providing a unified job submission interface across all sites, and low level data transfer between sites. These functions are provided via tried and true methods such as PKI infrastructure and protocols such as ftp. Given the large number of files that have to be tracked high level dataset transfer software such as SRM BeStMan (Berkeley

Storage Manager) is employed to keep track of all the files associated with one dataset. Datasets range between a few tens of gigabytes and tens of terabytes, broken up between a few hundred to a few tens of thousands of files.

The basic layout of a Grid site is illustrated in Figure 10. A user prepares jobs and initializes a Grid proxy secured by the PKI infrastructure. The jobs are submitted to a condorG job manager on the client machine. The job manager authenticates the user with the gatekeeper on the remote site and verifies that there virtual organization (VO) has the right to submit jobs to the site. The user is mapped to a user account on the remote site. This can be a generic multi-user account or an individual one to one user mapping. The jobs are pushed through. A script on the gatekeeper side converts the generic job description to one that is suitable for providing to the specific batch system running on the remote site. The script submits the job to the batch system on the remote site. The batch system queues the jobs and once a free slot becomes available, matching the job's resource requirements, on the batch farm the job is moved to the worker node and executed. The output streams are saved in files. The output files generated by the job are moved to a high level transfer server which caches the file for delegated transfer, still under the user's proxy. The job finishes execution and returns. Once bandwidth on the network path is available the file is pushed back to storage on the submitter's side.

Grid Model Caveats

At first sight the Grid model of Figure 10 seems fairly ideal. So what could be wrong? One of the main problems with the Grid model is lack of true virtualization and logic transparency. Grids offer organizational virtualization but poor systems virtualization. Even though jobs can be submitted to the remote site the environment on the foster site is usually not the same as the local site and the job exits in an error state. It is hard enough

Figure 10. Basic grid site setup

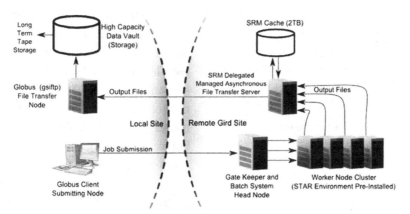

for interactive users to get software to run on a remote system without making adjustments and resolving dependences, environment variables, operating system incompatibilities and so forth, let alone to assume than a non-interactive script can do this all by itself, to many practitioners is shear fantasy. At first it was suggested that users try to write more self-contained software, however most of the software intended to run on the Grid is initially written, not for a Grid but for a standalone system. The code base in most cases can easily be over a million lines. In scientific computing, small changes in for example, how floating point numbers are handled, can have huge impacts and make big differences in the compounding of a result, especially when making very small critical measurements and comparison. By consistently using the same software for comparison the scientist's work is immunized from caveats of this sort. For a good example illustrating how dangerous it is to tinker with the initially working code just to accommodate Grid systems, consider Monte Carlo simulations, described above, where simulation software is changed to use new system libraries, where code in charge of random number generation does not exhibit good statistical randomness. Situations of this kind could be catastrophic, producing results of low integrity.

When the in-feasibility of just telling users to re-write code and make it more self-contained was realized, alternative "match making" option was considered. By characterizing data with respect to the sites and worker nodes, a high level scheduling system was concocted to match jobs to specific sites. Given the huge number of data parameters to take into an account, match making was not a great success. Some parameterizing problems would arise because of the inconsistencies caused by the updates and changes of the site description. Even with instant match-parameter synchronization, this solution could not accommodate jobs that would be already queued at a remote site.

To minimize the inconvenience of modifying software or parameterizing, some bartering may go on with foreign sites. For example, a foreign site may request that certain systems or library software be installed or upgraded to a newer version so that they can utilize the cluster. Whether such a demand is gratified depends on the effort required, (does it need to be adjusted on each node or just a network mounted disk), and the effect on local running jobs which take priority.

The main solution to all these problems was to only submit jobs on sites in which users would have full control of the software, in other words, computing facilities belonging to the experiment.

Computing systems associated with the experiment has a tiered structure. Table 3 shows the tiered system dividing computing into levels within an experiment.

Table 3. Experiment tiers

Tier	Description
0	A large computing facility located near the detector, e.g., the RHIC Computing Facility (RCF) indicated in Figure 8. Usually responsible for permanently storing the collected data.
1	A large computing facility located away from the Tier 1 site connected by a high speed network. For STAR such a facility is the National Energy Research Scientific Computing Center (NERSC) division of the Lawrence Berkeley National Laboratory, located in California.

Though Grid member sites are in general quite generous with run time, (because if it can't be used it is lost), they are less generous with storage space for output data. Because storage space must be dedicated for the purpose and high availability storage is costly. Ideally copying the data back directly from the worker node to the local site is desirable. However when this is tried in practice and a larger number of jobs start up at once they also finish their processing at approximately the same time, (distributed around some narrow normal Gaussian distribution mean value). If all of the jobs are allowed to copy the output data back within their run time intervals, they could saturate the pipe line back to the local site. This will extend the runtime of each job. Situations of this sort are undesirable in two ways, firstly, it wastes processor resource as the job is not doing very much except waiting for the remote side to respond, and secondly, the batch system puts a time limit on the wall clock of run time of jobs. If the job takes too long trying to get its output back to the remote site the batch system may forcibly terminate the idling job before it would be able to copy back all of its data. Essentially the output of a job would be lost and the processor time wasted.

The best solution that has been found for this problem is a delegated transfer that is done outside the jobs run time. Moving files around within a site is much faster then moving them between sites. So the output files of the job are moved from the scratch directory of the worker node to a cache elsewhere. The files are registered with the file mover, and then the job terminates. The files would still remain at the local site. But once there is network capacity between the sites the files are moved serially back to the registered site and location. This is also beneficial if the network contact to the requester site is lost (The mover will keep the file for some period of time before giving-up). The only negative part of this setup is that the remote site must provide the file mover service. If the site does not respond properly, the submitter must default back to less desirable options with all of the related shortfalls. The other option is to pack fewer events per job, which is easier to do with simulated events where the submitter formulating the job has control. This allows for more run time for the transfer. The other option is to temporarily copy the output files to a location somewhere on the site and then copy the data back later. This involves getting such an allocation in the first place, by agreement with the local site, if possible. If the site provides a generic location the submitter must try to assure that no other Grid or local user will fill the site with their own data. Then the transfer must be done manually by hand.

In concluding Grid technology is of great importance for computation driven experiments such as STAR, which is a collaboration of a tightly knit groups of sites which have similar objectives and are willing to provide all needed accommodating services, to provide support and resources to each other.

STAR EXPERIMENT IN THE CLOUD ERA

Virtualization and Cloud Computing

After Grids, the next scientific computing leap forward was introduction of cloud computing. Scientific computing using clouds is still in its relative infancy, so models, software stacks, and resource providers are still evolving and being explored. However it is fair to say that there are certain advantages over Grids that make this option appealing.

The old Grid framework suffered from the heterogeneous nature of worker nodes, where an experiment's jobs had difficulty running on a foreign site. The Grid framework never attempted to resolve the problem via virtualization though there is no technical impediment, only lack of community will. Virtualization allows the home site to bundle a copy of one of its own worker nodes into a virtual machine image. This can then be replicated across a group of worker nodes on the cloud to instantiate, or boot-up, several nodes which resemble an extension of nodes on the local sites batch system. The job is run inside the VM, so the job is encapsulated inside its native environment regardless of the underlying system.

This resolves the problem of not being able to utilize sites because of their environment. However it introduces new problems as well. Namely, there is a lack of standardization in this abstraction process. Different clouds use different virtual machine software (e.g., Xen, KVM, VirtualBox, VMware, etc.), so the image needs to be created and repackaged based on what brand of virtual machine the cloud supports. Lack of standardization also applies to the uploading of the image file(s) and the deployment of VM images. With each site the same tasks must be performed, images must be uploaded, the number of instances to be deployed must be specified, the address of the started instances must be recovered, when finished the instances must be shut-down, and so forth.

A few models have been tried, e.g., a full virtualized cluster including a separate batch system. Another model involves discarding the conventional batch system and using such a model where the image is prepared with start-up scripts to pull in its own workload.

The system works as follows; the user submits (prepares), jobs on a workload distribution server. The image is then uploaded to the remote site.

Next a request is passed to the cloud software stack to start n instances of the image. The cloud software stack propagates the requester's image to the nodes on its physical cluster. The cluster nodes receive a signal from the cloud software stack and start booting up instances of the image. Execution of scripts inside the boot sequence starts a process, which in turn makes a request to a workload server on the local site. The workload server passes back one unique job to each virtual node. Once a job is claimed by a worker node no other node may claim it. The script executes the job. As soon as the job finishes its files may be copied back, (there is some variation on how this can be done). The previous model, where the file is cached and transferred later, is possible and has been used by STAR. Because there is no runtime limit as with the batch system this method can be used according to the model shown in Figure 11, however the inefficiency of bottle-necking still applies.

Nonvolatile storage space may also be purchased on a cloud, so that when the virtualized cluster is down the data still exist on the cloud and can be copied back asynchronously at some later date.

To Own It or Not to Own It?

It is clear that STAR must use and consume computing resources to process its workload. Having a local supercomputing farm and the Grid to compare with new cloud option, a valid question is: "What solution is more efficient and which is less costly?" Clouds have some benefits, location is one. Supercomputing clusters consume large amounts of power. For instance, in 2011, the RHIC Computing Facility operating at roughly 2MW of power had huge electrical energy consumption of 17.52TWh with the yearly bill of 1.752 million USD, (Electric Power Monthly Report: DOE/EIA-0226 (2011/12), 2011).

According to Ernst report (Ernst, 2007), about half to one fourth of this is used by STAR. Power

Figure 11. High trhoughput cloud computing model

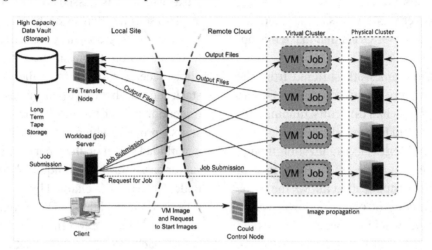

must be used to cool the cluster as virtually all its power consumption is dissipated as heat. Currently (end of 2011), the industrial electric rate in the state of New York is 96.8 USD/MWh, if the clusters were located in Washington state instead, the power cost would be 39.8 USD/MWh which would change the power cost from 1.7 Million USD to 0.68 Million USD per year. The figures quoted are relatively small when compared to power consumption of the accelerator itself, which is not included in this figure. Unfortunately, the accelerator is not as easy to relocate as it is the case with data and computing. It is reasonable to locate supercomputing facilities as close as possible to the power sources of the lowest cost. A valid remark would be also, that the location of the supercomputing clusters can be selected in the areas providing the lowest high tech labor rates.

Economy of rapid dynamic scale is another benefit of cloud computing. By aggregating many computing facilities into one location, hardware cost could be reduced as well as the cost of labor needed to service the consolidated, virtualized and "cloudified" computing site.

It should be noted that STAR and the other RHIC experiments consolidate the bulk of the on-site computing into one facility known as the RCF.

Other experiments at different interaction regions along the accelerator ring share the resources of the computing facility and pool personnel for operating the facility to minimize redundancy.

There are also down sides to outsourcing hardware and computing cycles. The in-house computing facility only has to worry about providing services and its own costs in contrast a commercial cloud has to produce a profit for its owners or operators and pass on any costs it incurs to its customers. For example an in-house computing center pays for floor space directly out of its own funds, and a computing center adds the cost of floor space to the hourly rate of running on their clusters and marks-up the cost to insure it makes a profit. It should be pointed out that besides commercial sites, academic sites and national research institutions are also experimenting with the technology and software stacks to be used in wider sharing, and possible sale of resources.

Economics of scientific computing is a multi-dimensional problem. Without a local facility an experiment could be subjected to market trends and price fluctuations in the cost of computing resources. Estimated STAR's planned life time is approximately 20 years. It could contract with a cloud provider to get resources for a fix amount of time at a fixed cost, however if new technology would emerge offering to reduce the cost of computing, locked into the contract, STAR would not be able to benefit from positive technological and market trends. Alternatively if the price of computing would rise, for example, if the cost of power would go up, the cloud site clients would be "safely" protected behind their contracts. One should not fail to observe that in extreme cases of violent electrical power market fluctuations, unable to pass power costs to its clients, cloud site could fail financially and be forced to shut its doors for business, translating client "safety" and protection into a disaster.

Direct support from the local administrators is also a benefit of an in-house computing facility. The whole facility is optimized for scientific workloads. For example when different hardware is available from different vendors samples may be provided, so that STAR's applications may be benchmarked allowing for the best hardware to be selected. Problems are addressed promptly because administrators are literally down the hallway.

As mentioned earlier, the added inefficiency, an overhead of running application on a VM instead of natively, must be considered as well. Technologies such as para-virtualization and binary translation, as seen on more modern VMs such as Xen and VMware, used on COTS hardware platforms, are considerably more efficient than older machine emulators. In addition, remote public or hybrid clouds may be frequently oversold and their inner network structure may further reduce the overall cloud performance.

Having scalable computation performance as the primary optimization parameter, STAR currently retains an in-house computing facility. When resource demand outstrips available reserves workload can be offloaded to STAR collaboration Grid sites such as PDSF. If there is even a larger need then a cloud can be used, preferably private cloud.

Tests of Cloud Facilities

With so many promises and claims it is hard to compare cloud software stacks and facilities. If possible, the best thing to do is to run productions on each of the Grid and cloud implementations, to evaluate the benefits of each and build up expertise on what is available, (Lauret, Walker, Goasguen, & Hajdu, 2010; Lauret, Keahey, & Levente, 2011; Hazelhurst, 2008; Jackson et al., 2010). We have tested the following systems:

- Amazon+Nimbus or Nimbus+Grid resources;
- Amazon/EC2 native interface;
- Clemson Virtual Organization Cluster (VOC) model;
- Condor/VM scheduling (GLOW);
- Clemson Kestrel model.

STAR's first cloud adventure came by way of the Nimbus infrastructure used as a front end to Amazon's Elastic Compute Cloud (Amazon EC2). At the time when STAR ran production on Nimbus (Lauret, Walker, Goasguen & Hajdu, 2010; Lauret, Keahey & Levente, 2011), the software was relatively new. Since then it has been upgraded with additional and improved existing functionality.

The Nimbus software allows a user to launch essentially a full Grid site virtualized (Figure 12). There are worker node images, having the Portable Batch System (PBS) client software, and a gatekeeper image, using the Globus VDT software stack, acting as the PBS batch head, (Urban, 2010). The requester authenticates to the Nimbus client tools via a regular Grid proxy using the Globus grid-proxy-init command. They can upload or download Zen VM images, launch clusters and when finished teardown virtualized clusters all using command line commands on the client side.

Figure 12. Organization of Amazon EC2 with Nimbus interface model

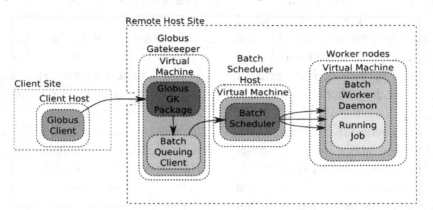

Once the user deploys a cluster, the cluster contextualizes. Contextualization is the initialization that is required at or after the VM image boots, before jobs can be submitted, involving actions such as:

- Nodes acquiring an IP addresses (dhcp);
- The download of updated information from the grid infrastructure, such as the Certificate Revocation Lists (or CRL);
- Worker nodes registering with the head node to receive jobs;
- Nodes mounting network disks, etc.

Host sites prepare site specific base images with different operating systems with contextualization pre-configured. On some models jobs cannot start running until the whole cluster is contextualized. Contextualization adds runtime overhead to the startup of the virtual computing cluster.

Because this site is essentially a fully virtualized Grid site, knowledge of Grid site operations and administration is simply transferred because responsibility for administrating the batch system and gatekeeper is transferred to the submitters. This function is in the non-virtualized traditional Grid model the responsibility of the facility operators. The benefit of this model is that the sites can be customized by the submitters to accommodate their needs. Unlike the traditional Grid sites

where use is opportunistic this model provides guaranteed dedicated slots.

STAR was able to use this site practically. Initially tests were done on a small 16 node cluster at the University of Chicago. For the Quark Matter conference a large simulation was required. It was decided that local resources were not available (busy with other tasks) to get the simulation done on time. The small cluster was seamlessly scaled-up to a 300-node cluster by changing the target location to Amazon's Elastic Compute Cloud for the production of 1 million Monte Carlo physics events. This production consumed over 25,000 processor hours (2 CPU years). At first the Amazon "Small Instance" nodes were used at a cost of 0.10 USD per node per hour (at the time of that production) however a "Medium Instance" was tested and it was determined to be a better value providing a little over twice the performance at 0.20 USD per node per hour. So a second cluster instance was prepared and while the cluster with the "Small Instance" nodes drained of jobs the "Medium Instance" cluster was filled. To complete the migration the "Small Instance" cluster nodes were released. Although the underlying hardware was not known an estimate was made that the "Small Instance" allocated two VMs per node. For jobs using only a fraction of the processor's capacity this is practical however as these jobs consume virtually all processor capacity, the performance can be divided by the number of VM instances with addition of some overhead. The data required for the conference was produced on time. This activity demonstrated the concept of offloading peak demand to the supporting cloud.

Important cloud production done by STAR used resources at Clemson University in a different model (Figure 13). The model would appear as a normal Grid site from the outside, presenting a standard Globus gatekeeper. However STAR would provide a custom image, into which Clemson would install a batch system client. When a job arrived at the site the submitter would be identified as requiring special action and instead of submitting the job to the batch system directly the batch system would start up the supplied VM (Figure 14). The client inside the VM would reg-

ister with the batch system head node and expect the job of the submitter. Once the job finished the sites software stack stops the VM and returns the node to normal native use. This cluster functioned as a hybrid in that it ran local native jobs as well as jobs requiring specialized infrastructure. From the end users perspective it models the Grid site perfectly, so there is no new learning of software required. The model allows for opportunistic use and does not require pre-allocation of nodes. From the site operators perspective the site proved more difficult to maintain because of the requirement to install clients and configure each image. So the model was tweaked and no client was installed.

Instead it would be the submitting sides (STAR's) responsibility to handle batch feeding of jobs. The allocation of nodes would still be

Figure 13. Clemson cloud (experimental model)

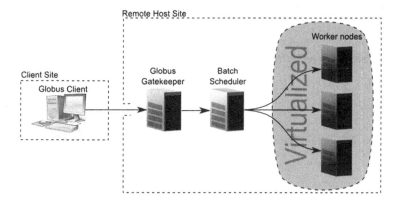

Figure 14. Condor: VM model

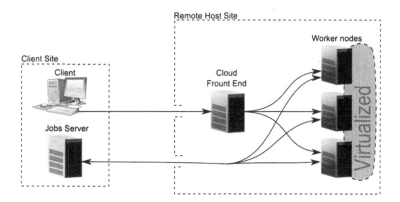

opportunistic (based on sites free capacity). This model was used to produce one of the largest Monte Carlo physics event productions ever recorded.

Next the same model was used for a reconstruction to fast-track the search for W-particles in newly taken raw detector data. This time two sites were used. Normally if two sites are used in a conventional Grid model the submitter makes a best guess estimate at the capacity of each site and splits up the workload in the appropriate ratio and submits the jobs to the batch system queues of each site. Because conditions on the site change dynamically the capacity estimate, even if based off current benchmarks will be off to some degree. This usually results in one site finishing its workload before the other and the requester having to wait for jobs on the slower site(s) to finish running. The benefit, when running with two or more sites, of having the batch system or job feeder on the submitting side is that work is

allocated as the jobs run, and the batch head sees all nodes across all clouds. This insures a global feedback loop where one suddenly slow site will not be over-burdened with excessive jobs. The better distribution provides for more efficient resource use and a quicker finish time for the last job to run (Figure 15).

The sites provided a hard allocation instead of working opportunistically. The model works in both modes. The two facilities used for this test were temporary government facilities erected to test the feasibility of running clouds. The name of the facility was Magellan it was deployed both at NERSC (National Energy Research Scientific Computing Center at Lawrence Berkeley National Laboratory in California) and ALCF (Argonne Leadership Computing Facility at Argonne National Laboratory in Illinois). The jobs where submitted from Massachusetts Institute of Technology (MIT) a STAR member institution.

Figure 15. Job pull-in model used with two sites

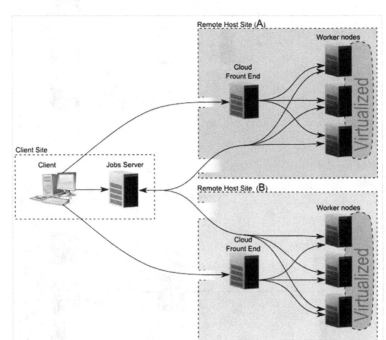

CONCLUSION

Faced with the massive data of more than one PB in size, and HPC processing problems, STAR experiment computing team is continuously working on the design and engineering of new more efficient and cost effective computing models, (The overall projected RHIC storage capacity for 2012 is over 30PB with processor capacity of over 60 MSI2k CPU metric units (Ernst, 2007).

Processing capacity of a cluster, Grid or cloud sites are commonly measured in referent units relative to Intel Pentium IV running at 3GHz (Marshall, 2010). The unit in question is known as kilo SpecInt2000 (kSI2k). Roughly, one modern quad-core processor has 2.1 kSI2k of computing capacity. For example, processor requirements at Tier-0 for first-pass reprocessing have been estimated therein to 3000 kSI2k or 3MSI2k, (rough computing work of 15kSI2k-seconds per event multiplied by 200 events per second).

Massive Monte Carlo simulation HPC jobs, such as STAR experiment, involve applications that generate extreme computing loads. Meeting the demands of such applications with the dedicated and permanently allocated massive computing infrastructure, would during the periods of low load shown in Figure 5, result in unnecessary waste. Optimal utilization and the economics of costly supercomputing sites justifies high level systems distribution solutions such as organization-virtualization Grid or system-virtualization of cloud computing.

Recent developmental efforts to better utilize and possibly optimize the use of available computing infrastructure have produced solutions such as clusters, Grid computing, virtualization and cloud computing. Widely advertised cloud computing has become a very attractive technology for rapid and flexible computing resource redistribution. On the higher end, the cloud has emerged as the next big trend after clusters and Grids Cloud computing numerous definitions, mostly high level and from the user interface point of view, to quote Winans

and Brown (Winans & Brown, 2009), frequently look "more nebulous than mnemonic." When contrasted to the concept of supercomputer Grid, this frequently not very well understood concept, is clarified in this chapter. No context can better be used to define cloud computing than Peta science computing such as the one employed by STAR experiment ar RHIC.

System size, computing power, distribution of resources and decentralized control, differentiates Grid computing from standalone cluster computing. Clusters are building blocks of supercomputers and Grid sites. Conceptually, cloud computing is not inclusive, not a substitute and not an extension of Grid computing. From the economics and computing job nature point of view, cloud computing can be viewed as complementary or sometimes as an alternative technology. Cloud dynamics of flexible acceptance of new loads of variable size (elasticity and granularity) is appealing to I/O bound enterprise applications, while efficient Grid solutions are more attractive for HPC processor-bound jobs.

With cloud computing as relatively new technology and well established Grid solutions, questions like "Is there a way to merge cloud and Grids?" or "Can Grid gain from virtual machine and cloud philosophy?" demand answers.

In this text we use computing power-hungry Monte Carlo simulation jobs of STAR experiment at RHIC, as one good illustrative example of Grid versus cloud computing puzzle resolution. Aside from many conveniences that cloud computing offers to mission and cost critical business enterprise jobs, in case of HPC scientific jobs, our current findings are that cloud based solutions have to complement the Grid of clusters. More precisely, recognizing cloud elasticity, we propose that cloud computing primarily serves as a backup or auxiliary support to Grid system for times when the peak computing power needs would exceed the free capacity of the Grid. Our point of view expressed here is, consistent with the IT market trends expressed by Gartner Inc., (The world leading IT market tracker). Namely, every year, during Gartner Symposium/ITxpo events, Gartner Inc. highlights and predicts the top 10 enterprise computing technologies and trends that will be strategic for most business organizations. Cloud computing, as the very first on the top 10 list of technologies for 2011 has lost in interest, ending as the last 10th on the list for 2012, (Gartner Newsroom, 2010; Gartner Newsroom, 2011). Our conservative acceptance of cloud computing as supporting auxiliary technology for HPC Peta scale scientific jobs is apparently accompanied by the sobering up of the IT market, and realistic recognition of cloud computing as maturing technology but not as a silver bullet for enterprise computing jobs.

ACKNOWLEDGMENT

The authors are thankful to their families for compassionate support during the production of this document.

REFERENCES

Amdahl, G. (1967). Validity of the single processor approach to achieving large scale computing capabilities. In *Proceedings of the AFIPS Spring Joint Computer Conference SE - AFIPS '67 (Spring)* (pp. 483-485). New York, NY: ACM.

Armbrust, M., Fox, A., Griffith, R., Joseph, A., et al. (2009). Above the clouds: A Berkeley view of cloud computing (Tech. Rep. UCB, 07-013). Berkeley, CA: University of California.

Bader, D. A. (Ed.). (2007). *Petascale computing: Algorithms and applications*. Boca Raton, FL: CRC Press. doi:10.1201/9781584889106

Buyya, R. (Ed.). (1999). *High performance cluster computing: Architectures and systems* (Vol. 1). Upper Saddle River, NJ: Prentice Hall.

Cary-1 Computer System. (1977). *Reference. Manual.*

(2011). *Electric Power Monthly Report: DOE/EIA-0226 (2011/12)*. Washington, DC: U.S. Energy Information Administration Office of Electricity, U.S. Department of Energy.

Ernst, M. (2007). *RHIC computing facility*. DOE/Nuclear Physics Review of RHIC Science and Technology.

Foster, I., & Kesselman, C. (1999). The globus toolkit. In *The grid: Blueprint for a new computing infrastructure* (pp. 259–278). San Francisco, CA: Morgan Kaufmann Publishers Inc.

Gartner Newsroom. (2010). *Gartner identifies the top 10 strategic technologies for 2011*. Gartner Symposium/ITxpo. Retrieved April 15, 2013, from http://www.gartner.com/it/page.jsp?id=1454221

Gartner Newsroom. (2011). *Gartner identifies the top 10 strategic technologies for 2012*. Gartner Symposium/ITxpo. Retrieved April 15, 2013, from http://www.gartner.com/it/page.jsp?id=1826214

Graham, S. L., Snir, M., & Patterson, C. A. (Eds.). (2005). *Getting up to speed: The future of supercomputing*. Washington, DC: National Academies Press.

Grimshaw, A. S., & Wulf, W. A. (1997). The legion vision of a worldwide virtual computer. *Communications of the ACM, 40*(1), 39–45. doi:10.1145/242857.242867

Gustafson, J. L. (1988). Reevaluating Amdahl's law. *Communications of the ACM, 31*(5), 532–533. doi:10.1145/42411.42415

Hazelhurst, S. (2008, October). Scientific computing using virtual high-performance computing: A case study using the Amazon elastic computing cloud. In *Proceedings of the 2008 Annual Research Conference of the South African Institute of Computer Scientists and Information Technologists on IT Research in Developing Countries: Riding the Wave of Technology* (pp. 94-103). New York, NY: ACM.

Jackson, K. R., Ramakrishnan, L., Muriki, K., Canon, S., Cholia, S., Shalf, J., & Wright, N. J. (2010, November). Performance analysis of high performance computing applications on the Amazon web services cloud. In *Proceedings of Cloud Computing Technology and Science (CloudCom), 2010 IEEE Second International Conference* (pp. 159-168). Washington, DC: IEEE Computer Society Press.

Kolmogoroff, A. (1931). Über die analytischen methoden in der wahrscheinlichkeitsrechnung. *Mathematische Annalen, 104*(1), 415–458. doi:10.1007/BF01457949

Lauret, J., Keahey, K., & Levente, H. (2011). *Clouds make way for STAR to shine, open science grid*. Retrieved April 15, 2013, from twiki.opensciencegrid.org/bin/view/Management/ResearchHighlight20

Lauret, J., Walker, M., Goasguen, S., & Hajdu, L. (2010). *From grid to cloud, the STAR experience*. Washington, DC: US Department of Energy, Office of Science.

Lo, J. L., Eggers, S. J., Levy, H. M., Parekh, S. S., & Tullsen, D. M. (1997). Tuning compiler optimizations for simultaneous multithreading. In *Proceedings of 30th Annual International Symposium on Microarchitecture*. Washington, DC: IEEE Computer Society Press.

Manhattan Project Hall of Fame Directory. (2005). The Manhattan Project Heritage Preservation Association, Inc. Retrieved April 15, 2013, from http://www.mphpa.org/classic/HICC/HICC_HF3.htm

Marshall, Z. (2010, April). Validation and performance studies for the ATLAS simulation. *Journal of Physics, 219*(3), 032016. doi:10.1088/1742-6596/219/3/032016

Message Passing Interface (MPI) Standard. (1995). *Message Passing Interface Forum*. The Physics of RHIC. Retrieved April 15, 2013, from www.bnl.gov/rhic/physics.asp

Metropolis, N. (1987). The beginning of the Monte Carlo method. *Los Alamos Science, 15*, 125–130.

Metropolis, N., & Ulam, S. (1949). The Monte Carlo method. *Journal of the American Statistical Association, 44*(247), 335–341. doi:10.1080/01621459.1949.10483310 PMID:18139350

Mihajlovic, R., Palande, U., & Mihajlovic, D. (2006, March). Practical approach to grid computing with multithreaded load balancing. In *Proceedings of YU INFO, XII Conference*. YU INFO.

Moore, G. E. (2006). Cramming more components onto integrated circuits. *Electronics, 38*(8).

Myhrvold, N. (1999). John von Neumann. *Time, 153*, 150–153.

Pfister, G. F. (1998). *In search of clusters* (Vol. 2). Englewood Cliffs, NJ: Prentice Hall PTR.

Popek, G. J., & Goldberg, R. P. (1974). Formal requirements for virtualizable third generation architectures. *Communications of the ACM, 17*(7), 412–421. doi:10.1145/361011.361073

Redin, J. (2012). *A brief history of mechanical calculators, part I: The age of the polymaths*. Retrieved from http://www.xnumber.com/xnumber/mechanical1.htm

Shi, Y. (1996). *Reevaluating Amdahl's law and Gustafson's law. Philadelphia* (pp. 38–24). MS: Computer Sciences Department, Temple University.

Sterling, T. L., & Zima, H. P. (2002). Gilgamesh: A multithreaded processor-in-memory architecture for petaflops computing. In *Proceedings of ACM/IEEE SC 2002 Conference* (SC'02). ACM/IEEE.

Strohmaier, E. (2011). *Japan reclaims top ranking on latest TOP500 list of world's supercomputers* (Press release). Retrieved from www.freerepublic.com/focus/f-chat/2737129/posts

Thomas, J. (2005). *The STAR detector at RHIC.* Berkeley, CA: Interdisciplinary Instrumentation Colloquium Lawrence Berkeley National Laboratory.

Urban, A. (2010). *PBS professional user's guide.* GridWorks, Altair Engineering, Inc.

IBM Virtual Machine Facility/370: Introduction. (1976). *IBM technical newsletters GN20-2677.* ILLIAC IV. (1974). Sumary Report.

Winans, T. B., & Brown, J. S. (2009). *Cloud computing: A collection of working papers.* Deloitte.

ADDITIONAL READING

Alford, T., & Morton, G. (2010). *The Economics of Cloud Computing - Addressing the Benefit of Infrastructure in the Cloud.* Retrieved September 15, 2013, from http://www.boozallen.com/media/file/Economics-of-Cloud-Computing.pdf

Balewski, J., Lauret, J., Olson, D., Sakrejda, I., Arkhipkin, D., & Bresnahan, J. etal. (2012). Offloading peak processing to virtual farm by STAR experiment at RHIC. [Bristol, UK: IOP Publishing.]. *Journal of Physics: Conference Series, 368*(1), 1–9.

Bell, K. L., Barrington, K. A., Crothers, D. S. F., Hibbert, A., & Taylor, K. T. (Eds.). (2002). *Supercomputing, Collision Processes, and Applications.* Dordrecht, Netherlands: Kluwer Academic Publishers. doi:10.1007/b100175

Christos Daillidis. (2004). *Establishing Linux Clusters for High-performance Computing (HPC) at NPS*, Thesis at Naval Postgraduate School Monterey. California.

Foster, I., & Kesselman, C. (Eds.). (1998). The Grid: Blueprint for a New Computing Infrastructure, 1st Ed. The Elsevier Series in Grid Computing. Burlington, MS: Morgan Kaufmann.

Hajdu, L., Didenko, L., & Lauret, J. (2010). Automation and Quality Assurance of the Production Cycle. [Bristol, UK: IOP Publishing.]. *Journal of Physics: Conference Series, 219*, 1–9.

Hajdu, L., & Lauret, J. (2006). Meta-Configuration for Dynamic Resource Brokering the SUMS Approach. *Tata Institiute of Fundamental Research, CHEP 06.* Retrieved April 15, 2013, from http://indico.cern.ch/contributionDisplay.py?contribId=144&sessionId=7&confId=048

Hwang, K., Fox, G. C., & Dongarra, J. J. (Eds.). (2012). *Distributed and Cloud Computing.* Burlington, MS: Morgan Kaufmann.

Johnson, F. (2007). Software Enabling Technologies for Petascale Science. *CT Watch Quarterly, 3(4),* Retrieved April 15, 2013, from http://science.energy.gov/~/media/ascr/pdf/program-documents/docs/Ctwatch_quarterly_13.pdf

Josyula, V., Orr, M., & Page, G. (Eds.). (2011). Cloud Computing: Automating the Virtualized Data Center, Networking Technology, 1 Ed. Indianapolis, In Cisco Press.

Lauret, J., Walker, M., Goasguen, S., Stout, L., Fenn, M., & Balewski, J. etal. (2011). When STAR meets the Clouds – Virtualization & Cloud Computing Experiences. *Journal of Physics: Conference Series, 368*(1), 1–8.

Lowendahl, J.-M. (2012). *A Quick Look at Cloud Computing in Higher Education.* Gartner Industry Research, ID:G00232738. Retrieved April 15, 2013, from http://blogs.darden.virginia.edu/cts/files/2012/05/Gartner-Cloud-Computing-in-Higher-Education-2012.pdf

Magoules, F. (Ed.). (2009). Fundamentals of Grid Computing: Theory, Algorithms and Technologies, 1 Ed. Chapman & Hall/CRC Numerical Analysis and Scientific Computing Series. Boca Raton, FL: CRC Press.

Magoules, F., Pan, J., Tan, K.-A., & Kumar, A. (Eds.). (2009). Introduction to Grid Computing, 1st Ed, Chapman & Hall/CRC Numerical Analysis and Scientific Computing Series. Boca Raton, FL: CRC Press.

Nadeau, T., & Gray, K. (Eds.). (2013). SDN: Software Defined Networks, 1 Ed. O'Reilly Media.

PRABHU. C.S.R. (Ed.) (2013). Grid and Cluster Computing. New Delhi, India: PHI Learning Private Limited.

Shukla, V. (Ed.). (2013). *Introduction to Software Defined Networking - OpenFlow & VxLAN.* CreateSpace Independent Publishing Platform.

Silva, V. (Ed.). (2005). Grid Computing for Developers (Programming Series), 1 Ed. Paperback. Stamford, CT: Cengage Learning.

Smith, J., & Nair, R. (Eds.). (2005). *Virtual Machines: Versatile Platforms for Systems and Processes. The Morgan Kaufmann Series in Computer Architecture and Design.* Burlington, MS: Morgan Kaufmann. doi:10.1016/B978-155860910-5/50002-1

Smoot, S. R., & Tan, N. K. (Eds.). (2012). Private Cloud Computing, - Consolidation, Virtualization, and Service-Oriented Infrastructure. Burlington, MS: Morgan Kaufmann.

Stout, L., Walker, M., Lauret, J., Goasguen, S., & Murphy, M. A. (2013). Using Kestrel and XMPP. to Support the STAR Experiment in the Cloud. *Journal of Grid Computing, 11*(2), 249–264. doi:10.1007/s10723-013-9253-8

The National Security Agency. (2009). An Overview of Cloud. *The Next Wave, 17*(4), 6–18.

Wilkinson, B. (Ed.). (2009). Grid Computing: Techniques and Applications, 1 Ed. Chapman & Hall/CRC Computational Science. Boca Raton, FL: CRC Press.

World Economic Forum. (2010). *Exploring the Future of Cloud Computing: Riding the Next Wave of Technology-Driven Transformation.* Retrieved September 15, 2013, from http://www.weforum.org/pdf/ip/ittc/Exploring-the-future-of-cloud-computing.pdf

Zerola, M., Barták, R., Lauret, J., & Šumbera, M. (2009). Using Constraint Programming to Plan Efficient Data Movement on the Grid. *In Proceedings of the 21st IEEE International Conference on Tools with Artificial Intelligence (ICTAI)* (pp. 729-733). Washington, DC: IEEE Computer Society Press.

KEY TERMS AND DEFINITIONS

Cloud Computing: Is on-demand general-purpose dynamic computing service distribution system. This definition generalizes Cloud computing previously defined as being service-based computing, scalable and elastic, shared, metered by use, and delivered using internet technologies.

Cluster: Is the preconfigured computing service distribution system powered by the computing and networking resources at one physical site.

Grid Computing: Is the preconfigured general-purpose static computing services distribution system powered by the managed computing resources from multiple physical locations.

High Performance Computing (HPC): Is a computing environment capable of delivering large processing capacity with low-latency large data storage in a form of a supercomputer, computer cluster, grid or cloud computing system. HPC also refers to a supercomputing environment in the teraflops (Trillion floating point operations per second) processing and the petabyte (1024 terabyte) storage range.

Multi-Core Processor: Is a single processing unit containing two or more single computing thread servicing units known as cores.

Petascale Science: Refers to the computation intensive scientific research requiring hardware performance in excess of one petaflops (i.e. one quadrillion floating point operations per second). Alternative definition assumes that the petascale science hardware performance must be sufficient to execute the standard LINPACK benchmark.

Power Wall: Is used to describe the limitation of CPU clock rate, CPU design, and CPU performance improvements due to the thermal and electrical power constraints, i.e., technological inability to use higher clock rates, more transistor switching elements, to use higher volumes of electrical energy and inability to maintain overall thermal stability.

Semiconductor Wall: Is a CPU capacity limitation factor representing semiconductor technology problems in manufacturing of switching transistor devices of reduced dimensions, able to use lower signal voltage levels and higher signaling rates.

Software Pressure (Sp) Factor: Is a modern computing technology market driving phenomena, manifested as almost exponential market demand for higher throughput and lower cost systems, running software of increased complexity and processing larger volumes of data.

Von Neumann Bottleneck (VNB): Is the computing system throughput limitation due to inadequate rate of data transfer between memory and the CPU. The VNB causes CPU to wait and idle for a certain amount of time while low speed memory is being accessed. The VNB is named after John von Neumann, a computer scientist who was credited with the invention of the bus based computer architecture. To allow faster memory access, various distributed memory "non-von" systems were proposed.

Chapter 14
Model of Interoperable E–Business in Traffic Sector based on Cloud Computing Concepts

Slađana Janković
University of Belgrade, Serbia

Snežana Mladenović
University of Belgrade, Serbia

Slavko Vesković
University of Belgrade, Serbia

ABSTRACT

This chapter analyzes the possibilities of applying the cloud concepts in the realization of the interoperable electronic business of traffic and transport subjects. Special attention is paid to defining the Business-to-Business (B2B) model of integrating the traffic business subjects in cloud computing technological environment. It describes the design, implementation, and application of the cloud concepts on the examples of B2B integration in the field of traffic. The examples demonstrate the usage of Platform-as-a-Service (PaaS) and Software-as-a-Service (SaaS) by traffic business subjects in the Republic of Serbia. The examples of PaaS are the databases created and hosted on Microsoft SQL Azure platform. The examples of SaaS are Web services hosted on Microsoft Windows Azure platform. The defined model of B2B integration allows interoperability of the traffic business subjects on the syntactic, conceptual, and semantic level.

INTRODUCTION

The notion of interoperability, in general, refers to the possibility of two systems to exchange information, as well as to make use of the exchanged

DOI: 10.4018/978-1-4666-5784-7.ch014

information. The interoperability is not a product; it is a property of a system (Janković, 2010). In the context of business systems and applications the interoperability has been defined as the capability of a system or a product to work seamlessly with other system or product not requiring any special efforts by the customer or user (Naudet, Latour,

Guedria, & Chen, 2010). The applications that have been developed independently (at a different time, by different teams, using different technologies) even within the same enterprise experience problems in exchanging data (Janković et al., 2011). The problem is of the same nature, but significantly magnified, when interoperability of e-business of several different organizations needs to be realized (Mladenović & Janković, 2011; Sehgal, Erdelyi, Merzky, & Jha, 2011).

Traffic and transport systems are heterogeneous systems which share information in their operation. Therefore, it is necessary to achieve the interoperability of their information systems (Janković, Mladenović, Radonjić, Kostić-Ljubisavljević, & Uzelac, 2011). The subject of research in this chapter is the definition of the model of interoperable electronic business of traffic business systems. The model has been based on the combination of the known methods of Business-to-Business (B2B) integration: integration of information, integration on the basis of services and portal integration (Radonjic, Jankovic, Mladenovic, Veskovic, & Kostic-Ljubisavljevic, 2011). The methods of B2B integration have been implemented within the cloud computing technological environment. A case study has been done as part of this chapter using as example organizations from the domain of traffic safety in the Republic of Serbia. A solution has been developed as the result of the case study, on Microsoft Windows Azure platform (Jennings, 2009; Li, 2010), which allows B2B integration of three traffic business subjects.

The following sections present the structure of the model of interoperable electronic business and the scenarios of B2B integration based on the proposed model. The implementation of the B2B integration methods based on the use of the cloud computing concepts has been described. The chapter is concluded with the analysis of the proposed model.

BACKGROUND

Traffic and transport systems are the very complex systems, so they are organizationally divided into a great number of units, such as directorates, sectors, services, etc. (Lee, Tseng, & Shieh, 2010). Each organizational unit uses applications and databases designed to meet their specific needs. It is not uncommon that one particular entity from the real system is modelled in multiple databases that are used in different organizational units (Radonjic, Jankovic, Mladenovic, Veskovic, & Kostic-Ljubisavljevic, 2011). An organizational unit of one transport systems often use the data generated and updated by another organizational unit. On the railways, for example, work of the Sector for transportation of goods and passengers is based on the data given by the Directorate of Infrastructure (data on construction, electrotechnical, telecommunication and transport infrastructure and its maintenance), the Department for maintenance of rolling stock and the Department for towing trains (Janković & Mladenović, 2012). In addition, each unit uses its own databases and applications. This creates redundancy and inconsistency of data. This means that cooperation between organizations and/or organizational units are often based on reports that have different syntax and semantics. To avoid redundancy and inconsistency of data and to avoid incompatible reports, it is necessary to enable the B2B integration of organizations and different organizational units of one traffic and transport system.

In defining the legal and institutional frames of integration, two basic types of B2B integrations are distinguished:

- **Horizontal B2B Integrations:**
  Integrations of entities which consider the common domain with approximately equal level of abstraction.

- **Vertical B2B Integrations:** Integrations of entities which consider the common domain with significantly different levels of abstraction (Lampathaki et al., 2009).

In practice, during B2B integration of two organizations usually the horizontal and the vertical integration are combined (Janković & Mladenović, 2012). The reason for this is that the organizations usually consider in one segment of their business the common domain with approximately the same level of abstraction, whereas in other segments of their operation the view of the real system differs significantly.

Depending on whether pure horizontal integration, pure vertical integration, or combined – hybrid integration is meant, also the frames of B2B integration are distinguished. Horizontal B2B integration is suitable in case of:

- Integration of organizations that belong to the same level within the same sector (commercial, public, or government sector);
- Integration of organizations that belong to the same level, within different sectors.

Vertical B2B integration is suitable in case of integration of organizations that belong to different levels within the same sector. Hybrid B2B integration is suitable in case of integration of organizations that belong to different levels within different sectors.

B2B Integration Model

We propose the B2B integration model of traffic business systems which consists of the following components:

C1: B2B integration system architecture;
C2: Development activities of B2B integration systems;
C3: Software architecture of B2B integration systems;

C4: Scenarios of B2B integration of traffic business systems;
C5: Methods of B2B integration of traffic business systems;
C6: Time planning of model realization.

Figure 1 presents the detailed structure of each of the components of B2B integration model, as well as their interrelations.

Creation of Common Information Model

The analysis of the existing information systems is the first step in the development of a new, common information model. The analysis of the current information system consists of the following activities: analysis of hardware and software infrastructure, analysis of the real system, analysis of the relations of the business system and other subjects from the domain, defining of the requirements regarding B2B integration (Janković, Milojković, Mladenović, Despotović-Zrakić, & Bogdanović, 2012). The process of creating an information model starts by getting familiar with the data. The objective is to understand the existing state of the data, and then the final future data architecture, which let us understand which data need to be located on local servers, and which on the cloud computing platform (Li, Chen, & Wang, 2011). The entire analysis is performed from the aspect of applying the service-oriented architecture (Erl, 2009) with new architectural options of cloud computing (Linthicum, 2010). This means that the following needs to be determined: where the data are currently located, the structure of the data, the logic model, the physical model, the solving of the security issues, etc.

The first step in identifying and locating the information about the data is to make a list of the systems in the domain of the issue. This list makes it possible to determine what types of databases exist within these systems. The next step requires determination of the database owners, their physi-

Figure 1. Structure of the proposed model of B2B integration of traffic business systems

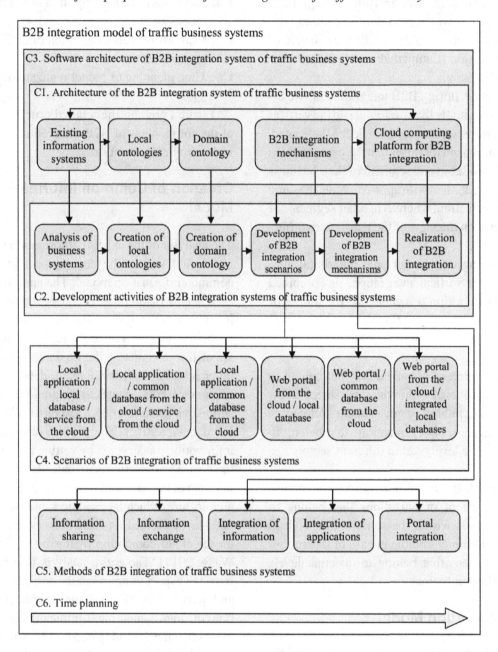

cal locations, etc. A traffic data glossary for each single system individually has to be created.

When analyzing the database which is a candidate for cloud computing, questions come up regarding the integrity of data. Data delay is yet another characteristic of data which has to be determined before the transfer to cloud com-

puting. Such information allows the architect to determine when the information should be copied or transferred from cloud to the local server of the company, or from the local server to the cloud, and how fast.

The cataloguing of traffic data represents formalization of information collected in the previous two steps. The data glossaries refer to one system or application, whereas the data catalogue contains all the systems in a domain. The data catalogue means the list of potential solutions of the observed architectural problem, and the information model means the final solution of the data architecture.

Creation of Local Ontologies and Domain Ontology

The aim of local ontology is to describe the knowledge relevant to the business domain of the studied traffic business system (Janković, Mladenović, Vesković, Mitrović, & Milinković, 2012). The phase of creating local ontologies is equivalent to the phase of creating the glossary and the catalogue of the traffic data. Therefore, these two phases are best realized simultaneously. One of the ways that allows efficient creation of local ontology is on the basis of the local database scheme (Gardner, 2005). If a certain system uses several databases, they have to be modelled within the local ontology.

The domain ontology is created with the aim of presenting the knowledge relevant to the studied domain (Staab & Studer, 2009). The activities that are part of the domain ontology creation are identical to the activities that make up the creation of local ontologies. The only difference lies in the choice of the method of creating the ontology. The most efficient method of creating

the local ontologies is the mapping of the database schemes (Kalfoglou & Schorlemmer, 2003). The domain ontology is created by integrating the existing local ontologies (Gelernter, 2011). When creating the domain ontology, one has to take into account the classes from all the local ontologies, links between them and all the properties of the classes. The domain ontology should represent also the relations that exist in real world between the concepts of local ontologies.

Development of B2B Integration Scenarios

Scenario 1: Local application of one traffic business system downloads data from the local base of another traffic business system by calling the service from the cloud (Figure 2).

Scenario 2: Local application of traffic system downloads data from the common database by calling the service (Figure 3).

Scenario 3: The user accesses data from the common base via user interface of the local application (Figure 4).

Scenario 4: The user accesses data from the local base via common user interface - Web portal in the cloud (Figure 5).

Scenario 5: The user accesses data from the common base via Web portal in the cloud (Figure 6).

Figure 2. Diagram of sequences: Scenario 1 of B2B integration of traffic business systems

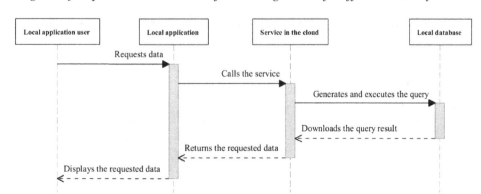

Figure 3. Diagram of sequences: Scenario 2 of B2B integration of traffic business systems

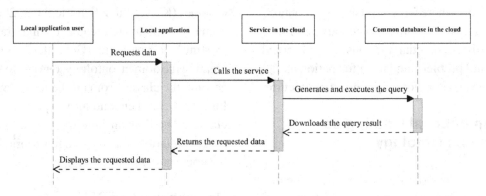

Figure 4. Diagram of sequences: Scenario 3 of B2B integration of traffic business systems

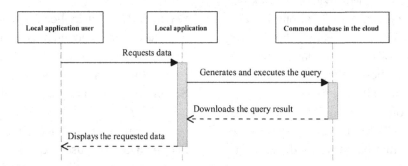

Figure 5. Diagram of sequences: Scenario 4 of B2B integration of traffic business systems

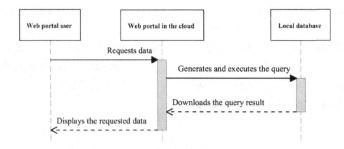

Figure 6. Diagram of sequences: Scenario 5 of B2B integration of traffic business systems

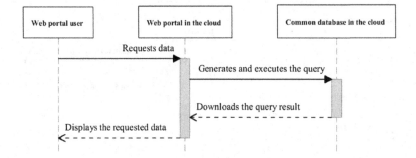

Scenario 6: Using Web portal in the cloud the user creates queries that are executed over the integrated data which originate from several local databases (Figure 7).

Two traffic business systems can select even several scenarios of B2B integration. The selection of the integration scenario depends on the nature of the business relations and interdependence of two traffic business subjects, i.e. on the defined requirements of the B2B integration. If there are several B2B integration requirements between two traffic business subjects, the most favourable integration scenario will be selected for each requirement.

Architecture of Cloud Computing Platform for B2B Integration

Architecture of cloud computing platform for B2B integration of traffic business systems has been presented in Figure 8. It consists of:

- Common database hosted on SQL Azure platform;
- Web portal hosted on Windows Azure platform;

- Windows Communication Foundation (WCF) Data services (Sharp, 2010) for downloading data from the common database, hosted on Windows Azure platform;
- WCF Data services for downloading data from the local databases, hosted on Windows Azure platform;
- WCF Data services for the transformation of queries hosted on Windows Azure.

Defining of Solution Development Phases

All the solutions of the B2B integration of traffic-transport business subjects can be classified into three big classes:

- Solutions based on the integration of the existing information and applications,
- Solutions based on the development of new databases and applications,
- Solutions based on the integration of the existing and new applications.

The approaches to solving and the development phases are different for the three classes of solutions. Regardless of the class to which the solution

Figure 7. Diagram of sequences: Scenario 6 of B2B integration of traffic business systems

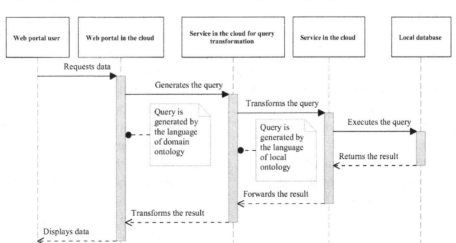

Figure 8. Architecture of cloud computing platform for B2B integration of traffic subjects

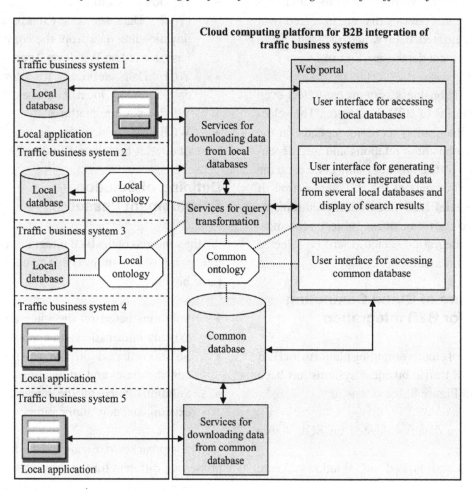

belongs, the proposed model of B2B integration means the development of the service-oriented solution in the cloud computing environment.

For the solutions based on the integration of the existing information and applications, the "bottom-up" approach is suitable. The integration of the existing applications requires the development of Web services as required. Therefore, the development of this category of solutions begins with the analysis of the application services. The modeling of application services should result in the definition of the requirements by the applications that can be fulfilled by using Web services.

For the solutions based on the development of new databases and applications the "top-down" approach is suitable. In this approach, first comes the analysis of the requests and business models of B2B integration subjects. It promotes not only the service-oriented development of the business processes, but also the creation (or harmonization) of the overall business organization model. This process has been derived from the existing business organization logics, and it results in the creation of a large number of business and application services. The part of the process that has the formation of ontology as consequence, represents the classification of the sets of information processed by one organization. This results in the creation of a common glossary, as well as in defining the relations existing between certain groups of data.

After having established the ontology, the existing business models have to be adapted and harmonized with ontology, and in many cases completely new business models need to be created, for the glossary defined by ontology to be validly represented by the business modelling terminology (Janković, Kostić-Ljubisavljević, Radonjić, & Mladenović, 2012).

The solutions of B2B integration based on the integration of the existing and new applications are the most complicated ones. For the solutions based on the integration of the existing and new applications the agile strategy is suitable. In comparison with the previous two approaches, this approach is the most complex one since it has the task to fulfil two sets of opposed requirements. The agile strategy is based on the parallel analysis of the business processes and service development. The biggest challenge is to find the balance in the implementation of the principle of service-oriented design in the business analysis environment. This strategy is also called "meeting-in-the-middle" approach.

Example of B2B Integration Solution in Traffic Sector According to the Proposed Model

Based on the proposed model of B2B integration of traffic business systems a solution of B2B integration of subjects in the field of traffic safety in the Republic of Serbia has been realized. The solution that has been realized as an example of the implementation of the proposed model allows interoperable electronic operation of the following subjects: Ministry of the Interior (MUP), Public enterprise "Putevi Srbije" (JPPS) and "Železnice Srbije" (Serbian Railways).

The organizations that work on raising the traffic safety level must have at their disposal data about the road infrastructure. JPPS has the most complete database about the road infrastructure. In order to have an insight into the spatial distribution of traffic accidents, MUP has to use the database about the road infrastructure. The "Železnice Srbije" have the need for the data about the road

infrastructure in order to raise the level of traffic safety on the railroad crossings. The development and implementation of the B2B integration solutions according to the proposed model enables the mentioned organizations to share and exchange data and services.

The essence of the proposed solution lies in the fact that every pair of business systems should select the scenario, or those scenarios of B2B integration which best satisfy their needs, and which are realized on the basis of the following principles:

- The existing databases that are used by the studied business systems, which have a similar structure and purpose, will be integrated into one common base located on the cloud computing platform;
- The Web portal is set on the cloud computing platform and it contains the user interface for updating the common base and for setting the queries over it. The tasks of updating the base will be divided among the studied business systems, in compliance with their jurisdiction and competence. The authorizations regarding query generation over the common base will be defined for every business system;
- The existing applications that are used by the studied business systems, currently operate over local databases set on their servers and generate diverse reports that represent the decision-making support. The proposed solution plans for some of these applications to download in the future the necessary data from the common database from the cloud;
- The existing local applications will download data from the common database which is located in the cloud, using the WCF Data services hosted in the cloud;
- The local databases that have not been integrated in the common base, and whose data the business systems want to share, will be

accessed by means of the Web portal hosted on the cloud computing platform;

- The local application of one business system will use the data from the local database of another business system, by calling WCF Data services hosted in the cloud;
- The local applications will be improved by the development of the user interface for accessing the common database in the cloud.

WCF Data services are elegant Microsoft technology for data publishing, either from the database from the local servers or from the databases in the cloud (Betts et al., 2010). They may be hosted on local Web servers or on the servers from the cloud. The application which uses the WCF Data service can be Desktop application, Web application hosted on the local Web server, or Web application hosted as a service in the cloud (Chou et al., 2010).

The phases in the development of the solution of the B2B integration of traffic business systems:

- Identification of business subjects that need to be included in the B2B integrations;
- Analysis of institutional and business relations between the selected subjects;
- Defining of the solution requirement of the B2B integration for every pair of traffic systems that needs to realize the integration;
- Development of local ontologies that represent the business domain of every single organization;
- Development of the common domain ontology;
- Defining of one or several scenarios of B2B integration for every pair of the traffic systems that need to realize the integration;
- Defining of mechanisms for the realization of the selected scenarios of B2B integration for every pair of traffic business systems;

- Implementation of components that allow the realization of the selected mechanisms of B2B integration;
- Analysis of the realization effects of B2B integration for every single traffic business system;
- Analysis of the realization effects of B2B integration for the entire safety domain in traffic.

The railroad crossings are controlled from the aspect of infrastructure and from the aspect of traffic safety. In order to determine correctly the adequate type of security for a crossing one needs to have data on the current condition of the crossing, traffic volume and crossing safety parameters. All the listed categories of data about the railroad crossings are unified in the SQL Azure database Serbian railroad crossings (Figure 9).

The Web portal Serbian Railroad Crossings is hosted on the Windows Azure platform and it is intended for updating and using of data about the traffic safety on the railroad crossings in the Republic of Serbia. The Web portal Serbian Railroad Crossings has been developed in the integrated development environment Visual Studio 2010, as WindowsAzureProject. By publishing the WindowsAzureProject, the service serbian railroad crossings of WebRole type has been created (Figure 10).

Serbian Railroad Crossings Web portal allows:

- Centralized updating and preview of data about the crossings;
- Centralized updating and preview of data about the volume and structure of the traffic on the railroad crossings;
- Calculation of safety parameters of the railroad crossings.

In accordance with the purpose, Web portal contains the common user interface for updating data about the railroad crossings as well as for the

Figure 9. Table traffic accident from SQL Azure database Serbian railroad crossings

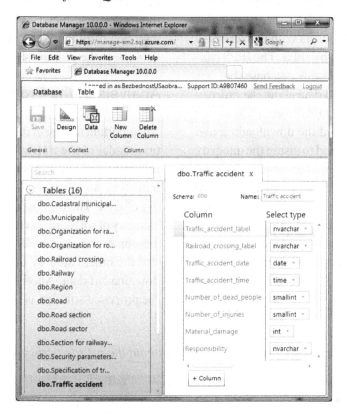

Figure 10. Service Serbian railroad crossings hosted on Windows Azure platform

generation of queries about the safety parameters of the railroad crossings. The user interface of Web portal provides the users with the access to the local database owned by JPPS. The JPPS cannot independently update this database, but has to occasionally download data about the railroad crossings from the Serbian Railways ("Železnice Srbije"). In order to avoid the downloading and the redundancy of data, and to insure the integrity of data, Web portal allows the employed at the "Železnice Srbije" to access the database on the JPPS server and to update this local base in compliance with the authorization. In this way every organization updates those data about the railroad crossings for which it has been authorized, without the need for mutual data exchange. Web portal allows also other interested subjects to access the data about the railroad crossings, to generate their safety parameters. Figure 11 shows the user interface from the Web portal for the preview of data about the crossings.

Analysis of the Proposed Model

An important feature of the proposed B2B integration model of the traffic business systems is the reliability and nearly complete elimination of the human factor in making errors during the updating of data. The proposed model means that one category of software services downloads data from a common base, as well as local databases, and that the other category of services processes the downloaded data. Another significant feature of the proposed solution is the centralized updating

Figure 11. User interface for the presentation of data about the railroad crossings

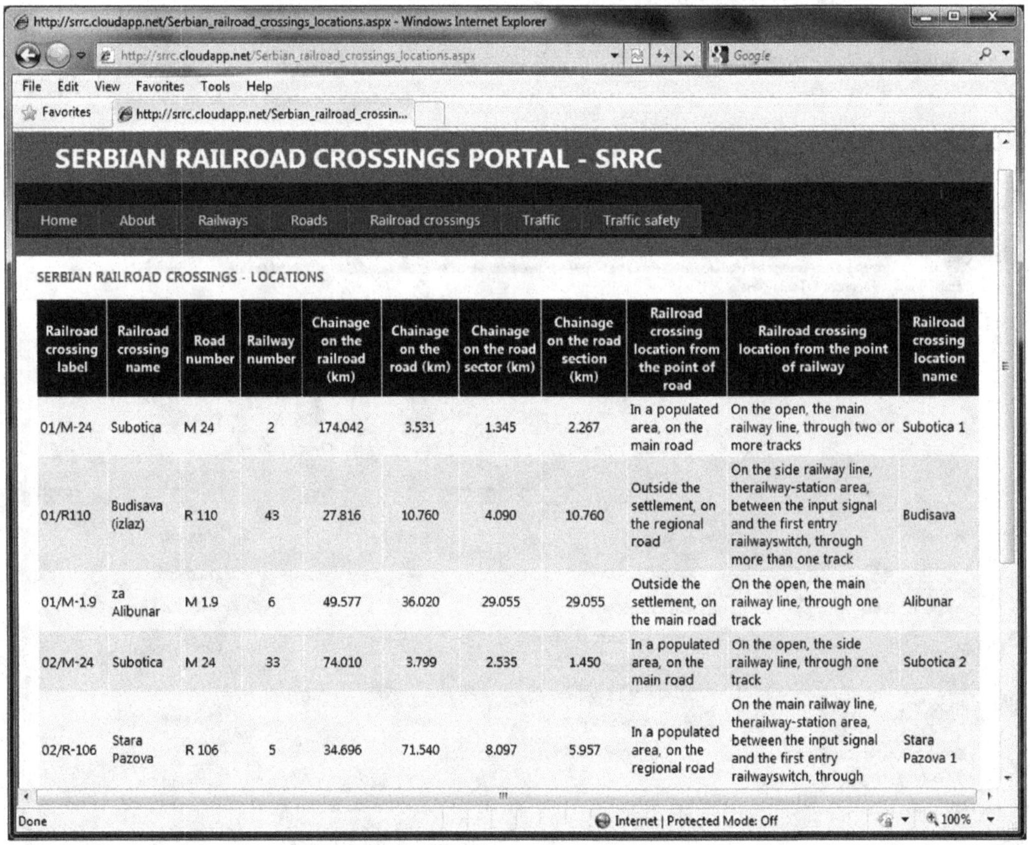

Railroad crossing label	Railroad crossing name	Road number	Railway number	Chainage on the railroad (km)	Chainage on the road (km)	Chainage on the road sector (km)	Chainage on the road section (km)	Railroad crossing location from the point of road	Railroad crossing location from the point of railway	Railroad crossing location name
01/M-24	Subotica	M 24	2	174.042	3.531	1.345	2.267	In a populated area, on the main road	On the open, the main railway line, through two or more tracks	Subotica 1
01/R110	Budisava (izlaz)	R 110	43	27.816	10.760	4.090	10.760	Outside the settlement, on the regional road	On the side railway line, therailway-station area, between the input signal and the first entry railwayswitch, through more than one track	Budisava
01/M-1.9	za Alibunar	M 1.9	6	49.577	36.020	29.055	29.055	Outside the settlement, on the main road	On the open, the main railway line, through one track	Alibunar
02/M-24	Subotica	M 24	33	74.010	3.799	2.535	1.450	In a populated area, on the main road	On the open, the side railway line, through one track	Subotica 2
02/R-106	Stara Pazova	R 106	5	34.696	71.540	8.097	5.957	In a populated area, on the regional road	On the main railway line, therailway-station area, between the input signal and the first entry railwayswitch, through	Stara Pazova 1

and sharing of data by means of a common user interface, which reduces to a large extent the need for data exchange.

The proposed solution allows semantically interoperable electronic business (Kalfoglou, 2010), since it is based on the common information model. The common information model is based on the common data model. The common data model has been developed on the basis of the common shared glossary and domain ontology. The domain ontology is the basis for consistent interpretation of the meaning of meta-data and data values (Verstichel et al., 2011).

Regarding hardware and software infrastructure, the proposed solution means the usage of information infrastructure from the cloud. This means that the users of the proposed solution are not obliged to purchase any additional hardware, nor do they have to buy any software licences (Rimal, Choi, & Lumb, 2010). The service-oriented architecture, which is the basis of the solution, allows the integration of the applications developed on different platforms. It may be concluded that the proposed solution does not require development of new local applications and databases, but rather allows the usage of the existing information systems. The integration of applications requires initialization and calling of WCF services, which does not require any major interventions in their code.

The proposed solution is based on the usage of two types of services from the cloud: platform as a service and software as a service. All types of services that may be used within cloud computing technological environment, have in common that they are paid "per usage" and that only the part that is actually used and to the extent to which it is used is charged (Furht, 2010).

For each proposed B2B integration scenario, experiments have been carried out. The first group of experiments consisted in the testing of the Web portal functionality. The access to the common data integrated in the SQL Azure database by means of the common user interface integrated in

the Web portal has been tested. It has been shown that the portal is reliable and that the data located in the cloud can be accessed instantly. The user subjective perception while using the portal in the cloud does not differ from the perception when using Web applications hosted on the application servers outside the cloud. The reason lies also in the fact that the portal has been developed in a development environment that has a long tradition and generates a recognizable visual setting. The accessibility of the database from the cloud did not show any problems either throughout the duration of portal developing and testing.

Also, the access to local SQL Server databases has been tested, directly from the Web portal in the cloud via common user interface. Web portal generates the SQL query and forwards it to the local SQL Server database. The data which represent the result of the query are displayed within the user interface of the Web portal. The duration of the response of the local base to the set queries does not differ significantly from the duration of the response of the database from the cloud.

The integration of the application from the cloud and the standard Web application by means of the WCF Data service has been tested as well. The response of the WCF Data services to the request from the mentioned application has been tested. No problems have been noted in this scenario of B2B integration either. The application shows data downloaded by the WCF Data services from the local base, as well as from the database from the cloud, within a unique user interface. It has been noted that the data from the cloud appear a little faster than the data from the local base.

The results of the experimental analysis are positive. All the components of the information infrastructure from the cloud have proven to be reliable. The speed at which the common database from the cloud generates the query results is also satisfactory. However, two downsides have nevertheless been noted. One lies in the fact that the usage of the SQL Azure platform for the needs of database testing is being charged. The second problem refers to the hosting of the services in the cloud. This procedure may take even up to several hours, and the result is uncertain. The speed of setting services on the cloud computing platform depends on the current busyness of the hardware in the cloud.

The proposed solution has been implemented on the Microsoft development platform. Web portal and all the Web services have been developed in the integrated development environment Microsoft Visual Studio 2010. The existing applications that have been integrated with new applications have been developed in the development environment Microsoft Visual Studio 2008. The existing local databases have been created in the relation system for database management Microsoft SQL Server 2008. The common database has been developed on Microsoft SQL Azure platform, which represents the relation system for database management in the cloud (Krishnaswamy, 2010). The conclusion is that all Microsoft tools and development environments allow the development of software components that feature excellent cooperation. The ease with which the connection between either Windows or Web application with SQL Azure database is established is encouraging. The connection is created in the same way in which the connection with the local SQL Server databases is created. From the aspect of implementation, the fact that SQL Azure databases can be created by the migration of the existing SQL Server databases is especially useful. It is only necessary to create the database script and to run it on the SQL Azure platform.

Another important feature of the proposed solution from the aspect of implementation is that during the development of the applications of the type WindowsAzureProject, which are hosted in the cloud, Visual Studio 2010 offers support for testing the applications locally. This support has been realized through Windows Azure SDK. By installing this tool the Visual Studio 2010 receives the support in the form of components:

Compute Emulator and Storage Emulator. These two components simulate the components with the same names on the Windows Azure platform. This allows the programmer to test the applications in the integrated development environment in the same way as in the case of any other type of application, without any additional efforts.

The implementation of the proposed solution of B2B integration allows interoperability of the traffic business systems at the level of: data, services, business processes, and operation. The interoperability of data is realized by sharing the information from the heterogeneous sources of data, stored on different machines, under different operating systems, and in different database management systems. The interoperability of the services is enabled by composing different applicative functions to work together, although they had been designed and implemented independently. The interoperability of the business processes has been realized by unifying the service sequences in order to realize a certain business activity. The interoperability of operation has been enabled by the harmonization of cooperation of organizations in the domain of traffic, regardless of the differences in: the decision-making method, working methods, legal acts on the basis of which they function.

The proposed solution exceeds all three categories of barriers to business system interoperability: conceptual, technological, and organizational barriers. The conceptual barriers refer to the syntactic and semantic differences of information that are being exchanged (Vernadat, 2010). These problems have been solved by unifying different models of data, used by the studied traffic business systems, into a unique domain data model. The technological barriers refer to the impossibility to connect the information technologies. These problems have been solved by using common standards for presenting, storing, exchange, and processing of data. The organizational barriers refer to the definition of responsibilities and authorities, and they are solved by defining the legal and contractual frame. The common database and the services in the cloud are used in accordance with the pre-determined user authorities.

FUTURE RESEARCH DIRECTIONS

The traffic business systems here do not include only the enterprises that perform transportation services, but rather also all non-traffic subjects that in some way enable and insure the realization of the transportation service. All the subjects that have the need for B2B integration in the field of traffic in the Republic of Serbia can be classified into the following categories:

- Traffic and transport companies,
- Public enterprises managing traffic infrastructure,
- Authorized ministries and other relevant Government organizations for handling business of the government administration in the field of traffic and transport.

Figure 12 shows the frame of B2B integrations in the sector of traffic and transport. Our future research will be in the area of developing models of interoperable e-business on the following types of relations:

- Commercial Sector-Commercial Sector (C-C),
- Commercial Sector-Public Sector (C-P),

Figure 12. Frame of B2B integrations in the sector of traffic and transport

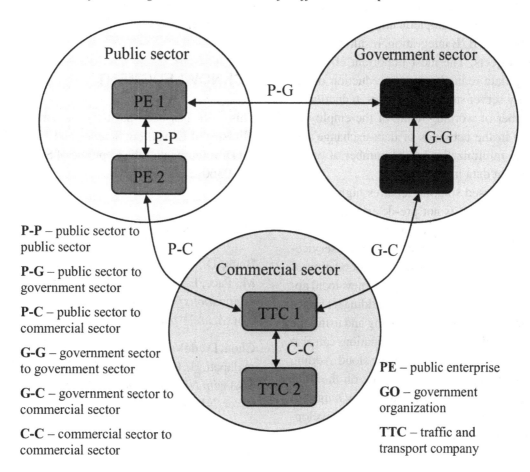

P-P – public sector to public sector

P-G – public sector to government sector

P-C – public sector to commercial sector

G-G – government sector to government sector

G-C – government sector to commercial sector

C-C – commercial sector to commercial sector

PE – public enterprise

GO – government organization

TTC – traffic and transport company

- Commercial Sector-Government Sector (C-G),
- Public Sector-Public Sector (P-P),
- Public Sector-Government Sector (P-G),
- Government Sector-Government Sector (G-G).

CONCLUSION

The most significant effect of implementing the proposed solution of the B2B integration is more efficient, more reliable and semantically interoperable electronic business of the B2B integration participants. The implementation of the proposed B2B integration model will improve the efficiency of electronic business by replacing the manual exchange of information by the automated exchange of information at the level of information systems. Reducing the redundancy of data is the basic effect of implementing the proposed solution of the B2B integration, resulting also in the side effects. The most important effects of reducing data redundancy are: reduction of the necessary server storage capacities, reduction of the number of working hours of the employees involved in the activities of data exchange and updating, minimization of the number of errors occurring at data input.

The proposed solution features high level of flexibility since it is not pre-determined by the number of B2B integration participants. The flexibility is the basic characteristic of the service-oriented architecture which is the foundation of this solution. Both the existing and new local applications can use this solution by adding reference to the adequate service, initializing and using the service from the cloud. New applications can also access the common database in the cloud. Adding new applications – database users, on the SQL Azure platform is done by adding new ranges of IP addresses from which the application developers can access the database.

The B2B integration model that has been proposed in this chapter can be used both for the needs of B2B integration of the Government organizations and the organizations from the public sector. Many small and mid-size enterprises that form a part of the transportation chains have no possibility of investing into ready-made commercial solutions that allow efficient data exchange. On the other hand, their need to exchange data is no less than the need shown by the big companies. The solution based on the usage of cloud computing services does not require high initial financial investments, which makes it applicable for the small and mid-size enterprises as well.

Every scientific and expert research requires the availability of huge amounts of data, usually from heterogeneous sources. The application of the proposed solution in the sphere of scientific and expert research in the field of traffic would significantly improve the efficiency of the research teams.

ACKNOWLEDGMENT

This work has been partially supported by the Ministry of Education, Science and Technological Development of the Republic of Serbia under No. 036012.

REFERENCES

Betts, D., Densmore, S., Dunn, R., Narumoto, M., Pace, E., & Woloski, M. (2010). *Developing applications for the cloud on the Microsoft® Windows Azure™ platform*. Redmond, WA: Microsoft.

Chou, D., deVadoss, J., Erl, T., Gandhi, N., Kommalapati, H., Loesgen, B., & Williams, M. (2010). *SOA with .NET and Windows Azure*. Upper Saddle River, NJ: Prentice Hall.

Erl, T. (Ed.). (2009). *SOA design patterns*. Boston: Prentice Hall.

Furht, B. (Ed.). (2010). *Handbook of cloud computing*. New York: Springer. doi:10.1007/978-1-4419-6524-0

Gardner, P. S. (2005). Ontologies and semantic data integration. *Drug Discovery Today*, *10*(14), 1001–1007. doi:10.1016/S1359-6446(05)03504-X PMID:16023059

Gelernter, J. (2011). Use of ontologies for data integration and curation. *International Journal of Digital Curation*, *6*(1), 70–78. doi:10.2218/ijdc.v6i1.173

Janković, S. (2010). Interoperability of transport business systems based on the integration of service-oriented B2B applications. *Info M*, *36*, 4–12.

Janković, S., Kostić-Ljubisavljević, A., Radonjić, V., & Mladenović, S. (2012). Semantic interoperability models in B2B integrations. In B. Zajc & A. Trost (Ed.), *The 21st international electrotechnical and computer science conference – ERK 2012* (vol. 2, pp. 71-74). Ljubljana, Slovenia: IEEE Region 8, Slovenia Section IEEE.

Janković, S., Milojković, J., Mladenović, S., Despotović-Zrakić, M., & Bogdanović, Z. (2012). Cloud computing framework for B2B integrations in the traffic safety area. *Metalurgia International*, *17*(9), 166–173.

Janković, S., & Mladenović, S. (2012). B2B integration models in cloud computing environment. *Info M*, *43*, 26–32.

Janković, S., Mladenović, S., Mitrović, S., Pavlović, N., & Aćimović, S. (2011). A model for integration of railway information systems based on cloud computing technology. In B. D. Milovanović (Ed.), *ICEST 2011 - XLVI international scientific conference on information, communication and energy systems and technologies* (vol. 3, pp. 833-836). Niš, Serbia: Faculty of Electronic Engineering University of Niš.

Janković, S., Mladenović, S., Radonjić, V., Kostić-Ljubisavljević, A., & Uzelac, A. (2011). Integration platform-as-a-service in the traffic safety area. In M. Banat (Ed.), MIC-CNIT 2011 - Mosharaka international conference on communications, networking and information technology (pp. 70-75). Dubai, UAE: Mosharaka for Researches and Studies.

Janković, S., Mladenović, S., Vesković, S., Mitrović, S., & Milinković, S. (2012). A model of semantic interoperable e-business of traffic business systems. In G. Ćirović (Ed.), *XXXIX symposium on operational research - SYM-OP-IS '12* (pp. 75-78). Belgrade, Serbia: Visoka Građevinsko-Geodetska Škola, Belgrade.

Jennings, R. (Ed.). (2009). *Cloud computing with the Windows® Azure™ platform*. Indianapolis, IN: Wiley Publishing, Inc.

Kalfoglou, Y. (Ed.). (2010). *Cases on semantic interoperability for information systems integration: Practices and applications*. New York: Information Science Reference.

Kalfoglou, Y., & Schorlemmer, M. (2003). Ontology mapping: The state of the art. *The Knowledge Engineering Review*, *18*(1), 1–31. doi:10.1017/S0269888903000651

Krishnaswamy, J. (Ed.). (2010). *Microsoft SQL Azure: Enterprise application development*. Birmingham, UK: Packt Publishing.

Lampathaki, F., Mouzakitis, S., Gionis, G., Charalabidis, Y., & Askounis, D. (2009). Business to business interoperability: A current review of XML data integration standards. *Computer Standards & Interfaces*, *31*(6), 1045–1055. doi:10.1016/j.csi.2008.12.006

Lee, W.-H., Tseng, S.-S., & Shieh, W.-Y. (2010). Collaborative real-time traffic information generation and sharing framework for the intelligent transportation system. *Information Sciences*, *180*(1), 62–70. doi:10.1016/j.ins.2009.09.004

Li, H. (Ed.). (2010). *Introduction to Windows Azure*. New York: Apress.

Li, Z. J., Chen, C., & Wang, K. (2011). Cloud computing for agent-based urban transportation systems. *IEEE Intelligent Systems, 26*(1), 73–79. doi:10.1109/MIS.2011.10

Linthicum, D. (Ed.). (2010). *Cloud computing and SOA convergence in your enterprise*. Boston: Pearson Education.

Mladenović, S., & Janković, S. (2011). Integration of traffic information systems in cloud computing environment. In M. Bakmaz et al. (Ed.), *XXIX symposium on novel technologies in postal and telecommunication traffic - PosTel 2011* (pp. 305-314). Belgrade, Serbia: Faculty of Transport and Traffic Engineering University of Belgrade.

Naudet, Y., Latour, T., Guedria, W., & Chen, D. (2010). Towards a systemic formalisation of interoperability. *Computers in Industry, 61*, 176–185. doi:10.1016/j.compind.2009.10.014

Radonjic, V., Jankovic, S., Mladenovic, S., Veskovic, S., & Kostic-Ljubisavljevic, A. (2011). B2B integration of rail transport systems in cloud computing environment. In N. Marchetti (Ed.), *The 4th international symposium on applied sciences in biomedical and communication technologies - ISABEL '11*. New York: ACM Digital Library.

Rimal, B. P., Choi, E., & Lumb, I. (2010). A taxonomy, survey, and issues of cloud computing ecosystems. In N. Antonopoulos, & L. Gillam (Eds.), *Cloud computing: Principles, systems and applications* (pp. 21–46). London, UK: Springer. doi:10.1007/978-1-84996-241-4_2

Sehgal, S., Erdelyi, M., Merzky, A., & Jha, S. (2011). Understanding application-level interoperability: Scaling-out MapReduce over high-performance grids and clouds. *Future Generation Computer Systems, 27*(5), 590–599. doi:10.1016/j.future.2010.11.001

Sharp, J. (Ed.). (2010). *Windows® communication foundation 4 step by step*. Sebastopol, CA: O'Reilly Media, Inc.

Staab, S., & Studer, R. (Eds.). (2009). *Handbook on ontologies*. Berlin, Germany: Springer-Verlag. doi:10.1007/978-3-540-92673-3

Vernadat, F. B. (2010). Technical, semantic and organizational issues of enterprise interoperability and networking. *Annual Reviews in Control, 34*(1), 139–144. doi:10.1016/j.arcontrol.2010.02.009

Verstichel, S., Ongenae, F., Loeve, L., Vermeulen, F., Dings, P., & Dhoedt, B. et al. (2011). Efficient data integration in the railway domain through an ontology-based methodology. *Transportation Research Part C, Emerging Technologies, 19*(4), 617–643. doi:10.1016/j.trc.2010.10.003

ADDITIONAL READING

Acuña, C. J., Minoli, M., & Marcos, E. (2010). Integrating Web Portals with Semantic Web Services. *International Journal of Enterprise Information Systems, 6*(1), 57–67. doi:10.4018/jeis.2010120205

Batarliene, N., & Jarašūniene, A. (2009). Research on advanced technologies and their efficiency in the process of interactions between different transport modes in the terminal. *Transport, 24*(2), 129–134. doi:10.3846/1648-4142.2009.24.129-134

Bean, J. (Ed.). (2010). *SOA and Web Services Interface Design: Principles, Techniques, and Standards*. Burlington, USA: Elsevier Inc.

Bhatia, R., & Wier, M. (2011). Safety in Numbers re-examined: can we make valid or practical inferences from available evidence? *Accident; Analysis and Prevention, 43*(1), 235–240. doi:10.1016/j.aap.2010.08.015 PMID:21094319

Buccella, A., & Cechich, A. (2003). An Ontology Approach to Data Integration. *Journal of Computer Science & Technology*, 3(2), 62–68.

Buyya, R., Yeo, C. S., Venugopal, S., Broberg, J., & Brandic, I. (2009). Cloud computing and emerging IT platforms: Vision, hype, and reality for delivering computing as the 5th utility. *Future Generation Computer Systems*, 25(6), 599–616. doi:10.1016/j.future.2008.12.001

Cardoso, J., & Bussler, C. (2011). Mapping between heterogeneous XML and OWL transaction representations in B2B integration. *Data & Knowledge Engineering*, 70(12), 1046–1069. doi:10.1016/j.datak.2011.07.005

Chen, D., Doumeingts, G., & Vernadat, F. (2008). Architectures for enterprise integration and interoperability: Past, present and future. *Computers in Industry*, 59(7), 647–659. doi:10.1016/j.compind.2007.12.016

Cheng, S. (Ed.). (2010). *Microsoft Windows Communication Foundation 4.0 Cookbook for Developing SOA Applications*. Birmingham, UK: Packt Publishing.

Chituc, C.-M., Azevedo, A., & Toscano, C. (2009). A framework proposal for seamless interoperability in a collaborative networked environment. *Computers in Industry*, 60(5), 317–338. doi:10.1016/j.compind.2009.01.009

Cruz, I., & Xiao, H. (2005). The role of ontologies in data integration. *Jounal of Engineering Intelligent Systems*, 13(4), 1–18.

Erl, T. (Ed.). (2005). *Service-Oriented Architecture: Concepts, Technology, and Design*. New Jersey, USA: Prentice Hall.

Erl, T. (Ed.). (2008). *SOA: Principles of Service Design*. Boston, USA: Prentice Hall.

Juric, M. B., Loganathan, R., Sarang, P., & Jennings, F. (2007). *SOA Approach to Integration XML, Web services, ESB, and BPEL in real-world SOA projects*. Birmingham, UK: Packt Publishing.

Karacapilidis, N., Lazanas, A., Megalokonomos, G., & Moraïtis, P. (2006). On the development of a web-based system for transportation services. *Information Sciences*, 176(13), 1801–1828. doi:10.1016/j.ins.2005.05.007

Marston, S., Li, Z., Bandyopadhyay, S., Zhang, J., & Ghalsasi, A. (2011). Cloud computing - The business perspective. *Decision Support Systems*, 51(1), 176–189. doi:10.1016/j.dss.2010.12.006

Mentzas, G. (Ed.). (2010). *Semantic enterprise application integration for business processes: service-oriented frameworks*. New York, USA: Business Science Reference.

Panetto, H., & Molina, A. (2008). Enterprise integration and interoperability in manufacturing systems: Trends and issues. *Computers in Industry*, 59(7), 641–646. doi:10.1016/j.compind.2007.12.010

Peng, Z.-R., & Kim, E. (2008). A Standard-Based Integration Framework for Distributed Transit Trip Planning Systems. *Journal of Intelligent Transportation Systems*, 12(1), 13–28. doi:10.1080/15472450701849642

Puustjärvi, J. (2010). Semantic Interoperability in Electronic Business. *International Journal of Computer Science Issues*, 7(5), 51–63.

Rimal, B. P., Jukan, A., Katsaros, D., & Goeleven, Y. (2010). Architectural Requirements for Cloud Computing Systems: An Enterprise Cloud Approach. *Journal of Grid Computing*, 9(1), 3–26. doi:10.1007/s10723-010-9171-y

Rodero-Merino, L., Vaquero, L. M., Gil, V., Galán, F., Fontán, J., Montero, R. S., & Llorente, I. M. (2010). From infrastructure delivery to service management in clouds. *Future Generation Computer Systems*, *26*(8), 1226–1240. doi:10.1016/j.future.2010.02.013

Rosen, M., Lublinsky, B., Smith, K. T., & Balcer, M. J. (Eds.). (2008). *Applied SOA: Service-Oriented Architecture and Design Strategies*. Indianapolis, USA: Wiley Publishing.

Roshen, W. (Ed.). (2009). *SOA-Based Enterprise Integration: A Step-by-Step Guide to Services-Based Application Integration*. New York, USA: The McGraw-Hill Companies.

Scale, M.-S. E. (2009). Cloud computing and collaboration. *Library Hi Tech News*, *26*(9), 10–13. doi:10.1108/07419050911010741

Serrano Orozco, J. M. (Ed.). (2012). *Applied Ontology Engineering in Cloud Services, Networks and Management Systems*. London, UK: Springer. doi:10.1007/978-1-4614-2236-5

Shariati, M., Bahmani, F., & Shams, F. (2011). Enterprise information security, a review of architectures and frameworks from interoperability perspective. *Procedia Computer Science*, *3*, 537–543. doi:10.1016/j.procs.2010.12.089

Stanoevska-Slabeva, K., Wozniak, T., & Ristol, S. (Eds.). (2010). *Grid and Cloud Computing*. Berlin, Germany: Springer-Verlag. doi:10.1007/978-3-642-05193-7

Subashini, S., & Kavitha, V. (2011). A survey on security issues in service delivery models of cloud computing. *Journal of Network and Computer Applications*, *34*(1), 1–11. doi:10.1016/j.jnca.2010.07.006

Vetere, G., & Lenzerini, M. (2005). Models for semantic interoperability in service-oriented architectures. *IBM Systems Journal*, *44*(4), 887–903. doi:10.1147/sj.444.0887

Vidal, V., Pinheiro, J., & Sacramento, E. (2009). An Ontology-Based Framework for Heterogeneous Data Sources Integration. *Revista de Informática Teórica e Aplicada*, *16*(2), 61–64.

Vujasinovic, M., Barkmeyer, E., Ivezic, N., & Marjanovic, Z. (2010). Interoperable Supply-Chain Applications: Message Metamodel-Based Semantic Reconciliation of B2B Messages. *International Journal of Cooperative Information Systems*, *19*(01 & 02), 31–69.

Vujasinovic, M., Ivezic, N., Kulvatunyou, B., Barkmeyer, E., Missikoff, M., & Taglino, F. et al. (2010). Semantic mediation for standard-based B2B interoperability. *IEEE Internet Computing*, *14*(1), 52–63. doi:10.1109/MIC.2010.17

Zhu, Y., Wang, J., & Wang, C. (2011). Ripple: A publish/subscribe service for multidata item updates propagation in the cloud. *Journal of Network and Computer Applications*, *34*(4), 1054–1067. doi:10.1016/j.jnca.2010.06.002

KEY TERMS AND DEFINITIONS

Application Integration: The process of bringing data or a function from one application together with that of another application.

B2B Integration Technology: The software technology that is the infrastructure to connect any back-end application system within enterprises to all its trading partners.

Cloud Computing Concepts: Involve a large number of computers connected through a real-time communication network such as the Internet.

E-Business: The application of information and communication technologies in support of all the activities of business.

Interoperability: The ability of diverse systems and organizations to work together.

Ontology: A formally representation of knowledge as a set of concepts within a domain, and the relationships between those concepts.

Semantic Interoperability: The ability of computer systems to transmit data with unambiguous, shared meaning.

Service-Oriented Architecture (SOA): A software design and software architecture design pattern based on discrete pieces of software that provide application functionality as services.

Software-as-a-Service (SaaS): A software delivery model in which software and associated data are centrally hosted on the cloud.

Traffic Sector: The enterprises that perform traffic and transportation services, but rather also all non-traffic subjects that in some way enable and insure the realization of the transportation service.

Chapter 15
Dot Net Platform for Distributed Evolutionary Algorithms with Application in Hydroinformatics

Boban Stojanović
Faculty of Science, University of Kragujevac, Serbia

Miloš Ivanović
Faculty of Science, University of Kragujevac, Serbia

Nikola Milivojević
"Jaroslav Černi" Institute for the Development of Water Resources, Serbia

Dejan Divac
"Jaroslav Černi" Institute for the Development of Water Resources, Serbia

ABSTRACT

Real-world problems often contain nonlinearities, relationships, and uncertainties that are too complex to be modeled analytically. In these scenarios, simulation-based optimization is a powerful tool to determine optimal system parameters. Evolutionary Algorithms (EAs) are robust and powerful techniques for optimization of complex systems that perfectly fit into this concept. Since evolutionary algorithms require a large number of time expensive evaluations of candidate solutions, the whole process of optimization can take huge CPU time. In this chapter, .NET platform for distributed evaluation using WCF (Windows Communication Foundation) Web services is presented in order to reduce computational time. This concept provides parallelization of evolutionary algorithms independently of geographic location and platform where evaluation is performed. Hydroinformatics is a typical representative of fields where complex systems with many uncertainties are studied. Application of the developed platform in hydroinformatics is also presented in this chapter.

1. INTRODUCTION

The evolutionary algorithms (EAs) are stochastic search methods that simulate the process of natural evolution. These algorithms have proven themselves as a robust and powerful mechanism when it comes to solving challenging optimization problems.

DOI: 10.4018/978-1-4666-5784-7.ch015

Evolutionary algorithm mimics the process of natural evolution, by modifying the set of potential solutions, called population, through selection, crossover and mutation of individuals. In order to select best candidates for reproduction, one has to determine the fitness of each individual in the population by evaluating it with respect to each objective. Each evaluation of the solution for the real-world problem usually requires running a complex, time consuming computer simulation, and so the use of distributed computing is a necessity.

Different approaches for the use of parallelism in evolutionary algorithms for optimization have been proposed in the literature and surveys have been written (Jaimes & Coello, 2009; Talbi et al., 2008). Three major parallel models of EAs exist: the master-slave model, the island model and the diffusion model.

In the master-slave model the objective functions evaluations are distributed among several slave processors, while a master processor executes the rest of EA. In the island model, the population is divided into several sub-populations (islands) and serial EA is executed in each of these islands for a number of generations called an epoch. At the end of each epoch, the individuals migrate between the neighboring islands along migration paths. Inter-processor communication frequency in this model is low, but modeling requires many parameters and design decisions. In the diffusion model, the population is spatially distributed onto a neighborhood structure which is usually a two-dimensional rectangular grid. There is a single individual per grid point and ideally, one processor per individual. Therefore, this model is called fine grained. The selection and mating is confined to a small neighborhood around each individual, and since individuals which take part in the selection are distributed among several processors, the communication costs tend to be high.

The purpose of this chapter is to introduce a platform for distributed evaluation of individuals in evolutionary algorithms based on the master-slave model. The evaluations of the individuals are performed by Windows Communication Foundation (WCF) web services. WCF is a part of .NET Framework which provides unified programming model for rapidly building service-oriented applications that communicate across the web. Although the platform is developed using .NET technology, mainly as a support to the existing .NET hidroinformation system widely used in leading hydro-energetic institutions in Serbia and

Republic of Srpska, it can be seamlessly integrated into any existing evolutionary framework.

The rest of the hapter is organized as follows: in section 2 we review related work, while section 3 describes the proposed platform. Application of the platform in hydroinformatics and discussion of achieved performances improvements are given in Section 4. Some concluding remarks are presented in the last section.

2. RELATED WORK

There are several protocols and libraries which provide aid in the development of parallel systems, by hiding some of the network connection and transmission details. The most important are MPI and OpenMP. MPI, the Message Passing Interface, is the standard for development of parallel codes on the distributed memory systems, whereas OpenMP (Open Multi-Processing) is the standard in shared memory systems (Dagum & Menon, 1998; Message Passing Interface Forum, 2009). The parallelization and distribution functionality in evolutionary software packages is often built on top of libraries implementing MPI, like in Simdist (Hoverstad, 2010) and ParadisEO (Cahon, Melab, & Talbi, 2004).

Grid technologies support the sharing and coordinated use of diverse resources in dynamic virtual organizations. The Globus toolkit is an open-source, community-based set of software tools to enable the aggregation of compute, data, and other resources to form computational grids. Multi population algorithm using master-slave parallel model in a Globus toolkit based grid environment was implemented in (Limmer & Fey, 2010). Implementation of the framework requires selection of certain parameters: the number of subpopulations, the size of the subpopulations, the number of migrants in an optimization step, and the number of the generations that are computed in a single optimization step. ParadisEO-CMW (Cahon, Melab, & Talbi, 2005), which is re-designed ParadisEO, provides a rich set of parallelization strategies. But it is only intended for grids consisting of multiple Condor pools combined via flocking. This form of grid is not as popular as Globus based grids and it is questionable if it can be seen as a grid in the commonly accepted meaning at all. JG2A (Bernal, Ramirez, Castro, Walteros, & Medaglia, 2009) was created as an extension of JGA (Medaglia & Gutiérrez, 2006) to take advantage of grid technologies, allowing instances parallelization and population evaluation parallelization. JG2A uses the Globus Toolkit 4 grid middleware, but requires Condor as underlying scheduler on the different sites. This makes it inflexible because, in general, other local resource managers than Condor are used at different computing sites of a grid and these sites may be under different administrative control (which makes it hard to enforce the deployment of Condor on all those sites). In (Shenfield & Fleming, 2005) authors implement grid-enabled framework MOGA-G for multi-objective optimization in a Service-Oriented Architecture using the Globus Toolkit. In the implementation of the MOGA-G framework there are two different services. One service exposes the operations of the multi-objective genetic algorithm to the client, and the other provides operations for running evaluations of the objective function on the computational grid. Another SOA approach to the implementation of parallel evolutionary algorithms can be found in (Lim, Ong, Jin, Sendhoff, & Lee, 2007). Two-level hierarchical parallel genetic algorithm has been implemented in a distributed computational Grid, with multiple subpopulations distributed across the Grid resources. The evaluation of candidate solutions in these subpopulations is then performed using the Master-Slave paradigm. In (Luna, Nebro, & Alba, 2006), Globus was used to develop gPAES, a Grid extension of the PAES algorithm. In the gPAES, the search model of consists in remotely executing a number of sequential PAES algorithms (separately exploring the whole search space) on machines of the Grid

and locating the best solutions according to a previously defined metrics. In (Mostaghim, Branke, Lewis, & Schmeck, 2008), the authors propose hybrid method using Multi-objective Particle Swarm optimization and Binary search methods in order to overcome the problem of long waiting time of the master processor in a heterogeneous environment. However, the implementation of the method requires selecting certain parameter, which depends on the heterogeneous resources and the estimated load on them.

To the best of our knowledge, there exists no previous framework for distributed evaluation in EAs that uses WCF web services.

3. PROPOSED PLATFORM

The service-oriented distribution of evaluation imposed the use of master-slave model as the most convenient way to parallelize the evolutionary algorithm. This model aims at distributing the (objective function) evaluation of the individuals to several slave computing resources, while the master node executes the rest of the algorithm in sequential fashion. In terms of web services, the client acts the role of the master node (by generating and varying the population), and the service acts the role of the worker (by evaluating the individuals). One drawback of the master-slave model is the communication overhead between the processors. Here, we ignore this issue, as we aim to solve very expensive optimization problems.

We developed a distribution subsystem to be inserted as an intermediate layer between the main evolutionary loop on the master, and the evaluation of individuals which takes place on slaves. The master is unaware of the number of slaves evaluating individuals, and which slave evaluates which individual. Each time the generation has to be evaluated, the distribution subsystem is started in a separate thread.

The main part of distribution subsystem is the evaluation pool. When master sends individuals to evaluation, they are being queued in the evaluation pool, and its job is to distribute them to the available web services and to assign evaluation result to the corresponding individual.

EvaluationPool is an abstract class that serves as the base for deriving specific classes, which perform evaluation out of main thread. Every evaluation pool contains queue where solutions sent to evaluation are collected. It also has various methods for manipulating the queue. Evaluation pool can be in one of three states: *idle*, *busy* and *error*.

For evaluation using distributed web services, the class *EvaluationPoolMultiWS* was developed. This class inherits class *EvaluationPool* and represents intermediate between software that performs evaluations and available web services. The role of this class is to take solutions from the evaluation queue and send them to free web services. It also has duty to receive values of fitness functions from the web services and to store them into collections inside each solution.

Every instance of *EvaluationPoolMultiWS* class receives list of available web services as an argument of the constructor. All web services must implement interface *IEvaluate*. The class uses the *thread* pool provided by the .NET Framework through the *ThreadPool* class (How to: Use a Thread Pool (C# Programming Guide). A thread pool is a collection of threads that can be used to perform a number of tasks in the background. As many individuals as there is available web services are assigned to those web services in the separate threads from the thread pool (Figure 1). That way, evaluations can be processed asynchronously, without tying up the primary thread of evaluation pool or delaying the processing of subsequent requests. Each thread calls web service on network computer and sends to it the solution that has to be evaluated. When evaluation of the solution is done, the result is returned to the client application and assigned to the solution. Once a thread in the pool completes its task, it is returned to a queue of waiting threads and can be reused later

Figure 1. Structure of the proposed platform

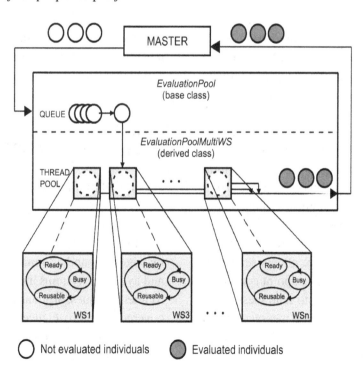

as well as the corresponding web service which completed the evaluation. This reuse enables applications to avoid the cost of creating a new thread for each task. The evaluation pool remains in the *busy* state as long as there are solutions waiting for evaluation in the queue. Once all web services return results and there are no more solutions in the queue, the evaluation pool changes its state to *idle* and send signal to the main thread that all evaluations are done.

If any of web services raises exception and evaluation of the solution fails, the same solution is sent to the first free web service. In order to avoid repetitive errors on problematic web service, the evaluation pool does not send solutions to that service for some time. This way, problematic web service is not fully eliminated from the evaluation, but is given a chance to be recovered.

The developer of the evolutionary system has to separate the evaluation step from the rest of the evolutionary algorithm loop, but has no concern with the details of distributing individuals and retrieving evaluations results. It is the task of the distribution subsystem to distribute individuals as efficiently as possible among the slave nodes, and gather the results. Calling method *Wait* of the *EvaluationPool* class it is provided to set synchronization points in the main algorithm. This way, the main thread of the algorithm remains on hold until all the solutions sent to evaluation are evaluated.

Web services we use for evaluation are set up using Windows Communication Foundation (WCF). WCF is a framework for building service-oriented applications (Chappell, 2010; Skonnard, 2006). It is designed to support distributed computing, where remote services can be consumed by multiple clients. Services expose one or more endpoints where clients send messages to request work. Each endpoint consists of an address specifying where to send messages, a binding describing how to send messages, and a contract describing what the messages contain. WCF includes predefined bindings for most com-

mon communication protocols such as SOAP over HTTP, SOAP over TCP, and SOAP over Message Queues, etc. Interaction between WCF endpoint and client is performed using a SOAP envelope. SOAP envelopes comply with a simple XML form that makes WCF platform independent.

Services use Web Services Description Language (WSDL) to share endpoint descriptions with clients, so any WCF client can consume the service, regardless of which platform the service is hosted on. WCF supports interoperability with WCF applications running on the same Windows machine or WCF running on a various Windows machines or standard Web services built on platforms such as Java running on Windows or other operating systems.

We defined a .NET interface *IWcfEvaluationService* to serve as the service contract and implemented the service contract in a .NET class *WcfEvaluationService*, known as the service type, to configure its behavior. The task our web service is to be able to perform evaluation of an individual it receives from client. The method Evaluate that serves as the operation contract accepts *JobParameters* – individual to evaluate, and returns *EvaluationResult*. Complex types that we used for the method parameters and return values must have a data contract defined for them to be serializable.

4. APPLICATION IN HYDROINFORMATICS

Hydroinformatics

Wide area of different tasks related to sustainable development, maintenance, improvement, control, management and administration of hydrological and hydraulic systems including the related environmental issues, of aquatic systems in general are covered by hydroscience and hydroengineering. Utilizing modern Information and Communication Technology (ICT), Hydroinformatics gives support to hydroscience and hydroengineering (Cunge, 1998). The theoretical foundation of Hydroinformatics has been given by Abbott (Abbott, 1991; Abbott, 1994) and other authors (Price, Ahmad, & Holz, 1998).

Hydroinformatics uses simulation modeling, and information and communication technology to help in solving problems of hydraulics (Grujović, Divac, Stojanović, Stojanović, & Milivojević, 2009), hydrology (Simić, Milivojević, Prodanović, Milivojević, & Perović, 2009) and environmental engineering for better management of water-based systems (Kojic et al., 2007). It provides the computer based decision-support systems that now enter increasingly into the offices of engineers, water authorities and government agencies. Many of water-related issues require solving an optimization problem, and some of the real-world examples follow.

Current advances in modeling point out that it is essential to take into account multiple fitting criteria, which correspond to different observed responses or to different aspects of the same response. This can be achieved through multi-objective optimization tools, thus providing a set of solutions rather than a single global optimum. There are some examples of multi-objective optimization problems in hydroinformatics:

- Find such release of the reservoir(s) with a hydropower dam that would lead to a maximum yearly production of the electrical power, and satisfy the water consumers downstream (Labadie, 2004; Milivojević, Divac, Vukosavić, Vučković, & Milivojević, 2009).
- Identify and present to a decision maker several rehabilitation plans for a drainage (or combined sewer) system that would a) lead to smaller (ideally, minimum) flood damages in case of heavy rain falls, and b) keep within the budget constraints (the lower the costs the better) (Barreto, Vojinovic, Price, & Solomatine, 2009).

- Find an optimal groundwater remediation strategy leading to a smallest possible concentration of a pollutant (or concentration below a certain limit) in a given time frame (smaller the better) (Maskey, Jonoski, & Solomatine, 2002).
- Find a combination of models, knowledge sources and human experts that would solve a particular water management problem in an optimal way.

Optimization techniques and tools complement the arsenal of the modeling tools, and play an important role in Hydroinformatics. Hydroinformatics serves the various stakeholders and integrates various data sources (remote sensing, ground measurements etc.), various types of models, and management and decision support processes. Future use of hydroinformation systems depends of further development of the software tools making this whole process effective and efficient. Using High Performance Computing and even computational grids is not a new topic in the field of hydrology and hydroinformatics. The volume of data to exploit and the modeling require more and more computing resources (CPUs and storage). Many data centers have developed service tools based on Web services for basic research activities like searching, discovering, browsing and downloading of datasets, but applications need not only to access various geographically-distributed data sets, but also to access directly the needed computing resources (Lecca et al., 2011).

Calibration of Hydrological Models

One of the possible applications of the platform for distributed evolutionary algorithms is calibration of hydrological models for rainfall-runoff calculations. Problem of hydrological model calibration can be defined as follows: for a hydrologic model, find the values of the parameters (which cannot be measured) which would lead to the smallest possible error of this model (Solomatine, Dibike,

& Kukuric, 1999; Milivojević, Simić, Orlić, Milivojević, & Stojanović, 2009). Theoretical background of the hydrological model applied in hydro-information system Drina (HIS Drina) (Divac, Grujović, Milivojević, Stojanović, & Simić, 2009; Divac, Prodanovic, & Milivojević, 2009) as well as the methodology and results of calibration of the proposed model using distributed evolutionary algorithms will be presented in this section.

Theoretical Background

For the purposes of HIS Drina, physically based, hydrodynamic hydrological model has been developed based on SWAT model (Arnold & Fohrer, 2005). The model requires a large number of input parameters: meteorological, topographic, pedological, parameters regarding vegetation, etc. In this model a watershed is divided into multiple subwatersheds, which are then further subdivided into hydrologic response units (HRUs) that consist of homogeneous land use, management, and soil characteristics (Figure 2). The HRUs represent percentages of the subwatershed area and are not identified spatially within a simulation. Spatial

and temporal discretization depends on input parameters accuracy. Climatic inputs used in the model include daily precipitation, maximum and minimum temperature, solar radiation data, relative humidity, and wind speed data, which can be input from the measured records and/or generated. The overall hydrologic balance is simulated for each HRU, including canopy interception of precipitation, partitioning of precipitation, snowmelt water, and irrigation water between surface runoff and infiltration, redistribution of water within the soil profile, evapotranspiration, lateral subsurface flow from the soil profile, and return flow from shallow aquifers.

In the Figure 2, distributed hydrological model based on network of HRUs is presented schematicaly. Basic hydrologic elements (HRUs) are parts of the system where basic vertical water balance components are calculated. Calculated surface flow Qsurf and percolation Wperc, are drained to adjacent linear reservoirs which are components of the horizontal water flow that transfer water to the outlet junction. Details of vertical and horizontal water balance calculation are given in (Simić, Milivojević, Prodanović, Milivojević, & Perović, 2009).

Figure 2. Schematic view of the distributed hydrological model

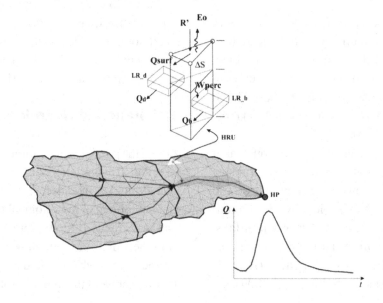

Calibration Methodology

Presented hydrological model is based on mathematical relationships with large number of parameters. Although most of parameters represent physical characteristics of the model and can be determined based on vegetation, pedology, and so on, some of them cannot be observed or measured. Also, measured parameters can have a low level of reliability, so they cannot be considered accurate enough to be applied in the calculation without additional adjustment. This is the reason why all unknown or uncertain parameter values have to be determined before using the model, in order that calculated results fit measurements as good as possible under the same conditions. This process is called parameter estimation or model calibration (Milivojević, Simić, Orlić, Milivojević, & Stojanović, 2009).

The best set of parameter values is systematically sought according to procedure given in Figure 3. Parameter estimation is performed in few steps:

- Choosing parameters to be calibrated, parameter value ranges and initial values;

Figure 3. Calibration algorithm

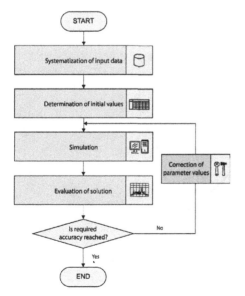

- Simulation;
- Solution evaluation;
- Parameter corrections and new simulation if necessary.

In case of calibration of Drina basin hydrological model, estimation of the following 11 parameters was performed:

- The maximum water volume to remain on plants in a given day;
- Soil porosity;
- Filtration coefficient;
- The maximum water volume to remain on fully grown plants;
- Surface runoff linear reservoir time constant;
- Ground water discharge linear reservoir time constant;
- Time constant of linear reservoir representing rivers;
- Base temperature for the start of formation of the snow pack;
- Rainfall gradient;
- Gradient of temperature drop with an increase in altitude;
- Snow melting factor.

Meanings of these parameters are given in (Arnold & Fohrer, 2005) and (Simić, Milivojević, Prodanović, Milivojević, & Perović, 2009). Initial parameter values are chosen from the range of possible solutions. In order to determine fitness of chosen set of values, it is necessary to perform simulation of model behavior with that parameter values.

Rainfall-runoff simulation is performed in such way that vertical balance is calculated for each HRU, and then horizontal flow through rivers and junctions is calculated. As a result of the simulation, hydrograms at all junctions are obtained. The most important hydrograms are those on junctions where reliable flow measurements exist, therefore the model results can be compared to the real observed values.

Afterwards, the comparison of calculated and measured hydrograms is performed (Figure 4). The aim of the comparison is to evaluate how well the model fits the real hydrological system. Depending on fitness of assumed parameter values, it can be decided whether the model satisfies desired accuracy. If accuracy criterion is not satisfied, values of the model parameters are corrected and whole process of simulation, evaluation and parameter correction repeats until predefined accuracy is achieved.

Distributed hydrological model of Drina basin was calibrated based on historical data. Measured temperatures and precipitations from chosen historical period are used as an input data for the model. After the simulation of the model behavior, calculated watershed outflows were compared to historical measurements in the same period. Based on deviation of calculated results compared to measurements, certain parameters of the model were corrected in order to improve model behavior.

Difference between outflows calculated using model and measured outflows was assessed based on two criteria:

- Root mean square error (RMSE) and
- Logarithmic error (LOGE).

RMSE is probably the most widely used criterion in calibration and can be written as:

$$RMSE = \sqrt{\frac{1}{N}\sum_{j=1}^{N}\left(O_j - S_j\right)^2} \qquad (1)$$

where O_j and S_j are measured and calculated watershed outflows, respectively, while N represents the total number of samples. While RMSE uses absolute errors which on relative scale tend to better fit higher outflows, on the other hand LOGE fitness function uses logarithms of outflows, rather than their original values, which favors lower (basic) outflows.

Figure 4. Comparison between measured and calculated hydrograms

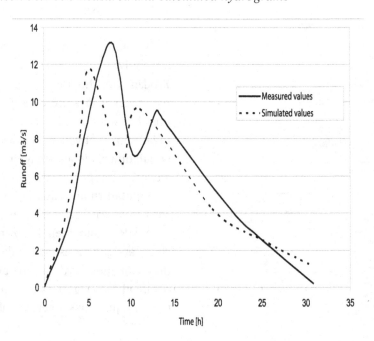

$$LOGE = \sqrt{\frac{1}{N} \sum_{j=1}^{N} \left(\log \left(O_j \; / \; S_j \right) \right)^2} \qquad (2)$$

Calculation of mean square and logarithmic errors is performed for each assumed set of values of eleven parameters. The aim of hydrological model calibration is to find such set of values which gain to minimizing square and logarithmic errors. Having in mind that both of errors have to be minimized simultaneously, the calibration of hydrological model can be considered as a multi-objective optimization problem. Mathematically speaking, the goal is to find a set of potential solutions in form $\vec{x} = \left(x_1, x_2, ..., x_{11} \right)$. Constraints in the form of ranges from which coordinates x_i, $i=1,...,11$ can take values represent allowable search space, where solutions of multi-objective optimization problem are sought.

Optimization of these two fitness functions cannot be represented as an analytical form due to high nonlinearity and discontinuity of the proposed hydrological model. Therefore, genetic algorithms were employed to minimize errors of the Drina basin distributed hydrological model. In the theory of genetic algorithms, allowable search space is represented by population consisting of individuals or chromosomes that actually represent solutions. Chromosomes are made from genes (in our case array of 11 real numbers), where each element of the array corresponds to the related coordinate from solution vector $\vec{x}$. In the following text, terms chromosome, individual and solution will be used as synonyms.

In order to solve the problem of hydrological model calibration, .NET application for multi-objective optimization using NSGA-II algorithm (Deb, Pratap, Agarwal, & Meyarivan, 2002) has been developed.

Performance Analysis

In NSGA-II algorithm evaluation of all individuals (calculation of fitness functions) is performed in every single generation. In case of hydrological model calibration, each evaluation can take more than a minute, depending on model complexity, simulated period duration and computer configuration. Having in mind that hundreds of individuals in tens of generations have to be evaluated, it is clear that a single calibration can take days or even months, which is unacceptable in the real-world applications.

Therefore, for the calibration of hydrological model, developed platform for distributed evolutionary algorithms has been employed. Evaluation of the individuals in a single generation is distributed to a number of network computers. The evaluation of every single individual is performed calling web service for evaluation installed on each computer. This way, in time frame needed to perform evaluation of a single individual, it is possible to evaluate as many individuals as there are web services available. Thanks to simultaneous evaluation of a number of individuals, the total duration of the optimization process is significantly reduced. Once all individuals from one generation are evaluated, evolutionary algorithm continues further.

In the case of developed application for hydrological model calibration, evaluation process is left to the class *EvaluationPoolMultiWS*. The task of this class is to take individuals sent to evaluation and to distribute them to the available web services for evaluation.

The first real hardware/software platform to implement the distributed NSGA-2 algorithm was an ordinary LAN of office Windows PCs. The main reason of this decision was an availability and ease of use in testing purposes, of course when there is a small number of PCs. In case that number of worker nodes (WNs) outgrows few dozens, one must invest some work into automation of the installation and configuration process, perhaps using scripting techniques. Besides that, due to the fact that the locality principle is respected – all WNs were connected to the same passive network device with 100Mbps speed, drastic effects of

371

latency due to communication events were not expected to occur. The test configuration was homogeneous regarding hardware and each worker node was equipped with modern dual core CPU with equal operating frequency as all others. The total number of WNs was 12, which means that one could count on 24 web services, because each WN runs double instance (one per core). Different instances listen on different TCP ports, in order to avoid collisions. The average duration of a single evaluation on described WN configuration was 54 seconds, when only one CPU core is employed, but it increases to 62 seconds when both cores are employed, which usually is the case. The reason for worse performance is the fact that both cores share a single system bus.

Besides the results verification, it was of significant interest to measure the speedup effects of the entire system, depending on the number of web services employed and how much the effects of Amdahl's law are going to show up (Quinn, 2003). Therefore, directly measured quantity was the duration of the evaluation of the entire generation which counts 500 individuals, depending on the number of engaged web services (workers). The evaluation speedup diagram is given on the Figure 5.

According to Figure 5, it is perfectly clear that the work invested into development of the distributed architecture for EA evaluation is worthwhile it. Almost perfect scalability was obtained thanks to:

- Relatively complex single evaluation (~1min duration),
- Homogeneous hardware platform.

Time-consuming evaluation leads to an increase of calculation to communication ratio, which always reflects favorably on the measure of speedup (Amdahl's effect). Homogeneous hardware platform leads to decrease of the waiting effect (when evaluations have to wait at the synchronization point), since all the evaluations finish their tasks at the same time.

Results

In the Figure 6, comparison between measured and calculated outflows at Prijepolje hydroprofile is shown.

From the Figure 6 it can be seen that calculated hydrogram fits measurements in periods of base flows relatively well. In the periods of peak

Figure 5. The scalability analysis of the distributed EA applied to calibration of Drina basin hydrological model. The speedup is calculated as a ratio between experimentally measured duration and theoretically projected duration of sequential run on a single CPU. Perfect speedup is a theoretical limit, obtained by neglecting all communications and synchronizations.

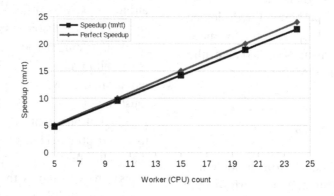

Figure 6. Comparison between measured and calculated outflows at Prijepolje hydroprofile

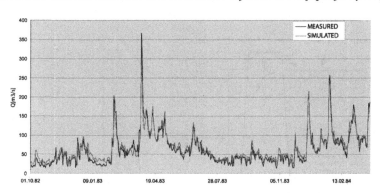

flows there are noticeable differences, which can be explained by inaccuracy of input data (temperatures and precipitations) in those periods. All other common phenomena such as snow melt and base outflow were simulated appropriately.

Water Management Optimization

Another application of the developed platform is the optimization of water management with the aim to increase profit according to given physical, ecological and social constraints. In the following text, optimization of the system of hydropower plants on Drina River is presented.

Model Description

The system modeled consists of two hydropower plants: HPP "Buk Bijela" and HPP "Foca" on the compensation basin located downstream of HPP "Buk Bijela ." Inputs in the system are inflows at the main stream at Scepan Polje and inflows from tributaries Sutjeska, Bistrica and Cehotina. Lateral inflows represent unpredictable influence on regulation.

In order to provide adequate simulation of hydropower plant system HPP "Buk Bijela" and HPP "Foca," hydraulic model (Grujović, Divac, Stojanović, Stojanović, & Milivojević, 2009) has been enriched with inner boundary conditions that

represent behavior of these two hydropower plants and their influence to water flow in the system. These boundary conditions are represented by equations that give correlation between the flow through the point on the river on one side and upstream and downstream water elevation at the same point on the other side. In case of passive system regulation, such as spillways, this kind of correlation is applicable for modeling water flow over dams. However, in case of active regulation, the flow through the dam is controlled in the more sophisticated manner, in order to fulfill request for power production optimization and with the respect to prescribed constraints. Consequently, the flow can have very complex dependency on more variables, which usually cannot be expressed in analytical form.

The model of the system HPP "Buk Bijela" and HPP "Foca" is given as a composite model of regulation, consisting of two submodels (Figure 7):

- **HPP "Buk Bijela":** Control of HPP "Buk Bijela" is based on daily planning of water consumption. Planned discharge is continuously monitored and corrected by controller if needed. Daily plan is defined as a total water volume that has to be spent for power production. The volume calculation is modeled according to three-days forecast of inflow into the system.

Figure 7. Schematic view of the system of hydropower plants "Buk Bijela" and "Foca"

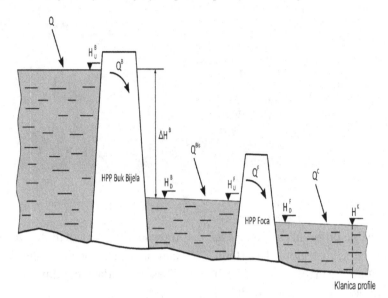

- **HPP "Foca":** Foca basin is a compensation basin with the role to control hydropower plant "Foca" in such manner to avoid violation of maximal allowed daily elevation oscillation at Klanica profile.

Dam Model

Two dams in the presented system have been modeled using modified PI controller with a feed-forward term. In the basic form of this kind of controller, dam discharge is defined by following expression:

$$Q(t) = k_p e(t) + k_i \int_0^t e(t)\, dt + Q_{FF}(t) \qquad (3)$$

with $e(t) = H_U(t) - H_R$, where $H_U(t)$ is headwater, H_R is the reference level, k_p and k_i are proportional and integral coefficients of PI controller, and $Q_{FF}(t)$ is the average expected inflow in the following period.

Various types of proportional-integral-differential (PID) controllers are widely used in the control theory. Proportional-integral controller tends to minimize difference between headwater and some reference level by correction of flow proportionally to the current difference, where proportionality factor is k_p. However, too small values of this coefficient lead to the weak response to the error appearance, while too large values can produce overreactions and system instability. Therefore, integral term which amplifies the flow correction when it is not eliminated by proportional term is introduced. This way, additional stability is added to the system.

Feed-forward term $Q_{FF}(t)$ in this setup represents an anticipation of the disturbances in the river and if it was ideal it would more or less make the PI controller useless. In that case, it would be possible to calculate exactly how to answer forecasted disturbances in order to maintain desired headwater. As the $Q_{FF}(t)$ term in reality is often represented by a low pass filter to account for the wave damping and a time delay to account for the retention, this is hardly the case. Therefore, the PI controller have to account for the error in the $Q_{FF}(t)$ feed-forward estimation by locally watch over the headwater $H_U(t)$ and adjust the outflow $Q(t)$ as the headwater differ from the reference value H_R.

Model of HPP "Buk Bijela"

The performance of the system HPP "Buk Bijela" and HPP "Foca" depends mainly on the estimation of water volume that has to be discharged through HPP "Buk Bijela" during one day, starting from 8:00 AM of the current day to 8:00 AM of the following day. Volume estimation takes into account expected inflows into basin in the following 72 hours and difference between headwater and normal level.

Mathematical model of HPP "Buk Bijela" has been developed based on PI controller with a feed-forward term, so total volume that has to be discharged can be expressed as:

$$V = \int_0^{72h} Q\big(t+\tau\big)W\big(\tau\big)d\tau + k_p^B e^B\big(t\big) + k_i^B \int_0^t e^B\big(t\big)dt$$

$$(4)$$

where:

- $Q(t+\tau)$ is the expected inflow into basin in time $t+\tau$,

- $W(\tau)$ is the weight function of expected inflows that represents influence of inflows at various times to the current discharge. Weight function $W(\tau)$ is unknown, and is approximated by parametric multilinear function (Figure 8), with the vertices at $(0h, w_1)$, $(36h, w_2)$ and $(72h, w_3)$,

- $e^B\big(t\big) = H_U^B\big(t\big) - H_R^B$, where $H_U^B\big(t\big)$ is headwater and H_R^B is normal level of the Buk Bijela basin, and

- k_p^B and k_i^B are proportional and integral coefficients of PI controller.

Thanks to forecast of the expected inflow into basin for the following three days $Q(t)$, HPP "Buk Bijela" can estimate discharge that leads to the desired headwater. Having in mind that this term, due to inaccuracy of the forecast, gives only approximate estimation of the inflow, proportional and integral term of PI controller will make an additional correction of possible level deviation. Forecast confidence level for each of three fol-

Figure 8. Expected inflows weight function

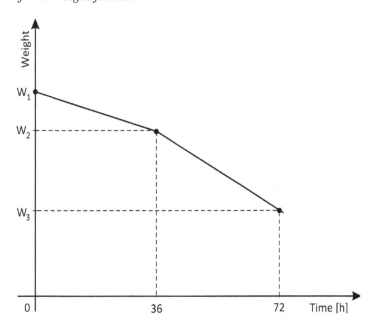

lowing days is defined by three weight coefficients w_1, w_2 and w_3.

Additional constraints of calculated daily water volume are:

- Total daily volume must be nonnegative.
- Total volume must ensure that average flow needed to fulfill planned volume discharge cannot exceed design flow.
- Total volume should not lead to overflow.
- Total volume cannot lead to level lowering below minimal working level of the power plant.

If the volume calculated by controller violates some of the specified constraints, the total volume is corrected to satisfy all prescribed constraints.

Once the total volume that has to be discharged is obtained, optimal hourly discharges for the whole day have to be determined. The aims of optimization are minimization of the intake head loss, maximization of the generator efficiency and maximization of the profit according to different energy prices during the day.

The first step in determining optimal hourly discharge is transformation of the intake head loss curve and turbine efficiency curve into aggregate efficiency curve, according to current gross head. The flows on the curve are sorted by efficiency, and then tested as possible solutions, beginning from those with maximal efficiency. Every possible solution is evaluated by profit criterion. The best solutions are those that provide power production in the period of expensive energy, while the worst solutions are those that produces overflow.

Presented algorithm for optimization of hourly discharges maximizes efficiency and profit that consequently maximizes work in the period of expensive energy and minimizes work in the period of cheap energy. However, such work can produce too big daily flow oscillations that cannot be compensated, due to capacity of the Foca basin. Without adequate compensation, daily level oscillations at Klanica profile would exceed allowed

values. Therefore, constraint of maximal daily flow oscillation ΔQ was incorporated into the algorithm for optimization of hourly discharges.

Model of HPP "Foca"

Water management on the "Foca" dam is defined by PI controller, where the flow through HPP "Foca" is calculated as:

$$Q(t) = k_p^F e^F(t) + k_i^F \int_0^t e^F(t) dt + Q_{FF}(t) + Q^{Bis}(t)$$

(5)

with:

- $e^F(t) = H_U^F(t) - H_R^F$, where $H_U^F(t)$ is headwater, and H_R^F is normal level of the Foca basin,
- k_p^F and k_i^F are proportional and integral coefficients of PI controller,
- $Q_{FF}(t)$ average discharge from HPP "Buk Bijela" in the following T_{FF} minutes,
- $Q^{Bis}(t)$ inflow from Bistrica River.

The term $Q_{FF}(t)$ represents average discharge from HPP "Buk Bijela" in the certain following period. Existence of this term is possible because daily working plan of HPP "Buk Bijela" is made at the beginning of the day and is known several hours forward. This way, when daily working plan is known for upstream hydropower plant, as well as its influence propagation time, HPP "Foca" is able to estimate discharge needed to reach desired headwater. This term gives only approximate estimation of the upstream hydropower plant, thus proportional and integral term of the controller are employed to correct possible headwater deviation, as described previously. Due to the additional influence of the Bistrica River, it is necessary to include inflow from that river into controller logic.

Controller Parameters Optimization

For the optimization of controllers on HPP "Buk Bijela" and HPP "Foca," described hydraulic model was used. The goals of the optimization were maximization of:

- The total income achieved through: selling base energy, selling peak energy, and through power fee.
- The daily level oscillations at Klanica profile in the Foca city.

Although the second criterion is eliminatory, it was assessed using continuous function:

$$f\left(x\right) = \begin{cases} 1 - \dfrac{1}{100\left(x-a\right)^2} + b, & 0 \le x \le c \\ k \cdot \left(x - c\right), & x > c \end{cases}$$

(6)

where c is allowed daily oscillation, and a and b are determined so the evaluation of the zero oscillation is 1 and the evaluation of the maximal oscillation is 0. It can be seen from the Figure 9 that oscillations around zero are evaluated with almost the same marks and marks rapidly decline when oscillations approach allowed level oscillation. Oscillations greater than allowed are evaluated as negative.

Due to the nature of evolutionary algorithms, continuous function $f(x)$ was chosen rather than discrete function that would evaluate positively only solutions giving daily oscillations less then allowed, while all other solutions are eliminated. As a consequence, all solutions giving acceptable oscillations are equally desirable, while their quality rapidly declines nearby the maximum allowed value. Having in mind that optimization is performed based on historical data, with smooth discrimination of critical oscillations, such function gives additional reserve of exceeding limits in possible hydrological situations that vary from historical ones. On the other hand, solutions that slightly violate constraint have small negative evaluations, but are not totally eliminated. Through the crossover with other solutions and through mutation, these solutions have a chance to give new solutions that fit constraints. Marks of those solutions that drastically violate allowed oscillations rapidly decline as the oscillations grow, so most of them are totally eliminated from further consideration.

Figure 9. Daily level oscillations evaluation function

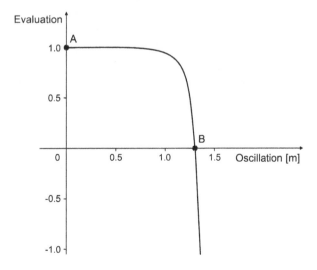

At the end of each day, difference between maximal and minimal daily water level at the Klanica profile is calculated. The difference is then evaluated using described function. Final mark is calculated as average mark of all daily oscillations in the simulated period.

Through the process of multi-objective optimization, values of 9 parameters

$$\left(k_p^B, k_i^B, w_1, w_2, w_3, \Delta Q, k_p^F, k_i^F, T_{FF} \right)$$

have been estimated. Parameters value ranges define the feasible search space. Two objective functions - the total income and the evaluation of daily level oscillations constitute the objective space. For each solution in the feasible search space there is a point (feasible point) in the objective space. The objective functions map the feasible search space to the objective space. The set of solutions that cannot be improved with respect to any objective without worsening at least one other objective is called Pareto set. The corresponding objective function values in the objective space are

called the Pareto front. In Figure 10, the red line represents the Pareto front. If we compare either two solutions from the Pareto set, one is better in terms of the total income objective, but has worse evaluation of the daily level oscillations and vice versa. The utopia point is defined as the point in objective space that is the best in every objective; this point is necessarily infeasible whenever the objectives compete.

For the purpose of multi-objective optimization, NSGA-II evolutionary algorithm was used (Deb, Pratap, Agarwal, & Meyarivan, 2002). In this algorithm, every single solution has to be evaluated by every optimization criterion. Evaluation was performed as follows (Figure 11). Simulation of the system behavior was performed using described hydraulic model and historical data about inflows into the system during the period of 63 years. As a result from the module for hydraulic calculation, flows and water levels along the river were being obtained, as well as discharges and levels at dams. Once the simulation is done, energy production and oscillations at Klanica profile were calculated from obtained

Figure 10. Pareto front

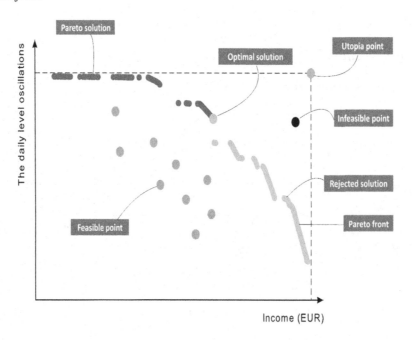

Figure 11. Evaluation workflow

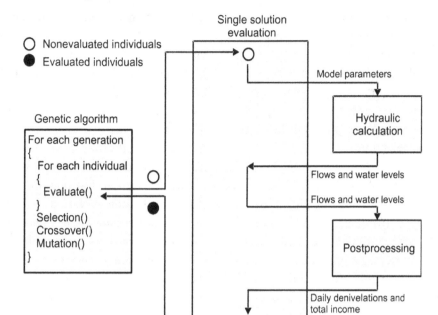

flows and levels. Based on these values, the total income and evaluation of daily oscillations at Klanica profile were calculated.

According to the fact that maximal daily oscillation of 1.3 meters at Klanica profile is set as constraint, but in genetic algorithm is evaluated by the continuous function, all solutions at the obtained Pareto front that violate this constraint were rejected at the end of the optimization process. Finally, among remaining solutions on the front, the solution that gives the largest income was chosen as the best one.

Performance Analysis

Due to inherent complexity of the optimization system of HPP "Buk Bijela" and HPP "Foca," there was a need for even more processing resources than a local network of office PCs. It is well known that the resources for high performance computing are grouped into so called computational clusters. This calculation has been performed on a Beowulf type cluster consisting of 14 nodes, each with a single 2.4GHz Intel Core2Quad Q6600 nodes with 8GB RAM memory, totaling to 56 CPUs with 112GB RAM memory. All nodes run Scientific Linux 5.7 in x86_64 architecture. PBS Torque batching system has been deployed for resource management purpose. The main issue to overcome was the platform incompatibility. Since the original MS .Net Framework is not available for UNIX platforms, we employed the open source implementation of .NET Framework – Mono v2.10.5 which almost completely complies with .NET 3.5 standard. After a couple of tweaks, the web services were ready and capable of performing evaluations on all Linux cluster worker nodes. Since a single node is equipped with 4 CPU cores, 4 web services were deployed on each of them.

As in the previous case, the duration of the evaluation of the complete generation which counts 500 individuals was measured. This time, a single evaluation lasts significantly less; 3.8s if the evaluation runs alone at the WN, but increases to 4.2s if 3 additional evaluations run on the same node (quite common case), due to already explained effects. The evaluation speedup diagram is given in Figure 12.

According to the diagram on Figure 12, it is obvious that the scalability of this problem is not exactly on the same level as in the case of hydrologic model calibration. Deeper analysis leads to two causes of this behavior:

- Relatively short evaluation leads to the amplification of the slowing effect caused by communication overhead, since evolution algorithm now communicates with web services at shorter time intervals.
- The locality principle wasn't fully satisfied, because, although all WNs belong to the same LAN, the management node (where all sequential parts of the EA run) is a remote system and uses standard Internet connection for all communication purposes.

Since it's now perfectly clear that the complexity of a single evaluation (duration) plays a big role in distributed system scalability level, an additional analysis has been performed. The results of this

analysis are meant to be used as a guideline for the estimation of the algorithm time consumption, since these runs usually last few days, even on large clusters. The quantity of a special interest is the estimated number of computed generations per unit time. Also, it's interesting to find out in which cases the parallel system is worth enough to be employed.

Therefore, the time needed to fulfill the evaluation of the entire generation of 500 individuals was measured, but now the duration of the single evaluation is varied. Hardware/software platform is the same Linux cluster equipped with Mono framework used in previous analysis. For the benchmarking purposes, we replace the real individual evaluation code with underlying operating system function sleep. Moreover, in order to simulate the real load conditions on the WN, we add a random variation of up to 5% of evaluation duration. The results of the analysis are shown on Figure 13.

As can be seen from the Figure 13, there is a significant difference in scalability of the calculations with different inherent complexity (quantified by the evaluation duration). The curves denoting more complex evaluations approach to the perfect scalability curve very closely, while the

Figure 12. The scalability analysis of the distributed EA applied to the system of hydropower plants. The speedup is calculated as a ratio between experimentally measured duration and theoretically projected duration of sequential run on a single CPU.

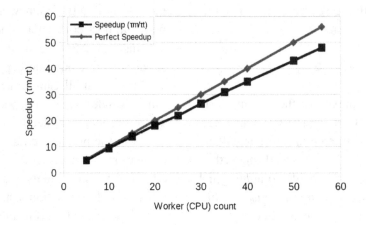

Figure 13. The scalability of the distributed EA depending on the duration of the single evaluation. The speedup is calculated as a ratio between experimentally measured duration and theoretically projected duration of sequential run on a single CPU.

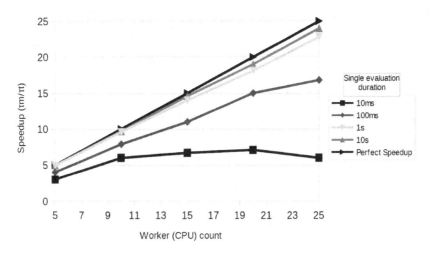

curves denoting less complex evaluations tend to reach their maximum at a certain number of workers and then even start declining. This behavior can be explained in the light of Amdahl's effect; the parallelization is not worthwhile in cases when management and communication costs overcome useful computation effort.

5. CONCLUSION

The platform for distributed evolutionary algorithms has been developed based on .NET WCF web services. It can be seamlessly integrated into any existing evolutionary framework due to its inherent modularity and full object orientation. Since the evaluation part of EA turns to be the most computationally expensive, the proposed framework provides API for efficient distribution of the evaluations, monitoring and gathering results.

Two real-world benchmarks were performed with different single individual evaluation complexity and different hardware/software platform to run on. The first one used relatively complex individual evaluation in the environment of ordinary LAN of office PCs. The second used a bit

less complex individual evaluation on the real HPC (High Performance Computing) resource – a computational cluster running Mono on top of Linux kernel and libraries. Both benchmarks have shown a significant speedup and good scalability potential. As expected, the more expensive evaluation leads to the better overall speedup and greater scalability potential. In order to properly quantify how the expense of a single evaluation affects speedup and scalability, the additional benchmarks has been performed, this time with quasi-evaluators simulating various durations. The results of this additional analysis are of practical use – one can take them as a guideline to estimate the duration of a very long EA run in heuristic fashion.

The future work will include the transition to even larger distributed platform – EGI (European Grid Infrastructure), a computational grid based on Globus toolkit and gLite middleware services. The preliminary tests have been performed, but general issue faced was the security setup on the large grid sites, which are mostly behind firewalls in private networks with strict access rules. A possible solution would be swapping roles of master and worker in the sense of communication. In this scenario, instead of remote web services possibly behind firewalls, the only callable WCF web service is a master itself. The master performs a sequential part of EA, while the remote workers on the grid invoke it in order to be given a new evaluation immediately when they reach ready state.

Another possible issue of such a large distributed system is the fact that sometimes, due to the batching systems principles, the shared grid resources are kept in busy state even if the workers are not supplied by any evaluation from their responsible master (job manager). This is not an example of a good and collaborative behavior, since the other grid users' jobs may wait queued while there is no actual load. The solution to described problem can be found in some kind of „elastic" behavior (Marović & Jovanović, 2006), when the master component is also responsible to submit sufficient number of worker jobs to the grid, but when load decreases, to reduce their number using heuristics.

ACKNOWLEDGMENT

The authors are thankful to Ministry of Education and Science of the Republic of Serbia for financial support, grant numbers III41007, OI174028, and TR37013, and to FP7 ICT-2007-2-5.3 (224297) ARTreat project.

REFERENCES

Abbott, M. B. (1991). *Hydroinformatics: Information technology and the aquatic environment.* Adlershot, UK: Avebury Technical Books.

Abbott, M. B. (1994). Hydroinformatics: A Copernican revolution in hydraulics. *Journal of Hydraulic Research, 32*(S1), 3–13. doi:10.1080/00221689409498800

Arnold, J. G., & Fohrer, N. (2005). SWAT2000: Current capabilities and research opportunities in applied watershed modelling. *Hydrological Processes, 19*(3), 563–572. doi:10.1002/hyp.5611

Barreto, W., Vojinovic, Z., Price, R., & Solomatine, D. (2009). Multiobjective evolutionary approach to rehabilitation of urban drainage systems. *Journal of Water Resources Planning and Management, 136*(5), 547–554. doi:10.1061/(ASCE)WR.1943-5452.0000070

Bernal, A., Ramirez, M. A., Castro, H., Walteros, J. L., & Medaglia, A. L. (2009). JG2A: A grid-enabled object-oriented framework for developing genetic algorithms. In *Proceedings of 2009 Systems and Information Engineering Design Symposium.* Retrieved from http://www.scopus.com/inward/record.url?eid=2-s2.0-77950273380&partnerID=40&md5=1308cf163301b8874f9b64363989f0b1

Cahon, S., Melab, N., & Talbi, E. G. (2004). ParadisEO: A framework for the reusable design of parallel and distributed metaheuristics. *Journal of Heuristics, 10*(3), 357–380. doi:10.1023/B:HEUR.0000026900.92269.ec

Cahon, S., Melab, N., & Talbi, E. G. (2005). An enabling framework for parallel optimization on the computational grid. In *Proceedings of CCGrid 2005 IEEE International Symposium on Cluster Computing and the Grid 2005.* Washington, DC: IEEE Computer Society Press. Retrieved from http://ieeexplore.ieee.org/lpdocs/epic03/wrapper.htm?arnumber=1558632

Chappell, D. (2010), MSDN library. *Introducing Windows Communication Foundation in .NET Framework 4.* Retrieved from http://msdn.microsoft.com/en-us/library/ee958158.aspx

Cunge, J. A. (1998). From hydraulics to hydroinformatics. In *Proceedings 3rd Int. Conference. Hydro--Science and--Engineering, Cottbus.* Academic Press.

Dagum, L., & Menon, R. (1998). OpenMP: An industry standard API for shared-memory programming. *IEEE Computational Science & Engineering*, *5*(1), 46–55. doi:10.1109/99.660313

Deb, K., Pratap, A., Agarwal, S., & Meyarivan, T. A. M. T. (2002). A fast and elitist multiobjective genetic algorithm: NSGA-II. *IEEE Transactions on Evolutionary Computation*, *6*(2), 182–197. doi:10.1109/4235.996017

Divac, D., Grujović, N., Milivojević, N., Stojanović, Z., & Simić, Z. (2009). Hydro-information systems and management of hydropower resources in Serbia. *Journal of the Serbian Society for Computational Mechanics*, *3*(1), 1–37.

Divac, D., Prodanovic, D., & Milivojević, N. (2009). Hydro-information systems for management of hydropower resources in Serbia. Belgrade, Serbia: Jaroslav Cerni Institute for the Development of Water Resources.

Grujović, N., Divac, D., Stojanović, B., Stojanović, Z., & Milivojević, N. (2009). Modeling of one-dimensional unsteady open channel flows in interaction with reservoirs, dams and hydropower plant objects. *Journal of the Serbian Society for Computational Mechanics*, *3*(1), 154–181.

Hoverstad, B. A. (2010). Simdist: A distribution system for easy parallelization of evolutionary computation. *Genetic Programming and Evolvable Machines*, *11*(2), 185–203. doi:10.1007/s10710-009-9100-7

Jaimes, A. L., & Coello, C. A. C. (2009). Applications of parallel platforms and models in evolutionary multi-objective optimization. In *Biologically-inspired optimisation methods* (pp. 23–49). Berlin: Springer Verlag. doi:10.1007/978-3-642-01262-4_2

Kojic, M., Filipovic, N., Stojanovic, B., Rankovic, V., Krstic, L., & Ivanovic, M. et al. (2007). Finite element modeling of underground water flow with Ranney wells. *Water Science & Technology: Water Supply*, *7*(3), 41–50.

Labadie, J. W. (2004). Optimal operation of multi-reservoir systems: State-of-the-art review. *Journal of Water Resources Planning and Management*, *130*(2), 93–111. doi:10.1061/(ASCE)0733-9496(2004)130:2(93)

Lecca, G., Petitdidier, M., Hluchy, L., Ivanovic, M., Kussul, N., Ray, N., & Thieron, V. (2011). Grid computing technology for hydrological applications. *Journal of Hydrology (Amsterdam)*, *403*(1), 186–199. doi:10.1016/j.jhydrol.2011.04.003

Lim, D., Ong, Y.-S., Jin, Y., Sendhoff, B., & Lee, B.-S. (2007). Efficient hierarchical parallel genetic algorithms using grid computing. *Future Generation Computer Systems*, *23*(4), 658–670. doi:10.1016/j.future.2006.10.008

Limmer, S., & Fey, D. (2010). Framework for distributed evolutionary algorithms in computational grids. *Advances in Computation and Intelligence*, *6378*, 170–180. doi:10.1007/978-3-642-16493-4_18

Luna, F., Nebro, A. J., & Alba, E. (2006). Observations in using grid-enabled technologies for solving multi-objective optimization problems. *Parallel Computing*, *32*(5), 377–393. doi:10.1016/j.parco.2006.06.004

Marović, B., & Jovanović, Z. (2006). Web-based grid-enabled interaction with 3D medical data. *Future Generation Computer Systems*, *22*(4), 385–392. doi:10.1016/j.future.2005.10.002

Maskey, S., Jonoski, A., & Solomatine, D. P. (2002). Groundwater remediation strategy using global optimization algorithms. *Journal of Water Resources Planning and Management*, *128*(6), 431–440. doi:10.1061/(ASCE)0733-9496(2002)128:6(431)

Medaglia, A. L., & Gutiérrez, E. (2006). An object-oriented framework for rapid development of genetic algorithms. In J. P. Rennard (Ed.), *Handbook of research on nature inspired computing for economics and management* (pp. 608–624). Hershey, PA: IGI Global. doi:10.4018/978-1-59140-984-7.ch040

Message Passing Interface Forum. (2009). *MPI: A Message-Passing Interface Standard Version 2.2*. Retrieved from http://www.mpi-forum.org/docs/mpi-2.2/mpi22-report.pdf

Microsoft. (n.d.). *How To: Use a Thread Pool (C# Programming Guide)*. Retrieved from http://msdn. microsoft.com/en-us/library/3dasc8as(v=VS.90). aspx

Milivojević, N., Divac, D., Vukosavić, D., Vučković, D., & Milivojević, V. (2009). Computer-aided optimization in operation planning of hydropower plants: Algorithms and examples. *Journal of Serbian Society for Computational Mechanics*, *3*(1), 273–297.

Milivojević, N., Simić, Z., Orlić, A., Milivojević, V., & Stojanović, B. (2009). Parameter estimation and validation of the proposed SWAT based rainfall-runoff model: Methods and outcomes. *Journal of Serbian Society for Computational Mechanics*, *3*(1), 86–110.

Mostaghim, S., Branke, J., Lewis, A., & Schmeck, H. (2008). Parallel multi-objective optimization using master-slave model on heterogeneous resources. In *Proceedings of 2008 IEEE Congress on Evolutionary Computation IEEE World Congress on Computational Intelligence*. Washington, DC: IEEE Computer Society Press. Retrieved from http://ieeexplore.ieee.org/lpdocs/epic03/wrapper. htm?arnumber=4631060

Price, R. K., Ahmad, K., & Holz, K. P. (1998). Hydroinformatic concepts. In J. Marsalek, C. Maksimovic, E. Zeman, & R. Price (Eds.), *Hydroinformatics tools for planning, design, operation and rehabilitation of sewer systems*. Dordrecht, The Netherlands: Kluwer Academic Publishers. doi:10.1007/978-94-017-1818-9_3

Quinn, M. J. (2003). *Parallel programming in C with MPI and OpenMP*. New York, NY: McGraw-Hill.

Shenfield, A., & Fleming, P. J. (2005). A service oriented architecture for decision making in engineering design. In *Advances in grid computing-EGC 2005* (pp. 334–343). Berlin: Springer Verlag. doi:10.1007/11508380_35

Simić, Z., Milivojević, N., Prodanović, D., Milivojević, V., & Perović, N. (2009). SWAT-based runoff modeling in complex catchment areas: Theoretical background and numerical procedures. *Journal of Serbian Society for Computational Mechanics*, *3*(1), 38–63.

Skonnard, A. (2006). *Learn the ABCs of programming windows communication foundation*. MSDN Magazine. Retrieved from http://msdn.microsoft. com/en-us/magazine/cc163647.aspx

Solomatine, D. P., Dibike, Y. B., & Kukuric, N. (1999). Automatic calibration of groundwater models using global optimization techniques. *Hydrological Sciences Journal*, *44*(6), 879–894. doi:10.1080/02626669909492287

Talbi, E.-G., Mostaghim, S., Okabe, T., Ishibuchi, H., Rudolph, G., & Coello, C. A. C. (2008). Parallel approaches for multiobjective optimization. In H. Braun & J. Branke (Eds.), *Multiobjective optimization* (Vol. 5252, pp. 349-372). Berlin: Springer. Retrieved from http://www.springerlink. com/index/F433U42G7Q041617.pdf

ADDITIONAL READING

Abbott, M. B. (1991). *Hydroinformatics: information technology and the aquatic environment*. Adlershot, UK: Avebury Technical Books.

Abbott, M. B. (1994). Hydroinformatics: a Copernican revolution in hydraulics. *Journal of Hydraulic Research*, *32*(S1), 3–13. doi:10.1080/00221689409498800

Abramson, D., Giddy, J., & Kotler, L. (2000). High performance parametric modeling with Nimrod/G: killer application for the global grid? *Proceedings 14th International Parallel and Distributed Processing Symposium*. IPDPS 2000. 520-528, Washington, DC: IEEE Computer Society Press.

Arajo, A. P., Boeres, C., Rebello, V. E., & Ribeiro, C. C. (2011). A distributed and hierarchical strategy for autonomic grid-enabled cooperative metaheuristics with applications. [Hoboken, NJ: Blackwell Publishing Ltd.]. *International Transactions in Operational Research*, *18*(6), 679–705. doi:10.1111/j.1475-3995.2011.00823.x

Buyya, R., Abramson, D., & Giddy, J. (2000). Nimrod/G: An architecture for a resource management and scheduling system in a global computational grid. *Proceedings Fourth International Conference/Exhibition on High Performance Computing in the Asia-Pacific Region*, 1(1), 283-289, Washington, DC: IEEE Computer Society Press.

Cahon, S., Melab, N., & Talbi, E. G. (2004). ParadisEO: A Framework for the Reusable Design of Parallel and Distributed Metaheuristics. *Journal of Heuristics, 10*(3), 357-380. Retrieved from http://www.springerlink.com/openurl. asp?id=doi:10.1023/B:HEUR.00000900.92269. ec

Cahon, S., Melab, N., & Talbi, E. G. (2005). An enabling framework for parallel optimization on the computational grid. *CCGrid 2005 IEEE International Symposium on Cluster Computing and the Grid 2005*. Washington, DC: IEEE Computer Society Press. Retrieved from http://ieeexplore.ieee.org/lpdocs/epic03/wrapper. htm?arnumber=1558632

Chappell, D. (2010), MSDN Library. *Introducing Windows Communication Foundation in.NET Framework 4*. Retrieved from http://msdn.microsoft.com/en-us/library/ee958158.aspx.

Divac, D., Stojanovic, Z., & Milivojevic, N. (2012). National and regional experiences and prospects related to use of hydropower. Energy and environment, 402-423, Serbian Academy of Sciences and Arts, Belgrade.

Dolan, E. D., Fourer, R., Moré, J. J., & Munson, T. S. (2009). The NEOS Server for Optimization: Version 4 and Beyond. Retrieved from http://www.mcs.anl.gov/papers/P947.pdf

Fletcher, R. (2000). *Practical Methods of Optimization*. Hoboken, NJ: Wiley. doi:10.1002/9781118723203

Garrett, D. (2010). PMF: A Multicore-Enabled Framework for the Construction of Metaheuristics for Single and Multiobjective Optimization. *Lecture Notes in Computer Science*, 6239, 351-360, Conference on Parallel Problem Solving from Nature, - PPSN XI, 11th, Conference on Parallel Problem Solving from Nature, - PPSN XI, Berlin Heidelberg: Springer Verlag.

Hardt, M., Seymour, K., Dongarra, J., Zapf, M., & Ruiter, N. V. (2008). Interactive grid-access using gridsolve and giggle. *Computing and informatics*, 27(2), 233-248.

He, K., Zheng, L., Dong, S., Tang, L., Wu, J., & Zheng, C. (2006). PGO: A parallel computing platform for global optimization based on genetic algorithm. [Elsevier Ltd.]. *Computers & Geosciences*, *33*(3), 357–366. doi:10.1016/j. cageo.2006.09.002

Imade, H., Morishita, R., Ono, I., Ono, N., & Okamoto, M. (2004). A Grid-Oriented Genetic Algorithm Framework for Bioinformatics. New Generation Computing –Tokyo, 22, 177-186. Berling Heidelberg: Springer Verlag.

Li, T., Wang, G., Chen, J., & Wang, H. (2011). Dynamic parallelization of hydrological model simulations [Amsterdam, Netherlands: Elsevier Science B.V.]. *Environmental Modelling & Software*, *26*(12), 1736–1746. doi:10.1016/j. envsoft.2011.07.015

Lim, D., Ong, Y.-S., Jin, Y., Sendhoff, B., & Lee, B.-S. (2006). Efficient Hierarchical Parallel Genetic Algorithms using Grid computing. *Future Generation Computer Systems*, 23(4), 658–670. doi:10.1016/j.future.2006.10.008

Luckow, A., Lacinski, L., & Jha, S. (2010). SAGA BigJob: An extensible and interoperable pilot-job abstraction for distributed applications and systems. *In Proceedings of the 2010 10th IEEE/ACM International Conference on Cluster, Cloud and Grid Computing, CCGRID '10*, 135–144, Washington, DC: IEEE Computer Society Press.

Mateos, C., Zunino, A., & Campo, M. (2010). On the evaluation of gridification effort and runtime aspects of JGRIM applications. *Future Generation Computer Systems*, 26(6), 797–819. doi:10.1016/j.future.2010.02.014

Munawar, A., Wahib, M., Munetomo, M., & Akama, K. (2009). The design, usage, and performance of GridUFO: A Grid based Unified Framework for Optimization. *Future Generation Computer Systems*, 26(4), 633–644. doi:10.1016/j.future.2009.12.001

Ng, H.-K., Lim, D., Ong, Y.-S., Lee, B.-S., Freund, L., Parvez, S., & Sendhoff, B. (2005). A Multi-cluster Grid Enabled Evolution Framework for Aerodynamic Airfoil Design Optimization. Lecture Notes in Computer Science, 3611, 1112-1121, Advances in natural computation, ICNC 2005, Advances in natural computation, Berlin Heidelberg: Springer Verlag.

Quinn, M. J. (2003). *Parallel programming in C with MPI and OpenMP*. New York, NY: McGraw-Hill.

Singiresu, S. R. (2009). *Engineering Optimization: Theory and Practice*. Hoboken, NJ: Wiley.

Solomatine, D. P., Dibike, Y. B., & Kukuric, N. (1999). Automatic calibration of groundwater models using global optimization techniques. *Hydrological Sciences Journal*, 44(6), 879–894. doi:10.1080/02626669909492287

Talbi, E.-G., Mostaghim, S., Okabe, T., Ishibuchi, H., Rudolph, G., & Coello, C. A. C. (2008). Parallel Approaches for Multiobjective Optimization. In H. Braun & J. Branke (Eds.), *Multiobjective Optimization* (Vol. 5252/2008, pp. 349-372). Retrieved from http://www.springerlink.com/index/F433U42G7Q041617.pdf

KEY TERMS AND DEFINITIONS

Calibration: Is the process of determination of model parameter values in order that calculated results fit measurements as good as possible under the same conditions.

Distributed Evaluation: Parallel evaluation of individuals (solutions) in an evolutionary algorithm using distributed computing resources.

Evolutionary Algorithms: In artificial intelligence, an evolutionary algorithm is a subset of evolutionary computation, a generic population-based metaheuristic optimization algorithm.

Hydroinformatics: Is a branch of informatics which concentrates on the application of information and communications technologies in addressing the increasingly serious problems of the equitable and efficient use of water for many different purposes.

Hydrology: Is the study of the movement, distribution, and quality of water on Earth and other planets, including the hydrologic cycle, water resources and environmental watershed sustainability.

Optimization: Is the selection of a best element from some set of available alternatives with regard to some criteria.

Water Resource Management: Is the activity of planning, developing, distributing and managing the optimum use of water resources.

Section 4
Security Issues

Chapter 16
Security Issues of Cloud Computing and an Encryption Approach

Miodrag J. Mihaljević
Mathematical Institute, Serbian Academy of Sciences and Arts, Serbia & Chuo University, Japan

Hideki Imai
Chuo University, Japan

ABSTRACT

The main security and privacy issues of cloud computing as well as the related implications are addressed, and a general framework for achieving the goals is summarized. This chapter basically considers scientific and educational employment of a cloud as a particular instance of a public cloud and its security, and as a potentially specific issue, a request for a heavy minimization of the costs implied by security is pointed out. Consequently, the problem of minimization of the overheads implied by security/privacy mechanisms is addressed. The main security requirements are given as well as the main recommendations, providing a framework for the security management. As a particular issue, data protection is considered and significance of data access control and encryption are discussed. Accordingly, an illustrative approach for achieving lightweight and provable secure encryption is shown. The considered encryption is based on joint employment of cryptographic and coding methods.

INTRODUCTION

On one hand side, cloud computing benefits are very exciting ones, but on the other hand side, security and privacy concerns are also very high. Cloud computing creates a large number of security issues and challenges. These issues range from the required trust in the cloud provider and attacks on cloud interfaces to misusing the cloud services for attacks on other systems. As an introduction regarding cloud computing security and privacy issues, following (Cloud Security Alliance, 2009; Borenstein & Blake, 2011; Ren, Wang, & Wang, 2012; Mell, 2012; Bohli, Gruschka, Jensen, Iacono, & Marnau, 2013; Xiao & Xiao, 2013), we outline several critical security and privacy challenges, point out their importance, and motivate need for further investigation of security solutions.

DOI: 10.4018/978-1-4666-5784-7.ch016

Privacy addresses the confidentiality of data for specific entities, and it carries legal and liability concerns, and should be viewed not only as a technical challenge but also as a legal and ethical concern. Protecting privacy in any computing system is a technical challenge, and in a cloud setting this challenge is complicated by the distributed nature of clouds and the possible lack of user awareness over where data are stored and who has or can have access.

From the security and privacy point of view the following two features of cloud computing appears as the top important ones: data service outsourcing, and computation outsourcing. The main problem that the cloud computing paradigm implicitly contains is that of secure outsourcing of sensitive as well as critical data and processes. When considering using a cloud service, the user must be aware of the fact that all data given to the cloud provider leave the own control and protection sphere. Even more, if deploys data-processing applications to the cloud, a cloud provider gains full control on these processes.

As illustrations of the problems and adequate solutions, note the following. Traditionally, to control the dissemination of privacy-sensitive data, users establish a trusted server to store data locally in clear, and then control that server to check whether requesting users present proper certification before letting them access the data. From a security standpoint, this access control architecture is no longer applicable when we outsource data to the cloud because data users and cloud servers aren't in the same trusted domain: the server might no longer be fully trusted as a reference monitor for defining and enforcing access control policies and managing user details. In the event of either server compromise or potential insider attacks, users' private data might even be exposed. One possible approach to enforce data access without relying on cloud servers could be to encrypt data in a differentiated manner and disclose the corresponding decryption keys only to authorized users. This approach usually suffers from severe performance issues, and doesn't scale, especially when a potentially large number of on-demand users desire fine-grained data access control.

Data encryption before outsourcing is the simplest way to protect data privacy and combat illegal access in the cloud, but encryption also makes deploying traditional data utilization services such as plaintext keyword search over textual data or query over database as a difficult task. The trivial solution of downloading all the data and decrypting data locally is impractical, due to the communications and processing costs. Also, an important issue that arises when outsourcing data service to the cloud is protecting data integrity and long-term storage correctness.

Security and Overheads

Cloud computing requires a lot of security measures in order to avoid heavy impacts if the security is compromised. On the other hand side, each security measure implies certain overhead to the cloud functions, and the cumulative overhead could jeopardize the main functionality. So, although embedding the security into the cloud is necessary and provides benefits to users and cloud system providers, it inevitably increases overhead for both. For users in particular, such overheads could offset the cloud's economical attractions, and might conflict with their reasons for using the cloud in the first place. How to quantitatively explore the trade-offs between security overhead and cloud benefit is another interesting and important problem.

The cumulative overhead appears as the implication of the particular ones among which the main are the following:

- Implementation overheads;
- Power consumption overheads;
- Computational overheads.

These overheads could significantly affect the costs of using cloud computing paradigms.

Deployment Models and Security Challenges

As discussed in (Jansen & Grance, 2011; Badger, Grance, Patt-Coner, & Voas, 2012), from the deployment models point of view, which could be considered as a starting point regarding the cloud computing security issues, the clouds can be classified into the following three main categories: private cloud, public cloud, and hybrid cloud. In a private cloud, the cloud infrastructure is provisioned for exclusive use by a single organization comprising multiple consumers (e.g., business units). It may be owned, managed, and operated by the organization, a third party, or some combination of them, and it may exist on or off premises. As a subclass of the private clouds or an intermediate class between the private and public cloud, we can consider the community cloud where the cloud infrastructure is provisioned for exclusive use by a specific community of consumers from organizations that have shared concerns (e.g., mission, security requirements, policy, and compliance considerations). In a public cloud, the cloud infrastructure is provisioned for open use by the general public. It may be owned, managed, and operated by a business, academic, or government organization, or some combination of them. In the third main approach of deployment, a hybrid cloud, the cloud infrastructure is a composition of private and public cloud infrastructures that remain unique entities, but are bound together by standardized or proprietary technology.

From the security point of view the most serious challenges are related to the scenarios where public cloud is employed. While one of the biggest obstacles facing public cloud computing is security, the cloud computing paradigm provides opportunities for innovation in provisioning security services that hold the prospect of improving the overall security of some organizations. The biggest beneficiaries are likely to be smaller organizations that have limited numbers of information technology administrators and

security personnel, and can gain by transitioning to a public cloud. One idea on reducing the risk for data and applications in a public cloud is the simultaneous usage of multiple clouds. Several approaches employing this paradigm have been proposed recently. They differ in partitioning and distribution patterns, technologies, cryptographic methods, and targeted scenarios as well as security levels (see for example (Bohli, Gruschka, Jensen, Iacono, & Marnau, 2013) for a discussion on multiple clouds).

Opportunities for improved security also benefit privacy. That is, effective privacy can exist only upon a sound foundation of information security. However, privacy, just as security, has broad organizational, operational, and technical implications. While some aspects of privacy are closely related to the confidentiality, integrity, and availability objectives of security, other aspects are not. Instead, they involve important privacy-related principles and considerations that are addressed in law, regulations, and guidance.

On Security of a Cloud for Scientific and Educational Computing

A natural question related to this book is: Does Cloud Computing dedicated to scientific and educational purposes implies specific security requirements. This chapter basically considers scientific and educational employment of a cloud as a particular instance of a public cloud and consequently addresses the security issues. This consideration provides a framework for establishing security and performing the security management within a cloud dedicated to scientific and educational purposes. As a potentially specific issue regarding security for scientific and educational purposes, a request for a heavy minimization of the costs (which could be more important than in some other scenarios) implied by security, and accordingly minimization of the security overheads, could appear. Accordingly, this chapter first discusses general issues of the cloud security and in the second part points out to a cryptographic technique for encryption which provides potential for achieving high security and low overheads.

GENERAL ISSUES OF CLOUD SECURITY

Basically, we could consider the cloud environment as a new computing platform to which the classic methodology of security can be applied as well. According to (Xiao & Xiao, 2013), an attribute-driven methodology can be employed to address the issue via consideration of an ecosystem of cloud security and privacy based on the following five security/privacy attributes which are currently the most representative ones:

- Confidentiality,
- Integrity,
- Availability,
- Accountability,
- Privacy-Preservability.

On the other hand side, a number of specific features of the cloud environment require a dedicated approach regarding the above issues. The Cloud Security Alliance (2009) has summarized the following five essential characteristics that illustrate the relation to, and differences from, traditional computing paradigm:

- **On-Demand Self-Service:** A cloud user may unilaterally obtain computing capabilities, like the usage of various servers and network storage, as on demand, without interacting with the cloud provider.
- **Broad Network Access:** Services are delivered across the Internet via a standard mechanism that allows users to access the services through heterogeneous thin or thick client tools (e.g., PCs, mobile phones, and PDAs).

- **Resource Pooling:** The cloud provider employs a multi-tenant model to serve multiple users by pooling computing resources, which are different physical and virtual resources dynamically assigned or reassigned according to users demand. Examples of resources include storage, processing, memory, network bandwidth, and virtual machines.
- **Rapid Elasticity:** Capabilities may be rapidly and elastically provisioned in order to quickly scale out or rapidly released to quickly scale in. From users' point of view, the available capabilities should appear to be unlimited and have the ability to be available in any quantity at any time.
- **Measured Service:** The service purchased by users can be quantified and measured. For both the provider and users, resource usage will be monitored, controlled, metered, and reported.

Taking into account the above preliminaries which are the "starting points" for more in details considerations, this section yields an overview of the challenges and approaches for providing security and privacy within public cloud systems, as well as the recommendations for achieving the goals employing the claims given in (Jansen & Grance, 2011; Badger, Grance, Patt-Coner, & Voas, 2012).

Main Topics Regarding Security and Privacy

Cloud computing originates from a number of previously existing technologies including service oriented architecture, virtualization, Web, and utility computing, and accordingly many of the privacy and security issues involved can be viewed as known problems in a new aggregating setting. On the other hand side the aggregation implies certain consequences, and the impact of their combined effect in the new joint setting should be taken into account. Public cloud computing represent a paradigm which shifts from conventional norms to an open deperimeterized organizational infrastructure. The sections below point out a number of privacy and security-related issues which have long-term significance for public cloud computing, and in many cases, for other cloud computing service models.

Governance

Dealing with cloud services requires attention to the roles and responsibilities involved between the organization/users and cloud provider, particularly with respect to managing risks and ensuring organizational requirements are met. Ensuring that systems are secure and risk is managed are challenging issues in any environment and even more within cloud computing. Audit mechanisms and tools should be in place to determine how data is stored, protected, and used, to validate services, and to verify policy enforcement. A risk management program should also be in place that is flexible enough to deal with the continuously evolving and shifting risk landscape.

Compliance

Compliance refers to an organization's responsibility to operate in agreement with established laws, regulations, standards, and specifications. Various types of security and privacy laws and regulations exist within different countries at the national, state, and local levels, making compliance a potentially complicated issue for cloud computing.

Cloud providers are becoming more sensitive to legal and regulatory concerns, and may be willing to commit to store and process data in specific jurisdictions and apply required safeguards for security and privacy. Even so, organizations are ultimately accountable for the security and privacy of data held by a cloud provider on their behalf.

One of the most common compliance issues facing an organization is data location. Use of an in-house computing centre allows an organization to structure its computing environment and to know in detail where data is stored and what safeguards are used to protect the data. In contrast, a characteristic of many cloud computing services is that data is stored redundantly in multiple physical locations and detailed information about the location of an organization's data is unavailable or not disclosed to the service consumer. This situation makes it difficult to ascertain whether sufficient safeguards are in place and whether legal and regulatory compliance requirements are being met.

When information crosses borders, the governing legal, privacy, and regulatory regimes can be ambiguous and raise a variety of concerns. Consequently, constraints on the trans-border flow of sensitive data, as well as the requirements on the protection afforded the data, have become the subject of national and regional privacy and security laws and regulations.

The main compliance concerns with trans-border data flows include whether the laws in the jurisdiction where the data was collected permit the flow, whether those laws continue to apply to the data post transfer, and whether the laws at the destination present additional risks or benefits. Technical, physical and administrative safeguards, such as access controls, often apply. For example, European data protection laws may impose additional obligations on the handling and processing of data transferred to the U.S. These concerns can be alleviated if the cloud provider has some reliable means to ensure that an organization's data is stored and processed only within specific jurisdictions.

Trust

Under the cloud computing paradigm, an organization transfers a high level of trust onto the cloud provider. Moving data and applications to a cloud computing environment operated by a cloud provider expands the circle of insiders not only to the cloud provider's staff and subcontractors, but also potentially to other Users using the service, thereby increasing risk.

Data Ownership

The organization's ownership rights over the data must be firmly established in the service contract to enable a basis for trust and privacy of data. The continuing controversy over privacy and data ownership rights for social networking users illustrates the impact that ambiguous terms can have on the parties involved.

Composite Services

Cloud services themselves can be composed through nesting and layering with other cloud services. Cloud services that use third-party cloud providers to outsource or subcontract some of their services raise concerns, including the scope of control over the third party, the responsibilities involved (e.g., policy and licensing arrangements), and the remedies and recourse available should problems occur. Public cloud providers that host applications or services of other parties may involve other domains of control, but through transparent authentication mechanisms, appear to a consumer to be that of the cloud provider. Trust is often not transitive, requiring that third-party arrangements are disclosed in advance of reaching an agreement with the cloud provider, and that the terms of these arrangements are maintained throughout the agreement or until sufficient notification can be given of any anticipated changes.

Visibility

Transparency in the way the cloud provider operates, including the provisioning of composite services, is a vital issue for effective oversight over system security and privacy by an organization.

To ensure that policy and procedures are being enforced throughout the system lifecycle, service arrangements should include some means for the organization to gain visibility into the security controls and processes employed by the cloud provider and their performance over time. For example, the service agreement could include the right to audit controls via a third party, as a way to validate control aspects that are not otherwise accessible or assessable by the consumer. Ideally, the user would have control over aspects of the means of visibility to accommodate its needs, such as the threshold for alerts and notifications, and the level of detail and schedule of reports.

Supporting Data

While the focus of attention in cloud computing is mainly on protecting application data, cloud providers also hold significant details about the accounts of cloud consumers that could be compromised and used in subsequent attacks. Payment information is one example and other types of information, can also be involved.

Risk Management

With cloud-based services, some subsystems or subsystem components fall outside of the direct control of a client organization. Many organizations are more comfortable with risk when they have greater control over the processes and equipment involved. Risk management is the process of identifying and assessing risk to organizational operations, organizational assets, or individuals resulting from the operation of an information system, and taking the necessary steps to reduce it to an acceptable level.

Architecture of Hardware and Software

The architecture of the hardware and software used to deliver cloud services can vary significantly among public cloud providers for any specific service model. The physical location of the infrastructure is determined by the cloud provider as is the design and implementation of the reliability, resource pooling, scalability, and other logic needed in the support framework. Applications are built on the programming interfaces of Internet-accessible services, which typically involve multiple cloud components communicating with each other over application programming interfaces. Virtual machines typically serve as the abstract unit of deployment for certain clouds and are loosely coupled with the cloud storage architecture. Cloud providers may also use other computing abstractions of virtual machine technology to provision services for other service models.

It is important to understand the technologies the cloud provider uses to provision services and the implications the technical controls involved have on security and privacy of the system throughout its lifecycle. With such information, the underlying system architecture of a cloud can be decomposed and mapped to a framework of security and privacy controls that can be used to assess and manage risk.

Attack Surface

The virtual machine monitor, called hypervisor, is an additional layer of software between an operating system and hardware platform that is used to operate multi-tenant virtual machines. Besides virtualized resources, the hypervisor normally supports other application programming interfaces to conduct administrative operations, such as launching, migrating, and terminating virtual machine instances. Compared with a traditional, non-virtualized implementation, the addition of a hypervisor causes an increase in the attack surface. That is, there are additional methods (e.g., application programming interfaces), channels (e.g., sockets), and data items (e.g., input strings) an attacker can use to cause damage to the system.

Identity and Access Management

Data sensitivity and privacy of information have become increasingly an area of concern for organizations. The identity proofing and authentication aspects of identity management are related to maintenance, and protection of personal information collected from users. Preventing unauthorized access to information resources in the cloud is also a major consideration. One recurring issue is that the organizational identification and authentication framework may not naturally extend into a public cloud and extending or changing the existing framework to support cloud services may prove difficult. The alternative of employing two different authentication systems, one for the internal organizational systems and another for external cloud-based systems, is a complication that can become unworkable over time.

Identity federation, popularized with the introduction of service oriented architectures, is one solution. Identity federation allows the organization and cloud provider to trust and share digital identities and attributes across both domains, and to provide a means for single sign-on. For federation to succeed, identity and access management transactions must be interpreted carefully and unambiguously and protected against attacks. Clear separation of the managed identities of the cloud consumer from those of the cloud provider must also be ensured to protect the consumer's resources from provider-authenticated entities and vice versa.

Software Isolation

High degrees of multi-tenancy over large numbers of platforms are needed for cloud computing to achieve the envisioned flexibility of on-demand provisioning of reliable services and the cost benefits and efficiencies due to economies of scale. To reach the high scales of consumption desired, cloud providers have to ensure dynamic, flexible delivery of service and isolation of consumer resources.

The security of a computer system depends on the quality of the underlying software kernel that controls the confinement and execution of processes. A virtual machine monitor or hypervisor is designed to run multiple virtual machines, each hosting an operating system and applications, concurrently on a single host computer, and to provide isolation between the different guest virtual machines.

Data Protection

Data stored in a public cloud typically resides in a shared environment collocated with data from other users. Organizations placing sensitive and regulated data into a public cloud, therefore, must account for the means by which access to the data is controlled and the data is kept secure.

Data must be secured and access to the data must be controlled while: "at rest", "in transit", and "in use".

In order to secure data in transit employment of cryptographic techniques and particularly encryption is the main request. Procedures for protecting data at rest are also heavily based on employment of encryption and suitable cryptographic key management. Also the interoperability issues should be taken into account: The lack of interoperability affects the availability of data and complicates the portability of applications and data between cloud providers. Protecting data in use is an emerging area of cryptography and basically still an open challenge for practical results to offer.

Availability

In simple terms, availability is the extent to which an organization's full set of computational resources is accessible and usable. Availability can be affected temporarily or permanently, and a loss can be partial or complete. Denial of service attacks, equipment outages, and natural disasters are all threats to availability.

Incident Response

As the name implies, incident response involves an organized method for dealing with the consequences of an attack against the security of a computer system. The cloud provider's role is vital in performing incident response activities, including incident verification, attack analysis, containment, data collection and preservation, problem remediation, and service restoration. Each layer in a cloud application stack, including the application, operating system, network, and database, generates event logs, as do other cloud components, such as load balancers and intrusion detection systems. Many such event sources and the means of accessing them are under the control of the cloud provider.

A Summary of the Security Recommendations

According to the considerations in the previous section, this section lists and briefly addresses the main issues regarding cloud security and privacy through the following recommendations given in (Jansen & Grance, 2011).

User-Side Vulnerabilities

Users should minimize the potential for client devices to be attacked by employing best practices for the security and hardening of consumer platforms, and should seek to minimize browser exposure to possibly malicious web sites.

Encryption

Users should require that strong encryption be used for web sessions and other network communication whenever a rented application requires the confidentiality of application interactions with other applications or data transfers. Also users should require that the same diligence is applied to stored data.

Authentication

Users should consider the use of authentication tokens or other appropriate form of advanced authentication, which some providers offer, to mitigate the risk of account hijacking and other types of exploits.

Identity and Access Management

Users should have visibility into the following capabilities of a provider:

- The authentication and access control mechanisms that the provider infrastructure supports,
- The tools that are available for consumers to provision authentication information, and
- The tools to input and maintain authorizations for consumer users and applications without the intervention of the provider.

Performance Requirements

Users should benchmark current performance scores for an application, and then establish key performance score requirements before deploying that application to a provider's site. Key performance scores include responsiveness for interactive user applications, and bulk data transfer performance for applications that must input or output large quantities of data on an ongoing basis.

Visibility

Users should request that a provider allow visibility into the operating services that affect a specific consumer's data or operations on that data, including the monitoring.

Virtual Machines (VM) Vulnerabilities

When providers offer computing resources in the form of VMs, users should ensure that the provider has mechanisms to protect VMs from attacks by:

- Other VMs on the same physical host,
- The physical host itself, and
- The network.

Typical attack detection and prevention mechanisms include Virtual Firewalls, and network segmentation techniques such as VLANs.

Physical

Users should consider physical plant security practices and plans at provider sites as part of the overall risk considerations when selecting a provider. Physical attacks require backup plans just as cyber attacks do. Users should also investigate whether a candidate provider offers redundancy for the sites they operate, and opt for providers that are not tied to a specific geographic location in case of natural disasters or other disruptions.

DATA PROTECTION, ACCESS CONTROL AND ENCRYPTION

As pointed out in the previous sections, data protection is one of the key issues regarding establishing adequate cloud computing security. On the other hand side, data access control and data encryption are the key elements for achieving data protection. Accordingly, this section discusses the main generic issues regarding the data access control and encryption.

Basic Approach

As pointed out above, the data should be secure while they are in transit, storage/archive and processing, and accordingly data access control is the key issue and encryption is the main technique for achieving these goals but encryption should be combined with the related appropriate techniques in order to achieve all the goals. In continuation, we discuss some of the related issues, and as the first we point out to some statements from (Ren, Wang, & Wang, 2012; Mell, 2012).

In cloud computing, users have to give up their data to the cloud service provider for storage and other operations, while the cloud service provider is usually a commercial enterprise which cannot be totally trusted. Data represents an extremely important asset for any user or organization, and they will face serious consequences if the confidential data are non-vulnerary disclosed. Thus, cloud users in the first place want to make sure that their data are kept confidential to outsiders, including the cloud provider. This is the first data security requirement, but data confidentiality is not the only security requirement. Flexible and fine-grained access control is also strongly desired in the service-oriented cloud computing model. For example, a health-care information system on a cloud is required to restrict access of protected medical records to eligible doctors and a customer relation management system running on a cloud may allow.

On the other hand side, encrypted databases are nothing new. Various encryption technologies have existed for a long time. With the data sitting in storage, encryption seems like the perfect security solution. The biggest difference between the various methods of database encryption is granularity. Some methods encrypt a tuple, some a relation, and some the whole database.

However, cryptography has its costs. It takes considerably more computing power, and this is multiplied by several factors in the case of a database. Cryptography greatly affects database performance because each time a query is run, a large amount of data must be decrypted. Running queries is the database's primary purpose, thus decryption operations quickly become excessive. Although much research has focused on techniques to run queries on an encrypted database, we have yet to achieve solid and acceptable efficiency and performance.

Simple approaches of data access control based on encryption are based on extensions to the query language that simply applied encryption before writing a value and running a decryption function before reading a value. These types of extensions still exist in many commercial databases today, along with more advanced counterparts. Even these counter parts are based on certain absolute trust and in a cloud environment, this trust is absent. Some alternative solutions have been proposed, including homomorphic encryption, however, each solution has its own compromises and downsides: some involve the security of the data against certain attacks and others involve the operations available to the customer. For example, homomorphic encryption is effective for summations on encrypted values but too slow for other operations.

In continuation we address an alternative approach for controlling data access based on encryption known under the name "broadcast encryption". An overview of broadcast encryption can be found in (Lotspiech, Nusser, & Pestoni, 2002). An illustration of some generalizations and recent security evaluation of certain broadcast encryption schemes can be find respectively in (Mihaljevic, 2003, 2004; Mihaljevic, Fossorier, & Imai, 2007). When broadcast encryption approach is employed for controlling the data access, a session-encrypting key (SEK) is used to encrypt the data. Ensuring that only the valid members of the group have SEK at any given time instance is the key management problem of data access control. To make updating of SEK possible, another set of keys called the key-encrypting keys (KEKs) should be involved so that it can be used to encrypt and transmit the updated SEK to the valid members of the group. Hence, the key management problem reduces to the problem of distributing KEKs to the members such that at any given time instant all the valid members can be securely updated with the new SEK, and an approach is based on the principle of covering all non-revoked users by disjoint subsets from a predefined collection, together with a method for assigning KEKs to subsets in the collection.

On Certain Dedicated Approaches

The traditional method to protect sensitive data outsourced to third parties is to store encrypted data on servers, while the decryption keys are disclosed to authorize users only. However, there are several drawbacks about this trivial solution. First of all, such a solution requires an efficient key management mechanism to distribute decryption keys to authorized users. Next, this approach could face lacks of scalability and flexibility: as the number of authorized users becomes large, the solution will not be efficient anymore. In case a previously legitimate user needs to be revoked, related data has to be re-encrypted and new keys must be distributed to existing legitimate users again. Last but not least, in a number of settings, data owners need to be online all the time so as to encrypt or re-encrypt data and distribute keys to authorize users. Accordingly, as an illustration, we discuss the following advanced approaches that have been reported in (Wan, Liu, & Deng, 2012; Li, Yu, Zheng, Ren, & Lou, 2013).

A Hierarchical Approach

The cloud service provider manages a cloud to provide data storage service. Data owners encrypt their data files and store them in the cloud for sharing with data consumers. To access the shared data files, data consumers download encrypted data files of their interest from the cloud and then decrypt them. Each data owner/consumer is admin-

istrated by a domain authority. A domain authority is managed by its parent domain authority or the trusted authority. Data owners, data consumers, domain authorities, and the trusted authority are organized in a hierarchical manner. The trusted authority is the root authority and responsible for managing top-level domain authorities. Each top-level domain authority corresponds to a top-level organization, such as a federated enterprise, while each lower-level domain authority corresponds to a lower-level organization, such as an affiliated company in a federated enterprise. Each domain authority is responsible for managing the domain authorities at the next level or the data owners/consumers in its domain. In the considered system, neither data owners nor data consumers will be always online. They come online only when necessary, while the cloud service provider, the trusted authority, and domain authorities are always online. The cloud is assumed to have a sufficient storage capacity and computation power. In addition, we assume that data consumers can access data files for reading only.

Attribute Based Encryption (ABE) Approach

In the ABE scheme, ciphertexts are not encrypted to one particular user as in traditional cryptography. Rather, both ciphertexts and users' decryption keys are associated with a set of attributes or a policy over attributes. A user is able to decrypt a ciphertext only if there is a match between his decryption key and the ciphertext. ABE schemes are classified into key-policy attribute-based encryption (KP-ABE) and ciphertext-policy attribute-based encryption (CP-ABE), depending how attributes and policy are associated with ciphertexts and users' decryption keys. In a KP-ABE scheme, a ciphertext is associated with a set of attributes and a user's decryption key is associated with a monotonic tree access structure. Only if the attributes associated with the ciphertext satisfy the tree access structure, the user can decrypt the ciphertext. In a CP-ABE scheme, the roles of ciphertexts and decryption keys are switched; the ciphertext is encrypted based on a tree access policy chosen by an encryptor, while the corresponding decryption key is created with respect to a set of attributes. As long as the set of attributes associated with a decryption key satisfies the tree access policy associated with a given ciphertext, the key can be used to decrypt the ciphertext. Since users' decryption keys are associated with a set of attributes, CP-ABE is conceptually closer to traditional access control models such as Role-Based Access Control (RBAC). Thus, it is more natural to apply CP-ABE, instead of KP-ABE, to enforce access control of encrypted data. However, basic CP-ABE schemes are far from enough to support access control in modern organization environments, which require considerable flexibility and efficiency in specifying policies and managing user attributes. In a CP-ABE scheme, decryption keys only support user attributes that are organized logically as a single set, so users can only use all possible combinations of attributes in a single set issued in their keys to satisfy policies.

ENCRYPTION EMPLOYING PSEUDORANDOMNESS, RANDOMNESS AND DEDICATED CODING

Protection of data and data access control requires employment of encryption techniques, and their employment results in certain overheads which should be minimized. These overheads accumulate with processing of each data bit, and currently we face extremely high speeds of hardware operations and amounts of data involved in processing (see for example (Flynn et al., 2013)) implying that a reduction of the cumulative overheads becomes a high priority. A number of light-weight encryption techniques have proposed for achieving the desired reduction. Unfortunately, all these re-

ported light-weight encryption techniques suffer from certain weaknesses which open doors for potential or already detected vulnerabilities (see (Mihaljevic, Gangopadhyay, Paul, & Imai, 2012a, 2012b) for some recent illustrative examples), and accordingly developing frameworks which enhance cryptographic security preserving light-weightiness is an important topic.

This section discusses an illustrative framework reported in (Mihaljevic & Imai, 2009), which in certain scenarios provides the desired goals of enhancing the security and preserving the light-weightiness. The origins for this approach include the issues reported in (Mihaljevic, 2007; Fossorier, Mihaljevic, & Imai, 2007), and it has been a background for some related techniques recently reported in (Khiabani, Wei, Yuan, & Wang, 2012; Mihaljevic, 2012; Wei, Wang, Yin, & Yuan, 2013), for example.

Underlying Ideas

The novel design assumes the following:

- A source of pure randomness is available (for example, as an efficient hardware module); and
- A suitable error-correcting coding (ECC) technique is available.

The availability means that the implementation complexities of the source of randomness and ECC do not imply a heavy implementation overhead in suitable implementation scenarios.

The main design goal is the following one: any method for cryptanalysis of a novel stream cipher scheme should have complexity close to the complexity of the exhaustive search. Particular origins for achieving the design goals include the results reported in (Mihaljevic, 2009; Fossorier, Mihaljevic, Imai, Cui, & Matsuura, 2006; Mihaljevic, Fossorier, & Imai, 2007), where certain issues regarding coding and randomness, complexity of the Learning Parity in Noise (LPN) problem, and generic time-memory-data trade-off method for recovering the secret key, respectively, are considered.

The novel approach for design of stream ciphers is based on the following:

- Employment of the pure randomness for the intentional data degradation;
- Employment of a dedicated homophonic-like coding which involves pure randomness.

Note that in the considered scenario, the homophonic coding does not have the same role as in its traditional applications where the role is to provide randomness of the plaintext. Here, a homophonic coding is employed to provide additional confusion at the attacker's side. So, the main underlying ideas of a framework for stream ciphers which involves pure randomness and provide low-complexity implementation include the following:

- Encoding/Decoding of the plaintext;
- Encryption/Decryption of the encoded plaintext/ciphertext;
- Homophonic encoding via embedding random bits and an intentional degradation of the code-words before transmission.

Accordingly, the framework of the main operations at the sender's and receiver's sides is given in Table 1.

Finally, regarding a comparison with some other approaches, note that the underlying ideas of the design given in this section include joint employment of randomness via the embedding and the additive degradation, as well as employment of the dedicated error-correction coding.

Components, Roles, and Architecture

In comparison with a traditional stream cipher which performs "encoding & encryption", the structure of the proposing one has the following three additional components:

1. A source of pure randomness called RAND-box;
2. A component, which at the encryption side performs homophonic encoding of the ciphertext via embedding the random bits and at the decryption side performs "decoding" via the (corresponding) decimation which provides splitting of the embedded bits;
3. A component at the encryption side which simulates a binary symmetric channel with controllable crossover probability.

Let's call ECC-box a box which encodes the plaintext in order to provide correction of the random errors. Note that, in the proposing stream cipher, ECC-box encodes the plaintext so that it can be recovered correctly after corruption due to the errors introduced intentionally in the ciphertext (in a general setting, certain noise in the public channel can be involved as well).

Block scheme of the novel stream cipher family is depicted in Figure 1. The "white" boxes in Figure 1 correspond to the boxes in a traditional stream

Table 1. The framework of the main operations at the sender's and receiver's sides: "embedding" assumes interleaving of the effective and random (dummy) bits and "splitting" assumes separation of the effective and dummy bits

Sender: Encode → Encrypt → Embedding & additive nose degradation
Receiver: Splitting (Decimation) → Decrypt → Decode

Figure 1. Encryption and decryption block scheme

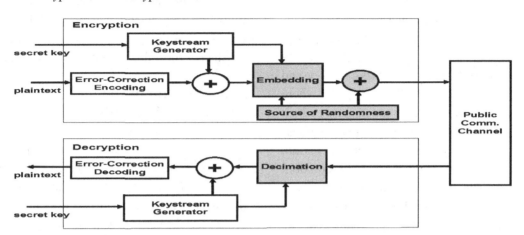

cipher which performs "encoding + encryption" in order to perform reliable operation over a noisy communication channel, and the "gray" boxes are the additional ones.

The role of the employed homophonic encoding, implemented via the embedding of the random bits, is to provide a heavy masking of the keystream generator sequences so that they appear as very uncertain for a given ciphertext even when the plaintext is known.

Accordingly, the main features of the proposed stream ciphers framework are as follows:

- The resulting ciphertext consists of effective bits and dummy ones embedded in a manner controlled by the secret key.
- At the receiving part, the dummy bits are simply discarded and the effective bits are those which are employed for the deciphering. The decimation assumes splitting of the effective and dummy bits.

The security is based on the impossibility of correct separation of effective bits from the dummy ones via the decimation of the available (embedded) sequence without the secret key.

Encryption and Decryption Algorithms

This section specifies the encryption and decryption algorithms in the proposed class of stream ciphers.

Encryption Algorithm

- **Input:** The message organized as a string of l-dimensional binary vectors $\{\mathbf{x}_t\}_t$, the secret key and non-secret initial vector which control the keystream generator, and the algorithm parameters m, n and η.
- **Encryption Steps:** For each t do the following:
  1. Encode $\mathbf{x}_t$ into the codeword $C(\mathbf{x}_t)$ (an m-dimensional binary vector) employing the selected ECC suitable for a binary symmetric channel with the crossover probability η.
  2. Employing the output, m-dimensional binary vector $\mathbf{y}_t$, from the keystream generator compute $C(\mathbf{x}_t)+ \mathbf{y}_t$, where "+" denotes bit-by-bit mod2 addition.

3. Generate by the RAND-box a random $(n-m)$-dimensional vector ρ_t and perform pseudorandom embedding (controlled by the keystream generator) of the bits from the vectors $C(\mathbf{x}_t) + \mathbf{y}_t$ and ρ_t as follows: $[C(\mathbf{x}_t) + \mathbf{y}_t \| \rho_t]\mathbf{P}_t$, where $\mathbf{P}_t$ is an $n \times n$ permutation matrix which corresponds to the considered embedding and $\|$ denotes the concatenation.

4. Generate by the RAND-box a random n-dimensional vector $\mathbf{v}_t \leftarrow \text{Ber}(n,\eta)$ (according to Bernoulli distribution with the parameters n,η) and generate the ciphertext vector as follows: $\mathbf{z}_t = [C(\mathbf{x}_t) + \mathbf{y}_t \| \rho_t]\mathbf{P}_t + \mathbf{v}_t$

- **Output:** The ciphertext $\{\mathbf{z}_t\}_t$.

Decryption Algorithm

- **Input:** The ciphertext organized as a string of n-dimensional binary vectors $\{z_t\}_t$, the secret key and non-secret initial vector which control the keystream generator, and the algorithm parameters m, n and η.

- **Decryption Steps**: For each t do the following:
  1. Perform decimation of $\mathbf{z}_t$ corresponding to the embedding performed in the encryption step 3 as follows: $\mathbf{z}_t\mathbf{P}_t^{-1} = [C(\mathbf{x}_t) + \mathbf{y}_t \| \rho_t] + \mathbf{v}_t\mathbf{P}_t^{-1}$ and $tcat_m(\mathbf{z}_t\mathbf{P}_t^{-1}) = [C(\mathbf{x}_t) + \mathbf{y}_t] + tcat_m(\mathbf{v}_t\mathbf{P}_t^{-1})$, where $\mathbf{P}_t^{-1}$ denotes the inverse permutation of $\mathbf{P}_t$ (which is the transpose of $\mathbf{P}_t$), and $tcat_m(.)$ denotes the truncating of the argument to the first m bits.
  2. Employing the output vector $\mathbf{y}_t$ from the keystream generator compute $tcat_m(\mathbf{z}_t\mathbf{P}_t^{-1}) + \mathbf{y}_t = C(\mathbf{x}_t) + tcat_m(\mathbf{v}_t\mathbf{P}_t^{-1})$.
  3. Perform decoding $C^{-1}(\cdot)$ according to the employed ECC and recover $\mathbf{x}_t$ as follows: $\mathbf{x}_t = C^{-1}(tcat_m(\mathbf{z}_t\mathbf{P}_t^{-1}) + \mathbf{y}_t) = C^{-1}(C(\mathbf{x}_t) + tcat_m(\mathbf{v}_t\mathbf{P}_t^{-1}))$.

- **Output:** The message in the form of the string $\{\mathbf{x}_t\}_t$.

Regarding the employed ECC we assume the following. It should be such that provides reliable decoding for the given parameter η and characteristics of the public communication channel.

A Discussion of the Encryption Security

This section yields a preliminary and informal discussion on the security of the proposed stream ciphers framework which points out to the security origins. For a formal security evaluation and the proofs see (Mihaljevic & Imai, 2009).

The role of the employed homophonic encoding, implemented via the random bits embedding, is to provide a heavy masking of the keystream generator sequences so that they appear as very uncertain for a given ciphertext even when the plaintext is known.

The proposed paradigm for providing the security is based on the following:

- Impossibility of correct decimation i.e. splitting of the effective from the dummy bits of the ciphertext without the secret key; and
- Availability of the noisy sample only, due to the employed additive noise degradation of the ciphertext before its transmission via a public communications channel.

The main role of the additive random degradation of the ciphertext is to introduce uncertainty into a sample available for cryptanalysis preventing a possibility of mounting the generic time-memory trade-off approaches for cryptanalysis in order to employ a generic approach more efficient than the exhaustive search. When an error-free sample is available the time-memory (and time-memory-data) trade-off based attacks can be directly mounted in order to recover the secret key **K**. On the other hand side, when the sample for cryptanalysis is not error-free, the time-memory trade-off approach, in a general case, does not work.

The above arguments are a background for the security evaluation of the proposed framework and for a conjecture that the complexity of cryptanalysis is determined by the complexity of exhaustive secret keys search. Note that the following are basic approaches for cryptanalysis of any stream cipher: (i) the generic key recovery attacks based on different search techniques (including the trade-off ones); (ii) the dedicated key recovery attacks based on particular weaknesses of the underlying structure; (iii) a number of different not key recovery oriented attacks (distinguishing attacks, ...).

In a known plaintext attack scenario, the goal of cryptanalysis is to recover the key **K**. There are the following two basic approaches for achieving this goal:

- Recovering **K** based on the given ciphertext $\{\mathbf{z}_t\}_t$,
- Recovering certain pseudorandom sequences specified by **K** based on $\{\mathbf{z}_t\}_t$ and then recovering **K** based on these sequences.

For achieving any of these goals, an attacker faces the following two main problems:

- The inverse mapping without knowledge of the secret key in order to recover the considered pseudorandom sequences based on $\{\mathbf{z}_t\}_t$;
- Impact of the noise sequence $\{\mathbf{v}_t\}_t$ to complexity of any generic technique for recovering the secret key beside the exhaustive search over the space of all possible keys which has complexity $O(2^K)$.

Hardness of the above problems is elaborated by the following. Note that even in the case of a noiseless public communication channel, there are the following two problems at the attacker's side:

- Removing the dummy bits from the ciphertext without knowledge of the secret key;

- Uncertainty due to effect of the binary symmetric channel with the crossover probability p <1/2 which corrupts the data before theirs availability to the attacker.

The uncertainty at the attacker's side can be considered as a consequence of a noise corresponding to a channel with the bits insertion and complementing which corrupts the sample for cryptanalysis. Because, the legitimate parties share the secret key, they face a lower noise (corresponding only to the bits complementing) in comparison with the noise which an attacker faces.

Accordingly, security of the scheme appears as consequence of the employed wiretap channel like encoding which provides confusion of an attacker which faces much heavier equivalent noise in comparison with the legitimate receiver because the attacker does not possess the employed secret key. This heavy noise implies that the attacker cannot learn about the keystream generator output sequences.

Without knowledge about the employed secret, it is not possible to efficiently remove dummy bits and to learn about (noisy) sequences from the keystream generator. On the other hand side, without reliable knowledge on the keystream generator output sequences, it is not possible to construct a more efficient approach for cryptanalysis than a hypothesis testing. Accordingly, the corruption of the output sequences by the noise $\{\mathbf{v}_t\}_t$ implies (as discussed above) that the time-memory trade-off hypotheses testing based attacks are not feasible because the entire system appears as a stochastic one which makes the algebraic approaches not feasible. So, the exhaustive search over the space of all possible keys appears as the only one option.

The above discussion implies that the security appears as a consequence of the uncertainty at the attacker's side which is jointly implied by: pseudorandom homophonic encoding, and effect of the intentional corruption of the data which are available only via a binary symmetric channel.

CONCLUSION

This chapter basically considers scientific and educational employment of a cloud as a particular instance of a public cloud and its security, and as a potentially specific issue, a request for a heavy minimization of the costs implied by security is pointed out and discussed.

Data processed in a public cloud and applications running in a public cloud may experience different security exposures in comparison with the case in an onsite hosted environment. A number of issues affect security of data and processing conducted in a cloud. For example, the quality of a cloud's implementation, the attack surface of a cloud, the likely pool of attackers, system complexity, and the expertise level of cloud administrators are a few considerations that affect cloud system security.

According to (Badger, Grance, Patt-Coner, & Voas, 2012), one aspect that is pervasive in cloud systems is reliance on "logical separation", as opposed to "physical separation" of user workloads, and the use of logical mechanisms to protect subscriber resources. Although more traditional systems employ logical separation also, they also employ physical separation (e.g., physically separated networks or systems) and logical separation has not been shown to be as reliable as physical separation; e.g., some virtualization systems have experienced heavy impacts of the dedicated attacks.

Consequently, establishing high security of cloud computing is recognized as one of the main requests. On the other hand side, the security mechanisms imply certain overhead – this overhead includes the following main components:

- Overhead regarding implementation of the security mechanisms;
- Computational overhead regarding operations of the security mechanisms; and
- Power consumption overhead of the security mechanisms.

Reduction of these security overheads is an active challenge. The security overheads reduction becomes more and more significant in the context of increasing the speed of processing and amount of involved data, so that each reduction of the per-bit normalized overhead appears as very important.

This chapter yields an overview of the cloud computing security issues and particularly addresses ones regarding the data protection based on data access control and encryption. The discussed encryption framework is an illustrative approach for providing reduction of certain security overheads and enhancing cryptographic security of compact light-weight encryption techniques.

ACKNOWLEDGMENT

The work has received partial financial support by the grants III 174006 and ON174008 of the Ministry for Education, Science and Technological Development, Government of Serbia.

REFERENCES

Badger, L., Grance, T., Patt-Coner, R., & Voas, J. (2012). *DRAFT cloud computing synopsis and recommendations (Special Publication 800-146)*. Gaithersburg, MD: NIST.

Bohli, J.-M., Gruschka, N., Jensen, M., Iacono, L. L., & Marnau, N. (2013). Security and privacy-enhancing multicloud architectures. *IEEE Transactions on Dependable and Secure Computing, 10*(4), 212–224. doi:10.1109/TDSC.2013.6

Borenstein, N., & Blake, J. (2011). Cloud computing standards: Where's the beef? *IEEE Internet Computing, 16*(2), 74–78. doi:10.1109/MIC.2011.58

Cloud Security Alliance. (2009). Security guidance for critical areas of focus in cloud computing V2.1. *Cloud Security Alliance*. Retrieved September 12, 2013, from https://cloudsecurityalliance.org/csaguide.pdf

Flynn, M., Mencer, O., Milutinovic, V., Rakocevi, G., Stenstrom, P., Trobec, R., & Valerio, M. (2013). Moving from Petaflops to Petadata. *Communications of the ACM, 56*(5), 39–42. doi:10.1145/2447976.2447989

Fossorier, M., Mihaljevic, M., & Imai, H. (2007). Modeling block coding approaches for fast correlation attack. *IEEE Transactions on Information Theory, 53*(12), 4728–4737. doi:10.1109/TIT.2007.909164

Fossorier, M., Mihaljevic, M., Imai, H., Cui, Y., & Matsuura, K. (2006). An algorithm for solving the LPN problem and its application to security evaluation of the HB protocols for RFID authentication. *Lecture Notes in Computer Science, 4329*, 48–62. doi:10.1007/11941378_5

Jansen, W., & Grance, T. (2011). *Guidelines on security and privacy in public cloud computing (Special Publication 800-144)*. Gaithersburg, MD: NIST.

Khiabani, Y., Wei, S., Yuan, J., & Wang, J. (2012). Enhancement of secrecy of block ciphered systems by deliberate noise. *IEEE Transactions on Information Forensics and Security, 7*(5), 1604–1613. doi:10.1109/TIFS.2012.2204983

Li, M., Yu, S., Zheng, Y., Ren, K., & Lou, W. (2013). Scalable and secure sharing of personal health records in cloud computing using attribute-based encryption. *IEEE Transactions on Information Forensics and Security, 8*(1), 131–143.

Lotspiech, J., Nusser, S., & Pestoni, F. (2002). Broadcast encryption's bright future. *Computer, 35*(8), 57–63. doi:10.1109/MC.2002.1023789

Mell, P. (2012). What's special about cloud security? *IT Professional, 14*(4), 6–8. doi:10.1109/MITP.2012.84

Mihaljevic, M. (2003). Key management schemes for stateless receivers based on time varying heterogeneous logical key hierarchy. *Lecture Notes in Computer Science, 2894*, 137–154. doi:10.1007/978-3-540-40061-5_9

Mihaljevic, M. (2004). Reconfigurable key management for broadcast encryption. *IEEE Communications Letters, 8*(7), 440–442. doi:10.1109/LCOMM.2004.832774

Mihaljevic, M. (2007). Generic framework for secure Yuan 2000 quantum encryption protocol employing the wire-tap channel approach. *Physical Review A., 75*(5), 052334-1–5. doi:10.1103/PhysRevA.75.052334

Mihaljevic, M. (2009). A framework for stream ciphers based on pseudorandomness, randomness and error correcting coding. In B. Preneel, S. Dodunekov, V. Rijmen, & S. Nikova (Eds.), *Enhancing cryptographic primitives with techniques from error correcting codes* (pp. 117–139). Amsterdam, The Netherlands: IOS Press.

Mihaljevic, M. (2012). An approach for lightweight encryption employing dedicated coding. In *Proceedings of 2012 IEEE Global Communications Conference (GLOBECOM)* (pp. 874-880). New York, NY: IEEE Communications Society.

Mihaljevic, M., Fossorier, M., & Imai, H. (2007). Security evaluation of certain broadcast encryption schemes employing a generalized time-memory-data trade-off. *IEEE Communications Letters, 11*(12), 988–990. doi:10.1109/LCOMM.2007.071029

Mihaljevic, M., Gangopadhyay, S., Paul, G., & Imai, H. (2012a). Internal state recovery of grain-v1: Employing normality order of the filter function. *IET Information Security, 6*(2), 55–64. doi:10.1049/iet-ifs.2011.0107

Mihaljevic, M., Gangopadhyay, S., Paul, G., & Imai, H. (2012b). Internal state recovery of keystream generator LILI-128 based on a novel weakness of the employed Boolean function. *Information Processing Letters*, *112*(21), 805–810. doi:10.1016/j.ipl.2012.07.013

Mihaljevic, M., & Imai, H. (2009). An approach for stream ciphers design based on joint computing over random and secret data. *Computing*, *85*(1-2), 153–168. doi:10.1007/s00607-009-0035-x

Ren, K., Wang, C., & Wang, Q. (2012). Security challenges for the public cloud. *IEEE Internet Computing*, *16*(1), 69–73. doi:10.1109/MIC.2012.14

Wan, Z., Liu, J., & Deng, R. (2012). HASBE: A hierarchical attribute-based solution for flexible and scalable access control in cloud computing. *IEEE Transactions on Information Forensics and Security*, *7*(2), 743–754. doi:10.1109/TIFS.2011.2172209

Wci, S., Wang, J., Yin, R., & Yuan, J. (2013). Trade-off between security and performance in block ciphered systems with erroneous ciphertexts. *IEEE Transactions on Information Forensics and Security*, *8*(4), 636–645. doi:10.1109/TIFS.2013.2248724

Xiao, Z., & Xiao, Y. (2013). Security and privacy in cloud computing. *IEEE Communications Surveys & Tutotials*, *15*(2), 843–859. doi:10.1109/SURV.2012.060912.00182

ADDITIONAL READING

Barua, M., Liang, X., Lu, R., & Shen, X. (2011). ESPAC: Enabling Security and Patient-centric Access Control for eHealth in Cloud Computing. *International Journal on Security and Networks*, *6*(2/3), 67–76. doi:10.1504/IJSN.2011.043666

Basu, S., Karp, A., Li, J., Pruyne, J., Rolia, J., & Singhal, S. et al. (2012). Fusion: Managing Healthcare Records at Cloud Scale. *Computer*, (November Issue), 42–49. doi:10.1109/MC.2012.291

Bernstein, D., & Vij, D. (2010). Intercloud Security Considerations. In *2nd International Conference on Cloud Computing* - CloudCom 10 (pp. 537-544). Washington, DC: IEEE Computer Society Press.

Chai, Q., & Gong, G. (2011). On the (in) security of two Joint Encryption and Error Correction schemes. *International Journal on Security and Networks*, *6*(4), 191–200. doi:10.1504/IJSN.2011.045227

Giannotti, F., Lakshmanan, L., Monreale, A., Pedreschi, D., & Wang, H. (2013). Privacy-Preserving Mining of Association Rules from Outsourced Transaction Databases. *IEEE Systems Journal*, *7*(3), 385–395. doi:10.1109/JSYST.2012.2221854

Grobauer, B., Walloschek, T., & Stocker, E. (2011). Understanding cloud computing vulnerabilities. *IEEE Security and Privacy*, *9*(2), 50–57. doi:10.1109/MSP.2010.115

Gruschka, N., & Jensen, M. (2010). Attack Surfaces: A Taxonomy for Attacks on Cloud Services. In *2010 IEEE 3rd International Conference on Cloud Computing*, (pp. 276-279). Washington, DC: IEEE Computer Society Press.

Idziorek, J., Tannian, M., & Jacobson, D. (2011). Detecting fraudulent use of cloud resources. In *3rd ACM workshop on Cloud computing security* (pp. 61-72). New York City, NY: ACM.

Kao, Y., Huang, K., Gu, H., & Yuan, S. (2013). uCloud: a user-centric key management scheme for cloud data protection. *IET Information Security*, *7*(2), 144–154. doi:10.1049/iet-ifs.2012.0198

Lin, H., & Tzeng, W. (2010). A Secure Decentralized Erasure Code for Distributed Network Storage. *IEEE Transactions on Parallel and Distributed Systems*, *21*(11), 1586–1594. doi:10.1109/TPDS.2010.27

Lombardi, P., & Di Pietro, R. (2010). Transparent security for cloud. In 2010 ACM Symposium on Applied Computing (pp. 414-415). New York City, NY: ACM.

Michael, J. (2013). Empowering Users through Secure On-Demand Data Provisioning. *Computer*, (June Issue), 84–85. doi:10.1109/MC.2013.203

Moreno-Vozmediano, R., Montero, R., & Llorente, I. (2013). Key Challenges in Cloud Computing: Enabling the Future Internet of Services. *IEEE Internet Computing. July/August Issue*, 18-25.

Naehrig, M., Lauter, K., & Vaikuntanathan, V. (2011). Can homomorphic encryption be practical? *In 3rd ACM Workshop on Cloud Computing Security* (pp. 113-124), New York City, NY: ACM.

Qiang, W., Zou, D., Wang, S., Yang, L. T., Jin, H., & Shi, L. (2013). CloudAC: a cloud-oriented multilayer access control system for logic virtual domain. *IET Information Security*, *7*(1), 51–59. doi:10.1049/iet-ifs.2012.0094

Saripalli, P., & Walters, B. (2010). QUIRC: A Quantitative Impact and Risk Assessment Framework for Cloud Security. In *2010 IEEE 3rd International Conference on Cloud Computing* (pp. 280-288). Washington, DC: IEEE Computer Society Press.

Singhal, M., Chandrasekhar, S., Ge, T., Sandhu, E., Krishnan, R., Ahn, G., & Bertino, R. (2013). Collaboration in Multicloud Computing Environments: Framework and Security Issues. *Computer*, (February Issue), 76–84. doi:10.1109/MC.2013.46

Subashini, S., & Kavitha, V. (2011). A survey on security issues in service delivery models of cloud computing. *Journal of Network and Computer Applications*, *34*(1), 1–11. doi:10.1016/j.jnca.2010.07.006

Szefer, J., Keller, E., Lee, R., & Rexford, J. (2011). Eliminating the hypervisor attack surface for a more secure cloud. In *18th ACM conference on Computer and communications security* (pp. 401-412). New York City, NY: ACM.

Tang, Y., Lee, P., Lui, J., & Perlman, R. (2013). Secure Overlay Cloud Storage with Access Control and Assured Deletion. *IEEE Transactions on Dependable and Secure Computing*, *9*(6), 903–916. doi:10.1109/TDSC.2012.49

Tordsson, J. et al. (2012). Cloud Brokering Mechanisms for Optimized Placement of Virtual Machines across Multiple Providers. *Future Generation Computer Systems*, *28*(2), 358–367. doi:10.1016/j.future.2011.07.003

Vattikonda, B., Das, S., & Shacham, H. (2011). Eliminating fine grained timers in Xen. In *3rd ACM workshop on Cloud computing security* (pp. 41-46). New York City, NY: ACM.

Weis, J., & Alves-Foss, J. (2011). Securing Database as a Service Issues and Compromises. *IEEE Security & Privacy, November/December Issue*, 49-55.

Zhang, Y., Juels, A., Oprea, A., & Reiter, M. (2011). HomeAlone: Co-residency Detection in the Cloud via Side-Channel Analysis. In *IEEE Symposium on Security and Privacy* (pp. 313-328). Washington, DC: IEEE Computer Society Press.

Zissis, D., & Lekkas, D. (2012). Addressing Cloud Computing Security Issues. *Future Generation Computer Systems*, *28*(3), 583–592. doi:10.1016/j.future.2010.12.006

KEY TERMS AND DEFINITIONS

Cloud Computing: Processing of data in a virtual environment within a complex and remote computer system.

Coding: Direct (Encoding) and inverse (Decoding) mapping of a data vector.

Cryptography: Scientific discipline dedicated to fundamental techniques for information security.

Data Access Control: A cryptographic approach for preventing unauthorized use of data.

Encryption: A cryptographic approach for providing data confidentiality.

Privacy: A request for preventing unauthorized disclosure of data.

Security: Un-breakability of the data protection.

Compilation of References

110. *Stat. 1936 - Health Insurance Portability and Accountability Act of 1996*. (1996). Retrieved October 10, 2013, from http://www.gpo.gov/fdsys/pkg/STATUTE-110/pdf/STATUTE-110-Pg1936.pdf

Aaron, W. (2007). Computing in the cloud. *netWorker*, *11*(4), 16–25. doi:10.1145/1327512.1327513

Abbott, M. B. (1991). *Hydroinformatics: Information technology and the aquatic environment*. Adlershot, UK: Avebury Technical Books.

Abbott, M. B. (1994). Hydroinformatics: A Copernican revolution in hydraulics. *Journal of Hydraulic Research*, *32*(S1), 3–13. doi:10.1080/00221689409498800

Abbott, R. (1983). Program design by informal English descriptions. *Communications of the ACM*, *26*(11), 882–894. doi:10.1145/182.358441

Abelson, H. (1999). *Architects of the information society: Thirty-five years of the laboratory for computer science at MIT*. Cambridge, MA: MIT Press.

Advanced Distributed Learning. (2009). *SCORM 2004 content aggregation model* [CAM]. 4th ed.). Alexandria, VA: ADL Initiative.

Alba, E. (Ed.). (2005). *Parallel metaheuristics: A new class of algorithms*. Hoboken, NJ: John Wiley & Sons. doi:10.1002/0471739383

Ally, M. (2009). *Mobile learning: Transforming the delivery of education and training*. Retrieved from http://www.aupress.ca/books/120155/ebook/99Z_Mohamed_Ally_2009-MobileLearning.pdf

Amdahl, G. (1967). Validity of the single processor approach to achieving large scale computing capabilities. In *Proceedings of the AFIPS Spring Joint Computer Conference SE - AFIPS '67* (Spring) (pp. 483-485). New York, NY: ACM.

Anand, N., & Daft, R. (2007). What is the right organization design? *Organizational Dynamics*, *36*(4), 329–344.

Anderson, C. (Ed.). (2009). *Free: The future of a radical price*. New York: Hyperion.

Anderson, D. P., Cobb, J., Korpela, E., Lebofsky, M., & Werthimer, D. (2002). SETI@home: An experiment in public-resource computing. *Communications of the ACM*, *45*(11), 56–61. doi:10.1145/581571.581573 PMID:12238525

Andreas, B., Gelenbe, E., Di Girolamo, M., Giuliani, G., De Meer, H., Dang, M. Q., & Pentikousis, K. (2010). Energy-efficient cloud computing. *The Computer Journal*, *53*(7), 1045–1051. doi:10.1093/comjnl/bxp080

Andrikopoulos, V., Binz, T., Leymann, F., & Strauch, S. (2013). How to adapt applications for the cloud environment - Challenges and solutions in migrating applications to the cloud. *Computing*, *95*(6), 493–535. doi:10.1007/s00607-012-0248-2

Angin, P., & Bhargava, B. K. (2011). Real-time mobile-cloud computing for context-aware blind navigation. *International Journal of Next Generation Computing*, *2*(2).

Angiuoli, S. V., White, J. R., Matalka, M., White, O., & Fricke, F. W. (2011). Resources and costs for microbial sequence analysis evaluated using virtual machines and cloud computing. *PLoS ONE*, *6*(10), 1–10. PMID:22028928

Antović, I., Vlajić, S., Savić, D., Milić, M., & Stanojević, V. (2012). Model and software tool for automatic generation of user interface based on use case and data model. *IET Software*, *6*(6), 559–573. doi:10.1049/iet-sen.2011.0060

Armbrust, M., Fox, A., Griffith, R., Joseph, A., Katz, R., & Konwinski, A. ... Zaharia, M. (2009). *Above the clouds: A Berkeley view of cloud computing* (Technical Report No. UCB/EECS-2009-28). Berkeley, CA: University of California at Berkley.

Arnold, J. G., & Fohrer, N. (2005). SWAT2000: Current capabilities and research opportunities in applied watershed modelling. *Hydrological Processes*, *19*(3), 563–572. doi:10.1002/hyp.5611

Atanassov, E. I., Dimov, I. T., & Durchova, M. K. (2004). A new quasi-Monte Carlo algorithm for numerical integration of smooth functions. *Lecture Notes in Computer Science*, *2907*, 128–135. doi:10.1007/978-3-540-24588-9_13

Aydin, M., & Sevkli, M. (2008). Sequential and parallel variable neighborhood search algorithms for job shop scheduling. In F. Xhafa, & A. Abraham (Eds.), *Metaheuristics for scheduling in industrial and manufacturing applications* (Vol. 128, pp. 125–144). Berlin: Springer. doi:10.1007/978-3-540-78985-7_6

Aymerich, F. M., Fenu, G., & Surcis, S. (2008). An approach to a cloud computing network. In *Applications of digital information and web technologies* (pp. 113–118). IEEE. doi:10.1109/ICADIWT.2008.4664329

Bader, D. A. (Ed.). (2007). *Petascale computing: Algorithms and applications*. Boca Raton, FL: CRC Press. doi:10.1201/9781584889106

Badger, L., Grance, T., Patt-Coner, R., & Voas, J. (2012). *DRAFT cloud computing synopsis and recommendations (Special Publication 800-146)*. Gaithersburg, MD: NIST.

Baer, J. L., & Wang, W. H. (1988). On the inclusion properties for multi-level cache hierarchies: Vol. 16. *No. 2* (pp. 73–80). IEEE Computer Society Press.

Bai, X. B. X. (2010). Affordance of ubiquitous learning through cloud computing. In *Proceedings of Frontier of Computer Science and Technology FCST 2010 Fifth International Conference on*. IEEE Computer Society.

Baker, M. (2009). *Cloud computing*. Retrieved October 10, 2013, from http://www.cse.unr.edu/~mgunes/cpe401/lect15_cloud.ppt

Balaž, A., Bogojević, A., Vidanović, I., & Pelster, A. (2009). Recursive Schroedinger equation approach to faster converging path integrals. *Physical Review E: Statistical, Nonlinear, and Soft Matter Physics*, *79*, 036701. doi:10.1103/PhysRevE.79.036701

Balaž, A., Prnjat, O., Vudragović, D., Slavnic, V., Liabotis, I., & Atanassov, E. et al. (2011). Development of grid e-infrastructure in South-Eastern Europe. *Journal of Grid Computing*, *9*(2), 135–154. doi:10.1007/s10723-011-9185-0

Balaž, A., Vidanović, I., Bogojević, A., & Pelster, A. (2010). Ultra-fast converging path-integral approach for rotating ideal Bose-Einstein condensates. *Physics Letters. [Part A]*, *374*(13-14), 1539–1549. doi:10.1016/j.physleta.2010.01.034

Balaž, A., Vidanović, I., Stojiljković, D., Vudragović, D., Belić, A., & Bogojević, A. (2012). SPEEDUP code for calculation of transition amplitudes via the effective action approach. *Computer Physics Communications*, *11*(3), 739–755.

Banharnsakun, A., Achalakul, T., & Sirinaovakul, B. (2010). Artificial bee colony algorithm on distributed environments. In H. Takagi, A. Abraham, M. Koppen, K. Yoshida, & A. C. P. L. F. de Carvalho (Eds.), *Second world congress on nature and biologically inspired computing (NaBIC'10)* (pp. 13-18). The Institute of Electrical and Electronics Engineers, Inc.

Barbosa, J., Hahn, R., Barbosa, D. N. F., & Geyer, C. F. R. (2008). Learning in small and large ubiquitous computing environments. In *Proceedings of 2008 IEEEIFIP International Conference on Embedded and Ubiquitous Computing*. IEEE. Retrieved from http://ieeexplore.ieee.org/lpdocs/epic03/wrapper.htm?arnumber=4756367

Barjaktarović-Rakočević, S., Marković, A., & Čavoški, S. (2006). Common stocks valuation using simulation models - Case of Serbian capital market. In Proceedings of International Scientific Days 2006, Competitivness in the EU - Challenge for the V4 Countries (pp. 1110-1116). Nitra: Faculty of Economic and Management SAU in Nitra.

Barreto, W., Vojinovic, Z., Price, R., & Solomatine, D. (2009). Multiobjective evolutionary approach to rehabilitation of urban drainage systems. *Journal of Water Resources Planning and Management, 136*(5), 547–554. doi:10.1061/(ASCE)WR.1943-5452.0000070

Basaeed, E., Berri, J., Zemerly, M. J., & Benlamri, R. (2007). Learner-centric context-aware mobile learning. *IEEE Multidisciplinary Engineering Education Magazine, 2*(2), 30–33.

Bateman, A., & Wood, M. (2009). Cloud computing. *Bioinformatics (Oxford, England), 25*(12), 1475. PMID:19435745

Baun, C., & Kunze, M. (2009). Performance measurement of a private cloud in the opencirrus (TM) testbed. In H.-X. Lin, M. Alexander, M. Forsell, A. Knüpfer, R. Prodan, L. Sousa, & A. Streit (Eds.), *Euro-Par 2009 - Parallel Processing Workshops* (pp. 434–443). Berlin: Springer-Verlag.

Bernal, A., Ramirez, M. A., Castro, H., Walteros, J. L., & Medaglia, A. L. (2009). JG2A: A grid-enabled object-oriented framework for developing genetic algorithms. In *Proceedings of 2009 Systems and Information Engineering Design Symposium*. Retrieved from http://www.scopus.com/inward/record.url?eid=2-s2.0-77950273380&partnerID=40&md5=1308cf163301b8874f9b64363989f0b1

Bernd, B., & Allen, D. (2004). *Object-oriented software engineering using UML, patterns, and Java* (2nd ed.). Upper Saddle River, NJ: Prentice Hall.

Bertino, E., Paci, F., Ferrini, R., & Shang, N. (2009). Privacy-preserving digital identity management for cloud computing. *IEEE Data Eng. Bull., 32*(1), 21–27.

Betts, D., Densmore, S., Dunn, R., Narumoto, M., Pace, E., & Woloski, M. (2010). *Developing applications for the cloud on the Microsoft® Windows Azure™ platform*. Redmond, WA: Microsoft.

Beyou, D. (2005, March/April). Treating students like customers. *BizEd Magazine*, 44-47.

Binkert, N. L., Dreslinski, R. G., Hsu, L. R., Lim, K. T., Saidi, A. G., & Reinhardt, S. K. (2006). The M5 simulator: Modeling networked systems. *IEEE Micro, 26*(4), 52–60. doi:10.1109/MM.2006.82

Bishop, M. (2003). What is computer security? *IEEE Security & Privacy, 1*(1), 67–69. doi:10.1109/MSECP.2003.1176998

Blakley, B., & Reeves, D. (Eds.). (2010). *Defining cloud computing*. Washington, DC: Gartner Inc.

Bogdanovic, Z., Jovanic, B., Barac, D., Milic, A., & Despotovic-Zrakic, M. (2011). An application of cloud computing as infrastructure for Eeducation. In L. Gómez Chova, D. Martí Belenguer, & A. López Martínez (Ed.), *Edulearn11 International Conference on Education and new Learning Technologies* (pp. 4699-4707). International Association of Technology, Education and Development (IATED).

Bogojević, A., Balaž, A., & Belić, A. (2005b). Systematic speedup of path integrals of a generic n-fold discretized theory. *Physical Review Letters, B 72*, 064302:1-8.

Bogojević, A., Balaž, A., & Belić, A. (2005a). Systematically accelerated convergence of path integrals. *Physical Review Letters, 94*(18), 180403–180407. doi:10.1103/PhysRevLett.94.180403 PMID:15904348

Bogojević, A., Balaž, A., & Belić, A. (2005c). Generalization of Euler's summation formula to path integrals. *Physics Letters. [Part A], 344*, 84–90. doi:10.1016/j.physleta.2005.06.053

Bogojević, A., Balaž, A., & Belić, A. (2005d). Asymptotic properties of path integral ideals. *Physical Review E: Statistical, Nonlinear, and Soft Matter Physics, 72*(036128), 1–4.

Bogojević, A., Vidanović, I., Balaž, A., & Belić, A. (2008). Fast convergence of path integrals for many-body systems. *Physics Letters. [Part A], 372*(19), 3341–3349. doi:10.1016/j.physleta.2008.01.079

Bohli, J.-M., Gruschka, N., Jensen, M., Iacono, L. L., & Marnau, N. (2013). Security and privacy-enhancing multicloud architectures. *IEEE Transactions on Dependable and Secure Computing, 10*(4), 212–224. doi:10.1109/TDSC.2013.6

Borenstein, N., & Blake, J. (2011). Cloud computing standards: Where's the beef? *IEEE Internet Computing, 16*(2), 74–78. doi:10.1109/MIC.2011.58

Boss, G., Malladi, P., Quan, S., Legregni, L., & Hall, H. (2007). *Cloud computing (Technical Report, IBM high performance on demand solutions, version 1.0a)*. IBM.

Boyd, D. M., & Ellison, N. B. (2007). Social network sites: Definition, history, and scholarship. *Journal of Computer-Mediated Communication, 13*(1), 210–230. doi:10.1111/j.1083-6101.2007.00393.x

Bradley, A. J., & McDonald, M. P. (Eds.). (2011). *The social organization: How to use social media to tap the collective genius of your customers and employees.* Boston: Harvard Business Review Press.

Bradley, C., Haynes, R., Cook, J., Boyle, T., & Smith, C. (2008). Design and development of multimedia learning objects for mobile phones. In M. Ally (Ed.), *Mobile learning in education and training* (pp. 158–181). Edmonton, Canada: AU Press.

Buchanan, M. (2003). *Nexus: Small worlds and the groundbreaking science of networks.* New York: W. W. Norton & Company, Inc.

Buss, A. H., & Stork, K. A. (1996). Discrete-event simulation on the world wide web using Java. In *Proceedings of the 28th Conference on Winter Simulation* (pp. 780-785). Washington, DC: IEEE Computer Society.

Butenhof, D. R. (Ed.). (1997). *Programming with POSIX threads.* Reading, MA: Addison-Wesley Professional.

Buyya, R. (2009). Market-oriented cloud computing: Vision, hype, and reality of delivering computing as the 5th utility. In F. Cappello, C.-L. Wang, & R. Buyya (Eds.), *10th IEEE International Conference on High Performance Computing and Communications* (pp. 1-1). Los Alamitos, CA: IEEE Computer Society.

Buyya, R. (Ed.). (1999). *High performance cluster computing: Architectures and systems* (Vol. 1). Upper Saddle River, NJ: Prentice Hall.

Buyya, R., Yeo, C. S., Venugopal, S., Broberg, J., & Brandic, I. (2009). Cloud computing and emerging IT platforms: Vision, hype, and reality for delivering computing as the 5th utility. *Future Generation Computer Systems, 25*(6), 599–616. doi:10.1016/j.future.2008.12.001

Byrne, J., Heavey, C., & Byrne, P. J. (2010). A review of web-based simulation and supporting tools. *Simulation Modelling Practice and Theory, 18*(3), 253–404. doi:10.1016/j.simpat.2009.09.013

Cahon, S., Melab, N., & Talbi, E. G. (2005). An enabling framework for parallel optimization on the computational grid. In *Proceedings of CCGrid 2005 IEEE International Symposium on Cluster Computing and the Grid 2005.* Washington, DC: IEEE Computer Society Press. Retrieved from http://ieeexplore.ieee.org/lpdocs/epic03/wrapper.htm?arnumber=1558632

Cahon, S., Melab, N., & Talbi, E. G. (2004). ParadisEO: A framework for the reusable design of parallel and distributed metaheuristics. *Journal of Heuristics, 10*(3), 357–380. doi:10.1023/B:HEUR.0000026900.92269.ec

Calheiros, R. N., Ranjan, R., De Rose, C. A. F., & Buyya, R. (2009). *CloudSim: A novel framework for modeling and simulation of cloud computing* (CoRR, abs/0903.2525). Retrieved October 10, 2013, from http://arxiv.org/abs/0903.2525

Calsoft. (2013). *Infrastructure-as-a-service.* Retrieved October 10, 2013, from http://www.calsoftinc.com/IaaS-new.aspx

Cardos, N. (2011). *Virtual clusters sustained by cloud computing infrastructures.* (Master Thesis). Faculdade De Engenharia Da Universidade Do Porto.

Cardoso, J., Binz, T., Breitenbücher, U., Kopp, O., & Leymann, F. (2013). Cloud computing automation: Integrating USDL and TOSCA.[CAiSE.]. *Proceedings of CAiSE, 2013*, 1–16.

Carlin, S., & Curran, K. (2011). Cloud computing security. *International Journal of Ambient Computing and Intelligence, 3*(1), 14–19. doi:10.4018/jaci.2011010102

Caron, E., Desprez, F., Loureiro, D., & Muresan, A. (2009). Cloud computing resource management through a grid middleware: A case study with DIET and eucalyptus. In J. E. Guerrero (Ed.), *2009 IEEE International Conference on Cloud Computing* (pp. 151-154). Los Alamitos, CA: IEEE Computer Society.

Cary-1 Computer System. (1977). *Reference*. Manual.

Catteddu, D., & Hogben, G. (2009). *Cloud computing security risk assessment*. Retrieved April 13, 2013, from http://www.enisa.europa.eu/activities/risk-management/files/deliverables/cloud-computing-risk-assessment/at_download/fullReport

Cearley, D. W. (2010). *Cloud computing: Key initiative overview*. Retrieved April 13, 2013, from http://www.gartner.com/it/initiatives/pdf/KeyInitiativeOverview_CloudComputing.pdf

Cearley, D., & Smith, D. M. (2010, November). *The cloud computing scenario*. Paper presented at the Gartner Symposium/ITxpo 2010. Cannes, France.

Ceperley, D. M. (1995). Path integrals in the theory of condensed helium. *Reviews of Modern Physics, 67*(2), 279–355. doi:10.1103/RevModPhys.67.279

Cerbelaud, D., Garg, S., & Huylebroeck, J. (2009). Opening the clouds: Qualitative overview of the state-of-the-art open source Vmbased cloud management platforms. In *Proceedings of the 10th ACM/IFIP/USENIX International Conference on Middleware*, (pp. 1-8). New York: Springer-Verlag.

Chang, H., & Tang, X. (2011). A load-balance based resource-scheduling algorithm under cloud computing environment. In *New Horizons in Web-Based Learning - ICWL 2010 Workshops* (pp. 85–90). Berlin: Springer-Verlag. doi:10.1007/978-3-642-20539-2_10

Chao, L. (2012). *Cloud computing for teaching and learning: Strategies for design and implementation*. Hershey, PA: IGI Global. doi:10.4018/978-1-4666-0957-0

Chappell, D. (2010), MSDN library. *Introducing Windows Communication Foundation in.NET Framework 4*. Retrieved from http://msdn.microsoft.com/en-us/library/ee958158.aspx

Chard, K., Caton, S., Rana, O., & Bubendorfer, K. (2010). *Social cloud: Cloud computing in social networks*. Paper presented at IEEE 3rd International Conference on Cloud Computing (CLOUD). doi: 10.1109/CLOUD.2010.28

Chellappa, R. K. (1997, October). *Intermediaries in cloud-computing: A new computing paradigm*. Paper presented at the INFORMS National Meeting. Dallas, TX.

Chen, W. (2002). Web services - What do they mean to web-based education? In *Proceedings of International Conference on Computers in Education* (vol. 1, pp. 707-708). Washington, DC: IEEE Computer. Society Press.

Chen, C.-M. (2009). Ontology-based concept map for planning a personalised learning path. *British Journal of Educational Technology, 40*(6), 1028–1058. doi:10.1111/j.1467-8535.2008.00892.x

Chen, G. D., Chang, C. K., & Wang, C. Y. (2008). Ubiquitous learning website: Scaffold learners by mobile devices with information-aware techniques. *Computers & Education, 50*(1), 77–90. doi:10.1016/j.compedu.2006.03.004

Chen, H., & Huang, H. (2010). User acceptance of mobile knowledge management learning system: Design and analysis. *Journal of Educational Technology & Society, 13*(3), 70–77.

Chen, I. J., & Popovich, K. (2003). Understanding customer relationship management (CRM), people, process and technology. *Business Process Management Journal, 9*(5), 672–688. doi:10.1108/14637150310496758

Chen, Y. S., Kao, T. C., & Sheu, J. P. (2003). A mobile learning system for scaffolding bird watching learning. *Journal of Computer Assisted Learning, 19*(3), 347–359. doi:10.1046/j.0266-4909.2003.00036.x

Chorfi, H. O., Sevkli, A. Z., & Bousbahi, F. (2012). Mobile learning adaption through a device based reasoning. *Procedia - Social and Behavioral Sciences, 47*, 1707-1712.

Chou, D., deVadoss, J., Erl, T., Gandhi, N., Kommalapati, H., Loesgen, B., & Williams, M. (2010). *SOA with.NET and Windows Azure*. Upper Saddle River, NJ: Prentice Hall.

Christensen, J. H. (2009). Using RESTful web-services and cloud computing to create next generation mobile applications. In *Proceeding of the 24th ACM SIGPLAN Conference Companion on Object Oriented Programming Systems Languages and Applications OOPSLA 09*. ACM Press. Retrieved from http://portal.acm.org/citation.cfm?doid=1639950.1639958

Chu, H.-C., Hwang, G.-J., Tsai, C.-C., & Tseng, J. C. R. (2010). A two-tier test approach to developing location-aware mobile learning systems for natural science courses. *Computers & Education, 55*(4), 1618–1627. doi:10.1016/j.compedu.2010.07.004

Chun, B., & Maniatis, P. (2009). Augmented smartphone applications through clone cloud execution. *Heart (British Cardiac Society)*, *43*(5), 8.

Chun, B., & Patti, A. (2011). CloneCloud: Elastic execution between mobile device and cloud. *Most*, *17*, 301–314.

Churchill, D., & Hedberg, J. (2008). Learning object design considerations for small-screen handheld devices. *Computers & Education*, *50*(3), 881–893. doi:10.1016/j.compedu.2006.09.004

Cloud Security Alliance. (2009). Security guidance for critical areas of focus in cloud computing V2.1. *Cloud Security Alliance*. Retrieved September 12, 2013, from https://cloudsecurityalliance.org/csaguide.pdf

Cloud Security Alliance. (2011). *Security guidance for critical areas of focus in cloud computing v3.0*. Retrieved from https://cloudsecurityalliance.org/guidance/csaguide.v3.0.pdf

Clough, G., Jones, A. C., McAndrew, P., & Scanlon, E. (2007). Informal learning with PDAs and smartphones. *Journal of Computer Assisted Learning*, *24*(5), 359–371. doi:10.1111/j.1365-2729.2007.00268.x

Cockburn, A. (Ed.). (2000). *Writing effective use cases*. New York: Addison-Wesley.

Costanzo, A., Assuncao, M., & Buyya, R. (2009). Harnessing cloud technologies for a virtualized distributed computing infrastructure. *IEEE Internet Computing*, *13*(5), 24–33. doi:10.1109/MIC.2009.108

Coulby, C., Hennessey, S., Davies, N., & Fuller, R. (2011). The use of mobile technology for work-based assessment: The student experience. *British Journal of Educational Technology*, *42*(2), 251–265. doi:10.1111/j.1467-8535.2009.01022.x

Cowhey, P., & Aronson, J. (Eds.). (2009). *Transforming global information and communication markets*. Boston: MIT Press.

Crainic, T. G., & Toulouse, M. (2010). Parallel metaheuristics. In M. Gendreau & J.Y. Potvin (Eds.), Handbook of metaheuristics (pp. 497-541). New York: Springer Science+Business Media.

Crainic, T. G., Gendreau, M., Hansen, P., & Mladenović, N. (2004). Cooperative parallel variable neighborhood search for the p-median. *Journal of Heuristics*, *10*(3), 293–314. doi:10.1023/B:HEUR.0000026897.40171.1a

Crainic, T. G., & Hail, N. (2005). Parallel meta-heuristics applications. In E. Alba (Ed.), *Parallel metaheuristics: A new class of algorithms* (pp. 447–494). Hoboken, NJ: John Wiley & Sons. doi:10.1002/0471739383.ch19

Čudanov, M., Krivokapić, J., & Krunić, J. (2011). The influence of cloud computing concept on organizational performance and structure. *Management – Journal for Management Theory and Practice, 16*(60), 19-25.

Čudanov, M. (Ed.). (2007). *Projektovanje organizacije i IKT*. Beograd: Zadužbina Andrejević.

Čudanov, M. (Ed.). (2011). *Organizacija i strateška primena informacionih i komunikacionih tehnologija*. Belgrade: Zadužbina Andrejević.

Čudanov, M., & Jaško, O. (2010). Adoption of information and communication technologies and dominant management orientation in organisations. *Behaviour & Information Technology*, *31*(5), 509–523.

Čudanov, M., Jaško, O., & Jevtić, M. (2009). Influence of information and communication technologies on decentralization of organizational structure. *Computer Science and Information Systems Journal, 6*(1), 93–108.

Čudanov, M., Jaško, O., & Savoiu, G. (2010). Interrelationships of organization size and information and communication technology adoption. *Journal of Applied Quantitative Methods, 5*(1), 29–40.

Čudanov, M., Săvoiu, G., & Jaško, O. (2012). New link in bioinformatics services value chain: Position, organization and business model. *The Amfiteatru Economic Journal, 14*(6), 680–697.

Cuervo, E., Balasubramanian, A., & Cho, D. (2010). MAUI: Making smartphones last longer with code offload. *Energy, 17*(1), 49–62.

Cunge, J. A. (1998). From hydraulics to hydroinformatics. In *Proceedings 3rd Int. Conference. Hydro--Science and--Engineering, Cottbus*. Academic Press.

Cung, V.-D., Martins, S. L., Ribeiro, C. C., & Roucairol, C. (2002). Strategies for the parallel implementations of metaheuristics. In C. C. Ribeiro, & P. Hansen (Eds.), *Essays and surveys in metaheuristics* (pp. 263–308). Norwell, MA: Kluwer Academic Publishers. doi:10.1007/978-1-4615-1507-4_13

Cvetković, D., & Davidović, T. (2011). Multiprocessor interconnection networks. In D. Cvetković & I. Gutman (Eds.), Selected topics on applications of graph spectra (pp. 35-62). Serbia: Mathematical Institute SANU.

Dagum, L., & Menon, R. (1998). OpenMP: An industry standard api for shared-memory programming. *IEEE Computational Science & Engineering*, *5*(1), 46–55. doi:10.1109/99.660313

Daly, D. M., Goodman, B. L., Powell, S. J., Sawdey, A. C., & Stuecheli, J. A. (2013). *U.S. patent no. 20,130,151,780*. Washington, DC: U.S. Patent and Trademark Office.

Danfeng, Y., Fangchun, Y., & Yeap, T. (2011). Service security architecture and access control model for cloud computing. *China Communication*, *8*(6), 44–50.

Dastjerdi, A. V., Bakar, K. A., & Tabatabaei, S. G. H. (2009). Distributed intrusion detection in clouds using mobile agents. In *Proceedings of Third International Conference on Advanced Engineering Computing and Applications in Sciences* (pp. 175-180). IEEE, Inc.

Davidović, T., & Crainic, T. G. (2013a). *Parallelization strategies for variable neighborhood search, CIRRELT-2013-47*. Retrieved September 10, 2013, from https://www.cirrelt.ca/DocumentsTravail/CIRRELT-2013-47.pdf

Davidović, T., & Crainic, T. G. (2013b). Parallel local search to schedule communicating tasks on identical processors. *CIRRELT-2013-54*. Retrieved September 10, 2013, from https://www.cirrelt.ca/DocumentsTravail/CIRRELT-2013-54.pdf

Davidović, T., Jakšić, T., Ramljak, D., Šelmić, M., & Teodorović, D. (2013). Parallelization strategies for bee colony optimization based on message passing communication protocol. *Optimization: A Journal of Mathematical Programming and Operations Research*, *62*(8), 1113-1142.

Davidović, T., Ramljak, D., Šelmić, M., & Teodorović, D. (2011). MPI parallelization of bee colony optimization. In *Proceedings of 1st International Symposium & 10th Balkan Conference on Operational Research*, (vol. 2, pp. 193-200). Thessaloniki, Greece: University of Macedonia, Economic and Social Sciences.

De Alfonso, C., Caballer, M., Alvarruiz, F., Molto, G., & Hernandez, V. (2011). Infrastructure deployment over the cloud. In B. Werner (Ed.), *Third IEEE International Conference on Coud Computing Technology and Science* (pp. 517-521). Los Alamitos, CA: IEEE Computer Society.

De Raedt, H., & De Raedt, B. (1983). Applications of the generalized Trotter formula. *Physical Review A.*, *28*(6), 3575–3580. doi:10.1103/PhysRevA.28.3575

DeAndrea, D. C., Ellison, N. B., LaRose, R., Steinfield, C., & Fiore, A. (2012). Serious social media: On the use of social media for improving students' adjustment to college. *The Internet and Higher Education*, *15*(1), 15–23. doi:10.1016/j.iheduc.2011.05.009

Deb, K., Pratap, A., Agarwal, S., & Meyarivan, T. A. M. T. (2002). A fast and elitist multiobjective genetic algorithm: NSGA-II. *IEEE Transactions on Evolutionary Computation*, *6*(2), 182–197. doi:10.1109/4235.996017

Demont, C., Breitenbücher, U., Kopp, O., Leymann, F., & Wettinger, J. (2013). Towards integrating TOSCA and ITIL. In O. Kopp & N. Lohmann (Eds.), *Proceedings of the 5th Central-European Workshop on Services and their Composition (ZEUS 2013)* (pp. 28-31). ZEUS.

Derrick, K., Javadi, B., Malecot, P., Cappello, F., & Anderson, D. P. (2009). Cost-benefit analysis of cloud computing versus desktop grids. In *Proceedings of IPDPS 2009. IEEE International Symposium on Parallel & Distributed Processing* (pp. 1-12). IEEE.

Despotović, M., Savić, A., & Bogdanović, Z. (2006). System components' integration within the portal for postgraduate distance education.[SymOrg.]. *Proceedings of SymOrg*, *2006*, 1–9.

Despotovic-Zrakić, M., Marković, A., Bogdanović, Z., Barać, D., & Krčo, S. (2012). Providing adaptivity in moodle LMS courses. *Journal of Educational Technology & Society*, *15*(1), 326–338.

Devetaković, M., Gajin, S., & Mitrović, B. (2010). Amres e-learning portal.[YuInfo.]. *Proceedings of YuInfo, 2010*, 1–6.

Dias, M. De A., Di Costanzo, A., & Buyya, R. (2009). Evaluating the cost-benefit of using cloud computing to extend the capacity of clusters. In *Proceedings of the 18th ACM International Symposium on High Performance Distributed Computing* (pp. 141-150). New York: ACM.

Dinh, H. T., Lee, C., Niyato, D., & Wang, P. (2011). A survey of mobile cloud computing: Architecture, applications, and approaches. *Computer*, 1–38. Retrieved from http://onlinelibrary.wiley.com/doi/10.1002/wcm.1203/full

Divac, D., Prodanovic, D., & Milivojević, N. (2009). Hydro-information systems for management of hydropower resources in Serbia. Belgrade, Serbia: Jaroslav Cerni Institute for the Development of Water Resources.

Divac, D., Grujović, N., Milivojević, N., Stojanović, Z., & Simić, Z. (2009). Hydro-information systems and management of hydropower resources in Serbia. *Journal of the Serbian Society for Computational Mechanics, 3*(1), 1–37.

Doelitzscher, F., Sulistio, A., Reich, C., Kuijs, H., & Wolf, D. (2011). Private cloud for collaboration and e-learning services: From IaaS to SaaS. *Computing, 91*(1), 23–42. doi:10.1007/s00607-010-0106-z

Doering, N. M. (2007). The mainstreaming of mobile learning at a German university. In *Proceedings of Proceedings of the Fifth IEEE International Conference on Pervasive Computing and Communications Workshops* (pp. 159-164). IEEE. doi: 10.1109/PERCOMW.2007.114

Domenico, T. (2011). Cloud computing and software agents: Towards cloud intelligent services. In G. Fortino, A. Garro, L. Palopoli, W. Russo, & G. Spezzano (Eds.), WOA (pp. 2-6). CEUR-WS.org.

Dong, B., Qinghua, Z., Yang, J., Haifei, L., & Qiao, M. (2009). An e-learning ecosystem based on cloud computing infrastructure. In I. Aedo, N-S. Chen, Kinshuk, D. Sampson, & L. Zaitseva (Eds.), *Ninth IEEE International Conference on Advanced Learning Technologies, ICALT 2009* (pp. 125-127). Los Alamitos, CA: IEEE.

Dong, B., Zheng, Q., Qiao, M., Shu, J., & Yang, J. (2009). BlueSky cloud framework: An e-learning framework embracing cloud computing. In M. G. Jaatun, G. Zhao, & C. Rong (Eds.), *The 1st International Conference on Cloud Computing (CloudCom 2009)* (pp. 577-582). Berlin: Springer.

Dong, B., Zheng, Q., Yang, J., Li, H., & Qiao, M. (2009). Jampots: A mashup system towards an e-learning ecosystem. In L. O'Conner (Ed.), *Fifth International Joint Conference on INC, IMS and IDC* (pp. 200-205). Los Alamitos, CA: IEEE Computer Society.

Dongarra, J. J., Luszczek, P., & Petitet, A. (2003). The LINPACK benchmark: Past, present and future. *Concurrency and Computation, 15*, 803–820. doi:10.1002/cpe.728

Dorigo, M., & Stützle, T. (2010). Ant colony optimization: Overview and recent advances. In M. Gendreau & J-Y. Potvin (Eds.), Handbook of metaheuristics (2nd ed.), (pp. 227-263). New York: Springer Science+Business Media.

Dudley, J. T., Pouliot, Y., Chen, R., Morgan, A. A., & Butte, A. J. (2010). Translational bioinformatics in the cloud: An affordable alternative. *Genome Medicine, 2*(51), 1–6. PMID:20193046

Elbendak, M., Vickers, P., & Rossiter, N. (2011). Parsed use case descriptions as a basis for object-oriented class model generation. *Journal of Systems and Software, 84*(7), 1209–1223. doi:10.1016/j.jss.2011.02.025

El-Hussein, M. O. M., & Cronje, J. C. (2010). Defining mobile learning in the higher education landscape research method. *Higher Education, 13*(3), 12–21.

Eludiora, S., Abiona, O., Oluwatope, A., Oluwaranti, A., Onime, C., & Kehinde, L. (2011). A user identity management protocol for cloud computing paradigm. *International Journal of Communications. Network and System Sciences, 4*(3), 152–163. doi:10.4236/ijcns.2011.43019

Ercan, T. (2010). Effective use of cloud computing in educational institutions. *Procedia - Social and Behavioral Sciences, 2*(2), 938-942.

Erl, T. (Ed.). (2009). *SOA design patterns*. Boston: Prentice Hall.

Ernst, M. (2007). *RHIC computing facility*. DOE/Nuclear Physics Review of RHIC Science and Technology.

Etro, F. (2009). The economic impact of cloud computing on business creation, employment and output in Europe. *Review of Business and Economics*, *54*(2), 179–208.

Etsion, Y., & Feitelson, D. (2012). *Exploiting core working sets to filter the L1 cache with random sampling.*

European Network and Information Security Agency (ENISA). (2010). *Cloud computing: Benefits, risks and recommendations for information security*. Retrieved September 1, 2013, from http://www.coe.int/t/dghl/cooperation/economiccrime/cybercrime/cy-activity-interface-2010/presentations/Outlook/Udo%20Helmbrecht_ENISA_Cloud%20Computing_Outlook.pdf

Fan, X., Cao, J., & Mao, H. (2011). *A survey of mobile cloud computing*. ZTE Corporation.

Farzad, S. (2011, May). *Cloud computing security threats and responses*. Paper presented at IEEE 3rd International Conference on Communication Software and Networks (ICCSN). doi: 10.1109/ICCSN.2011.6014715

Faure, H. (1992). Good permutations for extreme discrepancy. *Journal of Number Theory*, *42*(1), 47–56. doi:10.1016/0022-314X(92)90107-Z

Fellbaum, C. (2010). WordNet. In R. Poli, M. Healy, & A. Kameas (Eds.), *Theory and applications of ontology: Computer applications* (pp. 231–243). Dordrecht, The Netherlands: Springer. doi:10.1007/978-90-481-8847-5_10

Feo, T. A., & Resende, M. G. C. (1995). Greedy randomized adaptive search procedures. *Journal of Global Optimization*, *6*(2), 109–133. doi:10.1007/BF01096763

Ferreira, A., & Morvan, M. (1997). Models for parallel algorithm design: An introduction. In A. Migdalas, P. Pardalos, & S. Storøy (Eds.), *Parallel computing in optimization* (pp. 1–26). Dordrecht, The Netherlands: Kluwer Academic Publishers. doi:10.1007/978-1-4613-3400-2_1

Ferzli, R., & Khalife, I. (2011). Mobile cloud computing educational tool for image/video processing algorithms. In *Proceedings of 2011 Digital Signal Processing and Signal Processing Education Meeting (DSP/SPE)* (pp. 529-533). Piscataway, NJ: IEEE Signal Processing Society.

Feynman, R. P., & Hibbs, A. R. (Eds.). (1965). *Quantum mechanics and path integrals*. New York: McGraw-Hill.

Fishwick, P. A. (1996). Web-based simulation: Some personal observations. In *Proceedings of the 28th Conference on Winter Simulation* (pp. 772-779). Washington, DC: IEEE Computer Society.

Flanders, W. H., & Khosa, V. (2013). *U.S. patent no. 20,130,024,629*. Washington, DC: U.S. Patent and Trademark Office.

Flynn, M., Mencer, O., Milutinovic, V., Rakocevi, G., Stenstrom, P., Trobec, R., & Valerio, M. (2013). Moving from Petaflops to Petadata. *Communications of the ACM*, *56*(5), 39–42. doi:10.1145/2447976.2447989

Fogel, R. (2010). *The education cloud: Delivering education as a service*. Intel Corporation.

Fossorier, M., Mihaljevic, M., & Imai, H. (2007). Modeling block coding approaches for fast correlation attack. *IEEE Transactions on Information Theory*, *53*(12), 4728–4737. doi:10.1109/TIT.2007.909164

Fossorier, M., Mihaljevic, M., Imai, H., Cui, Y., & Matsuura, K. (2006). An algorithm for solving the LPN problem and its application to security evaluation of the HB protocols for RFID authentication. *Lecture Notes in Computer Science*, *4329*, 48–62. doi:10.1007/11941378_5

Foster, I., & Kesselman, C. (1999). The globus toolkit. In *The grid: Blueprint for a new computing infrastructure* (pp. 259–278). San Francisco, CA: Morgan Kaufmann Publishers Inc.

Foster, I., & Kesselman, C. (2004). *The grid 2: Blueprint for a new computing infrastructure* (2nd ed.). San Francisco, CA: Morgan Kaufmann.

Foster, I., Kesselman, C., & Tuecke, S. (2001). The anatomy of the grid – Enabling scalable virtual organizations. *International Journal of High Performance Computing Applications*, *15*(3), 200–222. doi:10.1177/109434200101500302

Furht, B. (Ed.). (2010). *Handbook of cloud computing*. New York: Springer. doi:10.1007/978-1-4419-6524-0

Gad, S. H. (2011). Cloud computing and MapReduce for reliability and scalability of ubiquitous learning systems. In *Proceedings of the Compilation of the Colocated*, (pp. 273-277). ACM. Retrieved from http://dl.acm.org/citation.cfm?id=2095096

Gallard, J., Lèbre, A., Morina, C., Naughton, T., Scott, S. L., & Vallée, G. (2012). Architecture for the next generation system management tools. *Future Generation Computer Systems*, *28*(1), 136–146. doi:10.1016/j.future.2011.06.003

Garcia-Crespo, A., Colomo-Palacios, R., Gomez-Berbis, J. M., & Ruiz-Mezcua, B. (2010). SEMO: A framework for customer social networks analysis based on semantics. *Journal of Information Technology*, *25*(2), 178–188. doi:10.1057/jit.2010.1

García-López, F., Melión-Batista, B., Moreno-Pérez, J. A., & Moreno-Vega, J. M. (2002). The parallel variable neighborhood search for the p-median problem. *Journal of Heuristics*, *8*(3), 375–388. doi:10.1023/A:1015013919497

Gardner, P. S. (2005). Ontologies and semantic data integration. *Drug Discovery Today*, *10*(14), 1001–1007. doi:10.1016/S1359-6446(05)03504-X PMID:16023059

Garrison, D. R., & Kanuka, H. A. (2004). Blended learning: Uncovering its transformative potential in higher education. *The Internet and Higher Education*, *7*(2), 95–105. doi:10.1016/j.iheduc.2004.02.001

Gartner Newsroom. (2010). *Gartner identifies the top 10 strategic technologies for 2011*. Gartner Symposium/ITxpo. Retrieved April 15, 2013, from http://www.gartner.com/it/page.jsp?id=1454221

Gartner Newsroom. (2011). *Gartner identifies the top 10 strategic technologies for 2012*. Gartner Symposium/ITxpo. Retrieved April 15, 2013, from http://www.gartner.com/it/page.jsp?id=1826214

Gartner. (2013). *Gartner IT glossary - Cloud computing*. Retrieved October 10, 2013, from http://www.gartner.com/it-glossary/cloud-computing/

Gašić, M. (2007) A survey of split data caches [PowerPoint slides]. Belgrade, Serbia: University of Belgrade.

Gelernter, J. (2011). Use of ontologies for data integration and curation. *International Journal of Digital Curation*, *6*(1), 70–78. doi:10.2218/ijdc.v6i1.173

Gendreau, M., & Potvin, J.-Y. (2010). Tabu search. In M. Gendreau & J-Y. Potvin (Eds.), Handbook of metaheuristics (2nd ed.), (pp. 41-59). New York: Springer Science+Business Media.

Girone, M. (2011). *EGI-InSPIRE current requirements & outlook*. Retrieved September 11, 2013, from http://storageconference.org/2011/Presentations/MSST/15.Girone.pdf

Giurgiu, I., Riva, O., Juric, D., Krivulev, I., & Alonso, G. (2009). Calling the cloud: enabling mobile phones as interfaces to cloud applications. In *Proceedings of the 10th ACMIFIPUSENIX International Conference on Middleware*. Springer-Verlag. Retrieved from http://portal.acm.org/citation.cfm?id=1656987

Glover, F., & Laguna, M. (Eds.). (1997). *Tabu search*. Boston: Kluwer Academic Publishers. doi:10.1007/978-1-4615-6089-0

Godwin-Jones, R. (2011). Emerging technologies: Mobile apps for language learning. *Language Learning & Technology*, *15*(2), 2–11.

Goldberg, D. E. (Ed.). (1989). *Genetic algorithms in search, optimization, and machine learning*. Reading, MA: Addison-Wesley Longman Publishing Co., Inc.

Gollmann, D. (2010). *Computer security*. London: John Willey & Sons, Ltd.

González, A., Aliagas, C., & Valero, M. (1995). A data cache with multiple caching strategies tuned to different types of locality. In *Proceedings of the ACM 1995 International Conference on Supercomputing* (pp. 338-347). ACM. Retrieved from http://portal.acm.org/citation.cfm?id=224622

Graf, S. (2008). Adaptivity and personalization in ubiquitous learning systems. In *HCI and usability for education and work* (LNCS), (vol. 5298, pp. 331-338). Berlin: Springer. Retrieved from http://www.scopus.com/inward/record.url?eid=2-s2.0-70350656112&partnerID=40&md5=19c6ab266a19c8a127a145354ad8fab0

Graham, S. L., Snir, M., & Patterson, C. A. (Eds.). (2005). *Getting up to speed: The future of supercomputing*. Washington, DC: National Academies Press.

Gramm-Leach-Bliley Act. (2000). *U.S. government printing office*. Retrieved October 10, 2013, from http://www.gpo.gov/fdsys/pkg/PLAW-106publ102/pdf/PLAW-106publ102.pdf

Granovetter, M. (1983). The strength of weak ties: A network theory revisited. *Sociological Theory*, *1*, 201–233. doi:10.2307/202051

Granovetter, M. S. (1973). The strength of weak ties. *American Journal of Sociology*, *78*(6), 1360–1380. doi:10.1086/225469

Greenberg, P. (2010). The impact of CRM 2.0 on customer insight. *Journal of Business and Industrial Marketing*, *25*(6), 410–419. doi:10.1108/08858621011066008

Greenberg, P. (Ed.). (2010). *CRM at the speed of light: Social CRM strategies, tools, and techniques for engaging your customers* (4th ed.). New York: McGraw-Hill Companies, Inc.

Greene, S. S. (Ed.). (2006). *Security policies and procedures*. Upper Saddle River, NJ: Prentice Hall.

Grimshaw, A. S., & Wulf, W. A. (1997). The legion vision of a worldwide virtual computer. *Communications of the ACM*, *40*(1), 39–45. doi:10.1145/242857.242867

Grobauer, B., Walloschek, T., & Stocker, E. (2011). Understanding cloud computing vulnerabilities. *IEEE Security Privacy Magazine*, *9*(2), 50–57. doi:10.1109/MSP.2010.115

Gropp, W., Lusk, E., & Skjellum, A. (Eds.). (1994). Using MPI: Portable parallel programming with the message-passing interface. Cambridge, MA: The MIT Press.

Gropp, W., & Lusk, E. (1996). *Users guide for mpich a portable implementation of MPI*. New York: Mathematics and Computer Science Division. doi:10.2172/378910

Grossman, R. L. (2009). The case for cloud computing. *IT Professional*, *11*(2), 23–27. doi:10.1109/MITP.2009.40

Gruber, T. R. (1993). A translation approach to portable ontology specifications. *Knowledge Acquisition*, *5*(2), 199–220. doi:10.1006/knac.1993.1008

Grujić, J., Bogojević, A., & Balaž, A. (2006). Energy estimators and calculation of energy expectation values in the path integral formalism. *Physics Letters. [Part A]*, *360*(2), 217–223. doi:10.1016/j.physleta.2006.08.044

Grujović, N., Divac, D., Stojanović, B., Stojanović, Z., & Milivojević, N. (2009). Modeling of one-dimensional unsteady open channel flows in interaction with reservoirs, dams and hydropower plant objects. *Journal of the Serbian Society for Computational Mechanics*, *3*(1), 154–181.

Guo, S., Bai, F., & Hu, X. (2011). Simulation software as a service and service-oriented simulation experiment. In *Proceedings of 2011 IEEE International Conference on Information Reuse and Integration (IRI)* (pp. 113-116). IEEE Systems, Man, and Cybernetics Society (SMC).

Gustafson, J. L. (1988). Reevaluating Amdahl's law. *Communications of the ACM*, *31*(5), 532–533. doi:10.1145/42411.42415

Hada, P. S., Singh, R., & Manmohan, M. (2011). Security agents: A mobile agent based trust model for cloud computing. *International Journal of Computers and Applications*, *36*(12), 12–15.

Hansen, P., & Mladenović, N. (2005). Variable neighbourhood search. In E. K. Burke & G. Kendall (Eds.), Search methodologies: Introductory tutorials in optimization and decision support techniques (pp. 211-238). New York: Springer Science+Business Media.

Hansen, P., Mladenović, N., Brimberg, J., & Moreno-Pérez, J. A. (2010). Variable neighbourhood search. In M. Gendreau & J-Y. Potvin (Eds.), Handbook of metaheuristics (2nd ed.), (pp. 61-86). New York: Springer Science+Business Media.

Hansen, P., & Mladenović, N. (2003). Variable neighbourhood search. In F. Glover, & G. Kochenagen (Eds.), *Handbook of metaheuristics* (pp. 145–184). Boston: Kluwer Academic Publishers.

Hazelhurst, S. (2008, October). Scientific computing using virtual high-performance computing: A case study using the Amazon elastic computing cloud. In *Proceedings of the 2008 Annual Research Conference of the South African Institute of Computer Scientists and Information Technologists on IT Research in Developing Countries: Riding the Wave of Technology* (pp. 94-103). New York, NY: ACM.

Hechtman, B. A., & Sorin, D. J. (2013). Evaluating cache coherent shared virtual memory for heterogeneous multicore chips. In *Proceedings of the IEEE International Symposium on Performance Analysis of Systems and Software*. IEEE.

Henderson, J. C., & Venkatraman, V. N. (1993). Strategic alignment: Leveraging information technology for transforming organizations. *IBM Systems Journal, 32*(1), 4–16.

Herper, M. (2011, January 17). Gene machine. *Forbes Magazine*. Retrieved September 15, 2013, from http://www.forbes.com/forbes/2011/0117/features-jonathan-rothberg-medicine-tech-gene-machine_1.html

Hill, M. D., Jouppi, N. P., & Sohi, G. S. (2000). *Readings in computer architecture*. San Francisco: Morgan Kaufmann Publishers.

Hodgins, H. (2004). The future of learning objects. In *Proceedings of 2002 ECI Conference on e-Technologies in Engineering Education: Learning Outcomes Providing Future Possibilities*. ECI.

Hoffman, A. R., & Traub, J. F. (Eds.). (1989). *Supercomputers: Directions in technology and applications*. Washington, DC: National Academy Press.

Holzinger, A., Nischelwitzer, A., Friedl, S., & Hu, B. (2010). Towards life long learning: Three models for ubiquitous applications. *Wireless Communications and Mobile Computing, 10*(10), 1350–1365. doi:10.1002/wcm.715

Hoverstad, B. A. (2010). Simdist: A distribution system for easy parallelization of evolutionary computation. *Genetic Programming and Evolvable Machines, 11*(2), 185–203. doi:10.1007/s10710-009-9100-7

HP-SEE. (2013). *High-performance computing infrastructure for South East Europe's research communities*. Retrieved September 11, 2013, from http://www.hp-see.eu/

Hsu, J.-T., Hsieh, S.-H., Lo, C.-C., Hsu, C.-H., Cheng, P.-H., Chen, S.-J., & Lai, F.-P. (2011). Ubiquitous mobile personal health system based on cloud computing. In *Proceedings of TENCON 2011 2011 IEEE Region 10 Conference*. IEEE. Retrieved from http://ieeexplore.ieee.org/lpdocs/epic03/wrapper.htm?arnumber=6129036

Hugos, M., & Hulitzky, D. (Eds.). (2010). *Business in the cloud - What every business needs to know about cloud computing*. Hoboken, NJ: John Wiley & Sons.

Hwang, G.-J., & Tsai, C.-C. (2011). Research trends in mobile and ubiquitous learning: A review of publications in selected journals from 2001 to 2010. *British Journal of Educational Technology*. Wiley-Blackwell Publishing Ltd. Retrieved from http://ovidsp.ovid.com/ovidweb.cgi?T=JS&PAGE=reference&D=psyc7&NEWS=N&AN=2011-12000-017

IBM Virtual Machine Facility/370: Introduction. (1976). *IBM technical newsletters GN20-2677*. ILLIAC IV. (1974). Sumary Report.

IBM. (2007). Google and IBM announced university initiative to address internet-scale computing challenges. Retrieved from http://www-03.ibm.com/press/us/en/pressrelease/22414.wss

IEEE Learning Technology Standards Committee. (2002). *Draft standard for learning object metadata*. Institute of Electrical and Electronics Engineers, Inc. Retrieved from http://ltsc.ieee.org/wg12/files/LOM_1484_12_1_v1_Final_Draft.pdf

IMS Global Learning Consortium. (2007). *IMS content packaging specification primer*. Retrieved from http://www.imsglobal.org/content/packaging/cpv1p2pd2/imscp_primerv1p2pd2.html

Iosup, A., Ostermann, S., Yigitbasi, M. N., Prodan, R., Fahringer, T., & Epema, D. H. J. (2011). Performance analysis of cloud computing services for many-tasks scientic computing. *IEEE Transactions on Parallel and Distributed Systems, 22*(6), 931–945.

ISO/IEC 27036 - IT security - Security techniques - Information security for supplier relationships (Draft). (n.d.). Retrieved from http://www.iso27001security.com/html/27036.html

Jackson, K. R., Ramakrishnan, L., Muriki, K., Canon, S., Cholia, S., Shalf, J., & Wright, N. J. (2010, November). Performance analysis of high performance computing applications on the Amazon web services cloud. In *Proceedings of Cloud Computing Technology and Science (CloudCom), 2010 IEEE Second International Conference* (pp. 159-168). Washington, DC: IEEE Computer Society Press.

Jacobson, I., Christerson, M., Jonsson, P., & Overgaard, G. (1993). *Objectoriented software engineering – A use case driven approach.* Boston: Addison Wesley Longman Publishing Co. Inc.

Jaimes, A. L., & Coello, C. A. C. (2009). Applications of parallel platforms and models in evolutionary multi-objective optimization. In *Biologically-inspired optimisation methods* (pp. 23–49). Berlin: Springer Verlag. doi:10.1007/978-3-642-01262-4_2

Jamshidi, P., Khoshnevis, S., Teimourzadegan, R., Nikravesh, A., Khoshkbarforoushha, A., & Shams, F. (2009). ASSM: Toward an automated method for service specification. In *Proceedings of IEEE Asia-Pacific Services Computing Conference, APSCC 2009* (pp. 451-456). IEEE.

Janković, S., Kostić-Ljubisavljević, A., Radonjić, V., & Mladenović, S. (2012). Semantic interoperability models in B2B integrations. In B. Zajc & A. Trost (Ed.), *The 21st international electrotechnical and computer science conference – ERK 2012* (vol. 2, pp. 71-74). Ljubljana, Slovenia: IEEE Region 8, Slovenia Section IEEE.

Janković, S., Mladenović, S., Mitrović, S., Pavlović, N., & Aćimović, S. (2011). A model for integration of railway information systems based on cloud computing technology. In B. D. Milovanović (Ed.), *ICEST 2011 - XLVI international scientific conference on information, communication and energy systems and technologies* (vol. 3, pp. 833-836). Niš, Serbia: Faculty of Electronic Engineering University of Niš.

Janković, S., Mladenović, S., Radonjić, V., Kostić-Ljubisavljević, A., & Uzelac, A. (2011). Integration platform-as-a-service in the traffic safety area. In M. Banat (Ed.), MIC-CNIT 2011 - Mosharaka international conference on communications, networking and information technology (pp. 70-75). Dubai, UAE: Mosharaka for Researches and Studies.

Janković, S., Mladenović, S., Vesković, S., Mitrović, S., & Milinković, S. (2012). A model of semantic interoperable e-business of traffic business systems. In G. Ćirović (Ed.), *XXXIX symposium on operational research - SYM-OP-IS '12* (pp. 75-78). Belgrade, Serbia: Visoka Građevinsko-Geodetska Škola, Belgrade.

Janković, S. (2010). Interoperability of transport business systems based on the integration of service-oriented B2B applications. *Info M, 36,* 4–12.

Janković, S., Milojković, J., Mladenović, S., Despotović-Zrakić, M., & Bogdanović, Z. (2012). Cloud computing framework for B2B integrations in the traffic safety area. *Metalurgia International, 17*(9), 166–173.

Janković, S., & Mladenović, S. (2012). B2B integration models in cloud computing environment. *Info M, 43,* 26–32.

Jansen, W., & Grance, T. (2011). *Guidelines on security and privacy in public cloud computing (Special Publication 800-144).* Gaithersburg, MD: NIST.

Janssen, M., & Joha, A. (2011). Challenges for adopting cloud-based software as a service (SaaS) in the public sector. In *Proceedings of ECIS 2011.* ECIS.

Jaško, O., Jaško, A., & Čudanov, M. (2010). Impact of management upon organizational network effectiveness. *Management – Časopis za Teoriju i Praksu Menadžmenta, 56,* 5-13.

Jaško, O., Čudanov, M., & Jevtić, M. (2009). Structure and functions of virtual organization as a framework for strategy design. *The IPSI BgD Transactions on Advanced Research, 5*(2), 21–26.

Jeffery, K., & Neidecker-Lutz, B. (2010). *The future of cloud computing.* Retrieved October 10, 2013, from http://cordis.europa.eu/fp7/ict/ssai/docs/cloud-report-final.pdf

Jennings, R. (Ed.). (2009). *Cloud computing with the Windows® Azure™ platform.* Indianapolis, IN: Wiley Publishing, Inc.

Jie, W., Arshad, J., & Ekin, P. (2009). Authentication and authorization infrastructure for grids - Issues, technologies, trends and experiences. *The Journal of Supercomputing, 52*(1), 82–96. doi:10.1007/s11227-009-0267-8

Jin, H., Ibrahim, S., Bell, T., Gao, W., Huang, D., & Wu, S. (2010). Cloud types and services. In B. Furht & A. Escalante (Eds.), Handbook of cloud computing (pp. 335-355). Berlin: Springer Science+Business Media.

Jin, Z. P., Jian, X., Ming, X., & Ning, Z. (2010). An attribute-oriented model for identity management. In *Proceedings of International Conference on e-Education, e-Business, e-Management and e-Learning* (pp. 440-444). Los Alamitos, CA: IEEE Computer Society.

Jinhui, Y., Shiping, C., Chen, W., David, L., & Zic, J. (2010). Accountability as a service for the cloud - From concept to implementation with BPEL. In *Proceedings of 2010 IEEE 6th World Congress on Services* (pp. 91-98). IEEE Computer Society.

Johnes, N. (2012, April). *The mobile scenario: Confusion, complexity and opportunity through 2015*. Paper presented at the Gartner IT Infrastructure & Data Center Summit. Tokyo, Japan.

Jones, B. (2009). *Enabling grids for e-science*. Retrieved September 11, 2013, from http://ec.europa.eu/research/conferences/2009/rtd-2009/presentations/infrastructures/robert_jones_-_egee_enabling_grids_for_e-science.pdf

Jones, R. (Ed.). (2005). *Internet forensics using digital evidence to solve computer crime*. Farnham, MA: O'Reilly.

Jouppi, N. P. (1990, May). Improving direct-mapped cache performance by the addition of a small fully-associative cache and prefetch buffers. In *Proceedings of Computer Architecture* (pp. 364–373). IEEE. doi:10.1109/ISCA.1990.134547

Jovanović, J., Gašević, D., Knight, C., & Richards, G. (2007). Ontologies for effective use of context in e-learning settings. *Journal of Educational Technology & Society*, *10*(3), 47–59.

Kaku, M. (2010). *Physics of the future*. New York: Double Day.

Kalfoglou, Y. (Ed.). (2010). *Cases on semantic interoperability for information systems integration: Practices and applications*. New York: Information Science Reference.

Kalfoglou, Y., & Schorlemmer, M. (2003). Ontology mapping: The state of the art. *The Knowledge Engineering Review*, *18*(1), 1–31. doi:10.1017/S0269888903000651

Kalim, A. (2013). Clouds on the academic horizon. *International Journal of Computer Science and Management Research*, *2*(4), 2239–2243.

Kampe, M., Stenstrom, P., & Dubois, M. (2004). Self-correcting LRU replacement policies. In *Proceedings of the 1st Conference on Computing Frontiers* (pp. 181-191). ACM.

Karaboga, D. (2005). *An idea based on honey bee swarm for numerical optimization* (Technical report-TR06). Retrieved September 10, 2013, from http://mf.erciyes.edu.tr/abc/pub/tr06_2005.pdf

Karaboga, D., Akay, B., & Ozturk, C. (2007). Artificial bee colony (ABC) optimization algorithm for training feed-forward neural networks. In V. Torra, Y. Narukawa, & Y. Yoshida (Eds.), *Modeling decisions for artificial intelligence* (Vol. 4617, pp. 318–319). Berlin: Springer. doi:10.1007/978-3-540-73729-2_30

Katz, R. (Ed.). (2008). *The tower and the cloud*. New York: EDUCAUSE.

Kermeta. (2013). *Kermeta - Breathe life into your metamodels*. Retrieved April 11, 2013 from http://www.kermeta.org/

Khalidi, Y. (2011). Building a cloud computing platform for new possibilities. *IEEE Computer*. Retrieved from http://ieeexplore.ieee.org/xpls/abs_all.jsp?arnumber=5719573

Kherraf, S., Lefebvre, E., & Suryn, W. (2008). Transformation from CIM to PIM using patterns and archetypes. In *Proceedings of 19th Australian Conference on Software Engineering* (pp. 338-346). Academic Press.

Khiabani, Y., Wei, S., Yuan, J., & Wang, J. (2012). Enhancement of secrecy of block ciphered systems by deliberate noise. *IEEE Transactions on Information Forensics and Security*, *7*(5), 1604–1613. doi:10.1109/TIFS.2012.2204983

Khmelevsky, Y., & Voytenko, V. (2010). Cloud computing infrastructure prototype for university education and research. In *Proceedings of 15th Western Canadian Conference on Computing Education* (pp. 1-5). New York: ACM.

Kim, T. K., Hou, B. K., & Cho, W. S. (2011). Private cloud computing techniques for inter-processing bioinformatics tools. In *Convergence and hybrid information technology (LNCS)* (Vol. 6935, pp. 298–305). Berlin: Springer.

King, S. F., & Burgess, T. F. (2008). Understanding success and failure in customer relationship management. *Industrial Marketing Management, 37*(4), 421–431. doi:10.1016/j.indmarman.2007.02.005

Kirkpatrick, S., Gelatt, C. D., & Vecchi, M. P. (1983). Optimization by simulated annealing. *Science, 220*(4598), 671–680. doi:10.1126/science.220.4598.671 PMID:17813860

Kirsten, T., & Rahm, E. (2006). BioFuice: Mapping-based data integration in bioinformatics. In *Proceedings of 3rd International Workshop on Data Integration in the Life Sciences* (LNCS), (Vol. 4075, pp. 124-135). Berlin: Springer.

Kleinert, H. (Ed.). (2009). *Path integrals in quantum mechanics, statistics, polymer physics, and financial markets* (5th ed.). Singapore: World Scientific Publishing Co. Pte. Ltd. doi:10.1142/9789814273572

Knausz, M. (2008). *Parallel variable neighbourhood search for the car sequencing problem. Diplomarbeit zur Erlangung des akademischen Grades.* Fakultät für Informatik der Technischen Universität Wien.

Kocabicak, U., & Dural, D. (2012). Secure and interoperable e-learning platforms based on web services. *Procedia - Social and Behavioral Sciences, 55,* 1265-1271.

Kočović, P. (2011). *Informatica postmoderna.* Belgrade, Serbia: Petar Kočović

Kočović, P. (2012). Challenges in cloud computing. *IPSI Transactions of Internet Research, 8*(1), 24–29.

Kojic, M., Filipovic, N., Stojanovic, B., Rankovic, V., Krstic, L., & Ivanovic, M. et al. (2007). Finite element modeling of underground water flow with Ranney wells. *Water Science & Technology: Water Supply, 7*(3), 41–50.

Kolmogoroff, A. (1931). Über die analytischen methoden in der wahrscheinlichkeitsrechnung. *Mathematische Annalen, 104*(1), 415–458. doi:10.1007/BF01457949

Koufaty, D., & Torrellas, J. (1998). Comparing data forwarding and prefetching for communication-induced misses in shared-memory MPs. In *Proceedings of the 12th International Conference on Supercomputing* (pp. 53-60). ACM.

Kovachev, D., Cao, Y., & Klamma, R. (2011). Mobile cloud computing: A comparison of application models. *Information Systems Journal,* (4): 14–23. Retrieved from http://arxiv.org/abs/1107.4940

Kreger, H. (2003). Fulfilling the web services promise. *Communications of the ACM, 46*(6), 29. doi:10.1145/777313.777334

Krishnaswamy, J. (Ed.). (2010). *Microsoft SQL Azure: Enterprise application development.* Birmingham, UK: Packt Publishing.

Kumar, S., Zhao, H., Shriraman, A., Matthews, E., Dwarkadas, S., & Shannon, L. (2012). Amoeba-cache: Adaptive blocks for eliminating waste in the memory hierarchy. In *Proceedings of the 2012 45th Annual IEEE/ACM International Symposium on Microarchitecture* (pp. 376-388). IEEE Computer Society.

Kumar, M. (2008). *Customer relationship management in services, focus: Educational institutions. New Delhi.* Hyderabad: ICFAI Business School.

L'Allier, J. J. (1997). *Frame of reference: NETg's map to the products, their structure and core beliefs.* Retrieved October 13, 2013, from http://journals.tdl.org/jodi/index.php/jodi/article/viewArticle/89/88

Labadie, J. W. (2004). Optimal operation of multireservoir systems: State-of-the-art review. *Journal of Water Resources Planning and Management, 130*(2), 93–111. doi:10.1061/(ASCE)0733-9496(2004)130:2(93)

Lagar-Cavilla, A. H., Whitney, J. A., Scannell, A., Patchin, P., Rumble, S. M., & de Lara, E. … Satyanarayanan, M. (2009). SnowFlock: Rapid virtual machine cloning for cloud computing. In Proceedings of Eurosys (pp. 1-12). ACM.

Lampathaki, F., Mouzakitis, S., Gionis, G., Charalabidis, Y., & Askounis, D. (2009). Business to business interoperability: A current review of XML data integration standards. *Computer Standards & Interfaces, 31*(6), 1045–1055. doi:10.1016/j.csi.2008.12.006

Lang, U. (2010). OpenPMF SCaaS: Authorization as a service for cloud & SOA applications. In J. Qiu, G. Zhao, & C. Rong (Eds.), *2010 IEEE Second International Conference on Cloud Computing Technology and Science (CloudCom)* (pp. 634-643). Los Alamitos, CA: IEEE Computer Society.

Laouris, Y., & Eteokleous, N. (2005). We need an educationally relevant definition of mobile. In *Proceedings of mLearn*. Cyprus Neuroscience & Technology Institute. Retrieved from http://citeseerx.ist.psu.edu/viewdoc/download?doi=10.1.1.106.9650&rep=rep1&type=pdf

Larman, C. (Ed.). (2004). *Applying UML and patterns: An introduction to object-oriented analysis and design and iterative development* (3rd ed.). Upper Saddle River, NJ: Prentice Hall.

Laudel, G. (2001). Collaboration, creativity and rewards: Why and how scientists collaborate. *International Journal of Technology Management, 22*(7-8), 762–781.

Lauret, J., Keahey, K., & Levente, H. (2011). *Clouds make way for STAR to shine, open science grid*. Retrieved April 15, 2013, from twiki.opensciencegrid.org/bin/view/Management/ResearchHighlight20

Lauret, J., Walker, M., Goasguen, S., & Hajdu, L. (2010). *From grid to cloud, the STAR experience*. Washington, DC: US Department of Energy, Office of Science.

Law, A. M., & Kelton, W. D. (Eds.). (1982). *Simulation modeling and analysis*. New York: McGraw-Hill Book Co.

Lecca, G., Petitdidier, M., Hluchy, L., Ivanovic, M., Kussul, N., Ray, N., & Thieron, V. (2011). Grid computing technology for hydrological applications. *Journal of Hydrology (Amsterdam), 403*(1), 186–199. doi:10.1016/j.jhydrol.2011.04.003

Lederer, H. (2011). *DEISA: Six years of extreme computing*. Retrieved September 11, 2013, from http://www.deisa.eu/

Lee, W.-H., Tseng, S.-S., & Shieh, W.-Y. (2010). Collaborative real-time traffic information generation and sharing framework for the intelligent transportation system. *Information Sciences, 180*(1), 62–70. doi:10.1016/j.ins.2009.09.004

Leimeister, S., Böhm, M., Riedl, C., & Krcmar, H. (2010). The business perspective of cloud computing: Actors, roles, and value networks. In *Proceedings of 18th European Conference on Information Systems ECIS*. ECIS.

Lenggenhager, T., & Schnellmann, P. (2012). AAI - Authentication and authorization infrastructure. *SWITCHaai Attribute Specification*, 1-46. Retrieved September 1, 2013, from https://www.switch.ch/aai/docs/AAI_Attr_Specs.pdf

Lewis, K., & Lewis, J. (2009). Web single sign-on authentication using SAML. *International Journal of Computer Science Issues, 2*, 41–48.

Ley, D. (2007). *Ubiquitous computing*. Retrieved from http://dera.ioe.ac.uk/1502/2/becta_2007_emergingtechnologies_vol2_report.pdf

Leymann, F. (2009). Cloud computing: The next revolution in IT. In *Proceedings of the 52th Photogrammetric Week* (pp. 3-12). Stuttgart, Germany: Photogrammetric Week.

Leymann, F., Fehling, C., Mietzner, R., Nowak, A., & Dustdar, S. (2011). Moving applications to the cloud: An approach based on application model enrichment. *International Journal of Cooperative Information Systems, 20*(3), 307–356. doi:10.1142/S0218843011002250

Li, Z., & Wei, J. (2008). Transforming business requirements into BPEL: A MDA-based approach to web application development. In *Proceedings of WSCS'08: IEEE Int. Workshop on Semantic Computing and Systems* (pp. 61-66). IEEE.

Liang, P. H., & Yang, J. M. (2011). Virtual personalized learning environment (VPLE) on the cloud. In Z. Gong et al. (Eds.), *Web information systems and mining* (Vol. 6988, pp. 403–411). Berlin: Springer Berlin Heidelberg. doi:10.1007/978-3-642-23982-3_49

Li, H. (Ed.). (2010). *Introduction to Windows Azure*. New York: Apress.

Li, M., Yu, S., Zheng, Y., Ren, K., & Lou, W. (2013). Scalable and secure sharing of personal health records in cloud computing using attribute-based encryption. *IEEE Transactions on Information Forensics and Security, 8*(1), 131–143.

Lim, D., Ong, Y.-S., Jin, Y., Sendhoff, B., & Lee, B.-S. (2007). Efficient hierarchical parallel genetic algorithms using grid computing. *Future Generation Computer Systems*, *23*(4), 658–670. doi:10.1016/j.future.2006.10.008

Limmer, S., & Fey, D. (2010). Framework for distributed evolutionary algorithms in computational grids. *Advances in Computation and Intelligence*, *6378*, 170–180. doi:10.1007/978-3-642-16493-4_18

Linthicum, D. (Ed.). (2010). *Cloud computing and SOA convergence in your enterprise*. Boston: Pearson Education.

Lipasti, M. H., & Shen, J. P. (1996). Exceeding the dataflow limit via value prediction. In *Proceedings of the 29th Annual ACM/IEEE International Symposium on Microarchitecture* (pp. 226-237). IEEE Computer Society.

Liu, X., He, Q., Qiu, X., Chen, B., & Huang, K. (2012). Cloud-based simulation: The state-of-the-art computer simulation paradigm. In *Proceedings of ACM/IEEE/SCS 26th Workshop on Principles of Advanced and Distributed Simulation (PADS)* (pp. 71-74). Washington, DC: IEEE Computer Society.

Liu, X., He, Q., Qiu, X., Chen, B., & Huang, K. (2012). Cloud-based computer simulation: Towards planting existing simulation software into the cloud. *Simulation Modelling Practice and Theory*, *26*, 135–150. doi:10.1016/j.simpat.2012.05.001

Li, X. P., & Broughton, J. Q. (1987). High-order correction to the Trotter expansion for use in computer simulation. *The Journal of Chemical Physics*, *86*(9), 5094. doi:10.1063/1.452653

Li, Z. J., Chen, C., & Wang, K. (2011). Cloud computing for agent-based urban transportation systems. *IEEE Intelligent Systems*, *26*(1), 73–79. doi:10.1109/MIS.2011.10

Lo, J. L., Eggers, S. J., Levy, H. M., Parekh, S. S., & Tullsen, D. M. (1997). Tuning compiler optimizations for simultaneous multithreading. In *Proceedings of 30th Annual International Symposium on Microarchitecture*. Washington, DC: IEEE Computer Society Press.

Loke, S. W. (2012). Supporting ubiquitous sensor-cloudlets and context-cloudlets: Programming compositions of context-aware systems for mobile users. *Future Generation Computer Systems*, *28*(4), 619–632. doi:10.1016/j.future.2011.09.004

Loniewski, G., Armesto, A., & Insfran, E. (2011). Incorporating model-driven techniques into requirements engineering for the service-oriented development process. In *Proceedings of ME'11: Proceedings of the 2011 Conference on Method Engineering,* (vol. 351, pp. 102-107). Boston: Springer.

Looi, C.-K., Seow, P., Zhang, B., So, H.-J., Chen, W., & Wong, L.-H. (2010). Leveraging mobile technology for sustainable seamless learning: A research agenda. *British Journal of Educational Technology*, *41*(2), 154–169. doi:10.1111/j.1467-8535.2008.00912.x

Lotspiech, J., Nusser, S., & Pestoni, F. (2002). Broadcast encryption's bright future. *Computer*, *35*(8), 57–63. doi:10.1109/MC.2002.1023789

Lučić, P., & Teodorović, D. (2001). Bee system: Modeling combinatorial optimization transportation engineering problems by swarm intelligence. In *Preprints of the TRISTAN IV Triennial Symposium on Transportation Analysis* (pp. 441-445). Sao Miguel, Azores Islands.

Lučić, P., & Teodorović, D. (2003a). Computing with bees: attacking complex transportation engineering problems. *International Journal of Artificial Intelligence Tools*, *12*(3), 375–394. doi:10.1142/S0218213003001289

Lučić, P., & Teodorović, D. (2003b). Vehicle routing problem with uncertain demand at nodes: The bee system and fuzzy logic approach. In J. L. Verdegay (Ed.), *Fuzzy sets based heuristics for optimization* (pp. 67–82). Berlin: Springer-Verlag. doi:10.1007/978-3-540-36461-0_5

Luna, F., Nebro, A. J., & Alba, E. (2006). Observations in using grid-enabled technologies for solving multiobjective optimization problems. *Parallel Computing*, *32*(5), 377–393. doi:10.1016/j.parco.2006.06.004

Maggiani, R. (2009). Cloud computing is changing how we communicate. In *Proceedings of IEEE International Professional Communication Conference, IPCC 2009* (pp.1-4). IEEE.

Mahamad, S., Ibrahim, M. N., & Taib, S. M. (2010). *M-learning: A new paradigm of learning mathematics in Malaysia.* Retrieved from http://arxiv.org/abs/1009.1170

Mahapatra, S., & Banerjee, D. (2010). The new conversation: Taking social media from talk to action. *Business, 57*(3), 21.

Manhattan Project Hall of Fame Directory. (2005). The Manhattan Project Heritage Preservation Association, Inc. Retrieved April 15, 2013, from http://www.mphpa.org/classic/HICC/HICC_HF3.htm

Marin-Lopez, R., Pereñiguez-Garcia, F., Ohba, Y., Bernal-Hidalgo, F., & Gomez, A. (2010). A Kerberized architecture for fast re-authentication in heterogeneous wireless networks. *Mobile Networks and Applications, 15*(3), 392–412. doi:10.1007/s11036-009-0220-3

Marković, A., Barjaktarović-Rakočević, S., & Čavoški, S. (2005). Spreadsheet models in stock valuation. *Management – Časopis za Teoriju i Praksu Menadžmenta, 10*(38), 26-33.

Marković, A., & Čavoški, S. (2005). Primena ADD-in programa u finansijskoj spreadsheet simulaciji. *Info M, 4*(13), 32–37.

Marović, B., & Jovanović, Z. (2006). Web-based grid-enabled interaction with 3D medical data. *Future Generation Computer Systems, 22*(4), 385–392. doi:10.1016/j.future.2005.10.002

Marshall, Z. (2010, April). Validation and performance studies for the ATLAS simulation. *Journal of Physics, 219*(3), 032016. doi:10.1088/1742-6596/219/3/032016

Martin, S., Diaz, G., Sancristobal, E., Gil, R., Castro, M., & Peire, J. (2011). New technology trends in education: Seven years of forecasts and convergence. *Computers & Education, 57*(3), 1893–1906. doi:10.1016/j.compedu.2011.04.003

Maskey, S., Jonoski, A., & Solomatine, D. P. (2002). Groundwater remediation strategy using global optimization algorithms. *Journal of Water Resources Planning and Management, 128*(6), 431–440. doi:10.1061/(ASCE)0733-9496(2002)128:6(431)

Massie, M., Chun, B., & Culler, D. (2004). The ganglia distributed monitoring system: Design, implementation, and experience. *Parallel Computing, 30*(7), 817–840. doi:10.1016/j.parco.2004.04.001

Mat, H. (2012). *Kill the password: Why a string of characters can't protect us anymore.* Conde Nast Digital, 13 Nov.2012 Web. 06 July 2013.

McGreal, R. (2004). Learning objects: A practical definition. *The Internatonal Journal of Instruction Technology & Distance Learning, 1*(9), 21–32.

McKee, S. A. (2004). Reflections on the memory wall. In *Proceedings of the First Conference on Computing Frontiers CF04.* ACM Press. Retrieved from http://portal.acm.org/citation.cfm?doid=977091.977115

McKinney, J. (2003). Shareable content objects (SCORM), whole course design and implementation issues. *Learning Solutions Magazine.* Retrieved October 13, 2013, from http://www.learningsolutionsmag.com/articles/319/shareable-content-objects-scorm-whole-course-design-and-implementation-issues

Medaglia, A. L., & Gutiérrez, E. (2006). An object-oriented framework for rapid development of genetic algorithms. In J. P. Rennard (Ed.), *Handbook of research on nature inspired computing for economics and management* (pp. 608–624). Hershey, PA: IGI Global. doi:10.4018/978-1-59140-984-7.ch040

Mell, P., & Grance, T. (2009). *Effectively and securely using the cloud computing paradigm.* Retrieved October 10, 2013, from http://gat1.isoc.org.il/conf2010/handouts/Yesha_Sivan.pdf

Mell, P., & Grance, T. (2011). *The NIST definition of cloud computing.* Retrieved from http://csrc.nist.gov/publications/nistpubs/800-145/SP800-145.pdf

Mell, P. (2012). What's special about cloud security? *IT Professional, 14*(4), 6–8. doi:10.1109/MITP.2012.84

Message Passing Interface (MPI) Standard. (1995). *Message Passing Interface Forum.* The Physics of RHIC. Retrieved April 15, 2013, from www.bnl.gov/rhic/physics.asp

Message Passing Interface Forum. (2009). *MPI: A Message-Passing Interface Standard Version 2.2*. Retrieved from http://www.mpi-forum.org/docs/mpi-2.2/mpi22-report.pdf

Metropolis, N. (1987). The beginning of the Monte Carlo method. *Los Alamos Science, 15*, 125–130.

Metropolis, N., & Ulam, S. (1949). The Monte Carlo method. *Journal of the American Statistical Association, 44*(247), 335–341. doi:10.1080/01621459.1949.10483310 PMID:18139350

Microsoft. (n.d.). *How To: Use a Thread Pool (C# Programming Guide)*. Retrieved from http://msdn.microsoft.com/en-us/library/3dasc8as(v=VS.90).aspx

Mietzner, R., Unger, T., & Leymann, F. (2009). Cafe: A generic configurable customizable composite cloud application framework. *Lecture Notes in Computer Science, 5870*, 357–364. doi:10.1007/978-3-642-05148-7_24

Miguel, A. R. D., & Faria, J. P. (2009). Automatic generation of user interface models and prototypes from domain and use case models. In *Proceedings of the International Conference on Software Engineering and Data Technologies,* (pp. 169-176). Academic Press.

Mihajlovic, R., Palande, U., & Mihajlovic, D. (2006, March). Practical approach to grid computing with multithreaded load balancing. In *Proceedings of YU INFO, XII Conference*. YU INFO.

Mihaljevic, M. (2012). An approach for light-weight encryption employing dedicated coding. In *Proceedings of 2012 IEEE Global Communications Conference (GLOBECOM)* (pp. 874-880). New York, NY: IEEE Communications Society.

Mihaljevic, M. (2003). Key management schemes for stateless receivers based on time varying heterogeneous logical key hierarchy. *Lecture Notes in Computer Science, 2894*, 137–154. doi:10.1007/978-3-540-40061-5_9

Mihaljevic, M. (2004). Reconfigurable key management for broadcast encryption. *IEEE Communications Letters, 8*(7), 440–442. doi:10.1109/LCOMM.2004.832774

Mihaljevic, M. (2007). Generic framework for secure Yuan 2000 quantum encryption protocol employing the wire-tap channel approach. *Physical Review A., 75*(5), 052334-1–5. doi:10.1103/PhysRevA.75.052334

Mihaljevic, M. (2009). A framework for stream ciphers based on pseudorandomness, randomness and error correcting coding. In B. Preneel, S. Dodunekov, V. Rijmen, & S. Nikova (Eds.), *Enhancing cryptographic primitives with techniques from error correcting codes* (pp. 117–139). Amsterdam, The Netherlands: IOS Press.

Mihaljevic, M., Fossorier, M., & Imai, H. (2007). Security evaluation of certain broadcast encryption schemes employing a generalized time-memory-data trade-off. *IEEE Communications Letters, 11*(12), 988–990. doi:10.1109/LCOMM.2007.071029

Mihaljevic, M., Gangopadhyay, S., Paul, G., & Imai, H. (2012a). Internal state recovery of grain-v1: Employing normality order of the filter function. *IET Information Security, 6*(2), 55–64. doi:10.1049/iet-ifs.2011.0107

Mihaljevic, M., Gangopadhyay, S., Paul, G., & Imai, H. (2012b). Internal state recovery of keystream generator LILI-128 based on a novel weakness of the employed Boolean function. *Information Processing Letters, 112*(21), 805–810. doi:10.1016/j.ipl.2012.07.013

Mihaljevic, M., & Imai, H. (2009). An approach for stream ciphers design based on joint computing over random and secret data. *Computing, 85*(1-2), 153–168. doi:10.1007/s00607-009-0035-x

Milgram, S. (1967). The small world problem. *Psychology Today, 1*(1), 61–67.

Milivojević, N., Divac, D., Vukosavić, D., Vučković, D., & Milivojević, V. (2009). Computer-aided optimization in operation planning of hydropower plants: Algorithms and examples. *Journal of Serbian Society for Computational Mechanics, 3*(1), 273–297.

Milivojević, N., Simić, Z., Orlić, A., Milivojević, V., & Stojanović, B. (2009). Parameter estimation and validation of the proposed SWAT based rainfall-runoff model: Methods and outcomes. *Journal of Serbian Society for Computational Mechanics, 3*(1), 86–110.

Miller, G. A. (1995). WordNet: A lexical database for English. *Communications of the ACM, 38*(11), 39–41. doi:10.1145/219717.219748

Milutinovic, V., Markovic, B., Tomasevic, M., & Tremblay, M. (1996). The split temporal/spatial cache: A complexity analysis. In *Proceedings of the SCIzzL-6*. Santa Clara, CA: ACM.

Milutinovic, V., Tomasevic, M., Markovic, B., & Tremblay, M. (1996). A new cache architecture concept: The split temporal/spatial cache. In *Proceedings of 8th Mediterranean Electrotechnical Conference on Industrial Applications in Power Systems Computer Science and Telecommunications MELECON 96*. MELECON.

Milutinović, M., Labus, A., Stojiljković, V., Bogdanović, Z., & Despotović-Zrakić, M. (2013). Designing a mobile language learning system based on lightweight learning objects. *Multimedia Tools and Applications*. doi:10.1007/s11042-013-1704-5

Mladenović, S., & Janković, S. (2011). Integration of traffic information systems in cloud computing environment. In M. Bakmaz et al. (Ed.), *XXIX symposium on novel technologies in postal and telecommunication traffic - PosTel 2011* (pp. 305-314). Belgrade, Serbia: Faculty of Transport and Traffic Engineering University of Belgrade.

Mladenović, N., & Hansen, P. (1997). Variable neighborhood search. *Computers & Operations Research, 24*(11), 1097–1100. doi:10.1016/S0305-0548(97)00031-2

Moore, G. E. (2006). Cramming more components onto integrated circuits. *Electronics, 38*(8).

Moore, M. G. (1973). Grahame toward a theory of independent learning and teaching. *The Journal of Higher Education, 44*(9), 661–679. doi:10.2307/1980599

Moreno, E. (2011). The society of our out of Africa ancestors (I), the migrant warriors that colonized the world. *Communicative & Integrative Biology, 4*(2), 163–170. PMID:21655430

Morgan, R. L., Cantor, S., Carmody, S., Hoehn, W., & Klingenstein, K. (2004). Federated security: The shibboleth approach. *Educause Quarterly*, 1-6. Retrieved September 1, 2013, from http://net.educause.edu/ir/library/pdf/EQM0442.pdf

Mostaghim, S., Branke, J., Lewis, A., & Schmeck, H. (2008). Parallel multi-objective optimization using master-slave model on heterogeneous resources. In *Proceedings of 2008 IEEE Congress on Evolutionary Computation IEEE World Congress on Computational Intelligence*. Washington, DC: IEEE Computer Society Press. Retrieved from http://ieeexplore.ieee.org/lpdocs/epic03/wrapper.htm?arnumber=4631060

Mueller, M., Park, Y., Lee, J., & Kim, T.-Y. (2006). Digital identity: How users value the attributes of online identifiers. *Information Economics and Policy, 18*(4), 405–422. doi:10.1016/j.infoecopol.2006.04.002

Mun, J. (Ed.). (2006). *Modeling risk applying Monte Carlo simulation, real options analysis, forecasting and optimization techniques*. Hoboken, NJ: John Wiley & Sons, Inc.

Myhrvold, N. (1999). John von Neumann. *Time, 153*, 150–153.

Nair, R. S., Miller, J. A., & Zhang, Z. (1996). Java-based query driven simulation environment. In *Proceedings of the 28th Conference on Winter Simulation* (pp. 786-793). Washington, DC: IEEE Computer Society.

Narasimhan, H. (2009). Parallel artificial bee colony (PABC) algorithm. In A. Abraham, A. Carvalho, F. Herrera, & V. Pai (Eds.), *VIII International Conference on Computer Information Systems and Industrial Management (CISIM, 2009), World Congress on Nature and Biologically Inspired Computing (NaBIC'09)* (pp. 306-311). IEEE.

Nathani, A., Chaudharya, S., & Somani, G. (2012). Policy based resource allocation in IaaS cloud. *Future Generation Computer Systems, 28*(1), 94–103. doi:10.1016/j.future.2011.05.016

National Human Genome Research Institute. (2013). *DNA sequencing costs - Data from the NHGRI genome sequencing program (GSP)*. Retrieved September 15, 2013, from http://www.genome.gov/sequencingcosts/

Naudet, Y., Latour, T., Guedria, W., & Chen, D. (2010). Towards a systemic formalisation of interoperability. *Computers in Industry, 61*, 176–185. doi:10.1016/j.compind.2009.10.014

Navigli, R., & Ponzetto, S. P. (2012). BabelNet: The automatic construction, evaluation and application of a wide-coverage multilingual semantic network. *Artificial Intelligence, 193*, 217–250. doi:10.1016/j.artint.2012.07.001

Ng, S. B., Nickerson, D. A., Bamshad, M. J., & Shendure, J. (2010). Massively parallel sequencing and rare disease. *Human Molecular Genetics, 19*(2), 119–124. PMID:20846941

Nikolaev, A. G., & Jacobson, S. H. (2010). Simulated annealing. In M. Gendreau & J-Y. Potvin (Eds.), Handbook of metaheuristics (2nd ed.), (pp. 1-39). New York: Springer Science+Business Media.

Nolan, R., & McFarlan, W. F. (2005). Information technology and the board of directors. *Harvard Business Review, 83*(10), 96–106. PMID:16250628

Noy, N. F., & McGuinness, D. L. (2001). *Ontology development 101: A guide to creating your first ontology.* Academic Press.

Núñez, D., Agudo, I., Drogkaris, P., & Gritzalis, S. (2011). Identity management challenges for intercloud applications. *Communications in Computer and Information Science, 187*, 198–204. doi:10.1007/978-3-642-22365-5_24

Ogata, H., & Yano, Y. (2003). How ubiquitous computing can support language learning. In *Proceedings of KEST* (pp. 1-6). Retrieved October 13, 2013, from http://www-b4.is.tokushima-u.ac.jp/ogata/pdf/KEST2003ogata.pdf

Olden, E. (2011). Architecting a cloud-scale identity fabric. *Computer, 44*(3), 52–59. doi:10.1109/MC.2011.60

Osterwalder, A., & Pigneur, Y. (Eds.). (2010). *Business model generation.* Hoboken, NJ: John Wiley & Sons.

Ouf, S., Nasr, M., & Helmy, Y. (2010). An enhanced e-learning ecosystem based on an integration between cloud computing and web 2.0. In *Proceedings of Signal Processing and Information Technology IS-SPIT 2010 IEEE International Symposium on.* IEEE. Retrieved from http://ieeexplore.ieee.org/stamp/stamp.jsp?tp=&arnumber=5711721

Parpinelli, R. S., Benitez, C. M. V., & Lopes, H. S. (2011). Parallel approaches for the artificial bee colony algorithm. In B. K. Panigrahi, Y. Shi, & M.-H. Lim (Eds.), *Handbook of swarm intelligence: Concepts, principles and applications* (Vol. 8, pp. 329–346). Berlin: Springer. doi:10.1007/978-3-642-17390-5_14

Parviz, B. A. (2009). *Augmented reality in a contact lens.* Retrieved from http://spectrum.ieee.org/biomedical/bionics/augmented-reality-in-a-contact-lens

Peppers, D., & Rogers, M. (Eds.). (2011). *Managing customer relationships: A strategic framework* (2nd ed.). Hoboken, NJ: John Wiley & Sons, Inc.

Peredo, R., Canales, A., Menchaca, A., & Peredo, I. (2011). Intelligent web-based education system for adaptive learning. *Expert Systems with Applications, 38*(12), 14690–14702. doi:10.1016/j.eswa.2011.05.013

Pérez, A., López, G., Cánovas, O., & Gómez-Skarmeta, A. (2011). Formal description of the SWIFT identity management framework. *Future Generation Computer Systems, 27*(8), 1113–1123. doi:10.1016/j.future.2011.04.003

Peter, M., & Grance, T. (2011). *The NIST definition of cloud computing (NIST special publication 800-145: 7).* Washington, DC: NIST.

Pfister, G. F. (1998). *In search of clusters* (Vol. 2). Englewood Cliffs, NJ: Prentice Hall PTR.

Ping Identity. (2011). *Simple cloud identity management (SCIM).* Retrieved September 1, 2013, from http://www.enterprisemanagement360.com/wp-content/files_mf/white_paper/simple-cloud-identity-management-scim.pdf

Pirkwieser, S., & Raidl, G. (2009). Multiple variable neighborhood search enriched with ilp techniques for the periodic vehicle routing problem with time windows. In M. J. Blesa, C. Blum, L. Gaspero, A. Roli, M. Sampels, & A. Schaerf (Eds.), *Hybrid metaheuristics* (pp. 45–59). Berlin: Springer. doi:10.1007/978-3-642-04918-7_4

Plummer, D. C., Smith, D. M., Bittman, T. J., Cearley, D. W., Cappuccio, D. J., & Scott, D. et al. (2009, May). Five refining attributes of public and private cloud computing. *Reproduction (Cambridge, England)*, 1–5. Retrieved from http://my.gartner.com/portal/server.pt?open=512&objID=260&mode=2&PageID=3460702&docCode=167182&ref=docDisplay

Plummer, D. C., Smith, D. M., Reeves, D., Robertson, B., Austin, T., & McDonald, M. P. (Eds.). (2010). *Cloud computing, CIO desk reference*. New York: Gartner Inc.

Polacek, M., Benkner, S., Doerner, K. F., & Hartl, R. F. (2008). A cooperative and adaptive variable neighborhood search for the multi depot vehicle routing problem with time windows. *Business Research*, *1*(2), 1–12.

Poole, C. M., Cornelius, I., Trapp, J. V., & Langton, C. M. (2012). Radiotherapy Monte Carlo simulation using cloud computing technology. *Australasian Physical & Engineering Sciences in Medicine*, *35*(4), 497–502. doi:10.1007/s13246-012-0167-8 PMID:23188699

Popek, G. J., & Goldberg, R. P. (1974). Formal requirements for virtualizable third generation architectures. *Communications of the ACM*, *17*(7), 412–421. doi:10.1145/361011.361073

PRACE. (2012). *PRACE – The scientific case for HPC in Europe*. Retrieved September 11, 2013, from http://www.prace-ri.eu/

Price, R. K., Ahmad, K., & Holz, K. P. (1998). Hydroinformatic concepts. In J. Marsalek, C. Maksimovic, E. Zeman, & R. Price (Eds.), *Hydroinformatics tools for planning, design, operation and rehabilitation of sewer systems*. Dordrecht, The Netherlands: Kluwer Academic Publishers. doi:10.1007/978-94-017-1818-9_3

Qian, L., Luo, Z., Du, Y., & Guo, L. (2009). Cloud computing: An overview. *Lecture Notes in Computer Science*, *5931*, 626–631. doi:10.1007/978-3-642-10665-1_63

Quinn, M. J. (2003). *Parallel programming in C with MPI and OpenMP*. New York, NY: McGraw-Hill.

Radenković, B., Despotović-Zrakić, M., Labus, A., & Vulić, M. (2011). Enhancing e-education process with social networking. In *Proceedings of SED 2011, 4th International Conference Science and Higher Education in Function of Sustainble Development* (pp. 1-7). Užice: Visoka poslovno-tehnička škola strukovnih studija.

Radenković, B., Despotović, M., & Bogdanović, Z. (2006). Web portal for postgraduate e-education.[SymOpis.]. *Proceedings of SymOpis*, *2006*, 1–4.

Radenković, B., Stanojević, M., & Marković, A. (Eds.). (2010). *Računarska simulacija*. Faculty of Organizational Sciences and FON and Faculty of Transport and Traffic Engineering.

Radonjic, V., Jankovic, S., Mladenovic, S., Veskovic, S., & Kostic-Ljubisavljevic, A. (2011). B2B integration of rail transport systems in cloud computing environment. In N. Marchetti (Ed.), *The 4th international symposium on applied sciences in biomedical and communication technologies - ISABEL '11*. New York: ACM Digital Library.

Radovanović, D. (2010). Internet paradigma, struktura i dinamika onlajn društvenih mreža: Fejsbuk i mladi u Srbiji. In *Proceedings of International Interdisciplinary Conference Problems of Adolescence,* (pp. 20-26). Serbia: Pančevačko čitalište.

Raichura, B., & Agarwal, A. (2009). Service exchange @ cloud. *SetLabs Briefings Infosys*, *7*(7), 55–60.

Rak, M., Cuomo, A., & Villano, U. (2012). mJADES: Concurrent simulation in the cloud, complex. In *Proceedings of 2012 Sixth International Conference on Intelligent and Software Intensive Systems (CISIS)* (pp. 853-860). IEEE, Inc.

Redin, J. (2012). *A brief history of mechanical calculators, part I: The age of the polymaths*. Retrieved from http://www.xnumber.com/xnumber/mechanical1.htm

Reeves, C. R. (2010). Genetic algorithms. In M. Gendreau & J-Y. Potvin (Eds.), Handbook of metaheuristics (2nd ed.), (pp. 109-139). New York: Springer Science+Business Media.

Ren, K., Wang, C., & Wang, Q. (2012). Security challenges for the public cloud. *IEEE Internet Computing*, *16*(1), 69–73. doi:10.1109/MIC.2012.14

Resende, M. G. C., & Ribeiro, C. C. (2010). Greedy randomized adaptive search procedures: Advances, hybridizations, and applications. In M. Gendreau & J-Y. Potvin (Eds.), Handbook of metaheuristics (2nd ed.), (pp. 283-319). New York: Springer Science+Business Media.

Resnick, D. (2012). Ideas for future high performance CPU and system architectures (No. SAND2012-1717C). Albuquerque, NM: Sandia National Laboratories (SNL-NM).

Rimal, B. P., Choi, E., & Lumb, I. (2010). A taxonomy, survey, and issues of cloud computing ecosystems. In N. Antonopoulos, & L. Gillam (Eds.), *Cloud computing: Principles, systems and applications* (pp. 21–46). London, UK: Springer. doi:10.1007/978-1-84996-241-4_2

Rittinghouse, J., & Ransome, J. F. (Eds.). (2009). *Cloud computing: Implementation, management and security.* San Francisco: Taylor and Francis Group, LLC.

Rolf, H., & Yamartino, M. (2010). *The economics of the cloud* (Microsoft whitepaper). Retrieved October 10, 2013, from http://www.microsoft.com/en-us/news/presskits/cloud/docs/the-economics-of-the-cloud.pdf

Romero, C., Ventura, S., & De Bra, P. (2009). Using mobile and web-based computerized tests to evaluate university students. *Computer Applications in Engineering Education,* 17(4), 435–447. doi:10.1002/cae.20242

Royal, C. D., Novembre, J., Fullerton, S. M., Goldstein, D. B., Long, J. C., Bamshad, M. J., & Clark, A. G. (2010). The inferring genetic ancestry: Opportunities, challenges, and implications. *American Journal of Human Genetics,* 86(5), 661–673. PMID:20466090

Rubin, E. M. (2010). Genomics of cellulosic biofuels. *Nature,* 454, 841–845. PMID:18704079

Rusk, N. (2011). Torrents of sequence. *Nature Methods,* 8, 44.

Rusu, O. (Ed.). (2004). *Information societies technology (IST) programme: South Eastern European research & education networking.* Retrieved September 11, 2013, from http://www.seera-ei.eu/images/stories/seeren/SEEREN-WP4-RoEduNet-006-D14bConfAndPerf-b-2004-10-09.pdf

Samimi, F. A., Mckinley, P. K., & Sadjadi, S. M. (2006). Mobile service clouds: A self-managing infrastructure for autonomic mobile computing services. *Science,* 3996, 130–141.

Sánchez, J., & Olivares, R. (2011). Problem solving and collaboration using mobile serious games. *Computers & Education,* 57(3), 1943–1952. doi:10.1016/j.compedu.2011.04.012

Saraiva, J., & Silva, A. R. D. (2010). A reference model for the analysis and comparison of MDE approaches for web-application development. *Journal of Software Engineering and Applications,* 3, 419–425. doi:10.4236/jsea.2010.35047

Sarbanes-Oxley Act. (2002). Retrieved October 10, 2013, from http://www.sec.gov/about/laws/soa2002.pdf

Satyanarayanan, M., Bahl, V., Caceres, R., & Davies, N. (2009). The case for VM-based cloudlets in mobile computing. *IEEE Pervasive Computing/IEEE Computer Society [and] IEEE Communications Society,* 8(4), 14–23. doi:10.1109/MPRV.2009.82

Savić, D., Silva, A. R. D., Vlajić, S., Lazarević, S., Stanojević, V., Antović, I., & Milić, M. (2012). Use case specification at different levels of abstraction. In *Proceedings of Eighth International Conference on the Quality of Information and Communications Technology (QUATIC '12)* (pp. 187-192). Washington, DC: IEEE.

Savić, D., Vlajić, S., Antović, I., Stanojević, V., & Milić, M. (2012). Language for use case specification. In *Proceedings of 34th Annual IEEE Software Engineering Workshop.* Limerick, Ireland: IEEE.

Savić, D., Simić, D., & Vlajić, S. (2010). Extended software architecture based on security patterns. *Informatica,* 21(2), 229–246.

Sboner, A., Mu, X. J., Greenbaum, D., Auerbach, R. K., & Gerstein, M. B. (2011). The real cost of sequencing: Higher than you think! *Genome Biology,* 12(8), 1–12. PMID:21867570

Schaffer, H. E., Averitt, S. F., & Hoit, I. M. (2009). NCSU's virtual computing lab: A cloud computing solution. *IEEE Computer,* 42(7), 94–97. doi:10.1109/MC.2009.230

Schintke, F., Simon, J., & Reinefeld, A. (2001). A cache simulator for shared memory systems. In V. Alexandrov, J. Dongarra, B. Juliano, R. Renner, & K. Tan (Eds.), *Computational science - ICCS 2001 (LNCS)* (Vol. 2074, pp. 569–578). Berlin, Germany: Springer-Verlag. doi:10.1007/3-540-45718-6_62

Schwan, J. (2009). Open source software, cloud computing can save government money. *Government Technology.* Retrieved September 15, 2013, from http://www.govtech.com/pcio/Open-Source-Software-Cloud.html

Sehgal, S., Erdelyi, M., Merzky, A., & Jha, S. (2011). Understanding application-level interoperability: Scaling-out MapReduce over high-performance grids and clouds. *Future Generation Computer Systems*, 27(5), 590–599. doi:10.1016/j.future.2010.11.001

Sempolinski, P., & Thain, D. (2010). A comparison and critique of eucalyptus, OpenNebula and nimbus. In J. Qiu, G. Zhao, & C.G. Rong (Eds.), *2nd IEEE International Conference on Cloud Computing Technology and Science* (pp. 1-10). Los Alamitos, CA: IEEE Computer Society.

Seo, C., Han, Y., Lee, H., & Jung, J. J. (2010). Implementation of cloud computing environment for discrete event system simulation using service oriented architecture. In *Proceedings of 2010 IEEE/IFIP 8th International Conference on Embedded and Ubiquitous Computing (EUC)* (pp. 359-362). IEEE, Inc.

Sevkli, M., & Aydin, M. E. (2007). Parallel variable neighbourhood search algorithms for job shop scheduling problems. *IMA Journal of Management Mathematics*, 18(2), 117–133. doi:10.1093/imaman/dpm009

Sha, L., Looi, C.-K., Chen, W., & Zhang, B. H. (2012). Understanding mobile learning from the perspective of self-regulated learning. *Journal of Computer Assisted Learning*, 28(4), 366–378. doi:10.1111/j.1365-2729.2011.00461.x

Shanklin, M. (n.d.). *Mobile cloud computing*. Retrieved from: http://www.cse.wustl.edu/~jain/cse574-10/ftp/cloud/index.html

Sharp, J. (Ed.). (2010). *Windows® communication foundation 4 step by step*. Sebastopol, CA: O'Reilly Media, Inc.

Sharples, M. (2000). The design of personal mobile technologies for lifelong learning. *Computers & Education*, 34(3-4), 177–193. doi:10.1016/S0360-1315(99)00044-5

Shen, Z. S. Z., & Tong, Q. T. Q. (2010). The security of cloud computing system enabled by trusted computing technology. In *Proceedings of 2nd International Conference on Signal Processing Systems ICSPS 2010*. IEEE. Retrieved from http://ieeexplore.ieee.org/lpdocs/epic03/wrapper.htm?arnumber=5555234

Shenfield, A., & Fleming, P. J. (2005). A service oriented architecture for decision making in engineering design. In *Advances in grid computing-EGC 2005* (pp. 334–343). Berlin: Springer Verlag. doi:10.1007/11508380_35

Shi, Y. (1996). *Reevaluating Amdahl's law and Gustafson's law. Philadelphia* (pp. 38–24). MS: Computer Sciences Department, Temple University.

Shuai, Q. (2011). What will cloud computing provide for Chinese m-learning? In *Proceeding of the International Conference on eEducation Entertainment and eManagement*. IEEE.

Shuai, Q., & Ming-Quan, Z. (2011). Cloud computing promotes the progress of m-learning. In *Proceedings of 2011 International Conference on Uncertainty Reasoning and Knowledge Engineering*. IEEE.

Shuqiang, H., & Hongkuan, Y. (2012). A new mobile learning platform based on mobile cloud computing. *Advances in Intelligent and Soft Computing*, 159, 393–398. doi:10.1007/978-3-642-29387-0_59

Silva, A. R. D., Saraiva, J., Ferreira, D., Silva, R., & Videira, C. (2007). Integration of RE and MDE paradigms: The ProjectIT approach and tools. *IET Software*, 1(6), 294–314. doi:10.1049/iet-sen:20070012

Simić, K. (2011). *Usage of mobile technologies in the development of application for cloud computing infrastructure in e-education*. (Master Thesis). University of Belgrade, Belgrade, Serbia.

Simić, Z., Milivojević, N., Prodanović, D., Milivojević, V., & Perović, N. (2009). SWAT-based runoff modeling in complex catchment areas: Theoretical background and numerical procedures. *Journal of Serbian Society for Computational Mechanics*, 3(1), 38–63.

Skillicorn, D. (2002). The case for datacentric grids. In *Proceedings of the International Parallel and Distributed Processing Symposium*. Washington, DC: IEEE Computer Society.

Skilton, M. (2010). Building return on investment from cloud computing. *The Open Group*. Retrieved September 15, 2013, from http://www.opengroup.org/cloud/whitepapers/ccroi/intro.htm

Skonnard, A. (2006). *Learn the ABCs of programming windows communication foundation.* MSDN Magazine. Retrieved from http://msdn.microsoft.com/en-us/magazine/cc163647.aspx

Slook, B. (2009). *Cloud architecture and the need for an architectural perspective bobs technology briefs.* Retrieved October 10, 2013, from http://bslook.wordpress.com/2009/04/27/cloud-architecture-and-the-need-for-an-architecture-perspective/

Smaglik, P. (2011). Minnesota: Medicine and materials. *Nature, 475*(7356), 413–414. PMID:21786466

Smith, A. J. (1987). Line (block) size choice for CPU cache memories. *IEEE Transactions on Computers, 100*(9), 1063–1075. doi:10.1109/TC.1987.5009537

Smith, D. M., & Plummer, D. C. (Eds.). (2009). *Global class: The inspiration for cloud computing.* New York: Gartner Inc.

Sobol', I. M. (1967). On the distribution of points in a cube and the approximate evaluation of integrals. *U.S.S.R Comput. Maths. Math. Phys, 7*(4), 784–802.

Sohrabi, B., Haghighi, M., & Khanlari, A. (2010). Customer relationship management maturity model (CRM3): A model for stepwise implementation. *International Journal of Human Sciences, 7*(1), 1–20.

Solomatine, D. P., Dibike, Y. B., & Kukuric, N. (1999). Automatic calibration of groundwater models using global optimization techniques. *Hydrological Sciences Journal, 44*(6), 879–894. doi:10.1080/02626666909492287

Sotomayor, B., Montero, R., Llorente, I., & Foster, I. (2009). Virtual infrastructure management in private and hybrid clouds. *IEEE Internet Computing, 13*(5), 14–22. doi:10.1109/MIC.2009.119

Srinivasa, R. V., Nageswara, R. N. K., & Kumari, E. K. (2009). Cloud computing: An overview. *Journal of Theoretical and Applied Information Technology, 9*(1), 71–76.

Staab, S., & Studer, R. (Eds.). (2009). *Handbook on ontologies.* Berlin, Germany: Springer-Verlag. doi:10.1007/978-3-540-92673-3

Stanimirović, D., & Vintar, M. (2010). Decision making criteria for outsourcing or onsourcing of IT service provision in public sector. *Management – Časopis za Teoriju i Praksu Menadžmenta, 58*, 65-69.

Stein, L. D. (2010). The case for cloud computing in genome informatics. *Genome Biology, 11*(5), 1–7. PMID:20441614

Sterling, T. L., & Zima, H. P. (2002). Gilgamesh: A multithreaded processor-in-memory architecture for petaflops computing. In *Proceedings of ACM/IEEE SC 2002 Conference* (SC'02). ACM/IEEE.

Steven, H. R., Linton, M., & Spence, M. C. (2010). *Cloud computing architecture, IT security, & operational perspectives.* National Aeronautics and Space Administration. Retrieved October 10, 2013, from http://www.nasa.gov/ppt/482833main_2010_Tuesday_5_Hunt_Linton_ChweSpence.ppt

Stockwell, G. (2010). Using mobile phones for vocabulary activities: Examining the effect of the platform. *Language Learning & Technology, 14*(2), 95–110.

Strohmaier, E. (2011). *Japan reclaims top ranking on latest TOP500 list of world's supercomputers* (Press release). Retrieved from www.freerepublic.com/focus/f-chat/2737129/posts

Stuart, D. (2009). Social media metrics. *Online, 33*(6), 22–24.

Subashini, S., & Kavitha, V. (2011). A survey on security issues in service delivery models of cloud computing. *Journal of Network and Computer Applications, 34*(1), 1–11. doi:10.1016/j.jnca.2010.07.006

Subotić, M., Tuba, M., & Stanarević, N. (2011). Different approaches in parallelization of the artificial bee colony algorithm. *International Journal of Mathematical Models and Methods in Applied Sciences, 5*(4), 755–762.

Su, J.-M., Tseng, S.-S., Lin, H.-Y., & Chen, C.-H. (2011). A personalized learning content adaptation mechanism to meet diverse user needs in mobile learning environments. *User Modeling and User-Adapted Interaction, 21*(1-2), 5–49. doi:10.1007/s11257-010-9094-0

Sultan, N. (2010). Cloud computing for education: A new dawn? *International Journal of Information Management*, *30*(2), 101–182. doi:10.1016/j.ijinfomgt.2009.09.004

Sun, S., Hawkey, K., & Beznosov, K. (2012). Systematically breaking and fixing OpenID security: Formal analysis, semi-automated empirical evaluation, and practical countermeasures. *Computers & Security*, *31*(4), 465–483. doi:10.1016/j.cose.2012.02.005

Suriadi, S., Foo, E., & Jøsang, A. (2009). A user-centric federated single sign-on system. *Journal of Network and Computer Applications*, *32*(2), 388–401. doi:10.1016/j.jnca.2008.02.016

Takabi, H., Joshi, J., & Ahn, G. (2010). Security and privacy challenges in cloud computing environments. *IEEE Security & Privacy*, *8*(6), 24–31. doi:10.1109/MSP.2010.186

Takahashi, M., & Imada, M. (1984). Quantum Monte Carlo simulation of a two-dimensional electron system – Melting of Wigner crystal. *Journal of the Physical Society of Japan*, *53*(11), 3765–3769. doi:10.1143/JPSJ.53.3765

Talbi, E.-G., Mostaghim, S., Okabe, T., Ishibuchi, H., Rudolph, G., & Coello, C. A. C. (2008). Parallel approaches for multiobjective optimization. In H. Braun & J. Branke (Eds.), *Multiobjective optimization* (Vol. 5252, pp. 349-372). Berlin: Springer. Retrieved from http://www.springerlink.com/index/F433U42G7Q041617.pdf

Talbi, E.-G. (Ed.). (2009). *Metaheuristics: From design to implementation*. Hoboken, NJ: John Wiley & Sons, Inc. doi:10.1002/9780470496916

Talukder, A. K., Zimmerman, L., & Prahalad, H. A. (2010). Cloud economics: Principles, costs, and benefits. In N. Antonopoulos, & L. Gillam (Eds.), *Cloud computing: Principles, systems and applications* (pp. 343–360). London: Springer-Verlag. doi:10.1007/978-1-84996-241-4_20

Tan, G., Sreedhar, V. C., & Gao, G. R. (2011). Analysis and performance results of computing betweenness centrality on IBM Cyclops64. *The Journal of Supercomputing*, *56*(1), 1–24. doi:10.1007/s11227-009-0339-9

Tanimoto, S., Hiramoto, M., Iwashita, M., Sato, H., & Kanai, A. (2011). Risk management on the security problem in cloud computing. In Y. C. Byun, K. Akingbehin, P. Hnetynka, & R. Lee (Eds.), *Proceedings of the First ACIS/J International Conference on Computers, Networks, Systems and Industrial Engineering (CNSI)*. Los Alamitos, CA: IEEE Computer Society.

Tarjan, D., Thoziyoor, S., & Jouppi, N. P. (2006). *CACTI 4.0*. HP laboratories. Retrieved from http://www.hpl.hp.com/techreports/2006/HPL-2006-86.pdf

Tata, S., Patel, J. M., Friedman, J. S., & Swaroop, A. (2005). *Towards declarative querying for biological sequences* (Technical Report CSE-TR-508-05). Ann Arbor, MI: University of Michigan.

Teodorović, D. (2009). Bee colony optimization (BCO). In C. P. Lim, L. C. Jain, & S. Dehuri (Eds.), *Innovations in swarm intelligence* (pp. 39–60). Berlin: Springer-Verlag. doi:10.1007/978-3-642-04225-6_3

Thomas, J. (2005). *The STAR detector at RHIC*. Berkeley, CA: Interdisciplinary Instrumentation Colloquium Lawrence Berkeley National Laboratory.

Thompson, J. M. (1914). Post-modernism. *The Hibbert Journal*, *12*(4), 733.

Tian, W., Su, S., & Lu, G. (2010). Framework for implementing and managing platform as a service in a virtual cloud computing lab. In Z. Hu & Z. Ye (Eds.), *The Second International Workshop on Education Technology and Computer Science*. Los Alamitos, CA: IEEE Computer Society.

Tilborg, H. C. A., & Jajodia, S. (Eds.). (2005). *Encyclopedia of cryptography and security*. Berlin: Springer. doi:10.1007/0-387-23483-7

Tor-Morten, G. (2012). Cloud computing and context-awareness: A study of the adapted user experience. *Lecture Notes in Computer Science*, *6762*, 427–435.

Toulouse, M., Crainic, T. G., & Gendreau, M. (1996). Communication issues in designing cooperative multi thread parallel searches. In I. H. Osman, & J. P. Kelly (Eds.), *Meta-heuristics: Theory & applications* (pp. 501–522). Boston: Kluwer Academic Publishers. doi:10.1007/978-1-4613-1361-8_30

Tsai, W.-T., Sun, X., & Balasooriya, J. (2010). Service-oriented cloud computing architecture. In *Proceedings of 2010 Seventh International Conference on Information Technology: New Generations (ITNG)* (pp. 684-689). The Institute of Electrical and Electronics Engineers, Inc.

Tsai, W.-T., Wu, L., Sarjoughian, H., & Qihong, S. (2011). SimSaaS: Simulation software-as-a-service. In *Proceedings of the 44th Annual Simulation Symposium* (pp. 77-86). San Diego, CA: Society for Computer Simulation International.

Uden, L., Wangsa, T., & Damiani, E. (2007). The future of e-learning: E-learning ecosystem. In E. Chang, & K. Hussain (Eds.), *Digital EcoSystems and Technologies Conference, DEST '07: Inaugural IEEE-IES* (pp. 113–117). IEEE.

Urban, A. (2010). *PBS professional user's guide*. GridWorks, Altair Engineering, Inc.

Urbanskienė, R., Žostautienė, D., & Chreptavičienė, V. (2008). The model of creation of customer relationship management (CRM) system. *The Engineering Economist*, *3*(3), 51–59.

Uzunboylu, H., & Ozdamli, F. (2011). Teacher perception for m-learning: Scale development and teachers' perceptions. *Journal of Computer Assisted Learning*, *27*(6), 544–556. doi:10.1111/j.1365-2729.2011.00415.x

Uzzi, B., & Spiro, J. (2005). Collaboration and creativity: The small world problem. *American Journal of Sociology*, *111*(2), 447–504. doi: doi:10.1086/432782

Vaidya, J. (2009). Infrastructure management and monitoring. *SetLabs Briefings Infosys*, *7*(7), 79–88.

Vaquero, L. M., Rodero-Merino, L., & Morán, D. (2010). Locking the sky: A survey on IaaS cloud security. *Computing*, *91*(1), 93–118. doi:10.1007/s00607-010-0140-x

Vazquez-Briseno, M., Vincent, P., Nieto-Hipólito, J. I., & Sánchez-López, J. D. D. (2012). Applying a modular framework to develop mobile applications and services. *Journal of Universal Computer Science*, *18*(5), 704–727.

Velte, T., Velte, A., & Elsenpeter, R. (Eds.). (2010). *Cloud computing: A practical approach*. New York: The McGraw-Hill Companies.

Verhoeven, M. G. A., & Aarts, E. H. L. (1995). Parallel local search. *Journal of Heuristics*, *1*(1), 43–65. doi:10.1007/BF02430365

Vernadat, F. B. (2010). Technical, semantic and organizational issues of enterprise interoperability and networking. *Annual Reviews in Control*, *34*(1), 139–144. doi:10.1016/j.arcontrol.2010.02.009

Verstichel, S., Ongenae, F., Loeve, L., Vermeulen, F., Dings, P., & Dhoedt, B. et al. (2011). Efficient data integration in the railway domain through an ontology-based methodology. *Transportation Research Part C, Emerging Technologies*, *19*(4), 617–643. doi:10.1016/j.trc.2010.10.003

Vidanović, I., Bogojević, A., Balaž, A., & Belić, A. (2009). Properties of quantum systems via diagonalization of transition amplitudes: II: Systematic improvements of short-time propagation. *Physical Review E: Statistical, Nonlinear, and Soft Matter Physics*, *80*, 066706. doi:10.1103/PhysRevE.80.066706 PMID:20365301

Vidanović, I., Bogojević, A., & Belić, A. (2009). Properties of quantum systems via diagonalization of transition amplitudes: I: Discretization effects. *Physical Review E: Statistical, Nonlinear, and Soft Matter Physics*, *80*, 066705. doi:10.1103/PhysRevE.80.066705 PMID:20365300

Vossen, P. (2002). *EuroWordNet general document*. Retrieved October 13, 2013, from http://vossen.info/docs/2002/EWNGeneral.pdf

Vossen, G., & Westerkamp, P. (2006). Secure identity management in a service-based e-learning environment. *International Journal of Intelligent Information Technologies*, *2*(4), 57–76. doi:10.4018/jiit.2006100104

Vouk, M. A., Sills, E., & Dreher, P. (2010). Integration of high-performance computing into cloud computing services. In B. Furht, & A. Escalante (Eds.), *Handbook of cloud computing* (pp. 255–276). Berlin: Springer. doi:10.1007/978-1-4419-6524-0_11

Vudragović, D., Balaž, A., Slavnić, V., & Belić, A. (2009). Serbian participation in grid computing projects. In *Proceedings of the XXII International Symposium on Nuclear Electronics & Computing* (pp. 286-293). Academic Press.

Vujin, V. (2010). Cloud computing in science and higher education. *Management – Časopis za Teoriju i Praksu Menadžmenta, 59,* 65-69.

Vujin, V. (2012). *IT infrastructure model for e-learning.* (Doctoral dissertation). University of Belgrade, Belgrade, Serbia.

Vulić, M. (2013). *Student relationship management model in e-education.* (Doctoral dissertation). University of Belgrade, Belgrade, Serbia.

Vulić, M., Barać, D., & Bogdanović, Z. (2011). CRM as a cloud service in e-education. In *Proceedings of 19th Telecommunications Forum (TELFOR)* (pp. 1470-1473). Belgrade: Telecommunications Society and Academic Mind.

Vulić, M., Labus, A., & Milić, A. (2011). Application of mobile services for improving CRM concept in e-education. *InfoM, 10*(39), 55–60.

Walczak, K., Chmielewski, J., Wiza, W., Rumiński, D., & Skibiński, G. (2011). Adaptable mobile user interfaces for e-learning repositories. In *Proceedings of IADIS International Conference on Mobile Learning* (pp. 10-12). IADIS.

Wang, M., Shen, R., Novak, D., & Pan, X. (2009). The impact of mobile learning on students' learning behaviours and performance: Report from a large blended classroom. *British Journal of Educational Technology, 40*(4), 673–695. doi:10.1111/j.1467-8535.2008.00846.x

Wan, Z., Liu, J., & Deng, R. (2012). HASBE: A hierarchical attribute-based solution for flexible and scalable access control in cloud computing. *IEEE Transactions on Information Forensics and Security, 7*(2), 743–754. doi:10.1109/TIFS.2011.2172209

Ward, J., & Peppard, J. (Eds.). (2009). *Strategic planning for information systems.* Chichester, UK: John Wiley & Sons.

Weibel, S. (2005). The state of the Dublin core metadata initiative: April 1999. *Bulletin of the American Society for Information Science and Technology, 25*(5), 18–22. doi:10.1002/bult.127

Weinhardt, C., Arun, A., Benjamin, B., Nikolay, B., Thomas, M., Wibke, M., & Jochen, S. (2009). Cloud computing – A classification, business models, and research directions. *Business Information Systems Engineering, 1*(5), 391–399. doi:10.1007/s12599-009-0071-2

Wei, S., Wang, J., Yin, R., & Yuan, J. (2013). Trade-off between security and performance in block ciphered systems with erroneous ciphertexts. *IEEE Transactions on Information Forensics and Security, 8*(4), 636–645. doi:10.1109/TIFS.2013.2248724

Wilde, S. (Ed.). (2011). *Customer knowledge management: Improving customer relationship through knowledge application.* Berlin: Springer Verlag. doi:10.1007/978-3-642-16475-0

Wilson, R. J. (2001). *The European DataGrid project.* Retrieved September 11, 2013, from http://www.snowmass2001.org/e7/papers/wilson.pdf

Winans, T. B., & Brown, J. S. (2009). *Cloud computing: A collection of working papers.* Deloitte.

Wulf, W. A., & McKee, S. A. (1995). Hitting the memory wall: Implications of the obvious. *ACM SIGARCH Computer Architecture News, 23*(1), 20–24. doi:10.1145/216585.216588

Xiao, Z., & Xiao, Y. (2013). Security and privacy in cloud computing. *IEEE Communications Surveys & Tutorials, 15*(2), 843–859. doi:10.1109/SURV.2012.060912.00182

Xie, Y. (2013). Future memory and interconnect technologies. In Proceedings of Design, Automation & Test in Europe Conference & Exhibition (DATE), 2013 (pp. 964-969). IEEE.

Yazdani, M., Amiri, M., & Zandieh, M. (2010). Flexible job-shop scheduling with parallel variable neighborhood search algorithm. *Expert Systems with Applications, 37*(1), 678–687. doi:10.1016/j.eswa.2009.06.007

Yin, C. Y. C., David, B., & Chalon, R. (2009). Use your mobile computing devices to learn - Contextual mobile learning system design and case studies. In *Proceedings of 2009 2nd IEEE International Conference on Computer Science and Information Technology.* IEEE. Retrieved from http://ieeexplore.ieee.org/lpdocs/epic03/wrapper.htm?arnumber=5234816

Zeigler, B. P., Kim, T. G., & Praehofer, H. (Eds.). (2000). *Theory of modeling and simulation* (2nd ed.). New York: Academic Press.

Zhang, S., Zhang, S., Chen, X., & Huo, X. (2010). Cloud computing research and development trend. In B. Werner (Ed.), *Proceedings of the Second International Conference on Future Networks* (pp. 93-97). Los Alamitos, CA: IEEE Computer Society. doi: 10.1109/ICFN.2010.58

Zhang, X., Schiffman, J., Gibbs, S., Kunjithapatham, A., & Jeong, S. (2009). Securing elastic applications on mobile devices for cloud computing. In *Proceedings of the 2009 ACM Workshop on Cloud Computing Security CCSW 09*. ACM Press. Retrieved from http://portal.acm.org/citation.cfm?doid=1655008.1655026

Zhang, Y., & Chen, J.-L. (2010). Universal identity management model based on anonymous credentials. In L. O'Conner (Ed.), *2010 IEEE International Conference on Services Computing* (pp. 305-312). Miami, FL: IEEE, Inc.

Zhang, Y., & Chen, J.-L. (2011). A delegation solution for universal identity management in SOA. *IEEE Transactions on Services Computing*, *4*(1), 70–81. doi:10.1109/TSC.2010.9

Zhao, W. Z. W., Sun, Y. S. Y., & Dai, L. D. L. (2010). Improving computer basis teaching through mobile communication and cloud computing technology. In *Proceedings of Advanced Computer Theory and Engineering ICACTE 2010 3rd International Conference*. IEEE. Retrieved from http://ieeexplore.ieee.org/xpls/abs_all.jsp?arnumber=5578977

Zissis, D., & Lekkas, D. (2012). Addressing cloud computing security issues. *Future Generation Computer Systems*, *28*(3), 583–592. doi:10.1016/j.future.2010.12.006

About the Contributors

Marijana Despotović-Zrakić received her BS degree at the Faculty of Organizational Sciences, University of Belgrade, in 2001, and a MSc degree in 2003. She received her PhD degree with the thesis "Design of Methods for Postgraduate E-Education Based on Internet Technologies" in 2006. Since 2001, she has been teaching several courses at the Faculty of Organizational Sciences: E-business, E-education, Simulation and Simulation Languages, Internet Technologies, Internet Marketing, Risk Management in Information Systems, M-Business, and Internet of Things. She has been an associate professor since 2011. Her current professional and scientific interests include software project management, information systems, Internet technologies, and e-education.

Veljko Milutinović is a Doctor Professor at the School of Electrical Engineering, University of Belgrade, Serbia. During the 1980s, for about a decade, he was on the faculty of Purdue University in the USA, where he co-authored the architecture and design of the world's first DARPA GaAs microprocessor. During the 1990s, after returning to Serbia, he took part in teaching and research at a number of major EU schools. He also delivered lectures at Stanford and MIT and has about 20 books published by leading publishers in the USA. He is on the Scientific Advisory Boards (SAB) of Maxeler Supercomputing, London, England, and Technology Connect of Boston, USA. Dr. Milutinovic is a Fellow of the IEEE and a Member of Academia Europaea.

Aleksandar Belić is Research Professor and Director of Institute of Physics, University of Belgrade, Serbia. He received his PhD at University of Illinois at Urbana in 1991 with thesis "Deep Inelastic Scattering by Quantum Liquids," fellowships from Serbian Academy of Sciences and Arts, University of Illinois, and F. T. Adler Fellowship. He was vice-president of Serbian Physical Society and Assistant Minister in Ministry of Science of the Republic of Serbia from 2000 to 2004. Since 2004, he has been the Head of Scientific Computing Laboratory. The unifying theme in his research is the application of high performance computing resources as simulation tools used to gain insight into behaviour and evolution of complex many-body systems. His research interests include various topics in the investigation of complex systems with many degrees of freedom, quantum Monte Carlo simulations, novel methods of calculation of path integrals, compactification of granular systems, etc.

* * *

Dušan Barać received his BS degree at the Faculty of Organizational Sciences in 2007. As a PhD student, he received scholarship from the Ministry of Science and Technological Development, the Republic of Serbia. He received his PhD degree with the thesis "Developing Model and Services of Portal for Adaptive E-Learning" in 2011. As assistant professor at Faculty of Organizational Sciences, University of Belgrade, he is involved in teaching courses covering the area of mobile business, Internet technologies, and e-business. His current professional interests include Internet technologies, mobile technologies, e-business, and distance education.

Zorica Bogdanović received her BSc degree at the Faculty of Organizational Sciences in 2005 and MSc degree in 2007. She received her PhD degree with thesis "Business Intelligence in Adaptive E-Education" in 2011. As assistant professor at the Faculty of Organizational Sciences, she is involved in teaching courses covering the area of e-business, mobile business, simulation and simulation languages, Internet technologies, Internet marketing, e-education, e-government, e-health, and risk management in information systems. Her current professional interests include: e-business, m-business, Internet technologies, e-government, and e-education. Zorica Bogdanović is member of following organizations: IEEE Computer Society and Serbian Society for Informatics - DIS.

Sava Čavoški graduated from the Faculty of Mechanical Engineering, University of Belgrade. He obtained his MSc from Faculty of Organizational Science. He has an extensive experience as a software architect. The following projects are worth mentioning: the Development of KOSTMOD 4.0 software project (it included the cooperation between Forskningsinstitutt [FFI] within the Ministry of Defence of the Kingdom of Norway, the Ministry of Defence of Serbia, and the Faculty of Organisational Science, University of Belgrade) and the Billing software for Cisco IP Telephony. Sava also worked on the implementation of hardware projects, mainly with the server installation and storage installation for companies EMC and IBM. He published extensively in the field of simulation and simulation modelling in domestic and international journals. His main areas of interest are the simulation models in finances and agent-based simulation models, computer-based simulation, and cloud computing. He is currently finishing his PhD thesis titled: "Agent-Based Simulation Models as a Support in Decision-Making in E-Commerce."

Teodor Gabriel Crainic received his PhD from the Computer Science and Operations Research Department, Université de Montréal, in 1982. He is Professor of Operations Research, Transportation, and Logistics, and holds the Logistics Management Chair in the School of Management, Université du Québec à Montréal. He is also Adjunct Professor (U. de Montréal and Molde University, Norway) and senior scientist at CIRRELT, the Interuniversity Research Center for Enterprise Networks, Logistics, and Transportation. He is Associate Editor for *Transportation Science* and *Transportation Research Part C: Emerging Technologies*, Area Editor "Logistics and Supply Chain" for the *Journal of Heuristics*, and serves on several other editorial boards. He is a member of the Royal Society of Canada – The Academies of Arts, Humanities, and Sciences. His research interests are in network, integer, and combinatorial optimization, meta-heuristics, and parallel computing applied to the planning and management of complex systems, particularly in transportation and logistics.

Mladen Čudanov works as assistant professor at the Faculty of Organizational Sciences, University of Belgrade. He has been visiting for one semester as an assistant professor in joint programs of iVWA from Germany and Jiangsu College of Information Technology from Wuxi and Zhuhai City Polytechnics from Zhuhai in China. His major research interests are ICT and organizational design, restructuring of business systems, and organizational change. He has published more than 80 articles at scientific journals and conferences and works as an associate editor/reviewer in several scientific journals, some on Thomson-Reuters JCR.

Tatjana Davidović received her PhD from the Mathematical Department at the University of Belgrade in 2006. She is a Research Associate Professor at the Mathematical Institute of the Serbian Academy of Sciences and Arts engaged in several scientific projects founded by the NSF Serbia. She is also an Associate Professor for the doctoral courses on Parallel Programming, Meta-heuristics, and Optimization at the Faculty of Technical Sciences, University of Novi Sad, Serbia. Dr. Davidović is a member of the Editorial Board for *International Journal for Traffic and Transport Engineering (IJTTE)* and the reviewer for several international journals. As a member of the program or organizing committee, she participated in organization of several international and domestic scientific conferences. Her main research interests include parallel computing, scheduling, combinatorial optimization, mathematical programming, and meta-heuristics.

Dejan Divac is Managing Director of Department of Dams, Hydropower, Mines, and Roads at the "Jaroslav Černi" Institute for the Development of Water Resources, Belgrade, Serbia. He is also appointed as docent at the University of Belgrade, School of Civil Engineering (courses in: Rock Mechanics, Tunneling, and Underground Structures). He has authored and co-authored more than one hundred scientific and technical papers presented at national and international conferences and published in distinguished journals: design and engineering of dams, hydroelectric power plants; tunnels and underground structures; lithological research and investigations; software and hydroinformation systems; and project management. He is a member of several scientific and professional associations, including the International Committee on Large Dams (ICOLD) and the International Society for Rock Mechanics (ISRM). In 2010, he was appointed Chairman of the Serbian Tunneling Association (ITA Serbia).

Levente Hajdu is a scientific software developer researching parallelized high throughput computing technologies such as Grid and Cloud computing and developing tools in order to fulfill the computing requirements of nuclear and particle physicists working on data from the RHIC (Relativistic Heavy Ion Collider) on both online and offline sides of the experiment. He works to distribute workload to stakeholders such as the RHIC ATLAS computing facility and National Energy Research Scientific Computer Center (NERSC), among others. He has been working for 10 years in the software and computing group for the STAR experiment at Brookhaven National Laboratory. He holds a graduate degree in computer science from the New York Institute of Technology and is a member of the OSG (Open Science Grid) VO STAR. He has authored an coauthpred numerous papers and presentations at the Conference on Computing in High Energy and Nuclear Physics (CHEP).

Hideki Imai received the B.E., M.E., and Ph.D. degrees in electrical engineering from the University of Tokyo in 1966, 1968, and 1971, respectively. From 1971 to 1992, he was on the faculty of Yokohama National University. From 1992 to 2006, he was a Professor in the Institute of Industrial Science, the University of Tokyo. In 2006, he was appointed as an Emeritus Professor of the University of Tokyo and a Professor of Chuo University. Concurrently, he is serving as the Director of Research Center for Information Security, National Institute of Advanced Industrial Science and Technology. His current research interests include information theory, coding theory, cryptography, and information security. Dr. Imai is a member of the Science Council of Japan. He was elected a Fellow of IEEE, IEICE, and IACR (International Association for Cryptologic Research) in 1992, 2001, and 2007, respectively. He is currently the Chair of CRYPTREC (Cryptography Techniques Research and Evaluation Committee of Japan) and of the IEEE Tokyo Section.

Miloš Ivanović is an assistant professor of Parallel Computing and Computer Communications at the Department for Mathematics and Informatics, Faculty of Science, University of Kragujevac. He holds a basic degree in Physics and a PhD in computer science. His main research interests include numerical modeling using mesh-free methods, the application of shared and distributed memory parallelism, GP-GPU computing, Big Data, Grid, and Cloud Computing. He participated in several national, European, and US funded projects. EU funded projects include infrastructural SEEGRID-2 and SEEGRID-SCI, together with research project FP7-224297 ARTreat (2008-2012). He also participated in a project supported by the US: NHLBI Particles in Developing Lung: Bioengineering Approach (Harvard University, 2004-2008). Dr Ivanovic is an author of over 10 publications in international journals and numerous conference publications. He is also a cofounder of Serbian Society for Computational Mechanics.

Slađana Janković is an assistant professor for Informatics by the Faculty of Transport and Traffic Engineering, University of Belgrade, Serbia. She graduated at the Faculty of Transport and Traffic Engineering and received PhD at the Faculty of Organizational Sciences, University of Belgrade. Her subjects of interest are the information technologies in traffic, development and integration of applications, models and methods of B2B integration, and cloud computing concepts. She has been the author or co-author of approximately 40 scientific works, 10 papers of which are on the application of cloud computing technologies. She participated in more than 10 studies and projects. She has been the author of one national monograph, as well as one book for students of the Faculty where she works. She holds a PhD on the development of models for B2B integration of transport systems in cloud computing technological environment.

Branislav Jovanić received his MA degree at the Faculty of Mathematics in 1975. He received his PhD degree in 1990 at the Faculty of Physics. Since 1983, he has been working at the Institute of Physics in Belgrade. In 1984, he was elected to the position of Research Professor. He is Head of Laboratory for multidisciplinary research at Institute of Physics, University of Belgrade. His current professional research includes experimental physics, computer simulation in science, and scientific computing.

Petar Kočović received his B. Sci degree at Belgrade University at the Mechanical Faculty in 1982, M. Sci Degree in 1987, and PhD in 1990. His Disertation topic was: "Non-Uniform Rational B-Splines and Surfaces and their Implementaion on Complex Machine Part Modeling." Currently, he is country manager of Gartner Serbia and has more than 25 years of experience working in the IT industry in management and technical positions for end-user organizations and software companies. He has experience in all Internet-related technologies, as well as mathematical foundation for CAD/CAM. He worked in system management, account management, marketing, consulting and systems support, as well as a software developer. He was invited to serve as speaker in a few universities. He is associate professor at the Alfa University from Belgrade and member of: the Institute of Electrical and Electronic Engineers (IEEE), since 1988, and American Society of Mechanical Engineers (ASME), since 1989.

Borko Kovačević received his B.Sc. degree at the Faculty of organizational sciences in 2005. As marketing director for South Balkans region at Microsoft, and as acting M & O Lead, Borko is managing the execution across Corporate Marketing Group, PR and Citizenship, and all three MS business groups to ensure excellence in marketing execution, drive sales results, and ensure scorecard target attainment while enforcing 100% compliance and individual accountability in execution. As a part of regular business review with sales segments, Borko runs regular revenue and KPI review with business group leads and making sure subsidiary sustains strong and focused sales execution ensuring revenue quarterly financial accountability, summarizing cross segment and cross business group view through a comprehensive set of reports and business KPIs to actively drive business results. His current professional interests include business management, marketing management, business strategy and development, project management, cloud computing, etc.

Ivanka Kovačević was born in 1982 in Kosovska Mitrovica, Kosovo. She finished high school, Gymnasium natural sciences section also in Kosovska Mitrovica. Ivanka graduated on the Faculty of Organizational Sciences in Belgrade (section – information systems) in the year 2005. Her graduation thesis was "Application of SAP Software Systems in Modern Business Environment." Ivanka enrolled in postgraduate studies, specializing in e-business. During her studies, Ivanka was an active contributor and associate in a project team for designing and developing the information system of postgraduate studies of the Faculty. After graduating, she attended many seminars and conferences in Serbia as well as abroad. As of 2006, Ivanka is employed by CT Computers, member of Comtrade Group, currently holding a position of a country brand manager for Microsoft and Kaspersky products.

Jovan Krivokapić is a teaching assistant at the Faculty of Organizational Sciences in Belgrade, in the Department for Business Systems Organization. He graduated at this faculty in 2007, and in 2009, he became a master engineer of organizational sciences. Currently, he is a PhD student. His areas of interest are organizational design and restructuring, business consulting, and special events management. As the author or co-author, he has published 3 books and more than 25 papers in scientific journals and conferences. He has participated in more than 10 consulting and research projects and some of them were of wide social significance.

Aleksandra Labus received her BS degree at the Faculty of Organizational Sciences in 2009 and her MSc degree in 2010. As a PhD student, she received scholarship from the Ministry of Science and Technological Development, the Republic of Serbia. She received her PhD degree with thesis "Edutainment in Electronic Education" in 2012. As assistant professor at the Faculty of Organizational Sciences, she is involved in teaching courses covering the area of e-business, Internet marketing, Internet technologies, Internet of things, m-business, simulation and simulation languages, risk management in information systems, and e-education. Her current professional interests include e-education, edutainment, cloud computing, e-government, social media, and student relationship management.

Jérôme Lauret is a Dr. Scientist at the Brookhaven National Laboratory and the Relativistic Heavy Ion Collider (RHIC) Solenoidal Tracker at RHIC (STAR) Software and Computing project Leader. STAR is a collaboration of 58 institutions spanning over 12 countries with a total of 587 collaborators. As the S&C leader, he is responsible for architecting and coordinating all aspects of the software needs and lifecycle of the STAR experiment. He coordinates the software efforts of more than 250 physicists and 10 computing professionals in processing, registering and redistributing Peta-Bytes of physics data per year. This data is redistributed across computer centers across the world and IT processing has relied and leveraged Grid and Cloud technologies on both public and commercial clouds and national Grid infrastructure. Dr. Lauret is also the council representative for the STAR Virtual Organization on the OpenScience Grid council (OSG), a member of the Brookhaven National Laboratory Cyber Security Advisory, and a member of the STAR management board. As a scientist, he has published 260 refereed papers to date.

Saša Lazarević is an assistant professor of software engineering at University of Belgrade, Faculty of Organizational Sciences, Department of Software Engineering. His research interests include software construction, software engineering tools and techniques, domain specific languages, cloud computing software metrics, and e-learning. He has taught undergraduate and graduate level courses: Principles of Programming, Design of Information System, Software Design, Databases, Programming Languages and Compilers, Software Construction, etc. He is one of the founders of the SILab - Software Engineering Laboratory and KSI - Department of Software Engineering at Faculty of Organizational Sciences.

Mihailo Marinković was born in 1978 in Belgrade. During his studies, he was an active member of AIESEC, international organisation for students' exchange. He graduated at the Faculty of Organizational Sciences in Belgrade in April 2005, and in January 2008, received his MSc at the same faculty. He started his professional experience in 2001, working as developer in emerging company Infovision. Since 2004, he has worked for Mobtel, first mobile operator in Serbia as engineer for software development. Since 2006, he has worked for Telenor, as business systems engineer and Internet and integration senior expert. During his professional career, he was in charge of software development, architecture, systems integration, and business processes analysis. In addition, he was team leader of technical teams and project manager. Together, with team from Faculty of Organizational Sciences, he was part of KOST-MOD 4.0, financial simulation software for Forskningsinstitutt (FFI) within the Ministry of Defence of the Kingdom of Norway. His fields of interest are software and systems architecture, data modeling, SOA, Web services, Web-based applications security, computer-based simulation, and cloud computing.

Aleksandar Marković is a Full Professor at the Faculty of Organizational Sciences, University of Belgrade, Serbia, where he got his MSc and PhD degrees in the field of Computer Simulation. Areas of his research include computer simulation, business simulation, business dynamics, and e-business management. He is editor in chief of *Journal Management*, published by Faculty of Organizational Sciences of University of Belgrade. He has published more than 60 papers in the country and abroad, all in specialized editions from domestic and international journals, congresses, and meetings. He was project leader and member of project teams for more than ten international and national projects, including projects financed by the Serbian Ministry for Science and Technology.

Radomir A. Mihajlović has been a faculty member at New York Institute of Technology (NYIT) for over 25 years. In various academic positions, he has taught computer science and has been doing research in the area of secure high performance computation systems and networks. He is one of the founders of the Computer Science department at NYIT and the very first faculty member in that department. Besides NYIT, he was a faculty member at University of Texas Austin, Polytechnic Institute of New York Unoiversity (PolyNYU), New Jersey Institute of Technology (NJIT), and University of Belgrade. Radomir completed his Ph.D. at Polytechnic Institute of New York University. At Polytechnic, he completed his M.S. degrees in Electrical Engineering and Mathematics and his Graduate Engineering studies at School of Electrical Engineering of University of Belgrade. He is a member of Eta Kappa Nu and Upsilon Pi Epsilon.

Miodrag J. Mihaljević is a research professor and the projects leader at the Mathematical Institute, Serbian Academy of Sciences and Arts, Belgrade. His main research areas are cryptology and information security. He has published more than 90 research papers in the leading international journals and conference proceedings (including over 50 papers in IEEE journals, *Journal of Cryptology, Phys. Rev. A, Computing, IET Information Security, Inform. Process. Lett., LNCS, IEICE Transactions*, and as certain book chapters) and over 150 publications in total. He is co-inventor of 6 granted patents in the US, Japan, and China. His research results have been cited more than 1500 times in the leading international publications. He has participated in over 10 international research projects and has served over 150 times as the reviewer for the leading international journals and conferences. Since the year 1997, he has held long-term visiting positions at the universities and research institutes in Japan, including the University of Tokyo, Sony Research Labs, and the National Institute AIST.

Aleksandar Milić received his BSc degree at the Faculty of Organizational Sciences in 2007 and his M.Sc. degree with Master thesis "Cloud Computing as an Infrastructure for E-Education" in 2010. Presently, he attends his PhD studies in E-business. As teaching associate at the Faculty of Organizational Sciences, he is involved in teaching courses covering the area of e-business, mobile business, Internet technologies, Internet marketing, simulation and simulation languages, and risk management in information systems. His current professional interests include: Internet technologies, e-education, e-business, mobile business, cloud computing, and Internet marketing.

Nikola Milivojević is leading researcher at the Jaroslav Černi Institute for the Development of Water Resources, Belgrade, Serbia. He is also appointed as docent at the Metropolitan University, Belgrade, Serbia. Nikola Milivojevic has earned a PhD in technical sciences from the University of Kragujevac. He is expert on computer modeling and simulations, optimization, and software development. His research interests are in the area of hydroinformatics, applied optimization, and decision support systems in hydropower system planning and control. He has participated in several international scientific projects. He is co-author of one national monograph, several international publications in peer review journals, and a designer of a number of simulation software.

Dejan Milojičić is a senior researcher and senior manager at HP Labs, Palo Alto, CA (1998-), working in the technical areas of systems software, distributed systems, Cloud computing, high performance computing, and service management. He is IEEE Computer Society 2014 President. He has served on many program committees of conferences and on journal editorial boards. He has been a member of IEEE CS, ACM, and USENIX for over 20 years. He worked in OSF Research Institute, Cambridge, MA (1994-1998), and Institute "Mihajlo Pupin," Belgrade, Serbia (1983-1991). He is teaching a class on Cloud Management at SJSU, San Jose CA. He received his PhD from University of Kaiserslautern, Germany (1993) and MSc/BSc from Belgrade University, Serbia (1983/86). Dejan is an IEEE Fellow, ACM Distinguished Engineer, and USENIX member. Dejan has published over 130 papers and 2 books; he has 12 patents and 25 patent applications.

Miloš Milutinović received his BS degree at the Faculty of Organizational Sciences in 2011 and MSc degree with Master thesis "Developing a Mobile Application for Learning Japanese Language Based on Learning Objects" in 2012. As teaching associate, he is involved in teaching courses covering the area of e-business, Internet technologies, Internet marketing, Internet of things, and m-business. As a PhD student, he receives scholarship from the Ministry of Science and Technological Development, the Republic of Serbia. His current professional interests include Internet technologies, e-business, m-business, e-education, cloud computing, e-government, and digital identities.

Snežana Mladenović is an associate professor for Informatics by the Faculty of Transport and Traffic Engineering, University of Belgrade, Serbia. She graduated at the Department of Mathematics and received her PhD at the Faculty of Organizational Sciences, University of Belgrade. Her subjects of interest are the information technologies in traffic, development and optimization of software systems, artificial intelligence, and data management. She has been the author or co-author of approximately 80 scientific works. She participated in more than 20 studies and projects. She has been the author of one national monograph and a co-author of another one, as well as two books for students of her faculty. She is a member of the editorial board and a reviewer of *International Journal for Traffic and Transport Engineering (IJTTE)*. Her papers are cited in *International Scientific Journals (SCI)* 8 times.

Pavle Petrović was born in 1986 in Serbia, where he finished high school. He received his BS degree at the Faculty of Organizational Sciences in 2012, with a thesis "Integration of Edutainment Games on Social Network with Learning Management System." He is currently a Master's candidate at the Faculty of Organizational Sciences, department of E-Business and Systems Management, where he is actively involved in the development of edutainment software for students. He has a wide working experience in software development. His current professional interests include social media, e-business, e-education, edutainment, and cloud computing.

Božidar Radenković received his BS degree at the Faculty of Organizational Sciences in 1984 and MSc degree in 1987. He received his PhD degree with thesis "Interactive Simulation System for Discrete-Stochastic Simulation of Organization Systems and its Realization at Mini and Macro Computers" in 1989. He has been working at the Faculty of Organizational Sciences since 1987. Since 1999, he has been a professor. Professor Božidar Radenković is a full member of the following professional organizations: IEEE (The Institute of Electrical and Electronic Engineers, Inc), ACM (The Association for Computing), SCS (The Society for Computer Simulation International), YU-INFO (Society for Information Systems and Computer Networks), DOPIS (Society for Operational Researches), UNESCO.

Miloš Radenković was born in 1991, he attended the "Kosta Abrašević" elementary school, followed by the 8th Belgrade Gymnasium; he has finished both with exceptional grades. He is currently a student at the School of Computing (RAF), Union University, at the Computer Sciences department. Presently, in his 4th year of studies, his interests and fields of study include databases, data warehousing, and ERP systems.

Goran Rakočević graduated from the School of Electrical Engineering, University of Belgrade, in 2007. In 2008, he enrolled in the PhD studies at the same school. Since then, he has been working on industrial and research projects at the University. Since 2011, he has also been an assistant researcher with the Mathematical Institute of the Serbian Academy of Sciences and Arts. His research interests include AI in ubiquitous computing, data mining and machine learning in highly distributed systems, and sensor networks, as well as applications of machine learning to bio- and neuro-informatics.

Dušan Ramljak received his BS and MS degree in Systems Control at the School of Electrical Engineering, University of Belgrade. He is currently a PhD student in Computer Science at Temple University, Philadelphia, PA, USA. He is also working as a Research Assistant at the Center for Data, Analytics and Biomedical Informatics, Temple University and is engaged in several scientific projects founded by DARPA and NSF, USA. Having experience in both industry and academia and in a broad range of areas, he now serves as a reviewer for several international journals and conferences. His main research interests include machine learning, spatial and temporal data mining, social network analysis, parallel computing, optimization, and meta-heuristics.

Vanjica Ratković Živanović has graduated from the electrotechnical high school "Nikola Tesla" in Belgrade. In 1986, she enrolled in the Faculty of Transport and Traffic Engineering at the University in Belgrade, where she graduated in 1995. She continued postgraduate studies in Management in 1998/99 and defended her Master's thesis "Researching Human Resources Management Models in Electronic Media" in 2005. Her first work experience was in Radio Television of Serbia, TV Belgrade, where she specialized in news about traffic and telecommunication. She graduated from the UNS Web journalism school when RTS was transformed to the Public broadcaster of Serbia and from the BBC school of journalism. She has worked as a journalist, host, and editor of "Beogradska Hronika." During the last three years, she has worked as the editor of "Morning Program" show on RTS. She has been performing research and analysis of electronic measurements of TV ratings since 2005.

Dušan Savić received the Magistar degree in information system and technologies from the Faculty of Organization Sciences, University of Belgrade, in 2010. He is currently a postgraduate student and teaching assistant in the Faculty of Organizational Sciences at the Software Engineering Department. He has interests in the following areas: modeling and meta-modeling, model driven engineering, requirement engineering, software development, software design, domain specific languages, and cloud computing. He has taught undergraduate and graduate level courses in his area. He is the author or co-author of several publications on national and international conference and workshop and journal papers.

Konstantin Simić received his B.Sc. degree at the Faculty of organizational sciences in 2010, and M.Sc. degree with Master thesis "Usage of Mobile Technologies in the Development of Application for Cloud Computing Infrastructure in E-Education" in 2011. As teaching associate, he is involved in teaching courses covering the area of e-business, Internet technologies, Internet marketing, Internet of things, m-business, and concurrent programming. As a PhD student, he receives scholarship from the Ministry of Science and Technological Development, the Republic of Serbia. His current professional interests include Internet technologies, cloud computing, e-business, e-education, digital identities, e-government, and social media.

Boban Stojanović is assistant professor at the Department of Mathematics and Informatics, Faculty of Science, University of Kragujevac, Serbia. He is an expert on computer modeling and simulations, optimization, applied informatics, and software development. Boban Stojanovic has earned a PhD in technical sciences from the University of Kragujevac. His research interests are in the area of numerical simulation and optimization methods, bioengineering (especially muscle modeling), and hydroinformatics. He is author and co-author of one international monograph, several national monographs, more than ten international publications in peer review journals, and a number of simulation software. He has participated in several international scientific projects, FP7, and TEMPUS projects and is prime investigator in bioengineering project with Steward/St. Elizabeth Hospital, Boston, US. Boban Stojanovic is cofounder of Serbian Society for Computational Mechanics and also a member of Committee for Enterprise of University of Kragujevac.

Vukašin Stojiljković is a PhD student at the University of Belgrade and associate at the Institute for Serbian Language of the Serbian Academy of Sciences and Arts. He obtained his Bachelor and Master's degrees in Linguistics from the University of Belgrade. Before joining the institute, he worked as an associate journalist for the daily newspaper *Politika* (the Culture Section). He received scholarship from Serbian Ministry of Education, Science and Technological Development. He has authored and co-authored papers in national and international journals. His current areas of interest include applied linguistics and technology, sociolinguistics, and linguistic anthropology.

Slavko Vesković is a full time professor for organization and technology railway transportation by the Faculty of Transport and Traffic Engineering, University of Belgrade, Serbia. He graduated at the Department of Railway traffic on the Faculty of Transport and Traffic Engineering and received PhD at the same faculty, University of Belgrade. His subject of interest is the planning, modelling, exploitation, safety, and ecology in railway transport and traffic. He has been the author or co-author of approximately 110 scientific papers. He was a project leader of 10 and participant in more than 50 studies and projects.

He has been the co-author of two national monograph, as well as two books for students of the faculty. He is a member of the editorial board and a reviewer of International Scientific Conference "New Horizons" in Doboj and President of Society of Graduated Railway Engineers of Serbia. He published 7 papers in international scientific journals (SCI).

Siniša Vlajić is an associate professor of software engineering at University of Belgrade, Faculty of Organizational Sciences, Department of Information Systems. He has taught undergraduate and graduate level courses: introduction to programming, introduction to information system, software design, software patterns, programming methodology, and Java programming language. He wrote many books, scripts, and publications about C++, Java, software design, software patterns, and database and information systems. His main research interests include: software process, software design, software maintenance, software pattern formalization, and programming methodology. He is one of the founders of the Laboratory and Department of the Software Engineering at Faculty of Organizational Sciences.

Vladimir Vujin received his BSc degree at the Faculty of Organizational Sciences in 1989. He has been employed at the Faculty of Organizational Sciences since 1998 as a senior system administrator at Department for distance learning. He received his Specialist degree with Expert thesis "Computer Network and Internet Services at the Faculty of Organizational Sciences." Master's degree received with Master thesis "Model of Network Services of a Higher Education Institution" in 2009. He received his PhD degree with thesis "IT Infrastructure Model for E-Learning" in 2012. His current professional interests include e-business, Internet technologies, Cloud Computing, and E-education.

Marko Vulić received his BS degree at the Faculty of Organizational Sciences in 2009 and MSc degree in 2010. He received his PhD degree with thesis "Student Relationship Management Model in E-Education." As teaching associate at the Faculty of Organizational Sciences, he was involved in teaching courses covering the area of E-Business, Simulation and Simulation Languages, Internet Marketing, and E-Education. As a PhD student, he received scholarship from the Ministry of Science and Technological Development, the Republic of Serbia. His current professional interests include e-business, e-education, student relationship management, cloud computing, e-government, and social media.

Index

A

application integration 360

B

B2B integration technology 360
bioinformatics 31, 42, 48, 55
business model 31-32, 40, 42-43, 45, 47-51, 55, 84, 281

C

caching block size 259
caching hierarchy 259
caching strategy 259
cloud-based simulation 281-282, 307
Cloud Computing (CC) 146, 194, 323
    application 2, 31, 40, 148, 159, 171, 186, 202
    concepts 341-342, 360
    security 11-12, 14, 30, 388, 390, 396, 404, 407
cloud model 1, 3, 7, 30, 72, 82, 102, 155, 186
cloud platform 10, 102, 117
cloud services 3, 10, 13, 42, 45, 59-60, 72-74, 83, 105, 153, 156, 171, 186, 302, 388, 392-394
combinatorial optimization 260-262, 264, 273, 279
condensed matter physics 214-215, 227, 245
context aware computing 30
Customer Relationship Management (CRM) 72, 194
    social 175-177, 191, 194

D

data access control 388-389, 396-397, 399, 404, 408
data locality 248-249, 252, 259
discrete event system specification 298, 307
distributed evaluation 362-364, 386
domain ontology 199, 211, 345, 353

E

evolutionary algorithms 362-364, 367-368, 371, 377, 381, 386

G

grid computing 5, 83, 214-215, 221-222, 227, 240, 245, 322-323, 335, 339

H

High Performance Computing (HPC) 214-215, 309, 315, 340
high performce processor 259
HPP "Buk Bijela" 373, 375
HPP "Foca" 374, 376
hydroinformatics 362-363, 366-367, 386

I

Identity as a Service (IDaaS) 72, 81
identity federation 61-63, 70, 74-75, 81, 114, 394
Identity Management (IDM) 81
Identity Management Systems (IDM) 146
Identity Provider (IDP) 81
Infrastructure as a Service (IaaS) 30, 109, 146, 245, 282

L

Learning Management Systems (LMS) 114, 135, 146, 211
learning object 197-199, 203-204, 206-207, 211
learning object repository 199, 204, 206, 211

M

meta-heuristics 260-263, 265-266, 270, 273-274, 280